55 *Victorian Prose Writers Before 1867*, edited by William B. Thesing (1987)

56 *German Fiction Writers, 1914-1945*, edited by James Hardin (1987)

57 *Victorian Prose Writers After 1867*, edited by William B. Thesing (1987)

58 *Jacobean and Caroline Dramatists*, edited by Fredson Bowers (1987)

59 *American Literary Critics and Scholars, 1800-1850*, edited by John W. Rathbun and Monica M. Grecu (1987)

60 *Canadian Writers Since 1960*, Second Series, edited by W. H. New (1987)

61 *American Writers for Children Since 1960: Poets, Illustrators, and Nonfiction Authors*, edited by Glenn E. Estes (1987)

62 *Elizabethan Dramatists*, edited by Fredson Bowers (1987)

63 *Modern American Critics, 1920-1955*, edited by Gregory S. Jay (1988)

64 *American Literary Critics and Scholars, 1850-1880*, edited by John W. Rathbun and Monica M. Grecu (1988)

65 *French Novelists, 1900-1930*, edited by Catharine Savage Brosman (1988)

66 *German Fiction Writers, 1885-1913*, 2 parts, edited by James Hardin (1988)

67 *Modern American Critics Since 1955*, edited by Gregory S. Jay (1988)

68 *Canadian Writers, 1920-1959*, First Series, edited by W. H. New (1988)

69 *Contemporary German Fiction Writers*, First Series, edited by Wolfgang D. Elfe and James Hardin (1988)

70 *British Mystery Writers, 1860-1919*, edited by Bernard Benstock and Thomas F. Staley (1988)

71 *American Literary Critics and Scholars, 1880-1900*, edited by John W. Rathbun and Monica M. Grecu (1988)

72 *French Novelists, 1930-1960*, edited by Catharine Savage Brosman (1988)

73 *American Magazine Journalists, 1741-1850*, edited by Sam G. Riley (1988)

74 *American Short-Story Writers Before 1880*, edited by Bobby Ellen Kimbel, with the assistance of William E. Grant (1988)

75 *Contemporary German Fiction Writers*, Second Series, edited by Wolfgang D. Elfe and James Hardin (1988)

76 *Afro-American Writers, 1940-1955*, edited by Trudier Harris (1988)

77 *British Mystery Writers, 1920-1939*, edited by Bernard Benstock and Thomas F. Staley (1988)

78 *American Short-Story Writers, 1880-1910*, edited by Bobby Ellen Kimbel, with the assistance of William E. Grant (1988)

79 *American Magazine Journalists, 1850-1900*, edited by Sam G. Riley (1988)

80 *Restoration and Eighteenth-Century Dramatists*, First Series, edited by Paula R. Backscheider (1989)

81 *Austrian Fiction Writers, 1875-1913*, edited by James Hardin and Donald G. Daviau (1989)

82 *Chicano Writers*, First Series, edited by Francisco A. Lomelí and Carl R. Shirley (1989)

83 *French Novelists Since 1960*, edited by Catharine Savage Brosman (1989)

84 *Restoration and Eighteenth-Century Dramatists*, Second Series, edited by Paula R. Backscheider (1989)

85 *Austrian Fiction Writers After 1914*, edited by James Hardin and Donald G. Daviau (1989)

86 *American Short-Story Writers, 1910-1945*, First Series, edited by Bobby Ellen Kimbel (1989)

87 *British Mystery and Thriller Writers Since 1940*, First Series, edited by Bernard Benstock and Thomas F. Staley (1989)

88 *Canadian Writers, 1920-1959*, Second Series, edited by W. H. New (1989)

89 *Restoration and Eighteenth-Century Dramatists*, Third Series, edited by Paula R. Backscheider (1989)

90 *German Writers in the Age of Goethe, 1789-1832*, edited by James Hardin and Christoph E. Schweitzer (1989)

91 *American Magazine Journalists, 1900-1960*, First Series, edited by Sam G. Riley (1990)

92 *Canadian Writers, 1890-1920*, edited by W. H. New (1990)

93 *British Romantic Poets, 1789-1832*, First Series, edited by John R. Greenfield (1990)

94 *German Writers in the Age of Goethe: Sturm und Drang to Classicism*, edited by James Hardin and Christoph E. Schweitzer (1990)

95 *Eighteenth-Century British Poets*, First Series, edited by John Sitter (1990)

96 *British Romantic Poets, 1789-1832*, Second Series, edited by John R. Greenfield (1990)

97 *German Writers from the Enlightenment to Sturm und Drang, 1720-1764*, edited by James Hardin and Christoph E. Schweitzer (1990)

98 *Modern British Essayists*, First Series, edited by Robert Beum (1990)

99 *Canadian Writers Before 1890*, edited by W. H. New (1990)

100 *Modern British Essayists*, Second Series, edited by Robert Beum (1990)

101 *British Prose Writers, 1660-1800*, First Series, edited by Donald T. Siebert (1991)

102 *American Short-Story Writers, 1910-1945*, Second Series, edited by Bobby Ellen Kimbel (1991)

103 *American Literary Biographers*, First Series, edited by Steven Serafin (1991)

104 *British Prose Writers, 1660-1800*, Second Series, edited by Donald T. Siebert (1991)

105 *American Poets Since World War II*, Second Series, edited by R. S. Gwynn (1991)

106 *British Literary Publishing Houses, 1820-1880*, edited by Patricia J. Anderson and Jonathan Rose (1991)

107 *British Romantic Prose Writers, 1789-1832*, First Series, edited by John R. Greenfield (1991)

108 *Twentieth-Century Spanish Poets*, First Series, edited by Michael L. Perna (1991)

109 *Eighteenth-Century British Poets*, Second Series, edited by John Sitter (1991)

110 *British Romantic Prose Writers, 1789-1832*, Second Series, edited by John R. Greenfield (1991)

111 *American Literary Biographers*, Second Series, edited by Steven Serafin (1991)

112 *British Literary Publishing Houses, 1881-1965*, edited by Jonathan Rose and Patricia J. Anderson (1991)

113 *Modern Latin-American Fiction Writers*, First Series, edited by William Luis (1992)

114 *Twentieth-Century Italian Poets*, First Series, edited by Giovanna Wedel De Stasio, Glauco Cambon, and Antonio Illiano (1992)

115 *Medieval Philosophers*, edited by Jeremiah Hackett (1992)

**(Continued on back endsheets)**

# Modern Latin-American Fiction Writers

## Second Series

# Modern Latin-American Fiction Writers

## Second Series

Edited by
William Luis
*Vanderbilt University*
and
Ann González
*University of North Carolina at Charlotte*

A Bruccoli Clark Layman Book
Gale Research Inc.
Detroit, Washington, D.C., London

For Gabriel, Diego, Antonia, Eric, and Tammie and Brent's baby

To my husband, Daniel, and my children: Carolina, Gina, John, Daniel, and Ana

Printed in the United States of America

Published simultaneously in the United Kingdom
by Gale Research International Limited
(An affiliated company of Gale Research Inc.)

The paper used in this publication meets the minimum requirements
of American National Standard for Information Sciences—Permanence
Paper for Printed Library Materials, ANSI Z39.48-1984. ⊗™

Library of Congress Catalog Card Number 94–13061
ISBN 0–8103–5559–0

The trademark **ITP** is used under license.

10 9 8 7 6 5 4 3 2 1

# Contents

# Plan of the Series

*... Almost the most prodigious asset of a country, and perhaps its most precious possession, is its native literary product — when that product is fine and noble and enduring.*

Mark Twain\*

The advisory board, the editors, and the publisher of the *Dictionary of Literary Biography* are joined in endorsing Mark Twain's declaration. The literature of a nation provides an inexhaustible resource of permanent worth. We intend to make literature and its creators better understood and more accessible to students and the reading public, while satisfying the standards of teachers and scholars.

To meet these requirements, *literary biography* has been construed in terms of the author's achievement. The most important thing about a writer is his writing. Accordingly, the entries in *DLB* are career biographies, tracing the development of the author's canon and the evolution of his reputation.

The purpose of *DLB* is not only to provide reliable information in a convenient format but also to place the figures in the larger perspective of literary history and to offer appraisals of their accomplishments by qualified scholars.

The publication plan for *DLB* resulted from two years of preparation. The project was proposed to Bruccoli Clark by Frederick C. Ruffner, president of the Gale Research Company, in November 1975. After specimen entries were prepared and typeset, an advisory board was formed to refine the entry format and develop the series rationale. In meetings held during 1976, the publisher, series editors, and advisory board approved the scheme for a comprehensive biographical dictionary of persons who contributed to North American literature. Editorial work on the first volume began in January 1977, and it was published in 1978. In order to make *DLB* more than a reference tool and to compile volumes that individually have claim to status as literary history, it was decided to organize volumes by topic, period, or genre. Each of these free-standing volumes provides a biographical-bibliographical guide and overview for a particular area of literature. We are convinced that this organization — as opposed to a single alphabet method — constitutes a valuable innovation in the presentation of reference material. The volume plan necessarily requires many decisions for the placement and treatment of authors who might properly be included in two or three volumes. In some instances a major figure will be included in separate volumes, but with different entries emphasizing the aspect of his career appropriate to each volume. Ernest Hemingway, for example, is represented in *American Writers in Paris, 1920-1939* by an entry focusing on his expatriate apprenticeship; he is also in *American Novelists, 1910-1945* with an entry surveying his entire career. Each volume includes a cumulative index of the subject authors and articles. Comprehensive indexes to the entire series are planned.

With volume ten in 1982 it was decided to enlarge the scope of *DLB*. By the end of 1986 twenty-one volumes treating British literature had been published, and volumes for Commonwealth and Modern European literature were in progress. The series has been further augmented by the *DLB Yearbooks* (since 1981) which update published entries and add new entries to keep the *DLB* current with contemporary activity. There have also been *DLB Documentary Series* volumes which provide biographical and critical source materials for figures whose work is judged to have particular interest for students. One of these companion volumes is entirely devoted to Tennessee Williams.

We define literature as the *intellectual commerce of a nation:* not merely as belles lettres but as that ample and complex process by which ideas are generated, shaped, and transmitted. *DLB* entries are not limited to "creative writers" but extend to other figures who in their time and in their way influenced the mind of a people. Thus the series encompasses historians, journalists, publishers, and screenwriters. By this means readers of *DLB* may be aided to perceive literature not as cult scripture in the keeping of intellectual high priests but firmly positioned at the center of a nation's life.

\**From an unpublished section of Mark Twain's autobiography, copyright by the Mark Twain Company*

*DLB* includes the major writers appropriate to each volume and those standing in the ranks immediately behind them. Scholarly and critical counsel has been sought in deciding which minor figures to include and how full their entries should be. Wherever possible, useful references are made to figures who do not warrant separate entries.

Each *DLB* volume has a volume editor responsible for planning the volume, selecting the figures for inclusion, and assigning the entries. Volume editors are also responsible for preparing, where appropriate, appendices surveying the major periodicals and literary and intellectual movements for their volumes, as well as lists of further readings. Work on the series as a whole is coordinated at the Bruccoli Clark Layman editorial center in Columbia, South Carolina, where the editorial staff is responsible for accuracy of the published volumes.

One feature that distinguishes *DLB* is the illustration policy – its concern with the iconography of literature. Just as an author is influenced by his surroundings, so is the reader's understanding of the author enhanced by a knowledge of his environment. Therefore *DLB* volumes include not only drawings, paintings, and photographs of authors, often depicting them at various stages in their careers, but also illustrations of their families and places where they lived. Title pages are regularly reproduced in facsimile along with dust jackets for modern authors. The dust jackets are a special feature of *DLB* because they often document better than anything else the way in which an author's work was perceived in its own time. Specimens of the writers' manuscripts are included when feasible.

Samuel Johnson rightly decreed that "The chief glory of every people arises from its authors." The purpose of the *Dictionary of Literary Biography* is to compile literary history in the surest way available to us – by accurate and comprehensive treatment of the lives and work of those who contributed to it.

The *DLB* Advisory Board

# Introduction

The so-called Boom period of Latin-American literature of the 1960s — which saw the explosion of experimental fiction in the region in the publication of such celebrated novels as Carlos Fuentes's *La muerte de Artemio Cruz* (1962; translated as *The Death of Artemio Cruz,* 1964), Julio Cortázar's *Rayuela* (1963; translated as *Hopscotch,* 1966), Mario Vargas Llosa's *La casa verde* (1966; translated as *The Green House,* 1968), Guillermo Cabrera Infante's *Tres tristes tigres* (1967; translated as *Three Trapped Tigers,* 1971), and Gabriel García Márquez's *Cien años de soledad* (1967; translated as *One Hundred Years of Solitude,* 1970) — gave Latin-American literature instant recognition worldwide. These works reflect the local conditions of Mexico, Argentina, Peru, Cuba, and Colombia respectively but also narrate themes that transcend the concerns of any one country and appeal to a broader audience. The literary and commercial profusion of the 1960s produced works that were exciting, creative, innovative, and imaginative and that proposed theoretical issues pertaining to reading, writing, spoken language, translation, history, and fiction. Many of these works included their own criticism and even suggested to the reader how they should be read. In some cases they attempted to question the boundaries between the canny and the uncanny, the real and the magic, reality and dreams, and to reveal that knowledge is not a given but is subject to interpretation.

These works and numerous others, however, come from an earlier Latin-American literary tradition that can be traced to the moment Europeans began to write about the New World and, more precisely, to when the inhabitants of the New World began to document their own experiences from their own point of view. Spanish-American fiction as a self-conscious genre began early in the nineteenth century when authors set the groundwork for a truly modern literature. For example, in Cuba the antislavery narrative focused on the plight of the slave who worked on sugar plantations, describing the tension between but also the coming together of whites and blacks. In Argentina literary works took the form of a protest against Juan Manuel Rosas, the governor and dictator of the province of Buenos Aires, which engaged the country in a debate between civilization and barbarism.

Some critics have argued that modern Latin-American literature begins toward the end of the nineteenth century with Rubén Darío and *modernismo,* a literary current of and for a minority concerned with beauty, elegance, and urbanization. In Brazil the trend also may have been initiated with modernism, corresponding to the avant-garde of Spanish-American literature and adapting European ideas to a Brazilian context.

In Latin America modern fiction is in part a reaction to the regionalist novel, which included works such as José Eustasio Rivera's *La vorágine* (1924; translated as *The Vortex,* 1935), Rómulo Gallegos's *Doña Bárbara* (1929; translated 1931), Alejo Carpentier's *¡Ecue Yamba-O!* (Praised Be the Lord!, 1933), and Ricardo Güiraldes's *Don Segundo Sombra* (1926; translated as *Don Segundo Sombra: Shadow on the Pampas,* 1935). These novels describe the countryside — a symbol of the nation — and local scenes, characters, and traditions. The emergence of modern fiction was accompanied by a thematic shift from the country to the city, which soon became the center of national identity. Although the specific origin of Latin-American fiction may be in dispute, there is no doubt that these and other literary movements gave Latin-American literature a character of its own.

Modern Latin-American fiction can be traced to the 1930s and 1940s, the Spanish Civil War and World War II, a period that showed a dramatic increase in the number of foundational writers and works. During this period political leaders and writers were struggling with the question of national identity. Spain's civil war, which turned the country into an international battleground, affected Latin-American writers such as Nicolás Guillén of Cuba, Pablo Neruda of Chile, and Octavio Paz of Mexico, among many others, who supported the efforts of the republican government to combat fascism on the Iberian peninsula. The success of Gen. Francisco Franco's army over the republicans forced many Spanish intellectuals into exile, many to Spanish America, where they continued their literary production and contributed to an increasing dialogue among writers living in Spanish-speaking countries. The end of World War II marks a moment of liminality linked to a series of events that signaled the beginning of a new order stimulating the development of a modern Latin-American literature.

Many writers established themselves in the 1940s, including Clarice Lispector, who published her first novel, *Perto do coração selvagem* (translated as *Near to the Wild Heart,* 1990) in 1944, followed by *O lustre* (The Chandelier, 1946) and *A cidade sitiada* (The Besieged City, 1949). Adolfo Bioy Casares did the same with his novels *La invención de Morel* (1940; translated as *The Invention of Morel and Other Stories,* 1965) and *Plan de evasión* (1945; translated as *A Plan for Escape,* 1975) and the collection of stories *La trama celeste* (The Celestial Plot, 1948). Juan José Arreola published his collection *Varia invención* (Various Inventions) in 1949, and Lygia Fagundes Telles presented her stories in *Praia viva* (Living Beach, 1944) and *O cacto vermelho* (The Red Cactus, 1949).

In the postwar period Latin-American literature underwent significant development and captured the attention of the world. In 1954 the Chilean poet Gabriela Mistral became the first Latin-American writer to receive the much-coveted Nobel Prize for Literature, thus bringing international recognition to her and her regional counterparts. Since Mistral, Latin America has produced a Nobel laureate each decade: Guatemalan Miguel Angel Asturias in 1967, the Chilean Neruda in 1971, the Colombian García Márquez in 1982, and the Mexican Octavio Paz in 1990. In the contemporary period writers such as Jorge Luis Borges, Alejo Carpentier, and João Guimarães Rosa, to name three of the most influential, have been strong contenders for the same prize and have received numerous awards. The World War II period also marked the Brazilian postmodernist Generation of 1945, when as a result of the war authors returned to writing about international issues.

The 1930s and in particular the 1940s and the postwar period became the training ground for the master Latin-American writers, including Carpentier, Guimarães Rosa, Jorge Amado, José María Arguedas, Juan Rulfo, and writers who went on to produce even more important works in the 1950s and 1960s. A sample of the publication history of some of them helps illustrate this tendency. Carpentier published his first novel *¡Ecue Yamba-O!* in 1933, but he wrote his best short stories in the 1940s. He published "Oficio de tinieblas" (Morning Office) and *Viaje a la semilla* (translated as *Journey Back to the Source,* 1970) in 1944 and "Los fugitivos" (The Fugitives) in 1946. He later gathered "Viaje a la semilla" and other stories in *Guerra del tiempo* (translated as *War of Time,* 1970) in 1958. Like Carpentier, Rulfo published his first short stories – "La vida no es muy seria en sus cosas" (Life Is Not Very Serious about Things), "Nos han dado la tierra"

(translated as "They Gave Us the Land," 1965), and "Macario" (translated 1959) – in 1945. The latter two were included in *El llano en llamas* (1953; translated as *The Burning Plain and Other Stories,* 1967). Unlike the previous two writers, Guimarães Rosa wrote his first collection of stories, *Sagarana* (translated as *Sagarana: A Cycle of Stories,* 1966) in 1937, but he rewrote it five years later and, like Carpentier and Rulfo with their stories, published it in the same decade, in 1946; it was received with tremendous enthusiasm. Arguedas wrote and published his initial collection of short stories, *Agua* (Water), in 1935, but it was *Yawar fiesta* (1941; translated as *Yawar Fiesta,* 1985) that confirmed his importance as a writer.

Although these and other writers began to produce important works in the 1940s, it was in the 1950s that they wrote and published fiction that substantially contributed to their national and international reputation. Carpentier and Rulfo wrote important novels in the 1950s: Carpentier published *Los pasos perdidos* (1953; translated as *The Lost Steps,* 1956) and *El acoso* (1956; translated as *Manhunt,* 1959), and Rulfo his *Pedro Páramo* (1955; translated 1959). Other writers followed a similar pattern: Guimarães Rosa with *Granda Sertão: Veredas* (1956; translated as *The Devil to Pay in the Backlands,* 1963) and Arguedas with *Los ríos profundos* (1958; translated as *Deep Rivers,* 1978). The number of distinguished fiction writers increased in the 1960s with writers of the Boom and in the 1970s with those of the post-Boom. Some critics even argue that with the works of the younger writers, Latin-American fiction is on the threshold of a new style.

Many of these influential writers received their literary training in Europe, where they witnessed and participated in new literary and artistic trends. For example, in Paris writers such as Carpentier, Asturias, and Arturo Uslar Pietri had the opportunity to meet intellectuals such as André Breton, Paul Valéry, and Salvador Dalí. Upon returning to their native countries these Spanish-American authors brought back current literary trends illustrated by the books they read and the works they wrote.

World War II also increased contact between the United States and Latin America, and writers south of the Rio Grande became familiar with and were influenced by their North American counterparts in general and John Dos Passos, Ernest Hemingway, and William Faulkner in particular. Latin-American writers read these and other North American authors in the original and in translation; some even translated the works themselves, including

Lino Novás Calvo, who wrote articles about Faulkner and Hemingway and translated Hemingway's *The Old Man and the Sea* (1952) in the Cuban magazine *Bohemia* in 1955.

The Cuban revolution further contributed to the contact between European and Latin-American writers, and most importantly among Latin-American writers themselves. Early in the revolution intellectuals throughout the world, and in particular Latin America, identified with the goals of Fidel Castro's government. They were invited to visit Cuba by the newspaper *Revolución,* edited by Carlos Franqui, and by its weekly literary supplement, *Lunes de Revolución* (Revolution Monday), edited by Cabrera Infante. After the closing of *Lunes de Revolución* in November 1961, Casa de las Américas with its journal of the same name became the center of culture in Latin America. Writers such as Cortázar, García Márquez, Carlos Fuentes, Mario Vargas Llosa, and José Donoso, among many others, traveled to Cuba, met other Latin-American writers, and read each other's works. The cohesion among Latin-American writers and the unified support intellectuals had given the Cuban government and its policies, a characteristic of the 1960s in the Boom period, came to an end with the Padilla affair of 1971, in which poet Heberto Padilla was forced to confess his antirevolutionary position. Castro made it clear that writers would have to confirm their allegiance to the revolution or be declared its enemy. Whereas writers such as Fuentes, Vargas Llosa, and Cabrera Infante became critical of Cuban policy, others such as García Márquez remained loyal to the Castro government. Cuba also enjoyed the support of younger writers interested in radical reform in their countries, in particular those of Central American origin. The Padilla affair marks the end of the Boom and the start of the post-Boom period.

Since Latin-American literature is an expansive subject that covers various genres and literary and historical periods from its inception in the fifteenth century to the present, and in order to differentiate this series from other anthologies compiled on the same subject, this volume focuses on the fiction of the contemporary period: modern Latin-American fiction has opened the door to all of Latin-American literature. Although no one will dispute the talents of Neruda and Paz, two of the most important poets from the Americas, it was the modern novel that became an instant international literary and commercial success and has inspired critics to rediscover other writers, genres, and periods.

Even though the time frame used for the First and Second Series technically begins in 1945, the end of World War II, and gathers writers whose major fictional production flourished after that period, the two volumes also make exceptions to include writers such as Borges, a monumental figure in Latin-American literature. Borges's early contribution falls outside of the time frame since *Historia universal de la infamia* (translated as *A Universal History of Infamy,* 1972) and *Ficciones* were published in 1935 and 1944 respectively, but he and his fiction have had a profound and lasting effect on subsequent generations of Latin-American writers. Modern Latin-American literature and criticism is not possible without the presence of Borges.

*Modern Latin-American Fiction Writers, First Series* gathers major figures in Latin-American fiction: giants such as Borges, Carpentier, Guimarães Rosa, and José Lezama Lima and popular writers such as Cortázar, Fuentes, García Márquez, and Fagundes Telles. Some are controversial, such as Amado; others are prolific, such as Mario Benedetti; and still others have left their mark with one or two works, such as Rulfo. Even though *Modern Latin-American Fiction Writers* is dedicated to prose, many of the writers have not limited their literary production to the novel and the short story. Some have also distinguished themselves in the essay, theater, and poetry. Therefore, references to the authors' work in other genres have been included.

*Modern Latin-American Fiction Writers, Second Series* reflects a recent interest in postmodernist thought and includes many younger writers associated with the post-Boom, such as Reinaldo Arenas, Antonio Skármeta, Julio Escoto, and Mario Roberto Morales. In fact, it can be convincingly argued that contemporary Latin-American fiction *is* postmodern. Characteristic of this fiction is the decentering of discourse and the political questioning of dominant ideologies. Such opposition to reigning structures has a long tradition in Latin America and can be traced back to early Amerindian and slave rebellions in the New World.

Latin-American literature and politics are inextricably related, and in the postmodern period the decentering of discourse is present in literature as well as in politics and history. In Latin America and the Caribbean, Cuba in particular facilitated an understanding of the inner workings of political and literary discourses within the context of a postmodern era. With the presence of Communism in the New World, the Castro government played a central role in challenging U.S. dominance over the region. This was the case in areas contested by Cuba. Just as the Cuban missile crisis brought Latin America and the Caribbean to the attention of the world, Cuban intervention in Nicaragua and El Salvador did the same for Central America. The Cuban presence gave the region an unprecedented importance. Its support of the Sandinistas in Nicaragua and the Frente de Liberación Nacional Farabundo Martí (National Liberation Movement Farabundo Martí) in El Salvador became the object of concern not only among politicians but also among writers and critics.

The Cuban presence in Central America has been the primary reason that the region has received attention from scholars in Europe and the United States. The assassination of Bishop Oscar Romero in March 1980, President Ronald Reagan's unrelenting support of the Nicaraguan Contras, and President George Bush's invasion of Panama to oust Manuel Antonio Noriega in December 1989, combined with the outbreak of civil war in El Salvador in the late 1970s, shifted the focus of international attention to that part of the world. Many supporters of the policies of the Cuban government, but also critics of Castro, saw events in Central America as a legitimate outlet for their social and political concerns. It is no coincidence that two of the Nobel Peace Prize winners in the last decade have come from this region: Oscar Arias of Costa Rica and Rigoberta Menchú of Guatemala.

Events in Central America have questioned the Cuban discourse and forced the government to rethink some of its own national policies. The most obvious example is the Sandinista government's unique mixture of Marxism and Catholicism, as represented by Father Ernesto Cardenal, who was minister of education in the Sandinista government and a poet in his own right. Whereas early Cuban policy discouraged the practice of religion and even targeted some religious groups, the Nicaraguans and other Central Americans recognized that the church played an important role in the political, economic, social, and spiritual transformation of their societies. The unique form of revolution in Nicaragua, with its blend of Catholicism, began to displace the Cuban model in favor of a nationalist model that incorporated the traditions and culture of the people into a political and economic context. This type of successful blend, as well as other events in and outside the region, forced the Castro government to reexamine its economic, social, cultural, and religious policies.

Many Central American writers fighting for reform in their countries saw in the Cuban model an alternative. The Cuban government and Casa de las Américas in particular promoted writers committed to a political and revolutionary ideology in

their works, and the testimony became the dominant narrative expression of the Central American crisis. For example, El Salvadoran Manlio Argueta's *Caperucita en la Zona Roja* (Little Red Riding Hood in the Red Zone), about political repression in El Salvador and the urban resistance, won Casa de las Américas's prize for the novel in 1977; Guatemalan Arturo Arias's *Ideologías, literatura y sociedad durante la revolución guatemalteca: 1944–1954* (Ideologies, Literature, and Society during the Guatemalan Revolution: 1944–1954), a Marxist analysis of the revolutionary process of Guatemala, including the U.S. Central Intelligence Agency overthrow of the progressive Jacobo Arbenz, was awarded the same prize for the essay in 1979. Panamanian José de Jesús Martínez's *Mi general Torrijos* (My General Torrijos), about the chief of the Panamanian national guard, Omar Torrijos, who consistently challenged U.S. policy, received the prize for testimony in 1987; and Nicaraguan Gioconda Belli's *Línea de fuego* (Line of Fire), about love and politics, won the poetry prize in 1978.

Even with all of the international attention on Central American politics over the last decade, contemporary Central American writers have tended to be overlooked by North American and European critics for no other reason than that the quality of the region's literature is unknown to them. Local publication costs are exorbitant, and Central American writers have found it difficult to distribute their work on a large scale. A first edition of a novel often may have no more than five hundred copies and rarely boasts of more than two or three thousand. Thus the works are seldom sold beyond their own national boundaries and rarely receive international attention.

Human-rights atrocities in Central America, however, have focused concern on the area and have stimulated academic studies by North American scholars in particular. Increased study of the region has revealed a plethora of literature and cultural projects of high artistic merit. Scholars have seized on the same approaches used to give publicity to the novel of the Boom period. English translations often appear in the United States or Europe well before many of the same works are known to other Spanish-speaking countries outside their national boundaries, as can be seen in the recent burst of anthologies on Central American fiction in translation. Clearly, North American critics and translators are beginning to take note of the stature of these writers in Latin America.

The Second Series includes writers of international stature such as Vargas Llosa of Peru, Ernesto Sábato of Argentina, Isabel Allende of Chile, and

Lydia Cabrera and Novás Calvo of Cuba as well as younger writers such as Rosario Ferré and Edgardo Rodríguez Juliá of Puerto Rico, Alfredo Bryce Echenique of Peru, and Nélida Piñon of Brazil. Since Cuba, Argentina, Chile, and Mexico have contributed a disproportional number of major writers to the field of Latin-American literature and have received critical attention in many other sources, this volume includes more marginalized writers from less traditionally representative areas, such as Juan Bosch and Marcío Veloz Maggiolo of the Dominican Republic, Demetrio Aguilera Malta of Ecuador, Jaime Saenz of Bolivia, Argueta of El Salvador, Mario Roberto Morales of Guatemala, Roberto Sinán of Panama, and Julio Escoto of Honduras. These writers have not received the international attention that, for example, writers of the Boom period have. Nevertheless, they are well known regionally and have contributed significantly to the development of literature in their respective countries. Furthermore, in this postmodern era all discourses should be included within the context of other discourses, including those that propose only one type of modern Latin-American fiction.

The Second Series also suggests areas in which the field will develop. Certainly women writers will occupy an important space, and this volume includes a representative number of women fiction writers: Carmen Naranjo of Costa Rica, Claribel Alegría of El Salvador, Elena Garro of Mexico, and Lya Luft of Brazil, among others. Because of the recent interest in Afro-Hispanic writers and literature, there are also representative essays on Aguilera Malta of Ecuador and Quince Duncan of Costa Rica. It is hoped that future histories and studies of Latin-American literature will follow this example and take into account the contribution Afro-Hispanic writers have made in exploring the cultural and racial complexity of Latin America.

Most recently, there is a growing interest in Hispanic-American (Latino) writers born or raised in the United States who, for the most part, write in English about the Hispanic presence and culture in North America. Although there are already separate *Dictionary of Literary Biography* volumes on Chicano literature, the Second Series highlights this literary manifestation among Hispanic Caribbean writers, with essays on Oscar Hijuelos (of Cuban descent) and Nicholasa Mohr (of Puerto Rican descent). Hispanic-Caribbean people since the early nineteenth century have traveled to and lived in New York, where intellectuals and politicians gathered and conspired against the Spanish colonial government. While living there, many wrote important works in Spanish about their native countries that inevitably included a North American perspective. In the most recent period Hispanics from the Caribbean, for political or economic reasons, continue to make the United States their home, and as their stays become more permanent, they are writing in English. Their literature describes the life of Latinos in the United States and forms a bridge between Hispanic and North American literatures and cultures.

Contemporary literary concerns and events have also influenced the selection of authors for these volumes. With the breakthrough of the literature of the post-Boom period, which has profited from the publicity attained by the writers of the Boom, much-needed attention has been brought to women, black, and Hispanic-American writers and themes. The presence of such marginalized writers, however, is not new. Women have been represented by writers such as Sor Juana Inés de la Cruz in the eighteenth century, the Condesa de Merlín and Gertrudis Gómez de Avellaneda in the nineteenth, and María Luisa Bombal in the twentieth. Black writers such as Juan Francisco Manzano and Martín Morúa Delgado wrote in the nineteenth century, and Adalberto Ortiz, Nelson Estupiñán Bass, and Quince Duncan in the twentieth; and Hispanic writers living and writing in the United States can be traced to Cirilo Villaverde, José Martí, and Emeterio Betances in the nineteenth century, but with a more North American perspective to Nicolasa Mohr, Oscar Hijuelos, Julia Alvarez, and Cristina García in the twentieth. However, these writers have generally been overshadowed by the Boom period and only recently have begun receiving recognition long overdue.

Linguistically and geographically, Latin-American literature ideally should gather works and authors from the Francophone and Anglophone Caribbean, the Netherlands Antilles, and Creole areas. However, these two volumes limit the definition of Latin-American literature to the Spanish-speaking Caribbean, Central and South America, and Portuguese-speaking Brazil.

This two-volume series has attempted a fair representation of modern fiction from every Latin-American country, highlighting not only the great canonical figures of the internationally recognized Boom period but also the underrepresented, forgotten, and marginalized writers who have contributed to the development of the region's high quality of fiction during the last five decades and without whom a study of modern Latin-American fiction would be necessarily fragmented and incomplete.

Above all, these two volumes indicate the wealth and strength of fiction from Latin America since World War II and point toward promising things to come.

— *William Luis and Ann González*

## Acknowledgments

This book was produced by Bruccoli Clark Layman, Inc. Karen L. Rood is senior editor for the *Dictionary of Literary Biography* series. Darren Harris-Fain was the in-house editor.

Production coordinator is George F. Dodge. Photography editors are Josephine A. Bruccoli and Joseph Matthew Bruccoli. Layout and graphics supervisor is Penney L. Haughton. Copyediting supervisor is Bill Adams. Typesetting supervisor is Kathleen M. Flanagan. Julie E. Frick is editorial associate. The production staff includes Phyllis A. Avant, Ann M. Cheschi, Melody W. Clegg, Patricia Coate, Wilma Weant Dague, Brigitte B. de Guzman, Denise W. Edwards, Sarah A. Estes, Joyce Fowler, Laurel M. Gladden, Stephanie C. Hatchell, Leslie Haynesworth, John Lorio, Rebecca Mayo, Kathy Lawler Merlette, Pamela D. Norton, Delores I. Plas-tow, Patricia F. Salisbury, Paul Smith, and William L. Thomas, Jr.

Walter W. Ross, Deborah M. Chasteen, and Robert S. McConnell did library research. They were assisted by the following librarians at the Thomas Cooper Library of the University of South Carolina: Linda Holderfield and the interlibrary-loan staff; reference librarians Gwen Baxter, Daniel Boice, Faye Chadwell, Cathy Eckman, Gary Geer, Qun "Gerry" Jiao, Jean Rhyne, Carol Tobin, Carolyn Tyler, Virginia Weathers, Elizabeth Whiznant, and Connie Widney; circulation-department head Thomas Marcil; and acquisitions-searching supervisor David Haggard. Special thanks are due to Roger Mortimer and the staff of Special Collections at the Thomas Cooper Library. The following librarians generously provided material: William Cagle and Joel Silver of the Lilly Library, Indiana University, and Ann Freudenberg, Kendon Stubbs, and Edmund Berkeley, Jr., of the University of Virginia Library.

This work was supported in part by funds provided by the University of North Carolina at Charlotte.

Dictionary of Literary Biography® • Volume One Hundred Forty-Five

# Modern Latin-American Fiction Writers

## Second Series

# Dictionary of Literary Biography

## Adonias Filho
*(27 November 1915 – 2 August 1990)*

Fred P. Ellison
*University of Texas at Austin*

BOOKS: *Os servos da morte* (Rio de Janeiro: José Olympio, 1946);

*Memórias de Lázaro* (Rio de Janeiro: O Cruzeiro, 1952); translated by Fred P. Ellison as *Memories of Lazarus* (Austin: University of Texas Press, 1969);

*Jornal de um escritor* (Rio de Janeiro: Ministério de Educação e Cultura, 1954);

*Modernos ficcionistas brasileiros,* first series (Rio de Janeiro: O Cruzeiro, 1958);

*Cornélio Pena* (Rio de Janeiro: Agir, 1960);

*Corpo vivo* (Rio de Janeiro: Civilização Brasileira, 1962);

*O bloqueio cultural: O intelectual, a liberdade, a receptividade* (São Paulo: Livraria Martins, 1964);

*O Forte* (Rio de Janeiro: Civilização Brasileira, 1965);

*Modernos ficcionistas brasileiros,* second series (Rio de Janeiro: Tempo Brasileiro, 1965);

*A nação grapiuna: Adonias Filho na Academia,* by Adonias and Jorge Amado (Rio de Janeiro: Tempo Brasileiro, 1965);

*Léguas da promissão* (Rio de Janeiro: Civilização Brasileira, 1968);

*O romance brasileiro de trinta* (Rio de Janeiro: Bloch, 1969);

*Luanda, Beira, Bahia* (Rio de Janeiro: Civilização Brasileira, 1971);

*Volta Redonda: O processo brasileiro de mudança,* by Adonias and Octales Gonzalez (Rio de Janeiro: Image, 1972); translated by Richard J. Spock as *Volta Redonda: The Brazilian Process of Change* (Rio de Janeiro: Image, 1972);

*Uma nota de cem* (Rio de Janeiro: Ouro, 1973);

*As velhas* (Rio de Janeiro: Civilização Brasileira, 1975);

*Adonias Filho, 1977*

*Sul da Bahia, chão de cacau: Uma civilização regional* (Rio de Janeiro: Civilização Brasileira, 1976);

*Fora da pista* (Rio de Janeiro: Civilização Brasileira, 1978);

*O Auto dos Ilhéus* (Rio de Janeiro: Civilização Brasileira, 1981);

*O Largo da Palma* (Rio de Janeiro: Civilização
Brasileira, 1981);

*Noite sem madrugada* (São Paulo: Difel, 1983);

*O homem de branco* (Rio de Janeiro: Bertrand Brasil,
1987).

OTHER: Cornélio Penna, *Os romances completos de
Cornélio Penna,* introductory essay by Adonias
(Rio de Janeiro: Aguilar, 1958);

"Catete: Amor no Catete," in *A cidade e as ruas:
Novelas cariocas* (Rio de Janeiro: Lidador,
1964);

"O nosso Bispo," in *O assunto é padre* (Rio de Janeiro:
Agir, 1968);

"A ficção de Guimarães Rosa," in *Guimarães Rosa:
Estudos* (Lisbon: Instituto Luso-Brasileiro,
1969).

SELECTED PERIODICAL PUBLICATION –
UNCOLLECTED: "Experiência de um romancista," *Minas Gerais Suplemento Literário,* 9 (9 February 1974): 2–3.

Brazilian novelist and critic Adonias Filho was
one of a handful of innovative writers who set a
new course for fiction in his country after World
War II. Beginning in 1946, his "cacao trilogy" and
other works about the cacao-growing area of southern Bahia established him as a luminary of modern
fiction alongside such celebrated writers as Clarice
Lispector and João Guimarães Rosa. Comparable to
his novels in artistic value are his long short stories,
which he called *novelas.* In addition, he left an important body of literary criticism and theory. As an
intellectual leader he was also a respected public figure, able to mediate between the extremes of right
and left, especially from the mid 1960s to the early
1980s – the period of military dictatorship and a
difficult time in Brazilian history.

The son of Adonias Aguiar and Rachel Bastos
de Aguiar, Adonias Aguiar Filho ("filho" indicating
he was his father's namesake) was born on the family cacao *fazenda* (plantation) in the municipality of
Ilhéus on 27 November 1915. After primary schooling, he was sent away at age thirteen for further education at the Ginásio Ipiranga in Salvador, the
state capital of Bahia. There he began a lifelong
friendship with another boy from Ilhéus, Jorge
Amado, who also would write about the cacao region and become the most successful novelist of
Brazil. In Salvador, Adonias completed his education at age nineteen and embarked on a journalism
career. In Brazil newspaper work is often combined
with literary writing, which he also began. Moving

to the national capital, Rio de Janeiro, in 1936, the
young writer soon began work as a reporter for the
Rio dailies *Correio da Manhã* and *O Jornal.* In 1938 he
began to write literary criticism for newspapers and
literary magazines in both Rio and São Paulo and
like many fledgling writers also worked as a translator of European literature, notably of novels by the
German writer Jakob Wassermann. In 1942 Adonias received the bachelor of law degree from the
Faculdade de Direito do Distrito Federal (Federal
Law School) in Rio and two years later wed Rosita
Galiano, a native of Rio. Their dedicated and enduring marriage produced a daughter and a son,
Rachel and Adonias.

Adonias Filho belonged to a post–World War
II group that reached beyond the social novel of the
1930s for a new kind of expression. He admits owing something to the earlier modernism of Mário de
Andrade and Oswald de Andrade, who in the 1920s
and early 1930s had set literary language free from
bookishness, assimilated certain techniques of
James Joyce and other European avant-gardists, and
adapted methods from cinematography. As Jorge
Amado observed years later in a speech welcoming
Adonias to membership in the Academia Brasileira
de Letras and published in *A nação grapiuna* (The
Grapiuna Nation), the postwar novel probed a new
dimension in which "certos problemas interiores do
homem passassem a ocupar na estrutura do livro
um lugar proeminente, que nem sempre lhe era concedido pela novelística de 30" (certain inner problems of people would come to occupy, in the structure of the work, a prominence they were not always given by creators of the novel of 1930).

When he moved to Rio at the age of twenty-one, Adonias had brought with him a first novel entitled *Cachaça* (Rum). However, he destroyed it before showing it to anyone. Perhaps it was a regional
social novel of the type then widely successful, especially as practiced by his lifelong friend Rachel de
Queiroz. Certainly his first published novel, *Os servos da morte* (Servants of Death, 1946), shows an entirely different approach despite dealing with the
area where he was born. Adonias later called it the
"civilização de cacau" (cacao civilization). The novel was influenced by his associations in Rio with introspective Catholic novelists such as Cornélio
Penna, Lúcio Cardoso, and Otávio de Faria. They
introduced him to a new world of European writers: Joyce, Franz Kafka, Marcel Proust, Thomas
Hardy, and T. S. Eliot, among others.

The title of *Os servos da morte* adumbrates the
morbid and terrifying climate of the novel, whose
protagonists are a demented cacao planter, Paulino

Duarte, his wife Elisa, their five sons, the wife of one son, and various retainers and relatives. Angelo, the youngest child and perhaps the most vicious of all, is, unbeknownst to Paulino, Elisa's child by a decadent *fazendeiro* (landholder) whom she has seduced out of revenge for Paulino's brutality. The novel ends in a holocaust involving most of the central characters. *Os servos da morte* is neither a regional nor a social novel in the vein of the northeastern Brazilian writers; Adonias's inspiration came from elsewhere. Certainly he felt a kinship with William Faulkner, judging from the 22 November 1945 entry in his *Jornal de um escritor* (A Writer's Journal, 1954): "William Falkner [*sic*] é um ficcionista que utiliza o social apenas como um meio, a chave que abre a porta a esse mundo oculto que é o conflito interior dos homens" (Faulkner is a writer of fiction who uses the social merely as a means, a key that opens the door to the occult world that is people's inner conflict). In *Os servos da morte* the central characters are in constant psychological turmoil. Some have inherited insanity; others are driven mad in this environment of hatred, brutality, revenge, sexual violence, murder, mutilation, and degradation. The overarching theme is the struggle of evil with good, the novel suggesting that evil inevitably – at least at present and in the setting of the cacao zone – will prevail. One of the Duarte brothers, Rodrigo, a drunk and the murderer of an infant, surprises the reader on occasion with such utterances as "Não, ainda não evoluímos uma polegada" (No, we still have not evolved an inch). Curiously, his brother Angelo is also capable of an occasional thought of spirituality. The reader is thus reminded of the total absence of God from the hearts of any of these virtually subhuman characters.

If not an unlimited critical success, *Os servos da morte* nevertheless attracted favorable attention, surprising the modest and soft-spoken Adonias. As the first of what he early announced would be a "cacao trilogy" of novels, the work rejects many of the time-honored techniques of the social novel. Chronology is reordered. The all-knowing narrator is downplayed in favor of interior monologue and a variety of first-person narrators, which permits events to be seen from the perspectives of the characters. Adonias was still groping for the spare, cadenced, often poetic prose that would later be his trademark.

In 1946 Adonias was named director of the Rio daily *A Noite,* where he remained nearly four years. He continued to write a literary column for the newspaper *A Manhã,* and he never stopped making trips several times a year to the family planta-

tion in southern Bahia. There in 1950 he ran for election to the national chamber of deputies from Ilhéus but failed in his bid. Returning to the capital, he accepted an invitation from the prestigious *Jornal de Letras* to write a regular feature on literature, becoming one of a few practicing literary critics who were at the same time successful novelists.

The second of his promised "cacao trilogy," *Memórias de Lázaro* (1952; translated as *Memories of Lazarus,* 1969), is set in an arid, forbidding part of the interior of southern Bahia. The author visited its Ouro Valley as a young man. However, thanks to his Poesque imagination it seems almost too nightmarish to qualify as reality. There are few characters, the action is spare, and the valley is characterized essentially by its muddy slough, its dusty road, the hot crust of its earth, and the black sky. The narrator is Alexandre, a coarse, brutish man who, his mind now shattered, begins to tell his story to his herculean mentor Jerônimo deep inside Jerônimo's cavern. In his hard-hearted demeanor and adherence to a vengeful code of honor, Jerônimo typifies the valley and its people. Time is a function of Alexandre's hallucinations as he tells of his childhood and his brief, brutal courtship of the farm girl Rosália, who grew up amid brutality and crime. Violence escalates as Rosália herself is killed or kills herself – certainty is impossible – and Alexandre kills her brother Roberto, who may or may not have fathered the child with which she is alleged to be pregnant. Blaming Alexandre for the deaths, the valley people want to hang him. He escapes over a mountain and nearly dies. He wanders for perhaps two years in the well-watered plantation zone and for a brief time seems to find spiritual peace. However, the trauma of witnessing the birth of a monstrous child to the daughter of Natanael, his benefactor and the soul of goodness, unhinges his mind once more. Suddenly he is back in the valley in Jerônimo's cavern, conversing with him. The story has come full circle, with time for little more than the narration of his own suicide by suffocation in the muddy slough.

As in *Os servos da morte,* Adonias is interested in depicting the inner states of his protagonists, even if they are illiterate, inarticulate country people whose minds can hardly be expected to be the stage for such an existential tragedy. More successfully than in the earlier work, the novelist in *Memórias de Lázaro* renews his effort to probe such minds. The universal theme of evil, with its litany of violence, lust, hatred, and vengeance, continues to fascinate him. He implies that people, not only of this region but everywhere, are like their literary symbol, the

*Adonias at his induction into the Academia Brasileira de Letras, 28 April 1966*

Ouro Valley – forbidding, unforgiving, uncivilized, and inhuman.

Struck by the strangeness and seeming unreality of Adonias's fictional world with its larger-than-life, even prophetic characters depicted in a language more universal than regional, critics have begun to apply the concepts of mythic criticism to *Memórias de Lázaro* and other novels. A recent example interprets Alexandre as a schizophrenic attempting to heal himself, even though such healing is negated (perhaps temporarily) by his "suicide." Alexandre's narration is consistent with his inward "mythical journey" or journey of healing as posited by Jungian psychologists. Adonias said that William Shakespeare and the myths of the Greek tragedians were a significant influence on him. With its deranged and unreliable narrator, its ambiguous chantlike language and narrative structure, and its plethora of symbols, *Memórias de Lázaro* has understandably lent itself to a variety of interpretations. For example, some read the work as a moral preachment on good and evil; others, no doubt influenced by the biblical story of Lazarus, have seen in it the Christian themes of sin (in the valley), redemption (in the forests of the plantation zone), and death. *Memórias de Lázaro,* as an early landmark among

novels based on the post-1945 aesthetic, was a critical success and, as Adonias said, his favorite among his works. It was translated into Spanish in 1970.

In the ten years following *Memórias de Lázaro* – with national politics marked by the suicide of President Getúlio Vargas in 1954, the rise of President Juscelino Kubitschek in the mid 1950s, followed by the inauguration of the new capital at Brasília in 1958 – Adonias published fragments of his critical journal, *Jornal de um escritor.* Four years later came the important essay "O romance da humildade" (The Novel of Humility), which introduces his one-volume edition of the fiction of fellow Catholic and friend Cornélio Penna, who died that same year. In 1958 Adonias also published the first volume of *Modernos ficcionistas brasileiros* (Modern Brazilian Fiction Writers), a selection from his critical articles of the 1940s and 1950s. A fundamental study of Brazilian fiction of the time, it includes "A revolução na estrutura" (The Structural Revolution) and fifteen other studies of contemporary novelists; the second series in 1965 adds several more.

By the mid 1950s Adonias was embarked on what were to be thirty years of service in positions of high public trust: in 1954 he was named director of the Serviço Nacional de Teatro (National Theater Service), in the following year interim director of the Instituto Nacional do Livro (National Book Institute). In 1961 he began a ten-year directorship of the National Library in Rio, which he jointly held with the directorship of the National Information Agency until 1964.

Based on a sketch of a novel going back to 1938, the third of the "cacao trilogy," *Corpo vivo* (Life Redeemed, 1962), proved to be the most successful of all his works. It had reached its twentieth printing by 1983. It is also his most widely translated novel, with versions in German, European Portuguese, Spanish, and Slovakian. Had there been an English translation, it would have had to contend with the ambiguous title, literally "living body" or "body alive." "Redeemed" seems justified in the case of a novel about redemption through love and its triumph over violence, hatred, and the increasingly insane obsession with revenge. Overtly religious motifs, found in works such as *Memórias de Lázaro* and elsewhere in Adonias's work, are absent from *Corpo vivo*.

A massacre begins the story. The family of the boy Cajango, living on a remote cacao plantation in the still-undeveloped interior of Ilhéus, is killed by marauders bent on taking their land. The sole survivor, Cajango escapes death and comes to manhood under the tutelage of his father's half brother Inuri, who despite some white blood lives like an Indian. Inuri trains him to become not only an expert marksman and jungle warrior but also the single-minded, unrelenting avenger of the deaths of his family. In time Cajango and his small band begin to wreak the long-desired vengeance while fending off attacks by his enemies. Cajango is as cruel as the cruelest of these. Unexpectedly, at a new juncture of the story, he meets Malva, a girl of the backlands, and falls in love, and even before the reprisals are complete and with a price on his head he escapes with her to the mountains and to a new life, but not before he has killed his kinsman Inuri, the incarnation of the vengeful spirit.

The novel consists of dramatically structured episodes. Although other narrators speak in *Corpo vivo,* the account belongs to João Caio, a drover of pack animals who heard or participated in the events. The omniscient author's voice has all but disappeared. The often lyrical narration is conveyed throughout in language that suggests but does not ape the language of the drover. Adonias maintains an atmosphere of strangeness and mystery that has led some critics to label the book magic realism. A new note of optimism has entered his work here. The clash of good and evil and the themes of vengeance and redemption are strikingly personified in the two lovers, who are believable simple folk. Furthermore, Adonias's poetic language, along with the "magical" atmosphere in which the characters seem to move, have appealed to interpreters of universal myth. As an example, Cajango and Malva are reminiscent of Adam and Eve, mythical hero and heroine escaping into the "sacred" space of forest and mountain, with the implicit promise of a rebirth of the Brazilian race.

When Adonias was inducted into the Academia Brasileira de Letras on 28 April 1965 in Rio de Janeiro, his close friend Jorge Amado gave a welcoming address, to which Adonias responded. Their two speeches were published as *A nação grapiuna: Adonias Filho na Academia* (The Grapiuna Nation: Adonias Filho in Academe, 1965). (*Grapiuna* is an ironic term used to describe inhabitants of the coastal area of Ilhéus by those from the extreme interior of that region.) Both speeches shed an interesting light not only on their rather different literary careers but also on their political stances: in Amado's case liberalism, in Adonias's conservativism. Adonias's reply is also a major statement of his political philosophy organized around the idea of freedom, especially in the context of the 1964 coup, with its escalating curtailment of civil and human rights by the military. In the year of the coup Adonias had published *O bloqueio cultural: O intelectual, a liberdade, a receptividade* (The Cultural Blockade: The Intellectual, Liberty, and Reception), an indictment of totalitarian communism and its multifarious attempts to "blockade" or repress intellectuals and artists. However, Adonias's focus in the long essay is not Brazil, but rather the United States and Europe and the tradition of liberal democracy.

In *O Forte* (The Fort, 1965), his fourth novel, Adonias turns away from southern Bahia and calls up some of his memories of the state capital Salvador, where he spent eight years as an intern in the Ginásio Ipiranga. Its central focus is Fort São Pedro, where Adonias received military training during World War II. A lyrical, even magical four-hundred-year history, *O Forte* is narrated mainly by Olegário, a black murderer now deceased who had been imprisoned in the fort. His mulatto granddaughter Tibiti and her lover Jairo look back on their years with Olegário and bring his voice to life. The fort likewise has a "voice," which on occasion can be heard by old Olegário or which "speaks" through him to re-create lively episodes of its history since colonial times. In the mid twentieth century Jairo, an engineer, is commissioned to level the fort. Its demolition signals a similar destruction of Tibiti's and Jairo's past – long separated, each has been unhappily married to someone else. Oblivious even to their children, Tibiti and Jairo pledge love to each other and start their lives anew. Clearly Adonias meant for the novel to be read as a historical metaphor based on the fort rather than as a love story.

Transforming itself over time – now threatening, now sheltering human liberty – the hulking, mysterious fort is a complex literary symbol inviting the reader's interpretation. It can be identified not only with Olegário and his people but with Bahia and Brazil – above all with their past. The myth of new beginnings found in earlier works echoes again through *O Forte*. In frequent references to folk *cantadores* (singers), Adonias underlines his own connection with these popular poets, often maintaining them as the link between twentieth-century novelists and past narrators of colonial times. Adding to the value of the book as an epic re-creation of history is its musicality, which in the simple poetic prose of *O Forte* rises to perhaps the highest level of intensity to be found anywhere in Adonias's oeuvre. Markedly different though it may be from his cacao cycle of novels, especially in its downplaying of violence, *O Forte* is considered by critics to be one of his best.

After twenty years of success as a novelist Adonias next turned to a shorter form of fiction. But first he lectured and traveled in the United States in 1967 and that same year took a sea voyage with other writers at the invitation of the Portuguese government to attend the II Congresso de Comunidades Portuguesas (Second Congress of Portuguese Communities) in Beira, Mozambique. The ship followed the course of the fifteenth-century Portuguese navigators who first rounded the Cape of Good Hope. A few years later the trip resulted in an unusual novel combining Brazilian, Portuguese, and African themes.

In the mid 1960s Adonias had been experimenting with the short story, or, as he called it, the *novela*. The term is imprecise in Brazilian literary usage but refers here to stories usually having several episodes. Adonias's are set in what was then the undeveloped and sometimes lawless territory of Itajuípe, where he was born. He called the collection *Léguas da promissão* (Promised Leagues, 1968), *leguas* connoting vastness and *promissão,* among other things, the biblical notion of "Promised Land." Ironically, the stories are about a land of barbarity and aggression. Even so the title is apt, for the stories about the territory also include by implication the idea of renewal and future progress. Some of the *novelas* show a kinship with the earlier

cacao novels, especially those in which dramatic scenes and episodes dominate. The rhythmic language is again equal to the best of the cacao trilogy. As he does with most of his novels, Adonias frames these stories: here a father is pointing out the sights to his son as they begin a train trip into the territory. Thus unified in space and embracing some one hundred years prior to 1930, when cacao growing and near-domination of the world cacao market was achieved, the six stories offer a panorama of social and ethnic types of the period. Scenes are impressionistically sketched by an artist interested in the reality as well as the mystery of life.

The six stories can be grouped variously by theme – as stories of love ("Imboti," "Um anjo mau" [An Evil Angel], "Simoa"); animals ("O pai" [The Father], "O túmulo das aves" [The Tomb of the Birds], "O rei" [The King]); revenge ("Imboti," "O pai," "O túmulo das aves," "Um anjo mau," "O rei"); and the mystical ("O túmulo das aves," "Um anjo mau," "Simoa"). As an example of the first category, Imboti is a Camacã Indian girl whose father has been killed by marauders bent on forcing the settlers off the land. Some years later Imboti is raped and killed by three ruffians. Francisco, her husband, narrates the bloody stages of his revenge on the three murderers. After the bloodbath is the suggestion of a mythical "rebirth" as his people, of mixed Indian-European extraction, celebrate amid feasting and song. A story with an animal motif, "O rei," which is the shortest of the *novelas,* describes the combat between a *carcará* (large hawk) and a hunter. Both are killers, and each is supreme in his domain – earth and sky. The hunter, who narrates, fires his rifle, sadly and reluctantly, only to salve the conscience of an old man physically unable to revenge himself upon the hawk, which had dived down and killed his grandson playing near his house. The story asks us to consider which killer is, ironically, "the King." An example of the mystical stories is "Um anjo mau." Martinho, a herculean black man, is a woodcutter and sometime prizefighter who comes to the aid of a young black girl, Açucena. As a ten-year-old child she was sold into prostitution by her mother after the child's father was killed. Years later Açucena demands that her lover take revenge on the killers of her own husband and child. However, as a righteous man and perhaps a Christian – there is one passing reference to "a cruz" (the cross) – Martinho refuses, but he is soon provoked by the murderers to take swift revenge to save Açucena's life. In 1971 "Um anjo mau" was made into a film by the respected São Paulo director Roberto Santos.

*Adonias with students after a 1967 lecture at the University of Texas at Austin*

True to his artistic creed of rejecting social preachment, Adonias creates a space of violence and death that often contrasts with an ideal or mythic space of contemplation or redemption. Mute but eloquent symbols such as the wild horses in "O pai," the hawk in "O rei," and the dead birds falling out of the sky in "O túmulo das aves" add to the ambiguity he seeks. Another source of ambiguity – and one requiring the reader's special attention – arises from Adonias's cinematic technique of cutting back and forth from present to past as he juxtaposes nonsequential time segments in a montage effect. Whether in first-person accounts or in third-person omniscient narration, simplicity of vocabulary and syntax, including the frequent omission of verbs, make the various kinds of discourse seem more colloquial.

In 1969 Adonias published twelve short critical studies in *O romance brasileiro de trinta* (The Brazilian Novel of the 1930s). The title refers to the post-1930 group of novelists preceding his own generation. The introductory chapters offer an interesting theory for the development of the so-called novel of the 1930s. Adonias emphasizes that Brazilian novelists' roots go back to the *oralidade* (orality) of folktales, plays, and various forms of balladry, including the *romances velhos* (ancient ballads) of colonial times. In recent years he has challenged literary historians to investigate these antecedents, particularly in the colonial centuries.

The literary result of Adonias's 1967 sea voyage to Africa was his 1971 novel *Luanda, Beira, Bahia* (respectively the capital of Angola, a seaport in Mozambique, and the capital of Bahia, also called Salvador). The protagonists of the novel are twentieth-century descendants of Pedro Alvares Cabral, the discoverer who linked Portugal, Brazil, Africa, and India in his famous voyage of 1500. The character João Joanes is a freckled, blond Brazilian sailor whose ancestry is specifically traced to Portugal. With an Indian woman in Ilhéus he fathers the mestizo Caúla, who will become a sailor like his father. Another character closely linked with Portugal is Manuel Sete, a hunter of leopards in the jungles of Angola. Years before with an Angolan woman he fathered Corina Mulele, who becomes the mulatto wife of João Joanes when he sails to Angola. Their daughter Iuta is destined to fall in love with Caúla in Luanda. By an irony of fate, he is her own half brother. For an instant there is an aura of Greek tragedy when Iuta and Caúla learn the truth from

João Joanes. Their violent deaths in Ilhéus are accorded mythic rites: the three are buried in a single casket made of part of a symbolic *jindiba* tree hewn in the shape of a funeral barge.

Love and fate here contribute to the theme of miscegenation found so frequently in Adonias's work; predominantly white Portuguese explorers and settlers in foreign lands were not hesitant to mate with brown and black women. In its lyricism, its historical themes, and its downplaying of violence *Luanda, Beira, Bahia* displays certain resemblances to *O Forte*. As they face out to sea some seamen may even commune with God, for God and the deep are part of the immense web of the novel, along with sirens and sea goddesses and the only real demons of the sea, the sharks. This is the first Brazilian novel to link Brazil, Portugal, and Africa in an epic of seafarers. The common language of Portuguese Africa and Portuguese America gives it unity. Despite its brevity, the novel offers an intricate fabric of maritime imagery, seascapes, marine flora and fauna, shipboard language and lore, and religion and superstitions from two continents. Nonetheless, because it may have seemed anomalous to Brazilian critics in its choice of subject matter and possibly because it may appear to have been created in response to a "sponsored" voyage, critics have not rated the novel as highly as Adonias's earlier works about cacao. Indeed, at times the work reads like a travelogue, with too many exotic motifs – for example, a trip to see wild animals during Caúla's sojourn in Beira, Mozambique – and perhaps too many extraneous sea yarns.

Adonias next published his highly acclaimed sixth novel, *As velhas* (The Old Women, 1975). Reflecting his sure-handed control of narrative techniques developed over the years and told in the stylized rhythmic language that suggests the colloquial without resorting to regional speech (except for limited use of regional vocabulary), the novel interweaves the life stories of four women born in the second half of the nineteenth century. As the story begins, all the women, contemporaries in their eighties, inhabit different parts of the southern jungles of Bahia. Tari Januária is a Pataxó Indian, Zefa Cinco a descendent of European immigrants, Zonga the child of former slaves, and Lina de Todos probably a mestiza. The framing device of this circular plot involves Tari Januária, who asks her son Tonho Beré to locate and bring home the bones of his father, the jaguar hunter Pedro Cobra who disappeared twenty years ago, so that she can die in peace. The quest eventually takes Tonho Beré and his young nephew to meet the other three *velhas*,

whose absorbing stories of their harsh lives finally lead to solving the mystery of Pedro Cobra.

The universal themes of courage and vengeance, death and redemption, are in some respects comparable to those found in such works as *Corpo vivo* and *Léguas da promissão*. The motivation of the women protagonists is limited to certain of their obsessions – for example, the recovery of a husband's bones, the search for a lost child, and in two cases the wreaking of vengeance. Pioneers in their fashion, survivors of bubonic plague and other disasters, the women have witnessed horrors, including in some cases the killing of parents, husbands, children, or grandchildren. At the end, the quest complete though the bones are never found, a sense of peace settles over Tari Januária. Tonho Beré observes, "Todas as velhas têm os seus mortos. A questão é saber se esses mortos ficaram ou se estão esperando na frente" (All the old women have their dead. The question is to know whether those dead stayed behind or if they are waiting up ahead). It is not surprising that Adonias once more broaches the ultimate themes of death and redemption and fashions a peaceful conclusion.

In the early and middle 1970s, with no sign of any easing in the military's repressive hold on Brazil, Adonias, the trusted public servant and at that time a member of the Conselho Federal de Cultura (Federal Council on Culture), continued unobtrusively trying to help intellectuals and others thread their way through the mazes of the dictatorship. Adonias said in a 1988 interview in *Jornal de Letras* with José Lívio Dantas that he considered the Conselho – and he also pointed to the Academia Brasileira de Letras – "o exemplo da melhor prática democrática que conheço" (the best example of democratic practice that I know of).

In 1975 he began a fruitful ten years of writing columns on themes of national interest for the Rio de Janeiro *Jornal do Comércio*. For the previous twenty-five years he had written and spoken on a wide range of topics in the fields of communications, transportation, and government as well as literature. His major nonliterary interest over the years was the history of Brazil's armed forces. Another activity was writing children's literature, as seen in *Uma nota de cem* (A Hundred-Cruzeiro Bill, 1973) and *Fora da pista* (Off the Beaten Track, 1978), a rollicking tale of contemporary adventure in southern Bahia dedicated to his grandchildren. Adonias also published a nonliterary essay indispensable for a full understanding and interpretation of his four cacao novels and related stories: *Sul da Bahia, chão de cacau: Uma civilização regional* (The Bahian South: Cacao Country – A Regional Civilization, 1976). A scholarly synthesis of what he calls "the regional civilization" based on cacao, *Sul da Bahia* reflects the author's wide knowledge of the political, socio-economic, and cultural history of this increasingly important region since the founding of Ilhéus by the Portuguese in 1535. Perhaps the central idea is that, in the process of settlement of the Bahian South, "o democratismo . . . é de fato o comportamento" (democracy . . . is indeed the basis of its social behavior). He points out the factors working against feudalism, aristocracy, and slavery and gives credit for social progress to the existence of medium and small land holdings and to the settlers' cooperativeness and respect for law – despite, one might add, the violence of some phases of the process.

Though adept at infusing his novels and stories with drama, Adonias was not a dramatist. His sole attempt in this genre, *O Auto dos Ilhéus* (The Drama of Ilhéus, 1981), stands closer to folk pageant than to theater in the usual sense. Deriving its name from the medieval auto, a short play given at public spectacles religious or profane, *O Auto dos Ilhéus* presents ten brief tableaux, each depicting a moment in the historical development of the region from 1535 to the present. Lacking in conventional dramatic action or characters, the auto seems intended to serve a ceremonial function in popular observances in Ilhéus.

In *O Largo da Palma* (Palm Square, 1981) Adonias returns to the Salvador of his novel *O Forte,* this time with six *novelas* about people from the middle and lower classes perhaps remembered from his student days. The ancient square with its church and plaza on a busy street in a city still retaining vestiges of its brilliant colonial past provides unity. A sadness pervades the atmosphere, even though a story may have a happy ending, as when, in "A moça dos pãezinhos de queijo" (The Girl Who Sold Cheesecakes), a mute boy discovers love with a shop girl and is at last able to utter one word, "amor" (love); or when, in "O largo de branco" (The Square in White), a wife, for many years estranged from her spouse, returns to a changed and now-loving husband. The tragic tone returns in "Um avô muito velho" (An Old, Old Grandfather). A young black girl is raped and beaten by a street gang. Her grandfather eases her slow death by his loving presence. Even in the confines of stories averaging fifteen pages, Adonias is interested in his characters' inner conflicts. His sympathy with the underdog goes without saying. As in all his works, something implicit – call it God, or perhaps an in-

Cover for Adonias's fictionalized biography of Jean-Henri Dunant, the founder of the International Red Cross

sight into the authentic self – often seems to rise above the grating facts of life. Constructed by a master of technique and sharp observer of the human condition, the stories, with their urbanized view of such themes as love, marriage, family, prostitution, and crime, have been well received by critics. However, neither this work nor his final two books published before his death have received the critical attention he could count on once as a leader of the "structural revolution" after World War II.

When Adonias first went to Rio de Janeiro, he lived near Catete Street, the short bustling thoroughfare between Largo do Machado and the Catete Palace. Except for a short story, "Catete: Amor no Catete," published in 1964, *Noite sem madrugada* (Night without Dawn, 1983) is his first literary recognition of nearly fifty years of principal residence in the great metropolis. *Noite sem madrugada* is a detective story in which an elderly lawyer unsuccessfully attempts to solve a murder for which his client Eduardo, a bookkeeper, is wrongly accused. Eduardo's wife Vilma similarly fails. When Eduardo is sentenced to prison and there is no longer hope, the real criminal is suddenly found thanks to the intervention of Vilma's friend Gabininha, a kindly black woman whose late husband consorted with criminals. His departed spirit may have helped locate the real murderer, as some of the characters no doubt believe; even today spiritualism has many adherents in Brazil. But the ordinary reader is unprepared for the abrupt ending. Adonias's world in this novel is vastly different from any of his earlier works: the criminal justice system, lawyers, witnesses, investigators, judges, defendants, and jailers. Adonias moves his suspenseful story skillfully in this new milieu, which he obviously understood well. The novel implicitly denounces injustice, mistreatment of prisoners, and corruption in the court system.

In 1985, after the dictatorship was replaced by an elected democratic government, Adonias stepped down from the directorship of the Conselho Federal de Cultura, stopped writing his weekly column for the *Jornal do Comércio,* and while maintaining his residence in Copacabana spent more and more time at his *fazenda* near Itajuípe. Three years before he died he published *O homem de branco* (The Man in White, 1987), a novelized biography of Jean-Henri Dunant (1828–1910), the Swiss founder of the International Red Cross. The biography is well written, but with its European locale and personages it is uncharacteristic of any of his preceding works. It could have been intended as an inspirational work for young Brazilians.

In a questionnaire prepared for Edla Van Steen's *Viver e escrever,* Adonias was asked to what extent a writer should participate in the public life of a country. Answering that he should mainly participate through his own writing, "o mais público de todos os atos" (the most public of all acts), Adonias observed that "o importante é que, acima dos fanatismos e dos dogmas ideológicos, o escritor seja um lógico a serviço dos bens da vida e da cultura como, por exemplo, a liberdade" (what is important is that, rising above fanaticisms and ideological dogmas, the writer be a logical thinker in the service of

the values of life and of culture, for example liberty). This self-styled Catholic writer, a quietly patriotic intellectual, wise, soft-spoken – even "bravio e misterioso" (wild and mysterious) like some of his characters in the words of his friend Rachel de Queiroz – has left no doubt about his right to a permanent place among the most original Brazilian novelists of the twentieth century. He died in Itajuípe on his plantation in southern Bahia on 2 August 1990 and was buried in Rio de Janeiro.

**Interview:**

Edla Van Steen, "Adonias Filho," *Viver e escrever* (São Paulo: L&PM, 1981); pp. 241–248.

**References:**

M. Fátima Albuquerque, "The Brazilian Nationalist Myth in Adonias Filho's *Corpo vivo,*" *Portuguese Studies,* 3 (1987): 149–158;

Assis Brasil, *Adonias Filho* (Rio de Janeiro: Organização Simões, 1969);

Sílvio Castro, "A moderna prosa de ficção: Adonias Filho," in his *A revolução da palavra* (Petrópolis, Brazil: Vozes, 1976); pp. 252–263;

Susan Hill Connor, "From Anti-Hero to Hero: The Rebirth Archetype," *Luso-Brazilian Review,* 16 (Winter 1979): 224–232;

Thomas Deveny, "Narrative Techniques in Adonias Filho's *Memórias de Lázaro,*" *Hispania,* 63 (May 1980): 321–327;

Fred P. Ellison, "The Schizophrenic Narrator and the Myth of Renewal in *Memórias de Lázaro,*" in *From Linguistics to Literature: Romance Studies Offered to Francis M. Rogers,* edited by Bernard H. Bichakjian (Amsterdam: Benjamins, 1981), pp. 155–166;

Maria do Carmo Figueiredo, "Percorrendo as *Léguas da promissão,*" *Luso-Brazilian Review,* 22 (Summer 1985): 33–49;

Daphne Patai, "Adonias Filho: The Myth of Malevolence," in her *Myth and Ideology in Contemporary Brazilian Fiction* (Rutherford, N. J.: Fairleigh Dickinson University Press, 1983), pp. 167–190;

Manuel Simões, "Introduçào à narrativa de Adonias Filho," *Studi di Letteratura Ispano-americana,* 11 (1981): 73–89.

# Demetrio Aguilera Malta

*(24 May 1909 – 29 December 1981)*

C. Michael Waag
*Murray State University*

BOOKS: *Primavera interior,* by Aguilera Malta and Jorge Pérez Concha (Guayaquil, Ecuador: Sociedad Filantrópica del Guayas, 1927);

*El libro de los mangleros* (Guayaquil, Ecuador, 1929);

*Leticia-Notas y comentarios de un periodista ecuatoriano* (Panama City: Talleres Gráficos Benedetti, 1932);

*Don Goyo* (Madrid: Cenit, 1933); translated by Enid Eder Perkins as "Don Goyo" in *Fiesta in November: Stories from Latin America,* edited by Angel Flores (Boston: Houghton Mifflin, 1942), pp. 120–228; translated by John Brushwood and Carolyn Brushwood as *Don Goyo* (Clifton, N.J.: Humana Press, 1980);

*C. Z. (Canal Zone): Los yanquis en Panamá* (Santiago, Chile-Ercilla, 1935);

*¡Madrid! Reportaje novelado de una retaguardia heróica* (Barcelona: Orion, 1937);

*España leal: Tragedia en un prólogo y tres actos, el último dividido en tres cuadros* (Quito, Ecuador: Ministerio de Educación, 1938);

*La isla virgen* (Guayaquil, Ecuador: Vera y Cía, 1942);

*Sangre azul,* by Aguilera Malta and Willis Knapp Jones (Washington, D.C.: Pan American Union, 1948); translated by Aguilera Malta and Jones as *Blue Blood* (Washington, D.C.: Pan American Union, 1948);

*Dos comedias fáciles* (Boston: Houghton Mifflin, 1950) – includes *Sangre azul* and *El pirata fantasma*;

*No bastan los átomos y Dientes blancos* (Quito, Ecuador: Casa de la Cultura Ecuatoriana, 1955);

*Dientes blancos* (Quito, Ecuador: Casa de la Cultura Ecuatoriana, 1956); translated by Robert Losada, Jr., as "White Teeth: A Play in One Act," *Odyssey Review,* 3 (March 1963): 19–36;

*El tigre: Pieza en un acto dividido en tres cuadros* (Quito, Ecuador: Casa de la Cultura Ecuatoriana, 1956);

*Honorarios* (Quito, Ecuador: Casa de la Cultura Ecuatoriana, 1957);

*Demetrio Aguilera Malta in his office, circa 1977 (photograph by Velia Márquez)*

*Trilogía ecuatoriana: Teatro breve* (Mexico City: De Andrea, 1959) – includes *Honorarios, Dientes blancos,* and *El tigre*;

*Una cruz en la Sierra Maestra* (Buenos Aires: Sophos, 1960);

*El Quijote de El Dorado: Orellana y el río de las Amazonas* (Madrid: Guadarrama, 1964);

13

*La caballeresa del sol: El gran amor de Bolívar* (Madrid: Guadarrama, 1964); translated by Jones as *Manuela, la caballeresa del sol* (Carbondale: Southern Illinois University Press, 1967);

*Un nuevo mar para el rey: Balboa, Anayansi y el Océano Pacífico* (Madrid: Guadarrama, 1965);

*Infierno negro: Pieza en dos actos* (Xalapa: Universidad Veracruzana, 1967); translated by Elizabeth Lowe as *Black Hell* in *Modern International Drama*, 10 (Spring 1977): 9–42;

*Guayaquil 70: Metrópoli dinámica,* by Aguilera Malta, Juan Aguilera Malta, Fausto Aguilera Malta, and Fernando Aguilera Malta (Guayaquil: Publicaciones Aguilera Malta, 1970);

*Siete lunas y siete serpientes* (Mexico City: Fondo de Cultura Económica, 1970); translated by Gregory Rabassa as *Seven Serpents and Seven Moons* (Austin: University of Texas Press, 1979);

*Teatro completo* (Mexico City: Finisterre, 1970) – includes *España leal, Lázaro, No bastan los átomos, Honorarios, Dientes blancos, El tigre, Fantouche, Muerte, S.A., Infierno negro*;

*El cuento actual latino-americano,* by Aguilera Malta and Manuel Mejía Valera (Mexico City: De Andrea, 1973);

*El secuestro del general* (Mexico City: Joaquín Mortiz, 1973); translated by Peter G. Earle as *Babelandia* (Clifton, N.J.: Humana Press, 1985);

*Hechos y leyendas de nuestra América: Relatos hispanoamericanos* (Mexico City: Talleres Gráficos de la Nación, 1975);

*Jaguar* (Mexico City: Grijalbo, 1977);

*Réquiem para el diablo* (Mexico City: Joaquín Mortiz, 1978);

*Una pelota, un sueño y diez centavos* (Mexico City: Joaquín Mortiz, 1988).

MOTION PICTURES: *La cadena infinita,* screenplay by Aguilera Malta and Velia Márquez, produced by Aguilera Malta, 1948;

*Entre dos carnavales,* screenplay by Aguilera Malta and Márquez, produced by Aguilera Malta, Arco Iris, 1951;

*Dos ángeles y medio,* screenplay by Aguilera Malta and Márquez, produced by Aguilera Malta and Carlos Corredor Pardo, 1958.

OTHER: *Los que se van: Cuentos del cholo i del montuvio,* by Aguilera Malta, Joaquín Gallegos Lara and Enrique Gil Gilbert (Guayaquil, Ecuador: Zea y Paladines, 1930);

"Una mujer para cada acto," by Aguilera Malta and Velia Márquez, in Márquez, *Tres comedias* (Mexico City: Finisterre, 1970).

SELECTED PERIODICAL PUBLICATION – UNCOLLECTED: "Amor y vino," by Aguilera Malta and Willis Knapp Jones, *Revista de la Casa de la Cultura Ecuatoriana,* 2, no. 3 (1946): 292–311.

Demetrio Aguilera Malta was a man of great talent and energy who traveled widely and accumulated varied experiences. At the end of his long life he had been a businessman, painter, world traveler, diplomat, teacher, artist, poet, playwright, editor, essayist, critic, journalist, and filmmaker, as well as one of Ecuador's greatest writers of fiction. He was a member of the Grupo de Guayaquil, five young writers who achieved fame in the 1930s for their social-realist fiction about Ecuador's coastal campesinos. With the possible exception of Jorge Icaza's *Huasipungo* (1934; translated 1964), Aguilera Malta's literary works have received more international critical attention over the last sixty years than those of any other Ecuadoran writer. His plays and short stories have been extensively anthologized; four of his novels have been translated into English and other languages, and in the extensive critical literature on his works he has been cited as one of the initiators of the magic-realist mode in Latin-American fiction.

Demetrio Aguilera Malta was born in Guayaquil, Ecuador, on 24 May 1909 to Demetrio Flaviano Aguilera Sánchez and Teresa Malta Franco. He attended two primary schools, the Colegio San Jóse and the Escuela Municipal Nelson Mateus, and received his secondary education at the Colegio Nacional Vicente Rocafuerte in Guayaquil. In 1922 at age thirteen he witnessed the massacre of striking workers by the police and military in the streets of Guayaquil, an event that left a profound impression on him, as it did on many writers of his generation. He was among the founders of the Ecuadoran Socialist party in 1926. Aguilera Malta studied law for two years at the Universidad de Guayaquil while attending classes at the Escuela de Bellas Artes. He spent five years on San Ignacio, one of the many islands in the Guayas estuary in the Gulf of Guayaquil, living with the people of Native American and African descent he would write about throughout his career. In particular, he met a man, probably a shaman steeped in native tradition, who would be the inspiration for the protagonists of several of his best works.

Aguilera Malta began his literary career during his adolescence with a poem, "Páginas de amor," published in the journal *Cromos* in 1924. He continued to publish his poetry in newspapers and journals, most notably in *Savia,* which was directed by Gerardo Gallegos. Aguilera Malta worked on the journal *América,* which in the mid 1920s had an international reputation as the most important literary and ideological publication in Ecuador, and founded two literary journals, *Ideal* in 1924 and *Voluntad* in 1927. With a student, Jorge Pérez Concha, he published a slim volume of poetry called *Primavera interior* in 1927. Aguilera Malta published his own poetry, *El libro de los mangleros,* in 1929, adorned with his sketches.

Throughout the 1930s and most of the 1940s Aguilera Malta supported himself as an educator, librarian, and journalist while writing his most important literary works. In 1930 he went to Panama, where he had his own column, "Savia," in the *Diario de Panamá.* He also wrote for *La Estrella de Panamá* and *Hoy* while sending articles to *El Universo* in his native Guayaquil. In 1936 he was awarded a scholarship to study in Salamanca, Spain, but his academic plans were thwarted by the outbreak of the Spanish Civil War. Aguilera Malta joined the Republican forces and went to work as a reporter, sending off material on the war from Madrid. Later he went to Barcelona, where he stayed until he left Spain along with other international volunteers. He returned to Guayaquil, where he founded yet another journal, *Trópico,* in 1938. Aguilera Malta's essays and journalistic pieces have appeared in major newspapers and journals all over Latin America and in the United States. His nonfiction is largely literary criticism, but he has also written pieces on Latin-American history, philosophy, international relations, and politics. Perhaps his most important essay is "Leticia" (1932), in which he discusses a border dispute between Ecuador, Colombia, and Peru and denounces the policies of Peruvian president Sánchez Cerro. In the course of his career as a freelance writer and occasional professional journalist, Aguilera Malta published approximately two thousand articles.

When Aguilera Malta returned to Ecuador from Spain in 1937 he was appointed undersecretary for education. He held teaching positions at home and abroad. From 1937 to 1943 he taught at the Colegio Nacional Vicente Rocafuerte and was a visiting professor at universities in Guatemala, Mexico, Brazil, and the United States (Howard University and Scripps College). In the late 1940s he represented Ecuador at diplomatic posts in Argentina, Mexico, Brazil, Uruguay, and Chile. He also served with the Office for Intellectual Cooperation at the Pan American Union in Washington, D.C.

Aguilera Malta first came to international attention as a writer of fiction in 1930 through his contribution of eight stories to *Los que se van: Cuentos del cholo i del montuvio* (Those Who Go Away: Stories of the Coastal People). The volume, published with Enrique Gil Gilbert and Joaquín Gallegos Lara, was the point of departure for a major transformation in Ecuadoran letters. With José de la Cuadra and Alfredo Paraja Diezcanseco, these authors came to be known as the Grupo de Guayaquil, *cinco como un puño* (five like a fist). All five wrote major novels during Ecuador's socialrealist period of the 1930s and 1940s. *Los que se van* scandalized Ecuador but instantly caught the attention of international critics who recognized its innovative qualities. Twenty-four stories in a similar style compose the volume; eight works by each of the three authors are intermingled in order to emphasize the solidarity of the group. The stories are not propagandistic, and nowhere is there any heavy-handed presentation of a thesis. The tales are earthy accounts of dramatic incidents in the lives of rural coastal people and blacks. Often the incidents emphasize and even exaggerate brutality, violence, and crudity. The dialogue imitates coastal Ecuadoran Spanish, and its metaphors reflect the world and psychology of the characters. Most important, the tone is never patronizing or denigrating. Even in the most aberrant incidents people are portrayed as human and admirably vital. Aguilera Malta's "El cholo que se vengó" (The Cholo Who Avenged Himself) and "El cholo que odió la plata" (The Cholo Who Hated Money) are the two most frequently anthologized stories from the collection.

In the late 1930s Aguilera Malta began to work in the theater. He was inspired no doubt by his recent experience in Spain and the need to champion the Republican cause and wrote his first dramatic work, *España leal* (Loyal Spain), which deals with the Spanish Civil War. It was published and premiered in Guayaquil in 1938. In 1941 he was teaching literature at his alma mater, the Colegio Nacional Vicente Rocafuerte in Guayaquil. A new boys' high school was under construction in the city, but funds had run out before it could be completely furnished. Aguilera Malta was asked to write a play in order to raise money to buy equipment for the school theater. The result was *Lázaro,* the tragic story of an inspired schoolteacher who, out of personal penury and lack of resources for public education, is driven to forsake his calling and invest his time and energy in menial activities to eke out a living. The play was an immense success and has probably been staged more often than any other in Ecuador.

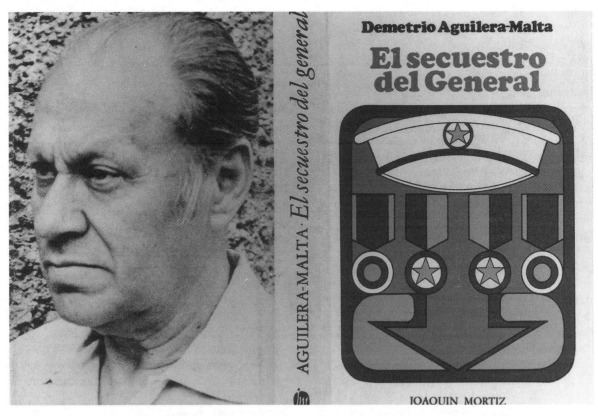

*Dust jacket for Aguilera Malta's 1973 novel, inspired by contemporary Ecuadoran politics*

In 1946 Aguilera Malta worked with North American professor Willis Knapp Jones on the drama *Sangre azul* (Blue Blood, 1948), which deals with the influence of North America on Latin-American culture. *El pirata fantasma* (The Ghost Pirate), a suspenseful comedy, and *Sangre azul* were published in the United States in *Dos comedias fáciles* (Two Easy Comedies) in 1950. *Dientes blancos* (White Teeth, 1956) marks a departure from his earlier plays and a tendency toward expressionism, which increasingly dominated his plays. The play denounces racism in an atmosphere reminiscent of the works of Eugene O'Neill. Other plays include *El tigre* (The Jaguar, 1956), *Honorarios* (1957), *Fantoche* (The Puppet, circa 1961), *Infierno negro* (Black Hell, 1967), *Muerte S.A.* (Death Inc., 1970), and *Una mujer para cada acto* (A Woman for Each Act, 1960, with Velia Márquez). The frequently anthologized *El tigre* is the most important of his plays. The situation, characters, and action are taken from an episode in the novel *La isla virgen* (The Virgin Island, 1942) and are expanded, still later, to form the basis for the novel *Jaguar* (1977). *Infierno negro* was also novelized as *Réquiem para el diablo* (Requiem for the Devil, 1978). According to Gerardo A. Luzuriaga, Aguilera Malta's plays become more expressionistic

beginning with *Dientes blancos* and culminating in *Infierno negro*.

It was during his diplomatic stay in Chile in the late 1940s that Aguilera Malta turned his time, energy, and savings to making a film. Together with Velia Márquez he wrote the script for *La cadena infinita* (The Infinite Chain, 1948), based on his unpublished novel "Tierra de esperanza" (Land of Hope). Actor José Bohr directed the film, which dealt with the plight of Spanish immigrants fleeing to Latin America. The project failed and left Aguilera Malta destitute. In 1951 he went to Brazil, where he made yet another feature film, *Entre dos carnavales* (Between Two Carnivals). He returned to Ecuador, where he made newsreels and short films about the churches of Quito and Ecuador's Salasaca and Colorado Indians.

Aguilera Malta's fame rests heavily on his career as a novelist. He published thirteen novels that fall into four categories: two early novels about people of the Ecuadoran coast, which are the most important works of his career; three novels written in response to specific political situations and events; three historical novels written in the 1960s; and five novels written in the 1970s influenced by the Latin-American New Novel.

After his initial success with *Los que se van*, Aguilera Malta abandoned the short story and published his first novel, *Don Goyo* (1933; translated as *Don Goyo,* 1942, 1980). His intention was to portray the beauty, vitality, and genius of a group of coastal dwellers steeped in indigenous tropical-forest culture and to expose the mechanisms through which implacable economic forces from Guayaquil and the developed world bring about deculturation and the destruction of a long-standing culture and viable way of life.

Don Goyo Quimí is the patriarch of an island community in the Guayas estuary. Being 150 years old, he has a vast knowledge of the intricate workings of the forest and guards the remnants of an ancient culture. He speaks with the mangrove trees and considers himself physically and spiritually associated with them in an intimate, symbiotic relationship. Don Goyo is both a real and a mythical figure to the islanders. His fleeting first appearance is preceded by the eerie sight of a glowing cigar ash that mysteriously moves across the black water on a tropical forest night. A humble "buenas noches de Dios" (God's good evening to you) spoken from an unseen canoe heralds an imposing figure.

The principal conflict in the novel develops with the appearance of Don Carlos, a white trader from Guayaquil, who wants the islanders to collect and sell him mangrove bark, which is valuable as a source of tannin. However, the mangrove tree is also important as a source of food to the island because of the marine life that attaches itself to its immersed roots, from which they are collected at low tide. Don Goyo does all he can to discourage Don Carlos's commercial exploitation and destruction of the mangrove, but in the end the old patriarch is unsuccessful. Don Goyo's concern stems not only from practical considerations but also from mythical prohibitions and insights learned through his communication with the great trees. He knows that serious consequences will result from abandoning the old ways and adopting an economy that abuses the delicate relationship between native man and his constant provider, nature. In the face of hard times, however, Don Carlos's short-term solution to economic difficulties is convenient, and the islanders are too far removed from the world of Don Goyo to be convinced by the patriarch's arguments. They do not see that in giving up their native means of sustenance and entering into the money economy, they are exchanging their dependence on their island habitat, a relatively reliable provider, for dependence on an economic system that will draw them in, strip away alternative means of sustenance,

and leave them vulnerable to exploitation as laborers. The process is irreversible: once the land, traditional technology, and unifying mythology are lost, they can never be recovered. Don Goyo is the repository of an ancient culture, the last high priest responsible for its continuation. When he dies the greatest mangrove in the estuary falls. His rejection by the islanders and his magical death symbolize the death of an indigenous culture.

Although classified as *criollista* fiction, *Don Goyo* constitutes a departure from novels such as José Eustacio Rivera's *La vorágine* (1924; translated as *The Vortex,* 1935). Rivera's protagonist, lost in Amazonia, struggles against a seemingly chaotic environment with which he is culturally unequipped to cope and ultimately is consumed, defeated, or devoured by it. Aguilera Malta's Don Goyo does not seek to dominate nature but to understand its complex laws and interact cooperatively with it. The tropical forest does not destroy or swallow up man but rather sustains him.

*Don Goyo* is also an important work in the history of the contemporary Spanish-American novel, for it is one of the earliest manifestations of magic realism (or *lo real maravilloso* to use the term coined by Alejo Carpentier). Essential to the literary mode is a non-Western cosmology embraced by narrator and characters with complete belief. What seems magical to Western readers is real, even mundane, to Don Goyo and others who populate the fictional world of the novel. Both magic realism and the portrayal of a symbiotic relationship between man and the tropical forest result from the work's vision of reality seen from a native rather than an exclusively European perspective. The non-Western worldview implied through the action and attitude of the characters in *Don Goyo* is what sets it apart from *criollista* fiction and makes it historically important.

*La isla virgen* is the second of Aguilera Malta's novels about Ecuadoran coastal people, and it differs from the first by presenting two protagonists with contrasting worldviews representative of the native and European cultural currents that coexist in much of Latin America. The counterpart of Don Goyo is Guayamabe. He is the faithful majordomo of an island plantation owned by Don Néstor, a white man from Guayaquil. Except for the island of San Pancracio, the once wealthy Néstor is destitute. In a desperate attempt to recover his fortune, he has come to the island hoping to get rich quickly and return to his accustomed high standard of living in Guayaquil and Paris. Don Néstor is somewhat like Rivera's protagonist, a man of European cultural origins thrust by adverse circumstances into the tropical forest and forced to cope with an alien environment. Time and again Guayamabe warns Nestor against pursuing schemes to make the island profitable. At first Nestor ignores Guayamabe's advice, and the projects consistently fail. With patience and self-assurance, Guayamabe remains at Nestor's side and does his bidding because he knows that Nestor depends on him for the knowledge required to cope with the tropical island, a microcosm of tropical America. Subservience in this case, however, is voluntary and reflects Guayamabe's heartfelt obligation to educate Nestor and other outsiders in the ways of the tropical forest. The relationship becomes more characteristic of a father and son than of a master and peon. Nestor becomes ever more aware of the inadequacy of his orientation and resolves to achieve a level of competence in dealing with the island.

The bicultural, egalitarian relationship portrayed in *La isla virgen* is the novel's innovation, and it indirectly denounces the denigration and destruction of native cultural traditions that hold the keys to adaptation in the New World. Successful colonization of the tropics must be a reeducation process for the colonizer in the alien but more appropriate ways of his new environment. As Guayamabe says to Nestor, "Nadie nace sabiendo, patrón. . . . Todos los hombres servimos para todo, patrón. Es cuestión de acostumbrarse. Y en estas tierras hay que saber de todo, si queremos vivir en ellas" ("Nobody is born knowing how, boss. . . . We can all do what needs to be done, boss. It's just a question of getting accustomed. In this country one has to know about everything if we want to live here").

In the final scene of the novel Nestor, distraught after a series of disasters and in an anxious state of mind, walks toward the center of the island. His symbolic walk signals his acquiescence to another view of reality and another way of life based on an acceptance of the island, in its unaltered form, as a habitable environment. He relinquishes his former self, which has remained firmly rooted in European culture, and completes a transformation to a hypothetical modern American man capable of adopting native tradition in adjusting to the New World.

While Aguilera Malta lived and worked as a journalist in Panama in the early 1930s, he wrote the first of three novels that deal with international situations. *C. Z. (Canal Zone): Los yanquis en Panamá* (C.Z. [Canal Zone]: The Yankees in Panama, 1935) evokes a collective identity crisis among the people of this isthmian republic due to the presence of the United States. Racial prejudice held by North American whites against blacks is a major theme

of the novel. The subject became a constant in Aguilera Malta's works, especially his plays.

In addition to his journalism and his first play, his experience in Spain at the time of the Spanish Civil War resulted in the novel *¡Madrid! Reportaje novelado de una retaguardia heróica* (Madrid!: A Fictional Account of a Heroic Rearguard, 1937), a passionate account of the struggle for the Spanish Republican cause. The first edition was published in Barcelona at the height of hostilities and came out in five subsequent printings, but like *Canal Zone,* even though it commanded great attention at the time of its publication, its importance has not endured. A similar fate befell *Una cruz en la Sierra Maestra* (A Cross in the Sierra Maestra, 1960), a fictionalized account set in Cuba of the revolutionary struggle to overthrow the Batista government in the late 1950s. The Cuban Revolution renewed Aguilera Malta's interest in the novel, which he had abandoned after 1942 in favor of film, theater, and other pursuits.

During the 1960s Aguilera Malta planned his *Episodios americanos* (American Episodes), a twelve-volume series of historical novels with artistic and didactic intent concerning the men, women, and events that make up Latin-American history. Only three volumes of the series were ever completed: *El Quijote de El Dorado: Orellana y el río de las Amazonas* (The Quixote of El Dorado, 1964), about Francisco de Orellana's descent down the Amazon River; *La caballeresa del sol: El gran amor de Bolívar* (1964; translated as *Manuela, la caballeresa del sol,* 1967, on the relationship between Manuela Sáenz and Simón Bolívar during and after the wars for independence; and *Un nuevo mar para el rey: Balboa, Anayansi y el Océano Pacífico* (A New Sea for the King: Balboa, Anayansi, and the Pacific Ocean, 1965), which tells of the discovery of the Pacific Ocean and the tragic fate of its discoverer, Núñez de Balboa. The small volume *Hechos y leyendas de nuestra América: Relatos hispánoamericanos* (Facts and Legends of Our America: Spanish-American Stories, 1975) — which contains very short versions of the above narratives as well as others titled "Pizarro y el Tahuantinsuyo" (Pizarro and the Tahuantinsuyo) and "Morelos, torrente incontenible" (Morelos, an Unstoppable Torrent) — provides some idea of the original conception of the series. Other figures from Latin-American history to be included in the series were La Malinche, Cortez's mistress during the conquest of Mexico; Domingo Faustino Sarmiento of Argentina; the liberator San Martín; Gen. Francisco Morazán of Honduras; and the imperial couple Maximilian and Carlota of Mexico.

No doubt what led Aguilera Malta to abandon his series of historical novels was the advent of the Latin-American New Novel. During the 1970s Aguilera Malta published four novels that mark a departure from the style of his earlier work and demonstrate an intense interest in the new forms, techniques, and vision that had shifted the attention of the international reading public to Latin-American fiction. However, he never lost his concern for authenticity and never abandoned Ecuadoran literary tradition. Most of what he wrote in the 1970s has strong links to his early work.

*Siete lunas y siete serpientes* (1970; translated as *Seven Serpents and Seven Moons,* 1979) brings Ecuadoran fiction into the mainstream of the Latin-American New Novel. Humor, especially exaggeration and overstatement, is the quality that most distinguishes this novel from the author's earlier work and from Ecuadoran fiction up to that time. The action is set in Santorontón, a village beyond time and geography but nevertheless reminiscent of the towns around the Guayas estuary, the setting of *Don Goyo* and *La isla virgen. Siete lunas y siete serpientes* uses multiple themes as well as flashbacks, internal monologue, temporal fragmentation, simultaneity of action, and mythical elements of African, Western, and Native American origin.

Various lines of action that develop multiple subthemes are unified by a main narrative concerning the brutal, homicidal Col. Candelario Mariscal. Against the wishes and interests of the Santorontón oligarchy, Candelario is to marry Dominga, the daughter of the black shaman, Bulu-Bulu. The shaman himself prescribed marriage for the colonel as the means of escaping the depredations of a phantom nymphomaniac, Chepa Quindales, who nightly seeks to avenge the victimization of her family. Candelario is the adopted godson of village priest Father Cándido, whose constant companion is a partially burned, living, speaking crucifix. Cristo Quemado, as it is called, suffered disfigurement when Candelario, a delinquent youth at the time, burned down the priest's palm-thatched church, the last of many pranks the old priest endured before disowning and banishing his godson from Santorontón. Reconciliation between godfather and godson and Candelario's marriage are the two potential events that unify the novel. A series of secondary conflicts reflects the main conflict and gives breadth to the narrative: Father Cándido with his social ministry is pitted against the traditional Father Gaudencio, for whom the church and the oligarchy are one; a humane doctor comes into conflict with an exploitative practitioner who profits from his

Cover for Aguilera Malta's 1977 novel, an expansion of his play El tigre (1956), about a beast that represents the magic of its tropical setting

mistakes by doubling as the town's only undertaker; and a pathological capitalist, Chalena, seeks to monopolize all access to water in order to gain total control over the people of Santorontón.

At the thematic core of the novel is the universal struggle between good and evil, with both Christ and the devil as symbolic characters fulfilling their respective roles in Western cosmology. Added to the traditional conflict, however, is a third role, the powerful shaman Bulu-Bulu and the non-Western cosmological forces he controls and represents. There is no major resolution to the plot; the action of the last few chapters paints a tableau much like a chessboard in midgame, offering a vision of existing powers, tensions, conflicts, and potentials, but without any clear indication of what will happen next. The critical move, however, falls to Bulu-Bulu. He assumes the form of a jaguar and ascends to the top of a great tree in order to consult with the magical forces at his disposal about his decision to marry his

19

daughter to Candelario. The marriage had seemed a hideous prospect to many at first, but the logic behind it now becomes clear: only the colonel's formidable image carries sufficient power to offset the malevolent forces of Chalena and the oligarchy. Evil as Candelario is, he has one saving grace: his respect for his godfather, Father Cándido, and his heartfelt yearning for a reconciliation with him. Thus the colonel is potentially linked to the positive forces represented by Father Cándido and a resistance movement in Santorontón.

In *Siete lunas y siete serpientes* Aguilera Malta focuses on contemporary problems common to all Latin America and plays them out in a magical microcosm set in a milieu similar to the Ecuadoran coast. It is given over to his own artifice, recombining various cultural and mythical elements from multiple cultural sources. He is not so much concerned with an authentic portrayal of life in the novel as with the creation of a parable about economics, politics, and culture in contemporary Latin America, cast in an archetypal thematic framework of apocalyptic struggle. Nearly forty years after *Don Goyo,* Aguilera Malta interprets Ecuadoran reality with much greater distance and from many points of view, including politics, morality, psychology, and myth.

*El secuestro del general* (The Kidnapping of the General, 1973; translated as *Babelandia,* 1985) is a satire that uses grotesque caricature as the principal device for achieving a humorous but nevertheless bitter denunciation of oppression in various forms. Seeking to portray the causes of revolution and the rise of popular guerrilla forces, the novel was inspired by political events in Ecuador around 1970, including the dictatorship of perennial populist José María Velasco Ibarra, the prominence and heavy-handed behavior of the military during his regime, and the kidnapping of a general that was probably a sham but was never explained to the public's satisfaction. Still, it is not merely a political novel, since it easily transcends history and unfolds a story, laden with symbolism, in the eternal moment and remote setting of myth.

Holofernes Verbofilia, the dictator, rules over the republic of Babelandia from his palace in the capital city of the same name. He is not a flesh-and-blood person but a robotlike *Esqueleto-disfrazado-de-hombre* (skeleton disguised as a man) with a special aperture in his chest for inserting cassette tape recordings of rousing public speeches for almost every occasion. He is especially fond of making speeches and sending his slithering ophidian spies through the crowd to keep an eye on any *anti-verbofilistas*. When he needs a general he pulls one out of a closet, where he keeps a large supply of them. He depends on the military, the *gorilas* (gorillas), and especially on the brutish and brutal Jonás Pitecántropo, to put down any opposition. The grotesque caricature of the dictator is typical of the novel's style and is also applied to the dictator's collaborators, beginning with their names: Baco Alfombra, the dictator's ingratiating private secretary; the urbane Fofo Opíparo; Equino Cascabel, the servile but treacherous secretary of defense; and Cerdo Rigoletto, the voracious secretary of state. Aguilera Malta considered the technique he employed similar to a comic strip, and indeed the narrative has the unreal, expressionistic flavor of a distorted Dick Tracy world somewhere between reality and fantasy.

The action develops in three settings, each with its distinct atmosphere: Babelandia, the comic domain of the dictator and his regime; Laberinto, a lugubrious provincial village where oppression of the spirit is a way of life; and the crater of a volcano where guerrilla fighters of all past ages reincarnate from time to time just as the volcano itself periodically becomes active. Through fragmentation of the narrative, the action in all three settings is presented simultaneously. The kidnapping of the general eventually brings the characters of all three together in the crater of the volcano.

The Amautas, or revolutionaries, live in the village of Laberinto, where prejudice, fear, and narrow-mindedness fester and suffocate the spirit of all trapped within the "pueblo de mil vericuetos, fácil entrada, difícil salida, enredadera de estómagos hambrientosos y cerebros cautivos" (town of a thousand alleys, of easy entry and difficult escape, a trap for empty stomachs and captive minds). Laberinto is a microcosm of Babelandia, but here the narrative focuses on characterization rather than on quickly sketched caricatures. Humor gives way to dark, macabre Goyaesque tones while oppression and abuse of power give rise to ignorance, superstition, violence, and sexual perversion. In Laberinto the Amautas Fúlgido Estrella, Eneas Roturante, Teófilo Brillo, and María suffer, resist, and are stoned to death at the hands of the Laberínticos, urged on by the salacious, narrow-minded priest Padre Polígamo. Nevertheless, we meet the Amautas again in the crater, where the general is held prisoner and where the dictator's allies have come to seek a compromise with the Amautas to reestablish themselves in the imminent new regime. The Amautas explain that they have no interest in changing the personnel in the existing system but intend to create a new, just, and viable society.

Ecuadorans speculated wildly about the mysterious unexplained kidnapping of a general in 1970. In writing *El secuestro del general,* Aguilera Malta laid aside verisimilitude and tapped into a rich current of popular fantasy to produce a work at once humorous and bitterly remonstrative, yet marked with Aguilera Malta's indomitable hope for the future of Ecuador and Latin America.

With *Jaguar* Aguilera Malta abandoned the purely mythical space of Santorontón or Babelandia and returned to the geographically identifiable but no less mysterious island-choked mouth of the Guayas River, the setting of *Don Goyo* and *La isla virgen.* The place, situation, and characters of *Jaguar* that fascinated Aguilera Malta throughout his literary career first appeared as an episode in *La isla virgen.* The episode was then extracted from the 1942 novel and developed into the drama *El tigre.* *Jaguar* is the same story amplified into a novel.

As in the play the action begins with three men who sit before a smoldering fire in the tropical forest as darkness steals over them. They talk about a fourth man, Zambo Aguayo, who lives in fear of El Tigre. This dreaded adversary may be two animals, one that lives in reality and another existing only in Aguayo's mind, or it may be just one animal occupying both physical and metaphysical space. The exact identity of the tiger is never made clear. Standing in contrast to Aguayo is the old majordomo Guayamabe, El Hombre-del-Cigarro (The Man with the Cigar). Guayamabe knows the ways of the mysterious tropical archipelago; he comprehends its order and does not fear the jaguar. Zambo Aguayo has fallen victim either to his own hysteria or to the terrifying powers of the animal, depending on the reader's interpretation. Not even the love of the beautiful Domitila can save him. Attempts to trap the jaguar are fruitless even when Aguayo himself courageously waits all night as the human bait in the trap. The cooperation of all the inhabitants of the island is insufficient to track down the beast. Aguayo's attempt to flee with Domitila to Guayaquil is thwarted by the intervention of the jaguar himself, and the incident serves to underscore the hopelessness of Aguayo's situation and to establish the impossibility of escaping his horrible fate.

The story is fleshed out with character development and background. The love affair between Aguayo and Domitila is expanded into a secondary plot complicated by a rival suitor, Domitila's cousin, Seberón Mite. Mite and his band of *Mala-Almas* are waterborne cattle rustlers or pirates who prey on the island landowners and successfully elude the pursuing rural police with magical deftness. Aguilera Malta achieves simultaneity of action by shifting from one character and plot line to another and suspense by cutting scenes at a point when tension has reached a maximum and begs for resolution.

With *Jaguar* Aguilera Malta reviews his earlier work armed with the techniques of the New Novel. The magical element subtly portrayed in his earlier novels is deliberately exploited in *Jaguar.* However, the unreal rings with greater authenticity in the earlier novels for having been taken directly from reality and put into literature with the naiveté of youth at the risk that always accompanies innovation.

Like *Jaguar, Réquiem para el diablo* is a novelization of one of Aguilera Malta's dramas, *Infierno negro.* The central character in *Réquiem para el diablo* is Hórridus Nabus, an ingenious inventor who has abandoned his youthful ideals in favor of acquiring material wealth and power. To achieve this end he proffers his genius to a corrupt oligarchy, Los Mandamás (the Big Shots), and develops schemes and devices that permit them increased control and more-efficient exploitation of the citizenry. Los Mandamás are made up of allegorical figures with suggestive names and sarcastic epithets: the banker, Crespo Topo, "El Depositario-del-oro-de-casi-toda-la Nación" (the Depository-of-all-the-wealth-in-the-nation); the unscrupulous industrialist, Arácnido Mefítico; the presumptuous, inarticulate General Pim-pam-pum, "Bonaparte de bolsillo" (Pocket Bonaparte); the effeminate Feto Eunuco, "Pico de Rubí" (Ruby Beak), the silver-tongued orator who defends with unctuous rhetoric the actions of the oligarchy, no matter how immoral or absurd they might be; and Mater Salamandra, an enormous jewel-laden woman who represents the notion that one's level of consumption is the perfect indicator of human worth. A group of characters called Los Cuatro Silenciosos Vestidos de Momias (The Four Silent Ones Dressed as Mummies) sit in a corner of the room under the influence of sedatives. By doing the bidding of the oligarchy, often to the detriment of their own interests, they represent an apathetic, compliant public.

The action is set in two distinct domains: Nylónpolis, an Orwellian state where Hórridus has lived out his life; and an extraterrestrial domain where the inventor faces judgment for his earthly conduct. Here four black youths recite excerpts of black verse by poets from all over the Americas, including Nicolás Guillén, Luis Palés Matos, and Langston Hughes, among others. The poetry

Cover for Aguilera Malta's 1978 novel, based on his play Infierno negro (1967),
about a Faustian inventor who allows a corrupt government to use
his creations to exploit its citizens

evokes the black experience in the Americas and links it to the absurd abuses and racist values of Nylónpolis. Hórridus is condemned to the Black Hell, where he will suffer all the horrors that have been the fate of blacks in the Americas.

Of all Aguilera Malta's novels, *Réquiem para el diablo* is the most experimental in its form, just as the expressionistic *Infierno negro* was his most experimental play. Among his perennial themes – such as racial prejudice, speculation and monopolization of essential resources, the evils of oligarchy and international economic dependency – are some new concerns, such as environmental pollution and the malaise known as *que-me-importismo,* or apathy born of a self-serving attitude that undercuts the potential for national solidarity and leaves the nation open to international exploitation and dependency.

Aguilera Malta updated the story to include two chapters treating Ecuador's experience since 1972 as an oil-producing nation. Magnus Skatos is

the agent of a transnational corporation who comes to Nylónpolis to develop and export the nation's oil reserves. Just as Hórridus has provided the oligarchy with devices with which to exploit the Nylónpolitanos in the past, he now allies himself with the foreign technocrats hoping to share in the impending oil wealth. With the author's typical irony, a radio announcer urges the Nylónpolitanos to ignore what they see, hear, and think and to trust blindly in the foreigners who have come to exploit the nation's natural resources, which will soon cause money to rain down in such quantities that the Nylónpolitanos will be able to paper their walls with bills. The marvelous foreign technocrats will not only build an oil pipeline around the world but will transport the tropical nation to a temperate latitude in the north more propitious for oil exploitation. In *Réquiem para el diablo,* the final novel of his career, Aguilera Malta once again focused on aspects of Ecuadoran reality that are taken for granted and amplified them to their absurd extreme in order to expose the contradictions of Ecuadoran life.

Aguilera Malta died in Mexico in 1981, where he had made his home with his second wife and collaborator, Velia Márquez, since 1958. *Una pelota, un sueño y diez centavos* (A Ball, a Dream, and Ten Cents) is a novel published posthumously in 1988 from a manuscript that Aguilera Malta left unfinished. As in most of the novels of the 1970s, the action takes place in a distorted setting, Macrópolis, where the familiar and mundane are mixed with the futuristic and unreal. The flavor of the work has much in common with *Réquiem para el diablo,* and one character appears in both novels. The story deals with soccer, "the sport of the multitudes." The truncated main plot takes place over the course of four or five hours, interrupted by multiple flashbacks and simultaneous action throughout its fourteen chapters. The central characters are two brothers. The older, Juan Angel (Rumba Eterna [Eternal Rumba]), is a hunchback who has raised his younger brother, Luis Ernesto or Pata de Aguila (Eagle Foot), to excel as a soccer player and become the national sports hero. Luis Ernesto makes an extraordinary goal to win a critical match. His instant fame attracts the Mandamás who seek to buy Luis Ernesto. Tension builds in anticipation of Luis's decisions on how to handle fame and fortune: will he be co-opted by the powerful manipulators of El Palacio de las Pelotas (Soccer Ball Palace) located in the Los Ricachos (the Rich Folks) suburb, or will he return to his own poor neighborhood and maintain allegiance to those who helped him rise in a static class society? According to the *nota final* (final note) by Velia Márquez, the manuscript lacked only eight pages to be finished. Certainly Aguilera Malta intended to say something about exploiting society's need for idols and the lot of the idols themselves. Still, with an unfinished work, one can only speculate about its intended theme.

Demetrio Aguilera Malta's early fiction – *Don Goyo, La isla virgen,* and his short stories in *Los que se van* – is his most important contribution to Ecuadoran and Latin-American literature. The innovations in his early work charted new ground and pointed the way for other Latin-American writers. His later novels and especially *Siete lunas y siete serpientes* owe much to the formal innovations associated with the Latin-American New Novel. That is, Aguilera Malta's later works are inspired by literature while the earlier ones take their inspiration directly from the reality he personally observed on the islands of the Guayas River. It is ironic that in his later years Aguilera Malta followed in the wake of an established tradition, the Latin-American New Novel, while in his youth he took innovative steps that led to the establishment of the very tradition he was to model. Nevertheless, *Siete lunas y siete serpientes* is an especially important novel, since its publication in 1970 seems to have empowered a new generation of Ecuadoran writers to embrace the Latin-American New Novel and embark on what may turn out to be the richest decade of the century for Ecuadoran fiction.

**Interviews:**

Orlando Cabrera Leyva, "Entrevista a Demetrio Aguilera Malta," *Letras del Ecuador,* 33 (1948): 14;

D. L. Pitty, "Ser antiimperialista resulta una actividad vital: Aguilera-Malta, entrevista," *El Gallo Ilustrado,* supplement of *El Día,* 26 October 1975;

Anthony Fama, "Entrevista con Demetrio Aguilera-Malta," *Chasqui: Revista de Literatura Latinoamericana,* 7 (May 1978): 16–23;

Elide Pittarello, "Conversando con Demetrio Aguilera Malta," *Studi de Letteratura Ispano-Americana,* 12 (1982): 31–47.

**Bibliography:**

Pedro Frank de Andrea, "Demetrio Aguilera Malta: Bibliografía," *Boletín de la Comunidad Latinoamericana de Escritores,* 5 (September 1969): 23–58.

**References:**

Allen, "El simbolismo empleado en *El secuestro del general,*" *Explicación de Textos Literarios,* 8 (1979–1980): 145–151;

Allen, "La obra literaria de Demetrio Aguilera Malta," *Mundo Nuevo,* 41 (1969): 53–62;

Giuseppe Bellini, "Magia e realtà nella narrativa di Demetrio Aguilera Malta," *Studi di Letteratura Ispano-Americana,* 4 (1972): 7–53;

Alejandro Carrión, "Demetrio Aguilera Malta," in *Diccionario de la literatura latinoamericana: Ecuador,* by Carrión and Isaac J. Barrera (Washington, D.C.: Union Panamericana, 1962), pp. 75–78;

Boyd G. Carter, "La novelística de Aguilera-Malta: Enfoques y pareceres," *Chasqui: Revista de Literatura Latinoamericana,* 3 (May 1974): 66–70;

"Demetrio Aguilera-Malta: Breves datos sobre su vida y obra," in Aguilera Malta's *C. Z.*

*(Canal Zone),* second edition (Mexico City: Andrea, 1966), pp. 5–9;

Luis A. Díez, "The Apocalyptic Tropics of Aguilera Malta," *Latin American Literary Review,* 10 (Spring–Summer 1982): 31–40;

Nora Eidelberg, "La ritualización de la violencia en cuatro obras teatrales hispanoamericanas," *Latin American Theater Review,* 13 (1979): 29–37;

Anthony Fama, *Realismo mágico en la narrativa de Aguilera-Malta* (Madrid: Playor, 1977);

Renán Flores Jaramillo, "Demetrio Aguilera-Malta," *Cuadernos Hispanoamericanos,* no. 348 (1979): 623–637;

Michael H. Handelsman, *"El secuestro del general, El pueblo soy yo* y la desmitificación del Caudillo," *Revista Interamericana,* 10 (Summer 1980): 135–142;

Karl H. Heise, *El grupo de Guayaquil: Arte y técnica de sus novelas sociales* (Madrid: Playor, 1975);

Phillip Koldewyn, "Protesta guerrillera y mitología: Novela nueva de Aguilera Malta," *Nueva Narrativa Hispanoamericana,* 5 (1975): 199–205;

Gerardo A. Luzuriaga, "Aguilera-Malta se incorpora a la nueva narrativa," *Nueva Narrativa Hispanoamericana,* 1 (1971): 219–224;

Luzuriaga, *Del realismo al expresionismo: El teatro de Aguilera Malta* (Madrid: Plaza Mayor, 1971);

Marta Morello-Frosch, "El realismo integrador de *Siete lunas y siete serpientes* de Demetrio Aguilera Malta," in *Otros mundos otros fuegos: Fantasía y realismo mágico en Iberoamérica,* edited by Donald A. Yates (East Lansing: Michigan State University Press, 1975), pp. 385–390;

Clementine Christos Rabassa, *Demetrio Aguilera-Malta and Social Justice* (Rutherford, N.J.: Fairleigh Dickinson University Press, 1980);

Rabassa, "Materia literaria: La épica, la narrativa, y Demetrio Aguilera Malta," *Nueva Narrativa Hispanoamericana,* 4 (1974): 261–268;

William L. Siemens, "The Antichrist-Figure in Three Latin American Novels," in *The Power of Myth in Literature and Film,* edited by Victor Carrabino (Tallahassee: Florida University Press, 1980), pp. 113–121;

Guillermo Antonio Villegas, "Mecanismo de dramatización de un mito: *El tigre* de Aguilera-Malta," *Thesaurus,* 33 (1978): 247–253;

C. Michael Waag, "Absurdity, Hyperbole and the Grotesque in Demetrio Aguilera Malta's Last Novel, *Réquiem para el diablo,*" *SECOLAS Annals,* 20 (March 1989): 56–62;

Waag, "Sátira política a través de la historia mitificada: *El secuestro del general* de Demetrio Aguilera Malta," *Revista Iberoamericana,* 55 (1988): 771–778.

# Claribel Alegría

## (12 May 1924 – )

### Margaret B. Crosby
*University of New Mexico*

BOOKS: *Anillo de silencio* (Mexico City: Botas, 1948);

*Suite de amor, angustia y soledad* (Mendoza, Argentina: Brigadas Líricas, 1950);

*Vigilias* (Mexico City: Poesía de América, 1953);

*Acuario* (Santiago: Universitario, 1955);

*Tres cuentos* (San Salvador: Ministerio de Cultura, 1958);

*Huésped de mi tiempo* (Buenos Aires: Américalee, 1961);

*Vía única* (Montevideo: Alfa, 1965);

*Cenizas de Izalco,* by Alegría and Darwin J. Flakoll (Barcelona: Seix Barral, 1966); translated by Flakoll as *Ashes of Izalco* (Willimantic, Conn.: Curbstone Press, 1989);

*Aprendizaje* (San Salvador: Universitaria de El Salvador, 1970);

*Pagaré a cobrar* (Barcelona: Ocnos, 1973);

*El detén* (Barcelona: Lúmen, 1977); translated by Amanda Hopkinson as "The Talisman" in Alegría's *Family Album* (Willimantic, Conn.: Curbstone Press, 1991);

*Sobrevivo* (Havana: Casa de las Américas, 1978);

*La encrucijada salvadoreña,* by Alegría and Flakoll (Barcelona: CIDOB, 1980);

*Suma y sigue* (Madrid: Visor, 1981);

*Album familiar* (San José, Costa Rica: Editorial Universitaria Centroamericana, 1982); translated by Hopkinson as "Family Album" in Alegría's *Family Album*;

*Nicaragua: La revolución sandinista – Una crónica política, 1855-1979,* by Alegría and Flakoll (Mexico City: Era, 1982);

*No me agarran viva: La mujer salvadoreña en lucha,* by Alegría and Flakoll (Mexico City: Era, 1983; San Salvador: UCA, 1987); translated by Hopkinson as *They Won't Take Me Alive: Salvadoran Women in Struggle for National Liberation* (London: Women's Press, 1987);

*Poesía viva* (London: Blackrose Press, 1983);

*Claribel Alegría, 1987 (photograph by Lars Hansen)*

*Para romper el silencio: Resistencia y lucha en las cárceles salvadoreñas,* by Alegría and Flakoll (Mexico City: Era, 1984);

*Pueblo de Dios y de Mandinga* (Mexico City: Era, 1985); translated by Hopkinson as "Village of God and the Devil" in Alegría's *Family Album*;

*Petit pays* (Paris: Editions des Femmes, 1985);

*Despierta, mi bien, despierta* (San Salvador: UCA, 1986);

*Luisa en el país de la realidad* (Mexico City: Universidad Autónoma de Zacatecas, 1987); translated by Flakoll as *Luisa in Realityland* (Willimantic, Conn.: Curbstone Press, 1987);

*Mujer del río* (Colombia: Museo Rayo, 1987); translated by Flakoll as *Woman of the River* (Pittsburgh: University of Pittsburgh Press, 1989);

*Y este poema río* (Managua: Nueva Nicaragua, 1988).

**Edition in English:** *Flores del volcán/Flowers from the Volcano,* bilingual edition, translated by Carolyn Forché (Pittsburgh: University of Pittsburgh Press, 1982).

OTHER: *New Voices of Hispanic America,* edited and translated by Alegría and Darwin J. Flakoll (Boston: Beacon, 1962);

Miguel Angel Asturias, *The Cyclone,* translated by Alegría and Flakoll (London: Peter Owen, 1967);

Morris West, *El hereje,* translated by Alegría and Flakoll (Barcelona: Pomaire, 1969);

*Unstill Life: An Introduction to the Spanish Poetry of Latin America,* edited by Mario Benedetti, translated by Alegría and Flakoll (New York: Harcourt, Brace & World, 1969);

*Homenaje a El Salvador,* edited by Alberto Corazón, with an introductory essay by Alegría (Madrid: Visor, 1981);

*Nuevas voces de norteamérica,* bilingual edition, edited and translated by Alegría and Flakoll (Barcelona: Plaza y Janés, 1981);

Robert Graves, *Cien poemas de Robert Graves,* translated by Alegría and Flakoll (Barcelona: Lumen, 1982);

Carlos Fonseca, *Viva Sandino,* translated by Alegría and Flakoll (Managua: Vanguardia, 1985);

"The Writer's Commitment," in *Lives on the Line: The Testimony of Contemporary Latin American Authors,* edited by Doris Meyer (Berkeley, Los Angeles & London: University of California Press, 1988), pp. 306–311;

"The Politics of Exile," in *You Can't Drown the Fire: Latin American Women Writing in Exile,* edited by Alicia Portnoy (Pittsburgh & San Francisco: Cleis Press, 1988), pp. 171–177;

*On the Front Line: Guerrilla Poems of El Salvador,* edited and translated by Alegría and Flakoll (Willimantic, Conn.: Curbstone Press, 1989);

Noam Chomsky, *Nuestra pequeña región de por aquí: Política de seguridad de los Estados Unidos,* translated by Alegría and Flakoll (Nicaragua: Nueva Nicaragua, 1989);

Salman Rushdie, *La sonrisa del Jaguar,* translated by Alegría and Flakoll (Managua: Vanguardia, 1989);

"Our Little Region," in *Being América: Essays on Art, Literature, and Identity from Latin America,* edited by Rachel Weiss and Alan West (Fredonia, N.Y.: White Pine Press, 1991), pp. 41–50.

SELECTED PERIODICAL PUBLICATIONS – UNCOLLECTED: "Literatura y liberación nacional en El Salvador," *Casa de las Américas,* 21 (1981): 12–16;

"The Two Cultures of El Salvador," *Massachusetts Review,* 27 (Fall–Winter 1986): 493–502.

"My main concern, rather than to talk about me, is to talk about my countries," says Claribel Alegría in the Fall 1989 issue of *Curbstone Ink.* "To talk about what is happening in El Salvador and Nicaragua is important," she continues. "Just to let people know what is happening right there, right then: that's my main concern. Nicaragua and El Salvador. I consider them both my countries."

Alegría, who was born in Nicaragua on 12 May 1924 and grew up in El Salvador, is one of the major contemporary voices in the struggle for liberation in Central America. As a poet, novelist, essayist, storyteller, translator, and indefatigable human-rights activist, she combines both love and revolution, the personal and the political, in her work. It reflects not only a strong commitment to Latin-American social change, but also her concern for the status of Latin-American women. As Nancy Saporta Sternbach observes, "Women of all ages and stages of growth and personal evolution populate her work. Whether Alegría is writing testimony or fiction, poetry or essay, the voice, the heart, the mind of women – Latin American women – are central and omnipresent. From an early age, Alegría defined herself as a feminist, as her work amply demonstrates."

Alegría divides her work into two categories: literary-poetic and *letras de emergencia* (emergency letters). The first category refers to the sentimental, introspective, lyrical poetry that typifies her early collections published from 1948 to 1961. The second category describes her politically conscious poetry and prose, published from 1965 to the present. These works address the prevailing realities and problems in her Central American homeland. As she explains in her 1988 essay "The Writer's Commitment," *letras de emergencia* is a phrase that captures "the double meaning of urgency and the emerging spirit of her work" and is a response to a crisis situation. She further defines this concept in her essay "Our Little Region" (1991), where she says that it "is any book, poem, article or speech that openly defends a cause or situation in which [the writer] deeply believes, such as the Nicaraguan Sandinista revolution or the necessity for a thorough political revolution in El Salvador." Whether her reply to the political crisis in her countries is expressed by writing or by speaking at international

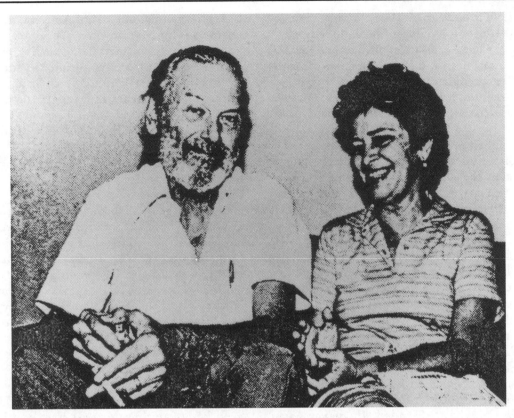

*Alegría with Darwin J. Flakoll, her husband and occasional collaborator and translator (photograph by Margaret Randall)*

symposia about Central America, it is a heartfelt response that characterizes all of her work.

Alegría believes it is crucial for artists to take sides and commit themselves to the struggle for liberation. In commenting on the role of the artist, she adamantly states in "Our Little Region" that "Any artist who avoids commitment in the struggle is guilty at least of ivory tower escapism and at worst of complicity with the Squadrons of Death and the total militarization of society." Furthermore, in "The Writer's Commitment" and also in an interview with American poet Carolyn Forché she admits that if she were to meet a Central American writer who sidestepped political commitment and favored the Latin-American Right, she would refuse to be his or her friend.

Born in Estelí, Nicaragua, Alegría is the daughter of a Salvadoran mother, Ana María Vides, and a Nicaraguan exile. Her father, Daniel Alegría, was a medical doctor and an anti-interventionist during the U.S. Marine occupation of Nicaragua in 1924. Since he openly opposed the marines' presence in his country, they terrorized him and his family by aiming and firing at his wife and six-month-old daughter. Three months later the family

fled Nicaragua and settled in Santa Ana, El Salvador where Alegría was raised and educated. From El Salvador her father helped Augusto César Sandino, who initiated the Sandinista movement in 1927 and who led the peasant uprising against the U.S. occupation of Nicaragua. In 1934 Sandino was assassinated. After that there was a price on Daniel Alegría's head, and he could only return to Nicaragua clandestinely.

In 1943 Alegría came to the United States, where she received a bachelor of arts degree in philosophy and letters from George Washington University. During this time she was the protégée of Juan Ramón Jiménez, the renowned Spanish poet and recipient of the 1956 Nobel Prize for literature. Jiménez taught Alegría the rigor, discipline, and craft of writing, and his influence can be seen in her early volumes of poetry. In 1947 Alegría married Darwin J. ("Bud") Flakoll, a U.S.-born journalist she met at George Washington University.

Alegría published *Anillo de silencio* (Ring of Silence), her first collection of poems, in 1948. This book marked the beginning of several collections of subjective, lyrical, and somewhat introspective and self-searching poetry. Her first narrative piece was

*Tres cuentos* (Three Stories, 1958), a collection of three short stories for children. In all three stories, according to Diane E. Marting in *Women Writers of Spanish America,* "flora and fauna communicate with children, revealing a special fantasy world. . . . [T]he impossible becomes the possible . . . and the fine line between dreams and reality is temporarily banished."

The Cuban revolution in 1959 represented a turning point in Alegría's life. To her the revolution demonstrated that social and political change in Latin America as well as an end to U.S. imperialism and oppression in Cuba were possible. The events of the revolution also raised her political consciousness and caused her to depart from what she calls the egotistical navel gazing and childhood nostalgia of her earlier works. As her global perspective expanded, her poetry began to change, focusing more on the misery, injustice, and brutal repression in El Salvador and Nicaragua.

During the course of their life together, Alegría and Flakoll have traveled, lived, and worked in the United States, Argentina, Chile, Mexico, Nicaragua, France, and Spain. In 1961 they lived in Uruguay, where he worked for the American embassy. During this time they befriended Uruguayan writers such as Mario Benedetti, Carlos Martínez Moreno, Carlos Real de Azúa, Idea Vilariño, and Manolo Claps.

From 1962 to 1966 they lived in Paris, where they associated regularly with the Latin-American Boom novelists Julio Cortázar (Argentina), Carlos Fuentes (Mexico), and Mario Vargas Llosa (Peru) – all of whom were at that time committed political leftists. In addition, Alegría and her husband began a lifelong friendship with Cortázar and his two wives, first Aurora Bernárdez and later Carol Dunlop.

During this period Alegría became obsessed with Latin-American politics and literature as well as her childhood memories. Fuentes urged her to write a novel based on her memories of the 1932 peasant uprising at Izalco, El Salvador, where dictator Gen. Maximiliano Hernández Martínez and his army slaughtered thirty thousand peasants and Indians in the name of anticommunism. Since writing about the massacre was both painful and difficult for her, Flakoll suggested they write the novel together. The result was *Cenizas de Izalco* (1966; translated as *Ashes of Izalco,* 1989). Published by Seix Barral, a major Barcelona press, the novel was a finalist for the publisher's annual literary prize.

The novel anticipates Alegría's subsequent recurring themes: mother-daughter relationships, U.S. intervention in Central America, female/male relations, Third World–First World relations, political repression as reality and metaphor, and revolution as the eruption of a volcano. In addition, the *matanza* (massacre) of 1932, which forms the setting in this novel, appears as a regular motif in other works. As a historical novel, *Cenizas de Izalco* is one of the first El Salvadoran novels to deal with the horror of the 1932 insurrection.

The relationship between mother and daughter forms the nucleus around which all other conflicts in the novel revolve. The protagonist, Carmen, a bourgeois El Salvadoran woman who lives in Washington, D.C., returns to El Salvador for her mother's funeral. Married to a conservative gringo, Carmen experiences an identity crisis roused by her mother's death and her reading of the diary her mother left to her. The diary, which belongs to her mother's secret North American lover, "serves as a bridge between the cultural, social revolution (the political sphere) and the private, intimate one (the personal) of one woman's life," according to Sternbach. Carmen realizes that she has never known her mother and that they both have been stifled by the same cultural constraints. They have lived lonely and meaningless lives restricted by a lack of personal autonomy and intellectual freedom. The novel also critiques the sexist and racist social structure that subordinates women and peasants.

In order to write the novel, Alegría and Flakoll traveled to El Salvador in 1964 to do research on the massacre. There they discovered that General Hernández Martínez had performed what *Curbstone Ink* termed a "cultural lobotomy on the Salvadoran people." In a 1986 essay, "The Two Cultures of El Salvador," Alegría explains that in 1932 General Hernández Martínez "ordered the destruction of all newspaper files in the country that dealt with the bloody events of those days. Libraries were ransacked to make sure no documentation of the massacre remained . . . the only documentation we could find consisted of three yellowed newspaper clippings a friend had hidden in his private library and a brief account in William Krehm's book *Democracies and Tyrannies in the Caribbean.* All the rest we had to reconstruct from my childhood memories of when I was seven years old and what grown-ups had told me in hushed tones as I grew older."

The events of 1932 have had a profound effect on Alegría. In talking with Forché she recalls, "I remember the Guardias Nacionales (National Guard) bringing dozens of prisoners into the fortress across the street from my home with their thumbs tied behind them with bits of cord, shoving them along with rifle butts. I remember the shots at night." "And then," she says in an excerpt from *Curbstone Ink,* "I started learning at a tender age about the terrible injustices."

When *Cenizas de Izalco* was first published, the Alegría family did not like its criticism of their upper-class standing and burned most of the first edition. Consequently, the novel did not reach El Salvador until ten years later. According to Alegría, Col. Arturo Armando Molina, the El Salvadoran dictator at the time, wanted to leave office as a great liberal. Shortly before the end of his term in 1976 he requested that all Salvadoran writers be included in the publications of the El Salvadoran ministry of culture. They published *Cenizas de Izalco* without reading it, classifying it as a high-school textbook because the title spoke of El Salvador. Alegría believes that since then the novel continues to be available in El Salvador because it has the seal of the ministry of culture. It has gone through twenty printings, and within El Salvador it is her best-known work.

In 1966 Alegría and her husband moved to the village of Deyá on the island of Majorca, Spain. There they spent twelve tranquil and productive years, resulting in the publication of several joint translations. In addition, Alegría published three volumes of poetry – *Aprendizaje* (Apprenticeship, 1970), *Pagaré a cobrar* (Installment Payments, 1973), and *Sobrevivo* (I Survive, 1978) – as well as a novella, *El detén* (1977; translated as "The Talisman" in *Family Album,* 1991). In this novella Alegría treats the shocking subject of a young woman's sexual abuse. Karen, the fifteen-year-old Central American protagonist, attends a Catholic boarding school in the United States, where she befriends the bitter and aloof Sister Mary Ann. Throughout their conversations, Karen shares her memories of her childhood friends as well as her sexual abuse by her mother's sadistic boyfriend. Karen learns that the nun is also a survivor of sexual abuse.

The novella is important for several reasons. First, Alegría makes central to the novel two themes that emerged in *Cenizas de Izalco:* the sexual oppression and powerlessness of women, and the relationship between mother and daughter. Second, she critiques Catholicism and its inherent condoning of physical abuse, personal suffering, and the denial of pain such as that experienced by the nuns and boarding school students who must prove their love for the Lord. Finally, by treating a rather taboo subject such as sexual abuse, she leads the El Salvadoran novel in a new direction: from an overt concern for linguistic experimentation, narrative technique, and social realism, all of which typified

*Cover for Alegría's 1977 novel, about sexual abuse and the Catholic church*

El Salvadoran fiction of the 1970s, to a preoccupation with feminist and women's issues.

The late 1970s represent a significant period in Alegría's life, characterized by a stronger political commitment on her part. In 1978 *Sobrevivo* won Cuba's prestigious Casa de las Américas prize for poetry. In this collection Alegría the "spokespoet" serves as an eyewitness to certain events. Through pre-Columbian myths and Central American history and geography Alegría addresses cultural imperialism, family relationships, exile, poverty, class differences, torture, disappearance, death, and the urgent need to change the political and social situation in her homeland. Electa Arenal contends that in *Sobrevivo* Alegría "asserts the strength of human life and mourns human suffering," adding that "the title refers both to the daily act of surviving and to the miracle and the guilt of surviving in our times."

In 1979, at age fifty-five, Alegría with her husband returned to Nicaragua for the first time since she fled the country as a small child. This visit represented another turning point in her life as she witnessed the triumph of the Sandinista movement and the end of Somocismo, the dictatorship of Anastasio Somoza and his two sons. As Arenal observes, "Alegría's [political] exile and return to Nicaragua run parallel to the history of the Sandinista [resistance] movement. This almost lifelong exile taught perseverance and gave perspective." For the next six months, Alegría and Flakoll traveled throughout Nicaragua gathering information and testimonies from people associated with the revolution for a five-hundred-page book of history and testimony entitled *Nicaragua: La revolución sandinista – Una crónica política, 1855–1979* (Nicaragua: The Sandinista Revolution – A Political Chronicle, 1855–1979). They did the actual writing in Majorca and published the book in 1982.

In 1982 Alegría also published *Flores del volcán/Flowers from the Volcano,* a book of previously published poems translated into English by Forché, and a novella, *Album familiar* (translated in *Family Album,* 1991). In the latter she returns to the theme of political awakening that had emerged earlier in *Cenizas de Izalco.* While the main action takes place in Paris, where the protagonist Ximena lives, a subplot occurs in Managua, Nicaragua, in 1978, on the day Edén Pastora seizes the national palace in a concerted effort to overthrow the Somoza regime. Alegría shows how Ximena, an upper-middle-class El Salvadoran–Nicaraguan wife and teacher, explores her relationships with her French husband, other family members, and nanny. When her politically active cousin confronts her fears and indifference as well as the disparity between her familial values and the nature of Central American reality, her political and social consciousness is awakened, and she commits to helping the revolutionary cause and the construction of a new Nicaraguan society.

During the 1980s testimonies dominated both El Salvadoran poetry and prose. With Flakoll, Alegría published two testimonial works that echo the voices of marginalized and oppressed people. The first work, *No me agarran viva: La mujer salvadoreña en lucha* (1983; translated as *They Won't Take Me Alive: Salvadoran Women in Struggle for National Liberation,* 1987), is dedicated to the thousands of Salvadoran girls and women who continue to fight courageously in the struggle for liberation. The book charts the politicization and militarization of Eugenia, a young woman from a bourgeois background who joins the guerrilla forces, becomes a

commanding officer, and later dies in the struggle. The reader learns about her through the testimonies of her sisters, friends, and other companions, at the same time learning about women of different social classes whose testimonies describe their experiences with war and their ability to survive hardship. In addition, the book describes Eugenia's relationship with her politically active husband, outlines and discusses the problem of machismo within the revolutionary organizations, and explores the role of the children of revolutionaries and their participation in the struggle. Eugenia incarnates the "new Salvadoran woman" and the new revolutionary subject. Her story speaks collectively for countless other women who have valiantly risked their lives so that others may live a life of peace.

The second work, *Para romper el silencio: Resistencia y lucha en las cárceles salvadoreñas* (Breaking the Silence: Resistance and Struggle in Salvadoran Prisons, 1984), is the testimony of Toño, a politically aware student leader who spent two years incarcerated as a political prisoner. The book recounts his ordeal as well as the tribulations and testimonies of many other political prisoners. Covering a six-year period, the book describes in detail the prisoners' daily suffering and the methods of torture the authorities used on them. While the book is painful to read at times, it also conveys hope. When the prisoners organize to demand more food as well as improvements in sanitary facilities and general living conditions, each request granted represents a small triumph. By singing collectively and scratching messages in a communal cork cup passed around the prison, they restore and maintain a sense of self while giving voice and dignity to their struggle.

Between 1985 and 1987 Alegría stopped writing poetry and testimonies to create three novels. The first of these, *Pueblo de Dios y de Mandinga* (1985; translated as "Village of God and the Devil" in *Family Album,* 1991), depicts the life of Slim and Marcia, a married couple who have recently moved from Paris to Deyá, Majorca. Their relationship suggests an autobiographical parallel to that of Alegría and Flakoll. In this work Alegría radically departs from some of the recurring themes seen in her previous novels to delve into magic realism. The novel humorously treats the idiosyncrasies of the local people, whose traditions and behavior are steeped in legends, folklore, superstitions, and rituals. Everyday life is a bizarre mixture of the supernatural and natural worlds, including the creation of a black hole that escapes from a rusted old bird cage where it is stored.

One of the major themes of the novel is nostalgia for life before tourists began to invade the island every summer. The town of Deyá is in a transition period in which the traditional way of life is dying out due to rapid population growth and construction. Sensing that things will never be the same as they once were, Slim and Marcia decide to return to Central America, where Marcia finds comfort in her ceiba tree.

The second novel Alegría published during this period was *Despierta, mi bien, despierta* (Wake Up, My Love, Wake Up, 1986). As Sternbach notes, "The intersection of a feminist and political consciousness in her female protagonists" is a recurring theme in novels such as *Cenizas de Izalco* and *Album familiar. Despierta, mi bien, despierta* also exemplifies this theme. Sternbach explains, "Speakers in the poems and protagonists in her fiction are often Central American women who have chosen a comfortable, bourgeois life outside their country. Furthermore, these women are not in a state of political exile, but rather are complacently content with their washing machines and other technological comforts."

The novel takes place in 1980, a few months before the assassination of El Salvadoran archbishop Oscar Romero. The protagonist, Lorena, is an upper-middle-class El Salvadoran woman married to a member of the oligarchy. Although her social class affords her many privileges, her life is virtually meaningless. She is lonely and bored, and her marriage is dull. When she has an affair with a young guerrilla poet she meets at a writer's workshop, she becomes more attuned to the political and social situation in her country. As a result, her consciousness is raised and her dormant sexuality awakened. Furthermore, she volunteers to help Archbishop Romero and the revolutionary cause by doing clerical work at his office.

*Despierta, mi bien, despierta* adheres to a formula that Alegría began in *Cenizas de Izalco,* and like *Album familiar* it falls into the category of resistance narrative, a term that describes much El Salvadoran prose fiction during the 1980s. According to literary critic Barbara Harlow, resistance narratives "propose specific historical analyses of the ideological and material conditions out of which they are generated, in Nicaragua, . . . El Salvador . . . or elsewhere. . . . [Moreover, they] contribute to a larger narrative, that of the passage from genealogical or hereditary bonds of filiation to the collective bonds of affiliation." In both *Album familiar* and *Despierta, mi bien, despierta,* Alegría criticizes upper-class values and shows how the protagonists, by their own ignorance and indifference, are complicit in the oppression of rural working-class people. As each protagonist looks critically at the values her fam-

*Alegría and Argentine writer Julio Cortázar, 1979 (photograph by Carlos Franco)*

ily and social class uphold, she decides to break the "hereditary bonds of filiation" and join the collective struggle to help her people effect social change in her country. Once her political and social consciousness is awakened, she is forever changed and can never go back to the way she once was.

Alegría's most recent novel is *Luisa en el país de la realidad* (1987; translated as *Luisa in Realityland,* 1987), which consists of alternating prose vignettes and poetry. The English translation, which includes two extra episodes and repeats seven key poems at the end, was published first because the Mexican publisher delayed production of the book.

Alegría gives a collagelike effect to the novel by weaving fiction, Central American history and folklore, Mayan mythology, testimony, and autobiographical memoir into the narrative structure. According to literary critics John Beverley and Marc Zimmerman, her objective is "to give some sense, through a montage of different literary forms, of the overall historical and political process Central America has gone through from the 1930s to the present, in her case presented, however, from within the intimate world of a particular woman's memories and experience."

Memories are central to this novel. Alegría uses the perspective of Luisa, the seven-year-old child protagonist, to reflect class struggle and keep alive the collective memory of the rural working people. Luisa learns her family history and the history of her country by observing what happens and by listening to the anecdotes, adventures, memories, and testimonies told by her parents, relatives, nanny, and others. One of the points Alegría makes in the novel is that without a sense of one's past, one cannot imagine a future. Furthermore, she ends the novel in the American edition with a long poem entitled "The Cartography of Memory," in which the poetic voice speaks from a position of exile. Lamenting her inability to return to El Salvador, the poetic voice remembers her country and its history and imagines a future of "rebellious, contagious peace." In short, as Sternbach contends, "more than any other aspect of Alegría's writing, the role and function of memory, especially that of female protagonists in fiction or speakers in poetry, serves as a powerful tool for self-realization, recognition, and determination."

Alegría's latest work is a bilingual collection of combat poetry she and Flakoll edited, *On the Front Line: Guerrilla Poems of El Salvador* (1989). The collection is comprised of poems by El Salvadoran revolutionaries on the different fighting fronts of the Farabundo Martí National Liberation front (FMLN) and includes poems by well-established poets as well as lesser-known poets. The poetry conveys the struggles, hopes, and dreams of writers whose greatest desire is the collective construction of a better future for El Salvador.

Despite Alegría's lengthy career and impressive list of publications, she has been until recently virtually unknown outside Latin America; criticism devoted to her work has been minimal. Her popularity is growing, however, as more of her work becomes available in translation and as more scholars study Central American literature. It is safe to project that within the next few years the critical attention paid her will steadily increase.

At present Alegría and her husband divide their time between their homes in Managua, Nicaragua, and Majorca, Spain. Since 1980 Alegría's commitment to social change and her opposition to suc-

cessive regimes have kept her in exile from El Salvador, where she cannot safely reside. Once she is able to return, however, she hopes to promote a national literacy campaign.

**Interviews:**

Carolyn Forché, "Interview with Claribel Alegría," *Index on Censorship*, 13 (April 1984): 11–14;

Gaspar Aguilera Díaz, "Claribel Alegría De Cronopios desaparecidos, encuentros y poesía nicaraguense de hoy," *Universidad de México*, December 1986, pp. 19–21.

**References:**

Electa Arenal, "Two Poets of the Sandinista Struggle," *Feminist Studies,* 7 (Spring 1981): 19–27;

John Beverley and Marc Zimmerman, "Testimonial Narrative," in their *Literature and Politics in the Central American Revolutions* (Austin: University of Texas Press, 1990), pp. 172–211;

Sandra M. Boschetto-Sandoval and Marcia Phillips McGowan, eds., *Claribel Alegría and Central American Literature* (Athens: Ohio University Press, 1994);

Carolyn Forché, "Preface: With Tears, Fingernails and Coal," in Alegría's *Flores del volcán* (Pittsburgh: University of Pittsburgh Press, 1982), pp. xi–xiv;

María Esther Gilio, "Con Claribel Alegría y Darwin Flakoll: Espejos y relámpagos," *Brecha,* 6 (November 1992): 20–21;

Barbara Harlow, "Narratives of Resistance," in her *Resistance Literature* (New York & London: Methuen, 1987), pp. 75–116;

Teresa Longo, "Claribel Alegría's Sorrow: In Defiance of the Space Which Separates," *Latin American Literary Review,* 39 (January–June 1992): 18–26;

Diane E. Marting, "Claribel Alegría," in her *Women Writers of Spanish America: An Annotated Bio-Bibliographical Guide* (New York: Greenwood Press, 1987), p. 16;

Nancy Saporta Sternbach, "Claribel Alegría," in *Spanish American Women Writers: A Bio-Bibliographical Source Book,* edited by Marting (New York: Greenwood Press, 1990), pp. 9–19;

George Yúdice, "Letras de emergencia: Claribel Alegría," *Revista Iberoamericana,* 51 (July–December 1985): 953–964.

# Isabel Allende

*(2 August 1942 – )*

Nora Erro-Peralta
*Florida Atlantic University*

BOOKS: *Civilice a su troglodita: Los impertinentes de Isabel Allende* (Santiago: Lord Cochran, 1974);
*La casa de los espíritus* (Barcelona: Plaza y Janés, 1982); translated by Magda Bogin as *The House of the Spirits* (New York: Knopf, 1985; London: Cape, 1985);
*La gorda de porcelana* (Madrid: Alfaguara, 1983);
*De amor y de sombra* (Barcelona: Plaza y Janés, 1984); translated by Margaret Sayers Peden as *Of Love and Shadows* (New York: Knopf, 1987);
*Eva Luna* (Barcelona: Plaza y Janés, 1987); translated by Peden as *Eva Luna* (New York: Knopf, 1988);
*Cuentos de Eva Luna* (Buenos Aires: Editorial Sudamericana, 1990); translated by Peden as *The Stories of Eva Luna* (New York: Atheneum, 1991);
*El plan infinito* (Buenos Aires: Editorial Sudamericana, 1991); translated by Peden as *The Infinite Plan* (New York: HarperCollins, 1993).

OTHER: "Los libros tienen sus propios espíritus," in *Los libros tienen sus propios espíritus: Estudios sobre Isabel Allende,* edited by Marcelo Coddou (Jalapa, Mexico: Universidad Veracruzana, 1986), pp. 15–20;
"Writing as an Act of Hope," in *Paths of Resistance,* edited by William Zinsser (Boston: Houghton Mifflin, 1989), pp. 39–63.

SELECTED PERIODICAL PUBLICATIONS – UNCOLLECTED: "Sobre *La casa de los espíritus,*" *Discurso Literario,* 2 (Autumn 1984): 67–73;
"La magia de las palabras," *Revista Iberoamericana,* 51 (July–December 1985): 447–452.

Isabel Allende is the best-known and most widely read woman writer from Latin America. When the English translation of her widely acclaimed first novel, *La casa de los espíritus* (1982), appeared in 1985 under the title *The House of the Spirits,* she became an immediate international success.

*Isabel Allende, 1992 (photograph by Marcia Lieberman)*

Since then, she has published three more novels and a book of short stories, all of which have been translated into several languages and many of which have been best-sellers in the countries where they are available. Allende is the first Latin-American woman writer to share in the worldwide fame and critical success of her male counterparts, popularized in the 1960s as representatives of the Latin-American literary Boom.

Allende was born in Lima, Peru, on 2 August 1942 to Chilean diplomat Tomás Allende and his wife Francisca Llona Barros. Her father was a first cousin of Salvador Allende, president of Chile, with whom Isabel and her family maintained a close, long-standing relationship. Her parents divorced when she was two years old, and she and her mother moved in with her maternal grandparents, whose presence and personalities exerted a powerful influence over her imagination and development, leaving a deep imprint later expressed in her writing. Her grandmother in particular was a great storyteller.

Allende's mother eventually remarried, again to a diplomat, whose assignments took the family – mother, stepfather, and two brothers – abroad. Thus, as an adolescent she lived in such widely scattered places as Bolivia, the Middle East, and Europe. Allende returned to Chile when she was fifteen, finished high school, and began working as a secretary for the Food and Agricultural Organization (FAO) of the United Nations. She found herself drawn to writing, however, and soon advanced into the field of journalism and communications, pursuing a variety of interests. During this period she wrote a column ("Impertinentes") for the radical women's magazine *Paula,* edited a leading magazine for children entitled *Mampato,* and even hosted a weekly television program. At the same time she was trying her hand at producing plays and writing short stories for children. In 1962, while still pursuing her career, Isabel Allende married Miguel Frías, with whom she had two children, Paula and Nicolás.

On 13 September 1973 a military coup in Chile led to the assassination of President Salvador Allende, the installation of a military government under the command of Gen. Augusto Pinochet Ugarte, and a period of widespread political change. These events had profound repercussions for Chilean society as a whole and for Allende in particular. Confronted with the repression and violence instituted by the military dictatorship, she joined the efforts of church-sponsored groups in providing food and aid to the needy and families of the victims of the regime. During the fifteen months that followed, she helped many of her compatriots escape military persecution. At the risk of her own life, she transported them to safety in her flower-painted Citronetta, witnessing events that she would later incorporate into her first novel.

In her 1984 essay "Sobre *La casa de los espíritus*" Allende made the connection between her personal experience and her writings: "Gracias a mi trabajo de periodista supe exactamente lo que sucedía en mi patria, lo viví de cerca y esos muertos, torturados, viudas y huérfanos, dejaron huellas imborrables en mi memoria. Los últimos capítulos de la *La casa de los espíritus* relatan esos acontecimientos. Me basé en lo que vieron mis ojos y en los testimonios directos de quienes vivieron la brutal experiencia de la represión" (Because of my work as a journalist I knew exactly what was happening in my country, I lived through it, and the dead, the tortured, the widows and orphans, left an unforgettable impression on my memory. The last chapters of *La casa de los espíritus* narrate those events. They are based on what I saw and on the direct testimonies of those who lived through the brutal experience of the repression).

Even after she was dismissed from *Paula* in 1974 Allende continued to write, gather information, interview people, and make recordings. By 1975 the heightened repression coupled with her own fear induced her to leave Chile. Settling in Caracas, Venezuela, with her husband and teenage children, she found it difficult to find work as a writer despite the fact that she had been a noted journalist in her native land. As a consequence, she turned to other avenues, working for a while as a teacher and administrator and neglecting her own creative writing for several years. After some time she was able to resume her work as a reporter and wrote satirical articles for *El nacional,* one of the leading newspapers in the country.

Isolated in this new country and concerned about her grandfather, who was then dying in Chile, she sat down to write him a letter that eventually became the manuscript for her first novel, *La casa de los espíritus.* It recounts the experiences of four generations of the del Valle–Trueba family, set against the background of Chilean politics from the turn of the century up to and including the coup that brought the military regime to power in 1973.

Although not autobiographical in the strictest sense of the word, *La casa de los espíritus* nevertheless derives much of its inspiration from her family's experiences and from her own memories of the house in which she was raised. Allende's maternal grandparents, with whom she lived during her most formative years, provided the models for two of the book's central characters: Esteban, the passionate, violent landowner-politician; and his clairvoyant, compassionate wife, Clara. In an interview with Marjorie Agosín, Allende pointed out the crucial role her childhood played in forming the basis for her first novel.

*La casa de los espíritus,* which is set in an unnamed South American country, traces the history of the del Valle–Trueba family through the first seventy-five years of the twentieth century. The fourteen chapters of the novel focus upon the lives of four women who successively serve as the central characters: Rosa, Clara, Blanca, and Alba. Weaving in and out of the narratives of their lives is Esteban Trueba, who is respectively lover, husband, father, and grandfather of the female protagonists. Born into poverty, Esteban is a self-made man who climbs the financial and social ladder, acquiring land, wealth, and political power as he goes. He epitomizes both strength and weakness, not only in his character but as a metaphor for the strengths and weaknesses of Latin-American society. In the end his brutal, violent behavior leads to the torture, mutilation, and rape of his beloved granddaughter, Alba, when the military, which he supports, takes over the country. Alba is saved from death when Clara, her dead grandmother, appears to remind her not to die but to survive and suggests that she accomplish this by writing the account of her misery. The text concludes with Alba chronicling the family's history as she awaits the birth of her own child and keeps vigil over the body of Esteban, her grandfather. The novel ends as it began, with the same sentence, thus bringing the narrative full circle.

*La casa de los espíritus* is constructed around that mixture of reality and fantasy that is sometimes termed magic realism. An aura of mystery and magic surrounds the Truebas' house, where the spirits of the past roam and mingle with the living. The characters are endowed with unusual physical and spiritual attributes: Rosa and Alba have green hair; Esteban shrinks; and Clara is endowed with mystical powers. She can predict the future, communicate with the spirits, play the piano with the cover closed, and move objects with the power of her mind.

On one level the novel creates a supernatural, fantastic universe peopled with characters who have semimagical gifts. On another level it bears witness to the tragic political history of Latin America, in which those who love their country well can also bring the most destruction upon it. Although the realistic events in the novel could have happened in many other Latin-American countries, references to well-known incidents and developments – the disastrous earthquake of 1933, the agrarian reform of the 1960s, the triumph of Salvador Allende, the death of Pablo Neruda, the assassination of Víctor Jara – clearly locate the action of the novel in Chile.

*La casa de los espíritus,* which Allende dedicated to her mother and grandmother, pays tribute to all the women of Latin America, as represented by the extraordinary characters in this novel, and thus offers a new feminine vision. The novelist presents a cast of women who are both strong and creative and who prove themselves able to resist the power of

Cover for the 1985 American edition of Allende's novel La casa de los espíritus (1982), which recounts the experiences of four generations of a family in Chile

convention and a patriarchal system through their own acts of will. Nívea del Valle fights for women's right to vote; Clara defies her husband and devotes herself to ministering to the poor; her daughter, Blanca, resists her father's authority by bringing up her illegitimate child and carrying on a long-standing love affair with a revolutionary peasant leader who opposes everything her father stands for; and Alba, Blanca's daughter, continues the independent path marked out by her female forebears by joining the student movement, becoming the lover of a guerrilla leader and later a victim of torture, and ultimately establishing her solidarity with ordinary women. Alba is the last in this series of luminous spirits to bring light to the world, and she heralds a new age. The novel concludes by suggesting the enormous capabilities that lie within the human spirit: its ability both to endure and to renew itself.

Alba reconstructs the history of her family by means of her grandmother Clara's journals, her mother's letters, and her grandfather Esteban's testimony, as well as her own experiences, assorted records, and family documents. Her story focuses on the lives of Nívea, Clara, Blanca, and herself. Alba identifies with her foremothers, finding in their writings a timeless reflection of the various aspects of female experience. This sense of the commonality of female experience across the boundaries of time and space, and of women's ability to create their own reality out of that experience, conveys a message of female empowerment that subverts the historical stereotype of the submissive woman.

Although *La casa de los espíritus* begins with a first-person narrative voice, this unnamed "I" soon disappears, and for the most part the rest of the story is related in the voice of a third-person omniscient observer. From then on, the narrative alternates between the voice of the third-person magic realist and the briefer, first-person testimony of Esteban. Only in the epilogue does the reader discover that the original narrator who began the story is actually Alba, the youngest member of the Trueba family and one of the main female characters in the novel. Aside from occasional subjective references, Alba's voice is essentially objective, relating the events in the tone of a detached bystander. A secondary voice is that of her grandfather Esteban, who presents his version of many of the same events but in so doing provides a window into his presumably masculine point of view. Allende's ingenious blending of the two narrative voices not only situates the female voice clearly within the context of a patriarchal culture but also displaces and subverts the power of that culture as well.

The novel employs many of the techniques of magic realism. The language is characterized by metaphors, oxymorons, and personification. Extensive use of both foreshadowing and flashbacks establishes verisimilitude and the discontinuity of time. The voice is detached and matter-of-fact when describing the most improbable events, which enables the author to develop her own style of magic realism in an effective, compelling way.

Allende conveys the story of the del Valles and Truebas through a masterful blending of the real and the unreal, in which imaginary characters, some with mystical or supernatural attributes, grapple with situations and events that inspire humor, pathos, and a sense of recognition in the reader. The author's skill in combining these elements has led many critics to place *La casa de los espíritus* squarely within the Latin-American literary current of magic realism.

Upon completing the novel Allende encountered numerous obstacles in trying to have it published. Editors rejected the manuscript due to the length of the text (five hundred pages) and to the fact that its author was both a woman and unknown. Finally accepted by Plaza y Janés of Barcelona, Spain, in 1982, *La casa de los espíritus* became an instant success. The author, in many interviews, has credited the spirit of her clairvoyant grandmother with protecting the fortune of the book.

Allende's fame and stature as an author rest largely on this first novel. Fourteen printings were issued during the first years following publication. It became a best-seller in Europe and was soon translated into fifteen languages. Its opening section appeared in *Vogue* in the United States in 1985. The novel was awarded the Grand Roman d'Evasion Prize in 1984 and the Quality Paperback Book Club New Voice Award Nomination in 1986.

In Chile the book was initially censored, and copies had to be smuggled into the country. In her 1985 essay "La magia de las palabras," Allende relates her astonishment at the ingenuity displayed by her compatriots: "Jamás imaginé que muchos chilenos desafiarían a la policía para introducir algunos ejemplares al país. Viajeros audaces lo disimularon en su equipaje; otros fueron enviados por correo sin tapas, o partidos en dos o tres pedazos para que no pudieran identificarlos al abrir los sobres. Conozco a una joven madre que pasó varios libros por la aduana ocultos en una bolsa de pañales de su recién nacido" (I never imagined how many Chileans would defy the police to bring books into the country. Bold travelers concealed them in their luggage; others were sent by mail without covers or cut in two or three pieces so they would not be able to identify them when the envelopes were opened. I know a young mother who smuggled several books in the diaper bag of her newborn baby).

Allende's second novel, *De amor y de sombra* (1984; translated as *Of Love and Shadows*, 1987), deals with the disappearance of fifteen peasants in the Lonquén region under the Pinochet military regime and confirms her skill as a storyteller. This time, however, she turned her talents to a story with a more limited historical perspective, choosing to focus on a transforming experience in the life of a young woman.

The novel begins with a journalist, Irene Beltrán, accompanied by freelance photographer Francisco Leal, on assignment to do a story about a fifteen-year-old peasant girl alleged to possess miraculous powers. Unexpectedly the pair find themselves involved in a confrontation with the military police,

*Allende, circa 1987 (photograph by Irmeli Jung)*

whereupon Evangelina, the peasant girl, disappears. Irene insists on trying to find the girl, and in the process she and Francisco uncover evidence of atrocities committed by military personnel. In an abandoned mine they find not only the body of Evangelina but also many others in various stages of decomposition. During their dangerous mission the couple fall in love, but their love is overshadowed by the violence and death around them. When they reveal their discovery, implicating the government in the mass murders, Irene is gunned down in the street. As soon as she is sufficiently recovered from her wounds to travel, she and Francisco flee into exile across the border. Though sad at having to leave, they are determined to return one day in the future.

Like *La casa de los espíritus*, *De amor y de sombra* also has elements of thinly disguised recent history. The setting is another unnamed country under the dictatorship of an unidentified general, which bears a strong resemblance to Chile under General Pinochet. The time is around 1978. Events in the novel closely follow those surrounding the 1978 discovery of fifteen bodies in two abandoned kilns near the village of Lonquén. Máximo Pacheco Gómez, a lawyer who took part in the investigation and was inspired by a desire to see justice done, published the principal documents in the case in a book entitled *Lonquén* (1980). In an interview with Magdalena García Pinto, Allende freely acknowledged the source of her material. Although Chile is never mentioned, the story comes from a highly publicized incident that occurred in 1978 in the Lonquén mine, an abandoned mine shaft fifty kilometers outside of Santiago, although segments of the story were fictionalized.

In *De amor y de sombra* Allende remains true to the moral imperative behind all her writing, which is to use literature as a way of bearing witness to a time and place in Latin-American history. In an epigraph to the novel, Allende explains that its inspiration came to her from a man and a woman who confided their lives to her.

*De amor y de sombra* employs its themes as structural counterpoints: the love story is inextricably entwined with the political story, each justifying and highlighting the other. The novel thus comprises a single unified action composed equally of the light of love and the shadow of violence, emphasizing the interplay between the two.

The novel is also the story of a woman's self-discovery. As in *La casa de los espíritus,* the female condition is Allende's underlying subject. Michael Moody, in an article entitled "Isabel Allende and the Testimonial Novel" (1986), highlights the continuing concerns of the author: "For just as Alba, the internal narrator of *La casa de los espíritus,* transcends her female ancestry, achieving illumination through her struggle against repression, so too Irene develops personal and social consciousness as a consequence of her evolving commitment against a state of repression that assumes both political and sexist forms."

This second novel, though considerably shorter, is carefully constructed, focusing on the events of one spring when two diametrically opposed events unfold. Nevertheless, *De amor y de sombra* received mixed reviews. Some critics felt that it was a more mature book, better written and structured than the first. This evaluation seems to correspond with the author's comment that she was conscious of its writing while the work was in progress. The novel was warmly received in Chile, but in Germany, despite the fact that *La casa de los espíritus* had been a runaway best-seller, reviewers were less kind, although *De amor y de sombra* still sold well. In *Narrative Magic in the Fiction of Isabel Allende* (1989), Patricia Hart suggests that the novel was less successful because it lacked suspense, its characters were superficial and oversimplistic, and the narrative voices were too similar. Despite these reservations, the English translation, *Of Love and Shadows,* was nominated for the Los Angeles Times Book Prize in 1987.

*Eva Luna* (1987; translated as *Eva Luna*, 1988), the story of a storyteller, is Allende's third novel, a modern, almost picaresque narrative about a twentieth-century Scheherazade who tells tales to survive in a politically unstable Latin-American society. Set in a country that closely resembles Venezuela, it tells the story of Eva Luna, born illegitimate to a mother who died when Eva was only six years old, and how she survived her orphan childhood and adolescence to find success and fulfillment eventually as a scriptwriter for television. Throughout this "autobiography" the stories of Eva's significant others, particularly that of her lover Rolf Carlé, are interwoven. His *historia* (story, history) recounts his life from his youth in Nazi Austria to his immigration to South America and his eventual fame as a controversial filmmaker.

The novel is basically a bildungsroman that contains many elements of the picaresque as it relates the life of an indomitable woman trying to sur-

vive in a hostile world. Like Scheherazade, who told tales to save her life and the lives of her loved ones, so Eva Luna learns the power of words and how to spin tales that first serve as an escape from a life of abject poverty and eventually pave the road to love, fame, and fortune.

From her mother, who had a gift for telling stories, Eva has learned that the power of language can be used to transform the world and create one's own reality: "Una palabra mía y, ¡lichas!, se transformaba la realidad" (One word from me and, abracadabra!, reality was transformed). Eva experiments, develops her talent for writing, and learns to re-create her life, reshaping it into a story and then making that story her life. Using elements from her own writing, she makes her own fate. As she actively molds her own reality, she creates the outcome she desires. Eva's unyielding will is most apparent when she uses the device of inventing another ending within the ending. The inconclusiveness of this strategy only serves to underscore the fact that she is not only creating her own destiny but is also capable of defining reality as she wishes.

The book throws into question the division between reality and fiction. Eva Luna, protagonist and narrator, relates the events of her own life and out of this material creates a *novela* (soap opera) for television within the novel — an upbeat form of the tale-within-a-tale structure. The life story of Eva Luna provides the framework for the soap opera *Bolero,* for which she writes the script. The memoirs of this fictional heroine are not only personal, however, but political. Eva Luna is a social critic in her stories, denouncing the cruelty and abuses of dictators, the violence of military repression, and the corruption that pervades all levels of government. The primary story, the history of Eva Luna, is also closely entwined with the history of Venezuela. When José Otero examined the historical background of the novel, he concluded that it covered seven decades of the twentieth century, with a focus on three particular periods: two dictatorships — those of Juan Vicente Gómez (1908–1935) and Marco Pérez Jiménez (1953–1958) — plus the time of the guerrilla movement that marked the presidencies of Rómulo Betancourt (1959–1964) and Raúl Leoni (1964–1969).

*Eva Luna* employs more than one kind of narrative: there is Eva Luna's "autobiography" narrated in the first person as well as the story related in the third person by the traditional omniscient observer. The latter is used to depict the stories of the three men in Eva's life — Rolf, Riad Halabí, and Huberto — which the reader assumes to be Eva's version. This complex structure, in which the various story lines intertwine and overlap, illuminates the evolution of Eva Luna's inner consciousness, both personal and social.

With *Eva Luna,* Allende returns to the lush narrative texture of her first novel. The marvelous, the strange, and the unusual are incorporated: Eva's mother, long dead, regularly shows up to keep her company in times of trouble; a phantasmagoric Palace of the Poor materializes and then vanishes for no apparent reason; on one occasion the evening sky is so transparently clear that angels can be seen floating in the air; the smell of desire is so strong at one point that it becomes visible, like a burning fire; and fictional characters, in the process of being developed by Eva herself, take human shape and disrupt the household routine.

After Allende's divorce from her first husband in 1987, she met her second, William Gordon, an American attorney, during a lecture tour in the United States. They were married on 17 July 1988 and settled in Marin County, north of San Francisco, California. Although her publisher worried that her new home outside Latin America might stifle her imagination, Allende found her new surroundings no less exotic.

Because the new marriage and environment made their own demands upon her, she adjusted by turning to the short story as a literary medium that would not require so much of her time. The result was a collection of short stories, *Cuentos de Eva Luna* (1990; translated as *The Stories of Eva Luna,* 1991). The twenty-three tales in the collection present an abundance of fascinating characters, some of whom had already appeared in *Eva Luna.*

The collection begins with a prologue from Eva's lover Rolf Carlé: "Cuéntame un cuento que no le hayas contado a nadie" (Tell me a story you have never told anyone before. Make it up for me). Like the famous tales from the *Arabian Nights Entertainments,* these stories combine fantasy, magic, biting social satire, and psychological insight as well as elements of magic realism – unlikely events presented as everyday occurrences.

Although Allende covers an array of themes and characters in *Cuentos de Eva Luna,* she excels in her portrayal of strong women. These include Dulce Rosa Orellano, who pledges to murder her father's assassin only to fall in love with him but who commits suicide rather than marry him; Casilda Hidalgo, who yields to an outlaw in order to protect her children; and Antonia Sierra, who makes friends with her husband's mistress and then connives to push him from both their lives.

Cover for the U.S. edition of Allende's 1987 novel, about a storyteller who creates her own life story

One of the most delightful stories, "Dos palabras" (Two Words), is a tribute to the magical power of language. Belisa Crepusculario, a poor girl with no material resources, makes her living selling stories, poems, and love letters. The words endow her with tremendous power. When she sells a political speech to the Coronel (Colonel), a savage fighting man, he becomes the most popular politician in the country overnight. However, Belisa grants him two secret words as a bonus, which then enslave him to her. She has enchanted the man with the power of her words.

Allende's latest novel, *El plan infinito* (1991; translated as *The Infinite Plan,* 1993), was well received when it was launched at the Santiago Book Fair in December 1991. The story of Gregory Reeves, a young man raised amid Chicanos in a Los Angeles barrio, it begins when he is four years old, traveling with his family while his father preaches his own philosophy of salvation, called the Infinite Plan. When his father becomes ill, the family is forced to settle in a Los Angeles suburb where the Morales family helps them to begin a new life. Struggling to overcome poverty, Gregory decides to study law at the University of California, Berkeley. Lonely and starved for affection, Gregory becomes infatuated with Samantha Ernst, daughter of a Hollywood tycoon, and marries her. When the marriage fails, he goes to Vietnam, where he confronts death and devastation. These memories continue to haunt him upon his return to the United States, but he plunges into his law career, concentrating on acquiring wealth and the power it brings. He leads a superficial life, concerned more with money than ethics, pursuing sex rather than love. Though he achieves his goals, happiness eludes him. His second marriage fails, his children have serious mental and emotional problems, and he becomes so painfully aware of his own difficulties that he is finally driven to seek psychiatric help. Slowly he finds his way to a stable, happy life. The novel follows Allende's familiar pattern of relating Gregory's life along with the various stories of his family and friends.

In November 1991 Allende stated in a lecture in Miami that *El plan infinito* is a story of survival, one of the major themes in her work. It is the external journey of a man who struggles to become successful at all costs, only to discover, upon reaching these goals, that everything important has been lost along the way. The second part of the book traces the internal journey, in which the man, now in search of his own soul, reverses his course and returns to his roots. Although the subject of *El plan infinito* clearly differs from Allende's previous works, it shares with them her fundamental values of love, solidarity, and hope and the concern with those qualities that enable the spirit to survive adversity. Again she employs the novelistic device of telling her story through two voices: the omniscient observer using the third person (in this case a feminine voice identified as the protagonist's lover); and the voice of Gregory, who tells his story in the first person. Gregory's story is told against a considerable historical background that incorporates real events over the past fifty years, primarily in California. Though the narrative voice follows a chronological path in relating the protagonist's life, it sometimes foreshadows future events, which is characteristic of much of Allende's work. The language is less elliptical and more direct than her earlier efforts, vividly depicting life in Berkeley during the 1960s as well as detailing the horrors of the Vietnam War.

Throughout her fiction women and politics are constant concerns. Much of Allende's work has utilized female-centered narratives. Allende continually endows and empowers her principal female characters with the gift of writing and telling stories as a way to preserve the past, organize the future, and gain control over their lives in the process. These characters are narrator-writers, recording their versions of the world. In *La casa de los espíritus* Alba tells the story of the del Valle–Trueba family by using the written accounts of those who have gone before in addition to her own account of events; in *De amor y de sombra* Irene, the journalist, uncovers a story of government violence and abuse; in *Eva Luna* Eva writes her own story in every sense of the word, creating, living, and writing her own script of life; and in *El plan infinito* both Gregory and his lover record his life story in order to give it meaning and ensure its survival.

Allende has defined her personal and literary philosophy in several interviews. In the November 1991 Miami lecture she emphasized: "Writing for me is the possibility of creating and recreating the world according to my own rules, fulfilling in those pages all my dreams and exorcising some of my demons." In her 1989 essay "Writing as an Act of Hope," she explains why she writes: "Maybe the most important reason for writing is to prevent the erosion of time, so that memories will not be blown away by the wind. Write to register history, and name each thing. Write what should not be forgotten." She essentially defines the novel as a vehicle for bearing witness, overcoming silence, and asserting the human values of love, justice, and reconciliation. She views the act of creation as an act of moral responsibility, as she states in "Sobre *La casa de los espíritus*": "Todos los que escribimos y tenemos la suerte de ser publicados, debemos asumir el compromiso de servir la causa de la libertad y la justicia" (All of us who write and are fortunate enough to be published ought to assume the responsibility of serving the cause of freedom and justice).

Deeply marked by historical events in her country, Allende perceives her writing as an honest attempt to improve the world. She wants to bear witness to the political and social situations in Latin America: its dictatorships, violent upheavals, torture, pain, and hunger. Despite this incredibly painful, difficult material, her works are not filled with a sense of pessimism or despair; on the contrary, her novels and short stories are uplifting and entertaining.

Allende's enormous appeal rests partly on the nature of her style: a dynamic combination of events and characters structured around a fast-paced narrative. Her work incorporates and integrates several stylistic devices: hyperbole, paradox, and the juxtaposition of the concrete with the abstract to convey a state of mind. The richness of her imagination both embellishes and reveals the seeming unreality of much of Latin-American reality, conveying not only the ostensible story but also her adroit use of fantasy as a metaphor for an underlying sociopolitical story.

Isabel Allende has successfully joined the ranks of some of the most distinguished writers of Latin America. She has won praise for her evocative use of language, her style, and her illumination of historical and social reality as well as her ability to entertain. Her works, now known throughout the world, testify to her well-earned reputation as a significant figure in contemporary literature.

**Interviews:**

Marjorie Agosín, "Entrevista a Isabel Allende/Interview with Isabel Allende," translated by Cola Frazen, *Imagine: International Chicano Poetry Journal,* 1 (Winter 1984): 42–56;

Michael Moody, "Entrevista con Isabel Allende," *Discurso Literario,* 4 (Autumn 1986): 41–53;

Moody, "Una conversación con Isabel Allende," *Chasqui,* 16 (November 1987): 51–59;

Verónica Cortínez, "Polifonía: Entrevista a Isabel Allende y Antonio Skármeta," *Revista Chilena de Literatura,* 32 (November 1988): 79–89;

Magdalena García Pinto, "Isabel Allende," in her *Historias íntimas: Conversaciones con diez escritoras latinoamericanas* (Hanover, N.H.: Ediciones del Norte, 1988), pp. 1–26;

Marie-Lise Gazarian Gautier, "Isabel Allende," in her *Interviews with Latin American Writers* (Elmwood Park, Ill.: Dalkey Archive Press, 1989), pp. 5–24;

Edith Dimo Gary and Claire Emilie Martin, "Entrevista con Isabel Allende," *Alba de América,* 8 (July 1990): 331–343.

**References:**

Lyana María Amaya and Aura María Fernández, "La desconstrucción y la crítica feminista: Lecturas posibles de *Cien años de soledad* y *La casa de los espíritus,*" *Nuevo Texto Crítico,* 2, no. 4 (1989): 189–195;

Andriana Castillo de Berchenko and Pablo Berchenko, *La narrativa de Isabel Allende: Claves de una marginalidad* (Perpignan, France: Université de Perpignan, 1990);

Marcelo Coddou, *Para leer a Isabel Allende: Introducción a "La casa de los espíritus"* (Concepción, Chile: LAR, 1988);

Coddou, ed., *Los libros tienen sus propios espíritus* (Jalapa, Mexico: Universidad Veracruzana, 1986);

Peter Earle, "De Lazarillo a Eva Luna metamórfosis de la picaresca," *Nueva Revista de Filología Hispánica,* 36, no. 2 (1988): 987–996;

Patricia Hart, *Narrative Magic in the Fiction of Isabel Allende* (Rutherford, N. J.: Fairleigh Dickinson University Press, 1989);

Linda Gould Levine, "Isabel Allende," in *Spanish American Women Writers: A Bio-Bibliographical Source Book,* edited by Diane E. Marting (New York: Greenwood Press, 1990), pp. 20–30;

Silvia Lorente-Murphy, "Isabel Allende: Una puerta abierta a la esperanza," in *La escritora hispánica,* edited by Nora Erro-Orthmann and Juan Cruz Mendizábal (Miami: Universal, 1990), pp. 93–100;

Doris Meyer, " 'Parenting the Text': Female Creativity and Dialogic Relationships in Isabel Allende's *La casa de los espíritus,*" *Hispania,* 73 (May 1990): 360–365;

Michael Moody, "Isabel Allende and the Testimonial Novel," *Confluencia: Revista Hispánica de Cultura y Literatura,* 2 (Fall 1986): 39–43;

José Otero, "La historia como ficción en *Eva Luna* de Isabel Allende," *Confluencia: Revista Hispánica de Cultura y Literatura,* 4 (Fall 1988): 61–67;

Sonia Riquelme Rojas and Edna Aguirre Rehbeim, eds., *Critical Approaches to Isabel Allende's Novels* (New York: Peter Lang, 1991);

Mario A. Rojas, "*La casa de los espíritus,* de Isabel Allende: Un caleidoscopio de espejos desordenados," *Revista Iberoamericana,* 51 (July–December 1985): 917–925.

# Reinaldo Arenas

*(16 July 1943 – 6 December 1990)*

Eduardo Béjar
*Middlebury College*

BOOKS: *Celestino antes del alba* (Havana: Unión de Escritores y Artistas de Cuba, 1967); revised as *Cantando en el pozo* (Barcelona: Argos Vergara, 1982); translated by Andrew Hurley as *Singing from the Well* (New York: Viking, 1987);

*Le monde hallucinant,* translated by Didier Coste (Paris: Editions du Sevil, 1969);

*El mundo alucinante* (Mexico City: Diógenes, 1969); translated by Gordon Brotherston as *Hallucinations* (New York: Harper & Row, 1971; London: Cape, 1971); translated by Hurley as *The Ill-Fated Peregrinations of Fray Servando* (New York: Avon, 1987);

*Con los ojos cerrados* (Montevideo: Arca, 1972); revised as *Termina el desfile* (Barcelona: Seix Barral, 1981);

*Le palais des très blanches mouffettes* (Paris: Seuil, 1975); translated by Coste; *El palacio de las blanquísimas mofetas* (Caracas: Monte Avila, 1980); translated by Hurley as *The Palace of the White Skunks* (New York: Viking, 1990);

*La vieja Rosa* (Caracas: Cruz del Sur, 1980); translated by Hurley as *Old Rosa* (New York: Grove, 1989);

*El central* (Barcelona: Seix Barral, 1981); translated by Anthony Kerrisa as *El central* (New York: Avon, 1984);

*Homenaje a Angel Cuadra* (Miami: Solar, 1981);

*Otra vez el mar* (Barcelona: Argos Vergara, 1982); translated by Hurley as *Farewell to the Sea* (New York: Viking/Penguin, 1986);

*Lazarillo de Tormes,* edited by José Olivio Jiménez (New York: Regents, 1984);

*Arturo, la estrella más brillante* (Barcelona: Montesinos, 1984);

*Necesidad de libertad* (Mexico City: Kosmos, 1986);

*Persecución* (Miami: Universal, 1986);

*La loma del ángel* (Miami: Mariel, 1987; Málaga, Spain: Dador, 1987); translated by Alfred J. MacAdam as *Graveyard of the Angels* (New York: Avon, 1987);

*El portero* (Málaga: Dador, 1987; Miami: Universal, 1990); translated by Dolores Koch as *The Doorman* (New York: Grove, 1991);

*Voluntad de vivir manifestándose* (Madrid: Betania, 1989);

*Viaje a La Habana* (Miami: Universal, 1990; Madrid: Mondadori, 1990);

*El asalto* (Miami: Universal, 1990);

*Leprosorio: Trilogía poética* (Madrid: Betania, 1990);

*Meditations de Saint-Nazaire,* bilingual edition, translated by Liliane Hasson (N.p.: Arcanes / MEET, 1990);

*Un plebiscito a Fidel Castro* (Madrid: Betania, 1990);

*El color del verano* (Miami: Universal, 1991);

*Final de un cuento* (Huelva, Spain: Diputación Provincional de Huelva, 1991);

*Antes que anochezca* (Barcelona: Tusquets, 1992); translated by Dolores Koch as *Before Night Falls* (New York: Viking, 1993).

SELECTED PERIODICAL PUBLICATIONS – UNCOLLECTED: "Celestino y yo," *Unión,* 3 (1967): 119.

A member of the generation of Cuban writers who emerged on the literary scene of the island during the 1960s, Reinaldo Arenas has been almost unanimously hailed as one of the most significant authors contributing to the formation of a "new writing" mode in Spanish America. His passionate and transgressive works are salient examples of the radical changes experienced by Cuban society and culture in the fervor of its first postrevolutionary years. His novels and short stories are notable additions to the ongoing experimentations of the most recent Spanish-American narrative, which found its impetus in the international recognition accorded to previous generations of writers. Within his group of younger authors, which has come to be broadly and imprecisely identified as the post-Boom generation, Arenas voiced staunch opposition to any discourse of power, be it political or cultural, that imposes an

42

*Reinaldo Arenas (photograph by Nestor Almendros)*

official ideology on the imagination, on its rights to a free interpretation of reality, and on the individual's social conduct. According to Arenas such restrictive limits tragically impoverish the wealth of experience and turn its artistic representation into a simplified design of reduced experiences and moral dictums: as he says in his 1967 essay "Celestino y yo" (Celestino and I), "la realidad es múltiple, es infinita, y además varía de acuerdo con la interpretación que queramos darle" (reality is multiple, infinite, and varies according to the interpretation we want to give it). The novelist or writer in general should not conform to the expression of one reality; the "máxima aspiración ha de ser la de poder expresar *todas las realidades*" (maximum aspiration is to express *all realities*).

For Arenas this pluralism could not be accomplished according to the traditional realist mode of representation, which purports a final and transcendental cognition of events, but instead it must incorporate disparity, indeterminacy, missing information, contradictory repetitions, and surrealistic visions. His fictions, consequently, are characterized by a labyrinthine and hallucinatory web of antithetical writings and rewritings, turns and returns, figurations and disfigurations that negate the totalizing presuppositions and objectives of nineteenth-century dialectical philosophy. For the centralizing official ideologues of the Cuban revolution, Arenas quickly became a subversive intellectual and a deviant writer, for which he suffered literary marginalization, political confinement, and finally exile. Since his stories are developed with quasi-autobiographical material – ranging from family oppression in childhood to adolescent repression in a hypocritical bourgeois society to coercive experiences as an adult within the Cuban revolutionary transformation – the corpus of his writings can be considered a postmodern allegory of striving against the constraints that power imposes on the individual. Like Jorge Luis Borges, Arenas likes to establish a paradoxical relationship between his life and its biographical textualization, faithfully undermining his own power position as authorial presence: "escribir sobre lo que he vivido o vivir lo que ya he escrito" (to write what I have lived or to live what I have already written).

Arenas was born on 16 July 1943 near Holguín, in the province of Oriente, Cuba. Shortly after

Arenas's birth his father abandoned the family, and his mother moved into her parents' home, which Arenas remembers as a *bohío* (gigantic, shabby palm hut). He lived there with eleven aunts, a grandmother who frequently interrupted her domestic chores to pray, and a reticent grandfather who, Arenas says, drank and would threaten to commit suicide every time he got drunk. Arenas learned to read and write from his mother and spent all of his childhood in this humble, rural family environment. By 1958 his mother had moved with him to Holguín, then a major agricultural center in western Cuba. At age fifteen he decided to join the rebel forces fighting in the nearby Sierra de Gibara against the army of dictator Fulgencio Batista. After the successful revolution Arenas returned to Holguín, where he received a scholarship from the new revolutionary government to study agricultural accounting. Upon completing this degree, he went to work at a poultry farm located in the Sierra Maestra, the southern mountain range of the province, but soon he became tired of pastoral life and left for Havana under the auspices of a national training program for economic planners. In 1962 he undertook this new specialization at the Universidad de la Habana but soon lost interest. The following year he began working as a staff member of the Biblioteca Nacional and decided to make writing central to his life.

Even though Arenas had been writing since age thirteen, it was not until 1964 that he was able to finish his first mature novel, *Celestino antes del alba* (Celestino before Dawn). In 1965 it received a Primera Mención at the Concurso Nacional de Novela Cirilo Villaverde, and it was published in Havana in 1967. The novel was well received by Cuban critics, including the then highly influential Alejo Carpentier, but shortly thereafter, under the tightening of the ideological parameters conceded to intellectual matters, Arenas's mode of writing fell out of favor, and the novel was prohibited from subsequent printings. Two years after Arenas's exile in 1980, a second and revised edition was published under the title *Cantando en el pozo* (translated as *Singing from the Well*, 1987). Early on Arenas also wrote a series of short stories, *Con los ojos cerrados* (With Closed Eyes), which was published by the critic Angel Rama in Uruguay in 1972. According to Arenas that edition was produced without his knowledge; a revision of the text was published in 1981 with a new title, *Termina el desfile* (End of the Parade).

In 1967, with the help of critic Carlos Franqui and painter Jorge Camacho, who were in Havana

attending the international exhibit known as Salon de Mai, Arenas managed to smuggle out of Cuba and into France the manuscript of his second novel, *El mundo alucinante* (translated as *Hallucinations*, 1971). It was published in French in 1969 and in Spanish the same year. The French journal *Le Monde* gave it the first prize as best foreign novel of the year, while Spanish-American critics also accorded Arenas favorable recognition. His name was from then on to appear in lists of significant new writers of Latin America. Similarly, his third novel, *El palacio de las blanquísimas mofetas* (translated as *The Palace of the White Skunks*, 1990), was taken out of Cuba clandestinely and appeared first in 1975 in a French version. According to Arenas the novel crossed the Cuban border under the disguised title of "Resumen científico de la flora cubana" (Scientific Summary of Cuban Flora) in the purse of French professor Paulette Paute. The Spanish version was published in 1980. Due to the censorship in Cuba, knowledge of his international fame never reached Arenas until his exile.

In 1973 Arenas was charged with ideological deviation and convicted for being extravagant, immoral, and a child corrupter and for publishing abroad without official consent. He was sent to prison in Havana, but after a few months he managed to escape and remained free under disguises. In 1974 he was rearrested and remained in the Morro Castle prison in Havana for almost a year. In 1976 he was sent to a so-called rehabilitation farm, from which he was finally set free later that year. During his time in the Morro Castle cell he arrived at the conclusion that he was destined to experience real-life situations similar to the ones he had previously fictionalized: by truculent twists of chance, Arenas found himself in the same position as Mexican friar Servando Teresa de Mier, the real-life hero of *El mundo alucinante*, who in the nineteenth century was persecuted by the Spanish Inquisition and sent to Morro Castle prison after having been a fugitive.

After Arenas's release in 1976, he began rewriting his fourth and most ambitious novel, *Otra vez el mar* (1982; translated as *Farewell to the Sea*, 1986). In 1971 Arenas had given the original 1969 manuscript to a close friend in order to avoid its confiscation. The friend, in turn, passed it on to some old women he knew for better security. The content of the novel apparently scandalized the traditional morals of the women, who proceeded to burn it. Months later Arenas requested it in order to send it secretly to France, as he had the previous ones, but the novel had disappeared. He then rewrote it, and just before his arrest in 1973 he hid the manuscript in the tile roof of his Havana home. His status as an ex-convict, however, did not allow him to return to the same house, and after a failed attempt to recover the bags from the roof, he considered the manuscript lost for a second time. Arenas spent 1976 through 1980 working on the third version of this novel and living a somewhat picaresque life in order to survive, doing a variety of menial jobs and constantly changing residences. On 5 May 1980, among the thousands of Cuban refugees who left the island from the port of Mariel, Arenas arrived in Florida, like Servando Teresa de Mier had done 150 years earlier. After a short stay in Miami, he moved to New York City, where he wrote the rest of his work without ever subsiding in his passionate denunciation of the repressive political system of Fidel Castro's revolution. His later works include *Arturo, la estrella más brillante* (Arturo, the Brightest Star, 1984) and *La loma del ángel* (1987; translated as *Graveyard of the Angels,* 1987). In addition he also published a long poem, *El central* (1981; translated as *El central,* 1984), and an experimental play, *Persecución* (1986), works that lyrically denounce the social, moral, and political oppression that has been a historical constant in Cuba.

*El mundo alucinante* is a surrealistic interpretation of the adventurous life of Friar de Mier. The novel uses as a pretext the friar's autobiographical accounts of his repeated persecutions, imprisonments, and escapes, a result of his wish for Mexican independence from Spanish colonial rule. The story follows the friar's original *Memorias* (Memoirs) in numbered episodes, spanning his childhood to his last days with the first Mexican president, Guadalupe Victoria. Arenas presents "hallucinatory" rewritings of de Mier's struggles for his country's emancipation, both in North America and Europe, down to his final disillusionment with the utopian revolutionary endeavor. As such, the novel is a critical commentary on historiographical claims to truth and an ironic portrayal that cautions the bureaucratic elements embedded in revolutionary societies.

Similarly, the triad constituted by *Celestino antes del alba, El palacio de las blanquísimas mofetas,* and *Otra vez el mar* can be considered as one continuous text that deals with the central theme of oppression at all levels of an individual's formation. The first novel is the story of a child who lives a cruel life of persecution and punishment at the hands of his grandparents for not conforming to their utilitarian demands. Instead, the young anonymous narrator tells in a lyrical manner of his liberating experiences with his alter ego, the young cousin Celestino,

*Cover of Arenas's 1980 novel, about a young man who escapes a repressive environment by joining rebel forces in the mountains*

whose predilection for poetic writing constitutes a major transgression from the grandfather's vision of order. The second novel of this group involves an interlude in the life of the same protagonist-narrator, now an adolescent living in Holguín; he is on the verge of sexual awakening and under the moral restrictions of a sanctimonious bourgeois society experiencing the crumbling effects of the insurgent fight against the forces of Batista. As a means of escape from the oppressive and stultifying environment created by the social mores of the provincial town, the maladjusted teenager takes to the surrounding mountains and joins the rebel forces, hoping to find there a redeeming cause to heal his existential anguish and bereavement. The death of the adolescent coincides with the end of the novel and confirms the allegorical dimension of the story.

*Otra vez el mar* has a different hero, a young poet living in Cuban revolutionary society, and the

*Arenas and his mother, Oneida Fuentes Arenas, in Miami during the early 1980s*

novel presents a day-to-day account of a one-week vacation at the seashore with his wife. The first half of the book comprises the wife's seven-entry diary, and the second half is a long poem written by the young man. The wife writes of the asphyxiating space in which she feels she is only man's specular representation; the husband's lyrical voice acts as an indictment of the limits of orthodox sexuality in its relation to the political goals of a moralizing patriarchal society in which homosexuality is forbidden. As in the previous novel, the final enunciations of the "double" text announce death as the only feasible escape, but this time in the form of the husband's suicide, which transcends the polarity of the voices.

*Arturo, la estrella más brillante* further explores the poignant narcissistic and Freudian dimensions present in Arenas's previous novels. The story takes place in one of the rehabilitation centers established by the Cuban revolutionary government during the 1960s for the confinement and reeducation of homosexuals and other social dissidents. The name of the protagonist recalls the French poet Ar-

thur Rimbaud, who suffered incarceration for his homosexual behavior and whose poetic transformations of reality always served Arenas well as inspirations. The hero, once again, is a writer suffering the repressive weight of a political apparatus from which he tries unsuccessfully to escape. This time his death comes at the hands of a tyrannical guardian with whom he has had sexual encounters and who metamorphoses as his mother in a transvestite mutation at the moment of his execution. The novel, therefore, goes beyond the mere fictionalization of Arenas's own experiences in political detention to become a metaphorical rendering of the Oedipus complex and the thwarting of desire by a patriarchal society.

*La loma del ángel* is a rewriting of a Cuban romantic classic, Cirilo Villaverde's *Cecilia Valdés* (1882), a novel of customs that denounces slavery. As in *El mundo alucinante,* Arenas's new version ironically subverts the traditional readings of the original, bringing out in a defamatory tone the evil and selfish nature of Villaverde's characters and of their love for each other. Arenas revokes the romantic celebration of love and family relations as a means of human transcendence and fulfillment, redefining them, in postmodern fashion, as an eternal quest for an imaginary realm that is never achieved.

His poem *El central* is a lyrical exposition of a Cuban topic of epic dimension: the forced labor in sugar plantations. Arenas presents in a recurrent manner three instances of obligatory work that represent the permanence of exploitative institutions in Cuban history: the system of *encomiendas* (land-grant system) of the Indians, the slavery of African-Cubans, and the organization of volunteer workers by the Cuban revolutionary government. These three institutions are poetically analogized, creating a complex play of reflections by which Arenas attempts to invalidate, as in *El mundo alucinante,* the traditional progressive conceptualization of history and its eschatological presuppositions.

His final work, *Antes que anochezca* (1992; translated as *Before Night Falls,* 1993), is an autobiography that covers, both tragically and humorously, key episodes of his life from early childhood to his last days in the United States. More than an autobiographical work, the book is a dramatic example of a poetic memoir and testimony. In it Arenas exposes the corruption and evil that have dominated Cuban political history and that finally led the nation into the iron grip of Castro and "political suicide." It is also a universal indictment of the basic hypocrisy and dishonesty of society, which through its power-oriented set of moral rules stifles individual self-realization. In order to denounce and fight this social oppression, Arenas irreverently brings forward his own homosexuality and the latent homosexuality of all people, underscoring at the same time the liberating dimension of writing as an erotic expression.

Throughout Arenas's works the leitmotiv of "no escape" keeps reminding the reader that the search for absolute freedom and truth, with the ensuing quenching of desire, is illusory, and that all seemingly expiatory or clarifying creations are nothing but rhetorical constructs marked by contingency and derived from a cultural and linguistic legacy. In this sense Arenas's writing falls within the "negative" philosophical tradition of Friedrich Nietzsche, Theodor Adorno, Borges, and postmodern thinkers such as Jacques Derrida. But the ironic consciousness of fragmentation is offset by the passionate longing for harmony in all of Arenas's works. In the face of divine silence and human blindness, liberating insight may be found in an agonistic act of constant writing and rewriting, which reveals the precariousness of the figures proposed as well as their glory as symbols of the imagination's boundless interpretive capacity.

Two of Arenas's texts, El mundo alucinante and La loma del ángel, explicitly make use of previous literary works as pretexts. In both the textual transformation results in a parody that satirizes the logical, semantic, and rhetorical structures of the originals. This satire is executed with double intentionality: as an indication of the artificiality of the reality represented in the initial works and as a means to expand that partial reality – that is, a parodic deconstruction. With El mundo alucinante the reader encounters a multifarious narrative, a parodic textual hyperbole of history, rather than its faithful literary re-creation.

This rich act of representational disfiguration is also found in the rest of Arenas's works, but without the initial prefatory identification of the text parodied. The pretextual models silently lie under the disguise of Arenas's own ironic style. Parts of Celestino antes del alba closely follow some of André Breton's surrealistic poetical formulas, while others draw on verses by Borges, Rimbaud, Federico García Lorca, and Eliseo Diego, among others. In Otra vez el mar there are parodic reminiscences of works by Homer, Walt Whitman, and José Martí. And in El central the subversive imitative act dismantles the linguistic conventions and idealist intentions of two Cuban antislavery subtexts, Bartolomé de las Casas's well-known Brevísima relación de la

destrucción de las Indias (1552; translated as Devastation of the Indies, 1924) and Lino Novás Calvo's El negrero (The Slave Trader, 1933). In general, the parodic function of Arenas's works undermines the normative powers of certain discourses consecrated by traditional consent or official manipulation in order to continue their control over individual self-assertion.

The use of intertextual allusions and insertions, which goes hand in hand with the satirical travesty of existing texts, is one of the most prevalent structural components of Arenas's textual fabrications, alongside the carnivalesque nature of the parodic strategy. This intertexuality used by Arenas follows Borges's understanding of language as a depository of collective history. Celestino antes del alba, for example, appears as a collection of intertexts – overt and covert, authentic and apocryphal. Some of them appear detached from the main narrative, while the remaining ones are syntactically integrated into it. Among the latter type few are identified by footnotes, whereas the others require literary competence in order to establish their textual or authorial origin. Explicitly present in this intertextual web are quotes from Sophocles, Shakespeare, Rimbaud, Lorca, Borges, Diego, La chanson de Roland (eleventh century) and a popular Hispanic folk song, "Mambrú se fue a la guerra" (Mambrú Went to War). Arenas also plays with intratextual segments, that is, he grafts together elements in a parodic manner. The possibilities of this narrative device appear with a greater degree of development in El palacio de las blanquísimas mofetas and Otra vez el mar.

In addition to this interweaving of material, Celestino antes del alba contains long sections exhibiting the conventions of other genres. Almost one-third of the text is rendered in the mimetic mode of the drama, and various poemlike segments of epic and lyrical nature are interspersed throughout. A similar "generic excess" is present in El mundo alucinante, which purports to be an autobiography, a historiographical account, a testimonial narrative, and a picaresque adventure novel all at once. In El palacio de las blanquísimas mofetas one of the three parts of the novel is a drama under the heading of "Función" (Function), while the other sections rely heavily on journalistic excerpts. Otra vez el mar couples a diary and a poem. The second half, in the form of Homeric "chants," is traversed by a multiplicity of fragments conforming to essay, short-story, and dramatic writing styles. The experimental play Persecución is made up of four short dramas in which the actors need to enunciate long recitative and narrative lines in such a degree of complexity that the performance

*Arenas in 1990, one month before his death (photograph ©
Lázaro Gómez Carriles)*

is negated by the privileged role of the narrative discourse.

In the parodic mode of writing and through the inscriptional system of grafting, Reinaldo Arenas found a literary strategy for the indictment of established power, be it epistemological, political, or moral, without becoming trapped by the delusive thought of a totally emancipated and unmarred future. Although there is no escape, his unyieldingly romantic upholding of human freedom and justice drove him to a passionate search for an existential condition not opposed to the full unfolding of the imagination's creative wealth. Arenas used a paradoxical, dazzling, twisting, ever-expansive, and self-subversive writing style that allowed him to escape from the official conventions of representation and to say, as in the last words of Persecución, "Mi triunfo" (My triumph). For this type of liberating textuality, Arenas gained an indisputable place of honor in the list of significant Spanish-American writers. On 6 December 1990, after several years of suffering from AIDS, he ended his life in his humble New York apartment.

**Interviews:**

Christina Guzmán, Interview with Arenas, in Arenas's *La vieja Rosa* (Caracas: Cruz del Sur, 1980), pp. 103–114;

Ana Roa, Interview with Arenas, *Américas,* 33 (September 1981): 36–38.

**References:**

Pedro Barreda, "Vestirse al desnudo, borrando escribirse: *El central* de Reinaldo Arenas," *Boletín de la Academia Puertorriqueña de la Lengua Española,* 12 (1984): 25–37;

Eduardo C. Béjar, *La textualidad de Reinaldo Arenas: Juegos de la escritura posmoderna* (Madrid: Playor, 1987);

Alicia Borinsky, "Re-escribir y escribir: Arenas, Menard, Borges, Cervantes, Fray Servando," *Revista Iberoamericana,* 41, nos. 92–93 (1975): 605–616;

Andrew Bush, "The Riddled Text: Borges and Arenas," *Modern Language Notes,* 103 (March 1988): 374–397;

Eliseo Diego, "Sobre *Celestino antes del alba*," *Casa de las Américas,* 45 (1967): 162–166;

Ottmar Ette, ed., *La escritura de la memoria: Reinaldo Arenas – Textos, estudios y documentación* (Frankfurt am Main: Vervuert, 1991);

Claude Fell, "Un neobarroco del desequilibrio: *El mundo alucinante* de Reinaldo Arenas," in *XVII Congreso: Instituto Internacional de Literatura* (Madrid: Cultura Hispánica del Centro Iberoamericano de Cooperación, 1978), pp. 25–31;

Angel L. Fernández-Guerra, "Recurrencias obsesivas y variantes alucinantes en la obra de Reinaldo Arenas," *Caravelle,* 16 (1970): 133–140;

Julio Hernández-Miyares and Perla Rozencvaig, eds., *Reinaldo Arenas: Alucinaciones, fantasía y realidad* (Glenview, Ill.: Scott, Foresman/Montesinos, 1990);

William Luis, "Present and Future Antislavery Narratives: Reinaldo Arenas's *Graveyard of the Angels*," in his *Literary Bondage: Slavery in Cuban Narrative* (Austin: University of Texas Press, 1990), pp. 238–247;

Jorge Olivares, "Carnival and the Novel: Reinaldo Arenas' *El palacio de las blanquísimas mofetas*," *Hispanic Review,* 53 (Autumn 1985): 467–476;

Julio Ortega, "El mundo alucinante de Fray Servando," *Revista de la Universidad de México,* 26, no. 4 (1971): 25–27;

Emir Rodríquez Monegal, "The Labyrinthine World of Reinaldo Arenas," *Latin American Literary Review,* 8, no. 16 (1980): 126–131;

Rozencvaig, *Reinaldo Arenas: Narrativa de la transgresión* (Miami: Universal, 1986);

Roberto Valero, *El desamparado humor de Reinaldo Arenas* (Miami: University of Miami Press, 1991);

Emil Volek, "La carnavalización y la alegoría en *El mundo alucinante,* de Reinaldo Arenas," *Revista Iberoamericana,* 130–131 (1985): 125–148.

# Manlio Argueta
*(24 November 1936 – )*

Ineke Phaf
*University of Maryland*

BOOKS: *En el costado de la luz* (San Salvador: Editorial Universitaria de El Salvador, 1968);
*El valle de las hamacas* (Buenos Aires: Sudamericana, 1970);
*Caperucita en la Zona Roja* (Havana: Casa de las Américas, 1977);
*Un día en la vida* (San Salvador: UCA, 1980); translated by Bill Brow as *One Day of Life* (New York: Vintage, 1983; London: Chatto & Windus, 1984);
*Cuzcatlán donde bate la mar del sur* (Tegucigalpa, Honduras: Guaymuras, 1986); translated by Clark Hansen as *Cuzcatlán: Where the Southern Sea Beats* (New York: Vintage, 1987);
*El Salvador,* with photographs by Adam Kufeld (New York: Norton, 1990).

MOTION PICTURE: *Cuzcatlán Stories,* screenplay by Argueta.

OTHER: *Poesía en El Salvador,* edited by Argueta (San José, Costa Rica: Editorial Universitaria Centroamericana, 1983);
Contributor, *Recopilación de textos sobre Roque Dalton,* edited by Horatio García Verzi (Havana: Casa de las Américas, 1986), pp. 580–584;
"Autovaloración literaria," in *Cambios estéticos y nuevos proyectos culturales en Centroamérica: Testimonios, entrevistas y ensayos,* edited by Amelia Mondragón (Washington, D.C.: Literal, 1994), pp. 27–33.

SELECTED PERIODICAL PUBLICATIONS –
UNCOLLECTED: "Rosario a las seis: Operación gaviota de ojos azules" and "La excusa," *Revista Bimestral de la Universidad de El Salvador,* 2 (March–April 1969): 107–116;
"La noche de los niños," *La Nación,* 12 July 1992, pp. 2D–3D.

Criticism on the work of Salvadoran novelist and poet Manlio Argueta is increasingly focusing on his relationship with the intellectual tradition in El Salvador and the other countries of Central America since the late 1950s. In those years young poets and students began to perceive the impact of a new era, the process of modernization of daily life which was to have dramatic consequences on the future of politics and completely transform the notion of contemporary cultural history.

Manlio Argueta was born on 24 November 1936. After growing up in San Miguel, a city he characterizes as a forgotten and marginal place in the province, Argueta went to the capital of El Salvador, San Salvador, for his university studies. The difference between these two towns was enormous. In order to explain the cultural environment in which he was brought up, Argueta tells the following anecdote in "Autovaloración literaria" (1994):

> Fue en 1955 cuando un amigo y profesor del liceo donde estudiaba recibió amonestación y separación del cargo de la sección literaria por haber concedido para mis poemas las dos páginas centrales del periódico. Los propietarios no aceptaban que se le concediera espacio a un joven desconocido y que, según ellos, no escribía poesía. No sé si influyó el contenido de los poemas, pues decían sobre los ríos de mi país y la muerte navegando en ellos.

> (It was in 1955 when a friend and teacher in the high school I attended was warned and dismissed from his job in charge of the literary section of the newspaper because of having published my poems on the centerfold. The owners did not want this space to be given to a young unknown author who, in their opinion, did not write poetry at all. I do not know if the content of the poems influenced them, because they spoke about the rivers in my country and death navigating in them.)

With this anecdote Argueta describes the existing ignorance toward literature in his native region and the consequent intolerance that forced him to hide his early passion for fiction and poetry, known exclusively to the members of his own family. Only after leaving for San Salvador a few months later could he begin discussing his ideas and interests with other people. Soon he was able to vindicate the honor of his

*Manlio Argueta, 1992 (photograph by Fiona Neill)*

friend in San Miguel by winning the national poetry prize.

Argueta entered law school like many other students of his generation who belonged to those "privilegiados universitarios en un país con el 76 por ciento de analfabetismo, cero prestaciones sociales, cero libertades y derechos" (privileged university students in a country with a 76 percent illiteracy rate, zero social welfare, zero freedom and justice). This encounter with new ideas in the capital had a decisive impact on his life and work. The capital at that time was undergoing a period of rapid modernization, and in the Literary University Circle, founded in 1956, young intellectuals such as Argueta and other writers – including Roque Dalton, Roberto Armijo, and Otto René Castillo from Guatemala, who later became well known – discussed how to express this transformation in an appropriate literary form. The members of this circle became highly active in cultural organizations as well as in politics. Their role model was lawyer and poet Oswaldo Escobar V, one of the initiators of the "poesía de denuncia" (poetry of social criticism) in El Salvador and the founder of the Asociación de Escritores Antifascistas (Association of Antifascist

Writers) in 1944. His house was a center for discussion, and in the cultural page of the newspaper the students published poetry in which the "national problem" was questioned from diverse perspectives. In a country where the military had ruled and determined education since 1931, these voices were considered subversive, anarchistic, and a potential danger to the public order.

For a long time after his graduation Argueta headed the university press in El Salvador, but after the military intervention at the university by the national army in 1972 he had to leave the country. For the next twenty-one years Argueta lived with his wife and children in San José, Costa Rica, where he founded and directed the Cultural Institute of El Salvador. He also had an important function in the Editorial Universitaria Centroamericana (EDUCA) and was president of the Association of Central American Writers. In 1993 Argueta was able to return to El Salvador, where he teaches literature at the National University and is director of its library.

Although Argueta considers himself mainly a poet, he has become known more for his four novels. With the manuscript of his first novel, *El valle de las hamacas* (The Valley of the Hammocks), published in 1970 in Buenos Aires, he won the national literary prize in El Salvador in 1968. The jury included renowned literary figures such as Angel Rama, Emmanuel Carballo, and Guillermo Sucre. Argueta's second novel, *Caperucita en la Zona Roja* (Red Riding Hood in the Red Zone), received the Casa de las Américas Prize in Havana in 1977. *Un día en la vida* (1980; translated as *One Day of Life,* 1983) not only was awarded the national prize from the Catholic University of San Salvador but also became the first best-seller in Central America and was translated into English, German, Dutch, Greek, and Turkish. His latest work, *Cuzcatlán donde bate la mar del sur* (1986; translated as *Cuzcatlán: Where the Southern Sea Beats,* 1987), also has received international attention. In addition Argueta has written the script for the film *Cuzcatlán Stories.*

Notwithstanding his success, Argueta has scarcely been studied within the literary tradition of his own country. This absence of interest in this aspect of Argueta's work may be due to his explicit involvement in the political situation in El Salvador and in the problems of other countries of Central America. Apparently his political involvement has precluded concentration on his national background as a writer. However, if one reads Argueta's poetry and prose from the point of view of the specific interest of the Literary Circle in social conditions and modern urban life, San Salvador projects itself throughout his work as an outstanding feature. In a sense Argueta shows readers how to imagine contemporary history from the perspective of the capital of El Salvador, with casual excursions to Honduras, Nicaragua, or France. This historical overview goes as far back as the colonization of Cuzcatlán by the Spaniards, the first military confrontation with indigenous groups and the precedent for the 1932 massacre, when the national army killed more than thirty thousand Salvadoran citizens. This confrontation in turn is connected to the civil war that broke out in 1980 between the Salvadoran government, supported by war material and capital coming from the United States, and the Farabundo Martí Front for National Liberation (FMLN). Since then approximately seventy-five thousand lives have been lost, and more than one million citizens have had to leave the country. (This historical framework marks exceptionally violent moments in the history of El Salvador.)

This historical focus also determines most of Argueta's poetry. For example, in the poem "Ciudad" (Town) – the last in a 1963 series of eight compositions entitled "El viajero" (The Traveler),

and included in his first book, *En el costado de la luz* (On the Side of the Light, 1968) – Argueta describes a trip leading from the metro stations at Gare de Lyon and Puerta de Lilas in Paris to Managua and the Villa Elena, ending in the "Calle de Lapa, cinturón de barrio pobre" (Lapa Street, belt of a poor neighborhood). The poet implies that the nucleus of the national life is condensed in this belt close to the city center, the sea, and the bay. However, this poverty is not understood as a natural or God-given situation.

Argueta states that his oeuvre is centered around an encounter with San Salvador in its function as the capital. In his first novel, *El valle de las hamacas,* this situation is already prominent. Argueta focuses on the problems of Salvadoran intellectuals, who see themselves confronted with the specific implications of metropolitan life. His collage technique constructs a fragmented perception of the environment of San Salvador, presenting various voices and personal testimonies mixed with quotations from books, newspapers, and magazines. This presentation of a highly active civic space involves the reader in a mixture of impressions.

In terms of structure, Argueta's novel follows the classical model of a Greek drama with its division into three parts. In the third and last section, the capital is placed at the center of the narrative. With the opening sentence, "Aquí comienza la ciudad" (Here begins the city), the author introduces San Salvador as an "esclava fiel, siervo que encenderá todas las teas que necesita el amo para no tropezar" (loyal slave, a serf who will light all the torches to prevent his master from falling).

The main character crosses the capital in a bus on Route 7, now a part of this "terrible" valley of hammocks, the Central American region. The title refers to a description of the valley from 1524, when it was already densely populated. Argueta constructs a link with the contemporary situation by quoting from a letter-report by Pedro de Alvarado to Hernán Cortés in which Alvarado refers to the conquest of the city of Cuzcatlán. All its inhabitants fled to the mountains and proved hard to conquer. Argueta makes the point that Alvarado was the first writer to document the violence of the colonial encounter, a "civilizing" trace whose consequences are still evident today.

The image of the bus reappears but with different connotations in Argueta's second novel. *Caperucita en la Zona Roja* is about the narrator, a *guerrillero* and "poor little poet" – an allusion to the title of a major work by Roque Dalton, *Pobrecito poeta que era yo . . .* (Poor Little Poet That I Was . . . ) –

and his girlfriend, Red Riding Hood, who lives with him in the dangerous urban area, alias the Red Zone, the favorite place where the wolf (the modern Salvadoran state and its repressive system) resides. Argueta's intellectuals, generally students, are involved in organizing the urban resistance while the guerrilla war focused activity in the mountains. The students plan a brief demonstration around a bus, and some of the demonstrators are taken prisoner and have a long debate with a high official who tries to instruct them in the rules of justice.

While mingling this dangerous urban world with a fairy tale about a young girl and a wolf, Argueta presents the role of the feminine throughout as a passive factor in the historical action, not as its vital element. In his two most recent novels, however, this panorama changes completely. Guadalupe Fuentes de Guardado in *Un día en la vida* and Lucía Martínez/Beatriz in *Cuzcatlán donde bate la mar del sur* tell the events in each novel in their own words. Argueta places their lives respectively in the period immediately before the assassination of Archbishop Oscar Romero on 24 March 1980 and on 9 January 1981, one day before the first successful offensive from the FMLN against the government.

This active role of the feminine as necessary to democratic forces in El Salvador is not surprising. According to sociologists and feminists, in the classical model of democracy the female personifies urban life in its intimate and welcoming form, offering its citizens privacy and domestic peace. In contrast, the male is associated with an abstract and aggressive public atmosphere and its military manifestations. In Argueta's novels this male aspect is represented by the soldier or police officer, well prepared against the danger of communism thanks to the instruction of foreign professors, mostly gringos in the military academy. Of humble origins, the young officers are completely alienated from the daily life within the pleasant neighborhoods of the urban middle class whose interests they defend. The intellectuals, peasants, and workers are opposed to this male role, and in accordance with the transformation of El Salvador, Argueta has to display a heroine who suits this scenario. She is a modest working person from the countryside who has experienced the repression of her whole family. By describing her situation the author highlights the formerly "invisible human beings" living in El Salvador and Central America. Thus critics such as John Beverley and Marc Zimmerman speak of the feminization of Central American literature, in which women take on new roles in the course of social struggle and new bonds of affiliation between men and women appear.

Cover for Argueta's 1977 novel, which comments on El Salvadoran society by placing the story of Little Red Riding Hood in a contemporary setting

Argueta often refers to his intellectual debt to his friend and colleague Rogue Dalton, who, with the novel-diary *Pobrecito poeta que era yo . . . ,* described his love-hate relationship with his country, the smallest in Central America. In his prologue Dalton expresses this ambivalent feeling: "Es una obligación de todo patriota odiar a su país de una manera creadora" (It is an obligation for every patriot to hate his country in a creative way). From the perspectives and testimonies of different men Dalton reflects on various episodes and experiences that document the social struggle for democracy in Central America.

To this male-centered view of El Salvadoran history Argueta adds the female perspective in his last two novels. In a 1981 interview with Ivonne Jiménez he stated that testimony goes beyond literature and that the role of women is particularly relevant. In another interview, with Zulma Nelly Martínez in 1985, Argueta explained that he got the idea for *Un día en la vida* after interviewing a peasant woman, the wife of an important leader, for an article in a magazine he worked for:

Y lo hice: pero después, tiempo después, en un momento en que decidí escribir una novela recordé que tenía una grabación de esa campesina, la volví a escuchar y me empezó a gustar: su voz, la ternura, la humildad con que hablaba y la seguridad con que decía las cosas, la serenidad con que planteaba su tragedia. Porque era una tragedia. La conversación con la campesina es bastante breve, de unos cuarenta y cinco minutos ... durante este breve lapso me cuenta cómo matan a su compañero y me refiere esa escena que reproduzco en la novela y que describe a los guardias llevando a su compañero ya moribundo al pueblo donde viven y, más específicamente, a la casa que comparten. Una escena, por cierto, muy dramática ya que toda la gente (los parientes y amigos e incluso ella misma) niegan conocerlo. Es decir, tienen que negarse a reconocerlo ...

(And I did it: but afterward, only afterward, at that moment that I decided to write a novel, I remembered that I had a tape recording of this woman. I listened to it over and over again and I began to like it: her voice, the tender and modest way she spoke and the conviction with which she said things, the serenity with which she explained her tragedy. Because it really was a tragedy. The conversation with her is rather short, only some forty-five minutes ... during this short time she tells me how they killed her companion, and I refer to this scene in the novel where she describes how the police brought him already dying to the village where they live and, more specifically, to the house where they lived together. It's very dramatic because everyone – the parents and friends and she herself – denies knowing him. That is to say, they have to deny knowing him ... ).

*Un día en la vida* was published in 1980, three years before the most well-known Central American testimony, *Me llamo Rigoberta Menchú* (translated as *I, Rigoberta Menchú*, 1984) by Mayan-Guatemalan Rigoberta Menchú and Venezuelan anthropologist Elizabeth Burgos Debray, came out. Menchú's testimony relates to an agricultural tradition full of local knowledge and centuries of life experiences, which contrasts with moments when violence manifests itself as the companion of modernization. The characteristics of this rural landscape and its daily occurrences also determine the rhythms of Argueta's two most recent narrative works. In *Un día en la vida* modern life is evidenced by the omnipresence of the Western clock and calendar. For Guadelupe Fuentes de Guardado, the main character, the day begins at 5:30 A.M. and

ends at 5:00 P.M., as is indicated in the headings of most of the chapters. Life is hard, but fortunately "sólo maíz no necesitamos comprar pues sembramos lo suficiente para el año y todavía sobran para venderles unas libritas a los vecinos" (the only thing we do not have to buy is corn, because we sow enough for the whole year and still have some left to sell to the neighbors). Argueta stresses the role of corn, for at least a thousand years the basic food in this region and devalued at present as the food of the poor.

The metaphor of the bus in Argueta's work becomes increasingly linked to the question of the struggle for better social conditions and against cultural discrimination. Adolfina Fuentes, the granddaughter of Guadelupe Fuentes de Guardado in *Un día en la vida,* takes the Number 38 bus for the route between Chalate (an abbreviation of Chalatenango) and El Salvador. There she meets María Romelia and her nephew Arturo, who participated in the demonstration organized by the Christian farmers' trade union in front of the bank in the capital. They had asked for loans to be able to buy fertilizers and other products that help them cultivate their land. The army intervened with guns and helicopters, burning the bus down with most of the demonstrators inside.

The relevance of this military repression also determines the events in *Cuzcatlán donde bate la mar del sur,* illustrated with the helicopters flying above the sea on the title page. Argueta takes the letter-report of Pedro de Alvarado in 1524 as an epigraph, followed by a dialogue between a soldier and a foreign reporter about their different vision of the mountains: either as a beautiful panorama or as the hateful symbol of war. The author then proceeds to repeat the phrase Microbus to San Salvador, 9 January 1981, six consecutive times as the titles of those chapters that determine the argument. Lucía Martínez, who uses the name of her grandmother as a pseudonym, takes a similar route when she has to testify about the murder of her companion. The guerrilla army takes the police sergeant Martínez, who committed the crime, as a prisoner. He turns out to be Lucía's nephew, and she judges that he should remain alive, conscious of the fact that he has killed a member of his own family.

In the course of the trips in these two novels a broad panorama of the material world appears framed around the connotations implied by little houses in the village, children, pigs, stones to grind maize, tortillas, cooperatives, trade unions, or the mesón (house divided in modest apartments for poor people) called Las Flores in San Miguel. Other terms relate to the hostile urban environment with which the peasants find themselves confronted:

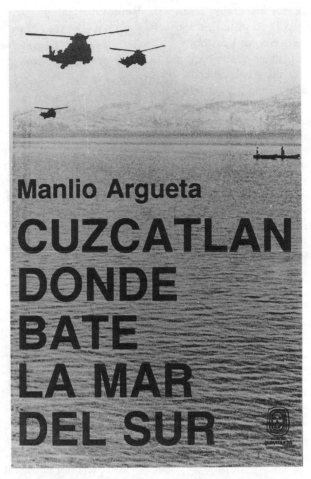

Cover for Argueta's 1986 novel, about the impact of war on
El Salvador

working conditions as in the times of slavery, unhealthy textile factories, sickness, unemployment, overpopulation, big airplanes, army helicopters, trucks, and so on.

It is remarkable that little by little in Argueta's works the members of the police and military receive more attention. In his 1987 interview with Dan Bellm, Argueta argued that national guardsmen also suffer. Typically born as sons of farmers, they have to leave home early in their lives and receive their education in a completely different environment. Sharp contradictions in the same family are precisely at the base of the national violence. Argueta predicts, however, that this situation will not persist. His forthcoming novel bears the title "La noche de los niños" (Night of the Children), and in a 1992 discussion with Victoria García Serrano the author revealed his future plans: "I would prefer to continue doing the work that I do, that is cultural work which I believe I could do well in El Salvador. In other words, [I would like to] fill

in those [cultural] gaps that I am always talking about. That's [a responsibility] that the government has not met, that has not been met through any other organization. For example, making books for schools, and above all for children."

Argueta's attitude is clear when one combines the meaning of several photographs taken by Adam Kufeld for which Argueta wrote the corresponding text in their book *El Salvador* (1990). A boy is in one photo and in another one a girl sitting in a bus, Argueta's repeated metaphor, on which is painted the slogan "Let's go." They are leaving the refugee camp in Honduras to return home with their families. If these children were to look out the window after having passed the border of El Salvador they would have seen soldiers standing there, more or less of the same age, who watch them with big rifles in their hands. This position of children whom the military has exploited to fulfill its role of repressing democratic movements in El Salvador as well as other countries of Central America becomes

Argueta's main thesis. He is not interested in increasing polarization but intends to give this violence a historical dimension, centered in a history El Salvador shares with other countries of the region. In this quality resides his outstanding relevance as a writer. Argueta's poems that accompany Kufeld's photos underline his intention of giving hope for a better future in El Salvador without forgetting to explain the inner meaning of its violent past:

> For children, the years ahead glitter like stars,
> almost visible.          Their dreams
>                                   no longer hopeless.
> Things are better these days, especially
> if we measure our era in terms of galactic years.
> All of the effort of the past is justified
>            by this awakening
> of radiant thoughts and welcome feelings.
> We can hardly sleep
>            reaching
> to take the stars in our hands.          Eyes
> open to a growing humanity.

## Interviews:

Ivonne Jiménez, "Manlio Argueta: Centroamérica está haciendo la literatura de America Latina," *Suplemento del Periódico Universidad,* 64 (November 1981): 7–8;

Zulma Nelly Martínez, *Hispamérica,* 15, no. 42 (1985): 41–54;

Dan Bellm, "Children of the Corn: Manlio Argueta's Rescue Mission," *Village Voice* (22 September 1987);

Victoria García Serrano, "Exiled Salvadoran Author Prays for Peace," *Voice* [Emory University], 9, no. 9 (1992): 3.

## References:

John Beverley and Marc Zimmerman, *Literature and Politics in the Central American Revolutions* (Austin: University of Texas Press, 1990), pp. 115–143, 189–196;

Myriam Bustos Arratia, "El cuento de Alegría y el de Argueta," *Literatura Chilena en el Exilio,* 11 (July 1979): 7–12;

Wilfrido H. Corral, "La hamaca contestataria o la posibilidad de varios paneles acerca de Manlio Argueta," in *Cambios estéticos y nuevos proyectos culturales en Centroamérica,* edited by Amelia Mondragón (Washington, D.C.: Literal, 1994), pp. 35–38;

Silvia L. López, "Argueta, Dalton y la crítica de la historia," in *Cambios estéticos y nuevos proyectos culturales en Centroamérica,* pp. 39–45;

Claire Pailler, "El reportaje del guerrillero: Una narrativa ambigua," *Studi de Letteratura Ispano-Americana,* 24 (1993): 67–82;

Raúl Rodríguez Hernández, " 'Nueva novela histórica' hispanoamericana: La insurrección y *Un día en la vida,*" *Texto Crítico,* 8, nos. 36–37 (1987): 153–163;

Monique Sarfati-Arnaud, "Le discours testimonial et le je(u) de l'autre dans 'Un día en la vida' de Manlio Argueta," in *Parole exclusive, parole exclué, parole transgressive: Marginalisation et marginalité dans les pratiques discursives,* edited by Antonio Gómez-Moriana and Catharine Poupeney Hart (Longueuil, Quebec: Préamble, 1990);

Nicasio Urbina, "Novela y testimonio en la narrativa de Manlio Argueta: El contrato autorial," in *Cambios estéticos y nuevos proyectos culturales en Centroamérica,* pp. 57–63.

# Miguel Barnet

*(28 January 1940 –    )*

Elzbieta Sklodowska
*Washington University*

BOOKS: *La piedra fina y el pavorreal* (Havana: Unión de Escritores y Artistas de Cuba, 1963);

*Isla de güijes* (Havana: El Puente, 1964);

*Biografía de un cimarrón* (Havana: Instituto de Etnología y Folklore, 1966); translated by Jocasta Innes as *The Autobiography of a Runaway Slave* (New York: Pantheon, 1968);

*La sagrada familia* (Havana: Casa de las Américas, 1967);

*Canción de Rachel* (Havana: Instituto del Libro, 1969); partially translated and annotated by Jill Netchinsky as "Song of Rachel," *Latin American Literary Review*, 8, no. 16 (1981): 119–125;

*Akeké y la jutía* (Havana: Unión de Escritores y Artistas de Cuba, 1978);

*Orikis y otros poemas* (Havana: Letras Cubanas, 1980);

*Gallego* (Madrid: Alfaguara, 1981);

*Carta de noche* (Havana: Unión de Escritores y Artistas de Cuba, 1982);

*La fuente viva* (Havana: Letras Cubanas, 1983);

*La vida real* (Havana: Letras Cubanas, 1986);

*Claves por Rita Montaner* (Matanzas, Cuba, 1987);

*Viendo mi vida pasar* (Havana: Letras Cubanas, 1987);

*Oficio de ángel* (Madrid: Alfaguara, 1989).

OTHER: Fernando Ortiz, *Ensayos etnográficos,* edited by Barnet (Havana: Editorial de Ciencias Sociales, 1984).

SELECTED PERIODICAL PUBLICATIONS – UNCOLLECTED: "Testimonio y comunicación: Una vía hacia la identidad," *Unión,* 17, no. 4 (1980): 131–143; translated as "The Documentary Novel," *Cuban Studies/Estudios Cubanos,* 11, no. 1 (1981): 19–32;

"The Culture That Sugar Created," translated by Naomi Lindstrom, *Latin American Literary Review,* 8, (Spring-Summer 1981): 38–46;

*Miguel Barnet, circa 1980*

"Nicolás Guillén: La sabiduría del Taita," *Unión,* 19, no. 2 (1982): 160–162.

Miguel Barnet is one of the most original writers of Latin America. His fiction, poetry, and essays derive their energy from the cultural diversity of Cuba while providing varied and often ambivalent responses to the shifting political demands of the Socialist regime after 1959. Within the broader framework of contemporary Latin-American literature, Barnet's most distinctive and enduring contribution lies in the *testimonio* (testimony). He coined the term to describe a novel-length first-person narrative based on eyewitness accounts, edited from transcripts and molded into a work of literary merit by a professional writer. *Testimonio* is essentially a hybrid: aesthetic aspirations to literariness combine with scientific claims of objectivity; stylistic devices of fiction merge with research and documentation borrowed from the social sciences.

Miguel Barnet was born on 28 January 1940. His "official" biography in the *Diccionario de literatura cubana* (Dictionary of Cuban Literature, 1984) is laconic and elusive: even the facts mentioned by the author himself in various interviews or alluded to in his creative writings cannot be pieced together easily. Barnet repeatedly refers to his bourgeois family background and mentions having been educated in American schools in his native Havana. In retrospect, however, he considers his formal education far less important than his childhood in the socially and ethnically diverse neighborhood of El Vedado. In a 1988 interview with Mariano Navarro, Barnet elaborated more specifically on his first encounters with the African customs and traditions that heightened his class awareness and later helped him overcome his alienation from the social realities of prerevolutionary Cuba. "He lived in a prosperous household, but in front of their house there was a five-story building turned into what in Cuba is called a *solar*, where poor people used to live. He would visit there and get to know a fabulous, utterly different world. It bewildered him at first, but he came to realize that this was also his world and that people of his class had simply been indifferent to this facet of Cuban culture.

The revolution of 1959 not only divided Barnet's life between his middle-class roots and his commitment to social and political change; it also separated his adolescence from his maturity. On the eve of the revolution Barnet was pursuing a career in advertising at the Escuela de Publicidad (School of Advertising) in Havana. At about the same time, he started writing his first poems, inspired by Afro-Cuban folktales and religious beliefs, later compiled by his friends and published as *La piedra fina y el pavorreal* (The Fine Stone and the Peacock, 1963). Barnet dedicated this book to Tonde, a *santero* (healer/diviner) from Palmira with whom he had first visited a *lucumí* temple. Although the new dominant ideology favored a materialistic interpretation of Cuban past and present, in the early 1960s the constraints of Marxist doctrine were not yet so in-

flexible as to ban the exploration of Barnet's main interest: Afro-Cuban folklore, with all its magic, "irrational" cults, beliefs, and myths.

During their first years in power the new ideologues favored revolutionary epics, but they also endorsed literary, historiographical, and anthropological projects that, as Seymour Menton puts it in *Prose Fiction of the Cuban Revolution* (1975), "exorcised" the past through a critique of prerevolutionary texts. And the history of black people – previously either distorted or simply unexplored – lent itself particularly well to such polemical rewriting. The most enduring projects of this nature, as Roberto González Echevarría suggests in "Criticism and Literature in Revolutionary Cuba," ventured beyond the limits of the revolutionary orthodoxy. Examples of this include Barnet's *Biografía de un cimarrón* (translated as *The Autobiography of a Runaway Slave,* 1968); Manuel Moreno Fraginal's monumental study of the slave economy, *El ingenio* (The Sugar Mill, 1964); and the research project "History of the People without History," conducted from 1963 to 1971 by Juan Pérez de la Riva and Pedro Deschamps Chapeaux under the auspices of the National Library. However, none of these works fully fits the areas so clearly mapped by Fidel Castro in his slogan addressed to the intellectuals: "Dentro de la Revolución, todo; fuera de la Revolución, nada" (Within the Revolution, everything; against the Revolution, nothing).

Barnet coped well with his own initial bewilderment and self-questioning during the first years of revolutionary enthusiasm. In 1960 he enrolled in a seminar on ethnology and folklore and soon began working as a professor of folklore at the Escuela de Instructores de Arte (School for Art Instructors) in Havana (1961–1966). In 1963 his first volume of poetry, *La piedra fina y el pavorreal,* was published, followed by *Isla de güijes* (Island of Pebbles, 1964). According to most critics as well as Barnet, these poems prefigure his future poetic and narrative work in their attempt to render exhaustively researched anthropological matter into a perfectly crafted, readable literary form.

At the same time, Barnet was also gaining research experience at the Institute of Ethnology and Folklore of the Academy of Science as an apprentice of Luis Argeliers, María Teresa Linares y Barreal, and Fernando Ortiz. Barnet has affirmed Ortiz's crucial role in his intellectual formation as a young ethnologist.

At this important stage in his search for identity, both as a poet and a social scientist, Barnet was also fortunate to become acquainted with many of the leading Cuban writers: Roberto Fernández Retamar prefaced *La piedra fina y el pavorreal;* Alejo Carpentier was his superior at the publishing house Editorial Nacional, where he worked for a time; and José Lezama Lima provided him both artistic guidance and close friendship. But it was Ortiz's vision and method – which detractors claimed was too eclectic and admirers praised as interdisciplinary – that helped to nourish Barnet's testimonial narrative.

Much like his mentor, Barnet moves beyond established genres and disciplines and can thus be perceived as an anomaly: a poet-novelist-ethnologist. As he stated in a 1980 interview with Barry B. Levine, "One has to go towards a fusion of the disciplines towards integration." Some critics nonetheless insist on a perfect harmony between different facets of Barnet's work. Angel Luis Fernández Guerra, for example, undertakes to demonstrate the continuity running through Barnet's discourse and even illustrates his point with intricate graphs in "Edipo y Cayo Graco (Para leer a Miguel Barnet)."

But this neat image is questioned by William Luis in the portion of his book *Literary Bondage: Slavery in Cuban Narrative* (1990) that focuses on the various ambiguities at the heart of Barnet's work. Safely avoiding the "biographical fallacy," Luis suggests that Barnet's decision to embark on the testimonial project was in a way a political one. When the rapidly shifting rules of the political game made Barnet's poetic activities difficult, it was the testimonial narrative that helped him to navigate "within" the discourse of the revolution and yet past the traps of ideologically aggressive jargon. Luis provides some background facts to substantiate his hypothesis: "Barnet was associated with a second-generation group of poets known as El Puente after a private publishing house of the same name which operated between 1960 and 1965. In 1964 El Puente published his second book of poetry, *Isla de güijes*. But the El Puente group fell from grace and was accused of stressing the aesthetic over the political. Regardless of their revolutionary commitment, group members were considered antisocial, and some were sent to rehabilitation camps known as . . . Military Units of Aid to Production. Those under detention and others were excluded from cultural and literary activities. During these years Barnet had gone unpublished in Cuba."

This analysis sheds light on Barnet's search for his own style of political commitment. What can be challenged is Luis's chronology. The testimonial

project seems to have been at least partly fueled by experiences prior to the El Puente incident. In his introduction to *Biografía de un cimarrón* – the prototype of testimonial narrative – Barnet explains that he had found out about his "protagonist," Esteban Montejo, as early as 1963 from a newspaper interview with a group of centenarians, including some former slaves. At that time Barnet was involved in researching "a monograph on slave life that a group of young Cuban writers were to put together," as he told Levine. According to the same interview, Barnet became fascinated with Montejo's magnetism and enchanting personality and decided to focus exclusively on the old man's story.

Given this sequence of events, Barnet's idea to commit Montejo's voice to paper might also have been inspired by Castro's "Palabras a los intelectuales" (Words to the Intellectuals). In one of his three well-publicized speeches addressed to intellectuals (June 1961), as quoted by Raúl González de Cascorro in "El género testimonio en Cuba" (1978), the Cuban leader recalled talking to an old woman, a former slave; then he confronted his audience at the National Library with the following rhetorical question: "Who could describe life under slavery better than this woman, and who can describe the present better than you?"

Like many other intellectuals of his generation and background, Barnet preferred to eschew the present and still keep his place "within the Revolution." Unlike Heberto Padilla or Virgilio Piñera, who quickly found themselves "out of the game," Barnet devised an acceptable formula: he became, according to his own plea in "Testimonio y comunicación: Una vía hacia la identidad" (1980; translated as "The Documentary Novel," 1981), a mediator for the voice of others, a scribe unveiling and reinterpreting the past on behalf of the Cuban people who, like Montejo or the old woman from Castro's anecdote, had no recorded history.

Despite its title Montejo's "autobiography" – called *biografía* in the Spanish version – does not cover Montejo's entire life: Barnet organized the raw material delivered orally by Montejo and, for the most part, tape-recorded by Barnet in a way that makes the omissions evident. The book is divided according to the following periods or events in Cuban history: slavery, abolition, and the War of Independence (1895–1898). From the introduction to the Spanish (but not the English) edition one learns that Montejo was an ardent Socialist and supporter of the revolution, but one has to take Barnet's word for it, since the "autobiography" cannot support this assertion: it ends fifty years before

*Cover for the fifth Mexican printing of Barnet's best-known book, a testimonial novel based on interviews with a former slave*

miguel barnet
biografía
de un
cimarrón

5ª edición
colección mínima 16

the revolution with the founding of the Republic of Cuba in 1902 and a brief mention of the death of Máximo Gómez, a hero of Cuba's war for independence, in 1905. Montejo's further life is a ghost chapter that can only partly be reconstructed from Barnet's extratextual comments, allusions dispersed throughout *Biografía de un cimarrón,* and a second testimonial, *Canción de Rachel* (Song of Rachel, 1969), that features Montejo as one of the secondary narrators. Although it reads as a first-person account, *Biografía de un cimarrón* raises many ethical, formal, and political issues concerning the interaction between the research worker-writer and his interlocutor. The book shows subtle but substantial editorial manipulation by means of structuring, splicing, and erasing of biographical material.

Born around 1860, Montejo lived through the colonial and postcolonial eras, slavery and emanci-

pation, Spanish domination and the U.S. protectorate of Cuba. As a child he was separated from his mother and sold to work at a sugarcane plantation, from which he eventually escaped. As a runaway slave he journeyed both in time and space: from the slave quarters to the hills, explaining the subterfuges he devised in order to survive and maintain his independence. After the abolition of slavery in 1886 Montejo became a wage laborer, and during the War of Independence he joined the *mambises* (anti-Spanish insurgents).

Montejo's account gives invaluable insights into those aspects of everyday life under slavery that had remained largely unexplored by social scientists due to a scarcity of sources: syncretic religious practices, witchcraft, sports and games, sexual and family relations, and most of all the secret rituals of resistance to slavery and the resources employed by fugitive slaves to survive in the wilderness. Montejo's account is both ethnographical and historical, as he also bears witness to the confusion of the first years following the Cuban emancipation and gives a critical, often sarcastic assessment of the political maneuvering that would eventually lead to U.S. domination.

From a formal standpoint, *Biografía de un cimarrón* can be described only through the family resemblance it bears to less eclectic forms such as the classical autobiography and the realist novel. With the former it shares the split identity of the narrating/experiencing subject, while like the latter it assumes a solid, empirical reality. It further appropriates narrative conventions from the picaresque novel as well as the bildungsroman and makes creative use of the anthropological and sociological formula known as life history. While claiming to mirror life and emphasizing the highest fidelity to facts, Barnet does not forget about what he elsewhere calls the "superobjectivo estético" (aesthetic superobjective). This objective is achieved in *Biografía de un cimarrón,* but the reader does not know who should be credited for it, since there is no way of establishing who is really speaking: a 105-year-old illiterate former fugitive slave or a young intellectual?

The problem of the speaker's identity is acute in mediated testimonials and has become a matter of serious critical debate. But for readers not versed in critical methods – who are, in fact, the intended readers of Barnet's testimonials – this question hardly matters. Montejo's story reads like a novel despite the fact that it elicits emotional response on the strength of verifiable experience. Montejo appears as a gifted storyteller whose vivid idiom rich in proverbs and anecdotes, sense of humor, and perspicacious, almost satirical comments on social and political issues captivates the reader's attention. His remarkable memory and self-conscious method of certifying the most controversial and bizarre facts make him a reliable narrator even in those passages that would easily qualify as magic realism. In spite of his ethnic and sexist biases, Montejo inspires confidence and is a rather likable character. The reader identifies with his plight and admires his relentless pursuit of freedom and his inventiveness in the art of resistance.

For critics and readers familiar with the plethora of fictionalized autobiographies of fugitive slaves in the United States, Montejo's story and Barnet's project may not seem all that original. Moreover, many of the ideological, formal, and ethical questions pertinent to such collaboratively produced texts seem to have been exhausted in the United States in the 1960s and 1970s in the course of lively theoretical debates surrounding the novelistic nonfiction of Truman Capote and Norman Mailer, William Styron's fact-based novel *The Confessions of Nat Turner* (1967), and anthropologist Oscar Lewis's "life stories." However derivative, manipulated, and ideologically preconditioned *Biografía de un cimarrón* may seem in retrospect, it is still a remarkable literary text and a powerful human document. Also, in Latin America the only tradition of antislavery narratives firmly established in the nineteenth century were novels written by white intellectuals. The only known "autobiography" of a slave is the *Autobiography* of Juan Francisco Manzano (1797?–1854), written in 1835 and published in England in 1840 and in Cuba in 1937.

Following the publication of Barnet's book, Montejo became a popular figure in Cuba and abroad. According to Levine, by 1980 *Biografía de un cimarrón* had sold more copies than any other Cuban book published since the revolution and was translated into Czech, Danish, English, French, German, Hungarian, Italian, Japanese, Polish, Portuguese, Russian, and Swedish. Two documentary films – *Cimarrón* (A Runaway Slave) and *Hombres de mal tiempo* (Men in Bad Weather) – were made in Cuba with the materials from the book, and a successful radio serial about Montejo's life was broadcast for more than a year. Claude Couffon, a French critic and translator of Hispanic literatures, made a widely publicized trip to Havana to meet with Montejo and Barnet. A pantomime production was directed by Olga and Ramón Flores, and *El cimarrón,* a recital piece for baritone, flute,

guitar, and percussion, with music by Hans Werner Henze and libretto by Hans Magnus Enzensberger, was enthusiastically received in Cuba and several European countries in 1970.

The enormous international success of *Biografía de un cimarrón* helped Barnet in his dealings with the cultural establishment, especially considering the growing isolation of the Castro regime after 1968 and the limitations on artistic expression imposed around that time by new guidelines from the Unión de Escritores y Artistas de Cuba (Union of Cuban Writers and Artists). International recognition notwithstanding, the magic formula he had achieved with his first testimonial did not bring Barnet prominence within the Cuban literary establishment. In the late 1960s, as the government stepped up its attack on nonconformist intellectuals, the book just barely led Barnet past the impasse caused by the El Puente episode: it was reduced to a password for his "reintegration" within the revolution. Perhaps in an effort to define his ideological position in more unequivocal terms, in 1967 Barnet published *La sagrada familia* (The Sacred Family), a collection of thirty-four poems, arguably his most important to date, that gained him a prestigious award from Casa de las Américas.

Part of the book includes reworkings of Afro-Cuban themes from Barnet's previous collections of verse, but most of the poems in *La sagrada familia* invite autobiographical readings: they are cast in the first person, and the name Miguel appears occasionally. Barnet claims, however, that the book is in fact pseudo-autobiographical. In a highly ironic fashion – also captured by the title – the poet seems to be exorcising his bourgeois family background by editing his own life story just as he had done with Montejo's biography.

In 1969 Barnet published his most influential essay, "La novela-testimonio: Socio-literatura" (The Testimonial Novel: Socioliterature). Originally written as a lecture, the text was appended to Barnet's next book, *Canción de Rachel,* and later reprinted in various journals and anthologies. It was also translated into English, with some minor alterations. The essay abounds in antibourgeois and anti-imperialist clichés, but it also contains some original thoughts about the poetics of the testimonial narrative. The essay inspired further theoretical inquiries among critics, particularly ones pertaining to the relation of fact to fiction and the rewriting of the Latin-American past from the point of view of "the people without a history."

Barnet's second testimonial, *Canción de Rachel,* brings these issues to the fore. At the core of this novel is Rachel's pseudo-autobiography, which in fact is a collage of biographical facts drawn from several oral accounts. In his introduction Barnet explains that in order to achieve a unity of different things that typically happened he went beyond Rachel's story: he interviewed six Cuban women – all of them former actresses in cabaret-style theaters for men only – and supplemented these accounts with press clippings from Cuban journals from the republican period (1902–1930) and testimonies from others.

Formally this is a first-person historical novel, but it treats history in a peculiar way. Major sociopolitical events of the first thirty years of the Cuban republic are selectively chosen, such as the Race War of 1912, the economic boom after World War I known as the "Danza de los Millones" (Dance of the Millions), and the Machado dictatorship of the 1930s. These events serve merely as a backdrop for apparently insignificant facts recorded by sensationalist newspapers or confined to intimate diaries, such as Rachel's love affairs, her description of people's reactions to Halley's comet, or her recollection of the death and funeral of Yarini, a notorious underworld figure.

For many critics *Canción de Rachel* represents a structural and chronological continuation of Barnet's testimonial project since it deals with yet another marginalized figure – a lower-class woman born to immigrant parents – and begins when *Biografía de un cimarrón* ends, with the first years of the Cuban republic. There is also an intertextual link between the two testimonials: Montejo appears as a character in *Canción de Rachel* to contradict Rachel's racist opinions and to comment specifically on the Race War. This particular episode not only raises an ethical question about the limits of Barnet's editorial manipulation of Montejo, but also a political one: why was the discussion of the Race War not included in *Biografía de un cimarrón*? Luis offers a plausible explanation when referring to Barnet's peculiar selectiveness in the book: "It may have been politically expedient not to rekindle the racial debate and conclude the novel at the end of the Spanish-Cuban-American War, thus alluding to the triumph of the Cuban Revolution." By limiting the discussion of racism to *Canción de Rachel*, Barnet implies that ethnic hostilities were endemic to the republican epoch and were eradicated by the revolution. Barnet's testimonial narrative thus becomes a form of conscious deception, which – contrary to its theoretical claims and like any other form of discourse – incorporates subterfuges necessary to cope with prevailing ideological demands.

Formal characteristics of *Canción de Rachel* differ from the testimonial model epitomized by *Biografía de un cimarrón* and Barnet's seminal essay. *Canción de Rachel* charts the path of the testimonial toward a more fictional form as it intends to steer clear of meticulous research and painstaking transcription. In his earlier book Barnet had used other texts in the margins of Montejo's discourse, such as introduction, glossary, and scientific-style footnotes, only to attest to his witness's accuracy, whereas Rachel's "song" becomes demythologized when counterpointed with the "chorus" of other voices. Since Barnet chooses to show Rachel as "open to influences, flexible, docile" and as a woman "who did not think with her head," as he states in his interview with Levine, he exposes the protagonist's ideology as "false consciousness" and inverts the testimonial contract established in *Biografía de un cimarrón*. Before he was Montejo's ventriloquist; now he caricatures his informants in order to satirize the sociopolitical reality of the Cuban republic.

Even when analyzed by a well-meaning reader, *Canción de Rachel* discloses much more than the author intended to say in his prefatory remarks: it dismantles Barnet's theoretical claim that *testimonio* can avoid fiction. Unlike *Biografía de un cimarrón*, here Barnet already seems constrained by his chosen role of self-effacing editor. In his further narratives he gradually gained still more confidence and mastery as a novelist interested in reconstructing real lives into lively stories, even at the risk of breaking the illusion of the testimonial pact – that of joint authorship and a "common front" between the researcher-writer and his interlocutors.

For reasons still unexplained by either critics or the author, despite the international acclaim earned by *Canción de Rachel* Barnet was unpublished in Cuba for almost a decade except for occasional contributions to literary journals. The first books to appear after this prolonged silence were *Akeké y la jutía* (Akeké and the Jutía, 1978) and *Orikis y otros poemas* (Orikis and Other Poems, 1980), both inspired by legends, images, and characters from the Afro-Cuban oral tradition.

As Julia Cuervo-Hewitt shows in "Yoruba Presence: From Nigerian Oral Literature to Contemporary Cuban Narrative" (1984), her in-depth comparative analysis of Yoruba literary expression, Barnet's fables compiled in *Akeké y la jutía* were influenced by Lydia Cabrera's and Rómulo Lachatañaré's literary reconstructions of "a world of personified natural forces that the Yoruba call *orishas*." Barnet's work, she continues, reveals "the still present tendency toward a highly stylized poetic vision of an African pantheon, which is now more than ever, mostly Yoruba."

The intended readers of these fables and poems should be familiar with the myths and symbols that constitute the Afro-Cuban microcosm. Occasionally, however, Barnet assumes his readers' ignorance and acts like an ethnographer translating the exotic world into more familiar terms. Thus, from the authorial footnote in *Orikis y otros poemas* the reader learns that *orikis* are laudatory songs in Yoruba culture, composed in honor of gods or distinguished people. Following this pattern, Barnet dedicates most of his stylized *orikis* to Cubans representing different currents of the Afro-Cuban movement in arts and literature, including Nicolás Guillén, Nancy Morejón, Bola de Nieve, José Zacarías Tallet, and others.

After receiving special mention in a literary competition for *Carta de noche* (A Letter at Night, 1982), another collection of poems, Barnet as poet and Barnet as ethnologist seemed somewhat ambivalent toward testimonial narrative, as he told Levine: "My future projects include a second volume of Cuban fables, but I am not planning any other testimonials for the moment, although there are many themes, many characters, and much richness yet to be worked on. I am afraid of falling into a pattern, in search of success. . . . I think I should wait at least 10 years before I sit down again to produce another book of testimony. For the moment, I will write my fables, and continue doing my research into Cuban culture and lore." But once again his literary practice unsettled his theoretical claims. In 1981 Barnet published another testimonial project, this time choosing an immigrant from the Spanish province of Galicia as his subject. In his introduction to *Gallego* (A Man from Galicia) the author underscores his reliance on research and documented facts, but the social scientist is ultimately subsumed by the novelist. The narrator-protagonist Manuel Ruiz, explains Barnet, is a composite character whose name could have been Antonio, Fabián, or José. Manuel's account – just like Rachel's story, which came to represent an epoch, according to Barnet's preface – is thus more of an allegory of fortunes and misfortunes of European immigrants in America than an idiosyncratic human document.

While the monumental sociological study *The Polish Peasant in Europe and America* (1918), by W. I. Thomas and F. Znaniecki, may be considered a possible ancestor of *Gallego,* the novel's reliance on the generic conventions of the picaresque is certainly

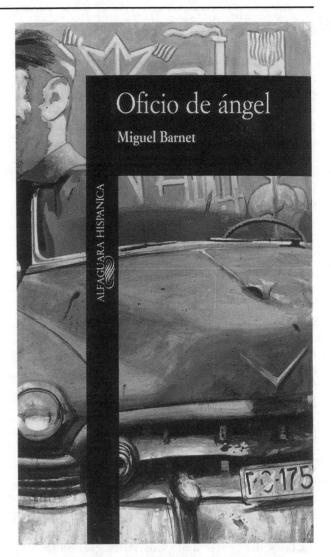

Cover for Barnet's 1989 novel, about a family in prerevolutionary Havana

more evident to literary critics, as Antonio Vera-León points out in "Montejo, Barnet, el cimarronaje y la escritura de la historia" (1989). But even though the topics of hunger and homelessness as well as repeated misfortunes and frustrating wanderings in search of work evoke the underworld of Spanish rogues, Manuel is not a picaresque hero. In fact, he becomes integrated into Cuban society when he marries a local woman. Individual destiny becomes a literary allegory when Barnet chooses the symbolic name América.

In *Gallego* there are only the vestiges of the testimonial contract, but this should not detract from our recognition of Barnet as a novelist. Much of the power of the novel lies in its symbolic significance and the lyrical quality of the protagonist's nostalgic language. Barnet should also be credited with the first novel dealing specifically with the Galician immigrant presence in Cuba.

Switching and merging ethnological, poetic, and novelistic modes continued to be a distinctive mark of Barnet's writings throughout the 1980s, even though he distanced himself more and more from the "pure" testimonial model. A collection of essays, *La fuente viva* (The Living Source, 1983), which followed the publication of *Carta de noche,* is an interesting amalgam of styles, formats, and topics. It includes ethnological studies of Afro-Cuban traditions along with previously published reviews of Oscar Lewis's *Children of Sánchez* (1961) and Reynaldo González's testimonial *La fiesta de los tiburones* (The Fiesta of the Sharks, 1983), as well as the 1969 essay on testimonial narrative and a more recent article elaborating on certain aspects of the same subject.

In 1986 Barnet published *La vida real* (Real Life), which according to his recent emphatic assertions is the last of his testimonials. Thoroughly researched during his nine-month stay in the United States, which was supported by a Guggenheim Fellowship, the book follows a pattern similar to *Gallego:* it tells the story of a Cuban immigrant to the United States, a peasant named Julián Mesa, who is actually a composite character based on twelve anonymous immigrants Barnet interviewed in New York. With Mesa's life story Barnet adds a few more chapters to his narrative synthesis of the last hundred years of Cuban political and cultural history, covering the era of the Batista rule and particularly the problem of Cuban immigration to the United States.

Barnet's inclination toward synthesis seems decisive in his novel *Oficio de ángel* (Angel's Job, 1989). Against the backdrop of prerevolutionary Havana he describes a family saga that bears some resemblance to the figures, conflicts, and anecdotes alluded to in *La sagrada familia.* Like that book, *Oficio de ángel* seems associated with Barnet's own life.

While the presence of memory draws together this novel and Barnet's previous testimonial texts, the poetics of remembrance in *Oficio de ángel* is notably different. As he shifts his focus away from the voices of others to what appears to be his own voice, his primary goal changes as well. As if responding to the postmodern debates surrounding the process of representation, Barnet seems to concentrate on an internal critique of language in the turbulent process of remembering and testifying and not as much on the task of rectifying the official history of neglected groups.

Although he might seem too elusive an author to be a prototype or a conventional authority, Barnet has decisively contributed to the recent flourishing of Latin-American testimonial narratives, which have been widely read as an alternative to some of the more difficult writings of the so-called Boom and perceived as a means of giving a voice to people otherwise silenced because of their subordinate condition.

**Interviews:**
"Miguel Barnet charla con los editores de *Vórtice,*" *Vórtice,* 2, nos. 2–3 (1979): 1–10;

Barry B. Levine, "Miguel Barnet on the Testimonial," translated by Lourdes A. Chedian, *Caribbean Review,* 9 (Fall 1980): 32–36;

Emilio Bejel, "Entrevista con Miguel Barnet," *Hispamérica,* 10, no. 29 (August 1981): 41–53;

Luis Iñigo Madrigal, "Entrevista con Miguel Barnet," *Araucaria,* 25 (1984): 116–123;

Alberto Batista Reyes, "Confesiones personales con palabras no escritas," *Letras Cubanas,* 3 (1987): 131–141;

Mariano Navarro, "Miguel Barnet: La voz de los otros," *El Urogallo,* 24 April 1988, pp. 28–34.

**References:**
John Beverley, "The Margin at the Center: On *Testimonio* (Testimonial Narrative)," *Modern Fiction Studies,* 35, no. 1 (Spring 1989): 11–28;

Andrew Bush, "Literature, History and Literary History: A Cuban Family Romance," *Latin American Literary Review,* 8, no. 16 (1980): 161–172;

Julia Cuervo-Hewitt, "El texto 'travesti': Narrativa y testimonio," *Estudios del Caribe,* 22, nos. 1–2 (1989): 53–66;

Cuervo-Hewitt, "Yoruba Presence: From Nigerian Oral Literature to Contemporary Cuban Narrative," in *Voices from Under: Black Narrative in Latin America and the Caribbean,* edited by William Luis (Westport, Conn.: Greenwood Press, 1984), pp. 65–88;

José B. Fernández, "*Gallego:* Novela de la inmigración," *Crítica Hispánica,* 7, no. 2 (1985): 121–127;

Angel Luis Fernández Guerra, "Cimarrón y Rachel: Un continuum," in *Nuevos críticos cubanos,* edited by José Prats Sariol (Havana: Letras Cubanas, 1983), pp. 530–537;

Fernández Guerra, "Edipo y Cayo Graco (Para leer a Miguel Barnet)," *Casa de las Américas,* 30 (May–June 1990): 45–54;

David William Foster, "Latin American Documentary Narrative," *PMLA,* 99, no. 1 ( January 1984): 41–55;

Bell Gale Chevigny, "Twice-Told Tales and the Meaning of History: Testimonial Novels by Miguel Barnet and Norman Mailer," *Centennial Review,* 30, no. 2 (Spring 1986): 181–195;

Reynaldo González, "*Biografía de un cimarrón:* El testimonio de un solitario," *Unión,* 4 (1966): 161–164;

Raúl González de Cascorro, "El género testimonio en Cuba," *Unión,* 4 (1978): 78–89;

Roberto González Echevarría, "*Biografía de un cimarrón* and the Novel of the Cuban Revolution," in his *The Voice of the Masters: Writing and Authority in Modern Latin American Literature* (Austin: University of Texas Press, 1985), pp. 110–124;

González Echevarría, "Criticism and Literature in Revolutionary Cuba," *Cuban Studies/Estudios cubanos,* 11, no. 1 (1981): 1–17;

González Echevarría, *Myth and Archive: A Theory of Latin American Narrative* (Cambridge & New York: Cambridge University Press, 1990);

Julio Huasi, "De gallegos, migraciones y testimonio americano," *Nueva Estafeta,* 31 (1982): 79–82;

William Luis, "The Politics of Memory: Miguel Barnet's *The Autobiography of a Runaway Slave* and César Leante's *Los guerrilleros negros,*" in his *Literary Bondage: Slavery in Cuban Narrative* (Austin: University of Texas Press, 1990), pp. 199–237;

Seymour Menton, *Prose Fiction of the Cuban Revolution* (Austin & London: University of Texas Press, 1975);

Alessandra Riccio, "Lo testimonial y la novela-testimonio," *Revista Iberoamericana,* 56 ( July–December 1990): 1055–1068;

Carlos Rincón, *El cambio de la noción de la literatura* (Bogotá: Instituto Colombiano de Cultura, 1978);

Marta Rojas, "El testimonio en la revolución cubana," in *Testimonio y literatura,* edited by René Jara and Hernán Vidal (Minneapolis: Institute for the Study of Ideologies and Literature, 1986), pp. 315–323;

Elzbieta Sklodowska, "La forma testimonial y la novelística de Miguel Barnet," *Revista/Review Interamericana,* 12 (Fall 1982): 375–384;

Sklodowska, "Miguel Barnet y la novela-testimonio," *Revista Iberoamericana,* 152–153 ( July–December 1990): 1069–1078;

Jean-Pierre Tardieu, "Religions et croyances populaires dans *Biografía de un cimarrón* de M. Barnet: Du refus a la tolerance," *Caravelle,* 43 (1984): 43–67;

Fanor Téllez, "Mediatización escrituraria y apropiación del discurso popular: *Biografía de un cimarrón* de Miguel Barnet," *Escritura,* 13 (January–December 1988): 47–75;

Antonio Vera-León, "Montejo, Barnet, el cimarronaje y la escritura de la historia," *Inti,* 29–30 (1989): 3–16.

# Juan Bosch

*(30 July 1909 –   )*

## Margarite Fernández Olmos
*Brooklyn College, City University of New York*

BOOKS: *Camino real* (La Vega, Dominican Republic: R. A. Ramos, 1933; revised edition, Santiago, Dominican Republic: El Diario, 1937);

*Indios, apuntes históricos y leyendas* (Santo Domingo: La Nación, 1935);

*La Mañosa: Novela de las revoluciones* (Santiago, Dominican Republic: El Diario, 1936; revised edition, Havana: La Verónica, 1940);

*Mujeres en la vida de Hostos, conferencia* (San Juan: Asociación de Mujeres Graduadas de la Universidad de Puerto Rico, 1938);

*Hostos, el sembrador* (Havana: Trópico, 1939);

*Dos pesos de agua* (Havana: A. Ríos, 1941);

*De espaldas a mí mismo: Conceptos laudatorios sobre la obra de gobierno del generalísimo Trujillo Molina* (Ciudad Trujillo, Dominican Republic: Partido Dominicano, 1942);

*Para la historia dos cartas* (Santiago, Dominican Republic: El Diario, 1943);

*Ocho cuentos* (Havana: Trópico, 1947);

*Cuba: La isla fascinante* (Santiago, Chile: Universitaria, 1955);

*Judas Iscariote: El calumniado* (Santiago, Chile: Prensa Latinoamericana, 1955);

*La muchacha de La Guaira* (Santiago, Chile: Nascimiento, 1955);

*Cuento de Navidad* (Santiago, Chile: Ercilla, 1956);

*Trujillo: Causas de una tiranía sin ejemplo* (Caracas: Librería Las Novedades, 1959);

*Simón Bolívar: Biografía para escolares* (Caracas: Escolar, 1960);

*Cuentos escritos en el exilio y apuntes sobre el arte de escribir cuentos* (Santo Domingo: Librería Dominicana, 1962);

*Apuntes para una interpretación de la historia costarricense* (San José, Costa Rica: Eloy Morúa Carrillo, 1963); revised and augmented as *Una interpretación de la historia costarricense* (San José, Costa Rica: Juricentro, 1980);

*David: Biografía de un rey* (Santo Domingo: Librería Dominicana, 1963); translated by John Marks as *David: The Biography of a King* (London:

*Juan Bosch*

Chatto & Windus, 1966; New York: Hawthorn Books, 1966);

*Un nuevo planteamiento de las relaciones entre México y la República Dominicana,* by Bosch and Adolfo López Mateos (Mexico City: La Justicia, 1963);

*Crisis de la democracia de América en la República Dominicana* (Guadalquivir, Spain: Centro de Estudios y Documentación Sociales, 1964); translated as *The Unfinished Experiment: Democracy in the Dominican Republic* (New York: Praeger, 1965; London: Pall Mall, 1966);

*Más cuentos escritos en el exilio* (Santo Domingo: Librería Dominicana, 1964);

*Páginas para la historia* (Santo Domingo: Librería Dominicana, 1965);

*Tres artículos sobre la revolución dominicana* (Mexico City: Partido Revolucionario Dominicano, 1965);

*Bolívar y la guerra social* (Buenos Aires: Jorge Alvarez, 1966);

*El pentagonismo: Sustituto del imperialismo* (Santo Domingo: Publicaciones Ahora, 1967); translated by Helen R. Lane as *Pentagonism: A Substitute for Imperialism* (New York: Grove, 1968);

*Teoría del cuento: Tres ensayos* (Mérida, Venezuela: Universidad de los Andes, 1967);

*El pentagonismo: Última etapa del capitalismo* (Montevideo: Katari, 1968);

*Composición social dominicana: Historia e interpretación* (Santo Domingo: Colección Pensamiento y Cultura, 1970);

*De Cristóbal Colón a Fidel Castro* (Madrid: Alfaguara, 1970);

*El próximo paso: Dictadura con respaldo popular* (Santo Domingo: Impresora Arte y Cine, 1970);

*Breve historia de la oligarquía* (Santo Domingo: Impresora Arte y Cine, 1971);

*Ecumenismo y mundo joven* (Madrid: P.P.C., 1971);

*Tres conferencias sobre el feudalismo* (Santo Domingo: Talleres Gráficos, 1971);

*Las mil y una sectas* (Madrid: P.P.C., 1973);

*Cuentos escritos antes del exilio* (Santo Domingo: Edición Especial, 1974);

*El oro y La Paz* (Santo Domingo: Edición Especial, 1975);

*Breve historia de la oligarquía y tres conferencias sobre el feudalismo* (Santo Domingo: Alfa y Omega, 1977);

*El Napoleón de las guerrillas* (Santo Domingo: Alfa y Omega, 1977);

*Viaje de los antípodas* (Santo Domingo: Alfa y Omega, 1978);

*Artículos y conferencias* (Santo Domingo: Alfa y Omega, 1980);

*La Revolución de Abril* (Santo Domingo: Impresora Mercedes, 1981);

*Clases sociales en la República Dominicana* (Santo Domingo: Corripio, 1982);

*La guerra y la restauración* (Santo Domingo: Corripio, 1982);

*Juan Vicente Gómez: Camino del poder,* by Bosch and Luis Cordero Velásquez (Caracas: Humboldt, 1982);

*Capitalismo, democracia y liberación nacional* (Santo Domingo: Alfa y Omega, 1983);

*Cuentos* (Havana: Casa de las Américas, 1983);

*El partido: Concepción, organización y desarrollo* (Santo Domingo: Alfa y Omega, 1983);

*El problema de las alianzas,* by Bosch and Narciso Isa Conde (Santo Domingo: Taller, 1983);

*La fortuna de Trujillo* (Santo Domingo: Alfa y Omega, 1985);

*La pequeña burguesía en la historia de la República Dominicana* (Santo Domingo: Alfa y Omega, 1985);

*Capitalismo tardío en la República Dominicana* (Santo Domingo: Alfa y Omega, 1986);

*Máximo Gómez: De Monte Cristi a la gloria – Tres años de guerra en Cuba* (Santo Domingo: Alfa y Omega, 1986);

*Las dictaduras dominicanas* (Santo Domingo: Alfa y Omega, 1988).

OTHER: Federico García Godoy, *El derrumbe,* prologue by Bosch (Santo Domingo: Universidad Autónoma de Santo Domingo, 1975).

Juan Bosch – novelist, essayist, political leader, and former president of the Dominican Republic – is also one of the most respected short-story writers of Latin America. Bosch is a member of the *criollismo* movement, which stressed Spanish-American themes and rural life in particular and had its greatest impact in the years following World War I until the late 1940s. Bosch's short stories have appeared in anthologies in several different languages and have influenced authors within and beyond the borders of his own country.

Born in La Vega, Dominican Republic, on 30 July 1909 of a Catalan father and a Puerto Rican mother, Bosch grew up in close contact with the campesinos that frequented his father's small business. The northern Cibao region of his youth was composed of small farms, mostly producing tobacco for export, in which semifeudal relationships predominated between landowners and peasants. This early experience played a fundamental role in his political and creative development, as the Dominican campesino later became the focus of his works. In interviews Bosch has stated that one of his motives for writing short stories was to vindicate the Dominican campesinos from the negative, unjust portrayal that had traditionally been ascribed to them by the middle and upper classes. Bosch wanted his stories to present a truer reflection of the Dominican masses: their capacity for hard work and for struggle and sacrifice as well as their rich oral traditions.

Historical events also had a strong impact on the direction of his creative work. As a young man Bosch witnessed the American armed intervention of the Dominican Republic (1916–1924), an event that had been repeated in many other Latin-American nations around the turn of the century. The emergence of U.S. hegemony in the region led many intellectuals to view their societies in a more critical light and examine more closely the landscape and peoples of their own countries in order to strengthen and affirm a national consciousness. Like others of his generation Bosch sought to present a renewed vision of Dominican popular culture in his writings. This linking of art and social responsibility is an integral aspect of Bosch's creative vision, a characteristic he shares with many other Latin-American authors.

As a young man Bosch participated in literary groups such as La Cueva (The Cave) in Santo Domingo, and in 1929 several of his stories were published in the newspaper *Listín Diario* and the journal *Bahoruco* in the Dominican Republic. In 1933 his first collection of stories, *Camino real* (King's Road), received critical acclaim. It was followed by another collection, *Indios, apuntes históricos y leyendas* (Indians, Historical Sketches and Legends, 1935), and the novel *La Mañosa: Novela de las revoluciones* (La Mañosa: A Novel of the Revolutions, 1936).

*Camino real* is representative of many of Bosch's works in its theme and narrative techniques: all the stories deal with the lives of campesinos in Bosch's native Cibao region of the Dominican Republic and depict the struggles of rural peasants to survive in a difficult environment in a straightforward and powerful narrative style. One of these stories, "La mujer" (The Woman), was among the author's first creative attempts and is still his best known and most anthologized. In his anthology *El cuento hispanoamericano* (The Hispanic-American Short Story, 1964), Seymour Menton refers to the story as "una sinfonía audiovisual del trópico" (an audiovisual tropical symphony). This brief but powerful tale concerns a woman who is exploited and physically abused by her brutish, tyrannical husband for having used their meager resources to feed their young son. A stranger intercedes to help the woman, and as the two men struggle silently, the woman kills the stranger who had intervened on her behalf. The story's brevity and symbolism permit various interpretations, as does its poetic language, with frequent, repeated references to a past that haunts the characters and a harsh natural environment that dehumanizes them.

For some critics the story reveals the brutalizing effects of poverty on human beings and the dependent psychology of women who defend, however illogically, their abusive partners. The poetic and sensual language used to describe the barren landscape and the repetition of the motif of violence and death in the characters and the setting of the tale, however, lend themselves to more complex interpretations.

In the sociohistorical interpretation found in Margarite Fernández Olmos's *La cuentística de Juan Bosch: Un análisis crítico-cultural* (Juan Bosch's Short-Story Technique: A Critical-Cultural Analysis) she notes, for example, the emphasis of the narrator on the *carretera* (road) that is the scene of much of the story's action. From the beginning it is depicted in human terms: it is a long mummy, with references made to the road's hind and the many years that have passed since its death. The narrator also describes the anonymous men who work on the road in a situation of forced labor or exploitation. The suggestive language expands the possibilities of interpretation. The action presented in the introduction – the death of the road and the struggle of the men who create it – is repeated throughout the story: life and death, creation and destruction define the relationships presented initially in a collective, historical context (the men on the road) and later in an individual relationship (the woman, her husband, and the stranger). The anonymous, collective characters evolve into the symbolic representation of mother, land, and nation in the character of the woman (also nameless in the story).

A historical interpretation might take into account, for example, the fact that Bosch lived during the U.S. occupation of the Dominican Republic after 1916. He has often commented on the personal humiliation and indignation he felt as a young boy and the nationalist sentiments that grew as a result of the U.S. intervention. The intervention of the stranger in this story, rather than helping the woman, aggravates the situation. The attempts of the stranger to be her benefactor results in her return to an abusive husband and implies a type of dependence on her part. It also ignores her ability to forge her own destiny. The woman's reaction can be seen as an unconscious process of affirmation; her identification with the road at the end of the story combines her efforts with those that came before, implying that history, like the road, is the collective creation of innumerable anonymous men and women. Her rejection of her husband and the stranger is another step toward a process to which she has contributed and of which she is now a part.

The story can therefore be considered a metaphor of Latin-American and Dominican history in several principal aspects: its themes of paralyzation and underdevelopment, exploitation and domination, and external and internal dependence. If one considers that the character of the woman represents the country itself, her rejection of the stranger is a rejection of traditional dependence and an affirmation of the process of national liberation.

In this story as in others in the collection, Bosch utilizes narrative techniques that appear in later works: symbolic and poetic descriptions of nature and the environment, indirect revelations, a brief denouement, and colloquial language in the dialogues that contrasts with the more poetic descriptions of the narrator. Symbols frame and thus unify the stories while emphasizing their significance. The stories are generally compact, and their climaxes usually coincide with the moment of epiphany or what Bosch refers to as the *hecho/tema* (episode/theme).

Bosch is often less concerned with character development than with plot. Many characters are anonymous, with little interiorization, and the conflict frequently revolves around a confrontation with others or within the characters themselves that obliges the protagonist to make a decision and act upon it. In these stories the narrator maintains an apparent objectivity that allows the reader to analyze and interpret the work.

Bosch's writings on the art of the short story reveal his great respect for the genre as well as his ideas about it. These ideas and the emphasis he places on certain aspects of the short story are reflected in his works in general. Bosch follows the traditional precepts of Edgar Allan Poe concerning the importance of unity of effect or impression and the need to maintain a structure that will produce a preconceived effect in the most efficient, direct manner. Ideas from Uruguayan author Horacio Quiroga's *Manual del perfecto cuentista* (Manuel for the Perfect Short-Story Writer, 1925) are also present in Bosch's essay, particularly the admonition to eliminate superfluous digressions or distractions. Quiroga insists on the importance of technique and discipline for the short-story writer, two qualities Bosch admires. In addition, Bosch stresses the importance of selecting an appropriate theme that places demands upon both writer and reader. Structurally, Bosch prefers to combine the *hecho/tema* so that the key detail will suddenly illuminate the larger meaning of the story. Thus the brevity of the short story, instead of a limitation, becomes an advantage in creating a carefully calculated effect.

Though best known for his short stories and his historical and political writings, Bosch combines these interests in his semi-autobiographical novel *La Mañosa,* widely considered a classic of Dominican literature. The action revolves around a young narrator, Juan, and the effects of a civil war on his family. La Mañosa is the name of the family's favorite mule, which, like everyone else in the novel, is a victim of the conflict. The story is filled with the senseless violence of the so-called revolution, which even the narrator cannot fully comprehend. Bosch does not attempt any rational interpretations but rather leaves them up to the reader's imagination.

Bosch's literary activities in the Dominican Republic after the publication of the novel were curtailed for political reasons. The repressive regime of Rafael Leonidas Trujillo had a decisive effect on Bosch and other Dominican intellectuals who opposed the dictator's rule. In 1933 Bosch was incarcerated for alleged anarchistic activities, and in 1937 he left for Puerto Rico with his wife and children to begin an exile that lasted twenty-four years. In 1939 he established himself in Havana, where he worked in radio and journalism. There he founded the Partido Revolucionario Dominicano (Revolutionary Dominican party) and worked with other exiled intellectuals to topple their country's dictatorial regime – without success.

In 1952, after Fulgencio Batista's successful coup in Cuba, Bosch left Havana for Costa Rica, where he taught at and later directed the Instituto de Educación Política in San José. During the 1950s Bosch traveled throughout Europe and Latin America, returning to Cuba in 1958 only to be incarcerated by the dictatorship. From there he traveled to Venezuela, where his close friend Rómulo Betancourt was president. The assassination of Trujillo in May 1961 finally allowed Bosch to return to his native country after a lengthy and active exile.

During his years outside the Dominican Republic, Bosch continued to publish: in Puerto Rico his stories appeared in the journals *Puerto Rico Ilustrado* and *Alma Latina;* in Cuba he published the biography *Hostos, el sembrador* (Hostos, the Sower, 1939) and the short-story collections *Dos pesos de agua* (Two Pesos of Water, 1941) and *Ocho cuentos* (Eight Stories, 1947). "Luis Pie," included in *Ocho cuentos,* received the Hernández Catá prize in 1943.

The collections published in Cuba reveal more literary experimentation and better structural development than his earlier work. Bosch was at this point a genuine master of the technique he so admired and felt freer to use fantasy, for example, within the general framework of *criollismo.* His

*Bosch in 1965, after an April coup attempt to return him to the Dominican Republic*

themes were no longer strictly *campesino,* although he never completely abandoned his interest in rural men and women. "Dos pesos de agua" is a good example of this evolution. In it a drought afflicts an old woman named Remigia and her neighbors, obliging them to abandon their lands. Remigia stubbornly refuses to leave, however, confident that the souls in purgatory will send her water if she buys candles in church for their sake. After ignoring her prayers for some time, the souls in purgatory discover that Remigia has accumulated the hefty sum of two pesos worth of candles. They immediately respond to her request for water, inadvertently causing a flood that destroys Remigia and the whole town.

With short, intense phrasing, the repetition of words and sounds, and the frenzied contrast between the prayers of Remigia and the cries of the souls in purgatory, the story ends with a powerful climax combined with effective dramatic irony. Bosch, always conscious of his reader and the cultural context of his stories, ably manipulates cultural stereotypes and value systems. During his youth a local belief in the power of the spiritual world was prevalent. His works, therefore, reflect what he has called "el mundo mental dominicano" (the mental world of the Dominican).

As in "La mujer" Bosch underscores the dependence of the protagonist. The souls send their

water down, reflecting their position of dominance over the protagonist, but this power is ironically unjustified and capricious. Therefore Remigia's dependence, rather than the drought, is the true cause of her final destruction. The mechanism of that dependence is her faith in an arbitrary power outside herself into whose hands she has placed her destiny.

In *Ocho cuentos* Bosch continues his literary experimentation while maintaining his social vision. One of the stories, "El socio" (The Fellow), combines traditional folk culture with local belief in a lighter tone than some of his earlier works. The reasons for the changes in style were not strictly literary; Bosch had entered the story under a pseudonym in the Juegos Florales Hispanoamericanos, which were celebrated in the Dominican Republic in 1940. He had disguised his style in order to conceal the true identity of the author at a time in which his name, under express orders of Trujillo, could not be mentioned favorably in the country. The story received first prize.

"El socio" concerns an abusive estate owner, Don Anselmo, and the campesinos who work for him and suffer due to his greed. The narrator discusses three neighbors in particular who have been victims of the landowner: "el Negro" Manzueta, whose land was unjustly taken by Don Anselmo; Dionisio Rojas, incarcerated for having denied Anselmo a part of his farm; and Adán Matías, whose granddaughter was kidnapped by Anselmo to become a member of his concubinage. Each one tries to get vengeance on the landowner, who the townspeople are convinced is aided by a pact with *el socio* — the devil. The story demonstrates that their belief is well founded, and only when one of the characters makes his own pact with *el socio* is he avenged.

This story, because of its humor combined with fantasy, is less typical of Bosch's work. It became highly celebrated, however, and once again the author managed to capture the essence of local popular belief and combine it with a sharp social critique. Many Dominicans believed, for example, that the length of Trujillo's power and success was due to supernatural circumstances.

While the marvelous and the fantastic can be found in other stories by Bosch, most deal with the human factors that cause more tangible nightmares. Suffering and real pain, the struggle of men and women against their environments, and their valor and courage in facing injustices are the themes found in the majority of his works. "Luis Pie," "La nochebuena de Encarnación Mendoza" (Encarnación Mendoza's Christmas Eve), and "El indio Manuel Sicuri" (The Indian Manuel Sicuri) are among the best examples of his artistry in the genre.

The award-winning "Luis Pie" demonstrates Bosch's talent in penetrating the tortuous inner world of the oppressed individual who searches for meaning and some sort of defense mechanism in dealing with a wretched, frustrating existence. It is also a daring critique of Dominican society's treatment of the Haitians that immigrate to their island neighbors' country in search of work, usually on the harsh sugarcane plantations. The abhorrent conditions of Haitian sugar workers and the abuses the Haitians had to suffer — the Trujillo regime massacred thousands of Haitians living on the border between the two countries in 1937 — were topics that few writers were willing to assume given existing political pressures. According to critics of Dominican literature, "Luis Pie" initiates a renewed vision of the Haitian in Dominican writing. Whereas previously Haitian characters were ridiculed and vilified, Bosch demythified the harmful stereotypes that have traditionally divided the two peoples and viewed the Haitians with empathy as equals.

Although Bosch is normally categorized as a neorealist or *criollista* writer, his works present more technical experimentation than usual for those movements. His later works, written in the 1950s, reflect a complex vision that is best noted in the narrative modes that are merged within the stories. For example, in "La nochebuena de Encarnación Mendoza," a suspenseful story of a rebel who attempts to return to his home in secret on Christmas Eve only to be fatally trapped by the police on the information innocently provided by his own son, the point of view of the narrator is skillfully intertwined with that of the protagonist, his pursuers, and the reader.

The concept of rebellion and resistance that is reiterated in Bosch's stories shifts from rural guerrillas to their urban counterparts in such stories as "Revolución" (Revolution) and "El hombre que lloró" (The Man Who Cried). The modernization of Latin America and the subsequent problems of campesinos living in its overcrowded capitals are among the social changes that Bosch incorporates into his works. It is fair to say, therefore, that Bosch is not only a literary predecessor of contemporary Dominican authors, but also an artistic link between writing from the beginning of the century — which in its portrayal of the rural masses occasionally presented a somewhat simplistic and paternalistic view of its subjects — and the more complex and collective perspective of the 1960s.

Of Bosch's works that do not treat Dominican themes, two merit particular note: "El indio Manuel Sicuri" and his last novel, *El oro y La Paz* (Gold and La Paz, 1975). The story of Manuel Sicuri resulted from one of Bosch's trips to Bolivia in the early 1950s and was written in Chile in 1956. It is one of the author's favorites, and many critics consider it one of his most accomplished works. Searching again for the type of profoundly human theme that could be expressed in his favorite genre, Bosch was so satisfied with his success that he abandoned the genre until several years later when he wrote his final story, "La mancha indeleble" (The Indelible Stain), a psychological tale of political repression.

"El indio Manuel Sicuri" concerns an Aymara Indian living peacefully with his family in a remote valley of Bolivia. One afternoon he receives a visit from a stranger who claims to be unjustly pursued by the Peruvian authorities. Manuel grants his request for shelter. The next day a *chasqui* (messenger) arrives, informing Manuel that he is searching for a Peruvian fugitive who has robbed a church. Manuel dares not tell him that he is harboring the man in his home and accompanies the *chasqui* into town after advising his wife to remove the fugitive in his absence. The stranger takes advantage of the situation and rapes Manuel's pregnant wife. Upon his return Manuel discovers the truth, pursues the offender, and kills him with an ax. The ending of the story finds Manuel in prison meditating over his actions, not comprehending why he should pay for an act he believes to have been totally justified.

The story utilizes dramatic techniques that may be described as cinematographic: flashbacks, focusing on certain objects for effect, alternating accelerated movements with slow-motion movements in the descriptions, and distant panoramas. In fact, the story was adapted for a Bolivian film that was presented at the Cannes Film Festival.

*El oro y La Paz* was also inspired by Bosch's visit to Bolivia and concerns adventurers who search for riches and for dreams of one type or another in the Bolivian jungles. The work poses the question of what humanity's ultimate search should be – wealth or, playing on the name of the Bolivian capital, peace (*la paz*), power, or beauty? The reply is not clearly given in the social terms normally found in Bosch's writing but is more enigmatic and perhaps more profound. The novel, less successful than his other works, was written in Puerto Rico in 1964 under circumstances that once again reflected the author's intimate involvement with the recent history of his country.

Two years after Bosch's return from exile to the Dominican Republic in 1961, he was elected president as a member of the Partido Revolucionario Dominicano, only to be toppled seven months later in a military coup and forced to leave the country. In April 1965 a civil war ensued between those who favored the restoration of the constitutional government and those who opposed it. The same month the U.S. Marines staged an armed intervention of the country in favor of the anticonstitutional forces with the rationale of saving the lives of U.S. citizens and preventing Communist forces from taking over the country. A transition government was formed, and in the following elections Joaquín Balaguer, the candidate favored by the United States, was victorious over Bosch.

Bosch's political and historical writings are also well known in Latin America and have been highly influential, as E. Bradford Burns has noted in *Latin America: A Concise Interpretive History* (1982). Bosch's political writings also demonstrate his ideological evolution from his earlier belief in representative democracy and reformist solutions to more recent radical positions. In 1974 he left the social-democratic Partido Revolucionario Dominicano to

form a new party, the Partido de la Liberación Dominicana (Dominican Liberation party), with a platform that rejects reformist policies and proposes socialism as the only solution to the country's problems. In the 1990s, despite his advanced age, Bosch is still the party's leader and continues to work for change and social justice. When asked in interviews if he plans to return to the short story or the novel, Bosch has stated that he will not return to the short story, although he desires to write another novel, given the time to do so.

Despite the importance of Bosch's writing in Dominican and Latin-American letters, his literary works have not received the critical attention they deserve in his own country due to political considerations. Bosch's stories were published and acclaimed outside the Dominican Republic in the countries in which he spent his long exile, but not until the mid 1960s did critics in his own country dare to include him in anthologies and critical texts. Today Bosch's literary contributions are widely recognized throughout the Spanish-speaking world, where he is respected as much for his courageous leadership as for the integrity and artistry of his words.

**Interview:**

Bruno Rosario Candelier, *Juan Bosch: Un texto, un análisis y una entrevista* (Santo Domingo: Editora Alfa y Omega, 1979), pp. 45–76.

**References:**

Efraín Barradas, "La seducción de las máscaras: José Alcántara Almánzar, Juan Bosch y la joven narrativa dominicana," *Revista Iberoamericana,* 142 (January–March 1988): 11–25;

Margarite Fernández Olmos, *La cuentística de Juan Bosch: Un análisis crítico-cultural* (Santo Domingo: Alfa y Omega, 1982);

Manuel Augusto Ossers Cabrera, *La expresividad en la cuentística de Juan Bosch* (Santo Domingo: Alfa y Omega, 1989);

Doris Sommer, *One Master for Another: Populism as Patriarchal Rhetoric in Dominican Novels* (Lanham, Md.: University Press of America, 1983), pp. 93–124.

# Alfredo Bryce Echenique

*(19 February 1939 – )*

César Ferreira
*University of North Texas*

BOOKS: *Huerto cerrado* (Havana: Casa de las Américas, 1968);

*Un mundo para Julius* (Barcelona: Barral, 1970); translated by Dick Gerdes as *A World for Julius* (Austin: University of Texas Press, 1992);

*Muerte de Sevilla en Madrid; Antes de la cita con los Linares* (Lima: Mosca Azul, 1972);

*La felicidad, ja, ja* (Barcelona: Barral, 1974);

*La pasión según San Pedro Balbuena que fue tantas veces Pedro, y que nunca pudo negar a nadie* (Lima: Libre–1, 1977); republished as *Tantas veces Pedro* (Madrid: Cátedra, 1981);

*A vuelo de buen cubero y otras crónicas* (Barcelona: Anagrama, 1977); revised and enlarged as *Crónicas personales* (Barcelona: Anagrama, 1988);

*Todos los cuentos* (Lima: Mosca Azul, 1979);

*Cuentos completos* (Madrid: Alianza, 1981);

*La vida exagerada de Martín Romaña* (Barcelona: Argos Vergara, 1981);

*El hombre que hablaba de Octavia de Cádiz* (Barcelona: Plaza y Janés, 1985);

*Magdalena peruana y otros cuentos* (Barcelona: Plaza y Janés, 1986);

*Goig* (Madrid: Debate, 1987);

*La última mudanza de Felipe Carrillo* (Barcelona: Plaza y Janés, 1988);

*Dos señoras conversan; Un sapo en el desierto; Los grandes hombres son así, y también asá* (Barcelona: Plaza y Janés, 1990).

SELECTED PERIODICAL PUBLICATIONS –
UNCOLLECTED: "Una actitud ante la literatura y el arte," *Oiga,* 25 January 1982, pp. 63–64;

"Confesiones sobre el arte de vivir y escribir novelas," *Cuadernos Hispanoamericanos,* 417 (March 1985): 65–76;

"El escritor latinoamericano," *Barcarola,* 25 (November 1987): 101–104;

"Instalar el humor en el corazón mismo de la tristeza," *Nuevo Texto Crítico,* 8 (1991): 55–72.

*Alfredo Bryce Echenique in Puerto Rico, 1991 ( photograph by José Peréz Mesa)*

For English-speaking audiences, Alfredo Bryce Echenique is in many ways an unknown celebrity among contemporary Latin-American writers. Widely read in Latin America and Europe – especially Spain and France, where his literary career began and where he has lived for the past twenty-five years – Bryce is one of the leading contemporary novelists of Peru along with Mario Vargas Llosa. Translated into some fifteen languages, with English the most recent, Bryce is the author of five novels, three books of short stories, a collection of novellas, and two volumes of journalism. More important, however, Bryce is the creator of a unique style of writing whose main traits are its conversational tone and humor, along with a personal fictional universe that ranges from themes such as the sentimental education of members of the Peruvian bourgeoisie to the experience of exile in Europe. He is considered a leading figure of the Spanish-American post-Boom generation.

Bryce was born in Lima on 19 February 1939 to a well-to-do aristocratic family. His father, Francisco Bryce, was a well-known banker, and his mother, Elena Echenique, was the granddaughter of a former president of Peru, José Rufino Echenique. The future writer was educated in exclusive upper-class schools of Peru, Inmaculado Corazón and Colegio Santa María, both run by American nuns and priests. He later attended a British boarding school set in the outskirts of Lima, Colegio San Pablo, from which he graduated in 1956.

Bryce claims that his interest in becoming a writer arose from his mother's admiration for French literature, particularly the works of Marcel Proust. His father, however, strongly opposed a career in literature, and against his better judgment Bryce halfheartedly entered the University of San Marcos in Lima to study law. At the same time he earned a degree in literature, graduating in 1964 after completing a thesis on Ernest Hemingway.

That same year, Bryce obtained a scholarship from the French government to continue his study of literature and to pursue a career in writing. Departing for Paris, he never permanently returned to Peru, a circumstance that had a profound effect on his creativity. Bryce's arrival in the French capital coincided with the emergence of the Latin-American Boom, led by such writers as Julio Cortázar, Guillermo Cabrera Infante, Mario Vargas Llosa, and Carlos Fuentes. In Paris he also befriended the Peruvian writer Julio Ramón Ribeyro. In 1965 Bryce spent several months in Perugia, Italy, where he wrote his first book, a collection of short stories entitled *Huerto cerrado* (Closed Garden, 1968). After his return to Paris in 1967 he married his girlfriend from Lima, Maggie Revilla, whom he later divorced, and began work as a lecturer in Spanish at the University of Nanterre in suburban Paris.

In 1968 *Huerto cerrado* received an award in a literary contest sponsored by publisher Casa de las Américas in Cuba and was published in Havana. *Huerto cerrado* is, without doubt, an important starting point in Bryce's literary career, for it announces themes that he developed later in his novels. The book is largely influenced by the works of Hemingway. In fact, the collection of twelve stories is mod-

eled after the Nick Adams stories that constitute much of *In Our Time* (1925). In these stories one main character is the protagonist in a variety of experiences that serve as an initiation into adulthood. Such is also the case with Manolo, the young hero of *Huerto cerrado*. In stories set among the Peruvian bourgeoisie, Manolo experiences various rites of passage in school and with his peers in stories such as "El camino es así" (The Road Is Like This) and "Un amigo de cuarenta y cuatro años" (A Forty-Four-Year-Old Friend). He discovers love and undergoes sexual initiation in "Una mano en las cuerdas" (A Hand on the Strings), "El descubrimiento de América" (The Discovery of America), and "Yo soy el rey" (I Am the King), and he acquires an awareness of class differences in "Su mejor negocio" (His Best Deal). Stylistically many of these stories pay tribute to Hemingway's concise use of dialogue and his "iceberg" technique, as in "El hombre, el cinema y el tranvía" (The Man, the Cinema, and the Streetcar), "Las notas que duermen en las cuerdas" (Notes That Sleep on Strings), and "Dos indios" (Two Indians). This last story is also his first look into the experience of exile, a central theme in Bryce's later novels.

Of all the stories in *Huerto cerrado*, particularly important is "Con Jimmy, en Paracas" (With Jimmy, in Paracas). In addition to its initiation theme, "Con Jimmy, en Paracas" represents a link with Bryce's first novel, *Un mundo para Julius* (1970; translated as *A World for Julius*, 1992). "Con Jimmy, en Paracas" narrates the story of Manolo, here a fourteen-year-old boy of the lower middle class who accompanies his father to Paracas, a beach resort outside Lima, on a weekend business trip. There he is confronted by his rich classmate Jimmy, whose father employs Manolo's father and who patronizes the lower classes. Though Manolo initially sees his father as a figure of authority, in the course of the story the boy discovers, much to his shame, his father's servile attitude toward his boss.

Bryce has always maintained that "Con Jimmy, en Paracas" represents the discovery of his narrative style. Indeed, the narrator stands out for his confessional tone, which is emphasized by the conversational quality of his storytelling. Bryce also shows a preference in his fiction for protagonists who are losers. Emotionally incapable of asserting themselves in the world, these characters painfully endure their weaknesses and failures but nevertheless demonstrate a true sense of humanity and compassion.

The publication of *Un mundo para Julius* placed Bryce in the front ranks of Latin-American literature. The novel quickly received critical acclaim for the author's distinctive ease in storytelling – the evident oral quality of the narrative and his ability to involve the readers in the novel in an intimate way, making them part of the narrator's actions. Critics also noted Bryce's preference for sentimentally fragile characters with a strong sense of their marginality. Peruvian critics in particular complimented Bryce on his ironic sense of humor. While humor has been an important trademark of Peruvian literature going back as far as Juan del Valle y Caviedes in the seventeenth century and Ricardo Palma in the late nineteenth century, it has largely been absent in the literature of this century except for José Diez-Canseco's little-known novel *Duque* (Duke, 1930). *Un mundo para Julius* shares with *Duque* another common denominator: an inside knowledge of Peru's upper class, a rare theme in Peruvian literature.

A tour de force of more than five hundred pages, *Un mundo para Julius* is the story of a sympathetic little rich boy of the priviliged world of the Peruvian bourgeoisie, growing up between the ages of five and eleven. The youngest child among two brothers, Santiago and Bobby, and a sister, Cinthia, Julius is largely ignored by his rich parents, Juan Lucas and Susan. As a result, he must turn to his many servants, particularly his Indian nanny Vilma, for the attention and affection he needs. Set in Lima in the 1950s, the novel illustrates Peru's transition from a colonial agrarian society to a more modern precapitalist state. In fact, the marriage of Juan Lucas, Julius's stepfather, to his widowed mother represents the merging of the traditional oligarchy with the new business technocrats who cater to the influence of the United States. The novel, however, is far from being so politically explicit. Instead, it chronicles the rich, happy life of an affluent social group that considers its privileged surroundings to be the natural order. In this environment Julius stands out as a child who possesses an enormous inquisitiveness and sensitivity and grows up innocently questioning the status quo of which he is part. His innocence is finally lost when, at the end of the novel, he learns that Vilma, to whom he has grown very attached, has been forced to make a living as a common prostitute shortly after being raped by Julius's older brother Santiago and dismissed from the family home.

The novel's greatest achievement clearly is Bryce's unique manipulation of language. He captures the reader's attention through his extraordinary use of humor and the rich orality of his style. *Un mundo para Julius* reproduces the language of the various social groups of Peru, particularly upper-

*Bryce in Paris, circa 1977*

class residents of Lima, and elicits a narrative tone that moves progressively from the hilariously funny to the utterly grotesque. The narrative point of view switches subtly, allowing the narrator to mix whimsically omniscient narration, interior monologue, memories recounted in conversation, and flashbacks. Language slowly emerges as the tool that unveils the sordid reality composing the frivolous world of the rich. In so doing, the narrator constantly appears and disappears from the story, slowly crafting his own personality and his presence. Although he never intends to condemn openly the unjust social order he portrays, his rich, ambiguous voice filled with poignant irony allows him to look at the world of the Peruvian upper class with nostalgia and pity. Through the aural quality and the tone of the speech of the rich reproduced by the narrator, the reader learns of the insensitive and selfish nature of such a class and in so doing must despise it.

When it first appeared, *Un mundo para Julius* had an important impact on the Peruvian cultural scene. It was published during the rule of a leftist revolutionary government in Peru led by Gen. Juan Velasco Alvarado. In 1968 Velasco had seized power, nationalized the country's U.S.-owned oil industry, and imposed a strong land reform. Such measures destroyed Peru's old ruling oligarchy, changing the country's social structure forever. Bryce's novel soon was perceived as the chronicle of a disappearing social elite, which earned him the National Literary Award of Peru in 1972. The novel outlived this first political reading, however, and is regarded today as a classic of Peruvian literature due to its unquestionable artistic value. The French translation received an award as best foreign novel in 1973.

Bryce continued to explore the world of the Peruvian upper class in his second collection of short stories, titled *La felicidad, ja, ja* (Happiness, Ha, Ha, 1974). The book insists that the happiness of the wealthy is frivolous and illusory. In most of the stories, the moral decadence of the upper social class is a main trait. Along with these themes, reflections of Bryce's Parisian exile permeates this work. In "Florence y nos tres" (Florence and Us), a young Latin American, a former student of the Sorbonne, is leading an unhappy life in Paris by trying to earn a living as a Spanish professor. In his loneliness he falls in love with one of his students, who slowly destroys his hopes for affection. For the first time in Bryce's work, Paris is here portrayed as a city that does not live up to its reputation of glamour and culture. Rather, it is a city that for Latin Americans leaves them lonely and marginal.

Solitude and marginality also characterize "Muerte de Sevilla en Madrid" (Death of Sevilla in Madrid), one of Bryce's short-story masterpieces. An orphan raised by two fervently religious spinster aunts in Lima, Sevilla is a boy whose life is destined for tragedy. Ugly, shy, and incapable of coping, Sevilla grows up to lead a mediocre and secluded existence as a bureaucrat. Totally unassertive, he expects nothing from life, wanting only to be left alone. However, in a contest organized by a new airline headed by an arrogant Spanish manager named Conde de la Avenida, he unexpectedly wins a free trip from Lima to Madrid. Although Sevilla's trip is intended to be a great public-relations campaign for the airline, it turns into a complete disaster. Distraught by having to deal with what proves to be an overwhelming experience, from the moment he steps on the plane in Lima and throughout his stay in Spain, Sevilla suffers from a chronic case of dysentery. Finally, he jumps out the window of his hotel room. Ironically, while Sevilla's corpse is shipped back to Peru, the formerly elegant and self-assured Conde de la Avenida is returning to Spain on another plane and is the victim of a nervous breakdown because of the failure of his public-relations campaign. While the story is narrated with an extraordinary display of humor, its tone ultimately turns grotesque and cruel. "Florence y nos tres" and "Muerte de Sevilla en Madrid" are also Bryce's first attempts to link two different geographical settings in his work, the Latin-American homeland and the foreign cultural space of Europe.

In 1977 Bryce published *A vuelo de buen cubero y otras crónicas* (Wayward Journeys and Other Chronicles). This collection of journalism chronicles a trip by the author through various cities of the South in the United States during the late 1970s. Bryce describes places such as Richmond, Memphis, Atlanta, and New Orleans with a personal slant. He is somewhat of a voyeur of American life, seeking to do away with the many myths that American culture exports, some of which owe their origins to American cinema. The presence of William Faulkner, however, is also felt in these texts, which often portray a less glamorized version of the country's marginal citizens. *A vuelo de buen cubero y otras crónicas* also includes various reflections on Bryce's European experience, particularly of Paris and the events of May 1968, as well as his admiration for Julio Cortázar, Thomas Wolfe, and Hemingway in literature and for Orson Welles in film. In 1988 the book was reissued as *Crónicas personales* (Personal Chronicles) in an expanded edition.

Tired of France, toward the end of 1977 Bryce returned to Peru for six months, his longest visit since his first departure in 1964. During his stay he completed a doctorate in literature from the University of San Marcos after writing a dissertation on the theater of the modern French writer Henry de Montherlant and published his second novel, *La pasión según San Pedro Balbuena que fue tantas veces Pedro, y que nunca pudo negar a nadie* (The Passion According to Saint Pedro Balbuena That Became the Many Lives of Pedro, Who Could Deny No One) which was later republished as *Tantas veces Pedro* (The Many Lives of Pedro, 1981). By then it was obvious that Bryce's European experience had had a heavy impact on his creative consciousness. *Tantas veces Pedro* is the story of a middle-aged Peruvian writer, Pedro Balbuena, who leads a vagabond life of amorous bohemian adventures in the United States and Europe. He is trying to overcome a tragic love affair conducted entirely in his mind with a French woman named Sophie, whose picture he had seen in his youth in a magazine. When Pedro finally meets the real Sophie, who proves to be a selfish and frivolous person, she eventually kills him.

*Tantas veces Pedro* is a novel about the writer as artist. Balbuena is a failed writer who claims to lack the necessary discipline because he instead prefers to enjoy life and talk with people. Ironically, it is his great skill as a conversationalist that produces a story in the form of a text in the novel. Thus the book also becomes a reflection of the artist's creative process in writing a novel. The most experimental of Bryce's books, *Tantas veces Pedro* is a novel of transition. The author's abandonment of Peru as a setting represents his first attempt to capture at length his own European exile told from the perspective of a Latin American, an idea central to his fictional world throughout the 1980s.

Meanwhile, tired of living in Paris and distraught by a failed love affair, Bryce abandoned the French capital for the southern city of Montpellier in 1980. There he taught Latin-American literature and culture at Université Paul Valéry and finished writing his third novel, *La vida exagerada de Martín Romaña* (The Exaggerated Life of Martín Romaña, 1981). One of Bryce's most ambitious and lengthy works, *La vida exagerada de Martín Romaña* is the first part of a diptych subtitled "Cuaderno de navegación en un sillón Voltaire" (Navigation Log in a Voltaire Chair) that was followed by *El hombre que hablaba de Octavia de Cádiz* (The Man Who Spoke of Octavia de Cádiz, 1985). Its protagonist is the son of an oligarchic Peruvian family who travels to Paris to break away from his privileged background in hope of becoming a writer. Martín Romaña is a kind of Peruvian Woody Allen whose experiences resemble many of Bryce's in Europe and who finds himself caught in several misadventures that underscore his personal insecurity and lack of assertiveness. Martín soon discovers that Paris is far from the romantic and mythical city of Hemingway's fiction in which he had so firmly believed while in Lima. Instead, he finds an insular place where Latin Americans are not particularly welcome.

In Paris Martín encounters a group of Latin-American student revolutionaries, known as El Grupo, who pretend to prepare the grand revolution of the proletariat upon their return to their respective countries. They constantly criticize Martín for his lack of revolutionary conviction. The strongest critic is his sweetheart from Lima, Inés. Although Inés marries Martín in Paris, she constantly threatens to abandon him, tired of his lack of assertiveness and of his ideological apathy. In an attempt to salvage his marriage, Martín tries to write a socially committed novel about a Peruvian fisherman's union, a reality of which he is totally ignorant, and of course he fails. His failure leads to Inés's departure

Cover for Bryce's 1977 book, La pasión según San Pedro Balbuena que fue tantas veces Pedro, y que nunca pudo negar a nadie, *an experimental novel about a middle-aged Peruvian writer in Europe and America*

from Paris, which triggers his nervous breakdown. But while Inés eventually grows out of her revolutionary phase, as do others of El Grupo, and marries a wealthy Brazilian, Martín on the other hand remains firm in his determination to become a writer. Years later he begins to write in a blue notebook the story of his life as he recalls it while sitting in his so-called Voltaire chair. As he attempts to reconstruct his misfortunes, he achieves the original ambition that had first brought him to Paris, becoming a writer.

A novel of literary apprenticeship, *La vida exagerada de Martín Romaña* further defines Bryce's narrative voice and thematic interests. Set in the framework of a fictional autobiography, the story is mainly narrated in the first person and has close ties with the narrative tradition of the picaresque, as well as with Laurence Sterne's *The Life and Opinions of Tristram Shandy, Gentleman* (1759–1767). As in the pica-

ALFREDO BRYCE
ECHENIQUE

LA VIDA
EXAGERADA
DE MARTIN
ROMAÑA

PLAZA&JANES
P&J
LITERARIA

Cover for Bryce's 1981 book, a picaresque novel that includes
the author as a character

resque and *Tristram Shandy,* Martín is an egotistical character who expresses a wide variety of emotions ranging from self-deprecation to self-pity, constantly manipulating the events of the narrative and seeking the reader's attention and complicity. But also, as in Miguel de Cervantes's *Don Quixote* (1605–1615) and François Rabelais's *Gargantua and Pantagruel* (1532–1564), two other important influences on the Peruvian novelist, Bryce seeks to expand the limits of reality, intermixing other stories in the course of the narration and using multiple points of view that ultimately create a large canvas of multifaceted perspectives on reality. In addition, the novel includes a character named Bryce Echenique, a successful writer also living in Paris, whom Martín envies, abhors, and during an encounter actually knocks down. Martín Romaña is Bryce's typical antihero marked by a sense of tragedy and absurdity and caught in a world of solitude and marginality. At the same time he is a Peruvian cosmopolitan who constantly moves about in the hope of finding affection and a sense of belonging in the world.

In *La vida exagerada de Martín Romaña* Bryce also comes to terms with Paris as a cultural capital. For many aspiring Latin-American artists since the nineteenth century, Paris has been a literary mecca. The novel's portrayal of Paris, however, seeks to destroy such a fiction. For Martín one such creator of that myth was Hemingway, cited throughout the novel, by whom he feels betrayed. Once the false image of the city is acknowledged and destroyed by Martín, Paris becomes a place that instead reinforces Latin-American cultural identity. Thanks to the experience of exile, Bryce's characters undergo self-evaluation of their Latin-American identity through a painful conflict with a different cultural code. As in the works of Henry James and Julio Cortázar, two authors whose exploration of a similar theme influenced Bryce's fiction, the confrontation with the "other" serves as an experience of apprenticeship and reaffirmation of self-identity in a foreign cultural space.

In 1984 Bryce abandoned teaching permanently and moved from France to Barcelona. There he published the second volume of Martín Romaña's saga, *El hombre que hablaba de Octavia de Cádiz.* Written in what Martín calls his "red notebook," the novel begins after Inés's departure from Paris and narrates his sentimental relationship with Octavia de Cádiz, an idealized woman who in his imagination fluctuates between reality and fiction. Often the line between reality and fantasy is erased by the author's ingenious use of language. The novel rehearses many of the themes of the first volume, particularly exile and the search for a Latin-American cultural identity. In the first book Martín was criticized by his compatriots for his bourgeois spirit and lack of revolutionary convictions; this time he is rejected by Octavia's aristocratic family, who sees him through European eyes as nothing but a subversive Third World revolutionary. The novel is a rejection of the frivolous world of money and modernity in which Martín suddenly finds himself immersed, remaining truthful to his vocation as a writer.

Bryce's most recent collection of short stories is *Magdalena peruana y otros cuentos* (Peruvian Magdalena and Other Stories, 1986). A heterogeneous volume of twelve stories, it repeats some of the same topics explored in previous books, such as solitude, exile, marginality, and social decadence. Many of the stories are based on a technique in which the events narrated occur in the same time and space, thereby erasing the dubious frontiers between reality and fiction. One of the singular traits of the collection is the reappearance of many characters from Bryce's previous books, including Manolo, Florence, and Martín Romaña. The art of storytelling itself is also a recurring theme, with several characters portrayed as writers or painters. Thus the concept of author as artist is reaffirmed as an important topic in his fiction.

By the late 1980s Bryce's reputation was well established both in Latin America and Europe. In 1987 the Instituto de Cooperación Iberoamericana in Madrid sponsored a symposium to discuss his works. He was also invited as a Tinker Visiting Professor to the University of Texas at Austin and lectured at several universities in the United States. In Texas he finished writing his fifth novel, *La última mudanza de Felipe Carrillo* (The Last Round of Felipe Carrillo, 1988). The shortest of his novels, it once again explores the conflict of exile and deracination. Felipe Carrillo is a successful Peruvian architect who has lived in Paris for many years, married to a French woman, Liliane. Distraught by Liliane's unexpected death, he questions his sense of belonging in Paris. Later he meets Genoveva, a divorced Spanish journalist with an adolescent son, Sebastián. The boy suffers from a profound Oedipus complex, making Felipe's relationship with Genoveva hard to bear. In a last attempt to salvage the relationship, all three travel from Spain to Colán, a beach resort in northern Peru, but once there the situation turns into an absurd ménage à trois.

Equally absurd are the novel's later events. Disillusioned with his relationship with Genoveva, Felipe gets involved with Eusebia, a mulatto woman who has been serving the guests during their visit to Colán and with whom he later elopes to the hacienda of a wealthy friend in the area. Like Alejo Carpentier's protagonist in *Los pasos perdidos* (1953), Felipe is caught between two worlds. He yearns to return to his Peruvian roots while also pretending that he will take Eusebia back to France. However, the cultural and social differences between them make this impossible. He finally returns to Paris, destroyed by his solitude and lack of belonging.

Perhaps Bryce's most experimental literary endeavor thus far, *La última mudanza de Felipe Carrillo* is the result of meticulous intertextual crafting. Language and the art of storytelling, rather than the plot, are the main focus of the novel. As in *La vida exagerada de Martín Romaña* it is the protagonist's painful memory that directs the story's narrative. As he digressively reassesses his sentimental failure with Genoveva and Eusebia, the narrator directly addresses the reader, commenting repeatedly on the creative process he is conducting. This time, however, his frankness reaches such levels that he explicitly confesses the names of the writers he is trying to emulate, even demanding that the reader share the same hatred he feels for Genoveva and her son. Bryce devises a fast-paced text that is psychologically intense in tone, for Felipe Carrillo is probably the character who most dramatically illustrates his concept of uprootedness and solitude.

While focusing on the fragile nature of the human condition and a strong display of emotions conveyed in the narrative, Bryce also parodies the scientific nature of psychoanalytic discourse and the rigidness of political ideology. Instead, a unifying factor in the narrative is Latin-American popular music, Bryce's latest stylistic novelty. Well blended with his conversational tone, the numerous references to music unite an otherwise seemingly chaotic storyline. Also, popular music makes Felipe and Eusebia's love affair possible because, thanks to its romantic nature, music becomes their only source of real communication, allowing them to overcome the social and cultural barriers that separate them. Through the narrator's final reconstruction of events, the reader once again witnesses the creative process that has unfolded. As with Octavia de Cádiz, the protagonist learns that Eusebia is nothing but the product of his imagination. Similarly, the act of writing reveals its therapeutic nature in the new self-awareness of Felipe's existential condition.

Shortly after publishing *La última mudanza de Felipe Carrillo*, Bryce left Barcelona and moved to Madrid in 1989 to marry Pilar de Vega, a professor of Spanish linguistics. In Madrid he is currently a regular contributor to various Spanish and Latin-American periodicals as well as an active participant in Spain's cultural scene.

Bryce's latest book, a collection of novellas titled *Dos señoras conversan; Un sapo en el desierto; Los grandes hombres son así, y también asá* (Two Ladies Converse; A Frog in the Desert; Great Men Are Like This and Also Like That, 1990) reveals a new dimension in his career. This book suggests the end of his European literary experience and a return to the national scene in Peru. In fact, Bryce uses recent historical events in Peru – the military government of the late 1960s and 1970s, the return of democratic rule, and the rise of terrorist activity in the 1980s – as the background for the three stories in the book.

In the first novella of the volume, "Dos señoras conversan," two elderly sisters, Carmela and Estela, reminisce about their aristocratic lifestyle in earlier twentieth-century Peru. Through their memories Bryce is able to give the reader a quick view of the country's contemporary history and hint at the conflicts that currently plague its society. A sharp exchange of dialogue between the two characters

Cover for Bryce's 1990 book, a collection of three novellas
drawing on recent events in Peru

slowly unveils the two sisters' solitude since the deaths of their husbands. The closed nature of Peru's elite is suggested by the fact that the husbands, Juan Bautista and Luis Pedro, were also brothers. The sisters' insulation from the outside world, in particular from the radical social experiments of the 1960s, becomes evident when they comment on the difficulty of finding good servants. The violent nature of the country's social conflict is portrayed as the reader learns that Jesús Comunión, the son of the family's long-time chauffeur, instead of following his father's footsteps as a servant, has entered a university, where he has become a member of a terrorist organization. Bryce once again focuses on the decadence of the Peruvian ruling class, reproducing a reality sentimentalized by nostalgia for the past while also addressing the dilemma presented by recent social developments in Peru.

Nostalgia also permeates the book's second novella, "Un sapo en el desierto." Its protagonist, Mañuco Cisneros, is a Peruvian literature professor in Austin, Texas. While drinking beer in a local bar called La Cucaracha with three friends, he tells them of his rare friendship when he was fifteen with Don Pancho Malkovich, an important executive for a U.S. mining company in Peru in the 1950s. With Don Pancho, Mañuco used to eat, drink, and play a Peruvian game called *sapo* (frog). Don Pancho invites Mañuco to spend time in the mining camp in the Peruvian Andes, and in spite of Don Pancho's apparent sympathy for the country's customs and its people, Mañuco also learns of his company's exploitation of the native workers. Later, when a rebellion takes place, Don Pancho is injured and eventually leaves Peru, aware of the social injustice of which he has been part. He moves to San Antonio, Texas, where he has retired and where now many years later Mañuco wants to visit him. When he does, he encounters an old, decrepit, lonely man, ignored by his son even though he lives next door to him. In his garden Mañuco spots the broken *sapo* game set that Don Pancho used while in Peru, now a symbol of his decadence. "Un sapo en el desierto" is a story of social apprenticeship and awareness as well as of a disillusioning encounter with the past. Like much of Bryce's work, it expresses the notion of a lost paradise that inhabits the psyches of many of his characters.

The third novella, "Los grandes hombres son así y también asá," presents an ironic view of the human contradictions of a left-wing Peruvian leader. Set in the wake of Peru's return to democratic rule in the late 1970s, it tells of the friendship from childhood of Raúl and Santiago, both of the upper-class Peruvian bourgeoisie. As a boy Santiago idolized Raúl, who early in school proved his leadership. But in adulthood Raúl has turned into a clandestine leftist revolutionary in Peru while Santiago, despite his phobia of insects, has become a spider researcher in Paris. Upon the sudden death of Raúl's wife Eugenia, Santiago returns to Peru to see his old friend. They had planned a trip to the Peruvian jungle to remember Eugenia together and cure Santiago's fear of spiders, but once in Lima, Santiago is forced to meet with Raúl in a slum in the outskirts of Lima where he carries out his secret political activities. There Santiago learns that Raúl has quickly suppressed his feelings for the loss of his wife and meets the beautiful Nani Peters, a mutual friend from adolescence and Raúl's new girlfriend. All three travel to the Amazon region of the Peruvian jungle, where their visit is marked by a series of burlesque adventures that include Raúl's obsession to remain anonymous throughout the trip while still carrying out his "heroic" revolutionary activities in a humorously covert manner as well as Santiago's neurotic fear of being bitten by insects – especially spiders. Raúl and Santiago's lifelong friendship is often narrated through Santiago's diary, which slowly accounts for the passing of time and the mutual respect for each man's particular way of dealing with reality in spite of their differing concerns. Eventually the friends meet once again in Paris, where Raúl is in exile and finally confronts Eugenia's loss.

Through all the characters in his fictional world, Bryce proves to be an outstanding chronicler of contemporary Peruvian society with its numerous contradictions. The act of writing becomes a survival tool for his many characters, who are marked by a deep sense of existential anguish reminiscent of picaresque heroes and more recently of Jewish-American writers such as J. D. Salinger and Philip Roth. But in the solitude of their displacement, Bryce's antiheroes are also acute explorers of their inner selves and critical observers of the worlds that surround them, carrying their personal quests to their limits.

A deep sense of the act of authorship permeates Bryce's writing, with orality and humor as trademark elements in his fiction for revealing the many faces of reality. Noted for its vitality, Bryce's work evinces an urge to recapture a lost paradise through the profound exercise of nostalgic imagination and a keen awareness of the many contradictions of the human condition. Unquestionably alteregos of the author, these characters prove capable of reasserting themselves in the world despite their weaknesses, loyal to their individual beliefs.

Bryce brings a renewed sense of cosmopolitanism to contemporary Peruvian literature. His characters embody the contradictions inherent in Peruvian identity through the experiences of exile and sense of displacement in European culture. But by the same token these characters experience a critical reassessment of their Latin-American idiosyncrasies that makes them in the long run natural citizens of the world. If the novel of the Boom was praised for its great verbal and structural experimentation, this trait of cosmopolitanism, along with the confessional storytelling voice, clearly distinguishes the latest narratives to come out of Latin America since the generation of the early 1960s. Along with the writings of Luis Rafael Sánchez, José Emilio Pacheco, and Antonio Skármeta, the work of Alfredo

Bryce Echenique undoubtedly points to a renewed sense of direction and a healthy future for the Spanish-American novel of the 1990s.

**Interviews:**

Augusto Ortíz de Zevallos and Abelardo Sánchez León, "Entrevista a Alfredo Bryce," *Debate*, 28 (1984): 8–23;

César Ferreira, "Entrevista con Afredo Bryce," *Antípodas*, 3 (July 1991): 41–47.

**References:**

*Co-textes*, special issue on Bryce, 9 (May 1985);

Jennifer Ann Duncan, "Language as Protagonist: Tradition and Innovation in Bryce Echenique's *Un mundo para Julius*," *Forum for Modern Language Studies*, 16 (1980): 120–135;

Tomás Escajadillo, "Bryce: Elogios varios y una objeción," *Revista de Crítica Literaria Latinoamericana*, 6 (1977): 137–148;

Luis Eyzaguirre, "*Tantas veces Pedro:* Culminación de ciclo en la narrativa de Alfredo Bryce Echenique," *Dactylus*, 8 (Fall 1987): 13–16;

Eyzaguirre, "La última mudanza de Bryce Echenique," *Hispamérica*, 18 (August–December 1989): 195–202;

Grazia Sanguineti de Ferrero, "Axiología del humor y la ironía en *Un mundo para Julius*," *Revista de la Universidad Católica*, 11–12 (1982): 257–285;

Ricardo Gutiérrez Mouat, "Travesía y regresos de Alfredo Bryce: *La última mudanza de Felipe Carrillo*," *Hispamérica*, 63 (1992): 73–79;

Fernando R. Lafuente, ed., *Semana de Autor: Alfredo Bryce Echenique* (Madrid: Ediciones de Cultura Hispánica, 1991);

Wolfgang Luchting, *Alfredo Bryce: Humores y malhumores* (Lima: Milla Batres, 1975);

Phyllis Rodríguez-Peralta, "Narrative Access to *Un mundo para Julius*," *Revista de Estudios Hispánicos*, 17 (October 1983): 407–418;

Rodríguez-Peralta, "The Subjective Narration of Bryce Echenique's *La vida exagerada de Martín Romaña*," *Hispanic Journal*, 10 (Spring 1989): 139–151;

Abelardo Sánchez León, "Un cierto imaginario oligárquico en la narrativa de Alfredo Bryce Echenique," in *Tiempos de ira y amor* (Lima: DESCO, 1990), pp. 9–45;

László Scholz, "Realidad e irrealidad en *Tantas veces Pedro* de Alfredo Bryce Echenique," *Revista Iberoamericana*, 155–156 (April–September 1991): 533–542.

# Lydia Cabrera
*(20 May 1900 – 18 September 1991)*

Julia Cuervo Hewitt
*Pennsylvania State University*

BOOKS: *Contes nègres de Cuba,* translated by Francis de Miomandre (Paris: Gallimard, 1936); *Cuentos negros de Cuba* (Havana: La Verónica, 1940);

*¿Por qué? Cuentos negros de Cuba* (Havana: Ediciones C.R., 1948);

*El monte: Igbo-finda, ewe orisha, vititi nfinda – Notas sobre las religiones, la magia, las supersticiones y el folklore de los negros criollos y del pueblo de Cuba* (Havana: Ediciones C.R., 1954);

*Anagó: Vocabulario lucumí – El yoruba que se habla en Cuba* (Havana: Ediciones C.R., 1957; revised edition, Miami: Ediciones C.R., 1970);

*La sociedad secreta Abakuá: Narrada por viejos adeptos* (Havana: Ediciones C.R., 1958; revised edition, Miami: Ediciones C.R., 1970);

*Otán iyebiyé: Las piedras preciosas* (Miami: Ediciones C.R., 1970);

*Ayapá: Cuentos de Jicotea* (Miami: Universal, 1971);

*La laguna sagrada de San Joaquín* (Madrid: R, 1973);

*Yemayá y Ochún: Kariocha, Iyalochas y Olorichas* (Madrid: Ediciones C.R., 1974);

*Anaforuana: Ritual y símbolos de la iniciación en la sociedad secreta Abakuá* (Madrid: R, 1975);

*Francisco y Francisca: Chascarrillos de negros viejos* (Miami, 1976);

*Itinerario del insomnio: Trinidad de Cuba* (N.p.: Ediciones C.R., 1977);

*La regla kimbisa del Santo Cristo del Buen Viaje* (Miami: Ediciones C.R., 1977);

*Reglas de congo: Palo monte mayombe* (Miami: Peninsular Printing, 1979);

*Koeko iyawó: Aprende novicia – Pequeño tratado de regla lucumí* (Miami: Ultra Graphics, 1980);

*Cuentos para adultos, niños y retrasados mentales* (Miami: Ediciones C.R., 1983);

*La medicina popular de Cuba: Médicos de antaño, curanderos, santeros y paleros de hogaño* (Miami, 1984);

*Vocabulario congo: El bantú que se habla en Cuba* (Miami: Ediciones C.R., 1984);

*Lydia Cabrera, 1980*

*Supersticiones y buenos consejos* (Miami: Universal, 1987);

*Los animales en el folklore y la magia de Cuba* (Miami: Ediciones C.R., Universal, 1988);

*La lengua sagrada de los ñáñigos* (Miami: Ediciones C.R., 1988).

OTHER: *Refranes de negros viejos,* compiled by Cabrera (Havana: Ediciones C.R., 1955; revised edition, Miami: Ediciones C.R., 1970);

Pierre Verger, *Cuba: 196 Photos,* preface and notes by Cabrera (Havana: Casa Belga, 1958).

SELECTED PERIODICAL PUBLICATIONS –
UNCOLLECTED: "El dueño de Ewe," *Memoire de
l'institut français de l'afrique noire,* 27 (1940);
"Eggüe o Vichichi finda," *Revista Bimestre Cubana,* 60
(1947).

At the time of her death, Lydia Cabrera was
widely considered a world authority on Afro-Cuban
cultures, religion, and folklore. Her prolific production, which includes short stories and detailed and
extensive ethnological research on the presence and
practices of African traditions in Cuban society,
combines documentation on Afro-Cuban folklore
and religions with her own fiction. Her work is a
clever interweaving of nonfiction and poetry, the
fantastic and the real, and unique characteristics of
Cuban society and universal aspects of the human
condition. Toward the last years of her life, Lydia
Cabrera worked diligently to edit and publish the
many notes she had collected during more than
thirty years of research in Cuba. Some of her later
work – especially her dictionaries of Spanish and
African languages spoken in Cuba as well as the
multitude of anecdotes, legends, and personal testimony from informants reproduced in "their voices"
– today constitutes an invaluable source of information for students of the Caribbean. The importance
of her research, however, lies not only in the monumental amount of data she collected, but also in the
testimonial nature of her work. The informants –
elders, medicine men and women, believers, and
initiates – constitute the main narrative voices.
Thus the writer becomes a scribe, an editor, and a
crafter whose purpose is to give the reader the opportunity of confronting the living sources which
have helped create Cuban society.

Close to half a million African slaves were taken
to Cuba from the early sixteenth century to the middle of the nineteenth century, most of them in the last
one hundred years of the slave trade. By the middle of
the nineteenth century more than half of the Cuban
population was of African descent. However, in the
latter part of the century with abolition, increasing
white immigration, mixed marriages, and a general
push to "improve" and "whiten" Cuban society, Afro-
Cuban traditions continued to be ignored or denied
by the ruling classes. Among the few Cuban writers
and researchers who dedicated their efforts to this sector of Cuban society, Cabrera was the one who practically single-handedly preserved elements of Afro-
Cuban lore that otherwise would have been lost. Due
to her innovation and documentation, Cabrera was
recognized for years mainly as a folklorist. However, recent studies of her creative writing have

begun to reveal the importance and the complexity
of her fiction. Several of her works have been translated into French and Italian and more recently into
English and German.

Lydia Cabrera was born 20 May 1900 in Havana, Cuba, to a prominent upper-class family, the
youngest of eight children. She was christened three
months later in Saint Patrick's Cathedral in New
York City during one of the many trips abroad her
family made. Her mother, Elisa Bilbao Marcaida y
Casanova, was an elegant woman who dedicated
her life to her husband and children. Her father,
Raimundo Cabrera, was a lawyer, writer, novelist,
and active defender of Cuban independence. After
the American intervention of 1898, he became a
strong supporter of the separation of Cuba from the
United States. As a young man he had participated
in the Ten Years' War (1868–1878) against Spain,
and as a writer and author of *Cuba y sus jueces* (Cuba
and Its Judges, 1897) he became an active spokesman for independence.

Lydia Cabrera was born during the transitional years in which Cuba, a former colony of
Spain, became an independent country. After the
two-year intervention by the United States following the 1898 Spanish-American War, Cuba was proclaimed independent on 20 May 1902, Cabrera's
second birthday. The first president of Cuba, Es-
trada Palma, told her jokingly that the festivities in
Havana on that day were in her honor, a tale the
young girl believed. Surrounded by a loving family,
especially her father and her sister Emma, Cabrera
grew up in a world of ideas, patriotic fervor, and devotion to her homeland. During her childhood and
adolescence Cabrera's home was a meeting place
for prominent figures, many of them close friends of
the family. Cabrera remembered meeting such legendary figures as Manuel Sanguilí; Enrique José
Varona, the mulatto writer and representative;
Martín Morúa Delgado, the prominent politician
and son of former slaves; Juan Gualberto Gómez;
and many others, including women such as Carmen
Zayas Bazán, widow of the fallen patriot José Martí.
The family also housed several servants, many of
them former slaves or descendants of slaves. From
seamstresses, cooks, and nannies Cabrera heard
many stories, especially from her Nana Tula, who
during Cabrera's childhood illnesses would entertain her with a repertory of anecdotes that she recalled as being a mixture of African traditions and
Western fairy stories.

Cabrera's father indulged all of her fantasies,
according to Ana Maria Simo in *Lydia Cabrera: An
Intimate Portrait* (1984), even "being a musketeer –

*Cabrera in 1925*

tended private school. Cabrera was educated mostly at home by tutors and her sister Emma and by using her father's library. There she read from an early age works by Lope de Vega, Francisco Gómez de Quevedo, Miguel de Cervantes, Victor Hugo, Alphonse-Marie-Louis de Lamartine, and Alexandre Dumas *pére,* her favorite. During these years the strong determination that characterized her entire life surfaced. Her dearest vocational interest was painting, especially oriental painting, but her father did not approve of her daughter's studying at an art school. Without her father's permission or knowledge she enrolled at and attended with her sister Emma the Art Academy of San Alejandro. Her interest in the pictorial arts, however, did not stifle her literary ability. By age fourteen she had published twenty-seven articles in *Cuba y América.* A few years later she published six illustrations in an article on oriental art, illustrated the cover for one of the issues, and published an article on Japanese art.

After the 1917 revolution known in Cuba as La Chambelona, Cabrera's father went into exile for a short time with his family, a period that she again dedicated mostly to reading. In 1918 she began to write articles for the prestigious *Diario de la Marina* that revealed another one of Lydia Cabrera's lifelong interests: the preservation of historical buildings, antiques, colonial architecture, and the nation's historical and cultural past. Cabrera finished her high school requirements and passed the difficult baccalaureate exam studying by herself at home.

By the time she was twenty the banality of bourgeois life in Havana had become intolerable to her. It enraged her that when the family traveled abroad she was allowed to live without the restrictive social limitations she experienced in Havana. One day, holding a gun to her head, she told her father that if he did not allow her to study at the Sorbonne in Paris, she would shoot herself. He promised that the whole family would move to France for five years so that she could attend school.

On the day of her twenty-third birthday, 20 May 1923, her father died before he could fulfill his promise. Determined to become financially independent and without the parental authority either to help or limit her, she broke with social expectations for a "proper" young lady of her social level. She organized an art exhibition and subsequently opened the first antique store and "antique" furniture factory in Havana. In 1927 she sold her part of the family business and went to Paris, settled in Montmartre, and enrolled in the Ecole du Louvre,

giving her an elaborate sword and taking her out at night on imaginary adventures." Also, her sister Emma introduced her to books of adventures and fantasy. Within this circle of friends, acquaintances, family, and servants, the perceptive young Cabrera was able to record social portraits of a wide spectrum of Cuban society; she later transformed these into the characters of her stories. Inspired by her father and the literary surroundings in which she spent her childhood, while still an adolescent Cabrera began to write long novels that she would read to the family servants in the kitchen or in back rooms of the house.

Being the youngest and her father's favorite, Cabrera was allowed to accompany him to gatherings of men in literary cafés and to meetings of the prominent Sociedad Económica de Amigos del País (Friends of the Country's Economic Society), of which he was president. As a literate and liberal man, Raimundo Cabrera raised his daughter to become his intellectual heir; however, he did not allow her to attend high school or a university. On two occasions, and only for a short time, she at-from which she graduated in 1930, having also taken courses at the Ecole des Beaux Arts. Soon after her arrival in Paris she came into contact with Venezuelan poet and novelist Teresa de la Parra, whom she had met in Cuba in 1924. From then on they were inseparable companions.

With the exception of short trips to Cuba, Cabrera stayed in Europe, mostly Paris, for seventeen years of great importance for her both as a writer and as a person. While studying oriental painting, she became interested in oriental religions. Her discoveries led her to become fully aware of the rich mythological and folkloric traditions in Cuban society and to understand the marvelous universal aspect of this heritage. She has often been quoted as saying that it was at the shores of the Seine that she discovered Cuba. Although this experience was her own, it is possible that she was influenced by Fernando Ortiz's monumental work on Afro-Cuban cultures. Ortiz was married to her sister Esther, whom he had met in Europe during one of the family's trips when Cabrera was only five years old. He also had rediscovered Cuba while studying in Europe. This awareness led him to research Afro-Cuban cultures. His first book, *Los negros brujos* (The Black Witch Doctors, 1906), which marks the beginning of his monumental career, was published when Cabrera was six. Although she often denied it, Ortiz's presence in the family possibly stirred Cabrera's curiosity and at least her awareness of the complex cultural wealth of the African heritage in Cuban society. If not yet fully conscious of the richness and universality of this legacy, Cabrera was involved with black communities before her years in Europe. In an article Alejo Carpentier wrote for *Carteles,* he recalled that while gathering material for his first novel in 1927, he unexpectedly met Cabrera at an Abakuá ceremony in a remote area of Marianao, Cuba.

The time Cabrera spent in Paris was an important gestation period for her literary career. There she read Marcel Proust and Albert Camus, came in contact with new art techniques and theories, experienced an escalating interest in aesthetics and ethnology, and more importantly was taken with the intense revival of African art and cultures sweeping France and other parts of Europe. This period marked a search for new modes of expression in the arts, such as surrealism and cubism, with which she would later experiment in her short stories. New discoveries in anthropology were published by Leo Frobenius and later by Cabrera's friends Pierre Verger, Alfred Metraux, and Roger Bastide. She befriended writers such as Lucien

Lévy-Bruhl, Paul Valéry, Rudyard Kipling, and Miguel Angel Asturias, who shared with Cabrera an interest in the indigenous mythologies of his native Guatemala. Cabrera also established a close friendship with the poet Gabriela Mistral. In Spain she cherished the close friendship of poet and playwright Federico García Lorca, whose work was inspired by Spanish folklore, mainly the Gypsy element of Spanish life.

With the arousal of her interest in Afro-Cuban folklore during brief visits to Havana in 1928 and in 1930 with de la Parra, Cabrera established permanent contact with the community of Pogolotti, a poor and predominantly black neighborhood that became one of the main sources of information for her research. When Cabrera shared the stories she had heard in the Afro-Cuban communities with de la Parra, the author of *Ifigenia* (1924) and *Las memorias de Mamá Blanca* (Mama Blanca's Memoirs, 1929) insisted that Cabrera write them down.

In 1932 Cabrera's mother died, and de la Parra found out she had contracted tuberculosis. Cabrera went with her to a sanatorium and accompanied her throughout most of her remaining years. During a short visit Cabrera made to Paris, she decided to entertain her friend as her nannie and sister had done for her during her illness as a child by writing a series of stories and sending them to de la Parra in Switzerland. These short stories, most of them witty, playful experiments with avant-garde techniques, recaptured anecdotes of African traditions garnished by Cabrera's lively imagination. She also shared them with friends in literary gatherings. The reception was positive, and they were soon translated into French by the poet Francis de Miomandre and published as *Contes nègres de Cuba* (Black Stories from Cuba, 1936). These early writings reveal Cabrera's poetic talent, her knowledge of Afro-Cuban lore, an ability to capture the rhythm and vitality of the African heritage in Cuba, and her skill in creating a verbal collage of cultural modes typically Cuban. Cabrera's successful lyrical accomplishment in prose in this collection is especially evident in the stories "Walo-Wila" and "El sapo guardiero" (The Guard Frog). Other stories, such as "Cheggue," "La loma de Mambiala" (Mambiala's Hill), and "El caballo de jicotea" (Tortoise's Horse), are re-creations of anecdotes from Africa and areas of the Americas where African folklore left its imprint. Most likely Cabrera heard different versions in Cuba. For the most part they are fictional compositions and recompositions of Cabrera's childhood fantasy world combined with the artistic modes and techniques in vogue rather than the result of ethno-

*Cabrera and her friend María Teresa de Rojas at the eighteenth-century Havana mansion they restored, 1947*

logical research. Nonetheless, the musical rhythm Cabrera often gives to her stories, in which the vitality of the Afro-Cuban legacy is recaptured, is already brilliantly evident in a short story from this early collection: "Suadende," a humorous anecdote that recalls, in an Afro-Cuban setting, García Lorca's "La casada infiel" (The Unfaithful Wife), a poem he dedicated to Cabrera and "su negrita" (her little black woman).

When *Contes nègres de Cuba,* which she dedicated to de la Parra, was published, Cabrera was in Spain accompanying her ailing friend, who died two months later. Cabrera returned to France, which was undergoing the political agitation leading to World War II. In 1936 the Spanish Civil War erupted, and Cabrera returned to Cuba seeking refuge and peace. There she became reacquainted with María Teresa de Rojas, a paleographer passionately interested, like Cabrera, in antiques, historical research, and the nation's colonial past. They collaborated in the restoration of the Pedroso Palace and bought a house in the old colonial town of Trinidad. Rojas also owned La Quinta San José, an abandoned eighteenth-century mansion close to the

Pogolotti community where Cabrera's informants lived. They both embarked on restoring the old mansion with the purpose of documenting the historical evolution of the Cuban colonial house and bequeathing it to the people of Cuba as a national museum. Gabriela Mistral visited Havana during this period and was shocked and distressed to find a bourgeois Cabrera surrounded by wealthy acquaintances.

In 1940 *Cuentos negros de Cuba* was published in Havana. Cabrera's growing interest in the African heritage of Cuba, the favorable reception her short stories had received in France, and Mistral's stinging remarks encouraged her to pursue her research. *Cuentos negros de Cuba,* however, did not receive the same positive reception in Havana, where it was either ignored or attacked by prejudiced traditional critics. In 1942, ignoring negative comments and determined to pursue serious research, she started an in-depth study of Afro-Cuban folklore and religions throughout the island: a long and sometimes arduous process of gathering materials, some of it in the African languages still spoken by the elders and utilized in ceremonies; talking for hours with informants; transcribing and editing stories, beliefs, ceremonies, and rituals; and trying to interpret and decipher contradictory and repetitious anecdotes in which, as she often explained, the starting point of an anecdote was not always the beginning of the story.

These years of research coincided with the increasing interest in popular and indigenous cultures and mythologies during the 1930s by writers inside and outside Cuba, among them Nicolás Guillén, Alejo Carpentier, Ramón Güirao, Rómulo Lachatañeré, and Emilio Ballaga. There was also the continuing research of Ortiz.

In 1948 Cabrera published a second collection of short stories, *¿Por qué? Cuentos negros de Cuba* (Why? Black Stories from Cuba). Continuing with the same subjects of her first collection, the twenty-eight anecdotes of the second book offer differences in style, the appearance of a philosophical humor, and a refined lyricism. Evident avant-garde techniques give way to a sophisticated blend of poetry, popular expressions, and careful documentation filtered through Cabrera's imagination. All of these stories are charged with complex religious symbolism: *orishas* (deities); African cosmological myths; ritual animals such as tortoises, vultures, and snakes; and trees such as the ceiba (in Africa the iroko) come together in Cabrera's re-creation of Afro-Cuban folklore. Some of the stories can be found in simpler versions in the Patakín, a collection of stories related to the oracle of Ifá, and the Dilogún, which in Yoruba (Lucumí) traditions is the channel by which man speaks to the forces of life, the *orishas*. Of these the religious anecdote most faithfully re-created by Cabrera is "Obbara miente y no miente" (Obbara lies and does not lie), a story that coincides with the religious anecdotes of the figure (or letter) and mythological character Obbara in the oracle. In general Cabrera works with a monumental oral and written archive of sayings, proverbs, and anecdotes extracted from the deep well of popular wisdom, the blending of two cultures, and the syncretic religious codes of the Cuban people. Many of these popular sayings, reconstructed and elaborated by Cabrera's imagination, are teachings from ancient oral traditions written down by Afro-Cuban priests in notebooks and handed down from *Babas* (fathers of the religion) to their initiates. At the same time they are Cabrera's own witty creations, in which the reader finds satire directed at all social types. Starting with *¿Por qué?* Cabrera called all her publications "Colección del Chicherekú" (Chicherekú's Collection), after a small demon who goes out at night to do mischief.

Her time-consuming efforts to document, compile, and edit (in the voice of her informants) a monumental amount of historical and religious anecdotes, religious practices, remedies, symbols, beliefs, proverbs, and in general the various aspects of Afro-Cuban lore culminated in Cabrera's most important work: *El monte: Igbo-finda, ewe orisha, vititi nfinda – Notas sobre las religiones, la magia, las supersticiones y el folklore de los negros criollos y del pueblo de Cuba* (Mountain, Bushland, or Forest: Igbo-Finda, Ewe Orisha, Vititi Nfinda – Notes on the Religion, Magic, Superstitions and Folklore of Black Creoles and Cuban People). Published in 1954, the book is a unique testimony to Afro-Cuban mythologies, culture, and history and is considered by experts in the field as the Afro-Cuban bible. The title summarizes the symbolic nature of its content and articulates the multiple meanings of *monte* for Afro-Cuban believers: not only forest, bushland, or any place where there is natural greenery, but mount, such as a high and sacred ground. For Afro-Cuban believers the forest, which can be any place, is the sacred zone of all life forces: the center of life, nature. As one informant says in *El monte,* because "everything can be found in the Monte . . . it gives us everything." This single text is in itself the most complete archive of the mythologies and folklore of the Cuban people.

Following the Spanish tradition of anthologizing and collecting sayings and proverbs in order to expose and preserve the popular wisdom of a particular group of people, in 1955 Cabrera published *Refranes de negros viejos* (Sayings and Proverbs of Black Elders). Two years later she published another monumental work, *Anagó: Vocabulario lucumí* (Anagó: Lucumí Vocabulary), a dictionary of the Yoruba (Lucumí) languages spoken in Cuba that not only revealed the extent to which African heritage can still be found on the island but also helped preserve for posterity a fragile aspect of Cuban society. A year later she published another revealing work, *La sociedad secreta Abakuá: Narrada por viejos adeptos* (The Secret Society of the Abakuá: Narrated by Old Adepts), the first detailed, objective account of the rites, ceremonies, and beliefs of a powerful and highly secret society commonly known in Cuba as *ñáñigos,* a Cubanized version of the traditions and myths of Carabalí tribes from the Cameroon area of Africa. In Cuba the *ñáñigos* were both feared and misunderstood. Cabrera's book was not only a testimonial and a carefully documented account of the religious practices and beliefs of this group, but also a daring project for a woman. The Abakuá is a closed, secret all-male society whose initiation rites center around the ritual remembrance of the immolation of Sikán, or Sikuanekua, a woman who heard the secret voice of the deity-fish Ekué and re-

Lydia Cabrera

AYAPA
Cuentos de Jicotea

Ediciones Universal
P. O. Box 353 (Shenandoah Station)
Miami, Florida, 33145. U.S.A.

*Title page for Cabrera's 1971 collection of short stories,
featuring a trickster figure from folklore*

vealed it. Ironically, Cabrera became the Sikua-nekua of Afro-Cuban lore, the one who revealed the inner secrets of a culture, its rites, magic, and potions, and also the poetry and myths that permeated Cuban society, still not fully aware of the wealth of its African heritage.

After the triumph of the Cuban revolution led by Fidel Castro in 1959, Cabrera and María Teresa de Rojas decided to leave Cuba for a time. On the eve of their departure Cabrera, following an intuition, took with her the notes she had gathered during nearly forty years. Soon after, for motives still unknown yet typical of the chaotic first years of the revolution, Quinta San José was seized and destroyed by the new government. Cabrera remained in exile for the rest of her life, mostly in Miami, Florida, except for a short period during which she lived in Madrid. In spite of her political differences with the revolutionary government, she was praised in Cuba by young writers also interested in Afro-Cuban cultures who saw her, like Ortiz, as a pioneer in the field. She had left behind the results of

her work, including a major enterprise she undertook between 1954 and 1958 of recording and editing the fourteen-record set *Música de los cultos africanos en Cuba* (Music of Afro-Cuban Cults).

Finally, after twelve years of silence, she published the first book of the second stage of her productive life: *Otán iyebiyé: Las piedras preciosas* (Otán iyebiyé: Precious Stones, 1970), an account of the ritual meanings Cuban experts give to precious stones and metals. In a conversational style she documented a specific element of Cuban lore at the same time that she gave it a universal character, for just like the Afro-Cuban *Baba,* she points out, Plato, the European alchemists, and many mythological traditions have shared the same beliefs. A year later she published a third book of short stories, *Ayapá: Cuentos de Jicotea* (Ayapá: Tortoise Stories, 1971). The twenty stories in this collection have the same protagonist in common, a small land turtle (*jicotea*) whose counterpart in Yoruba lore is the tortoise. She garnishes her stories with vivid imagination, wit, and humor but remains faithful to the African tradition in the context of Cuban society. Cabrera's Cuban land turtle differs from the African trickster-tortoise in that Jicotea is often female – a linguistic play, since *jicotea* in Spanish is a feminine word. Sometimes Jicotea is uniquely Cuban while at others it has African characteristics; sometimes it is a witty Cuban dandy, at others an old madam or a shady character corrupted by desire and power. Jicotea is a collage of universal human conditions and at the same time the incarnation of defined Cuban archetypes and the ritual magic and power that belong to the world of the *orishas.*

Although Jicotea, like the tortoise, is most often punished for wrongdoings, in Cabrera's stories goodness does not always triumph: Jicotea often gets away from those who are less astute and in so doing injures innocent victims. If the reader sometimes detects the hidden influence of existentialism in Cabrera's narratives, it is because goodness does not always win by default in her stories. Underneath its religious symbolism Cabrera's fictional world has been re-created with an irreverence she consciously nurtured toward all social types (especially the banality of the upper class), absolute truths, patriarchal authority, and snobbish intellectuality. Her fiction speaks of the world of the *orishas,* in which the dichotomy of good and evil does not exist and in which each deity is both many and one, incarnating both positive and negative forces against which human beings must act and react in a constant play of power and harmony. Cabrera mocks blacks and whites alike, rich and poor, animals and humans, men and women. If there is a didactic subtext in her stories, it is the unspoken condemnation of patriarchal authority, power, and corruption in a world in which human beings must be alert and astute or else perish. Unlike women characters in Western fairy tales, Cabrera's female protagonists are neither good nor bad. Unlike their counterparts in Western lore, they are the ones who outwit the enemy, rebel against unlimited power or abuse, and subvert it. A female Jicotea manages to ride a horse and make him her servant in "El caballo de jicotea," and Ochún seduces and domesticates Ogún, the owner of metals and the epitome of male strength, while also deceiving the power-hungry goat in "El chivo hiede" (The Goat Stinks).

At seventy-three years old Cabrera was racing against time to publish her still-unedited notes. In 1973 she published *La laguna sagrada de San Joaquín* (The Sacred Lagoon of San Joaquín), a testimonial account of a 1956 visit she made with friends to a black community in a central Cuban sugar mill town in the province of Matanzas. The short book is enhanced by photographs taken with a hidden camera. In 1974 Cabrera published another important book, *Yemayá y Ochún: Kariocha, Iyalochas y Olorichas* (Yemayá and Ochún: Kariocha, Iyalochas, and Olorichas), a collection of anecdotes, legends, and myths of the two Yoruba (Lucumí) feminine deities of water, Yemayá (Yemonja) and Ochún (Oshun). A year later, in 1975, Cabrera published *Anaforuana: Ritual y símbolos de la iniciación en la sociedad secreta Abakuá* (Anaforuana: Ritual and Initiation Symbols in the Secret Abakuá Society, 1975), an extensive pictorial book reproducing and explaining the religious symbols of the ritual drawings used in ceremonies and initiations of the Abakuá society. These symbolic drawings are in themselves testimony to the complex language and mythology of these rituals.

In 1977, deviating from her usual theme but not departing from her interests, Cabrera published *Itinerario del insomnio: Trinidad de Cuba* (Itinerary of Insomnia: Trinidad, Cuba), a marvelous imaginative journey to the past through the memories of an old woman who, rejecting modern sleeping pills, chooses instead to take advantage of her hours of sleeplessness. She lets her thoughts carry her freely to the past, rediscovering in the hidden crevices of her memory what she thought was forgotten. In this static journey the narrator returns to bygone years, visits people and places that have already ceased to exist, and peeps through stories and gossip into the simple everyday lives of the protagonists in this colonial town. This captivating chronicle and memoir,

written in Cabrera's conversational and testimonial style like most of her work, blends fact and fiction and in so doing recapitulates a favorite theme that has occupied Spanish-American narrative since early colonial times. While Cabrera gives an account of the history of Trinidad, she is also recalling the history of Spanish-American literature from its origins.

In 1977 Cabrera also published *La regla kimbisa del Santo Cristo del Buen Viaje* (The Kimbisa Cult of the Christian Saint of Good Travel), where she explains the history, rituals, and beliefs of an Afro-Cuban religious group that for Cabrera best exemplifies the religious syncretism – a mixture of Bantú and Lucumí beliefs, Catholicism, and spiritualism – that took place in Cuba. The uniqueness of the Kimbisa group, as Cabrera points out, is that it was founded in the nineteenth century by Andrés Petit, the Afro-Cuban priest who broke racial barriers imposed by the black secret fraternity when in 1863 he initiated the first white men in the Abakuá society.

Still working incessantly, Cabrera published an account of Bantu cults in Cuba, *Reglas de congo: Palo monte mayombe* (Congo Cult: Palo Monte Mayombe, 1979), an interesting and valuable document tinted by Cabrera's idealization of the colonial period, her irreverence for the present, and her constant search for harmony and equality. A year later she published another book about the Lucumí traditions: *Koeko iyawó: Aprende novicia – Pequeño tratado de regla lucumí* (Koeko Iyawó: Learn, Novice – Short Treatise on the Lucumí Cult), and in 1983, departing once more from the strict Afro-Cuban theme, *Cuentos para adultos, niños y retrasados mentales* (Stories for Adults, Children and the Mentally Retarded) gathered some of Cabrera's unpublished short stories, many of them her own witty re-creations of popular jokes and Cuban stereotypes.

By this time she was working on *Supersticiones y buenos consejos* (Superstitions and Good Counsel, 1987), and she had already finished other books: *La medicina popular de Cuba: Médicos de antaño, curanderos, santeros y paleros de hogaño* (Popular Medicine in Cuba: Yesterday's Doctors and Today's Healers, and Priests of the Santería and Palo Cults, 1984); and two other main works of research, *Vocabulario congo: El bantú que se habla en Cuba* (Congo Vocabulary: The Bantú Language Spoken in Cuba, 1984) and *La lengua sagrada de los ñáñigos* (The Sacred Language of the Ñáñigos, 1988), a dictionary of the ritual Abakuá language spoken among initiates. Cabrera's three dictionaries are invaluable references, allowing readers to understand the meanings of many words used in popular Cuban speech as well as the meanings of various rituals, sayings, and songs. They have also provided a means to uncode Cabrera's own fiction and have preserved a heritage that would otherwise have eroded under the pressures of unavoidable social transformations. *Los animales en el folklore y la magia de Cuba* (Animals in Cuban Folklore and Magic, 1988) is an encyclopedic account of the symbolic role of animals in Afro-Cuban lore. The text also decodes Cabrera's own use of animals in her stories and adds other levels of meaning and cultural significance to the folk stories Cabrera's informants provided.

Next to that of Fernando Ortiz, Lydia Cabrera's work offers the vastest, most prolific, and most detailed documentation available today on Afro-Cuban cultures. In spite of political differences, her work was recognized and praised in Castro's Cuba. Three times from 1966 to 1969 her stories were adapted into plays and presented by the Teatro Nacional Guiñol in Havana. In the United States she received several tributes and honorary degrees from Denison University, Redland University, Manhattan College, and Miami University. Her home in Miami was a place of pilgrimage for writers, academics, artists, and practitioners of Afro-Cuban religions drawn to Cabrera, who was simple and unpretentious, welcoming any curious reader, intellectual, or believer. Impish and determined, like the adolescent girl pursuing art classes, she continued her work in spite of age and loss of sight to become a marvelous blend of the small mischievous Chicherekú and Sikuanekua – the female voice that revealed the secret.

Different from traditional anthropological and ethnological studies, Cabrera's work combines her voice with that of the subject of her research. The testimonial nature of her work makes it possible for the reader to gain access, as much as possible in the transliteration of an oral tradition to writing, to the modes of speech, thought, and collective consciousness of one of the main cultural components of Cuban society. Cabrera's work, like the author herself, subverts traditional literary canons and resists the limited classifications of genre. Her stories are cross sections of Cuban society that cut through all social levels, gender, genre, and race. The protagonist of all of her stories, fictional and testimonial, is Cuba seen through the looking glass of the text and of Cabrera's imagination. Like the work of García Lorca, Cabrera's work is pregnant with myths, superstitions, legends, and national archetypes telling the history of the development of Cuban society. While critics have given scant attention to the aesthetic value of her fiction, Cabrera, a master storyteller, has earned a place among the best and most innovative short-story writers in Spanish America.

**Interview:**
Rosario Hiriart, *Más cerca de Teresa de la Parra: Diálogo con Lydia Cabrera* (Caracas: Monte Avila, 1980).

**References:**
Isabel Castellanos and Josefina Inclán, eds., *En torno a Lydia Cabrera* (Miami: Universal, 1987);

Congreso de Literatura Afro-Americana, *Homenaje a Lydia Cabrera* (Miami: Universal, 1978);

Mariela Gutiérrez, *Los cuentos negros de Lydia Cabrera: Un estudio morfológico* (Miami: Universal, 1986);

Rosario Hiriart, *Lydia Cabrera: Vida hecha arte* (Madrid & New York: Eliseo Torres and Sons, 1978);

Hiriart, ed., *Cartas a Lydia Cabrera: Correspondencia inédita de Gabriela Mistral y Teresa de la Parra* (Madrid: Torremozas, 1988);

Josefina Inclán, *"Ayapá" y otras "otán Iyebiye" de Lydia Cabrera* (Miami: Universal, 1976);

*Noticias de arte: Gaceta de las artes visuales, escénicas, musicales y literarias,* special issue on Cabrera (May 1982);

Lino Novás Calvo, "El monte," *Papeles de Son Armadans,* 150 (September 1968): 298–304;

Hilda Perera, *Idapo: El sincretismo en los cuentos negros de Lydia Cabrera* (Miami: Universal, 1971);

Ana María Simó, *Lydia Cabrera: An Intimate Portrait* (New York: Intar Latin American Gallery, 1984);

Sara Soto, *Magia e historia en los "Cuentos negros," "Por qué," y "Ayapá" de Lydia Cabrera* (Miami: Universal, 1988);

Rosa Valdez-Cruz, *Lo ancestral africano en la narrativa de Lydia Cabrera* (Barcelona: Vosgos, 1974);

María Zambrano, "Lydia Cabrera, poeta de la metamorfosis," *Orígenes,* 7, no. 25 (1950): 11–15.

# Autran Dourado

*(18 January 1926 – )*

M. Angélica Lopes
*University of South Carolina*

BOOKS: *Teia* (Belo Horizonte, Brazil: Edifício, 1947);

*Sombra e exílio* (Belo Horizonte, Brazil: João Calazans, 1950);

*Tempo de amar* (Rio de Janeiro: José Olympio, 1952);

*Três histórias na praia* (Rio de Janeiro: Ministério da Educação e Cultura, Serviço de Documentação, 1955);

*Nove histórias em grupos de três* (Rio de Janeiro: José Olympio, 1957);

*A barca dos homens* (Rio de Janeiro: Editôra do Autor, 1961; revised edition, Rio de Janeiro: Expressão e Cultura, 1975; revised edition, São Paulo: Difel, 1976);

*Uma vida em segrêdo* (Rio de Janeiro: Civilização Brasileira, 1964; revised edition, Rio de Janeiro: Expressão e Cultura, 1973; revised edition, Rio de Janeiro: Expressão e Cultura, 1975); translated by Edgar H. Miller, Jr., as *A Hidden Life* (New York: Knopf, 1969);

*Ópera dos mortos* (Rio de Janeiro: Civilização Brasileira, 1967); translated by John M. Parker as *The Voices of the Dead* (London: Owen, 1980; New York: Taplinger, 1981);

*O risco do bordado* (Rio de Janeiro: Expressão e Cultura, 1970; revised edition, Rio de Janeiro: Expressão e Cultura, 1973; revised edition, Rio de Janeiro: Difel, 1977); translated by Parker as *Pattern for a Tapestry* (London: Owen, 1984);

*Solidão solitude* (Rio de Janeiro: Civilização Brasileira, 1972);

*Uma poética de romance* (São Paulo: Perspectiva, 1973); revised and augmented as *Uma poética de romance: Matéria de carpintaria* (São Paulo: Difel, 1976);

*Os sinos da agonia* (Rio de Janeiro: Expressão e Cultura, 1974); translated by Parker as *The Bells of Agony* (London: Owen, 1989);

*Novelário de Donga Novais* (Rio de Janeiro: Difel, 1976);

*Armas e corações* (Rio de Janeiro: Difel, 1978);

*Três histórias no internato: Conto* (São Paulo: Editora Nacional, 1978);

*Novelas de aprendizado* (Rio de Janeiro: Nova Fronteira, 1980);

*As imaginações pecaminosas* (Rio de Janeiro: Record, 1981);

*O meu mestre imaginário* (Rio de Janeiro: Record, 1982);

*A serviço del-Rei* (Rio de Janeiro: Record, 1984);

*Lucas Procópio* (Rio de Janeiro: Record, 1984);

*Violetas e caracóis* (Rio de Janeiro: Guanabara, 1987);

*Um artista aprendiz* (Rio de Janeiro: José Olympio, 1989);

*Monte da Alegria* (Rio de Janeiro: Francisco Alves, 1990);

*Um cavalheiro de antigamente* (São Paulo: Siciliano, 1992).

Waldomiro Freitas Autran Dourado is a major Brazilian writer of the twentieth century. Among his thirteen novels, seven story collections, and critical essays are several masterpieces. During his forty-five-year career he has had consistent critical success and has received important literary prizes. Some of his novels have been translated into English and other languages, and a UNESCO panel chose *Ópera dos mortos* (1967; translated as *The Voices of the Dead,* 1980) as a representative universal work of literature. A conscientious practitioner of his art, Autran Dourado nevertheless considers himself an apprentice as he examines and builds his texts. He has studied the lessons of the masters he acknowledges: Gustave Flaubert, Henry James, Franz Kafka, William Faulkner, and Brazilian writer Joaquim Maria Machado de Assis. His combination of classical structure through pastiche and colloquial language makes for an admirable, fluid style. The author of more than twenty books, Dourado presents himself as both the heir of and speaker for the golden era of his native region, the eighteenth century, whose complexity and abundance he shares.

*Autran Dourado, circa 1984 (photograph by Ofélia Autran Dourado)*

Dourado was born in Patos de Minas, Minas Gerais, Brazil, the son of a judge, Telêmaco Autran Dourado, and his wife, Alice Freitas Autran Dourado. As a student at the University of Minas Law School in Belo Horizonte, he made friends whose interest in literary matters was as keen as his. The city, founded in 1897 as the state capital of Minas Gerais, had been a propitious starting place for writers. Among Dourado's contemporaries were other significant writers, including Fernando Sabino, Paulo Mendes Campos, Otto Lara Resende, and film critic Sábato Magaldi. Dourado's group of friends founded a literary magazine, *Edifício* (Building), which lasted only four issues, but they managed to publish some of their work, including Dourado's first effort, the novella *Teia* (Web, 1947), written four years earlier when the author was seventeen. He had decided against publishing an earlier story collection on the advice of Godofredo Rangel, a respected novelist who had seen the young author's talent as well as his need for technical improvement.

*Teia* is a somber book that has both the virtues and defects of 1940s and 1950s Brazilian fiction. Well constructed, with Dourado's excellent command of literary Portuguese, it presents situations and characters closer to allegory than to fiction. The novella takes place in a small town where the anonymous narrator is trying to escape the difficult memory of his father's murder in a brothel. The boardinghouse in which he takes refuge is as sinister as its owner. Only two other people live there, each seemingly carrying a secret as heavy as the narrator's. An example of Dourado's craft at an early age, *Teia* also points to the future integration in his work of both theme and mood. Like much of his later fiction, this early novella includes secrets gnawing away at family members, mystery, and a dark, oppressive atmosphere created by the dysfunctional family and reinforced by dangerous gossip. The title itself, connected with the idea of weaving, is related to themes apparent in other works, such as *O risco do bordado* (1970; translated as *Pattern for a Tapestry,* 1984) and his subtitle for his revised book of writing, *Matéria de carpintaria* (A Matter for Carpentry, 1976).

His second novel, *Sombra e exílio* (Shadow and Exile, 1950), was published a year after he graduated from law school. Like its predecessor, it was financed by the young author's mother. It was awarded the Mario Sette Prize from the *Jornal de Letras* — a good start for a twenty-four-year-old author. Dourado deals with the psyches of three characters: Rodrigo, the protagonist; his mother; and Marta, his estranged wife. The reader also encounters Artur, Rodrigo's prodigal brother. Here, as in *Teia,* the protagonist is young, spiritually drifting, and tormented by an unresolved Oedipus complex. His mother is ineffectual, and his dead, evil father still haunts him. The older son, Artur, resembles the father in his selfishness, cruelty, and sexual license. Stylistically and structurally, *Sombra e exílio* is a more ambitious and better novel than its predecessor because Dourado expanded his narrative devices. The character Silvia, for example, has a magnificent dream, upon her return to her husband's house, reminiscent of both Kafka and surrealist painting. Another important device is carried over from *Teia* and became a trademark of Dourado's fiction: gossip as a means of thickening both plot and atmosphere. Evil characters spread gossip and reveal secrets about people they dislike, often ruining their lives. Rodrigo's father did this to his wife, and the town does it to Rodrigo. Anguished and unable to find his path in life, Rodrigo is an existentialist character whose anxiety is caused by his late father and his brother's remembrance. Their unrelenting malevolence underlies the plot of the novel. *Teia* and *Sombra e exílio* were reprinted in one volume, *Novelas de aprendizado* (Apprentice Novels, 1980). The title again states his belief in the value of apprenticeship and of literary work as a continuum.

*Tempo de amar* (Time for Loving, 1952) received a prize from the city of Belo Horizonte. Considered by many critics to be the author's first important work of fiction, it continued with the features that have become associated with his work: the family with the rudderless, anguished intellectual son in the stifling small town where sex is shameful and hidden. A biblical subtext, also characteristic of Dourado's mythical approach, is evident in parallels between the protagonist, Ismael, and his father and the biblical Abraham and his firstborn son. With this novel and his previous efforts, Dourado placed himself in an important literary current in Brazil at the time along with writers such as Cornélio Penna and Lúcio Cardoso, who like Dourado dealt with moral scruples, budding sexual lives, and generational conflicts in an intense, minutely detailed way. Such psychologically focused stories about introverted characters reached a high aesthetic level and had come about partly as a reaction to the strong

regionalism of the 1930s and 1940s, which was a direct consequence of Brazilian modernism.

In 1954 Dourado became press secretary for President Juscelino Kubitschek de Oliveira, a position he held until 1959. In 1955 Dourado published *Três histórias na praia* (Three Stories on the Beach). Uncharacteristically, the setting is not landlocked Minas Gerais with its mountains of gold and iron, but the coast. A single episode witnessed by different people connects the three independent stories. The literary level is still high, but both the style and focus have changed from those of the earlier novels. Each of the three stories focuses on a different protagonist: a man, a child, and a young woman. All of the stories are written in a more straightforward narrative line than in his earlier work, and the intensity of the setting is less engulfing and inimical than in the novels.

Two years later Dourado included the three stories and six unpublished ones in a new volume, *Nove histórias em grupos de três* (Nine Stories in Groups of Three, 1957). The book received the major literary Artur Azevedo prize from the Instituto Nacional do Livro. Dourado chose not to revise the beach stories, as he points out in the preface of *Solidão solitude* (Lonely Solitude, 1972), because he believes in exploring old and new aspects in new works rather than reworking the same piece. The second group of stories in the collection shows a superb command of the first-person narrative. The most important of these is "A glória do ofício" (Labor's Glory), which Dourado has claimed is an allegory for the writing profession and his part in it. The last group of stories is "Histórias de internato" (Boarding School Stories). Well crafted and moving, they examine incidents in the lives of students at the Colégio São Mateus (also the setting of several later works): the young João Nogueira on his first day of class; the senior Martim on his last; and two misfits, a teacher and a perpetual student.

After Kubitschek's presidential term Dourado remained in Rio de Janeiro to work for the Ministry of Justice. His next books also received distinguished prizes. In 1961 *A barca dos homens* (The Ship of People) was awarded the Brazilian Union of Writers' Fernando Chinaglia Prize. The novel was also Dourado's first popular success. After *A barca dos homens* all his books sold well and were often reprinted. Like *Três histórias na praia,* this novel has a maritime rather than a mountain setting and weaves typical Dourado material in different, more complex ways. *A barca dos homens* marks the beginning of a major practice for Dourado: parody and homage as stylistic and structural de-

*Dourado, circa 1973 (photograph by Inês Autran Dourado Barbosa)*

vices. *A barca dos homens,* as the author explains, is a pastiche based on late medieval and Renaissance Portuguese literature, including anonymous sixteenth-century shipwreck accounts.

The novel's solidity, brilliance, and pathos firmly established Dourado as a major contemporary Brazilian novelist. It includes his usual combination – love and innocence, lust, distrust, anguish, and madness – in a plot loaded with mythical and religious connections in a realistically drawn Brazilian setting, an island off the Atlantic coast. The character of Fortunato represents one of the two major mythical figures in the novel. His name – the Fortunate One, or, from the original Greek, the Unfortunate One – points to his fate. A retarded young man, he is innocent and kindhearted. Hunted by the populace for a supposed crime, he will become Christ, the sacrificial lamb whose death will redeem the sins of the island. The other major mythic character is the satyr, a police lieutenant with a lust for Maria, a summer visitor. This novel is the first in which Dourado demonstrates his ability to create a powerfully erotic environment – a major feature in his later work.

Dourado's next novel, *Uma vida em segrêdo* (1964; translated as *A Hidden Life,* 1969), was his best-selling book and one of his masterpieces. In it he departs from the technique and themes of *A barca dos homens* and instead is closer to *Tempo de amar* in his focus on one protagonist and one major story line. The hidden life belongs to Gabriela Fernandes da Conceição, nicknamed Biela, a wealthy orphan who leaves the country to join her cousin and guardian and his family in the town of Duas Pontes. The narrative has led to comparisons with Flaubert's novella *Un Cœur simple* (1877). If a naive spinster's life makes for a simple and unified theme, the technique is quite the opposite, making the uneventful life of a shy small-town spinster a rich novel. Dourado creates Biela through her own consciousness as well as those of other characters. A self-proclaimed disciple of Henry James, Dourado shifts the viewpoint among the family members and other townspeople. His technical mastery is also evident in the novel's stylistic variety and his sureness in combining varied rhetorical devices and levels of speech. According to Dourado, *Uma vida em segrêdo,* unlike his other books, was written in one month.

In 1967 Dourado published *Ópera dos mortos* (translated as *The Voices of the Dead,* 1980). The title is significant since, like much of his fiction, the novel presents a variety of viewpoints as the narrator tells the story of another lonely, timid spinster, Rosalina. The setting is closely linked with the characters and at times becomes indistinguishable from them: the land mingles with people, whose extension it becomes. Dourado follows a classic symbology; for instance, house and character both inhabit and are inhabited by each other, as in Jungian psychology. The first chapter, on the mansion, refers to the Cota family seat whose decay is also evident in its last inhabitant, Rosalina. The densely textured novel examines family relationships, sexual anxiety, xenophobia, and conflicts between classes and races. Imagery and mythology, two of Dourado's trademarks, are represented by the protagonist's name and actions. Rosalina (small rose) and her female servant live retiring lives in the mansion in the main square of the old town. The servant connects her mistress to the outside world, communicating with townspeople only to buy food and sell the silk flowers her mistress makes. Their peaceful lives are disturbed by a stranger's arrival. He is not, however, a knight in armor (as foreseen by Rosalina) but a hired hand who seduces her and whom she seduces. Like *A barca dos homens,* *Ópera dos mortos* ends tragically, with the death of an innocent.

One reason for the importance of *Ópera dos mortos* is that it is Dourado's first work in which the Cota family appears. Like Faulkner with his Snopeses and Compsons, Dourado has developed the Cota family over more than one work. Similarly, Rosalina's town, Duas Pontes (Two Bridges), has become his Yoknapatawpha County, as Dourado has developed Rosalina's contemporaries and ancestors in his later work. *Ópera dos mortos* also marks Dourado's maturity as he produced his own style and dealt with more psychologically complex characters and situations.

*O risco do bordado* is not only the title for Dourado's next book but also a metaphor for his philosophy and opus. Primarily, this notion of pattern has to do with life itself and the attempt to capture the design of life in literature. Dourado elsewhere quotes the proverb "Only God knows the pattern of the entire embroidery," which relates to the several generations of families he has written about in his many books. As the author points out in *Uma poética de romance* (A Poetics of Fiction, 1973), *tecido* (woven cloth) is etymologically the same as the word *text*. Embroidery then is a metaphor for textuality. In particular, embroidery and other needlework such as sewing, knitting, and crocheting signify the female presence in Duas Pontes. Like cooking in a traditional society, it is women's work and is equated with patience, repetition, and boredom. But needlework is ambivalent in Dourado's work because it also represents creation and art. Thus, the characters' sewing, embroidering, knitting, or crocheting can be a metaphor for literary creation.

*O risco do bordado* reintroduces João da Fonseca Nogueira, the adolescent protagonist from Duas Pontes away at a boarding school in neighboring São Mateus. The book represents the "pattern of the embroidery" that the future writer is trying both to piece out and construct by remembering and eventually recording family stories, especially older ones. Slowly the forms of the family romance appear in the pattern; desire and admiration, hatred, sexual frustration and jealousy, and crime and remorse are inextricably linked in the character's memory. The design is predetermined as though traced by an unseen hand. At the end of the book the narrator reveals that he has returned to Duas Pontes twenty years after leaving it, and he then relates the effects of time on the situation. *O risco do bordado* is thus neither a set of stories nor a novel, but rather a succession of narratives, each the equivalent of a chapter or story narrating a self-contained episode.

Dourado added three more stories to *Nove histórias em grupos de três,* which already contained the earlier *Três histórias na praia,* in 1972. The title *Solidão solitude* is from a poem by Mário de Andrade, a few lines of which also serve as the epigraph of the book. The three new stories deal with a newspaper editor who as a young poet had met the great Andrade, a widower who leaves his favorite occasional mistress, and a man and woman who commit suicide because of their love for a dead airplane pilot. Written between 1950 and 1971, according to Dourado, these stories are technically superb and moving in their depiction of human despair.

Dourado published *Os sinos da agonia* (1974; translated as *The Bells of Agony,* 1989) after analyzing other books in *Uma poética de romance. Os sinos da agonia,* in turn, was extensively studied in the 1976 revision of *Uma poética de romance,* as was *Ópera dos mortos. Os sinos da agonia* is characteristic of Dourado's work in its careful construction and incorporation of modern techniques such as stream of consciousness and multiple points of view. It is also typical of Dourado's fiction in its baroque characteristics, including parody and open construction. Like *A barca dos homens* and *Ópera dos mortos,* it also deals with unexpected psychological turns concerning the mysteries of love, hatred, and sin, and innocence that can be more dangerous than evil.

In *Os sinos da agonia* symbol and reality, history and story, and classical and everyday Portuguese are interwoven masterfully. Unlike its immediate predecessors, however, *Os sinos da agonia* does not focus on a fictional family but on parallel events in a major period of Brazilian history: the golden age of the eighteenth century, when more gold was extracted from Minas Gerais (General Mines) than anywhere else in the world. There the author sets the Greek myth of Phaedra and Hippolytus through the perspectives of Euripides, Seneca, and Jean Racine. Not only do these characters work realistically in this setting, they also convey preoccupations unconnected with the Greek myth but central to Brazil then and now: the use and abuse of natural resources, class and color prejudices, and political revolt. Like Dourado's other fictional works, *Os sinos da agonia* proposes an enigma to be deciphered at the end of the book. It has to do in part with a double Hippolytus: one dark- and one light-skinned, which symbolizes instinct and reason as well as the racially mixed character of the country itself.

The 1976 publication of Dourado's book on literary theory, *Uma poética de romance — Matéria de carpintaria,* reveals much about his fictional practice.

*Cover for Dourado's 1987 novel, an ironic commentary on the line dividing sanity and madness*

Based on his notes from a course on fiction he taught at the Catholic University in Rio de Janeiro, the book also evinces his ample knowledge of other authors in Brazilian and foreign literatures. He looks at the literary work as both a tangible, explicable product and as a union of images. As both a technical construction and a mysterious constellation of metaphors, the fictional text is woven, a pattern to be deciphered, an embroidery to be read. As in his fiction, threadwork — whether weaving by spiders or humans — and needlework are a major trope. This trope is reminiscent of James's story "The Figure in the Carpet," and Dourado has often paid tribute to James as a great technician and rhetorician of the novel.

Dourado's notion of literature as a technical machine is also similar to Flaubert's and Edgar Allan Poe's conception of fiction, Paul Valéry's "thought machine," Gilles Deleuze's "machine of signs," and Le Corbusier's "machine for emotions."

Again alluding to a favorite proverb, the ultimate machine maker is God, whose universe is an enormous, mysterious tapestry.

*Novelário de Donga Novais* (Novelário of Donga Novais) was also published in 1976. Stylistically and structurally similar to the three novels immediately before it, it is an inquiry into memory, storytelling, and truth and lies. The narrative is privileged over the discontinuous plot. Dourado's coined word *novelário* announces the nature of the book and its rich multiplicity. *Novelário* is a collection of *novelas* and/or *novelos;* both nouns recur in the book, composing a motif. *Novelo* is a skein of string or wool, and *novela* is a story, novella, or radio or television soap opera. Making this wordplay even richer linguistically, the protagonist's surname, Novais, is etymologically related to "newness." When he tells a story, Donga Novais is unraveling a skein and also providing listeners with the melodramatic element found in everyday life that Brazilian television soap operas explore so well. Ageless, sleepless, and immensely wise, Donga Novais is a seer for whom past, present, and future appear as one. He never forgets anything but will change a story every time he tells it, although he keeps its essence intact.

The first-person narrator is in a dialogic position toward Donga Novais: he represents the town of Duas Pontes and its curiosity about secret lives and loves of its most eminent citizens. Among them is a young Helen of Troy with the childish nickname Lelena, temptress par excellence and the perfect subject for a soap opera. But even her conquests are incidental to the main narrative thread in *Novelário de Donga Novais.* The book sets up a narrative net in which echoes of major cultural works and other national experiences are combined with an ironic tone. Extremely parodic, the novel evokes bits and pieces of Brazilian history, Brazilian and Portuguese literature, and abundant aphorisms Donga Novais uses in the course of the narrative.

In 1978 Autran Dourado published *Armas e corações* (Arms and Hearts), a collection of four novellas dealing with crimes of the heart. In *Armas e corações* the narrative lines are more straightforward than in *Novelário de Donga Novais.* An outstanding work, *Armas e corações* offers various characters, climates, paces, and narrative tones for each novella while keeping the same thematic focus: passion, the narrator as chorus, ironic social commentary, and the acceptance of human foibles. Three of the stories tell of killings by firearms (*armas*) and the passions provoked (*corações*). The setting is Duas Pontes, and most of the characters are from earlier works. One is a father who unwittingly shoots his only son; another is a man shot by a stranger immediately after the man has killed his sister's seducer. The third story shows a gigantic millionaire in love with a tiny circus artist who later kills him. Only in the fourth story is death avoided, as a naive Protestant minister protects a famous bandit from the police.

*As imaginações pecaminosas* (Sinful Imaginations, 1981) was immediately recognized as one of Dourado's finest works. The collection combines his characteristic subjects of erotic interest, which provoke gossip from the "sinful imaginations" of Duas Pontes, with characters from earlier works. His irony is aimed at the melodramatic aspects of life and love. The third-person omniscient narrator often assumes the tone of a Greek chorus, reading and outguessing the town's "sinful imaginations." Stylistically these stories are closer to *Armas e corações* than to *O risco do bordado* because the narrative is less meandering and baroque than in the latter work. The narrator becomes more of a messenger than an "embroiderer," telling tales more directly. Still, the book offers Dourado's superb style and a flowing, rich narrative. Of the ten stories in the book, eight are interconnected. The first four also have a sexual scandal and violent end in common. The tone of the whole book, though, is compassionate in its examination of human failings.

Based on his experience as press secretary to Governor and later President Kubitschek, Dourado completed *A serviço del-Rei* (In the King's Service) in 1984. Always willing to explore new territory, he tackles a new challenge here; instead of limiting comic touches to a few aspects of the work, he produces a broad farce. The book starts in an uncharacteristic expository style but soon adds narrative voices. It alludes to myths such as Uranus devoured by his son Saturn and a host of other allusions, quotations, and puns. The complicated narrative thread leads to stream of consciousness. Political and literary tenets, literary history, and common beliefs are inserted at various points, interrupting the plot. A pessimistic though humorous novel, *A serviço del-Rei* uses patricide as a metaphor to denounce the corruption caused by ambition, including literary ambition. The "pattern of the embroidery" exposed here is the underpinning of Dourado's very political state of Minas Gerais. Farce is sustained throughout this novel, which cynically explores politics as an art in which treason, demagoguery, and sundry forms of lying are often major tools. The novel is pitiless in exposing both the political boss Saturniano de Brito and

his press secretary João, who learns treachery from him. The book weaves straight narrative about the multiple treasons that take Saturniano de Brito from small-town mayor of Duas Pontes to governor of Minas Gerais and president of Brazil with dream and hallucination sequences, thus representing an attempt at creating a carnivalesque work. Only a naive reader, however, would take it as autobiographical, directly referring to Dourado and the late Kubitschek.

Dourado's next novel, *Lucas Procópio* (1984), continues the saga of the Cota family in Duas Pontes. Its eponymous protagonist is the paternal grandfather of Rosalina from *Ópera dos mortos*. Structurally and stylistically, this is possibly Dourado's most direct work. The pared-down narrative represents the author's latest phase and is carried over in most of *Um artista aprendiz* (An Apprentice Artist, 1989) and all of *Monte da Alegria* (Mount Joy, 1990). *Lucas Procópio* deals with family influence, lust, love, the delicate border between madness and sanity, and small-town gossip. The novel is divided into two parts, "Person" and "Persona." The "person" Lucas Procópio is a dreamer in late-nineteenth-century Minas Gerais. A landed aristocrat, he is seeking to restore his province to the gold and diamond age of earlier centuries. To Lucas Procópio such splendor does not signify worldly wealth but the riches of the heart and mind. He longs for a society like that in the city of Ouro Prêto during the mid 1700s, in which poetry and music were of utmost importance as they were recited and played in magnificent baroque palaces and churches. The era he nostalgically would like to re-create is paramount to Brazilian history and culture and is the focus of Dourado's masterpiece *Os sinos da agonia*. In *Lucas Procópio,* however, the reader observes a gentle maniac's pathetic dream becoming ridiculous through its impossibility. The dream is a parody of something glorious. This ridiculousness becomes concrete in the protagonist, a figure of fun for the populace. He rides his horse to town dressed in an obsolete, ornate National Guard uniform. An apostle of beauty, he seeks converts to listen as he recites his poems.

The first part of *Lucas Procópio* pays tribute to an important subject in world fiction, the dreamer gone mad. Like Miguel de Cervantes's Don Quixote, Procópio occasionally regains his sanity and is often more sensible than those around him, but he is unable to distinguish between actual circumstances as opposed to the ideal ones of his own creation. The second part of *Lucas Procópio* deals with the character as a National Guard colonel and

*Cover for Dourado's 1989 novel, about the education of a young artist*

stories. A physically mature and wily fourteen-year-old girl, she fascinates the men around her, including the two physicians. Innocent Dr. Alcebíades temporarily cures her by having her cultivate violets, while satyrlike Dr. Viriato changes the prescription to snails. Other characters embroidered in the tapestry of *Violetas e caracóis* include the handsome banker Vitor Macedônio and the many male visitors to the Bridge House, the brothel that has been a constant feature of Duas Pontes since *Sombra e exílio,* published almost forty years before this novel. New characters make their first appearance in *Violetas e caracóis.* Among these are historical figures such as diplomat and writer Afonso Arinos, the protagonist of one story. Important politicians and statesmen also are named as background figures, providing an element of historical reality.

The book also pays homage to Brazilian literature, alluding to or quoting prominent writers from Minas Gerais, with its distinguished three-hundred-year-old literary tradition. The main character, Luisinha Porto, is based on a poem by well-known poet Carlos Drummond de Andrade. In the title story the reader finds lines from another major poet, the symbolist writer Alphonsus de Guimarães.

*Violetas e caracóis* takes up Dourado's concern with sanity and madness present in earlier books. The tone is ironic rather than farcical, and his attitude can be compared to that of Cervantes and Machado de Assis, for whom the dividing line between sanity and madness is often tenuous to the point of nonexistence. Like their characters, the aristocratic, generous Francisco Hermeto Carneiro Leão of "Os Lavoura" starts with solid ideas – in his case, agricultural diversification and a liberal newspaper. However, neither is practical for his time and place. Coffee, the monoculture, is lucrative beyond measure, and the city has enough newspapers. Eventually Francisco loses his fortune and his mind. His sisters also gently ease into madness. Like his predecessors, Dourado does not deride idealism so much as its misapplication caused by ignorance of actual circumstances.

*Um artista aprendiz* was dedicated to Artur Versiani Veloso, Dourado's high-school philosophy professor, and Godofredo Rangel, a respected novelist who advised the young Dourado on literary matters; both appear as characters in the book under fictional names. This novel is the "autobiography" of writer João da Fonseca Nogueira, an alter ego of Dourado who made his first appearance in *O risco do bordado. Um artista aprendiz* focuses on João's apprenticeship as a writer and partially borrows its title from James Joyce's *A Portrait of the Artist as a*

wealthy coffee planter near Duas Pontes. He has married a beautiful and unhappy aristocrat from Diamantina, the Diamond City, with whom he has had a daughter and a son. The latter is Rosalina Cota's grandfather João Capistrano Honório Cota. At the end of the novel the Lucas Procópio of this second part is unmasked and murdered by the real Lucas Procópio's former slave and friend Jerônimo, who has known for many years that Pedro Chaves – the "persona" of Lucas Procópio – had killed his friend and former master.

Dourado resumed a high literary level with his next work. Like *O risco do bordado, Violetas e caracóis* (Violets and Snails, 1987) can be read either as a collection of stories or as a novel in which protagonists from other of Dourado's works appear as supporting characters. The title refers to the contrasting methods that the Duas Pontes physicians choose to treat hysterical Luisinha Porto, the protagonist of several of these

*Young Man* (1915). Here the term *artist* can be taken as *craftsman,* the writer who builds his fiction as blocks, patiently working and reworking them. Compared to an artisan, however, a writer for Dourado produces on a loftier level, presenting a parallel to divine creation. However, given Dourado's ironic, parodic tone, *artist* here can also mean something less noble – in the popular sense of the word in Portuguese, a circus artist, a recurring figure in several stories. A second colloquial connotation of *artista* is frankly pejorative: an artist is a liar.

*Um artista aprendiz* starts in a Proustian manner: memory is involuntarily triggered by the motion of the train taken by a young João as he is leaving Duas Pontes for the capital of Belo Horizonte and senior high school. His father has lost everything. João's studies will be paid for by his grandfather Tomé. The narrative style changes: it becomes more direct, without digressions, as João settles himself in the new city and school. The protagonist relates the building of his life as an adult in fairly uncomplicated chronological order, ending with his marriage. Arriving in Belo Horizonte, he made friends, fell in and out of love, entered law school, joined and then left the Communist party, and published his first novel. *Um artista aprendiz* is then a bildungsroman as well as a portrait of a young artist. It can also be considered a roman à clef.

Always an artist and craftsman attempting new directions and challenges, Dourado published *Monte da Alegria* in 1990. In this novel, although the author continues the techniques he had experimented with since *Nove histórias em grupos de três,* he simplifies the narrative thread. In fact, *Monte da Alegria* is a minimalist work. It is also uneven: its second part is less carefully written than the beginning, both in characterization and structure. It is a curious work in which hagiography is treated as psychological fiction. Like many of Dourado's earlier novels, it is also strongly symbolic and clearly connected with Brazilian literature and history.

The story of the protagonist, Brother Francisco of Our Lady, parallels the life of Francis of Assisi, which in turn follows the life of Jesus. A rich young man like the Italian saint, this mid-nineteenth-century Brazilian character moves from riches to rags and penance and becomes a mendicant preacher. Unlike Francis, Brother Francisco remains a layman unrecognized by the official church. However, like Jesus and the medieval monk, the Brazilian performs miracles and is followed by holy women. Named Maria and Martha, they remind the reader of Lazarus's sisters. Like them, one is pragmatic, the other meditative.

Autran Dourado's latest novel, *Um cavalheiro de antigamente* (An Old-Time Gentleman, 1992), is more a literary exercise and an inquiry into philosophical and psychological matters than a dramatic piece. The old-time gentleman protagonist, João Capistrano Honório Cota (Lucas Procópio's son and Rosalina Cota's father), is a melancholy character who becomes obsessed and alienated upon receiving an anonymous letter accusing his mother of adultery thirty years before. This supposed indiscretion by Isaltina and the parish priest is the pretext for the novel. Through it Dourado examines his major concerns: love and death, change, reality and illusion, and gossip as danger and as the genesis of fiction. The adroitly handled multiple-viewpoint technique makes *Um cavalheiro de antigamente* an homage to two of its author's acknowledged masters, James and Faulkner.

Autran Dourado's opus is marked by talent, discipline, and experimentation soundly based on literary research. His awards have acted as incentives: Dourado has chosen not to rest on his brilliance or his laurels, but has instead always sought newer paths as he continued to perfect ones he had already chosen. Having created his own body of work and promoted the Brazilian literary tradition, Dourado may yet surprise his readers by taking a new path. After all, his latest books deviate from what had before been classified as the Dourado canon. Autran Dourado's development as a writer has been consistent with his early promise, making him one of the finest Brazilian authors of the modern era.

**References:**

M. Consuelo Cunha Campos, *Obras de Autran Dourado* (Rio de Janeiro: Difel, 1976);

M. Lúcia Lepecki, *Autran Dourado: Uma leitura mítica* (São Paulo: Quíron, 1976);

Daphne Patai, *Myth and Ideology in Contemporary Brazilian Fiction* (Rutherford, N. J.: Fairleigh Dickinson University Press, 1983);

Jeremy E. Pollock-Chagas, "Rosalina and Amelia: A Structural Approach to Narrative," *Luso-Brazilian Review* (Winter 1975): 263–272;

Angela Senra, *Autran Dourado: Seleção de textos, notas, estudo biográfico, histórico e crítico – Exercícios* (São Paulo: Abril, 1983);

Malcolm Silverman, "Autran Dourado and the Introspective-Regionalist Novel," *Revue des Langues Romanes,* 6 (1976): 609–619.

# Quince Duncan
*(5 December 1940 –    )*

Ian Isidore Smart
*Howard University*

BOOKS: *El pozo; Una carta* (Goicoechea, Costa Rica: D. L. E. H., 1969);

*Una canción en la madrugada* (San José: Costa Rica, 1970);

*Hombres curtidos* (San José: Cuadernos de Arte Popular, 1971);

*El negro en Costa Rica,* with Carlos Meléndez Chaverri (San José: Costa Rica, 1972);

*Los cuatro espejos* (San José: Costa Rica, 1973);

*El negro en la literatura costarricense* (San José: Costa Rica, 1975);

*Los cuentos del Hermano Araña* (San José: Territorio, 1975);

*La rebelión Pocomía y otros relatos* (San José: Costa Rica, 1976);

*La paz del pueblo* (San José: Costa Rica, 1978);

*Final de calle* (San José: Costa Rica, 1979);

*Los cuentos de Jack Mantorra* (San José: Nueva Década, 1988);

*Teoría y práctica del racismo,* with Lorein Powell (San José: Departamento Ecuménico de Investigaciones, 1988);

*Kimbo* (San José: Costa Rica, 1990).

OTHER: Contributor, *Justice for Aboriginal Australians: Report of the World Council of Churches Team Visit to the Aborigines, June 15 to July 3, 1981* (Geneva: World Council of Churches, 1981);

Contributor, *Cultura negra y teología* (San José: Departamento Ecuménico de Investigaciones, 1986).

SELECTED PERIODICAL PUBLICATIONS – UNCOLLECTED: *El trepasolo, Escena,* 11, nos. 22–23 (1979): 106–144;

"El modelo ideal de mujer: Un análisis ficciológico de estereotipos sexistas en la narrativa costarricense," *Káñina,* 9 (July–December 1985): 97–101;

*Quince Duncan, circa 1970*

"Visión panorámica de la narrativa costarricense," *Revista Iberamericana,* 53 (January–June 1987): 79–94.

Quince Duncan's fictional universe is built on roots as deep as the very beginnings of human self-consciousness articulated in the oldest and most pervasive myths. In "The African Presence in Caribbean Literature" Edward Kamau Brathwaite, perhaps the most distinguished living poet and scholar of the Caribbean, declared that African culture, from which Caribbean literature flows, is oriented toward religion. The most fruitful readings of Caribbean literature respect this spiritual centering.

Quince Duncan, born 5 December 1940 in San José, Costa Rica, to a second-generation Costa Rican with Jamaican roots and a Panamanian of Barbadian heritage, grew up in the eastern province of Limón. A trained teacher and at one time an Anglican priest, he earned a licentiate in Latin-American studies from the Universidad Nacional Heredia. His publications indicate the breadth of his scholarly interests and artistic focus. Nevertheless, Duncan has made his most lasting contribution in creative writing. As a man of letters he is as fully Caribbean as he is Hispanic and has used his talents to explore the presence of blacks of West Indian origin in his native Costa Rica. Indeed, according to Lisa E. Davis in "The World of the West Indian Black in Central America: The Recent Works of Quince Duncan": "Duncan has become the spokesman for an entire segment of the population whose history and culture are generally unknown both within the nation and to outsiders," particularly of "the descendants of those Blacks who began to emigrate in large numbers at the end of the nineteenth century from the bankrupt islands of the British Empire . . . to the republics of Central America, an emigration that mushroomed in the first decade of the twentieth century with the construction of the Panama Canal."

The author's first published creative work was a collection of short stories, *Una canción en la madrugada* (A Song in the Early Morning, 1970), in which Duncan depicts the lives of black Jamaican descendants living on the Costa Rican Atlantic coast. The stories become progressively pessimistic after the lighthearted slice-of-life title story as Duncan tackles sociopolitical themes and problems: poverty, the need for blacks to go to the capital to escape the hopelessness of their coastal existence, the psychological destruction and loss of those who migrate inland, and the individual black struggle against racism, exploitation, and difference. This dark social context ultimately translates itself into individual existential questions and doubts about personal value, identity, and purpose – themes central to Duncan's later work. In one of the bitterest stories in the collection, "Demasiado peso" (Too Heavy), the black protagonist, psychologically isolated from society, asks himself, "Qué valor tengo?" (What good am I?), only to answer himself with "debo tener lepra. Eso es: tengo lepra" (I must have leprosy. That is it: I have leprosy). The fact that blacks are not part of the mainstream of dominant

white culture, that is, the realities of their difference, causes pain, suffering, defeat, and humiliation. Not until his later and more-mature writing does Duncan begin to celebrate and reaffirm, rather than lament, black differences.

Duncan's first novel, *Hombres curtidos* (Chastened Men, 1971), is now out of print and unavailable, for as Duncan explained, it was published prematurely in an effort to preempt the plagiarizing designs of a white Costa Rican writer who was better known and ready to appropriate a black man's artistic product.

The first of Duncan's currently available novels is *Los cuatro espejos* (The Four Mirrors, 1973), the story of Charles Forbes, a West Indian involved in a complex resolution of the conflicts regarding his identity as a colonized person, both African and Hispanic. The novel is essentially about a black man's struggle to come to terms with his blackness. His efforts meet with some success; as Duncan explained, the protagonist's smile at the end indicates that he is again at peace with himself. Likewise Kimbo, the protagonist of *Kimbo* (1990), flashes a final smile to his wife an instant before he is killed in accordance with an established twentieth-century American ritual, gunned down by a rogue policeman: "Fue una sonrisa linda. . . . Nunca le había visto sonreir así" (It was a beautiful smile. . . . I had never seen him smile like that).

Duncan as a West Indian Costa Rican is a man of two worlds, just as the epigraph from A. Sivanandan that he uses for "Los mitos ancestrales" in *La rebelión Pocomía y otros relatos* (The Pukumina Rebellion and Other Stories, 1976) proclaims: "On the margin of European culture . . . the 'coloured' intellectual is an artifact of colonial history. . . . He is a creature of two worlds, and of none." Duncan, however, has resolved the conflict of the colonized person; he has affirmed his West Indianness as a neo-African cultural manifestation. *Los cuatro espejos* dramatizes this conflict, for Charles Forbes, while not a deliberately fashioned alter ego, mirrors Duncan's own experience in important ways. Like Duncan, he is a trained priest of the Anglican church who after a period of exercising his priesthood in rural and African West Indian Limón departs for the capital city San José, a modern Western urban center. The confrontation assumes crisis proportions when one morning Charles wakes to find that he is unable to see the color of his face in the mirror. The novel ends in an epiphanous moment. "Al entrar a casa fui directamente al baño para mirar mi rostro en el espejo. Una sonrisa profunda iluminó el color de mi piel" (When I got home I

QUINCE DUNCAN

UNA CANCION
EN LA MADRUGADA

*Cover for Duncan's 1970 collection of short stories, about black Jamaicans in Costa Rica*

went directly to the bathroom to look at my face in the mirror. A deep smile lit up the color in my skin). This is clearly a metaphor for the success in Duncan's own life.

According to Barbadian novelist George Lamming, one of the best-known authors of the Caribbean, the theme of the journey or voyage is a major principle of communality in the literature of the region. Following this pattern, Charles Forbes makes several journeys back and forth between opposing worlds before undertaking the final journey of "reaffirmation" back to the Limón of his neo-African West Indian roots. He had already undertaken the journey within, from country (Limón) to town (San José) as well as the interior journey of self-realization, rising above the limits of his original immediate socio-economic circumstances. In Duncan's later novels *La paz del pueblo* (The Peace of the Town, 1978) and *Kimbo,* the journey theme is also central. In both novels the protagonists attain their

full dimension as liberator/*cimarrón* (runaway slave) by journeying back to the sites of struggle and sacrifice.

In a collection of short stories called *La rebelión Pocomía y otros relatos,* Duncan begins to develop one of his most powerful symbols, the *samamfo.* Duncan himself explains in his interview with Ian I. Smart:

> I found [the term *samamfo*] in some book on African culture. I had been searching for a word that would express this idea we have at home that the spirits of our ancestors are alive, present all the time there with you. I well remember hearing my grandparents talking about the older people just as if they were still there. They really were there, the only problem was that they were, you know, still in Jamaica.... [T]he ones that had died in Costa Rica would be considered to be around. I remember many times, for example, at night when we arrived home after a walk through the dark, an animal or something might go by and the comment would be: "Your grandmother walks with you to protect you." So the spirits of the ancestors are here constantly with you. I couldn't find any way of expressing this in either Spanish or English until I ran across that term *samamfo,* which said exactly what I wanted to say.

Once he discovered the appropriate label, Duncan began to create a fictional universe that exactly matched the real world of his formative years by centering his narratives around the concept of *samamfo.*

In the tellingly titled short story "Los mitos ancestrales" (The Ancestral Myths), the last in *La rebelión Pocomía y otros relatos,* the concept appears on the first page. The story allegorically recounts the history of colonization in Africa as Duncan reconstructs an African mythology based on his familiarity with African philosophy and religions. The principal character and first-person narrator is an inhabitant of the *samamfo,* defined briefly in a footnote as "Espíritu y herencia de los antepasados" (Spirit and inheritance of the ancestors). Duncan leaves no room for doubt as to the legitimacy of the character's status as an "hijo del *samamfo,*" (son of the *samamfo*), for he has him declare, "Y nos ejecutaron a los dos, a mi valiente hijo y a mi, en la plaza pública, el día quinto, cuando para pena mía, el lunes encabezó la semana" (And they executed us both, my valiant son and myself, in the public square on the fifth day, when to my embarrassment, the week began on a Monday). In the bewildering complexities of this otherworldly narrative, the only certainty is the main character's passionately declared fidelity to the *samamfo* in the closing lines of the story: "Pero yo he contado la historia del Samamfo. Solo yo. Yo he adorado a Nyambe, y lo he encarnado en el Pueblo" (But I have told the tale of the *Samamfo*. I alone. I have worshipped Nyambe, and I have made him incarnate in the People). In this respect the protagonist prefigures Pedro, the main character of Duncan's next novel, *La paz del pueblo,* for Pedro can also be essentially defined by his fidelity to the *samamfo* and to a higher power, "god," or "orisha," whom he calls Cumina rather than Nyambe and whom he too makes incarnate in the people.

Duncan said in the 1985 interview with Smart that *La paz del pueblo,* which appeared two years after *La rebelión Pocomía y otros relatos,* "was just going to be a short story of about five pages or so. But when I sat down at my typewriter and started writing, I just couldn't stop." Later in the interview he revealed that the novel "marks a turning point in my writing." In this first *samamfo* novel the definition of *samamfo* has evolved somewhat and is placed in a glossary of terms at the end of the book rather than in a footnote: "palabra de origen ashanti que significa lugar o estado en que se encuentran los muertos, o los espíritus de los antepasados" (a word of Ashanti origin that signifies the place or state in which the dead find themselves, or the spirits of the ancestors). At an early stage in the development of the plot the *samamfo* is introduced in a particularly significant context. An unidentified, archetypal grandfather is conversing with his equally unidentified and archetypal grandchild:

> – Abuelo . . . ¿ cómo es eso del cielo y del infierno?
> – Eso es cuando termine todo. Al final, después del juicio. Pero por ahora nadie se muere, hijo: simplemente volvemos al samamfo.

> ("Grandfather . . . how does this business about heaven and hell go?"
> "That is when it is all over. At the end, after the judgment. But for now nobody dies, son: we simply return to the *samamfo*.")

The *samamfo* functions in the novel as a dynamic living presence active in all beings, maintaining a constructive continuity between them. Señora Mariot, one of the important secondary characters in the novel, undertakes as a young girl an act of rebellion that prefigures the fundamental rebellion-liberation act of the main character, Pedro Dull. Since Duncan's preferred style is the tortured realism of the most successful contemporary Latin-American novelists, the progeny of William Faulkner, at certain moments the narrative is grounded in certitude, albeit fleetingly. One such instance occurs with the narration of Señora Mariot's momentous

act: "Ese fue el motivo de su decisión. Aconsejada por quién sabe qué oculta fuerza del samamfo, que la hizo capaz del supremo acto de la rebelión" (That was the reason for her decision. Counseled by who knows what hidden forces of the *samamfo,* which made her capable of the supreme act of rebellion).

The primal connectedness between Señora Mariot and Pedro, her daughter Sitaira's lover, is established through the agency of the *samamfo,* clearly manifested in the narrative itself prior to the older woman's offer of herself to the young Pedro. The primeval coupling is pointedly recorded: "Te acordarás de ella, de sus convulsiones, de la alegría de su entrega, de su fanática fidelidad al samamfo, y del espasmo final seguido por un leve comentario: – Ya una está vieja, pero talvez . . . talvez . . . " (You will remember her, her convulsions, the joy with which she gave herself, her fanatic fidelity to the *samamfo,* the final spasm and then the casual remark: "I am old now, but maybe . . . maybe . . . "). The profound mythical significance of the event is highlighted through the use of the future tense to narrate a past action, a recollection. The great moments of mythical action are always beyond the limits of ordinary time, manifested in the sequential passage from past to present to future. The mythical moment is an eternal now.

Further, there is an almost sacred tone in the description of this event that replays one of humanity's earliest myths, that of the son-consort, the self-sacrificing vibrant young liberator-victim. For the Yoruba people, as Manuel Zapata Olivella reveals in his 1983 novel *Changó, el gran putas* (Shango, the Baddest), this myth is actualized in the story of Shango's father-brother Orungan, the son-consort of Yemayá. Shango himself is a hero who is hounded to death. For the ancient Africans the concept is enshrined in the myth of Horus/Osiris, the son/brother-consort of Isis. Indeed, not only is the figure of Osiris conflated with that of his and Isis's son Horus, but "the Egyptian name of Osiris, ASAR or WOSIR, means 'begotten of Isis,'" according to Charles S. Finch III. Thousands of years later the tragic Horus/Osiris-Isis-Seth triangle was retold by the Greeks in the story of Oedipus, Jocasta, and Creon. Charles Forbes, the protagonist of Duncan's first novel, *Los cuatro espejos,* also participates in the primevally significant act of mating with an older woman, Engracia, who is a form of the earth mother and whose legitimate spouse, as is the case with Señora Mariot, has passed his prime.

Pedro Dull, the first of the fully developed liberator manifestations in *La paz del pueblo,* is clearly a messiah figure. In one of the key passages of the

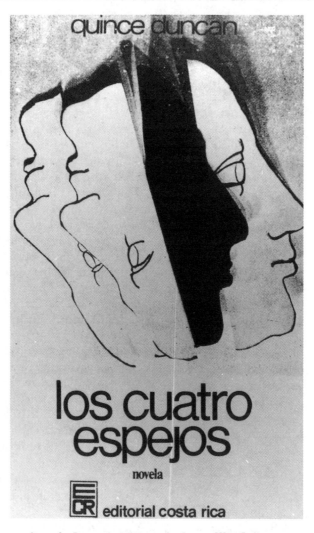

*Cover for Duncan's 1973 novel, about a West Indian man*
*seeking to resolve his African and Hispanic identities*

novel a Christian pastor, the official spokesman of the established religion, is made to proclaim Pedro's messianic role in a "sermón sin sentido" (a sermon without meaning):

> Jugando, esperaban. Como si esa noche fuese a nacer el mesías. Como si aquel sermón sin sentido, tantas veces predicado por el pastor "De entre mi pueblo levantaré a uno – dice el Señor – le quitaré el corazón de piedra y le daré uno de carne, y será la liberación de muchos y la gloria del pueblo." Cuando el pastor decía eso, los hombres se miraban unos a otros sin entender nada.

> (As they played, they waited. As if on that night the messiah were to be born. As if that sermon without meaning, preached so many times by the pastor "From among my people I will raise up one," says the Lord. "I will take away his heart of stone and will give him one of flesh, and he will be the liberation of many and the glory of his people." When the pastor would proclaim

this, the men would look at one another, not understanding anything.)

The text provides a clear "meaning" to the sermon, accessible to the people if not to the official church figure, three pages later on the final page of the novel in a richly epiphanous passage:

> Los hombres ya no esperaban nada. De pronto entendieron la obstinada predicación del pastor, y estaban seguros de que él mismo no lo entendería jamás. Y vieron con toda claridad, en el profundo silencio de la madrugada, el silencio del medio día. (Cuminá danzaba la paz del pueblo.)

> (The men did not wait for anything else. They immediately understood the pastor's insistent preaching, and they were sure that he himself would not ever understand what he was saying. And they saw in all clar-

ity, in the deep silence of the early morning, the noontime silence. [Cumina danced his peace to the people.]])

Pedro fully metamorphoses into the messiah announced by a spokesman of the official Euro-Christian church, who is incapable of understanding the fully African nature of his messiahship, which culminates in the myth of Cumina (a neo-African "god" invented by Afro-Christian Jamaicans) dancing "his peace to the people."

Duncan's creative intelligence, as he claims to be under the guidance of the *samamfo,* intuits the deepest levels of the central mythos of humanity articulated in the art and literature of ancient Africa. Pedro enters to a substantial degree into the role of the son-consort who fecundates his earth mother ritually by watering her with his blood. The rite can only be effected fully through the actual death and dismemberment of the virile young liberator, (as in the Asar/Osiris myth). Duncan's version of the myth respects the realities of its sociohistorical context by placing it in the most important arena of struggle and the real focus of liberation for the West Indian Costa Rican population, which is principally of Jamaican provenance – the banana plantation.

Duncan's 1979 novel, *Final de calle* (Dead End), sheds further light on his West Indian Costa Rican identity. With a firm reputation as a West Indian (that is, black) Costa Rican writer, Duncan wished to establish that he was simply a talented Costa Rican writer, not a "quota" artist. He has plainly indicated that his favorite writers are James Baldwin, William Faulkner, and John Steinbeck from North America and Mario Vargas Llosa and Gabriel García Márquez from South America. He considers himself part of the same artistic line as respected Costa Rican authors Fabián Dobles, Carlos Luis Fallas, and Joaquín Gutiérrez. Yet the national literary establishment persisted in viewing him as their "black" writer. Duncan thus composed *Final de calle* and submitted it anonymously in a national literary contest. It won the 1978 Editorial Costa Rica contest and the following year the prestigious Aquileo Echeverría literary prize.

Although the novel contains no reference to the West Indian Costa Rican experience, it is consistent with Duncan's neo-African aesthetic. Essentially an existential novel charged with a sense of the fundamental absurdity of the human condition symbolized in the title, this is the only one of Duncan's novels that plumbs the depths of pessimism without relief. By doing so the author gives indirect but unequivocal expression to his rejection of the Eurocentric hegemonic and racist ethos of the Costa Rican establishment.

Zapata Olivella's *Changó, el gran putas,* a prototypical Afrocentric text, places the destiny of African Americans, and by extension the entire race, squarely in the hands of the ancestor-gods. Liberation is the certain result and is in fact the very purpose for which the suffering of the race was imposed. In this reading of black history Shango only becomes the liberator through the agency of Legba, the god of the road.

In Duncan's fictional universe, the thrust toward liberation is also the fundamental driving force. The central protagonist is a liberator, a *cimarrón* (maroon) who resembles in every respect the multitude of characters in Olivella's novel marked with a sign of Legba and utterly dedicated to the work of liberation. Duncan, however, does not highlight the role played by Legba, a version of Hermes, and related to Thoth, the divine agent, facilitator, and empowerer in ancient Africa. Rather, Duncan focuses on the liberator/*cimarrón* figure himself.

In one of Duncan's more important short stories before *La paz del pueblo* in *La rebelion Pocomía y otros relatos,* the main character is also a liberator inspired by Cumina. This rebel figure, Jean Paul, who like Pedro Dull leads West Indian Costa Rican banana workers in industrial action against the exploiting owners, is a John the Baptist type. Like his prototype and unlike Pedro Dull, he attains the fullest level of sacrificial messiahship by giving up his life. Similarly, Duncan's liberator in *Kimbo* is made to conform fully to the model of this hero, actually giving his life for the good of the people.

Duncan is deliberate in his development of messianic imagery with respect to Kimbo. The text in the final pages of the novel declares pointedly and in the voice of one of the reliable narrators, "Sí, el devuele las esperanzas. No murió en vano. Vuelve de su tumba y el mundo va a creer su palabra" (Yes, he brings back hopes. He did not die in vain. He will come back from his grave, and the world will believe in his word). The biblical references are as clear as earlier with Pedro Dull and Jean Paul. Charles Forbes of *Los cuatro espejos* is the only major protagonist of the "black experience" novels who does not enter into the messiah paradigm in any substantive sense. He is, however, a representative of the conflict between the Eurocentric and Afrocentric worlds, as was the unnamed hero of "Los mitos ancestrales" in *La rebelión Pocomía.*

In addition to his messiah status bestowed by metaphor, Kimbo is explicitly identified in the text as an "hijo del samamfo," a concept significantly more evolved from earlier, as seen in the definition of *samamfo* presented in this work first completed in 1982, reworked by 1985, and published five years later. The glossary to the novel defines *samamfo* as "Espíritu y herencia de los Ancestros. En el samamfo están los valores y tradiciones del pueblo. Es la memoria colectiva de la raza-cultura que pasa de generación a generación y que se actualiza en los ritos religioso-seculares del pueblo, en sus luchas, en sus experiencias. Los Ancestros nunca han abandonado a sus herederos" (The spirit and inheritance of the Ancestors. It is in the *samamfo* that the values and traditions of the people reside. It is the collective memory of the race-culture that passes from generation to generation and that is actualized in the religious/secular rites of the people, in their struggles, in their experiences. The Ancestors have never abandoned their heirs).

Frantz Fanon, one of the best-known Caribbean intellectuals of the twentieth century, made it clear that the colonized person can achieve fullness of being only through a complete liberation, one that necessarily includes overcoming sociopolitical oppression. Fanon's theoretical framework in *Les damnés de la terre* (1961; translated as *The Wretched of the Earth,* 1967) describes the development of a full-blown revolutionary consciousness with particular emphasis on the metaphorical use of laughter. Duncan is clearly aware of the particular emphasis on laughter as a unique response in Afro-Caribbean culture, as he says in his interview with Smart:

> When you hear black people laugh . . . well, let us take, for example, the case of a play written by another author from Limón, based on Joaquín Gutiérrez's *Puerto Limón.* The author presents the situation of the complete breakdown of the system for those engaged in the banana industry on the Atlantic coast. After all those years of labor, the company is suddenly leaving and there is nobody to sell bananas to. . . . The black man starts laughing, whereas the Spaniards carry on with their "¡Ay! ¿Qué vamos a hacer?" [Oh, what are we to do?] lamentations. The black man's laughter erupts at that final moment [of *La paz del pueblo*] when this character, Sitaira, sees that an alliance has been formed, that there is a ray of hope.

Sitaira's laughter of triumph literally comes from the *samamfo,* for she has already been sacrificed, cut down in her prime of female fecundity and beauty, and she has returned to the waters of life. She shares with her mother La Señora Mariot the role of earth mother – she with her raw vitality and beauty, her mother with physical fecundity.

They both are clearly associated with the *samamfo.* Her laughter, coming forth from the river where she has been murdered, affirms the birth of the new liberator and hence sacrificial victim, the male *cimarrón* Pedro. At other epiphanous moments Duncan strikes the deep chord of laughter without evoking the river, as in the finale of *Los cuatro espejos.* Consciously or unconsciously, Duncan has intuited many of the rich dimensions of a fundamentally African mythos.

The question of language is perhaps the most important for any "word soldier," and it impinges on Duncan's creativity. It could be argued that non–West Indian precursors fail to penetrate the inner reaches of West Indian literature precisely on the basis of language. With Duncan the very language of narration is West Indian. It is fully Hispanic, for it is Spanish, but it exudes a peculiar and authentic Anglophone West Indian flavor, first and foremost through the use of what Stephen Henderson calls *mascon* terms, "certain words and constructions [which] seem to carry an inordinate charge of emotional and psychological weight, so that whenever they are used they set all kinds of bells ringing, all kinds of synapses snapping, on all kinds of levels." Duncan's narrative is charged with such terms as *yuca, bofe, cho!, obeahman, dopi, Pocomía, Cumina, Hermano Araña,* and *Kimbo.* The second mechanism through which the authentic West Indian flavor is generally inserted is the use of an artistic bilingualism. While Duncan's prose does not use this technique in any significant way, his still-unpublished poetry is in English.

Duncan and other authors of Anglophone Caribbean heritage have begun to create a literature in Spanish essentially similar in form and content to the Anglophone literature emanating from the region. The similarity, which can be labeled "West Indianness," is based on an essential thread of homogeneity that runs through all Caribbean cultures and hence all Caribbean literary expressions, no matter the language.

Along with fellow Costa Rican poet Eulalia Bernard and Panamanian poets Gerardo Maloney, Melvin Brown, and Carlos Guillermo Wilson, who is also a novelist and short-story writer, Duncan has created an impressive Central American West Indian literature that qualifies both as a new Hispanic literature and a Caribbean/West Indian expression. His four central tropes – the *samamfo,* the *cimarrón,* the river, and laughter – are integrally linked to the neo-African core of Caribbean creativity. Quince Duncan's work, therefore, is arguably one of the richest and most exciting cultural products of the

Caribbean region. A brilliant artist fully in tune with the resonances of all the traditions that make up his heritage, Duncan exemplifies the finest in late-twentieth-century Americanism.

## Interview:

Ian I. Smart, "The Literary World of Quince Duncan: An Interview," *College Language Association Journal,* 28 (March 1985): 281–298.

## References:

Roger D. Abrahams, *The Man-of-Words in the West Indies: Performance and the Emergence of Creole Culture* (Baltimore: Johns Hopkins University Press, 1983);

Edward Kamau Brathwaite, "The African Presence in Caribbean Literature," *Daedalus,* 103 (Spring 1974): 73–109;

Lisa E. Davis, "The World of the West Indian Black in Central America: The Recent Works of Quince Duncan," in *Voices from Under: Black Narrative in Latin America and the Caribbean,* edited by William Luis (Westport, Conn.: Greenwood Press, 1984), pp. 149–162;

Frantz Fanon, *The Wretched of the Earth,* translated by Constance Farrington (Suffolk: Penguin, 1967);

Charles S. Finch III, *Echoes of the Old Darkland: Themes from the African Eden* (Decatur, Ga.: Khenti, 1991);

Donald K. Gordon, *Lo jamaicano y lo universal en la obra del costarricense Quince Duncan* (San José: Costa Rica, 1989);

Gordon, "The Sociopolitical Thought and Literary Style of Quince Duncan," *Afro-Hispanic Review,* 7 (January–September 1988): 27–31;

Stephen Henderson, *Understanding the New Black Poetry* (New York: Morrow, 1973);

Dellita L. Martin-Ogunsola, "Translation as a Poetic Experience/Experiment: The Short Fiction of Quince Duncan," *Afro-Hispanic Review,* 10 (September 1991): 42–50;

Alan Persico, "Quince Duncan's *Los cuatro espejos:* Time, History, and a New Novel," *Afro-Hispanic Review,* 10 (January 1991): 15–20;

Edwin Salas Zamora, "La identidad cultural del negro en las novelas de Quince Duncan-Aspectos temáticos y técnicos," *Revista Iberoamericana,* 53 (January–June 1987): 377–390;

Ian I. Smart, *Central American Writers of West Indian Origin: A New Hispanic Literature* (Washington, D.C.: Three Continents, 1984);

Smart, "The Literary World of Quince Duncan," *College Language Association Journal,* 28 (March 1985): 281–298;

Smart, "Religious Elements in the Narrative of Quince Duncan," *Afro-Hispanic Review,* 1 (May 1982): 27–31;

Smart, "The West Indian Presence in the Works of Three New Central American Writers," in *Design and Intent in African Literature,* edited by David F. Dorsey and Stephen H. Arnold (Washington, D.C.: Three Continents, 1982), pp. 119–132.

# Salvador Elizondo

*(19 December 1932 –   )*

Steven M. Bell
*University of Arkansas*

BOOKS: *Poemas* (Mexico City: privately printed, 1960);

*Luchino Visconti* (Mexico City: Universidad Nacional Autónoma de México, 1963);

*Farabeuf, o La crónica de un instante* (Mexico City: Joaquín Mortiz, 1965);

*Narda o el verano* (Mexico City: Era, 1966);

*Salvador Elizondo* (Mexico City: Empresas Editoriales, 1966);

*El Hipogeo Secreto* (Mexico City: Joaquín Mortiz, 1968);

*Cuaderno de escritura* (Guanajuato, Mexico: Universidad de Guanajuato, 1969);

*El retrato de Zoe y otras mentiras* (Mexico City: Joaquín Mortiz, 1969);

*El grafógrafo* (Mexico City: Joaquín Mortiz, 1972);

*Contextos* (Mexico City: Secretaría de Educación Pública, 1973);

*Antología personal* (Mexico City: Fondo de Cultura Económica, 1974);

*Miscast, o, Ha llegado la señora Marquesa: Comedia opaca en tres actos* (Mexico City: Oasis, 1981);

*Regreso a casa* (Mexico City: Universidad Nacional Autónoma de México, 1982);

*Cámera lúcida* (Mexico City: Joaquín Mortiz, 1983);

*La luz que regresa* (Mexico City: Fondo de Cultura Económica, 1985);

*Elsinore: Un cuaderno* (Mexico City: Ediciones del Equilibrista, 1988);

*Teoría del infierno y otros ensayos* (Mexico City: El Colegio Nacional/Ediciones del Equilibrista, 1992).

OTHER: *Museo poético,* edited by Elizondo (Mexico City: Universidad Nacional Autónoma de México, 1974);

Paul Valéry, *Paul Valéry, obras escogidas,* translated by Elizondo (Mexico City: Sepsetentas Diana, 1982).

*Salvador Elizondo, circa 1969*

To read Salvador Elizondo Alcalde is to enter a dark, difficult, seemingly private realm that does not easily yield its secrets. The author is a stubbornly idiosyncratic and disruptive figure in Mexican and Latin-American literature. His works constitute a kind of intricate and arcane laboratory: they are like a stage upon which he reenacts some of the more radical fictional experiments in the Western tradition, or an operating table upon which he dissects philosophical issues such as pleasure versus pain, nature versus culture, and time and existence in life and in writing. On the surface Elizondo's compositions have very little Mexican or Latin-American about them. Yet he is paradoxically a representative Latin-American or Mexican writer to the degree that he has had to struggle against the imposition of limitations on his art because of his national origins and cultural identity. For the notoriety Elizondo's innovations in fiction have earned him, his work is often associated with the works of the contemporary Boom of Latin-American literature. However, Elizondo's writing implicitly rejects the often-romanticized and mythologizing view of Latin America characteristic of some representative works of the Boom; instead, it interrogates our myths and assumptions about literature and confronts the possibilities and limitations of literary expression. Elizondo's greatest virtue, and perhaps also his curse, is to have pursued the impossible ideal of a perfect or pure form of linguistic representation.

Salvador Elizondo was born on 19 December 1932 an only child to affluent parents in Mexico City, Josefina Alcalde y González Martínez and Salvador Elizondo Pani, a successful businessman and author of a book on commerce. Elizondo's childhood appears to have been at once opulent and anarchic. He had tutors and nannies and attended private schools. From 1936 to 1939 Elizondo lived with his family in Berlin, and after their return to Mexico City he entered the Colegio Alemán (the German School). Later he studied at a private academy in California and completed his college-preparatory work at the University of Ottawa.

Elizondo's education was typical of many Latin-American artists and intellectuals in its cosmopolitan flavor and its preference for informal education or self-instruction over systematic training. These characteristics were especially marked for Elizondo, who always was taking up a new interest or a new course of study with which he then became bored or disillusioned. Indeed, Elizondo's most characteristic works all have the air of stemming from impetuous sparks of intense but short-lived inspiration. In his typically self-conscious fashion, the vagaries of the human attention span themselves became the theme of a piece collected in *Cámera lúcida* (1983) called "Proyectos" (Projects).

Elizondo has stated privately that art in his family environment was simply "in the air." A well-known Mexican poet, Enrique González Martínez, was his uncle and an important figure in the family. As early as age ten, Elizondo dreamed of being a writer. His literary vocation, nonetheless, was reached only after frustrated attempts at painting and filmmaking.

Though he eventually fulfilled the requirements for a certificate of proficiency in English from the University of Cambridge, Elizondo's postsecondary education was fragmentary. In 1951 and from 1955 to 1958 he traveled and studied in Italy, France, and England, undertaking various programs of study, including architecture and cinema-

tography. Later Elizondo studied literature at the Universidad Nacional Autónoma de México.

Elizondo originally set out for Europe to pursue a career in painting begun in Mexico City at the National Art Institute, including the Escuela Nacional de Artes Plásticas, Academia de San Carlos. But while in Europe, Elizondo left off painting, developed a strong interest in film, and first began to cultivate his literary vocation seriously. His incursions into painting and film anticipate the importance of visual imagery in his writing. The contrasts between these two arts reflect the complexities his literary enterprise entails: while his attraction to film suggests the futuristic experimentalism of much of his writing, his efforts as a painter perhaps foreshadow the more classical and romantic aspects of his work, in which he defends the traditional value of high culture.

When Elizondo returned to Mexico in the late 1950s, he continued for a time to pursue his interest in film. A book on an Italian filmmaker, *Luchino Visconti* (1963); the journal of film criticism Elizondo helped to produce in the early 1960s, *Nuevo cine;* and an experimental film, *Apocalypse 1900,* are all products of this activity. But in part because of the poverty of the film industry in Mexico at the time, Elizondo came to concentrate his efforts in the literary arena.

It is clear from his youthful autobiography, *Salvador Elizondo* (1966), that he found it difficult and frustrating to break into the literary scene in Mexico. Though these difficulties are in part because of his numerous extended absences from Mexico, they are also due to his temperament and character. Emmanuel Carballo, who met Elizondo in 1953, recalls in his prologue to the autobiography the complexities of the young author's personality, making special note of his precocity.

The 1950s and 1960s were a turbulent period for Elizondo. He married and was divorced from his first wife, Michèle Alban, by whom he has two daughters, Mariana and Pía. In spite of certain complaints listed in the autobiography, however, he seems to have relished the life of the struggling artist, a role in his case taken on more by choice than from necessity. Yet if in these years Elizondo lived with reckless abandon, the 1960s still stand as a high point in his literary productivity.

Elizondo's career moved forward dramatically when he was awarded one of the inaugural scholarships from the Centro Mexicano de Escritores (Mexican Center for Writers) for 1963–1964 and another for 1967–1968. The scholarships partially underwrote the composition of Elizondo's two nov-

Salvador Elizondo
El retrato de Zoe
y otras mentiras

serie del volador

*Cover of Elizondo's 1969 collection of fifteen short stories that parody efforts to portray reality in fiction*

els, even while he continued to pursue his personal passions and uncommon interests. First with a scholarship from the Colegio de Mexico and later in New York and San Francisco in 1965 with a grant from the Ford Foundation, Elizondo undertook studies of written Chinese that influenced the writing of his novel *Farabeuf, o La crónica de un instante* (Farabeuf, or The Chronicle of an Instant, 1965). In the autobiography Elizondo gives his own summary of these early years, including a somewhat romanticized account of his problems with alcohol, his bouts of depression and melancholy, and certain self-destructive tendencies.

Although Elizondo's work does not seem to fit easily within Mexican and Latin-American contexts, he is by no means an unprecedented figure, and may even be considered a throwback to earlier periods. His rebelliousness and alienation make him a kind of romantic figure, similar to a prominent un-

dercurrent in the Western tradition that includes many authors he has recognized as inspirations, including Edgar Allan Poe, Ezra Pound, Paul Valéry, Stéphane Mallarmé, Gustave Flaubert, James Joyce, the Marquis de Sade, Georges Bataille, Johann Wolfgang von Goethe, Fyodor Dostoyevsky, and modern philosophers such as Edmund Husserl and Ludwig Wittgenstein. In contemporary Latin America Elizondo's work has few parallels. His clearest precursors in Mexico and Latin America would be Julio Torri and Jorge Luis Borges, who like Elizondo rejected the determination of literature by national culture and became obsessed with the problem of originality in the context of the Western literary tradition. Elizondo also shares their preference for minor forms such as the essay and short story or for unclassifiable texts of various invention.

Elizondo's work has always evinced a complex attraction and repulsion toward our animal and criminal instincts, a marked aversion to the mundane and the mediocre, and an obsession with perfection that perhaps belies an underlying fear of failure. The most striking of these paradoxes may be that though Elizondo has become a respected literary figure of Mexico, he is renowned for works largely inaccessible and even threatening to the general reading public, and he remains better known as an eccentric figure than as a writer.

Though he has written more than a dozen books, Elizondo earned his reputation primarily through two short novels from the early stages of his career, *Farabeuf, o La crónica de un instante* and *El Hipogeo Secreto* (The Secret Hypogeum, 1968) — works whose critical impact and originality Elizondo's subsequent books have not rivaled. With the exception of *Farabeuf,* which has been frequently reprinted and translated into French, Italian, Polish, and German, few of Elizondo's books have had more than a second or third printing.

Two stages are distinguishable in Elizondo's career to date. An extended period in the late 1970s and early 1980s, during which he published no substantially new works of fiction, separates the two stages. The first phase includes six books between 1964 and 1972, highlighted by the two early novels and a collection of short texts entitled *El grafógrafo* (The Graphographer, 1972). In this first phase Elizondo carries out a radical critique of traditional realistic fiction and tries to push written literary expression to its limits. The second phase of Elizondo's production, highlighted by *Cámera lúcida* and *Elsinore* (1988), has involved a painful and protracted effort to recover the motivation and inspiration to write, as the author himself admits. The works of the first period played the literary game with great earnestness; the works of the second phase are lighter, self-mocking, confessional, and resigned to the death of the original idealistic literary project. They signal a new beginning for Elizondo and mark a partial turn to a more conventional approach to language and representation.

Elizondo's style and concerns as a fiction writer take shape in *Narda o el verano* (Narda or the Summer, 1964), a collection of short stories. Critics have often viewed these five stories as preliminary sketches for the novels that followed since they essay many of the same themes, motifs, and preoccupations, but the stories deserve attention on their own. They exhibit a freshness and innocence mostly lacking elsewhere in Elizondo's work. The stories also present greater variety, as if the author were deliberately testing different styles and techniques. To some degree, this first book of fiction points down a road not taken by Elizondo.

More directly than any other work, *Narda o el verano* reveals Elizondo's debts to certain masters of short fiction: for its use of terror and suspense "En la playa" (On the Beach) suggests Elizondo's affinities with Poe, while "La historia según Pao Cheng" (History According to Pao Cheng), with its conceptual play on time, existence, and writing, proclaims Elizondo's admiration for Borges. Another story, "Puente de piedra" (Stone Bridge), draws out a problem central to Elizondo's literary enterprise, the consciousness of self that distances us from a nonreflexive state of being in the world. Its moral is never made explicit, but it still constitutes a sort of parable dramatizing our irreparable distance from nature. Elizondo has articulated this critique of the dilemma of civilized man forcefully in "Una conjetura" (A Conjecture), a satiric essay in his *Cuaderno de escritura* (Notebook of Writing, 1969). There he argues that language, writing, and the life of the mind, just like the articulated jaw and the jointed thumb, are shameless marks of our cowardice rather than signs of evolutionary progress. He further suggests that humanity still does not realize the impossibility of improving on nature.

*Farabeuf, o La crónica de un instante* and *El Hipogeo Secreto* could not appear on the surface more dissimilar, but they share many underlying conceptual obsessions and several prominent motifs. As avant-garde or experimental fiction, moreover, they share as well a formal and substantive opposition to traditional mimetic representation. Critics have correctly identified the nature of writing, its links to reality and its autonomous reality, as a central thread in both novels, and it is important to understand them in this light. The two novels have no conventional plot, characters, or settings, and to approach them with such expectations only invites frustration

and rejection. They matter, instead, for the alternative experiences they offer and for the metaphysical and literary concepts they enact.

*Farabeuf, o La crónica de un instante* is a renowned work of fiction. Difficult and disquieting though ultimately rewarding, the novel adopts a rigorously conjectural attitude: events are only "remembered" or "imagined"; they are "reflections," "hypotheses," or simply "lies." Through repetition and variation, the novel fuses and confuses a series of scenes and motifs seemingly distant in time and space. Elizondo's sources of inspiration for the novel – a heterogeneous mix of the arcane and the exotic, the erotic and the eschatological – include most prominently H. L. Farabeuf's nineteenth-century treatise on surgical techniques *Précis de Manuel Operatoire,* and Georges Bataille's *Les larmes d'Eros* (1961). Octavio Paz has explained *Farabeuf* as a work constructed around two series of parallel signs. The ideogram *liú* (death); the hexagrams of the *I ching,* an ancient text on divination; and a celebrated photograph taken in Peking in 1905, in which a condemned person is undergoing a form of torture called *Leng T'che,* constitute the first series, belonging to the Chinese world. The second series, the Western counterpart, includes a painting by Titian (*Sacred and Profane Love*); divination by means of the Ouija board; and the surgical operations of Farabeuf. These signs produce multiple variations of what may be a single situation, including a love story and possibly some sort of political conspiracy – a couple walking on a beach and Farabeuf's adventure with a woman, perhaps a nun, a spy, or a nurse. The times and places in which the events occur, then, as well as the number of characters involved, could alternately or simultaneously be four and/or two and/or one. The reduction of places and characters to one lies in the possibility that the four basic characters share the identity – or fate – of the person tortured in the famous photograph included in the novel. The gender of this person, significantly, is a point debated but never resolved in the novel.

*Farabeuf* is disturbing not because of the violent scenes it depicts, but rather because of its deliberate and relentless confusion of character identities and its conflations of time and space, which violate our notions of linear time, contiguous space, and unique individual consciousness. *Farabeuf* mystifies because it would all seem a senseless game, yet it is played out with apparently deadly seriousness. The majority of the motifs repeated across the text designate some form of writing or representation. Everything in the text repeats, reflects, re-presents every-

*Elizondo in the early 1970s*

thing else: the Chinese ideogram has the same physical form as a starfish on the beach, which in turn repeats the configuration of the torturers in the photograph. Yet while conventional mimetic representation is eliminated, the beings and the "instant" supposedly chronicled multiply infinitely, as in a series of mirrors. Indeed, the instant itself is finally indescribable; it can never truly be chronicled but only infinitely prepared and deferred. In the end we have made no progress, and the last word of the text repeats the first.

What the novel is about is not so important as what it does: it makes us live through the reading a form of ritualistic torture like that invoked in the novel. *Farabeuf* deals with the futility of the mind's operation in spite of itself since it shows the incredibly complex labyrinths the mind can weave to comfort, or in this case to frighten, itself. Anything expressible is an illusion or an image reflected in the mirror of language; yet *Farabeuf* stubbornly strives to express the inexpressible. The meaning communicated is the ultimate meaninglessness of the world of the living and of language, but to reduce the work to such an articulated meaning ignores the excitement and terror meant simply to be experienced.

*El Hipogeo Secreto* (The Secret Hypogeum), Elizondo's second novel and third book of fiction, has received less sustained attention and acclaim than its forerunner. Though it experiments with

equally rigorous insistence, it does not play its game with the same level of intensity as *Farabeuf,* making for a lighter reading experience. *Farabeuf* deals primarily with physical and metaphysical issues; *El Hipogeo Secreto,* in contrast, deals with mental and literary issues, concerning itself principally with space, time, identity, and the dimensions of reality in imaginative experience. The two books are complementary, but they present parallel universes that never cross.

*El Hipogeo Secreto* occurs in a fantastic, purely mental time and space invoked in the very first lines of the text, a setting that seeks insofar as possible to bear no relation to our normal physical world. Ideas, not actions, constitute the essence of *El Hipogeo Secreto,* in particular the metafictional discussions and metaphysical speculations of narrators and characters. The running self-commentary contrasts all of this, implicitly or explicitly, with that other writing – so-called realistic fiction – that pretends to transcribe experience and create lifelike characters. Frequently, then, *El Hipogeo Secreto* assumes the characteristics of a literary manifesto as each of the participants ponders the question of his or her identity, destiny, and ultimate reality as part of the project entitled El Hipogeo Secreto. The battle between the author and his characters for superiority and the incorporation of the figure of the creator into the text of his creation constitute the principal intrigue of the novel. The phantasmagoric quest for the Secret Hypogeum allegorizes or symbolizes the concepts debated by characters and narrators. Like *Farabeuf,* the novel prepares but never actually narrates the potentially transcendent moment itself, the characters' final entrance into the Secret Hypogeum. The text insinuates that the characters seek to murder their creator, thus achieving some sort of liberation. But the end also suggests the characters' fusion with the mind of their creator and thus a return to their point of origin.

Like all of Elizondo's fiction, *El Hipogeo Secreto* can be read as a dramatization of the essential paradox of human beings, the language animals. The novel succeeds to the degree that it becomes a self-engendering creation that escapes the supposed transparency of everyday language and realistic fiction. But it still cannot escape representation, and so Elizondo cannot finally transcend the limitations of conventional literary expression he illustrates.

The year after the publication of *El Hipogeo Secreto,* Elizondo published two other books: *El retrato de Zoe y otras mentiras* (The Portrait of Zoe and Other Lies, 1969) and *Cuaderno de escritura* (Notebook of Writing). In them the experimental nature of Elizondo's writing appears even in the external form the compositions take, individually and as collected. The concept of the writer's notebook that *Cuaderno de escritura* explores, for example, underscores Elizondo's rejection of traditional generic categories of literature in favor of "writing," while *El retrato de Zoe y otras mentiras* summarizes in its title his disaffection for traditional mimetic fiction. *Zoe* is the Greek word for life, making the title "the picture of life and other lies." The fifteen short stories in *El retrato de Zoe y otras mentiras* offer a playful parody of humanity and its representations and of its emotional and conceptual commonplaces, thus giving further, often-delightful elaboration to themes and concepts present in the novels.

*Cuaderno de escritura* collects essays and occasional writings that provide a kind of map of Elizondo's world. In the case of a writer as peculiar and difficult as Elizondo, such maps can be especially useful. In fact, Elizondo's most recently published work, *Teoría del infierno y otros ensayos* (Theory of Hell and Other Essays, 1992), provides an updating of this service; its title essay revises and expands a piece from *Cuaderno de escritura* and reprints it together with other essays previously unpublished in book form originally written between 1959 and 1972.

*Cuaderno de escritura* includes essays on several Mexican painters; essays on Joyce, Borges, Marcel Proust, and several short vignettes on literary concepts; and some longer anthropological or psychological essays, such as "Teoría del infierno" and "De la violencia" (On Violence). A kind of literary manifesto, "Teoría mínima del libro" (Minimal Theory of the Book) clarifies certain premises underlying Elizondo's experiments in writing. The volume concludes with a long selection of aphorisms, a form that fits Elizondo's style of thought.

The recent *Teoría del infierno* presents a similar array of styles and concerns. It includes several essays on Mexican poetry, including that of his uncle González Martínez, that serve to complement Elizondo's well-known anthology of Mexican poetry, *Museo poético* (Poetic Museum, 1974). It also includes multiple essays on Pound and Joyce – including Elizondo's much-discussed Spanish translation of the first page of Joyce's *Finnegans Wake* (1939), with extensive commentaries – together with essays on the devil in world literature, on the *I ching,* and on selected French literary figures such as Jean-Jacques Rousseau and Bataille. The most useful key to Elizondo's own work is provided here by "La autocrítica literaria" (Literary Self-Criticism), which originally appeared in his *Antología personal* (Personal Anthology, 1974) as "Parerga (Taller de autocrítica)" (Parerga [Self-Criticism Workshop]).

*El grafógrafo* is the last Elizondo work to take the project of a pure or higher form of literary representation seriously, completing the first stage of his literary career. For its failures as much as for its successes, *El grafógrafo* is arguably the most representative of Elizondo's books. *El grafógrafo* takes Elizondo's literary project to a point beyond which the writing must either fall silent or return to more traditional forms of literary expression.

The short texts collected in *El grafógrafo* resemble in varying degrees the essay, the short story, and the prose poem. These difficult texts can easily seem pointless or unbearably self-satisfied. As the book's title suggests, the graphographer himself provides the collection's central figure and principal unifying element, and writing, implicitly or explicitly, constitutes the writing's primary concern. Each word in *El grafógrafo* is first and foremost just a word; each composition is nothing more, and nothing less, than an exercise in composition.

Nonetheless, a certain method can be discerned in this madness. Generally the texts follow one of the two approaches in *Farabeuf* and *El Hipogeo Secreto,* different paths toward the same end of rejecting traditional realism and subverting conventional forms of reading and interpretation. At one extreme stand the compositions in *El grafógrafo* that

*Jorge Luis Borges, Octavio Paz, and Elizondo (photograph © Paulina Lavista)*

appear to invalidate interpretation and the traditional role of the reader: they mean just what they say, but what they say seems to mean nothing. These antirepresentational texts are generally the shorter ones closest to the prose poem, such as "El indio verde" (The Green Indian), "Los hijos de Sánchez" (The Children of Sánchez), and "Aviso" (Warning).

A series of self-conscious texts that constantly comment upon themselves and thus usurp the role of the critical reader exemplifies the other basic strategy in *El grafógrafo*. These texts include "Sistema de Babel" (System of Babel), "Tractatus retórico-pictóricus," "Novela conjetural" (Conjectural Novel), and "Futuro imperfecto" (Future Imperfect). "Mnemothreptos" carries this approach to its furthest extreme: it presents multiple variations of a single passage, each followed by its own commentary. Like all of Elizondo's writing, "Mnemothreptos" pursues the chimera of a pure and perfect literary realization. It also brings to fore the harsh self-criticism to which Elizondo has always subjected his writing.

The opening and title story of *El grafógrafo* is often quoted by other writers and has become a signature piece for Elizondo and his literary project. "El grafógrafo" begins with the narrator's consciousness of writing and continues to predicate a series of concentric circles upon the act of writing itself. This short text approximates perhaps better than any text in existence the ideal of pure self-referentiality.

*Narda o el verano, Farabeuf, o La crónica de un instante, El Hipogeo Secreto, El retrato de Zoe, Cuaderno de escritura,* and *El grafógrafo* were all produced between 1964 and 1972. In contrast, in the ten years following 1972 Elizondo published only three books: *Contextos* (Contexts, 1973), a collection of short periodical essays; *Antología personal,* the first of two anthologies of the author's writing to date, this one containing two new texts of special note, "El escriba" (The Scribe) and "Parerga (Taller de autocrítica)"; and *Miscast, o, Ha llegado la señora Marquesa: Comedia opaca en tres actos* (Miscast, or, The Marchioness Has Arrived: An Opaque Comedy in Three Acts, 1981), commissioned by the National Arts Institute in Mexico and a dramatic rendition of the struggle between the author and his characters in *El Hipogeo Secreto.* None of these three books, however enjoyable, has added significantly to Elizondo's fiction. Not until 1983 with the publication of *Cámera lúcida* and again in 1988 with *Elsinore* did Elizondo resume his career as fiction writer. His published work since has continued to be quite limited, dominated by the tendency confirmed with the recent compilation *Teoría del infierno* to recycle older materials as if to compensate for the lack of substantially new ones. Certainly, the ten years of virtual silence that separate *El grafógrafo* from *Cámera lúcida* cannot be overlooked or attributed simply to the vagaries of literary creativity.

*Cámera lúcida* marks a new beginning in Elizondo's development, signaling the adoption of a different style, tone, and approach. Elizondo achieved this return to fiction writing primarily by turning literature against itself and making the author and his career the object of self-conscious humor and parody. From the very first pages of *Cámera lúcida* the extended silence that preceded the publication of the new book is openly discussed and explained.

Like *El grafógrafo, Cámera lúcida* collects a series of short texts of various invention. While the texts in *El grafógrafo* seem composed and collected in a very premeditated and programmatic way, most of the texts in *Cámera lúcida* are more truly occasional writings: many were produced for a column in Octavio Paz's monthly literary review, *Vuelta,* and others were written for special occasions such as the author's inaugurations into the Academia Mexicana de la Lengua (Mexican Academy of Language) and the Colegio Nacional (National College). Elizondo's earlier works had fused aspects of poetry, prose fiction, and philosophical speculation into radical experiments in writing; the new texts collected in *Cámera lúcida* employ other combinations and constitute an alternative approach. Individually, the texts no longer defiantly resist classification. Now they freely mix fiction and biography into musings, memoirs, and confessions that may or may not be true.

Though most of the texts in *Cámera lúcida* could be made to fit traditional categories loosely, some element still seems to complicate the classificatory scheme, and many texts shift modes in midstream. "La luz que regresa" (The Light That Returns) is science fiction. "Ein Heldenleben" (A Hero's Life) is a memoir. The inaugural addresses, "Regreso a casa" (Return Home) and "Ida y vuelta" (Full Circle), are essays, as are other texts such as "Mi deuda con Flaubert" (My Debt to Flaubert).

Ultimately, the author himself, who has been silent for so long and now pretends not to know what to say or write, once again gives the collected texts a certain unity. Two of the texts written originally for *Vuelta,* "Vocaciones frustradas" (Frustrated Vocations) and "Poisson d'avril" (April Fool), ingeniously take as their theme the very problem of what to do when one has nothing to write yet faces a deadline. The collection and publication of the pieces appear justified not on their intrinsic merit, but as the idiosyncratic musings of an eccentric writer.

Fortunately the playful self-parody in *Cámera lúcida* does not mask the author's underlying nostalgia for the earlier period of confidence in the ideals of his experiments in writing. The self-parody can be read as a strategy of coping with the failure or impossibility of the original design. Previous works, dating back to the 1966 autobiography, prepared and anticipated Elizondo's use of the author as character, and the practice is self-consciously discussed in "Mi deuda con Flaubert." In such works as *El Hipogeo Secreto* and *El grafógrafo* the author-character had purely metafictional or metaphysical functions, but in this recent phase the figure functions more personally and autobiographically. In the new work the graphographer has become a sort of clown, with all the complex, tragicomic combinations of laughter and tears such a figure entails.

Elizondo's latest work of "fiction," *Elsinore: Un cuaderno* (Elsinore: A Notebook, 1988), would appear to have little connection to previous efforts. This elegant limited-edition novella/memoir offers a much more straightforward and conventional narrative than any Elizondo has produced to date and constitutes a refreshing change of pace. However, *Elsinore* is not entirely unprecedented, picking up the memorial vein initiated in "Ein Heldenleben" from *Cámera lúcida.* In his inaugural address to the Academia Mexicana de la Lengua Elizondo spoke of "Ein Heldenleben" with some affection as a unique piece in which he had never been so close to the truth. Both "Ein Heldenleben" and *Elsinore* are nostalgic evocations of the innocence of youth, the former recalling his days at the Colegio Alemán in Mexico, the latter treating adolescent adventures at a private military academy in California during World War II. *Elsinore* moves away from the radical critiques of the earlier works and hints at a certain longing for simpler human values.

In "Ein Heldenleben" as in *Elsinore* Elizondo represents a definable time and place beyond the material realm of the printed page and outside the space of pure thought for the first time in his work. *Elsinore* displays a recognizable social and political background and even documents the historical homelessness of Mexicans of different backgrounds and origins. The narrator-protagonist, a privileged youth and student at the school, confronts his distance from the Mexican immigrant laborers he meets who are called into service as soldiers in the war. *Elsinore* thus arguably reflects Elizondo's personal struggle to come to grips with the accidents of his fate, with his felt superiority over the tribe and his alienation and solitude in Mexico.

For all its difference from his previous work, *Elsinore* is an integral part of Elizondo's interrogations into literature and writing. Indeed, in the context of the creative silence into which Elizondo had fallen, the book's very existence is significant. Self-consciousness constitutes a minor but significant aspect of the text as a whole: it appears primarily in the narrative frame, in which the author-narrator reflects upon his present feelings and possible reasons for writing. The subtitle gives another indication that *Elsinore* still participates in the author's experiments in writing. Elizondo does not call the volume a memoir or a novella but a notebook, thus invoking the central motif in *Cuaderno de escritura* (1969) and once again emphasizing that writing can never be the mechanical transcription of a pre-ordained meaning, that it always implies a process and that the search for significance is itself a worthwhile end. *Elsinore* contains several thematic threads: love and desire, authority and rebellion, heroism and the social nature of personal esteem. But as if to insist that there can be no preconceived message or agenda, the author never allows any of these threads to coalesce into the point of the story.

Though Elizondo's motivation and inspiration have fallen off considerably in recent years and he has been unable to sustain the audacity of his original design, his renown in Mexico is undiminished. He continues to be a popular figure, which no doubt contributes to the peace of mind he has found in his private life since the early 1970s. In contrast to his formative years, Elizondo today leads a surprisingly domesticated existence in which he lives with his second wife, photographer Paulina Lavista, and their young son Pablo, Elizondo's third child, in the former colonial town of Coyoacán, a district of Mexico City and a haven for many artists and intellectuals. The author divides his attention between home and family and a variety of intellectual pursuits: writing, part-time teaching, speaking engagements, and service on editorial boards and honor societies. This may seem incongruous or even contradictory in the case of a writer so disruptive and unconventional, but Elizondo takes pride in his institutional acceptance in Mexico. Since 1976 he has held an associate professorship in literature at the Universidad Nacional Autónoma de México. That same year he occupied a seat on the Academia Mexicana de la Lengua, and in 1981 he was made a member of the prestigious society of Mexican scholars and intellectuals known as the Colegio Nacio-

nal. In these appointments perhaps he has found some measure of vindication for having dared to be different, for confronting the darker side of our existence in his writing, or for his early struggles and general isolation in Mexican culture.

**Interviews:**
Jorge Rufinelli, "Salvador Elizondo: Entrevista," *Hispamérica,* 4, no. 16 (1977): 33–47;

Margarita García Flores, "Salvador Elizondo: La novela del solipsismo," in her *Cartas marcadas* (Mexico City: Universidad Nacional Autónoma de México, 1979), pp. 289–300;

Danubio Torres Fierro, "Salvador Elizondo," in his *Memoria plural: Entrevistas a escritores latinoamericanos* (Buenos Aires: Sudamericana, 1986), pp. 142–151.

**References:**
Victorio G. Agüero, "El discurso grafocéntrico en *El grafógrafo,* de Salvador Elizondo," *Hispamérica,* 10, no. 29 (1981): 15–27;

Steven M. Bell, "Literatura crítica y crítica de la literatura: Teoría y práctica en la obra de Salvador Elizondo," *Chasqui,* 11, no. 1 (1981): 41–52;

Bell, "Postmodern Fiction in Spanish America: The Example of Salvador Elizondo and Néstor Sánchez," *Arizona Quarterly,* 42, no. 1 (1986): 5–16;

Bruce-Novoa, Introduction to Elizondo's "History According to Pao Cheng," *Latin American Literary Review,* 6, no. 12 (1978): 119–123;

Vicente Cabrera, "Tortura en cámara lenta: Salvador Elizondo, 'En la playa' y otras historias," *Revista Interamericana de Bibliografía,* 40, no. 4 (1990): 394–399;

Julieta Campos, "Una novela que llega a los límites de la novela: *El Hipogeo Secreto,*" in her *Oficio de leer* (Mexico City: Fondo de Cultura Económica, 1971), pp. 62–65;

Emmanuel Carballo, "Prólogo," in Elizondo's *Salvador Elizondo* (Mexico City: Empresas Editoriales, 1966), pp. 5–12;

Carol Clark D'Lugo, "Elizondo's *Farabeuf:* A Consideration of the Text as Text," *Symposium,* 39, no. 3 (1985): 155–166;

Russell Cluff, "La omisión conspicua en Juan Rulfo y Salvador Elizondo," in his *Siete acercamientos al relato mexicano actual* (Mexico City: Universidad Nacional Autónoma de México, 1987), pp. 149–157;

Dermot F. Curley, *En la isla desierta: Una lectura de la obra de Salvador Elizondo* (Mexico City: Fondo de Cultura Económica, 1989);

Manuel Durán, *Tríptico mexicano: Rulfo, Fuentes, Elizondo* (Mexico City: Sepsetentas, 1973);

Claude Fell, "*Farabeuf,* de Salvador Elizondo," in his *Estudios de literatura hispanoamericana contemporánea* (Mexico City: Sepsetentas, 1976), pp. 153–157;

Bernard Fouques, "*Farabeuf:* Entre l'anatheme et l'anamorphose," *Bulletin Hispanique,* 83, nos. 3–4 (1981): 399–431;

Margo Glantz, "*Farabeuf,* escritura barroca y novela mexicana," in her *Repeticiones* (Jalapa, Mexico: Universidad Veracruzana, 1974), pp. 17–26;

Magda Graniela Rodríguez, *El papel del lector en la novela mexicana contemporánea: José Emilio Pacheco y Salvador Elizondo* (Potomac, Md.: Scripta Humanistica, 1991);

Luz Elena Gutiérrez de Velasco, "El paso a la textualidad en *Cámera lúcida,*" *Revista Iberoamericana,* 150 (1990): 235–242;

René Jara, *Farabeuf: Estrategias de una inscripción narrativa* (Jalapa, Mexico: Universidad Veracruzana, 1982);

George R. MacMurray, "Salvador Elizondo's *Farabeuf,*" *Hispania,* 3 (1967): 596–601;

Lillian Manzor-Coats, "Problemas en *Farabeuf,* mayormente intertextuales," *Bulletin Hispanique,* 88, nos. 3–4 (1986): 465–474;

Octavio Paz, "El signo y el garabato," in his *El signo y el garabato* (Mexico City: Joaquín Mortiz, 1973), pp. 200–206;

Alicia Rivero Potter, "El erotismo en 'El desencarnado' de Salvador Elizondo," *Modern Language Studies,* 12, no. 1 (1982): 54–67;

Rolando Romero, "Ficción e historia en *Farabeuf,*" *Revista Iberoamericana,* 151 (1990): 403–418;

Severo Sarduy, "Del yin al yang (sobre Sade, Bataille, Marmori, Cortázar y Elizondo)," in his *Ensayos generales sobre el barroco* (Mexico City: Fondo de Cultura Económica, 1987), pp. 229–247;

Aurea M. Sotomayor, "*El Hipogeo Secreto*: La escritura como palíndromo," *Revista Iberoamericana,* 112–113 (1980): 299–313.

# Julio Escoto

(28 February 1944 –  )

Amanda Castro-Mitchell
*Westminster College*

BOOKS: *Los guerreros de Hibueras* (Tegucigalpa, Honduras: López, 1967);

*La balada del herido pájaro y otros relatos* (Tegucigalpa, Honduras: Universidad Nacional Autónoma de Honduras, 1968);

*El árbol de los pañuelos* (San José, Costa Rica: Editorial Universitaria Centroamericana, 1972);

*Casa del agua* (Tegucigalpa, Honduras: Banco Central de Honduras, 1975);

*Descubrimiento y conquista para niños,* with Gypsy Silverthorne Turcios (San José, Costa Rica: Editorial Universitaria Centroamericana, 1979);

*Los Mayas,* with Gypsy Silverthorne Turcios (San José, Costa Rica: Editorial Universitaria Centroamericana, 1979);

*Días de ventisca, noches de huracán* (San José, Costa Rica: Nueva Década, 1980);

*Bajo el almendro . . . junto al volcán* (San Pedro Sula, Honduras: Centro Editorial, 1988);

*José Cecilio del Valle: Una ética contemporánea* (Tegucigalpa, Honduras: Fundación para el Museo del Hombre Hondureño, 1990);

*El ojo santo: La ideología en las religiones y la televisión* (Tegucigalpa: Universidad Nacional Autónoma de Honduras, 1990);

*El general Morazán marcha a batallar desde la muerte* (San Pedro Sula, Honduras: Centro Editorial, 1992);

*Rey del albor: Madrugada* (San Pedro Sula, Honduras: Centro Editorial, 1993).

OTHER: "Resistir. No resistir. La resistencia. ¿Por qué la resistencia?" in *Antología del cuento hondureño,* edited by Oscar Acosta and Roberto Sosa (Tegucigalpa, Honduras: Universidad Nacional Autónoma de Honduras, 1968);

"Relato primero del fotógrafo loco," in *Antología del cuento centroamericano,* edited by Sergio Ramírez (San José, Costa Rica: Editorial Universitaria Centroamericana, 1973);

*Antología de la poesía amorosa en Honduras,* edited by Escoto (Tegucigalpa, Honduras: Banco Central de Honduras, 1974);

Juan Ramón Molina, *Tierras, mares y cielos,* preface by Escoto (San José, Costa Rica: Editorial Universitaria Centroamericana, 1976);

"Abril antes del mediodía," in *Premio "Gabriel Miró"* (Alicante, Spain, 1983); translated by Alberto Huerta as "High Noon in April" in *Clamor of Innocence: Stories from Central America,* edited by Barbara Paschke and David Volpendesta (San Francisco: City Lights Books, 1988); translated by Gregory Rabassa as "April in the Forenoon" in *And We Sold The Rain: Contemporary Fiction from Central America,* edited by Rosario Santos (New York: Four Walls Eight Windows, 1988; Petersborough, U.K.: Ryan, 1989).

The works of Julio Escoto comprise one of the most vital segments of Honduran fiction during the last three decades of the twentieth century. His novels and short stories have been a regular focus of attention for critics and have inspired countless young writers. Living in a country that continues to be wracked with political, economic, and class turmoil, Escoto consistently proposes through his writings that changes in society begin with changes in individuals. His work reveals the two sides — constructive and destructive — of human nature. Through a variety of techniques, themes, voices, characters, periods, and events, Escoto's writings continually explore the question of identity — of the individual Honduran, of Honduras as a nation, and of Hondurans as Latin Americans. Identity to Escoto is not an abstract concept but a journey that must be made with courage and honesty, a quest in which the seeker must be prepared to confront and overcome his or her own weaknesses and stupidities. At times Escoto addresses this quest in existential terms and at other times through basic issues of everyday life such as friendship, solidarity, inti-

*Julio Escoto*

macy, love, and passion. Seeking a better Honduras and a better world, Escoto proposes that this ideal can only be brought about by better people.

Born on 28 February 1944 in San Pedro Sula, Cortes, a part of Honduras that has always experienced industrial and economical development, Escoto is the son of Pedro Escoto López and Concepción Borjas de Escoto and the second child of eight. In an unpublished 1992 interview with Leticia de Oyuela, Escoto was asked to talk about his "traumas de infancia" (childhood traumas) and expressed that he had none. Though his father was severe, his childhood was happy and protected. His mother was a polite lady who always accepted everything but always ended up doing what she wanted. Escoto believes that the combined influence of his parents provided a balance for the family.

Escoto's father was originally from Santa Bárbara, Honduras, and was the son of a Lenca Indian. Escoto's mother was from Quimistán. However, a document in his mother's possession, dated 1756 and dealing with land division in Quimistán, has led Escoto to believe that his mother's ancestors might have come from the Spaniards who had tried to populate the Mosquito Coast of Honduras but,

discouraged by the great distance from other cities and the attacks made by Misquito Indians, moved to Quimistán. As a writer always looking for his own roots, Escoto has found these ethnic backgrounds important to his literary development.

Escoto attended grade school and high school in San Pedro Sula, graduating from high school in 1960. His father was strongly inclined toward journalism (in fact he owned a small newspaper in San Pedro Sula) and liked to read. Thus Escoto and his siblings became adept readers at an early age, although he was the one who took to it with more enthusiasm.

Respect for human life is essential to Escoto. He discovered this value through personal experience at an early age – a significant experience not only because it defined his ethical values but also because it led to his first short story. Aware of his interest in writing, the principal of his high school commissioned sixteen-year-old Escoto to contribute to the school magazine. After days of not being able to find a suitable topic, Escoto had the following experience, which he related in a 1992 interview with Amanda Castro-Mitchell. When he was learning how to drive, on one occasion he borrowed his father's car. When he was returning to the house he felt that the car had run over a soft object. He was frightened because he thought it could have been a child. It was one of the first experiences in which he confronted his own values about life. The next day he wrote his short story, about what had happened and the terror that the character had experienced.

Published in the school magazine in 1960, this story was received favorably by his classmates and provoked several enthusiastic comments from his teachers. This response motivated him, and he began writing small short stories based on personal experiences. One of these, "Los estornudos" (The Sneezes), was published in a magazine in Tegucigalpa. It was motivated by his physical reaction to the contrast between the hot weather of San Pedro and the water temperature when he took a shower. This reaction would cause him to sneeze up to fifteen times as soon as he stepped under the shower. In this short story the character jumps from the bed to the shower, starts sneezing, and continues sneezing until he disappears. This publication strengthened his motivation to write, and he moved to Tegucigalpa in 1961 to pursue undergraduate studies in languages and literatures in La Escuela Superior del Profesorado (the normal school for high-school teachers). He graduated in 1964 with an even stronger motivation to write.

In 1964 Escoto married Nohemí Córdova Santos and started a family life that lasted eleven years and gave him three sons: Julio Guillermo, Carlos Adolfo, and Jorge Enrique. He taught Spanish in several high schools from 1965 to 1969 to support his family but was never free from the urge to write. During these years he was particularly interested in his father's experiences as a revolutionary in the 1920s, fighting against the "gobernistas" (sympathizers with the dictatorial government). Escoto remembers his father as a tall, strong, and handsome man who liked to talk about what he had lived. His father's experience fascinated him, and he started writing a short story about revolutionaries trying to overthrow the dictatorial government. This interest came to fruition with the completion of *Los guerreros de Hibueras* (The Warriors of Hibueras) in early 1967. Upon its completion Escoto submitted *Los guerreros de Hibueras* to the national Froylán Turcios competition, sponsored by Escuela Superior del Profesorado. The book was awarded second prize and was published in March 1967.

In this book Escoto not only relates his father's experiences, he also displays his ethical values regarding life. War is seen firsthand; the characters – "los guerreros" (the warriors) – narrate and describe the battles they have fought during years

of trying to bring about a revolution. This violent and bloody book accentuates the cruelty rather than the glory of war. Its descriptions include brutal and shocking details, seeming at times deliberately formulated to provoke nausea in the reader. Shocking, too, are the reflections of the warriors themselves, who often seem to be enjoying the blood of their enemies and in their inner dialogues reveal that they have lost all capacity for human feeling.

In this early work Escoto attempts to understand human nature by accepting its capacity to create and its capacity to destroy. Even though the characters in *Los guerreros de Hibueras* are trying to achieve a social change that would bring better times for them and their families, their efforts are enormously destructive. These warriors have developed a strong sense of solidarity among themselves but at the same time are unaffected by the smell of their enemies' burning corpses. In *Los guerreros de Hibueras* Escoto portrays human nature as it is: loving, tender, and loyal on the one side but brutal and merciless on the other.

Following the completion of *Los guerreros de Hibueras,* Escoto began intensely reading authors from the Boom, largely through *Mundo Nuevo* (New World), a review edited by Emir Rodríguez Monegal in Paris. Here Escoto read the first chapter of Gabriel García Márquez's *Cien años de soledad* (1967; translated as *One Hundred Years of Solitude,* 1970), through which he was first exposed to the sense of the ludicrous in literature. Escoto himself points out, "todavía no había entendido cómo uno podía divertirse al mismo tiempo que estuviera escribiendo un libro" (I had not yet understood how one could amuse oneself at the same time that one was writing a book).

In a 1967 journey to Ilama, Honduras, Escoto found the topic for his next book: He was impressed by the town, and especially by its people, many of whom did not distinguish between reality and magic, between reality and imagination and dream. Thus the magic of Ilama, coupled with his paternal grandmother's ethnic background, motivated Escoto to write *El árbol de los pañuelos* (The Tree of Handkerchiefs, 1972). Escoto had always been interested in the ethnic groups of Honduras, and when he found out through a family photograph album and by information gathered through archives that his grandmother was in fact a "lenca pura" (pure Lenca Indian) from Ilama, he felt that he had found some of his roots. Escoto declares that "sentí un gozo porque era como encontrarme un poco conmigo mismo" (I felt a great joy because it was as if I were encountering myself a bit).

*El árbol de los pañuelos* has its genesis in Ramón Amaya Amador's novel *Los brujos de Ilamatepeque* (The Witches of Ilamatepeque, 1958), which in turn is based on the 1843 assassination of the Cano brothers, who had fought with Gen. Francisco Morazán during the period of independence and later during the formation of the Federación Centroamericana (Central American Federation), from the 1820s to the early 1840s.

In a 1986 analysis of *El árbol de los pañuelos,* Helen Umaña notes that it is a quest for roots, both individual and collective, that manages to address universal human concerns while dealing with specific instances. This search for his own roots – and by extension the roots of Honduras and Latin America – is found throughout Escoto's fiction and essays. In *El árbol de los pañuelos* the search is seen through the main character, Balam Cano, whose mother was an ordinary human and therefore mortal and whose father was a witch and therefore immortal. Balam is thus compelled to search through his Mayan ancestry to determine whether his own dominant characteristic is that of human or witch.

Balam's Indian background parallels Escoto's Indian roots. Through the voice of Balam Cano, Escoto poses questions regarding his own identity and roots, but these questions also refer to Latin America in general. *El árbol de los pañuelos* seems to challenge all Latin Americans to seek, with Balam, their deepest roots in Indian heritage.

From the very beginning *El árbol de los pañuelos* reveals conflicts of identity. The name of the main character, part Indian (Balam) and part Spanish (Cano), alludes to the conflicts of *mestizaje* (the mixing of Indians and Spaniards). Moreover, the name Balam reminds the reader of the ancient Mayan prophetic text *El libro de los libros de Chilam Balam* (The Book of the Books of Chilam Balam). According to Barrera-Vásquez and Silvia Rendón, "Balam es el nombre del más famoso de los Chilames que existieron poco antes de la venida de los blancos al continente. Balam es un nombre de familia, pero significa jaguar o brujo ... Chilam (o chilan) es el título que se daba a la clase sacerdotal que interpretaba los libros y la voluntad de los dioses. La palabra significa 'el que es boca ... ' " (Balam is the name of the most famous of the *Chilames* that lived before the arrival of whites on the continent. Balam is a family name, but it means jaguar or witch ... *Chilam* [or *chilan*] is the title that was given to the priest that interpreted the books as well as the will of the gods. The word means "the one who is mouth ... ").

Although Balam Cano is searching for his own identity, his name already suggests that he is a "brujo" (witch). But as narrator of *El árbol de los pañuelos,* Escoto's Balam is also a "mouth," the mouth of Honduran Indians as well as of the witches and even of the Cano brothers by telling their story. Through these many connections *El árbol de los pañuelos* becomes part of a larger story, a history of ethnicity, ancestry, and identity. At the same time, these connections with references to the Mayan cosmology also suggest a prophecy that is passed from voice to voice, from generation to generation. This need to "say" things rather than write them is another frequent Escoto theme.

*El árbol de los pañuelos* also proposes a series of questions that address the process of conquest and colonization and the problems of *mestizaje* that arise from the confrontation of two different cultures and religions in which one dominates the other. These questions are examined from two perspectives. The first is a general perspective, focusing on the identity problems of all Latin Americans, which addresses conflicts strictly related to issues of ethnicity and domination. The second is a personal perspective in which Balam Cano is trying to find out which of his two parts – human or witch – is dominant.

Balam's Indian ethnicity is crucial in determining his identity as a witch. These same two characteristics, however, bring Balam into serious conflict with the Spanish Catholic culture, which burned witches and slaughtered Indians in the Inquisition. But Balam is also partly white and human, thereby combining two contradictory ethnic backgrounds and religions. Balam is therefore the personification of the mestizo conflict. His real quest, in which he is "the mouth" of Latin America, is one that strives for reconciliation of these contradictory elements. Is he witch or human? His veins contain the blood of both, but is he Spanish killer or Indian victim?

This quest also relates to the ethical question of good and evil. At moments Balam appears to be "good," such as when he grants an old man's wish not to die without having seen the sea. There are also times when the novel suggests that Balam is evil, such as when his grandmother states in the beginning, "Balam, Balam, que quien nace de brujo gracia tiene del diablo" (Balam, Balam, one who is born from a witch has gifts from the devil). Thus the novel seeks a reconciliation between the good and evil sides of human nature.

By giving Balam these two opposite features, the novel seems to propose a Buddhist balance in which opposites exist together. Balam seeks a balance between his capacity to be good and his capacity to be evil, yet he must recognize that both elements exist inside him. He proposes that his witchlike nature does not make him evil per se: "Pero no puedo ser malo porque mi padre no lo era, aunque era brujo. O quizás sólo soy bueno porque mi madre lo era. . . . En ese caso mi padre tendría que haber sido malo para hacer el balance de brujo y de humano" (But I could not be evil because my father was not evil, although he was a witch. Or maybe I'm only good because my mother was good. . . . In which case my father must had been evil in order to make the balance between witch and human). On a philosophical level this search for balance also goes against the Catholic tradition of viewing these elements as mutually exclusive. In this view of Catholicism, one has to be all good or all evil but not both, yet Balam *is* both.

Here, as in many of his works, the novel reveals Escoto's distinctly anticlerical attitude and lack of respect for the church as a social institution, a position originating from his senior year of high school. After going through what he calls "la etapa mística" (the mystic stage) when he wanted to be a missionary, Escoto's attitude shifted to the point where he did not believe in anything, only in God, and developed an anticlerical attitude.

Escoto's anticlerical view becomes evident through the priest who appears at the beginning of *El árbol de los pañuelos* and executes Balam's father and uncle:

¡Señor Dios mío! Hágase tu voluntad conmigo y con ellos que la justicia llegue por la mano del hombre pero inspirada por ti. Sé que mi absolución no es posible pues soy juez pero también soy parte, el sacerdote, otros son ellos los brujos y ¿cuál de los dos tiene la razón? ¿El que dice que son brujos o los brujos que dicen que no lo son? ¿El que quiere dejarlos amarrados para fusilarlos o los que quieren que los suelten para escaparse? Que se haga la voluntad del cielo mas los brujos no deben vivir . . . pero el pueblo dice que tampoco pueden morir . . . y si aconsejo que los maten sólo será para hacerlos vivir. . . . Yo creo en ti Señor pero también sé que no todo nos lo has dicho y puede haber algo oculto en la hoja de la hierba o en la flor del maíz aún no comprendido porque la causa de que no nos digas todo es nuestra ignorancia y nuestra ignorancia se debe a que nos dices muy poco. . . . ahora te prometo que los quemaré vivos o los fusilaré con balas curadas . . .

(Lord my God! May your will be done with me and with them, may justice be in the hands of man but inspired by you. I know my absolution is impossible since I am not only judge but also part, the priest; the others are the witches, and which of the two is right? Those who say they are witches or those witches who say they are not? The one who wants to leave them there to be executed or those who want me to untie them so they can flee? May the will of heaven rule, but the witches must die . . . but the people say that they cannot die either . . . and if I advise that they be murdered it will only be to make them live. . . . I believe in you Lord, but I know that you have not said everything to us and there could be something hidden in the leaf of grass or in the corn flower, something not yet comprehended because the reason you don't tell us everything is our ignorance and our ignorance comes from the fact that you tell us so little. . . . now I promise you that I will burn them alive or I will kill them with blessed bullets . . .).

The priest's prayer contains hints of unpriestly agnosticism. In his prayer the priest admits that God has not yet revealed himself to him or to humans in general, and in having him do so the novel implies that God is unknowable. His prayer also shows that the priest, his personal doubts notwithstanding, was responsible for the "death" of the Cano brothers, and thus of Balam's father. While in the end even the priest recognized the immortality of the two witches, his statement "pero el pueblo dice que ellos tampoco pueden morir" (the people say that they cannot die either) carries important sociopolitical implications: it is the people who believe the witches cannot die. This belief represents a hope that Morazán's ideal of a unified Central America, to which the Canos were strongly committed, will share some of these witches' immortality. Furthermore, this prayer strengthens the possibility of Balam's own immortality and in so doing bestows upon the human Balam a godlike feature.

The novel proposes two different identities – Balam-witch-evil and Balam-human-good – and in manipulating them begets a broader dilemma: what if neither of these identities is correct? What if Balam is in fact a witch yet not evil? Could he be God himself? What if he is evil and at the same time godlike? From this the text proposes an infinite series of questions about identity.

*El árbol de los pañuelos* could be compared to Carlos Castañeda's *The Teachings of Don Juan* (1968) regarding the two elements mentioned by Don Juan, the *tonal* and the *nahual*. A human part, the *tonal,* allows human beings to be connected with "this" reality; a nonhuman part, the witchlike-godlike *nahual,* permits the perception of other realities. More importantly, the *nahual* allows humans to "transform" themselves into anything they want and at the same time allows them to "connect" with the source of life. It is also the part that transcends death.

Balam Cano has the capacity not only of perceiving a different reality but also of making others perceive such a reality. In his encounter with the old man who has never seen the sea, Balam shows it to him merely by pointing to the horizon. Balam's *nahual* feature — to borrow Castañeda's terminology — allows him to transcend time and space, as when he returns to Ilama even before Ilama is born. In addition, the text gives to itself the capacity to transcend and to suggest some prophetic elements. One could say that the text predicts the birth of Ilama; it could also be said that the text may seek to prophesy Balam's quest as well as the death of his father in the same way that *The Book of the Books of Chilam Balam* prophesied the arrival of whites onto the continent and the destruction of Indian ancestry.

By granting Balam the capacity to be immortal, however, the novel proposes that indigenous ancestry is also immortal, which is an inherent contradiction because the Spanish eliminated almost all Honduran Indians. In his personal quest Balam finds a resolution: a part of him is in fact witchlike and will never die while another part is human and mortal. This new contradiction recalls the issue of transcendency that surrounded Balam's father, who was killed but did not die. His father's continued existence is shown by the fact that Balam goes to Ilama because he is summoned there by his father and "un buen hijo no puede desobedecer la llamada de su padre" (a good son cannot disobey the call of his father).

At the plot level *El árbol de los pañuelos* was strongly influenced by Juan Rulfo's *Pedro Páramo* (1955; translated as *Pedro Páramo,* 1959); each novel narrates the story of a man who is looking for his father as a way of finding his own identity. *El árbol de los pañuelos* was written in 1968 and that same year was selected by critics Angel Rama, Emmanuel Carballo, and Guillermo Sucre as one of three finalist novels for the Primer Certamen Cultural Centroamericano (First Central American Cultural Contest); it was first published in 1972.

From 1969 to 1971 Escoto lived in Tampa and Gainesville, Florida, where he obtained a bachelor of arts degree in education from the University of Florida and was distinguished with membership on the president's honor roll. Escoto claims that the experience of living in the United States taught him many things, ranging from expanding his mind to protecting himself: "Yo sabía que iba a entrar a las entrañas del imperio y tenía que ciudarme que el imperio no me fuera a seducir y no cambiara mi mentalidad revolucionaria . . . al final me dí cuenta de que no había intensión de modificarme; la modificación era por el ejemplo . . . El imperio modifica no por represión, sino porque genera deseos" (I knew that I was entering into the entrails of the empire and that I had to take care of myself so that

the empire would not seduce me and I would not end up changing my revolutionary mentality . . . in the end I realized that there was no real intention of changing me; that the change came with the example . . . The empire modifies behavior not by repression, but by generating desires). Escoto believes that one of the things that helped him protect himself during his residency in America was his strong sense of respect for humanity, which he thought was lacking in the competitive and individualistic society of the United States.

In 1972 Escoto returned to Tegucigalpa, where he worked as a professor of grammar in the Escuela Superior del Profesorado. By the end of 1972 he began working in the Universidad Nacional Autónoma de Honduras (UNAH), where he taught Spanish, Latin-American, and Honduran literature, and by 1974 he was appointed chair of the department of languages and literatures. During this period Escoto was also appointed director of publications for the Banco Central de Honduras (Central Bank of Honduras), where he published his book of essays *Casa del agua* (House of Water, 1974) and *Antología de la poesía amorosa en Honduras* (Honduran Love Poetry: An Anthology, 1974), the first anthology of love poetry by Honduran writers. In this same year he was awarded the Premio Nacional de Literatura del Estado de Honduras (Honduran National Literary Prize). At the end of 1974 he accepted an invitation to return to the United States issued by the International Writing Program of the University of Iowa. He remained in Iowa until the middle of 1975, when he returned to Tegucigalpa.

In 1975 Escoto divorced Nohemí Córdova Santos and in the following year married Gypsy Silverthorne Turcios, a native of Tegucigalpa whose mother was from Tegucigalpa and father from the United States. During 1975 and 1976 Escoto continued as professor of literature at the UNAH, and toward the middle of 1976 he was offered the position of director of cultural development of CSUCA (Council of Universities of Central America), based in San José, Costa Rica. Escoto accepted the position because he was motivated by the opportunity to work in cultural programs and especially on the Central American level. Escoto and his family moved to San José in 1976, where they lived for ten years, during which time Escoto held different positions related with cultural, editing, or publishing programs. From 1977 to 1980 he served as director of the most important editorial house in Central America, EDUCA (Editorial Universitaria Centroamericana, an editorial house comprised of all the Central American universities).

From 1980 to 1986 Escoto and his family lived in Coronado, Costa Rica, where he worked for the Instituto Interamericano de Cooperación Agrícola (Inter-American Institute of Agricultural Cooperation), holding different positions that ranged from director of teaching tools to director of the editorial board. During this time Escoto was also editor of two reviews, *Turrialba* and *Desarrollo Rural de Centro América* (Rural Development in Central America). During this time Escoto also undertook graduate studies at the Universidad de Costa Rica, from which he received the degree of magister literarum with honors in 1984.

Although he wrote quite extensively, Escoto published very little during his years in Costa Rica. Particularly when he was working at EDUCA, Escoto had the opportunity to meet many prestigious writers and travel around Latin America. From these trips Escoto learned that the problems of human beings are shared throughout Latin America. Escoto's few publications during these years were largely concerned with these common problems.

In 1980 Escoto published *Días de ventisca, noches de huracán* (Days of Wind, Nights of Hurricane) in Costa Rica. This novel was not well received in Honduras because it includes a strong criticism of the Honduran–Latin-American left wing, accentuating the incapacity of the left-wing movement to bring about revolution. The movement prohibited its members from reading the book.

Escoto's broader vision gave him the ability to see what was really happening inside the Honduran left-wing movement, where factional leaders squandered their time criticizing other left-wing groups. Living outside Honduras, Escoto could see the artificiality of the leftist movements of Honduras, and he attempted to portray this vision in *Días de ventisca, noches de huracán*. This was not the first time Escoto had expressed misgivings regarding revolutionary movements. In his first book, *Los guerreros de Hibueras,* one of the revolutionary fighters questions the revolutionary ideal: "Ideal revolucionario – pensaba – y ¿qué era eso?.... Una justificación para llegar al poder allá en Tegucigalpa" (Revolutionary ideal – he thought – and what was that? ... An excuse to gain power there in Tegucigalpa).

Written and published during his residency in Costa Rica and included in his story collection *La balada del herido pájaro* (Dance of the Wounded Bird, 1985), "Abril antes del mediodía" (April in the Forenoon) was awarded the Gabriel Miró Prize in Spain in 1983. In this story Escoto proposes that one can betray everything during times of war – even one's best friend.

In 1986 Escoto returned to Honduras, motivated by the fact that his children were starting to lose their Honduran identity. This issue of identity and roots has been crucial for Escoto as well as for his wife. When they returned to Honduras, they decided to live in the industrial center of San Pedro Sula in order to contribute to cultural activity there.

Both Escoto and Silverthorne Turcios arrived in San Pedro Sula with many projects. Escoto established an editorial house in May 1987, while his wife's aim was the creation of a children's library in San Pedro Sula. In 1987 she initiated this project in conjunction with the municipality of San Pedro and the support of other interested people. Unfortunately, she was not able to see her dream finished due to her untimely death in April 1990. However, Escoto and the other members of the board have extended her project well beyond her original design. No longer limited to a children's library, it is evolving into the Centro Cultural Infantil (Cultural Center for Children). This center seeks to provide children of all ages and social classes not only with a library especially designed to meet their needs, but with dance, drawing, painting, ballet, and ceramic and handcraft classes as well as with theater presentations, puppets, conferences, and lectures – all designed for children. The center will also have a psychologist and a social worker along with scholarships to help poor children.

Escoto's own projects reflect a similar commitment to the people of Honduras. In 1989 Escoto founded the review *Imaginación* (Imagination), which has two principal goals: first, it provides new writers the opportunity to publish and become known; second, it allows young readers the opportunity to familiarize themselves with the work of older authors, particularly nineteenth-century Honduran writers who might be overlooked by the educational system. *Imaginación* publishes almost exclusively narrative written by Hondurans or about Honduras; occasionally it includes essays focusing on Honduras. In 1991 Escoto also initiated the annual Jornadas de Identidad Cultural (Workshops on Cultural Identity). The purpose of these encounters is to gather as many "trabajadores de la cultura" (cultural workers) as possible in order to update, discuss, examine, and design new guidelines for research being done in all areas of Honduran culture, from the social sciences to art.

Throughout his life Escoto has shown a strong concern for uncovering the past. In order to accomplish this he draws variously on historical charac-

*Honduran president Callejas presenting Escoto with a plaque that honored Escoto for his novel* El general Morazán
marcha a batallar desde la muerte *(1992), based on the life of a Central American hero*

ters, events, and sites that introduce elements in his works that go beyond literature, at times producing texts that become "testimony" and "oral history." By exploring Honduran and Central American historical events, his works update them; frequently he exposes events that do not appear in the "official" history but are part of the Honduran or Central American social and individual identity.

At times it is difficult to understand how Escoto — a passionate believer in the value of life — writes so often about war and killing. Such writings, however, reveal his respect for life as he seeks to understand those aspects of human nature that are particularly mystifying because of their brutality and inhumanity. By writing fiction based on real wars Escoto forces his readers to ask themselves the same questions that the characters have asked: was it necessary to kill all of these people just to attain some sort of power? Is it reasonable that two of the poorest countries in the continent engage in war at a time when their people are starving? Does the left wing want to see poor people achieving higher living standards, or does it care only to obtain power for itself? How can real social change be accomplished?

In 1988 Escoto published *Bajo el almendro . . . junto al volcán* (Under the Almond Tree . . . Next to the Volcano) in San Pedro Sula. *Bajo el almendro . . . junto al volcán* recalls "la guerra del fútbol" (the soc-

cer war) that took place between Honduras and El Salvador in 1969 after diplomatic relations were broken off following a fatal dispute at a soccer game between the two countries. Although it describes a war, *Bajo el almendro . . . junto al volcán* does not include the vivid descriptions of physical confrontations found in *Los guerreros de Hibueras*. Both, however, reveal the loss of humanity resulting from "guerras cochinas" (dirty wars) in *Los guerreros de Hibueras* and "guerra idiota" (stupid war) in *Bajo el almendro . . . junto al volcán*.

The immediate question posed by *Bajo el almendro . . . junto al volcán* is who is the real enemy? Is it the Salvadoran people who lived in Honduras at the time of the war and were assumed to be traitors only because they were Salvadorans? Or is it the politicians and military leaders whose fundamental motivation was to protect the interests of the oligarchy? The text proceeds from this overarching question to present some of the hidden issues that surround the reality of war. The novel starts by presenting the instinctive response of attacking when one feels threatened.

The main character in the first part of the novel, "El Capitán Centella" (Captain Spark), is an old "capitán de cerro" (a term used in Honduras to refer to those who are not soldiers in the traditional sense but are veterans of actual fighting.) Centella, who had fought in some of the revolutions of the

1920s, prepares a battalion with which he will defend his town from the expected invasion from El Salvador. Here the novel criticizes the Honduran social view, which expects one to be willing to die with dignity in defense of the land. Although initially Centella and his peasant warriors seem willing to die defending their country, the doubts they express early in *Bajo el almendro . . . junto al volcán* reveal that they are not in fact quite so willing either to kill or to die. Here the social criticism in the novel becomes evident: the "warriors" know what society expects from them in terms of defending the nation; however, such social expectations have nothing to which these peasants can relate. They have all been taught that they must defend the country when necessary, yet they were never asked if they wanted to die in a war. Had they been asked, their response would have been negative; humans, like any other animal, have a great fear of dying.

Furthermore, the novel seeks to present these peasant-warriors as humans who view cold-blooded murder as contrary to their moral and religious values. Centella and his warriors are acting based on their mechanical response to defend the nation when they prepare to attack the house of a Salvadoran tailor who had lived in their town for about a decade. They are drawn there because of the "clic-clic" they hear coming from the tailor's house, which they assume is a telegraph sending messages to the enemy. When they realize that they might have to kill the tailor, they hesitate:

Desde el interior de la casa emanaba el clic-clic . . . ordenó; atendieran el clic-clic y formaran en plan de ataque para entrar a degüello en la habitación. Contaría hasta tres y entonces . . . entonces se quedaron viendo, sumergidos y atónitos . . . aturdidos por el ramalazo de sangre que les despertaba en la memoria la palabra *degüello,* lo que hizo que al comandante se le entintara el rostro y tratara avergonzadamente de excusarse . . . se disculpó. ¿Qué tal si mejor llamaban a la puerta como personas civilizadas?

(From the interior of the house came the clic-clic . . . he ordered them to pay attention to the clic-clic, to line up in attack position and to get ready for the throat-cutting as soon as they entered the room. He would count to three and then . . . then they were startled, looking at him not knowing what to do . . . perturbed because of the visions of blood that the word *throat-cutting* brought back to their memories; this forced him to blush in shame, trying to apologize . . . he apologized. [Centella then asked,] "Why not knock at the door like civilized people?")

Here the novel employs sarcasm to establish the difference between "civilized" people and savages who can kill without remorse. Later, sarcasm and irony accentuate the stupidity of the war: the tailor and his wife are deeply moved by the peasants' "visit," wondering how their neighbors knew that this was the birthday of the tailor's wife. The warriors' consternation is compounded when they discover that the clic-clic was coming from the tailor's new sewing machine.

These peasant-warriors in *Bajo el almendro . . . junto al volcán* portray – at times ironically – Escoto's desire to reconcile the opposing creative and destructive sides of human nature. As the "warriors" approach the unsuspecting "traitor's" house on tiptoe, they are careful not to step on the tomato plants or disturb the rose petals. Realizing that they may have to kill the tailor, they are nevertheless careful not to damage his orange trees, because as peasants they know how much time and energy the tailor has invested in them. The peasant exists to nurture life, not to destroy it.

*Bajo el almendro . . . junto al volcán* is probably Escoto's most merciless social criticism; moral, religious, and ideological conventions of Honduran society are examined ironically and sarcastically and by juxtaposing differing concepts of nationalism, honesty, decency, and democracy. The young warriors have a social consciousness that differs from Centella's, while Centella's ideas regarding nationalism differ from those held by the representative of the Honduran army and government, Major Gavilán (Major Hawk). The sociopolitical discourse expressed by Guillermo, one of the young peasant-warriors, proposes that the war between Honduras and El Salvador was provoked in large part by the Salvadoran oligarchy to avoid a revolution: " 'si usted fuera campesino en El Salvador y le negaran la tierra, ¿qué hacía?' . . . 'Yo iniciaba una revolución,' aseguró el comandante" ("if you were a peasant in El Salvador and they denied you the land, what would you do? . . ." "I would start a revolution," assured the commandant). Although Centella is more conservative than Guillermo, he recognizes that he is capable of starting a revolution in order to get land. Guillermo, who has studied in Tegucigalpa, displays a different consciousness. Yet both can identify unfair land distribution as the basic problem. According to Guillermo, by creating a war the Salvadoran government could invade Honduras and place the angry Salvadoran peasants on the land that would be wrested from Honduras in such an invasion.

Here the novel introduces another set of differing values. Centella refuses to believe that the

Salvadoran army and government would be willing to be part of such a dishonest activity: "¿acaso el ejército de El Salvador se prestaba a semejante cosa?" (is it possible that the army of El Salvador would lend itself to such a project?) This suggests that Centella is an honest warrior who believes that the Salvadoran army should be equally honest. Later *Bajo el almendro . . . junto al volcán* emphasizes Centella's honesty by contrasting it with the attitude of Gavilán, who believes that power can only be gained through arms and therefore the use of arms is justified to insure "democracy." Here the reader is confronted with two different perspectives regarding nationalism and patriotism: the honesty of Centella versus the dishonesty of the major.

The stronger social criticism of *Bajo el almendro . . . junto al volcán* is shown when the novel exposes the war as a circus, a carnival, displaying the foolishness of the characters who participate. It also presents these characters as a product of "castigo divino" (divine punishment), strongly suggesting that the punishment is not war itself but the people who invent it.

Toward the end of the novel Centella undergoes certain changes. It is significant that up to this point the reader has not yet encountered any experiences of death or destruction. With the arrival of the Honduran army in Centella's town, however, the destruction, violence, and repression begin. Everything Centella has worked for as mayor in order to make his town beautiful and hospitable is destroyed. Pavement, trees, benches, gardens, and even his beautiful park are torn apart by the army encampment; a curfew is imposed, and the citizens are required to carry identification cards — all this imposed by his own government's army. Although old and stubborn, Centella is compelled to change his support for the army because of his confrontation with Major Gavilán and the destruction of his own town. Centella no longer wishes to be part of a "circus" war; rather, he and his wife will teach the younger generation how to win "la guerra de la paz" (the war of peace).

In July 1969 Escoto was living in El Loarque, a residential area of Tegucigalpa near the Honduran air force base. When he and his first wife heard explosions and shots on 14 July, they realized that their country was at war with El Salvador and proceeded to hide their children. After the first Salvadoran attack on Honduran territory, every neighborhood proceeded to create "comités de vigilancia" (watching committees). These committees were commissioned to guard against hostile activities on the part of Salvadorans living in their neighborhoods. Escoto and his group were patrolling the streets of El Loarque on the second night of the war when they heard some noises in the dark and received no response when they demanded identification. Assuming then that the noises came from a Salvadoran traitor running away, they prepared to open fire. Escoto recalls, "Yo me bajé el rifle del hombro y puse el dedo en el gatillo listo para disparar" (I took my rifle and put my finger in the trigger, ready to open fire). But since they did not hear any further noise, they did not fire. Patrolling the following morning, they discovered that the source of noise the previous evening was an enormous kerosene tank, and a single bullet would have incinerated the entire block. Escoto believes that their behavior the night before was an example of "la histeria que había" (the hysteria that reigned). The absurdity of the whole situation experienced by Escoto and all Hondurans during the war is reflected in *Bajo el almendro . . . junto al volcán*. For Escoto the only positive result of the war was the unification of the country.

*Bajo el almendro . . . junto al volcán* constitutes a testimony of the war in an almost scholastic manner; it seeks to inform young readers of those historical events as well as to present an ideological analysis of the motivations of such a war. In its conclusion *Bajo el almendro . . . junto al volcán* offers the younger generation an alternative resolution to social and political disagreement: learn how to maintain peace rather than how to wage war.

In 1990 Escoto published two volumes of nonfiction: *El ojo santo: La ideología en las religiones y la televisión* (The Holy Eye: Ideology in Religion and Television) and *José Cecilio del Valle: Una ética contemporánea* (José Cecilio del Valle: A Contemporary Ethic). Although Escoto has been a frequent critic of institutionalized religion, *El ojo santo* reveals that he is a deeply religious man. Lacking dogma and prescribed rules, his is a personal religion based upon his own harmonious relationship with God and with the universe and therefore with himself. The second of these books presents and analyzes the ethical values espoused by del Valle, a hero of Honduran and Central American independence. Here, as in many of his other writings, Escoto proposes a path that will allow Hondurans and Central Americans to learn more about their countries and their histories as well as about themselves.

In commemoration of the 200th anniversary of General Morazán's birth and the 150th anniversary of his death, Escoto published *El general Morazán marcha a batallar desde la muerte* (General

*Cover for Escoto's 1988 novel, based on a 1969 conflict
between Honduras and El Salvador*

clares, that his vision of Francisco Morazán was nurtured over many years, and that he had never been able to understand his extraordinary work until he conceived of him as a brother, not as the demigod that school had taught him.

*El general Morazán marcha a batallar desde la muerte* is an unconventional historical account of Morazán's life. The general himself begins the narration after his execution in San José, Costa Rica, and from this point on he develops a reflexive tone. Although the reader receives an enormous quantity of historical data, it is presented by Morazán in such a manner that the reader is drawn as much to Morazán's own views of the battles as to the historical events. The text is presented as testimony, an oral history, rather than mere literature. Morazán himself has come back from the dead to talk to the readers.

*El general Morazán marcha a batallar desde la muerte* proposes the possibility of existence after death. Morazán is dead, yet he is also alive; he has transcended time and space. Morazán narrates the past as well as foresees the future – a future beyond his death. Morazán himself claims that "la muerte . . . no existe y es sólo el paso de nuestras imperfectas cualidades al espacio de la verdad. . . . Sobrenadamos en una cósmica oquedad de amor que nos envuelve y nos materializa como transparentados por la luz" (death . . . does not exist; it is only a step taken by our imperfect qualities into the place where truth resides. . . . We swim in a cosmic emptiness where love surrounds us and gives us essence made transparent by the light).

*El general Morazán marcha a batallar desde la muerte* presents a reconciliation with death. No longer the enemy who devours loved ones, death becomes an essential part of the life cycle. In the novel both Morazán and his wife Doña María Josefa have accepted their fate. Their union is such that they will continue to be together forever, and they know it. Here the book reflects Escoto's personal experiences. When Escoto's wife died in 1990, he went through a deep depression. Following a period when Escoto wished only for his own death, he started to find an answer for her sudden departure: "me dediqué a leer libros de sicología, de siquiatría y hasta lecturas metafísicas . . . y así fue como descubrí que todos teníamos una misión en la vida, que no estábamos aquí sólo para andar viendo el ciprés" (I devoted myself to reading psychology, psychiatry, and even metaphysics . . . and it was in this way that I discovered that we all have a mission in life, that we are not here only to pass the time). This traumatic loss of his partner gave Escoto the

Morazán Comes Back to Fight from his Death) in March 1992. By June the book had sold ten thousand copies in two printings. No other novel by a Honduran author has provoked as broad a spectrum of commentary. *El general Morazán marcha a batallar desde la muerte* inspired articles by the most prominent Honduran critics as well as by readers expressing their gratitude to Escoto through letters to the press. In response to the novel Rafaél Leonardo Callejas, the president of Honduras, presented Escoto a plaque honoring his brilliant accomplishment in bringing the *paladín* (champion) of the Central American unification movement back to life.

In his newspaper account of the book Edgar Villamil described *El general Morazán marcha a batallar desde la muerte* as a "novela histórica o historia novelada" (historical novel or history-made-novel). The book presents General Morazán as a man, not as a legend, who fought for his beliefs and ideals as well as a man of flesh and blood. In an interview with the press of San Pedro Sula, Escoto himself de-capacity to transform pain into a work of art. One can see Escoto's own pain in that of Morazán when he realized that his ideal of unification in Central America had died, when he saw that the same people he had helped liberate were those who wanted him dead.

Both Escoto and Morazán come to terms with death in *El general Morazán marcha a batallar desde la muerte*. Morazán knows that despite his own death his ideas have not been extinguished. The novel also suggests that transcendence, existence beyond death, is only possible because of love – a love that comes from having achieved reconciliation with oneself and with humanity in general. The love expressed by Morazán – and by Escoto – arises from an ideal of unification with humanity and with the universe. This solidarity, according to Umaña in her 1992 review, can lead humanity to construct life based on a communal vision.

Julio Escoto resides in San Pedro Sula and continues to write. His new book, *Rey del albor: Madrugada* (King of the Dawn: Madrugada, 1993), is a novel about the history of Honduras that explores Honduran and Central American cultural identity based on historic and fictional facts and characters. Escoto continues to work in his publishing company and in the cultural projects that he and his second wife began when they moved back to Honduras in 1986. A gentle and sensitive person, Escoto talks about himself reluctantly because – to quote from Escoto in conversation with Amanda Castro-Mitchell – "es que es el trabajo lo que importa, yo no importo" (it is the work, not me, that is important).

**Interview:**

Unpublished interview with Amanda Castro-Mitchell, 1992.

**References:**

Ramón Amaya Amador, *Los brujos de Ilamatepeque,* third edition (Tegucigalpa, Honduras: Baktum, 1985);

Alfredo Barrera Vásquez and Silvia Rendón, eds. *El libro de los libros de Chilam Balam* (Mexico City: Fondo de Cultura Económica, 1948);

Helen Umaña, "El problema de la identidad en una novela de Julio Escoto," in her *Literatura hondureña contemporánea: Ensayos* (Tegucigalpa, Honduras: Guaymuras, 1986), pp. 275–286.

# Rosario Ferré

*(28 July 1942 –   )*

Carmen S. Rivera
*University of North Carolina at Charlotte*

BOOKS: *Papeles de Pandora* (Mexico City: Joaquín Mortiz, 1976); translated by Ferré as *The Youngest Doll* (Lincoln & London: University of Nebraska Press, 1991);

*El medio pollito: Siete cuentos infántiles* (Río Piedras, P.R.: Huracán, 1976);

*La caja de cristal* (Mexico City: La Máquina de Escribir, 1978);

*Los cuentos de Juan Bobo* (Río Piedras, P.R.: Huracán, 1980);

*La muñeca menor / The Youngest Doll* (Río Piedras, P.R.: Huracán, 1980);

*Sitio a Eros: Trece ensayos literarios* (Mexico City: Joaquín Mortiz, 1980); "La cocina de la escritura" translated by Ferré and Diana L. Vélez as "The Writer's Kitchen" in *Lives on the Line: The Testimony of Contemporary Latin American Authors,* edited by Doris Meyer (Berkeley: University of California Press, 1988);

*La mona que le pisaron la cola* (Río Piedras, P.R.: Huracán, 1981);

*Fábulas de la garza desangrada* (Mexico City: Joaquín Mortiz, 1982);

*"El acomodador": Una lectura fantástica de Felisberto Hernández* (Mexico City: Fondo de Cultura Económica, 1986);

*Maldito amor* (Mexico City: Joaquín Mortiz, 1986); translated by Ferré as *Sweet Diamond Dust* (New York: Ballantine, 1988);

*El árbol y sus sombras* (Mexico City: Fondo de Cultura Económica, 1989);

*Sonatinas* (Río Piedras, P.R.: Huracán, 1989);

*El coloquio de las perras* (San Juan: Cultural, 1990); "Ofelia a la deriva en las aguas de la memoria" translated by Ferré as "On Destiny, Language, and Translation; or, Ophelia Adrift in the C. & O. Canal" in *The Youngest Doll* (Lincoln & London: University of Nebraska Press, 1991);

*La cucarachita Martina* (Río Piedras, P.R.: Huracán, 1990);

*Cortázar* (Washington, D.C.: Literal / Río Piedras, P.R.: Cultural, 1991);

*Rosario Ferré, circa 1990 ( photograph by Juan E. Ortiz)*

*Las dos Venecias* (Mexico City: Joaquín Mortiz, 1992);

*Memorias de Ponce: Autobiografía de Luis A. Ferré* (Bogotá: Norma, 1992).

Rosario Ferré has become the "translator" of the reality of Puerto Rican women, opening the doors for the feminist movement on the island. By combining classical mythology with indigenous folktales that usurp the traditional actions of female characters, Ferré has interpreted, translated, and rewritten a more active and satisfying myth of Puerto Rican women. In so doing she breaks with the Puerto Rican literary tradition of women writing poetry about love. Ferré has published short stories, poems, critical essays, and a short novel dealing with a wide range of themes, from the oppressive situation of women in Puerto Rican society to the colonial status of the island. Her works underline with both humor and poignancy the different roles that women play in society while at the same time she attempts to construct a new identity. Many critics believe that with the publication of her first book, *Papeles de Pandora* (Pandora's Roles, 1976; translated as *The Youngest Doll,* 1991), Ferré began the feminist movement in Puerto Rico and became, if not its only voice, one of its most resonant and forceful spokepersons.

If anyone understands the dichotomy of roles imposed by society, it is Rosario Ferré. She was born on 28 July 1942 and grew up in Ponce, a city considered until recently the southern capital of the island because of its industrial and cosmopolitan nature. Her parents epitomize the dialectic of Puerto Rican society during the first half of the century. Her mother, Lorenza Ramírez Ferré, came from a family of the landowning elite who were fighting to maintain their way of life based on the dying economy of the sugarcane plantations. This group looked for its identity in the values and traditions of Spain, which until 1898 had ruled the island. Her father, Luis A. Ferré, was governor of Puerto Rico between 1968 and 1972; he represented the burgeoning new upper class based on an industrial and banking economy supported by American corporations. Many of her short stories capture the struggle between the agrarian and industrial classes for social and economic dominance and the precarious position of women in both societies.

For the most part Ferré attended a Catholic school for girls, where she was taught that as a woman she should be virtuous and silent. Fortunately, she had the opportunity to experience firsthand a boy's education. From first to fifth grade she attended a Jesuit school for boys where her brother was studying. Given the Jesuits' background and preparation, the education for boys was far superior.

During these years she was introduced to the fantastic world of fairy tales by the Brothers Grimm, Hans Christian Andersen, and E. T. A. Hoffmann, and to the exotic world of Scheherazade in *A Thousand and One Nights.* She also listened in-

tently to the stories told by Gela, her black nanny. It was then that she started writing, with the sole intention of preserving Gela's narrations. Many of these anecdotes were included later in her collections of children's stories.

After graduating from high school Ferré studied English literature in the United States. During the 1960s she married and had three children. The early 1970s, however, proved to be a turning point in her life. Her mother died while her father was still serving as governor, an event that forced her to perform as official hostess of La Fortaleza, the governor's residence. During that period she divorced her husband and embraced the cause of Puerto Rican independence, a political position totally opposed to that of her father. At the same time she was working on her master's degree in Spanish literature at the Universidad de Puerto Rico. It was then that she met Angel Rama and Mario Vargas Llosa, who both encouraged her to write and publish.

In 1970 Ferré started to publish a literary magazine entitled *Zona de Carga y Descarga* (Loading and Unloading Zone). In spite of its short life (1970–1976) this magazine had a definite impact on the literature and politics of the island. In it unknown and rising artists found the means to publish their works. The magazine also published political articles demanding social reforms without aligning itself with a specific political party. Thus the magazine came under attack from both the right and left wings. Here Ferré published her first short story, "La muñeca menor" (The Youngest Doll), later included in her first collection of short stories and poems, *Papeles de Pandora.* Ferré moved to Mexico in 1976, where this book was published. Considered a feminist manifesto, the book, as the title indicates, contains papers (short stories and poems) depicting the various *papeles* (roles) of women in Puerto Rican society. Since then, Ferré has published almost every year: collections of children's short stories, poetry collections, critical essays, and translations of her short stories in literary magazines and anthologies.

*Papeles de Pandora* immediately established Ferré as an influential Puerto Rican feminist writer. Together with her 1980 collection of essays, *Sitio a Eros* (Eros Besieged), and the poems in *Fábulas de la garza desangrada* (Fables of a Bleeding Crane, 1982), it forms a trilogy of feminist manifestos. With *Papeles de Pandora* Ferré, like the woman in the title, opened the literary world to a new scope of themes, myths, and language. "La muñeca menor," the first story of the collection, introduces one of the most

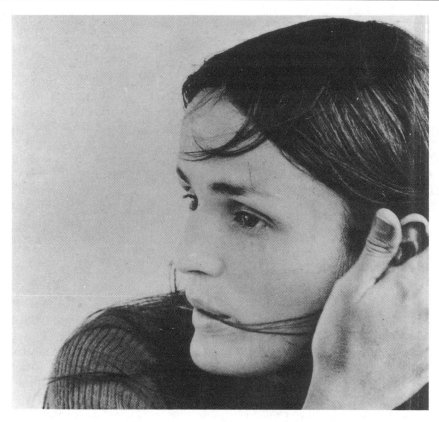

*Ferré at the time* Papeles de Pandora *was published in 1976*

devastating roles of women in society, that of social adornment. An aunt who has been bitten by a river prawn is confined to the house and devotes herself to making dolls of human scale in the image of her nieces. The youngest niece gets married to the young doctor attending the aunt and as a wedding gift receives a doll that has her baby teeth and her diamond earrings as eyes. The doctor, newly wealthy and all too aware of his wife's social prestige, positions his wife on the porch so people can see that he married into the old aristocracy. Little by little the girl transforms herself into a doll, until one day the doctor cannot even perceive her breathing. At the end he approaches her at night, and she opens her eyes to reveal the infuriated prawns within. Thus the feminine figures of aunt, wife, doll, and nature have all become one, and after years of frustrations they cannot hide their anger anymore.

Dolls are a constant motif in this book. In "Amalia" the child Amalia is confused with the doll named after her. In "Marina y el león" (Marina and the Lion) the protagonist decides to give a costume party and disguises herself as a doll wrapped in a box. In a complicated game of dressing and un-

dressing, women are depicted as they step into and out of the diverse roles imposed by society.

Solidarity among female characters becomes an essential element in the struggle against a patriarchal system. Ferré effectively uses the stream of consciousness of various female characters, thus interweaving their voices and identifying one with the other. By having characters that fuse with one another Ferré insists that the oppression of women takes place at all levels of society, regardless of class or race. The white lady of the house as well as the mulatto maid, the devoted wife and mother and the prostitute – all are abused by men. "Cuando las mujeres quieren a los hombres" (When Women Love Men) combines the stream of consciousness of Isabel Luberza, the widow of Ambrosio, and Isabel la Negra, his black mistress who runs a bordello in town. The wife wants to become the voluptuous and sensuous mistress while the prostitute wants to become a respectable lady. At times their respective monologues combine to form a "we" that recriminates Ambrosio for his mistreatment of them and for his final act of leaving the house to both of them. At the end the two women have the final laugh when they become partners and decide to make the house into a bordello and become rich at his expense.

Ferré also breaks with Puerto Rican literary tradition by using in her narratives the common and sometimes even vulgar speech of the working and poor classes of the island. In "The Writer's Kitchen," a translation of her essay "La cocina de la escritura" (from *Sitio a Eros*) by Ferré and Diana L. Vélez, she comments on her sexually explicit language: "I had wanted to turn the sexually humiliating insult – a weapon society had wielded against us for centuries – against society's own outworn and unacceptable biases." Language is used both to demystify and to attack the social and political structures that oppress women. Isabel la Negra's popular speech is not only a realistic feature but a weapon masterfully articulated to avenge her.

In "El collar de camándulas" (The Seed Necklace) Armantina the maid uses an old family recipe as a weapon against the family that has mistreated and abused her over the years, thus avenging not only herself but the dead lady of the house. The stream of consciousness of the wife and mother, mistreated because of her love for a poor guitarist, flows into and unites with that of the mulatto maid beaten because she knows the dirty secrets of the family. At the end Armantina takes revenge on the father and sons by poisoning them with a cake she prepares. In other stories Ferré rewrites folktales in which the female character finally rebels against oppression by wielding as a weapon domestic objects such as scissors or knitting needles.

The poems included in the book complement the short stories. Ferré, again departing from literary traditions, uses poetry to destroy the myth of love and to rewrite the role of women. Following "La muñeca menor" is the poem "Eva María," which combines the voices of the first woman, Eve, and the mother of Jesus, Mary, the example of virtue and submissiveness. The poem ends with a new voice, which insists that she will choose to be both, to create and to destroy, in order to become her own person.

*Fábulas de la garza desangrada* is a collection of poems that continue this motif of rewriting the roles of mythical, biblical, and literary female figures. Here Ariadne aborts the Minotaur, Daphne's lover runs away from her, Mary Magdalene seductively anoints the body of Christ, and Desdemona poisons Othello. In the essay "La prisionera" (The Prisoner), a young Medusa refuses to become an Andromeda to give birth to princesses and kings. In "Contracanto," the most accomplished poem in the collection, Helen of Troy complains about her fate, which has forced her to perform as Menelaus's wife and then as Paris's courtesan, rebels against her

third role as the cause of war and the annihilation of two armies, and kills herself.

Behind these poems is the struggle to find one's own identity, to authorize one's life. Ferré believes that a woman can forge her own identity through the creative process of writing, thus becoming the author of "her/story." Thus there are constant references throughout her work to the act of writing. The woman of "Fábula de la garza desangrada," who struggles to escape the bonds imposed by society, is identified with the bleeding crane that desperately tries to fly in order to soar above death. The flowing blood no longer feeds the placenta carrying a baby but becomes the ink with which her poems are written.

*Sitio a Eros* and *Fábulas de la garza desangrada* were written during the same period. Ferré declares that one book could not exist without the other since their themes are the same: the woman, whether historical or mythical, torn between the formulas imposed by society and her search for her own identity.

"La cocina de la escritura" is the first and most extensive essay in *Sitio a Eros*. Here Ferré talks about writing, especially how her stories come into being, and deals directly with controversial and current questions such as whether or not there is such a thing as feminine writing. In an extensive metaphor of writing as cooking, she explains how she uses the *palabra* – a feminine noun – and its creative power to beget her own identity. Ferré admits that this process has a binary function: it allows her to destroy the oppressive reality around her and to substitute a more compassionate one. She also recognizes the risks and dangers involved in the literary process; if not cooked right it can end up burning her.

When considering the matter of feminine as opposed to masculine writing, Ferré insists that there is no such distinction and no distinctive women's style. When one compares Jane Austen to Emily Brontë, for instance, one finds very little in common. What is different is the experience of women as opposed to that of men, and therefore the themes that obsess women. As she says in the English translation of the essay, "That is why women's literature has, much more so than men's literature, concerned itself with interior experiences, experiences that have little to do with the historical, the social, or the political. Women's literature is also more subversive than men's because it delves into forbidden zones – areas bordering on the irrational, madness, love, and death – zones that our rational and utilitarian society makes it dangerous to recognize."

ROSARIO FERRÉ

## Las dos Venecias

CUARTO CRECIENTE

*Cover for Ferré's 1992 collection of poems and essays dealing with her life, feminism, and politics*

The next thirteen essays are a sociohistorical retrospective of women artists who left a profound imprint on the spirit of the Puerto Rican writer. Ferré summarizes in concise yet warmhearted narratives the experiences of Mary Shelley, George Sand, Flora Tristán, Jean Rhys, Anaïs Nin, Tina Modotti, Alexandra Kollontai, Sylvia Plath, Julia de Burgos, Lillian Hellman, and Virginia Woolf. The essays describe their struggle to find their own identity while at the same time they realize how their sex, their bodies – specifically their uteruses – determine their roles as wives and mothers. Ferré describes the sexual discrimination characteristic of each artist's period even among liberal ideology groups and male literary contemporaries considered friends. Suicide, chosen by several of these women, is perceived then not as a defeat but as a final attempt to liberate themselves from

social oppression and win supremacy over their bodies and spirits.

Ferré borrows from Kollontai's essay "Winged Eros Besieged" for the title of her book. She agrees with the Russian activist that for a true political revolution to take place it would have to be based on a sexual revolution first. Kollontai's philosophy that a woman should define herself independently of her relation with men permeates all of Ferré's work. Kollontai, however, ended up criticized and ostracized by the Communist party she helped to empower.

The last essay, "De la ira a la ironía, o sobre cómo atemperar el acero candente del discurso" (From Ire to Irony, or How to Temper the Hot Steel of Discourse), is a short response to Woolf's claim that anger has no place in women's literature. Ferré argues that irony is the technique of disguising anger so that it can be turned into more effective discourse. This wrath tempered by irony allows Ferré's stories to deal with themes previously considered taboo.

*Maldito amor* (Cursed Love, 1986; translated as *Sweet Diamond Dust,* 1988) is a short novel composed of four stories in which women, oppressed by both the old sugarcane feudal system and the new industrial society, finally direct their anger at usurping the absurd reality that men insistently uphold. Each story takes place during an important period of Puerto Rican history: the first story occurs at the turn of the century, the second around the 1950s, the third around the end of the 1960s, and the last story in an unidentified near future. Ferré parodies novels about the land, a popular genre during the first half of the century, as she sets out to rewrite Puerto Rican history from a woman's perspective. She describes how the island (*isla* is a female noun in Spanish) is oppressed by the government and American businesses – both of which are rendered as masculine in Spanish – while drawing parallels to the situation of women.

The story "Maldito amor" is a play of perspectives and voices in which the authority of the narrator is finally disarmed by the intruding voices of female characters. Don Hermenegildo Martínez sets out to write the history of the mythical town of Guamaní and its hero, Ubaldino de la Valle. The story about how de la Valle saved a dying sugarcane plantation and defied American corporations is interrupted again and again by female characters such as Titina, the family maid; Doña Laura, the dying widow; and Gloria, nurse and mistress of the hero. By introducing conflicting accounts of the family history, the authority of the male narrator is called into question, and the heroism of Don Ubaldino is ultimately deflated. History then is no longer an objective truth but a limited and biased version that promotes a given ideology.

Aside from the obvious oppression of the land and of women, Ferré also delves into other themes, such as homosexuality, racial discrimination, the clash between criollos and North Americans, and the hypocrisy of the Catholic church. "El regalo" (The Gift), the second story, ends with the nuns' beating of a mulatto girl who defies their teachings of decency and propriety.

In the 1980s Ferré moved to the United States to complete her doctorate at the University of Maryland, writing her dissertation on the short stories of Julio Cortázar and their association with the Romantics. She taught for five years at Georgetown University in Washington, D.C., and lectured at other universities throughout the country. In 1990 Ferré decided to move back to the island in order to return to her roots. At present she resides in Puerto Rico with her husband, Mexican novelist Jorge Aguilar Mora.

*Las dos Venecias* (The Two Venices, 1992) is a compact, intimate collection of autobiographical essays and poems centered around the figure of her deceased mother and the city of Venice, where they each went on their honeymoons. Venice becomes Ponce, Puerto Rico, and Washington, D.C., a macrocosm of the female body with all its "canals" and mysteries. Here Ferré expands her themes to other social concerns, such as homelessness and Vietnam War veterans. She also introduces poems written originally in English.

A discussion of Ferré's work and her contribution to contemporary Latin-American fiction would be incomplete without reference to her collections of children's stories. These narratives are not literature for children, but rather stories written for adults from a child's point of view. Ferré's three collections of children's stories – *El medio pollito* (The Half Chicken, 1976), *Los cuentos de Juan Bobo* (The Tales of Juan Bobo, 1980), and *La mona que le pisaron la cola* (The Monkey Whose Tail Got Stepped On, 1981) – are consistent with the themes of her feminist trilogy. She uses allegory, personification of animals and objects, and animalization to depict the corruption of institutions and the breakdown of the social order.

Both "El medio pollito" and "El sombrero mágico" (The Magic Hat) ridicule and criticize the greed and absurdity of those in power. In the first story half a chicken, born out of half an egg given to a poor boy, finds a gold nugget. In order to help the generous boy who spared its life, the chicken decides to give the gold to the king in exchange for beans, rice, and flour. The king apparently accepts and asks the pitiful animal to come back the next day for the food. The next day, though, the king refuses to pay, and the half chicken opens its half beak to let the waters of a river it swallowed earlier flood the court. The stubborn king refuses to pay, and so he drowns. When the water goes back to the riverbank, the child and the half chicken give away all the wealth from the palace to the poor. The king is portrayed not only as stubborn but also as greedy, insensitive, and foolish. The child and the half chicken, on the other hand, represent the values of generosity, caring, and, in spite of their poor origins, ingenuity.

The whimsical and absurd nature of kings is once again seen in the last story of the collection. Ferré also uses fantastic elements in "El sombrero mágico" to tell the story of Pedro, a poor farmer boy who learns a lesson about the meaning of power. Before leaving his home, his mother gives him a straw hat and tells him to keep his head covered unless it is a matter of life and death. Pedro arrives in town at the moment when they are crowning the new king. The king furiously yells at Pedro to obey the royal mandate that all people remove their hats in the presence of the king. Pedro refuses, since he fails to understand the connection. When condemned to die, Pedro tries to take his hat off, but different hats keep growing out of his head. Just as he is climbing the scaffold, he feels a crown on his head and hears the king, on his knees, screaming and begging to give him back his crown. The people realize how stupid they have been for obeying the irrational mandates of a man who placed his source of power on outward appearances.

In "Arroz con Leche" (Rice Pudding), one of the most accomplished stories of this collection, Ferré borrows a children's rhyme of the same title and rewrites the story of a girl who rebels against the fate of marriage imposed on her by society. Arroz con Leche is a blond, refined young boy who wants to marry someone who, as the song says, "knows how to knit, to embroider, and can put a needle in its place." He searches for the perfect bride until finally he meets an intelligent girl who is not impressed by his wealth. He decides to marry her but realizes that he will never be able to manipulate her. Deciding to kill her on their wedding night, Arroz con Leche is found the next morning with a knitting needle stuck in his heart.

Allegory is a distinctive trait in Ferré's short stories, especially the ones about Juan Bobo, the is-

*Ferré with her father, Luis A. Ferré, circa 1992*

land bumpkin. *Los cuentos de Juan Bobo* subtly parodies the social, political, educational, and religious institutions of Puerto Rico. The stories are organized as a bildungsroman in which we see various attempts to educate Juan Bobo and the funny and sometimes disastrous consequences of such efforts. The first story, "Juan Bobo y las señoritas del manto prieto" (Juan Bobo and the Ladies of the Black Cloak), sets the tone for the rest. Juan Bobo's mother, following the advice of her neighbors, borrows some syrup from a sugar-mill worker and sends Juan Bobo to sell the syrup in town. Followed by some flies, Juan Bobo gets tired and goes back home, telling his mother that the Ladies of the Black Cloak took all the syrup from him. Assuming that he is referring to nuns, the mother sends him back to collect his money. Juan Bobo goes back to town and starts insulting the ladies for not paying, and he is arrested. The judge, realizing Juan Bobo's confusion, tells him to slap the ladies/flies the next time he sees them. Right then a fly lands on the judge's nose, and Juan Bobo punches him. Although a simple, entertaining story, the political implications are far-reaching. Many critics see the innocent and trusting Juan Bobo as the island abused by different groups, including the sugarcane industry, the church, and the judicial system.

Ferré shows how, with simplicity and country wisdom, the simpleminded can get ahead. Such is the result in the last story of this collection, "Juan

Bobo va a la capital" (Juan Bobo Goes to the Capital). Here Juan Bobo decides to try his fortune by going to the capital city, where he matches his wits against Don Mundo (Mr. World), a political leader running for governor. He convinces the corrupt old man that underneath his hat he has a bird that can anticipate the results of the elections. Don Mundo offers to buy the bird for one hundred dollars and holds the hat tightly while Juan Bobo supposedly goes to get a cage for the bird. After a few hours Don Mundo, suspecting the deception, lifts the hat only to find bird droppings in it. Pleased by the embarrassment caused to his archrival, the governor offers Juan Bobo his daughter in marriage. Such an alliance does not amount to anything because the king of Spain is about to name a new governor. Ferré poignantly reminds us here how the destiny of the island is in foreign hands.

In her last collection of children's short stories, *La mona que le pisaron la cola,* Ferré moves away from political criticism to adopt a definite feminist stance. "Pico Rico Mandorico," for example, depicts the sexual liberation of its female protagonists. Alicia and Elisa, two orphan sisters whose names are confused throughout the story, witness how the landowner poisons the people in town so they cannot sleep and wish only to work. Finally, one of the sisters falls for the landowner and is poisoned by the fruits he sells. Deciding to take revenge, the other sister cuts the nose off the gentleman in the middle of the night with her sewing scissors. The town is freed from the enchantment, and the land-owner can no longer sell his poisonous fruits be-cause now he can be easily identified. Sexual symbolism is developed throughout the stories of *La mona que le pisaron la cola.* Also predominant in the collection are children's rhymes that Ferré effectively incorporates while subverting their traditional meanings.

Ferré has also translated her own work. In her essay "Ofelia a la deriva en las aguas de la memoria" (Ophelia Adrift in the Waters of Memory; translated as "On Destiny, Language, and Translation; or, Ophelia Adrift in the C. & O. Canal" in *The Youngest Doll,* 1991) the Puerto Rican writer explains how she considers writing a form of translation, "a struggle to interpret the meaning of life, and in this sense the translator can be said to be a shaman, a person dedicated to deciphering conflicting human texts, searching for the final unity of meaning in speech." Ferré believes that her situation is unique because as a Puerto Rican writer she has grown up between two languages and two cultures. By insisting that a writer needs to break the boundaries of her own language and cultural reality, she thus advocates solidarity not only among women but among Latin-American nations.

Rosario Ferré has established herself as a writer setting the path for generations to come. Within each successive work she explores new themes, many of them traditionally taboo. While composing a new identity for herself, Ferré has re-written the history and identity of Puerto Rico.

## Interviews:

Andrew Bush, "'Señalar las discrepancias': Rosario Ferré y Antonio Skármeta hablan de Cortázar," *Revista de Estudios Hispánicos,* 21 (May 1987): 73–87;

Miguel Angel Zapata, "Rosario Ferré: La poesía de narrar," *Inti,* 26–27 (Fall-Spring 1987–1988): 133–140;

Magdalena García Pinto, *Historias íntimas* (Hanover, N.H.: Del Norte, 1988), pp. 67–96.

## References:

María I. Acosta Cruz, "Historia, ser e identidad femenina en 'El collar de camándulas' y 'Maldito amor' de Rosario Ferré," *Chasqui,* 19 (November 1990): 23–31;

Aida Apter Cragnolino, "El cuento de hadas y la 'bildungsroman': Modelo y subversión en 'La

Bella Durmiente,'" *Chasqui,* 20 (November 1991): 3–9;

Elsa R. Arroyo, "Contracultura y parodia en cuatro cuentos de Rosario Ferré y Ana Lydia Vega," *Caribbean Studies,* 22, nos. 3–4 (1989): 33–46;

María José Chaves, "La alegoría como método en los cuentos y ensayos de Rosario Ferré," *Third Woman,* 2, no. 2 (1984): 64–76;

Lisa E. Davis, "La puertorriqueña dócil y rebelde en los cuentos de Rosario Ferré," *Sin Nombre,* 9 (January–March 1979): 82–88;

Juan Escalera Ortiz, "Perspectivas del cuento 'Mercedes Benz 220SL,'" *Revista/Review Interamericana,* 12 (Fall 1982): 407–417;

Margarite Fernández Olmos, "Constructing Heroines: Rosario Ferré's *Cuentos Infantiles* and Feminine Instruments of Change," *The Lion and the Unicorn,* 10 (1986): 83–94;

Fernández Olmos, "Desde una perspectiva femenina: La cuentística de Rosario Ferré y Ana Lydia Vega," *Homines,* 10 (August 1986–February 1987): 330–338;

Fernández Olmos, "Luis Rafael Sánchez and Rosario Ferré: Sexual Politics and Contemporary Puerto Rican Narrative," *Hispania,* 70 (March 1987): 40–46;

Lucía Guerra-Cunningham, "Tensiones paradójicas de la feminidad en la narrativa de Rosario Ferré," *Chasqui,* 13 (February–May 1984): 13–25;

María-Inés Lagos-Pope, "Sumisión y rebeldía: El doble o la representación de la alienación femenina en narraciones de Marta Brunet y Rosario Ferré," *Revista Iberoamericana,* 51 (July–December 1985): 731–749;

Yvette López, "'La muñeca menor': Ceremonias y transformaciones en un cuento de Rosario Ferré," *Explicación de Textos Literarios,* 11, no. 1 (1982–1983): 49–58;

Luz María Umpierre, "De la protesta a la creación – Una nueva visión de la mujer puertorriqueña en la poesía," *Imagine,* 2 (Summer 1985): 134–142;

Umpierre, "Un manifiesto literario: *Papeles de Pandora* de Rosario Ferré," *The Bilingual Review/ La Revista Bilingüe,* 9 (May–August 1982): 120–126;

Carmen Vega Carney, "El amor como discurso político en Ana Lydia Vega y Rosario Ferré," *Letras Femeninas,* 17 (Spring-Fall 1991): 77–87;

Vega Carney, "Sexo y texto en Rosario Ferré," *Confluencia,* 4 (Fall 1988): 119–127.

# Elena Garro
*(11 December 1920 –   )*

Adriana Méndez Rodenas
*University of Iowa*

BOOKS: *Un hogar sólido, y otras piezas en un acto* (Jalapa, Mexico: Universidad Veracruzana, 1958);

*Los recuerdos del porvenir* (Mexico City: Joaquín Mortiz, 1963); translated by Ruth L. C. Simms as *Recollections of Things to Come* (Austin: University of Texas Press, 1969);

*La semana de colores* (Jalapa, Mexico: Universidad Veracruzana, 1964);

*El árbol* (Mexico City: Rafael Peregrina, 1967); translated by Evelyn Picón Garfield as "The Tree," in *Women's Fiction from Latin America,* edited by Garfield (Detroit: Wayne State University Press, 1988), pp. 70–86;

*Felipe Ángeles* (Mexico City: Difusión Cultural/UNAM, 1979);

*Andamos huyendo Lola* (Mexico City: Joaquín Mortiz, 1980);

*Testimonios sobre Mariana* (Mexico City: Grijalbo, 1981);

*Reencuentro de personajes* (Mexico City: Grijalbo, 1982);

*La casa junto al río* (Barcelona: Grijalbo, 1983);

*Y Matarazo no llamó . . .* (Mexico City: Grijalbo, 1989);

*Memorias de España* (Mexico City: Siglo Veintiuno, 1992).

OTHER: "Los perros," in *Doce obras en un acto,* edited by Wilberto Cantón (Mexico City: Ecuador, 1967); translated by Beth Miller as "The Dogs," *Latin American Literary Review,* 8 (Fall-Winter 1979): 68–85;

"La señora en su balcón," in *Teatro breve hispanoamericano contemporáneo,* edited by Carlos Solórzano (Madrid: Aguilar, 1969), pp. 347–358; translated by Miller as "The Lady on Her Balcony," *Shantih,* 3 (Fall-Winter 1976): 36–44;

"Perfecto Luna," in *Puerta abierta: La nueva escritora latinoamericana,* edited by Caridad L. Silva-

*Elena Garro*

Velázquez and Nora Erro-Orthman (Mexico City: Joaquín Mortiz, 1986), pp. 131–139.

SELECTED PERIODICAL PUBLICATIONS – UNCOLLECTED: "La dama boba," *Revista de la Escuela de Arte Teatral,* 6 (1963): 77–126;

"A mi me ha ocurrido todo al revés," *Cuadernos Hispanoamericanos,* 246 (April 1979): 38–51.

Elena Garro is one of the most innovative contemporary writers in Mexico. Garro developed her literary career in Europe, yet her works always

138

evoke the elusive and mysterious, qualities crucial to the mask that according to Octavio Paz comprises a Mexican identity. Garro's writings can be divided into two periods. The first is characterized by the search for the marvelous, the poetic treatment of time, and inquiry into the female imagination. In the second phase her works evince the psychological disintegration and societal breakup of the contemporary world. Though many of Garro's later works may have been conceived much earlier, there is undoubtedly a connection between an early Mexican period and a later postmodern style that seems to emerge from the author's exile in Europe.

Since the facts of Garro's biography are scarce, critics are left to speculate as to the correspondences between her creative work and her personal life. Born on 11 December 1920 in Puebla, Garro spent her youth in Mexico. She studied at the National Autonomous University of Mexico City and was active in Julio Bracho's theater group as both choreographer and actress. Her love of drama led Garro to her first career as a playwright and influenced her later development as a fiction writer.

In 1937 Garro married Mexican poet Octavio Paz, with whom she had a daughter, Helena Paz. The marriage was not only unsuccessful but had other unfortunate consequences as well. Garro claims that Paz blocked the aspiring actress's way to the stage, perhaps because of professional rivalry; according to Juan García Ponce, the couple wrote for the Poesía en Voz Alta theater group, the first of its kind in Mexico. This obstacle only intensified Garro's desire to write drama, for she later explained how her yearning for the lost paradise of the theater influenced her decision to recover that world by writing plays.

During her youth Garro was actively involved in the defense of Indian land rights and engaged in political journalism that denounced the marginal and impoverished condition to which Indians have been relegated in Mexico. As a result of her political activities during the turbulent year of 1968, the year of the Massacre of Tlatelolco under the presidency of Díaz Ordaz, Garro was driven out of Mexico for reasons that still remain obscure. In a brief, tragicomic personal portrait titled "A mi me ha ocurrido todo al revés" (Everything Has Always Happened to Me Backwards, April 1979) Garro bitterly complains of unjust accusations of political subversion. For example, she encountered difficulties in obtaining a Mexican passport when she tried to leave Mexico due to her daughter's health and hints that Paz's influence may have accounted for the many

bureaucratic tangles. After a trip to New York related to her journalistic activities, Garro has spent the last period of her life in exile, first in Madrid, where she fled in 1974, and then in France, where she resided until 1993.

Both in theater and fiction, Garro's constant theme is the contrast between imagination and reality, often depicted as a conflict between two types of characters who represent opposing worldviews: adult and child, male and female, white and Indian. If one represents the limited perspective of reason, logic, and strictly ordered chronology, the second allows access into a fantasy world unbound by time and created by the sheer force of the imagination. In *El árbol* (1967; translated as "The Tree," 1988) Garro depicts the imagination as a reservoir of hidden treasures. Garro privileges theater as the place that opens up the imaginary realm, so that in effect theater and fiction become inextricably linked. This is why in her later works theatrical representations play such an important role and, inversely, why her early drama highlights the celestial, otherworldly sphere of fiction over and above the dull appearance of everyday reality.

Garro's yearning for the transcendent is best dramatized in the dissonance between female and male views of the world. Woman's defense of the imaginary against man's prosaic, colorless world of production lines, rigid chronology, and purposeful activity is a life-and-death struggle to preserve her inner nature. In the play *Andarse por las ramas* (Beating around the Bush) included in the collection *Un hogar sólido, y otras piezas en un acto* (A Solid Home and Other Pieces in One Act, 1958), Garro comically depicts the husband as "Don Fernando de las Siete y Cinco" (7:05 Don Fernando), given his desire to be served dinner at that precise time. Don Fernando accuses his imaginative wife, Titina, of contaminating the order of the home with fantasy and madness since for him, as for most of the male characters in Garro's literary world, women live in another dimension: the lunar dimension, the unconscious zone of desire and active imagination. Titina rebels against her husband and finds refuge in the treetops, literally enacting the idiomatic title of the play. In contrast, the tyrannical Don Fernando represents the metaphorical meaning of the title *Andarse por las ramas,* a colloquial expression whose English equivalent is "to beat around the bush." Hence the conflict between the dominant male view of the world and the elusive and repressed female values arises in part from the difference in how men and women use language. When Titina attempts to escape with the enticing Lagartito, to her dismay she finds that despite his alluring appearance, he is as prosaic as her husband, and so she stays up in the tree in order to be at least physically closer to the ethereal region in her heart. In Garro's fictional world the tree is a symbol of an inner connectedness to nature, the root of life and woman's only source of support.

This positive vision is reversed, however, in Garro's dramatic version of *El árbol,* which depicts the conflict between the Indian and the white in Mexican society through the confrontation between two women, the rich Marta from Mexico City and a disheveled, unkempt Indian woman named Luisa. Whereas Luisa represents malevolent forces, Marta stands at the opposite end of the ethical spectrum, signifying both virtue and the emptiness of modern urban life. A psychological struggle gradually unfolds between the two characters as Marta becomes increasingly vulnerable to Luisa's infernal game of mastery over her class rival. The climax is reached when Luisa reveals a well-hidden secret from her turbulent past, the chilling tale of how she matter-of-factly murdered a woman in the marketplace. Years after her release, Luisa unburdens her guilt to a tree. She recalls that she threw her sins on top of it and it dried up, implying that perhaps her interlocutor will suffer the same fate. In a paroxysm of fear Marta calls out to Luisa, preferring the strange presence of the Indian over the vortex of her own aloneness. Later in the play the servant returns to find her mistress cruelly slaughtered. The short-story version included in *La semana de colores* (The Week of Colors, 1964) ends on a bitter note as Luisa, who thought her crime would guarantee a return to her "prison-paradise," the only place where she had experienced any kind of real camaraderie and comfort, discovers that the world she so nostalgically imagined no longer exists. In one of the few realistic treatments of time in Garro's fiction, Luisa sadly acknowledges that Martita was right: the past is never to be recovered.

Luisa's disillusionment and the inability to return to the past aptly illustrate the logic behind Garro's critique of time, by far the most insistent of her themes. Both *La semana de colores* and her first novel, *Los recuerdos del porvenir* (1963; translated as *Recollections of Things to Come,* 1969), properly form part of the Latin-American school of magic realism. Although Garro is regarded as a pioneer of this movement, so far there is no systematic study of the considerable debt that major Latin-American novelists owe to Garro. To begin with, her early theater pieces anticipate the blending of realistic and fictitious events in magic realism and fantastic literature. One example is the title play of *Un hogar sólido,*

which takes place inside a family crypt where the characters pass the time awaiting the visit of the next deceased relative. The "solid home" is a metaphor for both heaven and the underworld. Newly arrived at the crypt, Lidia wishes for something like the house they had as children. But since life brought her only the emptiness of a loveless marriage, Lidia is granted her last wish only after death: to come home to her own burial crypt. Garro's characters find their ultimate realization inside the cemetery walls.

Garro's theater and early fiction juxtapose mythic and chronological time, as does Gabriel García Márquez's *Cien años de soledad* (1967; translated as *One Hundred Years of Solitude,* 1970). Whereas the magic of García Márquez's novel resides in the construction of simultaneous time lines (the story of the Buendía family and the repetitious, circular time of Melquíades's storytelling), Garro's narrative magic upsets conventional time frames. Poetic reverie or "women's time" has to subvert the strict linear logic imposed by man in order to assure his dominion over nature.

Like women, children too reject the linear chronology imposed by patriarchy and defend an alternative time in which days can be combined in varied series and in which every moment is endowed with strange new possibilities. The sisters Eva and Leli in the story "La semana de colores" reshuffle the conventional unit of the week to fit their own magical beliefs. Instead of a succession of seven-day weeks, the girls believe that Monday could suddenly be turned into a Friday and Friday arbitrarily jump forward to Tuesday. Here the analogy to language is made clear. Like the multilayered time of childhood, dreams, and erotic reverie, words – and the poetic use of words – can evoke the magic kingdom lying behind our drab, too-familiar surroundings.

Eva and Leli discover in Don Flor's house on the hill his mysterious commerce with the Days of the Week. Each Day is a woman with a distinct erotic tendency who is kept, like a caged animal, in a locked room until Don Flor chooses to "occupy" one of them – a Mexican euphemism for sexual intercourse. Projecting onto the women his own perverse fantasies, Don Flor accuses the women/Days of every imaginable form of sadism and lust, vices disguised, however, as Christian virtues.

Don Flor's alternative calendar suggests the power of libido acting behind the facade of liturgical time, which is associated with the patriarchy. The girls' father explains that the days are white and that the only week is a Holy Week. Then one day

*Cover for Garro's 1982 novel, in which the protagonist sees herself as a character in F. Scott Fitzgerald's novel* The Great Gatsby *(1925)*

the entire Week escapes to the Feria de Teloloapan, a popular village feast marking the death of the black magician Don Flor. In contrast to the benevolent father figure, Don Flor represents the patriarchal control of time as a means to dominate feminine passion and erotic desire. Like the servant's testimony at the end of *El árbol,* here casual witnesses, the muleteers passing by, discover the dead Don Flor. The story ends with the suggestion that it was the women who killed him, finally avenging themselves on their sadistic master and causing the Week to vanish as if by magic. Thus, only the innocence of childhood, women's marginal status, or the Indian's connection to origins can recapture for us that "time without time" that according to Esther Seligson suspends everyday temporal categories and pushes ordinary reality to its outer limits.

Garro attacks historical time, the convention of time conceived by man to understand his own ex-

perience, and substitutes it with the atemporal structure of myth. "La culpa es de los tlaxcaltecas" (translated as "It's the Fault of the Tlaxcaltecas" in *Other Fires: Short Fiction by Latin American Women* [1986] edited by Alberto Manguel), the opening story in *La semana de colores,* remains one of Garro's better-known and most successful works. The story represents a retelling of Mexican history from a woman's perspective, a new *reverso de la conquista* (other side of the conquest) analogous to Miguel León-Portilla's well-known collection of Aztec poetry from the pre-Hispanic period. Carlos Fuentes's *tiempo mexicano* (Mexican time) is personified in Laura's ability to shift back and forth as an inhabitant of the famed Aztec capital Tenochtitlán and then as an upper-class woman from its modern version, Mexico City. Unhappy in her marriage to a government bureaucrat named Pablo, Laura escapes into the legendary past for periodic rendezvous with an enigmatic Indian warrior whom she honors as her cousin-husband. In this way Garro suggests a spiritual and historical kinship between the Creole descendants of the Spaniards and the original pre-Hispanic peoples that prevails over and beyond class and racial differences. The split in time thus corresponds to a strange spatial juxtaposition in which the "café Tacuba" in the heart of Mexico City is magically transformed into the "Calzada de Tacuba," precisely the place where the Spaniards built a fortification from which they directed their final attack against Tenochtitlán.

Garro's story reverses the traditional interpretation of the conquest as a result of two acts of betrayal, those of la Malinche, who acted as Hernán Cortés's mistress and translator, and the Tlaxcala Indians, who collaborated with the Spaniards in revenge for their age-old feud against the Aztecs. Instead, in "La culpa es de los tlaxcaltecas" the white woman systematically betrays her Indian lover, thus rendering ironic the title's pointed allusion to the Tlaxcaltecas' high treason. At another level, Laura's actions signify that the true fault lies in the Spaniards' rape of the Indian women and their destruction of pre-Columbian civilization. If, as Paz claims in his *El laberinto de la soledad* (1950; translated as *The Labyrinth of Solitude,* 1961), the Mexicans have never forgotten their fate as "sons of la Malinche" and have refused to forgive women's weakness for opening up to the conquistador, Garro shows instead the Indian's willingness to forgive the harm inflicted on him. When the mythic time of the defeat of Tenochtitlán draws to a close, Laura escapes with her phantom lover to the end of time, much like Titina's flight to the treetops in "Andarse por las ramas." In this way "La culpa es de los tlaxcaltecas" undermines not only a sense of historical progression and continuity but also implies woman's psychic liberation from the confines of the male view of the world.

From a psychological perspective Garro's theater and fiction portray psychological dichotomy between the real and the imaginary as a struggle between the male and female components of the human psyche. The plays in *Un hogar sólido* and the short stories in *La semana de colores* read as dramatic reenactments of the tensions between the conscious and unconscious sides of the personality. This is especially seen in the play *El Encanto, tendajón mixto* (Enchantment, Dry Goods Store, 1958), which reaffirms Garro's views of woman as the source of charm and magic. Three tired muleteers stop to rest after a long journey at a point eight leagues from their hometown. The men – Anselmo, Juventino,

and Ramiro – stand at the crossroads between their conscious and unconscious life, at the *camino real* (high road) where they confront ancestral man's repressed wish for complete union with the other and the abolition of solitude. In their night journey the men meet a woman with beautiful black hair, a phantasmagoric presence that induces them to enter her store of imaginary delights. A mysterious woman of water appears as the archetypal feminine, or man's eternal companion or helpmate. She seduces the men with a cup of sweet wine, but only young Anselmo is swayed by her charms, fearlessly entering the enchanted tent against the warnings of his older companions. The woman encourages Anselmo to drink, initiating him into mysteries associated with "the second sex." As soon as he takes the cup Anselmo disappears from view, rushed away forever along with the dark-haired enchantress and her heavenly store. The poetic juxtaposition of time frames typical of Garro's mature fiction surfaces at the end of the play when the men return to the magic spot one year later in an attempt to rescue Anselmo from the sorceress's spell. Once more the store appears on the scene, but time has been detained as if by magic. Whereas the men remain fixed within the confines of chronological time and male gender, Anselmo has embraced his *ánima,* or feminine side, in the prehistoric time of man's mythic origin. There woman reigns supreme and man can only grope in an unknown world where he has lost his ordinary bearings. Lacking words with which to express his newfound garden of sensory delights, Anselmo chooses to remain in the imaginary sphere rather than reenter the daily monotony to which his friends beckon him. Every third of May the same ritual is repeated, as if to show the simultaneity of two separate times, the present moment that marches with the rigorous chronology of the clock and the luminous past that belongs to all but from which we are cut off at birth.

Hence women's time would necessarily consist of the alteration of time frames in which a single instant can encompass all of time. The story "¿Qué hora es . . . ?" (What Time Is It . . . ?) depicts woman's circular destiny, trapped as she is in a tragic fate designed by man, a theme of Garro's pessimistic later fiction. Like "La culpa es de los tlaxcaltecas," it repeats the innovative counterpoint between a feminine or imaginary time, filled with desire and erotic fantasy, and a masculine or symbolic time of historical action and absolute power, anticipating the conflict of her first novel, *Los recuerdos del porvenir.* "¿Qué hora es . . . ?" starts with the mysterious arrival of a South American traveler,

Lucía Mitre, at a luxurious Parisian hotel. She takes a room in order to meet her Mexican lover, Gabriel Cortina, who is supposed to arrive that night on the 9:47 flight from London. Enveloped in a soft peach scarf, Lucía lives suspended in an atemporal dimension where the only meaningful moment is the longed-for embrace of her phantom lover. Unaware of ordinary reality, Lucía has no money to pay for her hotel room and lets the hotelkeeper, Brunier, periodically take one of her jewels in exchange for her board. Like her double Clara in "La Señora en su balcón" (1969; translated as "The Woman on Her Balcony," 1976), she longs to escape from the prison of the real world by a symbiotic fusion with the beloved. Hence her insistent question "¿Qué hora es?" floats in space through a timeless void. Time for her is an endless vacuum marked only by the minute that never comes and a lover who remains absent.

Lucía's time turns into an eternity of rock, Garro's metaphor for a monumental Kronos, the god of time, that destines women's time to the heaviness of unfulfilled desire, inactivity, and waiting. This contrasts with the memory of another time, the pristine time of childhood, an absolute present that flows without the arbitrary ticking of the clock. For eleven months Lucía waits, at first patiently, then desperately, for Cortina's arrival, and she finally dies in strict compliance with an obscure fate at the precise moment when her lover was meant to arrive, exactly at 9:47. When Brunier announces this ominous fact to Gilbert, the hotel owner, an athletic, handsome young man walks in with a preoccupied air and asks for room 410, where Lucía now lies dead. Carelessly bouncing a tennis racket, the young man goes up to the room before the amazed stares of the innkeepers, who realize that the young man's appearance must have been a hallucination and that Lucía's accumulated longing had finally brought him back from the high sierras of Mexico. The narrative magic is wrought when, upon opening Lucía's room to proceed with her burial, they find the tennis racket left behind by the ephemeral Cortina either as proof of his presence or as a trace of his absence. Like her double Isabel Moncada in *Los recuerdos del porvenir,* Lucía also disappears, yet she goes into a *nada* (nothingness) that erases the contours of a woman's face so that she cannot fathom her own image in the mirror.

Garro's first novel is an attempt to recover memory – the lost memory of women caught within the confines of a patriarchal order but also a historical memory that critically surveys the Mexican revolution. In a manner reminiscent of Jorge Luis

Borges's "El Aleph" (1949), memory is represented as a mirror or prism in which all times converge toward a single infinite point. This is the moment when Ixtepec, a small town in southern Mexico, begins to tell the story of its tragic fate under the military occupation of Gen. Francisco Rosas. Set during the Cristero Rebellion in Mexico (1926–1929), a civil war sparked by Plutarco Elías Calles's campaign of violence against the Catholic church, the novel plays with the genre of the historical novel by the presence of a collective narrator, the town of Ixtepec, which according to Robert K. Anderson means "a hill made out of obsidian" in the Aztec language Nahuatl. Just as the Aztec soothsayers used obsidian mirrors as a means of divination, Garro's Ixtepec meditates on its place in history and projects its past onto the future. Ixtepec's recollections order the cycles of time in a manner similar to the Aztecs' foretelling stone, emphasizing Garro's poetic analogy of memory as a mirror.

Written in Switzerland during Garro's long illness around 1950, *Los recuerdos del porvenir* was not published until 1963, when it won the prestigious Xavier Villaurrutia Prize in Mexico. Though Ixtepec's variegated reflections provide a historical critique of the Mexican revolution, at another level the mirror image serves as an organizing principle for fiction itself. *Los recuerdos del porvenir* is divided into two parts, each dominated by the image of a woman: the mysterious Julia Andrade in the first part and her double, Isabel Moncada, in the second. As lovers of Gen. Francisco Rosas, the two women mirror each other inversely: if Julia is the center around which the town revolves and comes to Ixtepec as a stranger, she is soon replaced by Isabel Moncada, the town's "decent" daughter, who fills the other's absence when, dressed in red, she enters the Hotel Jardín at the general's beck and call. Such a tragic repetition of fates indicates once again Garro's belief that women's destinies are out of their control, like a series of mirror images endlessly repeated.

The elusive Julia appears to have escaped this fate, since at the end of the first part of *Los recuerdos del porvenir* she manages to defy the general's strict vigilance and rides away in the night with the outsider Felipe Hurtado, who has come to rescue her. In a scene reminiscent of the magical erasure of time in *El Encanto, tendajón mixto,* time has apparently been detained to allow for the lovers' escape. The novel ends, however, with the metaphor of its own temporality, the rock on which Ixtepec sits to tell its story. In the second part of the novel the townspeople wage a lost battle against Rosas and his troops.

*Garro in 1986*

Even though Rosas is responsible for the deaths of her two brothers, Isabel cannot renounce her love for him and is turned into stone as a punishment for her guilt, literally carving her desire in the epitaph that an old woman inscribes on the rock. As a baroque inscription of death Isabel's petrified body also functions as the emblem of the textual memory that Ixtepec enacts as collective narrator. Like the polished obsidian of the Aztecs, the stone remains as a monument to the town's suffering and as the portent of prophecy and magic.

After *Los recuerdos del porvenir* Garro's postmodernist fiction is characterized by the apparent lack of connection to her native Mexico, a turn marked by the short story collection *Andamos huyendo Lola* (Let's Keep Running, Lola, 1980). The title story, centered on a white Russian woman and her daughter who are hiding in an abandoned New York apartment, captures the image of entrapment, paranoia, and sheer loss of direction shared by all female characters in Garro's later fiction.

The inability to return home, to recapture the past and seek a common source, is dramatized in the fate of the protagonist of the novel *La casa junto al río* (The House by the River, 1983). Young Consuelo, who journeys back to her native Spain hoping to find the solace of origins and the lost link to family and self, is mercilessly victimized and persecuted by a set of hostile relatives. Unlike Laura, the

protagonist of "La culpa es de los tlaxcaltecas" who finds happiness in a legendary past, Consuelo reenters the mythic house by the river at the moment of her death, thus resembling the tragic protagonist of "La Señora en su balcón," who reaches her beloved Nínive only after leaping to suicide.

Nowhere is woman's helplessness more tragically depicted than in *Testimonios sobre Mariana* (Testimonies about Mariana, 1981), Garro's most outstanding novel after *Los recuerdos del porvenir* and an important work of Latin-American post-Boom literature. At one level *Testimonios sobre Mariana* is a rewriting of the *novela de testimonio* (testimonial novel) centered on an individual character who represents a lost link with history, as theorized by Cuban writer Miguel Barnet with regard to his own *Biografía de un cimarrón* (1966; translated as *The Autobiography of a Runaway Slave,* 1968). Rather than representing a collective historical subject as in Elena Poniatowska's *La noche de Tlatelolco* (The Night of Tlatelolco, 1971; translated as *Massacre in Mexico,* 1975), which is based on the testimonies of anonymous witnesses who survived the massacre at Tlatelolco Square in 1968, *Testimonios sobre Mariana* testifies rather to a typical postmodern phenomenon, the loss of the subject, both in a historical and a personal sense. If *La noche de Tlatelolco* registers a historical trauma that left its mark on the collective unconscious of the Mexican people, Garro's *Testimonios sobre Mariana* appears as a direct inversion of Poniatowska's *novela de testimonio* since its protagonist Mariana never appears except as a trace in other people's memory. While Poniatowska erases her authorial presence in *La noche de Tlatelolco* in order to allow the historical witnesses to speak, Garro's absence in *Testimonios sobre Mariana* is a sign of the modern subject's alienation from history.

Garro's *testimonios* consist of three separate tales narrated by characters who verbally reconstruct their relationship to Mariana, an enigmatic woman without a past and without a future much like the mythical Julia Andrade in *Los recuerdos del porvenir*. Since Mariana is a fragmented subject who exists nowhere but in the fictional realm, the reader must piece together the three testimonies into a coherent story, thus endowing Mariana with a history or concrete existence despite its occurring in the imaginary world of narrative. As Kathleen Taylor has shown, the three narrators project themselves onto Mariana as if she were a mirror of their own subjectivity, providing dissonant and even discordant versions of Mariana's life in Paris after World War II. In truth, what the reader is told is not so much the story of Mariana herself but rather the intricate web of her relationships with the three narrators, who suffer either from unfulfilled desire, guilt, or unrequited love for the elusive woman. All of them fail to decipher the mystery of Mariana's existence, and each uniquely contributes to her ultimate destruction and to her disappearance from the text. Tied to her husband, Augusto, aptly named after the Roman emperor of similar wrath, Mariana is unable to break free of that circular destiny allotted women, condemned as they seem to economic dependency, emotional passivity, and a love bond dangerously akin to torture. Her fate seems to be that of a victim held captive by invisible and destructive forces; in effect, as Taylor puts it, "the mystery and irony of her life" is that "she has no control over her own destiny yet she controls the lives of others."

The novel presents the reader with the riddle of Mariana's identity, for she seems to have no identity of her own but rather represents the universal problem of identity. It is significant that Garro chooses a woman to symbolize this dilemma, which is resolved only with the reader's conclusion as to the meaning of Mariana's life. Whether we believe Gabrielle, who has seen her dancing in the Bolshoi Ballet, or André, who hopes for her eventual return, the truth of Mariana's story, if there is any, is that her husband, Augusto, purposely eliminated her, pushing her either to the brink of madness or suicide. *Testimonios sobre Mariana* not only effectively critiques patriarchal dominance but also undermines the validity of the notion of history in the modern age. As modern ideologues, Augusto and his group represent the false consciousness of the Latin-American bourgeois intellectual turned revolutionary, whereas Mariana, a fugitive from the Bolshevik Revolution, remains an outsider and victim to a history ruled by irrational forces. In a world that no longer experiences itself as unified, literature replaces history as the best memory of the past – a memory that paradoxically appears as the need to forget or imagine, thereby escaping the terror of history altogether.

After *Testimonios sobre Mariana,* Garro's fiction seems to follow the course of her own characters, caught as they are in a cycle of repetitions, destructive acts, and flights from reality. Her novel *Reencuentro de personajes* (Reunion of Characters, 1982), for example, takes up the prototypical Garro character of the unexpected traveler of *Testimonios sobre Mariana,* woman as an eternal exile who tries to escape the fate of a doomed yet interminable love affair. Hearkening back to the fragile Lucía Mitre of "¿Qué hora es? . . ." in *La semana de colores,*

Verónica, the protagonist of *Reencuentro de personajes,* goes from one European hotel to another in her intense wish to free herself from the controlling presence of her lover Frank, who is characterized as diabolic. Verónica can only repeat the set of words that bind her to a symbiotic and sadistic relationship. An echo of Mariana, Verónica never manages to escape Frank's psychological hold and gets caught in a cycle of persecutions, mistaken identities, and suspected assassinations from which she emerges as sole historical witness. Although Verónica swears to speak the truth after Frank is dead, thus freeing herself at last from the labyrinth of lies in which he has trapped her, one of the characters in Frank's circle cynically assures her that no one is interested in the truth.

Since the possibility of truth has been canceled, Verónica's life resembles fiction, and like Mariana her status is that of a purely fictional creation. More radical than *Testimonios sobre Mariana* in its undermining of what French literary theorist Roland Barthes has called the effect of the real, *Reencuentro de personajes* testifies to the Borgesian concept that our approaches to reality are no more than fictions. In fact, Verónica sees herself as an actor in F. Scott Fitzgerald's *The Great Gatsby* (1925), much like Borges's character in "Las ruinas circulares" (The Circular Ruins in *Ficciones* [Fictions], 1956), who discovers himself a creature of another god. In this later work Garro's female protagonist reaches the apex of powerlessness and passivity. If in *Testimonios sobre Mariana* the lack of control was due to psychological and social factors influencing the lives of women, in *Reencuentro de personajes* it is due rather to the fictional nature of the world itself, where, like Borges's Library of Babel, nothing can happen other than what has been prescribed by the letter.

The title *Reencuentro de personajes* not only refers to the regathering of Fitzgerald's characters within Garro's novel but also to her need to bring together a cast of characters from her own literary past. In this way Garro exorcises the function of authorship, as if to clear the way to a new stage in her literary work. At another level *Testimonios sobre Mariana* and *Reencuentro de personajes* beg a reading as romans à clef that exorcise Garro's troubled relationship with Octavio Paz.

Garro returned to Mexico for a three-week visit in November 1991 with a bag full of unpublished works. Her return was due to a great extent to the efforts of José María Fernández Unsaín, president of the Mexican Society of Writers, who wanted to bring Garro back to Mexico. During this trip she toured her native city in the company of

Elena Garro

Mexican playwright Héctor Azar and was warmly received by the mayor and other civic and intellectual figures. While in Mexico she was widely acclaimed by the Mexican press and the object of numerous tributes sponsored by the Mexican Institute of Fine Arts in Mexico City and the provinces. This public recognition culminated in a round-table discussion of Garro's work held in the Palacio de Bellas Artes (Palace of Fine Arts) on 28 November 1991. At this event younger women writers hailed Garro's work, and one of them, Carmen Boullosa, declared that Garro had been a constant inspiration to their generation of writers. Perhaps the most compelling tribute was the performance of her plays by the Teatro Campesino e Indígena (Indigenous and Rural Theater) of Oxolotán, Tabasco, which restored to Garro both her early interest in drama and the subversive thrust of her theater because the plays chosen dealt with agrarian conflicts and the fate of the Indians of Mexico. Garro left Mexico having earned the title of national writer long denied her by the years of oblivion spent in her self-proclaimed exile. In 1993 Garro returned to live in Cuernavaca, Mexico.

Her last stage is marked by two books: a novel, *Y Matarazo no llamó . . .* (And Matarazo Never Called Back . . . , 1989), and the autobiographical *Memorias de España* (Memoirs of Spain, 1992). Though originally written in 1960, *Y Matarazo no llamó . . .* was not published until the late 1980s, probably because of its provocative treatment of Mexico's highly charged political climate, as it anticipates the massacre of Tlatelolco and the cruel repression of the student movement in 1968 under President Díaz Ordaz. *Y Matarazo no llamó . . .* centers on the Kafkaesque experience of a divorced middle-aged man, Eugenio Yáñez, who becomes involved almost inadvertently with a workers' strike in Mexico City. The lonely Eugenio decides to assist the strikers by offering them some cigarettes as he casually strolls by in front of the station, thus entangling himself in a political plot beyond his control. First he assists two of the strikers, Pedro and Tito, a pair of idealistic youths accompanied by Ignacio and Eulalio, two other agitators depicted in the novel as seasoned revolutionaries. After the police break up the strike Pedro and Tito seek refuge in Yáñez's house, bringing with them a badly wounded companion and the mysterious Matarazo. While Tito and Pedro manage to escape the authorities by traveling clandestinely to Zacatecas in the north of Mexico, Yáñez is left alone in the house to care for the wounded man. A plot unfolds in which poor Yáñez comes to depend on Matarazo's nightly

visits and calls in order to cope with his heavy burden, the man agonizing on his bed. One night Matarazo does not call, and Yáñez panics when he sees plainclothes policemen march slowly toward his apartment. Fleeing to the north like Pedro and Tito before him, Yáñez finally confesses to a priest in Torreón, who tries to save him by driving him to nearby Durango. However, they are intercepted by the police, who torture Yáñez and take him prisoner. In a dark cell in Mexico City he meets none other than Matarazo, who turns out to be another innocent victim of a cruel political plot. While the government accuses the pair of political assassination, the sinister Eulalio dogmatically charges them with infiltrating the student movement. It is obvious that Eulalio and Ignacio had set up a trap for the innocent, well-meaning Yáñez and his silent friend Matarazo, most probably to save themselves. Garro's chilling tale leaves no doubt that a shadow of terror and treason creeps behind Mexico's modern facade.

The same questioning of political motives surfaces in Garro's most recent book, *Memorias de España,* a humorous autobiographical account of her experiences in Spain during the Spanish Civil War. Garro accompanied Octavio Paz to the Congress of Anti-Fascist Intellectuals held in Valencia in 1939. Garro's ironic style and air of assumed naiveté mocks the high seriousness of Latin-American leftist intellectuals committed to the Republican cause. She gives a corrosive view of the internal divisions within the Communist movement, noting particularly the effect of the Stalinist purges on the Latin-American Left. Though Paz apparently denied her any access to the hidden world of politics, she soon realized that to be a Communist was dramatic and dangerous. Playing on Paz's and the Mexican delegation's sexism, Garro presents herself as a naive female spectator of the epic male scenario of war. Garro debunks the prevailing discourse of the Left, including the shibboleth of the Soviet Union, presented ironically as the great mystery for the initiates of the new religion. Despite her mocking tone, she effectively describes the effect of the Spanish Civil War as an enormous tragedy. *Memorias de España* chronicles as well the European sojourn of major Latin-American writers such as Alejo Carpentier, Nicolas Guillén, and César Vallejo, along with dramatic views of the fate of Spanish intellectuals such as León Felipe, Antonio Machado, and Miguel Hernández. Lastly, the book documents the contradictions of Mexican politics; Mexico's ambassador in Spain refused to pay Silvestre Revueltas's passage home, forcing

Paz and Garro to split their tourist ticket three ways in order to cover the musician's and their own passage home in a third-class ship bound for Veracruz. *Memorias de España* thus stands as a healthy antidote to the idealistic view of the Spanish Civil War and of Stalinist Russia depicted in Elena Poniatowska's *Tinísima* (1992).

Now reintegrated both into her native country and into the canon of its literature, Garro no longer has to search for something beyond her reach. It is to be hoped that the many characters still hidden within the pages of her unpublished works find their homes in the republic of letters.

**Interview:**

Roberto Páramo, "Reconsideración de Elena Garro," *El Heraldo Cultural de México* (31 December 1967): 2.

**Bibliography:**

Diane E. Marting, ed., *Women Writers of Spanish America: An Annotated Bio-Bibliographical Guide* (Westport, Conn.: Greenwood Press, 1987), pp. 151–153.

**References:**

Robert K. Anderson, "La realidad temporal en *Los recuerdos del porvenir*," *Explicación de Textos Literarios*, 9 (1980–1981): 25–29;

Frank Dauster, "Elena Garro y sus recuerdos del porvenir," *Journal of Spanish Studies: Twentieth Century*, 8 (Spring–Fall 1980): 57–65;

Juan García Ponce, "Poesía en voz alta," *Revista de la Universidad de México*, 11 (August 1957): 29–32;

Suzanne Jill Levine, "House of Mist, House of Mirrors," in *María Luisa Bombal: Apreciaciones*

*críticas*, edited by Marjorie Agosín, Elena Garcón-Vera, and Joy Renjilian-Burgy (Tempe, Ariz.: Bilingual Press/Editorial Bilingüe, 1987), pp. 136–146;

Adriana Méndez Rodenas, "Tiempo femenino, tiempo ficticio: *Los recuerdos del porvenir* de Elena Garro," *Revista Iberoamericana*, 51 (July–December 1985): 843–851;

Doris Meyer, "Alienation and Escape in Elena Garro's *La semana de colores*," *Hispanic Review*, 55 (Spring 1987): 153–164;

Gabriela Mora, "A Thematic Exploration of the Works of Elena Garro," in *Latin American Women Writers: Yesterday and Today*, edited by Yvette E. Miller and Charles M. Tatum (Pittsburgh: Latin American Literary Review, 1977), pp. 91–97;

Lady Rojas-Trempe, "El brujo en *La semana de colores* de Elena Garro," in *Mitos en Hispanoamérica: Interpretación y literatura*, edited by Lucía Fox Lockert (East Lansing, Mich.: Imprenta la Nueva Crónica, 1989);

Harry L. Rosser, "Form and Content in Garro's *Los recuerdos del porvenir*," *Revista Canadiense de Estudios Hispánicos*, 2, no. 3 (1978): 282–294;

Esther Seligson, "*In illo tempore:* Aproximaciones a la obra de Elena Garro," *Revista de la Universidad de México*, 29 (August 1975): 9–10;

Caridad Silva-Velázquez and Nora Erro-Orthmann, eds., *Puerta abierta: La nueva escritora latinoamericana* (Mexico City: Joaquín Mortiz, 1968), pp. 131–139, 316–320;

Kathleen Taylor, "La nueva narrativa mexicana: Re-visiones y sub-versiones de la historia," Ph.D. dissertation, University of Iowa, 1988.

# Oscar Hijuelos

*(24 August 1951 – )*

## Gustavo Pérez Firmat
*Duke University*

BOOKS: *Our House in the Last World* (New York: Persea, 1983);

*The Mambo Kings Play Songs of Love* (New York: Farrar, Straus & Giroux, 1989);

*The Fourteen Sisters of Emilio Montez O'Brien* (New York: Farrar, Straus & Giroux, 1993).

SELECTED PERIODICAL PUBLICATION – UNCOLLECTED: "Columbus Discovering America," *Persea: An International Review,* 1 (1977): 105–109.

As the first Latino novelist to receive the Pulitzer Prize for fiction, Oscar Hijuelos is the best known of an increasing group of American Hispanic writers to reach a broad American audience. Born in New York on 24 August 1951 of Cuban parents, Hijuelos writes only in English. Although Cuban culture is his narrative point of departure, the voice that speaks in his novels, which may be close to Hijuelos himself, is that of a second-generation Cuban-American, someone whose ties to Cuban culture are becoming increasingly distant. Cuba provides Hijuelos with a subject, but it is not constitutive of his writerly stance, his choice of language, or his audience. Even when Hijuelos draws extensively on Spanish-American material, he weaves it into a work whose fabric is resolutely Anglocentric. Hijuelos pays tribute to things Cuban even as he bids them farewell. His work is a complex and moving valedictory to the Spanish language, to his Cuban parents, and to the island's mores and music.

His first novel, *Our House in the Last World* (1983), is an immigrant memoir that follows the fortunes of the Santinio family over several decades. Beginning with the meeting of Alejo Santinio and Mercedes Sorrea in Cuba in 1939, the novel narrates the couple's marriage, their immigration to the United States, the birth of their children, and the family's difficult life in Spanish Harlem. The central consciousness in the novel is Hector, the Santinios'

*Oscar Hijuelos, 1989 (photograph © Jerry Bauer)*

second son, who, like Hijuelos, was born in New York in 1951. Hector's father arrives in America with high hopes but can never go further than the kitchen of a restaurant. Hector's mother, Mercedes, is a manic-depressive who sees visions and talks to spirits. Resentful of her husband and unhappy with her lot, she becomes withdrawn and shrewish, finally retreating into a fantasy world of Cuban ghosts. Although Hector's older brother Horacio manages to escape the family's hellish life, Hector remains trapped until the end. When Alejo drops dead from a heart attack in 1969, the family all but collapses, going from poverty to near destitution.

The great theme of Hector's childhood and adolescence is Cuban manhood – what it means, what it costs, how to achieve it. Over and over Hector harps on the fact that he is not as "Cuban" as his father or older brother. He does not speak Spanish, he is blond, he is frail, and he is a mama's boy. Unlike Horacio, who follows in his father's footsteps by becoming *muy macho* – hard drinking, brawling, womanizing – Hector develops into an overweight and shy "American" teenager. As Horacio gloats at one point, "He's just dumb when it comes to being Cuban." Horacio's striking physical likeness to his father makes things worse. "They were like twins, separated by age, with the same eyes, faces, bodies. Except Alejo was from another world – *cubano, cubano.*"

As he grows up, Hector develops the sense that he is a defective replica of his father, exact in many outward details but lacking Alejo's Cuban spirit. Too Cuban to be American but hardly Cuban enough to resemble his father, Hector sees himself as a "freak, a hunchback, a man with a deformed face." He is a "Cuban Quasimodo," a phrase whose hybridity conveys Hector's sense of lacking a suitable cultural habitation. A French Quasimodo is strange enough; a Cuban Quasimodo is doubly monstrous.

But Hector is not the only monster in the family. His feelings of inadequacy are complicated by Alejo's habits of excess. Something of a dandy as a young man, Alejo never renounces his youthful Cuban ways. His wife's recriminations are not enough to stop him from spending most of his free time away from the house, drinking and womanizing. If Hector is a freak because he is not Cuban enough, perhaps Alejo is a freak for being too Cuban. At least this is what his son seems to think. "During the night Hector had screamed out because the monster was prowling in the hall. The monster was Alejo, hanging onto the walls to get from the kitchen to the bathroom."

When Horacio says that his brother is "dumb," the adjective's original meaning should not be overlooked, for Hector's feelings of inferiority have a great deal to do with his poor Spanish. The "real Cubans" are those who speak fluently, without groping for words or stuttering. He finds it impossible to generate a good Spanish sentence. When he tries to speak like his gregarious father, he feels that the words and phrases immobilize him, tie him in knots:

> He was sick at heart for being so Americanized, which he equated with being fearful and lonely. His

Spanish was unpracticed, practically nonexistent. He had a stutter, and saying a Spanish word made him think of drunkenness. A Spanish sentence wrapped around his face, threatened to peel off his skin and send him falling to the floor like Alejo. He avoided Spanish even though that was all he heard at home. He read it, understood it, but he grew paralyzed by the prospect of the slightest conversation.

Spanish is an artificial skin, a kind of mask that literally defaces him. If he has a "deformed face," as he remarks, it must be from peeling away the words. Hector is a sort of mummy, "part Cuban, part American – all wrapped up tightly inside a skin in which he sometimes could not move."

Because for Hector Spanish is his father's tongue, it is a language that he both desires and avoids. Curiously, even though Mercedes writes poetry, it is Alejo who comes to incarnate the maternal language. When Hector speaks Spanish, he becomes Alejo; but when he becomes Alejo, he turns into the "monster" who comes home drunk in the middle of the night. Since Spanish focalizes his ambivalent feelings toward his father, it is a wound, a handicap. Spanish is the hump in the hunchback, the twitch in the face. The problem is not only that Hector's Spanish is monstrous, but also that Spanish is the language of monsters.

His pathological view of language is decisively shaped by the circumstances in which he learns English. The most wrenching scenes in the book describe Hector's prolonged stay in a pediatric hospital when he is three or four years old. In 1954, shortly after returning to the United States from a trip to Cuba, Hector becomes seriously ill from a kidney infection and has to spend nearly a year convalescing in a hospital full of terminally ill children. During this period he sees his mother only intermittently and his father not at all. Separated from his parents, he comes under the care of a nurse who takes it upon herself not only to bring him back to health but also to teach him English. In order to force him to learn the new language, she tries all kinds of scare tactics, even locking him up in a closet from which he is not released until he says, in English, "Let me out!" At first recalcitrant, Hector eventually gives in. The result, however, is not only that he begins speaking English but that he develops a distrust for Spanish.

By the time he returns home Hector is a different person. "When we left Cuba," Mercedes says, "Hector was sick but so happy and fat that we didn't know anything. He came back saying *Cuba, Cuba* and spent a lot of time with Alejo. He was a little Cuban, spouting Spanish." A year later, when he

OUR HOUSE
IN THE
LAST WORLD

A NOVEL   OSCAR HIJUELOS

*Dust jacket for Hijuelos's 1983 novel, about a Cuban family in New York*

finally is released from the hospital, all of this has changed. Hector is healthy but thin, he no longer speaks Spanish, and he has become distanced from his father, who hardly recognizes him: "Alejo looked at Hector, wondering if this was his son. There he was, a little blondie, a sickly, fair-skinned Cuban who was not speaking Spanish. He patted the kid on the head, turned around, and took a swig of beer." At the hospital Hector undergoes a death and rebirth. He loses one identity and acquires another. That closet is a womb from which he is delivered by the American nurse, who is both mother and midwife, tender and terrible at the same time.

Immigrant memoirs are often conversion narratives. What is unusual about *Our House in the Last World* is the location of its conversion scene. For the young immigrant typically the school ushers him into the new language, and a teacher replaces the mother or the father. But in Hector's case the whole experience takes place in a hospital under the guidance of a nurse. His experience is not only a conversion but a cure. This means that Spanish is not merely a language but a disease. For the rest of his life Hector views Cuba, its language and its culture, with a mixture of awe and apprehension. "Cuba gave the bad disease. Cuba gave the drunk father. Cuba gave the crazy mother. Years later all these would entwine to make Hector think Cuba had something against him." In perhaps the most striking image in the book, Hector compares the X rays of his diseased kidneys to the map of Cuba. His mysterious illness, which his mother attributes to drinking puddled water, is labeled only a "Cuban infection" carried by the ever-present *microbios* (microbes), one of the few words in the novel almost always written in Spanish.

Hector's evaluation of Spanish and English helps one to understand the Anglocentric bias of the narration. *Our House in the Last World* evinces an almost ruthless effort of translation from Spanish to English. The initial sentence of the novel already makes clear that the "last world" of the title will be re-created according to Hector's peculiar sensibility. "Hector's mother met Alejo Santinio, his Pop, in 1939 when she was twenty-seven years old and working as a ticket girl in the Neptuna movie theater in Holguín, Cuba." Although Hector does not appear as a character for several chapters, the reader is made to realize right away that whatever is seen will be from his point of view. The possessive *Hector's* tells one that, even when Hector is offstage, the story belongs to him, which is why it is significant his father is labeled, somewhat incongruously, *Pop*. From first word to last, this sentence is filled with Cuban sounds – *Hector, Alejo Santinio, Neptuna, Holguín, Cuba.* Among them the colloquial American *Pop* sticks out like a hump. But given Alejo's importance in the novel, this initial act of naming is crucial. What does one call a Cuban father in English? Did Hector, as a child growing up in a Spanish-speaking home, call his father Pop? Or was it rather *papá* or *papi?* No, it was always Pop: "I remember my mother and father – 'Pop' always 'Pop.'" The conversion of a *papi* into a *Pop* entails a decisive act of translation. Mercedes, identified in the sentence by the colorless *mother,* does not undergo so radical a transformation. By calling Alejo Pop, Hector reduces his father to manageable proportions, removing or neutralizing some of his terror. The American name fends off the Cuban monster.

*Our House in the Last World* is haunted by the specter of the father, the father's land, and the father's language. After Hector recovers from his "Cuban illness," the narrator says, "Now he looked American and spoke mostly American. Cuba had become the mysterious and cruel phantasm standing behind the door." That cruel phantasm wears Alejo's size forty-six pants. In this novel Cuban culture is like Alejo's corpse, lifeless but imposing. Even though the novel succeeds as a subtle, sensitive study of Hector's struggles to achieve psychic health, to rid himself of spiritual *microbios,* one has the sense that the struggle is finally unresolved. Indeed, the problem may be Hector's excessively bacterial view of Cuba; his memorable image of the island as an infected kidney is a symptom of illness. To achieve health, those microbes need to be construed also as life-giving. Since Hector cannot deny that he is his father's son, so long as he sees Cuba as disease he will remain a cripple.

The issue of paternal presence is taken up again in Hijuelos's second novel, *The Mambo Kings Play Songs of Love* (1989), which was awarded the Pulitzer Prize for fiction in 1990. *The Mambo Kings* centers on another larger-than-life Cuban man, Cesar Castillo, the mambo king, and his nephew Eugenio, who serves as the vehicle for Cesar's story. In this novel the Alejo character is no longer a monster, and the Hector character is a nephew rather than a son. Not only is Cesar cast in a more favorable light than Alejo, but Eugenio enjoys an autonomy or distance that Hector never achieves. Uncles are like fathers one can love without fear. When Eugenio says that his project is "the resurrection of a man," his language evokes the ghosts and voices of the earlier novel. Yet Cesar is not a "mysterious and cruel phantasm," but a man. He is imposing but not such a problem. Although his portrait is by no means flattering, it is not as one-sided as that drawn in *Our House in the Last World.*

*The Mambo Kings* follows the lives of two Cuban brothers, Cesar and Nestor Castillo, who immigrate to New York in the late 1940s and form an orchestra called the Mambo Kings, achieving ephemeral fame one night in 1955 when they appear on television in an *I Love Lucy* episode as Ricky's Cuban cousins. In talent as well as temperament the two brothers are worlds apart. Nestor is moody and melancholy. His main claim to fame is having written the brothers' greatest hit, "Bellísima María de mi Alma" (Beautiful María of My Soul), a bolero or ballad about the girl who broke his heart in Cuba. For years Nestor works tirelessly on this tune, coming up with twenty-two different versions of the lyric; only his death in a car accident puts an end to his obsessive rewriting.

In contrast, Cesar is impulsive rather than melancholy. He is a consummate ladies' man with slicked-back hair, a melifluous voice, and an irre-

pressible libido. He is reminiscent not only of Alejo, who possesses many of these same qualities, but also of his idol, Desi Arnaz, who played Ricky on *I Love Lucy.* Like Arnaz, Cesar was born in Santiago de Cuba, has a thick Cuban accent, and "pretty-boy looks," and plays the conga drum. Like Arnaz, he spends a considerable part of his life chasing women and comes to regret it. By 1980 Cesar has ended up, broke and broken, in a seedy New York tenement. On the brink of death, he takes out a stack of old Mambo King records and opens a bottle of rye whiskey. He spends his last hours reminiscing, replaying melodies and memories, records and *recuerdos* (memories). As an account of Cesar's final recollections, the novel takes the form of a death watch in mambo time, an agony with words and music.

The first character seen, however, is not Cesar but Eugenio, the author of the book's fictional prologue and epilogue. The prologue gives his account of seeing a rerun of the *I Love Lucy* episode in which Cesar and Nestor appear, an "item of eternity" replayed throughout the book. The epilogue relates Eugenio's visit to Arnaz's ranch in California after his uncle's death. As they sit among the bougainvillea and sip Dos Equis beer, Eugenio and Desi reminisce about the Mambo Kings. The novel closes by rerunning once more the brothers' guest spot on *I Love Lucy.* Much as Hector was the sentient center of *Our House in the Last World,* Eugenio is the focalizing presence in this novel. Like Hector, Eugenio is the source of the novel's point of view, of its attitudes and values. Even though he appears only briefly in Cesar's recollections, his presence frames the whole story.

Cesar and Eugenio's relationship is crucial. Although it may seem strange that Eugenio shows more interest in his uncle than in his father, the reason is that spiritually and emotionally Cesar is Eugenio's real father. The anonymous third-person narration of Cesar's recollections functions as a filter for their parallel sensibilities. Cesar's voice can be heard in the nostalgic tone and in the narration's limitation to events that he witnessed. Indeed, there are moments when the narration lapses into the first person. Eugenio's voice is heard not only in the epilogue and prologue but in the interior story as well, which uncannily repeats some of his sentences word for word — and not just any sentences, but his description of the central *I Love Lucy* episode. It is not entirely clear what one should make of this duplication, which is inexplicable unless one posits that the entire account is Eugenio's fabulation, a possibility the text does not confirm.

Without going this far, however, one can at least venture the opinion that the duplication

*Hijuelos, circa 1983 (photograph by Ken Dean)*

virtually impossible. Although the novel bears a certain Hispanic family likeness, it is far from a chip off the old block.

The family resemblance is evident in two principal ways. Given its episodic plot and the explicitness with which Cesar's sexual exploits are recounted, *The Mambo Kings* links up with the Hispanic picaresque and particularly with the erotic picaresque, a genre that in Cuba includes such works as Carlos Loveira's *Juan Criollo* (1927) and Guillermo Cabrera Infante's *La Habana para un infante difunto* (1979; translated as *Infante's Inferno,* 1984). Like the protagonist of Loveira's novel, Cesar is a Don Juan *criollo,* a Creole translation of the Spanish literary type. In the classical picaresque the protagonist is driven by hunger and spends a large part of his life in the service of a succession of masters. In the erotic picaresque the moving force is a different kind of appetite, and instead of going from master to master the protagonist goes from mistress to mistress — not *de amo en amo* (from boss to boss) but rather *de amorío en amorío* (from affair to affair). Cesar's attitude is summed up in the motto "rum, rump and rumba," a Cuban version of "wine, women, and song."

If one token of tradition in the book is sex, the other is music, for *The Mambo Kings* places itself in the line of descent of a spate of recent Spanish-American novels also inspired by popular music, including works such as Severo Sarduy's *De donde son los cantantes* (1967; translated as *From Cuba with a Song,* 1972), Lisandro Otero's *Bolero* (1986), Luis Rafael Sánchez's *La importancia de llamarse Daniel Santos* (1989), and even Manuel Puig's *El beso de la mujer araña* (1976; translated as *Kiss of the Spider Woman,* 1984), with which Hijuelos's novel also shares the practice of providing explanatory footnotes. More concretely Hijuelos's novel is reminiscent of Cabrera Infante's *Tres tristes tigres* (1967; translated as *Three Trapped Tigers,* 1971) and Sánchez's *La guaracha del Macho Camacho* (1976; translated as *Macho Camacho's Beat,* 1980). Like *La guaracha del Macho Camacho,* which centers on a tune by the same name, *The Mambo Kings* revolves around one song, "Bellísima María de mi Alma," one of the cuts on an album from which the book takes its name. Both novels enact a kind of counterpoint between music and text, *música y letra,* that issues in the transcription of the lyric at the end of each book. Cabrera Infante's novel, which also draws heavily on popular music, includes a section entitled "Ella cantaba boleros" (She Sang Boleros), a phrase that Hijuelos transposes, since "songs of love" is his English translation of the Spanish "boleros." If "she sang boleros," the mambo kings play songs of love.

evinces the extent to which Eugenio "underwrites" Cesar's memoirs — to underwrite is both to write beneath something and to guarantee. Even if Eugenio is not always responsible for the specific verbal shape of Cesar's recollections, he is at least generally responsible for the memoirs as a whole. Eugenio's name already indicates that he is the source, the "genitor" of the account. As his uncle's closest relative and the author of the framing texts, he occupies a position halfway between the narrating *I* and the narrated *he.* Perhaps Eugenio is best seen as Cesar's translator; their two voices are formally separate but often hard to tell apart.

Eugenio and Cesar's complex filiation suggests the novel's ambivalent embrace of Cuban (and more generally Spanish-American) culture. In spite of its obvious concern with things Cuban, its connection to Hispanic culture in general and to Spanish-American literature in particular is far from simple. Even as *The Mambo Kings* evokes central works in the canon of contemporary Hispanic fiction, it distances itself from its Spanish-language pedigree. It is not easy to read *The Mambo Kings* as a "Hispanic book," because it makes such a reading

With its juxtaposition of mambo and bolero, Hijuelos's title alerts the reader to the importance of these two musical genres in the novel. The mambo and bolero serve as correlates for the two dominant but discordant emotions in the book, lust and melancholy. The mambo is a mixture of Afro-Cuban rhythms and American big-band instrumentation popularized by Dámaso Pérez Prado, whose nickname was "the king of mambo." Fast-paced, aggressive, and seductive, the mambo is Cesar's chant of conquest. By contrast, boleros are sad, even whining ballads whose speaker is typically passive and mournful. Like Nestor's "Bellísima María de mi Alma," the bolero is a medium for bemoaning unhappiness in love, for questioning the injustice of fate. If the mambo is about conquest, the bolero is about loss. The great theme of the bolero is separation anxiety, a male's often elaborate longing for a lost love.

The bolero's wordiness sharply contrasts with the mambo's laconism – most mambos were instrumental compositions. In fact, the lovely inarticulateness of the mambo makes it an odd choice as a model for literary composition. To the extent that *The Mambo Kings* takes inspiration from the mambo, it tends toward a kind of expressiveness whose medium is not language. Most literary transpositions of popular songs focus on their lyrics, as in *La guaracha del Macho Camacho* or *De donde son los cantantes*. But with the mambo, literary transposition is difficult because of the instrumental nature of the form.

For this reason, it is not surprising that what the mambo kings play are not mambos but songs of love, for in the novel songs of love fill the verbal void left by the mambo. In a bolero, rhythm and melody take a back seat to verbal elaboration, as suggested by Nestor's twenty-two versions of the lyrics of "Bellísima María de mi Alma." The nostalgic tone of the novel is a transposition of the sensibility of the bolero, which provides the narrator with structures of feeling and forms of expression. The theme of the novel can then be stated as a musical question: is life mambo or bolero? Is it a chronicle of conquest or a dirge?

The answer, of course, is that life is both, as the lives of the two brothers bear out. Cesar, with his "king-cock strut," is the mambo king; Nestor is the spirit of the *letra* of the bolero. As the narrator succinctly puts it, "Cesar was *un macho grande* [a great man]; Nestor, *un infeliz* [an unhappy man]." But the irony is that in the end the great *macho* turns out to be no less of an *infeliz* than his brother, for after Nestor's death Cesar gradually takes on his brother's temperament. Early in the novel Nestor is described as "the man plagued with memory, the way his brother Cesar Castillo would be twenty-five years later." The gradual merging of the two brothers culminates with Cesar's last act, which is to transcribe the lyric of his brother's composition. When he copies the lyric as if it were his own, Cesar becomes Nestor. This final gesture shows that Cesar has become another man "plagued by memory."

Cesar's impersonation of his brother summarizes the drift of the book. Like the title itself, the novel moves from mambo to bolero, from lust to loss, from conquest to relinquishment. Cesar lives in frenetic mambo time only to discover that life actually follows the languid measures of a bolero. His celebration of "rum, rump and rumba" is tempered by the reader's awareness that these chronicles of conquest are actually a derelict's last words. If Nestor composes his bolero in order to get María back, Cesar reminisces in order to recapture his life as a *macho grande*. The narration explicitly plays on the punning relationship between *member* and *remember* – at one point Cesar "remembered a whore struggling with a thick rubber on his member." For Cesar, remembering is a way of re-membering himself, a way of sleeping with the past. But the vitality thus achieved is illusory. Like the bolero composed by Nestor, the novel is very much "a song about lost pleasures, a song about youth."

Nestor's song of love is also an elegy to Cuba. The novel's relation to things Cuban in general and to the Spanish language in particular is affectionate but distant. In one sense Spanish is everywhere in the text: in the place and character names, in the characters' Hispanicized diction, and in the constant references to Cuban music. In another sense, however, Spanish is nowhere, for Hijuelos has rendered in English all of the characters' thoughts and words. Indeed, since Cesar's remembrances make up most of the novel and since these remembrances were almost certainly framed in Spanish, the text presupposes an invisible act of translation, somewhat in the manner of *Don Quixote* (1605–1615), which was supposedly translated by Miguel de Cervantes from Arabic. The mambo king's English needs to be read as Spanish in translation, and the source of this translation must of course be Eugenio, who then becomes, like Cervantes, the "second author" of the book. Eugenio's genius is to render his uncle's recollections in such a way that the reader tends to overlook the nephew's presence in the uncle's words.

Significantly, the only sustained Spanish passage in the book is the lyric of "Bellísima María de mi Alma," which appears at the very end. Nestor's song of love, the book's preeminent statement on

*Dust jacket for Hijuelos's Pulitzer Prize–winning novel, about two fictional Cuban-American musicians who appear with Desi Arnaz on* I Love Lucy

loss, is transcribed in a language that itself has been lost. The Spanish lyric is a testament to what is lost in translation. And Nestor's beautiful María may then be an emblem for the maternal language left behind in Cuba. Moreover, since Cesar's last act is to transcribe this lyric, this Spanish interpolation is literally a testament. When the reader finally comes upon these words, he finds himself at a loss. Like Ricky's Spanish outbursts in *I Love Lucy,* the lyric creates a kind of lacuna, a gap in the discursive flow of the novel. The bolero, one of the novel's principal links to Hispanic culture, is also the emblem for the loss of that culture, a loss whose most fundamental manifestation is linguistic.

In a narrow but significant sense, this linguistic loss is present throughout the novel in the surprisingly large number of errors in the spelling of Spanish words and names. For example, Antonio Arcaño, one of the seminal figures in the development of the mambo, becomes Antonio Arcana; the well-known singer Bola de Nieve is strangely transformed into a Pala de Nieve; the equally well-known Benny Moré loses his accent and becomes Beny More. The accentuation throughout is inconsistent: while Cesar and Nestor lose the accent on their names, other characters keep theirs. Misspelled words are not infrequent: *nalgita* for *nalguita, batida* for *batido, quatro* for *cuatro,* and so on. Although these errata may be evidence of sloppy editing, they are also typographical reminders of translation as loss, as displacement.

Like Hijuelos's first novel, *The Mambo Kings* is written "from" Cuba but "toward" the United States. This translational drift is already evident in the title, which goes from the Cuban "mambo" to the English "songs of love." But the beguiling richness of the novel, and what sets it apart from *Our House in the Last World,* stems from the fact that its Anglocentrism is not motivated by fear. From Eugenio's perspective, Cesar is not a threatening paternal ghost but a benign avuncular presence. He may be pathetic, but he is not horrific. The considerable achievement of *The Mambo Kings* is to stage the negotiation between cultures in such a way that the novel neither forsakes nor is enslaved by its family resemblance to things and texts Hispanic. Cuban culture figures in the novel as a distant relation, much as Cesar and Nestor appear on *I Love Lucy* as Ricky's Cuban cousins. The art of *The Mambo Kings* resides in knowing how to cultivate distant relations, which means also knowing how to put them in their place. *Our House in the Last World* was not able to achieve this distance, for Hector was able neither to slay nor to celebrate his father. Hijuelos's second novel is much more successful in staking out a territory – linguistic, cultural, and emotional – not overrun by Cuban ghosts. By distancing itself from its ancestry, the novel is able to occupy an eccentric space somewhere between Havana and Harlem, a kind of make-believe border ballroom where north meets south and mambo kings play songs of love forever.

References:

Enrique Fernández, "Exilados on Main Street," *Village Voice,* 1 May 1990, pp. 85–86;

Gustavo Pérez Firmat, "Rum, Rump, and Rumba: Cuban Contexts for *The Mambo Kings Play Songs of Love,*" *Dispositio,* no. 41 (1991): 75–86;

Ilán Stavans, "Oscar Hijuelos, novelista," *Revista Iberoamericana,* 155–156 (April–September 1991): 673–677.

# Osman Lins
## *(5 July 1924 – 8 July 1978)*

Ana Luiza Andrade
*Universidade Federal de Santa Catarina*

BOOKS: *O visitante* (Rio de Janeiro: José Olympio, 1955; revised edition, São Paulo: Martins, 1970);

*Os gestos* (Rio de Janeiro: José Olympiã, 1957);

*O fiel e a pedra* (Rio de Janeiro: Civilização Brasileira, 1961; revised edition, São Paulo: Martins, 1967; revised edition, São Paulo: Martins, 1971);

*Marinheiro de primeira viagem* (Rio de Janeiro: Civilização Brasileira, 1963);

*Lisbela e o prisioneiro* (Rio de Janeiro: Letras e Artes, 1964);

*Um mundo estagnado* (Recife, Brazil: Universidade Federal de Pernambuco, 1966);

*Nove, novena* (São Paulo: Martins, 1966);

*Guerra do "Cansa-Cavalo," peça em três atos* (Petrópolis, Brazil: Vozes, 1967);

*Capa-verde e o natal: Peça infantil em 2 atos* (São Paulo: Comissão Estadual de Teatro, 1968);

*Guerra sem testemunhas: O escritor, sua condição, e a realidade social* (São Paulo: Martins, 1969);

*Avalovara* (São Paulo: Melhoramentos, 1973); translated by Gregory Rabassa (New York: Knopf, 1980);

*Santa, automóvel e soldado* (São Paulo: Duas Cidades, 1975);

*Lima Barreto e o espaço romanesco* (São Paulo: Ática, 1976);

*A rainha dos cárceres da Grécia* (São Paulo: Melhoramentos, 1976);

*O diabo na noite de Natal* (São Paulo: Pioneira, 1977);

*Do ideal e da glória: Problemas inculturais brasileiros* (São Paulo: Summus, 1977);

*La Paz existe?*, by Lins and Julieta de Godoy Ladeira (São Paulo: Summus, 1977);

*Casos especiais de Osman Lins* (São Paulo: Summus, 1978);

*Evangelho na taba: Outros problemas inculturais brasileiros* (São Paulo: Summus, 1979);

*Mundo recusado, o mundo ace to e o mundo enfrentado* (São Paulo: Record, 1979).

*Osman Lins*

OTHER: Henrik Pontoppidan, *O urso polar e outras novelas,* translated by Lins (Rio de Janeiro: Delta, 1963);

*Missa do Galo: Variações sobre o mesma tema,* edited by Lins (São Paulo: Summus, 1977).

Osman Lins was always aware of the writer's professional problems of survival and acceptance in Brazilian society, which had been under military rule since 1964. During these difficult historical times, when centralization of power largely depended on the media, Lins became especially sensitive to the liberating function of literature in modern society, an underlying topic in his fiction.

155

Born on 5 July 1924 in Vitória de Santo Antão in the state of Pernambuco a few days before his mother's death and raised by his grandmother, who later appeared as one of his fictional characters in *Nove, novena* (Nine, Novena, 1966), Lins had a solitary childhood that gave him an introspective nature, which was to be developed in his literary career. This introspection, a distinctive mark that inextricably ties his life to his work, is evident in his unique tendency for self-reflexiveness. His critical approach to his own writing, according to his biographer, became unusually developed as he matured.

In *Osman Lins: Uma biografia literária* (Osman Lins: A Literary Biography, 1988) Regina Igel traces the writer's intellectual influences to his own explanations of his early tendencies. The first is about the absence of his mother, who died as a consequence of his birth. This deep vacuum was to be fulfilled in his literary searches. In his youth, with his heart already set on writing, he was forced to work for a living at the Banco do Brasil while completing his studies in economics at the Universidade de Recife. At the same time his admiration for his father, a tailor, explains his fascination with the techniques acquired in the art of craftsmanship: he began to see writing as a craft.

While Lins was living in Recife, the capital of Pernambuco, the gradual impositions of a secure, bourgeois lifestyle – his job at the bank, his marriage to Dona Maria do Carmo in 1947, and the births of his three daughters, Livânia, Leticia, and Angela – were not enough to restrain his exploring spirit. Important trips to Europe (1961) and São Paulo (1962) not only helped him expand this restless side but also became decisive turning points in his career. In Recife he found support in his uncle, the critic Alvaro Lins, who introduced him to several prominent intellectuals, such as Gilberto Freyre, Olivio Montenegro, Mario Sette, and Mario Motta. His first experience in France, as the result of a grant from the Academie Française, helped him decide to move to São Paulo, a city that could offer more to him in terms of culture. By then his marriage had failed, and he already had several books published, including the novel *O fiel e a pedra* (The Pointer and the Clock, 1961). From 1941 to 1978 he wrote plays (some of them adapted for television and radio), poems, and essays, but above all he published fiction.

Both as an introduction to all of Lins's fiction and as a preparation to the understanding of *Avalovara* (1973; translated, 1980), his best-known novel, *Guerra sem testemunhas: O escritor, sua condição, e a realidade social* (War without Witnesses, 1969),

serves as a bridge between essay and fiction in its peculiar combination of polemics and confession. The essay not only depicts the writer's marginalization but also lays the foundations for a personal poetics. On the one hand Lins establishes external factors related to a growing consumer-oriented mentality that pose an adverse cultural situation both to literary activity and to the contemporary writer. Ineffective criticism, escapist reading, obsolete academic institutions, consumer-oriented publishers, and repressive censorship are for Lins both conditioning and aggrieving factors, in Brazil as much as outside it, of the writer's occupation.

On the other hand, while discussing these conditioning factors Lins defines his cultural position, laying the basis for his own literary ideology. Two respective lines of procedure, the critical and the creative, are represented in Lins's fictive double, a partner and literary artifact called Willy Mompou, a name that already reflects a play between a pair of opposites in its initials, inversions of each other, W. M. This character's presence is explained through what Lins called a "dialogical" relationship between writer and society when the critical conscience of the artisan splits into writer/reader or creator/critic in a dialogue both with the world and with himself.

Both these narrative voices – the critic's and the creator's – express the dialogue of the writer with himself and with the world while sharing the weight of the pronoun *I*: the man and the writer are one but separate. As a critic of his own career, in the reflexive process of rewriting his own literary autobiography, he creates a writer. Lins's "partner" Willy Mompou functions as a representation of the writer's double voice from which the work becomes a war without witnesses.

The multiple fighting fronts in *Guerra sem testemunhas* reveal the critical contributions of the essayist through the intentions of the fiction writer represented in three stages of the struggle between artist and society – search, encounter, and plenitude – that not only anticipate *Avalovara* but also offer the guidelines for examining all of Lins's fictional work. These three stages in the writer's career, which are seen as phases in a process of apprenticeship, also offer a typology to examine the progressive stages of Lins's relationship with his own work.

In the first stage Lins's search moves from an inarticulate, inchoate form of expression – what he calls "gestures" in the collection of short stories *Os gestos* (Gestures, 1957) – to a more meaningful and conscious use of words in the novel *O visitante* (The

Visitor, 1955). Both gestures and words become a means to free characters from their social constraints. In each work the main characters acquire a creative or generative force through a critical view of themselves. Only then can the reason for their social impotence be seen as conditioned by a superficial repetition of ritualistic gestures and mechanical words.

*Os gestos* contrasts characters who are socially dependent by lack of discernment, which is expressed through meaningless gestures, and the autonomy of the critical gesture that liberates them from the previous situation. Nevertheless, the limitation in gestures is precisely what, later on, makes it possible for the character to have a poetic perception, acquired through a critical reading of his daughter's own gestures while they are describing her passage from childhood to adolescence. He then arrives at a new critical-creative conscience.

*O visitante* also belongs to the author's first searching stage. For most of the novel the main character remains subjected to adultery in the form of ritualistic visits that substitute for religious habit. A critical reading of the Bible not only puts an end to these rituals but also provokes a new perception of self and of the world in the character. The biblical epiphany, which means revelation, is like reading afresh: the change from the role of reader to that of writer, one who participates in the process, is equivalent to undergoing an epiphanic experience.

The novel *O fiel e a pedra* is, in the author's words, both the platform of arrival from his first stage and the exit to the next. As a synthesis of his first stage, the novel is the epic journey of a hero threatened by the domination of a hostile world. The reproduction of an extinct tradition is a threat equivalent to the same tendency, in the first stage, to repeat sterile gestures and mechanical words. As an exit to the next stage, the novel is a conquest, the epic journey of a hero whose power of resistance is derived from Virgil's Aeneas. In the transposition of the *Aeneid* to the novel's abandoned northeastern region of Brazil, Lins builds a social criticism on the same level as a new literary creation based on an old myth. The pointer that indicates a weighing machine in the title of the novel becomes a symbol for Lins's own oscillation at this stage. On the one hand, he breaks with a novelistic tradition centered in social problems; on the other, he opens up a new trend through a critical reading of Virgil's epic poem.

The short-story collection *Nove, novena* can be singled out as a transition between the first stage

Cover for Avalovara (1973), Lins's best-known work, about the art of fiction

(search) and the third (plenitude) in the author's career. At this particular stage the skilled craftsman and the writer converge in the common acceptance of a higher challenge that implicitly rejects the idea of "pleasurable" or "easy" reading exemplified by the best-seller. All of the narratives in *Nove, novena* introduce the reader directly to the here and now of the characters: they become narrative voices or threads that appear as literary constructions independent from an omniscient narrator. This new narrative technique allows both an intimate and a direct relationship between characters and narrative structures, their discourse and the reader. Moreover, the present tense of these voices releases them from a temporal dimension, projecting them in diverse spatial configurations in narratives that form geometrical designs as exemplified in their titles. These nine narratives bring together both ethics and aesthetics in Lins's work, not only through their innovative technique but also because they carry his critical-creative procedure further and deeper.

Sandra Nitrini's *Poéticas em confronto: Nove, novena e o novo romance* (A Poetics of Confrontation: Nine, Novena and the *Nouveau Roman,* 1987) traces Lins's new techniques in *Nove, novena* to the French novelists who became better known as the writers of the *nouveau roman* such as Alain Robbe-Grillet, Michel Butor, Nathalie Sarraute, Claude Simon, and others. In fact, there are close similarities between them and Lins, for like these writers Lins's techniques in these narratives are rooted, as Nitrini points out, in a Husserlian phenomenology that privileges "things in themselves" and the direct relationship with conscience. As a result, this type of discourse becomes nonchronological, nondramatized, and "writerly." Nitrini further explains that, by minimizing the plot both in its historical and causal conventions, both the *nouveau roman* and Lins's work question the idea of a ready-made story, enhance both incompleteness and ambiguity, and consequently change the role of a passive reader into an active one.

Two narratives in *Nove, novena* become good contrasting examples of Lins's new techniques in this transitional stage. In the first the spiritual power of the medieval bas-reliefs is recaptured as unifying the different narrative voices. In contrast, in the second the narrative units are fragmented or disassembled, showing alternative ways of reading rather than just one.

The first story is a written transcription or a description of a medieval construction, usually seen in cathedrals behind the altar, telling about the life of a saint. Joana Carolina's everyday life in northeast Brazil becomes the battle of an ordinary woman against domination, disease, and death. The different narrative voices become poetic engravings about her life, transforming Joana the character into a metaphor for a power that is eternal, cosmic, and regenerative: the power of the written word. Joana becomes the personification of the word as the result of the artist's power to transpose critical moments, his "second," "godlike" creation.

Instead of the reconstitutive unifying power of the word that shapes one story, another questions the idea of a single plot in three possible narrative versions of plots that are incomplete and ambiguous. The illusory distortions of the ornamental baroque style are noticeable when the structure of the Sacred Triangle – Father, Son, and Holy Ghost – is substituted for a structure of criminals: a murderer, an exploiter, and a prostitute. The occurrence of a series of deaths as a result of this substitution works like narrative cuts grouped in threes, indicating alternative impossibilities in metaphors for chaos and emptiness.

The coexistence of geometry and ornament, contrastive aesthetical poles that are indicators of the author's oscillation between the critical and the creative postures at this stage, represents a major advance as a preparation for the ambitious step taken with *Avalovara.* According to Lins, the novel is his most ambitious project, saying that few, particularly the translators, who are forced to do it in their own profession, have realized the fact that there is a vast universe inside it, with an infinity of human as well as literary problems, waiting to be deciphered.

Writing about the art of fiction can be detected very early in Lins's literary career. In 1963 he already aimed at the creation of a literary work able not only to transmit both a singular and intense vision of the universe but at the same time the living story of the conquering of this vision. It took him twenty-three years to achieve his purpose with the novel *Avalovara,* the climax of his career.

*Avalovara* is not only an allegory of the art of the novel but also the synthesis and epitome of all Lins's previous fiction. In *Avalovara,* through an extended metaphor of the sexual act, writing itself is represented as a necessary critical path for the regeneration of a dying world. Its geometrical structure, based on a play between two figures, a spiral and a square, tells the story of the spiral course of the novel in the transgressions of its own rational limitations imposed by the square.

For its ambitious aim at the universal, the critics of *Avalovara* tend to place Lins's work among the most modern literary trends in contemporary fiction. At times it appears related to an international Latin-American group led by Jorge Luis Borges, Cortázar, García Márquez, and José Lezama Lima; at other times it appears related to the French *nouveau roman.* Lins has rejected this last possibility on the grounds that he felt too primitive to fit into such an intellectual group of artists.

In a 1979 article in *World Literature Today* critic Gregory Rabassa, who translated *Avalovara* in 1980, observes certain parallel characteristics in the new Latin-American fiction, especially between Cortázar's *Rayuela* (1963; translated as *Hopscotch,* 1967) and *62: Modelo para armar* (1968; translated as *62: A Model Kit,* 1972), García Márquez's *Cien años de soledad* (1967; translated as *One Hundred Years of Solitude,* 1970), and *Avalovara,* ascribing to them an underlying epic trend in Latin-American contemporary fiction based on structure. Critics have traced common roots both in Lezama Lima's *Paradiso* (Paradise, 1966) and *Avalovara* in the European novel of the beginning of the twentieth century, particularly in James Joyce's *Ulysses* (1922). But Lins established a difference, saying that while Joyce explored the word, his work has more to do with the novel's structural problems and the building of characters.

In spite of not having specifically acknowledged the influence of Hispanic-American writers, Lins met many of them on his trips to Europe (he also met many French authors, including Michel Butor) and admits that they share a mythical conscience of identification, which is what makes them different from the Europeans. However, he denies their direct influence on *Avalovara,* quoting instead as major sources Dante and François Rabelais.

*Avalovara* represents Lins's search in his own literary career. While in *Guerra sem testemunhas* his career was defined in terms of the interaction between text and society, *Avalovara* is an actual fictional departure from the solitary but dialogic act between the creator and the critic inside him. In a preface to the novel, Antonio Cândido interprets the tendency to artifice in *Avalovara* as a courageous attitude.

In *Avalovara* the technical innovations in *Nove, novena* are radicalized. At the outset the novel unites the geometry of the square to the ornamental spiral as its structural foundations. The letters of the Latin sentence "Sator arepo tenet opera rotas" (The creator carefully maintains the world around its orbit) are contained in the square, forming the novel's chapters, which revolve around its plot, the spiral journey of its hero. The close relationship of plot and novel throughout all of its thematic variations shows the writer's continuous meditation on the progression of his own text.

*Avalovara* represents the return of the writer to the world, the final fulfillment of his creative function. The plot itself fictionalizes the author's stages in life: the journey of the hero Abel in *Avalovara* is also a search for a novel that results from his affairs (encounters) with three different women, who represent the stages in Lins's career as expressed in *Guerra sem testemunhas:* search, encounter, and plenitude.

Lins's self-reflexive route throughout his fiction was proposed by *Guerra sem testemunhas* when the writer expressed his need to penetrate appearances by writing. *Avalovara* is the act of writing represented in its penetration of appearances. Its title is the verbalization of an imaginary bird whose name was taken from oriental mythology, Avalokiteshvara. According to the author, *Avalovara* is a word composed of birds, which suggests the multiple verbal flights of a bird that proliferates narrative "imaginative" voices.

As an allegory of the novel, the critical-creative simultaneity resides precisely in the double act of folding and unfolding of the novel on itself, making it possible for a deeper critical approach to the world that incorporates the creative process. It is in this sense that the act of writing is the penetration of appearances, a game of experience expressed in a metaphoric dialogue between lovers. Their narrative movements are a writing of attractions and rejections.

The novel is a seductive game, making it closer to Cortázar's *Rayuela*. Both these novels resemble puzzles to be resolved by the reader, fragmented narratives that fit together according to their structural rules. They both offer the reader other possibilities of reading besides the conventionally linear one. As in *Rayuela,* where Cortázar indicates the pages that can be skipped, *Avalovara* can also be read either linearly or in isolated chapters by following each of its eight narrative lines. These correspond to the letters contained in the Sator-Rotas' magic square. Both the magic square and the spiral juxtaposed over it indicate the rules of a game that combines imagination and experience, a composition that shows the reversibility of literary creation. The square and the spiral are symbols of a game between a critical discourse that is rational within the limits of the square and a liberating discourse that is creative in the fight against all impositions, a discourse that erupts through imagination and breaks up the barriers of space and time like the bird Avalovara.

Both the flight of the bird and Abel's search are transgressive: the first breaks up narrative conventions of time and space, while the second has to do with social institutions. Abel's search is based on his adulterous relationship with a woman whose name he wants to find. It is a creative search that transgresses limited structures. His lover's voice is liberated through physical touch. Their relationship keeps an initial distance reflected in the flight of the bird. The physical relationship between lovers expresses the search of the writer as perceived by his lover: the cone — the vertex of the spiral — describes a converging point of the lovers that would be the encounter with the bird, a sexual/textual act that liberates the repressed voice in the word.

Abel's route is fragmented by the limitations imposed by the world — the authoritarian discourse of institutions — which interrupts the creative process in the critical moments of its course. The other

*Cover for Lins's 1978 collection of novellas*

own disappearance, each time it shows itself under a censored or geometric form. Geometry, like reason, is an imposition of limits. It exercises an aesthetic control over the narrative art, for it is the measure of humanity that fights through the imagination in order to break it up. It is in this sense that Abel's rebelliousness in his search is also a fight against the absurdity of death.

The sexual act between the lovers flows like the narrative process itself, like a "textual act" in which separation and union are both masculine and feminine. The desire to attach and to undo the narrative chain is expressive of its double search for integration and transgression. Through Abel the text expands – Avalovara's orbit grows larger – in a continuous unfolding of metaphors: words are transformed into flowers that color the surface of the text, into fish that leap from the sea, into animals that walk over the lovers' bodies. In short, the word is life, which explodes in a natural abundance of metaphors exceeding the limitations represented by Olavo Haiano, its obverse and deadly side.

Two opposites of the same literary process, Abel and Olavo Haiano reflect themselves in the feminine narrative voice: the first searches for a liberating identity while the second interferes and disaggregates. Consequently, both the images of the adulterous lover and the conforming wife explain the double existence of this woman whose body is transformed into a fighting ground where there is a confrontation between the image of the slave against the one that resists. The physical duel between these two feminine images – the conforming and the rebellious – is the drama of the writer in search of the original poetic word. The woman has no name, embodying the absence of creativity – oppression, obscurity, and the impossibility of identification of the artist and the world. She is named only through Abel's dialogue because she is the world in its transpositions to the novel, the poetry from which metaphors can be generated. As representative of the double voice of the word, she has two births: she is called "Twice-Born," which indicates the second birth of the word. In fact, she is ambiguity in its power to create and to destroy, to die and to live, in her metamorphosis from flesh to word, from a chaotic world to the cosmic order regenerated by the act of writing. Lins's fight with the word – a weapon hidden in itself – aims at recovering it from the degenerative erosion of modern mechanisms. His dialogical discourse unfolds into a discourse about the relationship of the artist with a historical time dominated by oppression. This time of oppression, a clear allusion to the Brazilian mili-

side of Abel is Olavo Haiano, who personifies the strategy of power and imposes himself as an interdiction, as the censor of language. In the plot Olavo Haiano is a military man and the husband of Abel's lover. In the text he is Abel's limitations, embodying the conventions that constantly threaten both the lovers' affair and the continuation of Abel's search. Olavo Haiano's power is perceived in the way he provokes the distance which disintegrates the metaphor, suppresses sexual desire, and destroys identity. He is perceived as the forbidden, the limitation of space. Power is defined by the imposition of limits. Thus the woman falls into mortal anonymity, the trap set by Olavo Haiano, like an obligatory and ritualistic descent into hell. Olavo Haiano is the inevitable mistake that silences her, which confines her within textual limits – coffers, vials, squares, a verbal prison. Unlike Abel, who fertilizes his lover's body through a metaphoric proliferation, Olavo Haiano's poison contaminates the narrative process each time language announces its tary dictatorship in Lins's time, is particularly represented in a narrative line about the historical function of art.

Similar to Abel's novel, the clock idealized by Julius indicates a discontinuous poetic time. It is devised to work in leaps that release certain phrases of a Domenico Scarlatti sonata from time to time. The whole sonata would be liberated only in the right historical moment. Nevertheless, Julius's historical time contradicts the purposes of his masterpiece. Continuously escaping authoritarian regimes that censor his art, the clock instead indicates a chronological time regulated by a tradition of oppression, a repetitive historical time. In *Avalovara* this machine works as a metaphor for the novel itself: it is not only critical of the enslavement of the artist, who has to surrender in times of tyranny, but it also becomes an incongruous product of his creation. Both Julius's poetic leap and the flight of the Avalovara create moments of exception that result from a cosmic conjugation of circumstances, ironic occurrences that could even pass unnoticed in the wrong historical context. This happy conjugation of circumstances coincides with the moment of integration of all eight of the narrative lines in the novel, a simulated convergence of its liberating mechanisms. As a literary artifact, the clock therefore serves a double purpose in the novel: while it controls its timing, the speed of its production, it is also seen as poetry when it breaks up the concept of time itself as a historical and linear convention.

The precision with which the novel is conceived (even the number of words obeys a certain pattern), in the sense that the eight narrative lines that compose it cross each other exactly during Abel's critical moments, offers fragments of his journey as aspects of the world along the way: one line describes his journey in Europe as preparation or "search"; another includes the "encounters" between Abel and Cecilia in Pernambuco, where he confronts Brazilian social problems. Others deal with the "discovery" of the word and its revelation to Abel and the stages preceding the achievement of "plenitude" in the integration of novel and world. Finally, two others respectively refer to the spatial and the temporal dimensions in the novel.

Yet, like the chronological time in Julius's clock, in one narrative line time is illusory because it obeys conventional linearity. Abel's final "revelations" are achieved only through a critical-creative type of reading, or a reversible moment in which the reader not only experiences what seems like chaos but also participates in the cre-

ative assembly of its parts. This passage from chaos to cosmos, from the critical to the creative moment, results in the aesthetic vision — its structure — in the coincidence of forms presented in the beginning: the spiral, evoking the sensitive, "matrix" force, and the square, evoking the spirit, "a blank sheet of paper."

This play of contrasts, typical of baroque architecture, is shown in Abel's use of language. His lover's body evokes the Renaissance feminine figures of Tintoretto or Titian, both painters of the Venetian golden age. The woman called "Twice-Born" combines, in both color and sound, the double-sided character of the word, its life and death: life is suggested not only by the European gold, symbolic of Abel's affair with Roos, but also by the element of fire, symbolic of his affair with Cecilia. In addition, black, the color of death, is the sign for the absence of language. Similarly, her sounds are either lifelike, in the scattered textual echoes of Scarlatti's sonata, or they die in words such as *shot* or *thunder* when they announce Olavo Haiano's presence.

The killing of the lovers by Olavo Haiano's shot at the end of the novel allows for the novel's multiple crossroads, or Abel's routes, to surface in the final scene. Both a scene of fusion and of transposition when writer and novel, or more specifically writer and word, rise from the dead like apocalyptic lovers, it is the transformation of the novel as a traditional form that expresses a decadent world and life to a new poetic form that expresses the world as fiction. In this poetic moment the world and the novel are one. Ironically, this is not yet a perfect moment, for the clock misses the next last group of musical notes and continues its "search." This critical failure in its timing is a break in the creative flow, the final expression of inadmissible historical times. This interruption can also be read as a simple human error, an imperfection that is hardly accounted for in a computerized modern society that trusts technology above all else.

Extreme intersections of life and death undercut Lins's text in a baroque language that tells about itself in a fashion reminiscent of the famous Portuguese baroque sermons of Padre Antonio Vieira. Just as *Avalovara* is a novel about a novel, the *Sermão da Sexagésima* is about the art of preaching. But beyond the common rationalist play in its artful devices, Vieira's sermon is based on the rhetoric of persuasion. Lins's artifice opens itself to criticism by expressing the language of what is really being said. His text provokes both the unfamiliar and the familiar feelings of the modern reader, caught between his own humanism and dehumanized technology.

Simultaneously attached to and alienated from his own times, Lins shows, as a conscious artisan, both the identification and the separation that typify modern society. Octavio Paz says that technical signs show the limits, always on the move, between humanity and the unknown. The double edge of technology is that it captures while it frees the imagination. Lins's writing technique is then both familiar and alienating in its appeal to modern humanity. Above all, his search for cosmic integration brings humanity back in touch with itself while making it free to choose a more human way of living.

## Biography:

Regina Igel, *Osman Lins: Uma biografia literária* (São Paulo: Queiroz/MINC, 1988).

## References:

Mary Lou Daniel, "Through the Looking Glass: Mirror Play in Two Works of João Guimarães Rosa and Osman Lins," *Luso-Brazilian Review,* 13 (Summer 1976): 19–34;

Sandra Nitrini, *Poéticas em confronto: Nove, novena e o novo romance* (São Paulo: Hucitec / Brasilia: Instituto Nacional do Livro, 1987);

Gregory Rabassa, "The Shape and Shaping of the Novel," *World Literature Today,* 53 (Winter 1979): 30–35;

Anatol Rosenfeld, "The Creative Narrative Processes of Osman Lins," *Studies in Short Fiction,* 8 (Winter 1971): 230–244;

Candace Slater, "A Play of Voices: The Theater of Osman Lins," *Hispanic Review,* 49 (Summer 1981): 285–295.

# Lya Luft

*(15 September 1938 –   )*

## Carmen Chaves Tesser
### *University of Georgia*

BOOKS: *Canções de limiar* (Pôrto Alegre, Brazil: Instituto Estadual do Livro, 1964);
*Flauta doce: Tema e variações* (Pôrto Alegre, Brazil: Sulina, 1972);
*Matéria do cotidiano* (Pôrto Alegre, Brazil: Grafosul/Instituto Estadual do Livro, 1978);
*As parceiras* (Rio de Janeiro: Nova Fronteira, 1980);
*A asa esquerda do anjo* (Rio de Janeiro: Nova Fronteira, 1981);
*Reunião de família* (Rio de Janeiro: Nova Fronteira, 1982);
*O quarto fechado* (Rio de Janeiro: Nova Fronteira, 1984); translated by Carmen Chaves McClendon and Betty Jean Craige as *The Island of the Dead* (Athens: University of Georgia Press, 1986);
*Mulher no palco* (Rio de Janeiro: Salamandra, 1984);
*Exílio* (Rio de Janeiro: Guanabara, 1987);
*O lado fatal* (Rio de Janeiro: Rocco, 1988).

In July 1980, amid the usual fanfare reserved for autograph parties for the publication of a new book, the publishing house Nova Fronteira in Rio de Janeiro introduced Lya Luft's novel *As parceiras* (The Players, or The Board Game). At the time Luft was already well-known in Brazilian literary circles as a gifted translator of German- and English-language fiction into Portuguese. In Pôrto Alegre, where she resided, she was also renowned for her essays and poetry published in the local newspapers and literary magazines. When asked why she turned to fiction, Luft explained to Claudia Nocchi in a 1980 interview: "duas coisas me levaran a escrever esse romance angustiado. Uma, assumir o lado trágico da vida. Outra, pôr para fora fantasmas que há tanto me atormentavam" (two things led me to writing this anguished novel. One, to take over the tragic side of life. Another, to exorcise ghosts that tormented me for so long). These two objectives still drive her writing. Critical reaction to *As parceiras* was immediate and positive, best summarized by Antônio Carlos Villaça on 8 November

1980 in the Pôrto Alegre newspaper *Correio do Povo:* "Se me perguntassem qual foi o acontecimento intelectual deste ano que mais me impressionou, diria sem receio que foi a estréia de Lya na ficção" (If I were asked what impressed me the most as an intellectual happening this year, I would say without hesitation that it was Lya's debut in fiction). Less than one year later, when her second novel, *A asa esquerda do anjo* (The Angel's Left Wing, 1981), appeared, *As parceiras* continued to be one of the best-selling works of fiction in Brazil. With the publication of each new novel, Luft's critical acclaim has made her one of the foremost Brazilian writers of the last decade.

Luft's contribution to Brazilian fiction stems from a systematic evolution from *As parceiras* to *Exílio* (Exile, 1987) of what may be termed a search or longing for meaning in a chaotic world. Luft's words express neither the irony found in Machado de Assis nor the metaphysical anguish found in Clarice Lispector. Rather, Luft follows the path of those who opted for stream of consciousness, such as William Faulkner, Marcel Proust, and Virginia Woolf. Josué Montello finds the key to Luft's fiction precisely in her profession as a translator. He concludes that her translations of Rainer Maria Rilke and of Woolf present in Portuguese "dois textos que gostaria de ter escrito. Ou melhor, para ser exact – que poderia ter escrito" (two texts she would have liked to have written. Or rather, to be exact – that she could have written). Luft's originality lies in a combination of subjective style, mysterious themes, magic realism, and a defiant questioning of accepted literary and social norms. The story of her own life reads much like one of her fictional plots, although none of her novels is strictly autobiographical.

Lya Fett Luft was born in Santa Cruz do Sul, a small town in the interior of the southernmost state of Brazil, Rio Grande do Sul, which was colonized by German immigrants during the late nineteenth century. The daughter of an attorney, Arthur

*Lya Luft, circa 1987 (photograph © Eduardo Vieira da Cunha)*

Germano Fett, who taught at the local law school, Luft grew up in a house full of books. She remembers that books were her friends as a child. Some of her earliest memories are of her mother, Wally Neumann Fett, her aunts, and local community women who gathered at her house and always spoke German. Luft and her brother, who was four years younger, had what she remembers as a happy childhood, although she vividly recalls knowing the difference between "us" and "them." The Silvas and Souzas – the Brazilians – were "them"; the Neumanns and Fetts – the Germans – were "us." While the harshness of this segregation does not appear in Luft's work for some time, her history certainly explains some of her preoccupations with being different and feeling alone.

As a child she had many fears. She explains in an interview published in *Autores gaúchos* (1984): "Eu era uma criança impressionada e vivia inutilmente grandes tormentos. Uma fantasia excessiva, alimentada por muita leitura e uma vida entre gente adulta. O universo adulto era para mim fascinante e assustador, uma coisa ambivalente. E porque esse universo não me era bem explicado, ele me assustava" (I was an impressionable child and I lived great torments uselessly. An excessive imagination, fed by much reading and a life among adults. The adult universe was for me fascinating and frightening, something ambiguous. And since that universe was not explained to me adequately, it scared me). Thus her formative years were filled with irrational

fears; the most critical, according to Luft, was fear of fear itself.

Luft developed a keen literary sense by reading from her father's vast library. She graduated from Colégio Mauá in 1953. In 1955 she moved to Pôrto Alegre, the capital city of Rio Grande do Sul, to attend normal school at the Colégio Americano (a Methodist missionary boarding school). Homesick and unhappy, Luft returned to Santa Cruz do Sul in 1957 to finish her studies at the normal school of the Colégio Sagrado Coração de Jesus. In 1958 she moved permanently to Pôrto Alegre, where she began to study pedagogy at Catholic University.

The 1960s, tumultuous times in Brazil, were also transitional times in Luft's life. In 1960 she completed her study of pedagogy and began studying Germanic languages at Catholic University. In 1962 she won her first literary prize in a contest sponsored by the Instituto Estadual do Livro (State Book Institute). Along with the recognition came the publication of her first book, *Canções de limiar* (Threshold Songs, 1964). During her studies she met the Marist brother Celso Pedro Luft, already known as one of the foremost linguists in Brazil. They fell in love, and, defying most accepted social norms and strong disapproval from the literary community, they were married in 1963. When Luft published her second volume of poetry, *Flauta doce* (Sweet Flute, 1972), she was the mother of three children: Susana, born in 1965; André, 1966; and

Eduardo, 1969. She was also a faculty member in linguistics at the Faculdade Pôrto-Alegrense de Ciências e Letras (Pôrto Alegre College of Arts and Sciences). In addition, she had a weekly column in *Correio do Povo* and began translating for the publishing house Editora Globo. Her life seemed perfect. But, as she indicates, fate hides in every corner. In 1973 her father suffered a fatal heart attack, and Luft for the first time was forced to confront her most secret fear – death. The fear of death and the playing of hide-and-seek with it is illustrated in all of Luft's fiction. As she said in the *Autores gaúchos* interview: "Minha vida se dividiu ao meio. Com ele perdi minha infância" (My life was divided in half. With him, I lost my childhood).

In 1974 Luft received national acclaim for her translation of Günter Grass and began her career as a translator for two other publishing houses, Record and Nova Fronteira. So successful were her translations that she decided to dedicate her intellectual energy toward bringing German- and English-language titles to Brazil. To this end she translated some fifty works by writers such as Woolf, Rilke, Doris Lessing, Hermann Hesse, Thomas Mann, Norman Mailer, and Robert Musil, among others. During this period, while translating thousands of pages of foreign fiction, she completed a master's degree in linguistics at Catholic University in 1975 and another master's degree in Brazilian literature from the Federal University of Rio Grande do Sul in 1978. Again life seemed to stabilize for Luft, and again it played a trick on her. She suffered a near-fatal automobile accident in 1977. Her brush with death and slow recovery gave Luft a new perspective on life. In her mind the accident was the turning point from seeing the world through rose-colored glasses and writing essays that reflected a world of appearances – acceptable middle-class values – to the kind of fiction that she writes today. In 1978 the Fundación Givré in Buenos Aires, Argentina, awarded her the Alfonsi Storni Poetry Prize for "Retrato a Dois" (Picture of a Couple). The same year, in a collection entitled *Matéria do cotidiano* (Daily Life Subjects), she published the last of her light essays and, in her words, turned another page in her existence. It was after this stage in her life that Luft the powerful fiction writer emerged.

*As parceiras,* structured in seven short chapters, each representing one day of the week, revolves around the meaningless life of the protagonist, Anelise, who during a week of solitude manages to unravel not only her own life but also the lives of those around her. The protagonist reflects on her life and compares herself to her grandmother, Catarina Von Sassen, who had been isolated in an attic room of the old family home. The story of Anelise is the story of many women who suddenly find themselves searching for meaning in their existence. Against a background of cliffs and the ocean reminiscent of the Torres beach where Luft and her family spent many summers, Anelise goes through a process of meditation on the theme of death. At the same time two "partners" are playing a board game. Because the narrative is written in a diarylike sequence, the reader has the impression of discovering reality at the same time as Anelise. As the days go by, Luft creates an atmosphere of shadows and moldy odors that both fascinate and repulse the reader. After seven days of meditation, Anelise meets the ghostlike figure that had haunted her, and they go down the cliffs.

The last sentence in this novel, "Descemos de mãos dadas" (We descended holding hands), is open and problematic. Not only is the reader not exactly sure who the woman in white is, but also the reader is left to imagine whether the descent means suicide, a walk back to the house, or a figurative descent into insanity. This kind of mind game has befuddled critics and amused the writer. In a 1991 interview published in *Brasil/Brazil,* Luft stated, "Everybody asks me, 'This last sentence, . . . did she commit suicide, did she go crazy, did she reconcile with life with the ghost of her grandmother?' I don't know, I don't know." Even in this first novel the reader finds, as is apparent in all other Luft narratives, a series of levels of reality presented in the form of a game. Because of the development of Luft's narrative, critics now can go back to *As parceiras* and describe the game as one between life and death, or perhaps as one between Eros and Thanatos.

In *A asa esquerda do anjo* Luft continues her exploration of an immigrant German family. Although the physical space described in this text is somewhat smaller – a house, a graveyard – the narrative dramatic space is larger than that portrayed in *As parceiras.* Lígia Averbuck, in a 1981 article in *Zero Hora,* describes this opening of the dramatic space as "destruição do mito familiar" (the destruction of the family myth). In this novel the figure of the grandmother, Frau Wolf, represents a strong controlling matriarchal force that commands respect based on the fear of those around her.

The protagonist, Guísela, unlike Anelise of *As parceiras,* must rid herself of the ghost. She is able to do so, but hers is not a descent holding hands. Luft employs in this narrative the elements of both magic realism and the fantastic. The narrative, written in the form of point/counterpoint, describes literally what goes on inside the protagonist and what goes

*Luft in 1981 (photograph by Lisete Guerra)*

on around her. The final birthing process – the one that transforms Guísela into Gisela – again leaves the narrative open-ended. Has Guísela now become rid of her irrational fears? Has she destroyed her inner self by giving birth to a milk-starved worm? Luft provides no answers. This novel is another step in the process of discovering "qual é a minha identidade?" (What is my identity?). The fine lines between love and hate, life and death, and nurture and malice are blurred. In *Autores gaúchos* José Onofre states, "Oútero e o tumulo se confundem, se tornam a mesma coisa híbrida, doente, assustadora" (Uterus and tomb are confused; they become the same hybrid thing, sick, frightening).

The third novel by Luft, *Reunião de família* (Family Gathering, 1982), continues the theme of the incomprehensible fact of death but discards the German immigrant family. Luft admits that it was a conscious process to stop being the writer of German descendants. Luft's preoccupation is much more universal than that of one group of immigrants in one country. *Reunião de família* depicts an uncommunicative family gathering together one weekend, during which two sisters, their brother, two of their spouses, their father, and a maid painfully relive their past, unearthing buried secrets as

well as buried emotions. As the characters one by one disclose their secrets, the apparently solid foundations of their personalities crack, like the brick patio floor that buckles with the intrusion of the roots of the recently felled poplar tree.

The drama, primarily stated from the point of view of Alice, the protagonist of *Reunião de família*, takes place in front of a large cracked mirror, which reflects mutilated images of the characters and which serves as a corridor to another world. Continuing the technique of counterpoint, Luft is masterful in her description of the game. This time the game is one in which each character has three realities: they are who they see as themselves; they are who others see; and they are reflections of the two. So careful is Luft in crafting the narrative that not only is the discourse level balanced from the beginning to end, but the narrative begins and ends with Alice's mention of wanting a large mirror. Thus the end of the narrative is merely a reflection of the beginning of the narrative. This time, although the meaning remains open, the narrative provides us with an unusual and ambiguous circularity. This ambiguity attracted Caio Fernando Abreu to adapt *Reunião de família* to the theater. The play opened 14 June 1984 in the Clube de Cultura in Pôrto Alegre.

The purposefully planned short run was applauded by packed audiences and praised by critical reviewers.

As critics increasingly began to notice the intricacies of Luft's narrative, the House of Representatives honored her with the Erico Veríssimo Prize for literature. The ceremony held in the chamber room of the House of Representatives included the presentation of a gold medallion and a certificate. Luft was moved by the ceremony and presented accolades of her own for the award's namesake, Erico Veríssimo, who had been a personal friend and, with his wife Mafalda, had served as godparent to her son André. In her acceptance speech she claimed to be aware of her role not only as a writer but also specifically as a Brazilian writer. Quoted in a news release published in *Folha da Tarde,* 8 April 1983, she says that "o escritor tem uma missão: expôr, através da ficção, realidades das gentes em geral, de forma séria, abordando desde o corriqueiro até as feridas da sociedade" (the writer has one mission: to show, through fiction, the reality of people in general in a serious fashion, covering [topics] from the mundane to society's wounds). In her concluding remarks she announced that her new novel, tentatively called "Ilha dos mortos" (Island of Death), was almost complete.

Anyone studying the ascending orbit of Luft's career and familiar with her personal history would at this time be braced for a dramatic change of some sort in the writer's life. Such was the case shortly after the publication of her fourth novel, *O quarto fechado* (The Island of the Dead, 1984). While attending the 1985 Congresso Brasileiro de Escritores (Brazilian Writers' Congress), she met for the first time Hélio Pellegrino, one of the foremost psychoanalysts of Brazil and a noted journalist. Their instant friendship continued for some time through the exchange of letters. The success of *O quarto fechado* led Luft to several visits to Rio de Janeiro and meetings with Pellegrino. Their friendship blossomed to love, and although both were middle-aged, Luft claims that they never felt older than twenty during their time together. While her personal life became chaotic, *O quarto fechado* continued to acquire critical accolades. In *World Literature Today* in 1985 Malcolm Silverman concluded that this novel, "together with her previous three pieces, completes a homogeneous mosaic in which emphasis on atmosphere and characterization reinforces the search for (female) self-identity."

As in Greek tragedy, time in this novel has been totally compressed to a twenty-four-hour period. The action takes place during the wake for an eighteen-year-old boy named Camilo who has taken his own life. The narrative consists almost entirely of the thoughts of the family members: the boy's mother, Renata, who has given up a career as a concert pianist for marriage and motherhood; his father, Martin; his maiden aunt Clara; his foster grandmother, whom everyone calls "Mother"; and his twin sister, Carolina. The point of view shifts from one mind to another, back and forth, as the characters through their separate memories together reconstruct the boy's past. Even the dead boy takes part, in sections headed by the phrase "Se ele pudesse falar ele diria . . ." (If he could speak, the dead boy would say . . .). Another character is both present and absent – by now a staple in Luft's fiction. This time the living/dead character is Ella, Mother's illegitimate daughter, who because of an accident that paralyzed her long ago has rotted in the locked room upstairs. For thirty years she is nothing but a huge mass of flesh, unable to speak, attended to by Mother and feared by Martin. This creature, like the woman in white in *As parceiras,* the angel in *A asa esquerda do anjo,* and the professor in *Reunião de família,* fascinates, frightens, and repulses each character in a different way. Like these other elusive characters, Ella is the only one whose point of view is not represented.

The continuous searching that the reader finds in Luft's narrative – the frustrating open-ended ambiguous search in *As parceiras,* the search for identity in *A asa esquerda do anjo,* the search for meaning of life in *Reunião de família* – in this novel becomes a search for the meaning of death. "What is death?" emerges as a constant query from every point of view. More than the others, this novel explores the struggle between life forces (Eros) and death forces (Thanatos). *O quarto fechado* reached a wide audience in Brazil. In 1986 the translation into English by Carmen Chaves McClendon and Betty Jean Craige as *The Island of the Dead* was published.

It was during this period of great professional growth for Luft that Hélio Pellegrino entered her life. It was an extremely difficult time for Luft. Her situation in Pôrto Alegre with her husband was comfortable, and her children were with her at this time. Once again her stable and predictable world was shattered. She astounded the literary and social communities in Pôrto Alegre and moved to Rio de Janeiro to be with Pellegrino.

Another collection of her poetry, *Mulher no palco* (Woman on Stage, 1984), appeared. The volume collects some reflections about being a woman and being what others want her to be. Luciano Alabarse adapted the poems from *Mulher no palco* for a

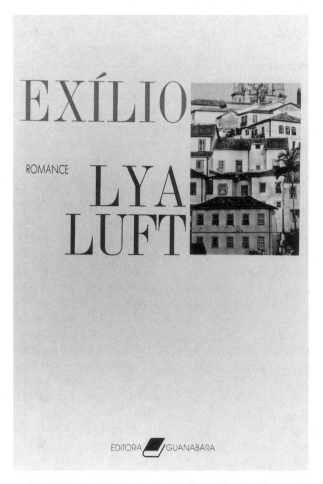

*Dust jacket for Luft's 1987 novel, about a boardinghouse and
its inhabitants*

reader's theater, and the result was staged at the Casa de Cultura Mario Quintana. The move to Rio de Janeiro was not an easy transition for Luft. She was literally living some of the dilemmas that she had so carefully described in her novels; her strong passion divided her. During this period she began working on her fifth novel, tentatively titled "Mulher dividida" (Divided Woman). The novel appeared in 1987 with the title *Exílio*.

In *Exílio*, written entirely during her stay in Rio de Janeiro, the reader finds again the intimate narrative characteristic of Luft's style. The spatial world is closed. The locked room of *O quarto fechado* has become a closed boardinghouse. The characters come and go in puppetlike fashion without expressing emotion. Ever present and ever elusive throughout the narrative is the character of the dwarf gnome, who in this text takes the place of the ghosts of the earlier stories. More so than in previous novels, the characters in *Exílio* are caricatures, and like Mother of *O quarto fechado* they are known only by their descriptions:

the brunette, the blonde, the fat one, the mother. An interesting twist to this text is the appearance of the house itself as a character.

*Exílio* is better understood in the context of all of Luft's works. It is a culmination in the process of human self-searching, giving answers to the questions posed in earlier texts. The exile is present in everyone's lives whether or not they connect with anything or anyone. Luft dismisses the autobiographical elements in *Exílio* in the *Brasil/Brazil* interview: "I think sometimes the reader fantasizes a lot about [autobiographical elements] and projects on the writer and the characters a lot of himself. I have only one book that is really autobiographical. That is *O lado fatal*."

On 23 March 1988, after two years of a "fascinating and frightening" life together, Hélio Pellegrino suffered a fatal heart attack, and Luft came face to face with death once more. Forced to leave her world of dreams and fantasy and make decisions concerning her future, Luft turned to the one escape that comforted her. She wrote *O lado fatal* (The Fatal Side, 1988), a collection of poems dedicated to the short life she shared with Pellegrino. *O lado fatal* became an instant best-seller and continued on the best-seller lists in some regions of Brazil into the early 1990s.

In 1988 Luft returned to Pôrto Alegre to be near her children. She continued to translate and began writing her sixth novel. In the spring of 1989 she made her first visit to the United States; less than a year later she was invited to participate in a meeting of world writers held in Canada. In the late 1980s she announced that she and Celso Pedro Luft had once again begun a life together. Shortly after their reconciliation Celso Pedro suffered a near-fatal stroke and became incapacitated. Today Luft is at peace and is happy with her children while she cares for their father. It is difficult, however, for a student of Luft's works and life to be perfectly at peace. But as she has often said when her work has been compared to that of Clarice Lispector, "she was a philosopher, I am a dreamer."

Luft represents those Brazilian writers preoccupied with universal fears – death, identity – that contribute to the struggle of life. In her fiction she depicts women protagonists, which places her among the best who describe the situation of women in Latin America in general and Brazil in particular. Her fiction goes beyond the definition of being female, however, attempting to define the existential struggle of being human. She has described her writing as compulsive; once she starts a project it is difficult for her to stop. In a 1987 interview with Walter Sebastião published in the *Tribuna de Minas,* she explained how she was able to write five well-crafted and beautifully executed novels from 1980 to 1987: "por ter desejado toda a minha vida escrever romance (e não ter tido coragem), começou a vir tudo de uma vez" (because all my life I wanted to write novels [and did not have the courage to do so], everything began to come to me at once).

Lya Luft's novels compel the reader to continue reading even as they frighten and repulse. Her narrative work set in motion with *As parceiras* has been described by critics as an approach-avoidance of death, a fictional game that may well place the reader in a posi-

tion of approach-avoidance of the text itself. The reader, though frightened by what the text may reveal, continues to read in morbid fascination representative of Luft's characters, and to await with anticipation the next novel by this gifted Brazilian writer.

**Interviews:**

Wilson Chagas, "O inquietante jogo da vida e da solidão," *O Estado de São Paulo* (21 June 1981): 27;

Lígia Averbuck, "Com a palavra a mulher: A novela de Lya Luft e a condição feminina," *Zero Hora,* 25 August 1981, n.p.;

Regina Zilberman, ed., *Autores gaúchos: Lya Luft* (Pôrto Alegre, Brazil: Instituto Estadual do Livro, 1984);

Walter Sebastião, "Inquieto mergulho nas profundezas da alma," *Tribuna de Minas,* 3 July 1987, n.p.;

Judith A. Payne, "Lya Luft: Fiction and the Possible Selves," *Brasil/Brazil,* 5 (1991): 104–114.

**References:**

Carmen Chaves McClendon, "O espelho e a realidade em *Reunião de Família*," *O Eixo e a Roda,* 4 (1985): 5–11;

Chaves McClendon, "Reflexos de reflexos e a narrativa femenina de Lya Luft," *Anais do primeiro simpósio de literatura comparada,* 1 (1987): 48–54;

Chaves McClendon, "Theoretical Dialogue in *O quarto fechado*," *Chasqui: Revista de literatura latinoamericana,* 17 (November 1988): 23–26;

Josué Montello, "Entre Rilke e Virginia Woolf," *Manchete,* 12 November 1983, p. 94;

Alberto Moreiras, "Símbolo, alegoria y temporalidad en *Reunião de família* de Lya Luft," *Hispania,* 70 (May 1987): 250–256;

Susan Canty Quinlan, *The Female Voice in Contemporary Brazilian Narrative* (New York: Peter Lang, 1991);

Malcolm Silverman, review of Luft's *O quarto fechado,* in *World Literature Today,* 59 (Spring 1985): 252–253;

Antônio Carlos Villaça, "Romance da ambiguidade: *As parceiras*," *Correio do Povo,* 8 November 1980, p. 16.

# Nicholasa Mohr

*(1 November 1938 – )*

John C. Miller
*University of Colorado, Colorado Springs*

BOOKS: *Nilda,* illustrated by Mohr (New York: Harper & Row, 1973);

*El Bronx Remembered,* illustrated by Mohr (New York: Harper & Row, 1975);

*In Nueva York* (New York: Dial, 1977);

*Felita* (New York: Dial, 1979);

*Rituals of Survival: A Woman's Portfolio* (Houston: Arte Público, 1985);

*Going Home* (New York: Dial, 1986);

*All for the Better* (Austin, Tex.: Raintree Stech-Vaughn, 1993);

*Old Letivia and the Mountain of Sorrows* (New York: Viking, 1993);

*In My Own Words: Growing Up inside the Sanctuary of My Imagination* (New York: Messner, 1994).

TELEVISION: "Aquí y Ahora" (five half-hour videotapes focusing on Caribbean Hispanic Americans living in the United States), Film Video Arts, 1975.

RADIO: "Inside the Monster – Latino Women Writers," Film Video Arts, 1981.

OTHER: "A Special Gift," in *Kikirikí: Stories and Poems in English and Spanish for Children,* edited by Sylvia Cavazos Peña (Houston: Arte Público, 1981), pp. 91–101;

"An Awakening – Summer 1956," in *Woman of Her Word: Hispanic Women Write,* edited by Evangelina Vigil (Houston: Arte Público, 1983), pp. 107–112;

"Puerto Ricans in New York: Cultural Evolution and Identity," in *Images and Identity: The Puerto Rican in Two World Cultures,* edited by Adela Rodríguez de Laguna (New Brunswick, N.J.: Transaction, 1985), pp. 157–160;

"Jaime and the Conch Shell," in *Tun-Ta-Ca-Tun: More Stories and Poems in English and Spanish for Children,* edited by Cavazos Peña (Houston: Arte Público, 1986), pp. 181–189;

*Nicholasa Mohr, circa 1977 (photograph by Richard Howard)*

"Uncle Nick's Gift," in *Passages* (New York: Holt Rinehart & Winston, 1988), pp. 376–391;

"Puerto Rican Writers in the U.S.; Puerto Rican Writers in Puerto Rico: A Separation Beyond Language (testimonio)," in *Breaking Boundaries: Latina Writing and Critical Reading,* edited by Asunción Horno Delgado, Eliana Ortega, Nina M. Scott, and Nancy Saporta Sternbach (Amherst: University of Massachusetts Press, 1989), pp. 111–116.

SELECTED PERIODICAL PUBLICATIONS – UNCOLLECTED: "On Being Authentic," *The Americas Review,* 15 (Fall–Winter 1986): 106–109;

"The Journey toward a Common Ground: Struggle and Identity of Hispanics in the USA," *The Americas Review,* 18 (Spring 1990): 81–85.

Nicholasa Mohr, a significant New York–Puerto Rican (Nuyorican) writer, focuses on life in the city with particular emphasis on the lives of adolescents and women. Her books reflect the psychological, spiritual, and physical experiences of the Nuyorican traveling between two cultures, island and mainland. Her novels and short stories span the time period from the 1940s to the 1980s, capturing the changing and evolving role of the Puerto Rican community in New York as it extends from the Bronx and the Barrio (Spanish Harlem) and as the generational ties weaken among members of extended families on the mainland and on the island. Her writing, based largely on her own experiences, explores the joys and sorrows of living in the Barrio, the Bronx, and Losaida, the Lower East Side. Mohr is also a distinguished teacher, lecturer, and visual artist whose stories are collected and anthologized in numerous textbooks.

With four young sons in Puerto Rico, her mother, Nicholasa Rivera, went to New York at age twenty-two in the 1930s to join her sister, another emigrant escaping the rugged economic conditions of the island. In New York Nicholasa Rivera met and married Pedro Golpe (probably originally Guelpi), a Basque merchant marine seaman from La Coruña, Spain, and reunited the family in New York with her four sons from Ponce, where they had been living with an aunt. This marriage produced two more sons and a daughter, Nicholasa, who was born on 1 November 1938 in an apartment in the Barrio on a kitchen table because her mother refused to leave her other children.

Mohr grew up in the Barrio and attended school on Prospect Avenue in the Bronx. Her father died when she was eight years old and her mother when she was in junior high school. She attended Stabermore High School, a textile high school in Manhattan. She married briefly just after high school and began attending the Art Students League and City College. After her annulment she went to Berkeley, California, and to Mexico, where she studied in the Taller de Gráficos. On her return in 1957 she met and married Irwin Mohr, a graduate student in psychology at Brooklyn College, and began to study at the Brooklyn Museum, the New School for Social Research, and the Pratt Institute of Technology. While living in Manhattan they had two children, David and Jason. After the death of her husband in 1978, Mohr moved from Teaneck, New Jersey, to Brooklyn. Descriptions of her family and their experiences in New York are recounted in her early work.

Mohr's mentors and studies were principally in the visual arts – Richard Mayhew and Ruben Tan at the Brooklyn Museum, Roberto Delamonica at Pratt, and Bob Conover at the New School. Her first show, "art densely laden with graffiti" in an East Side gallery in 1971, was successful. Her art agent suggested that she write something, preferably something similar to Piri Thomas's popular autobiography *Down These Mean Streets* (1967). Supported intellectually by her husband and her brother Vincent, who worked in publishing, she wrote and then typed fifty pages of memories – all painful events in her own life. In 1972, when contacted by a publisher to illustrate a book jacket, Mohr handed over her fifty pages and two weeks later received a book contract. Her visual artist fellowship at the MacDowell Colony was transformed, providing her the opportunity to write the first eighty-eight pages of *Nilda.*

Published in 1973, *Nilda* is dedicated to the children of El Barrio. As with many authors' first books, the novel is replete with autobiographical elements. The book details growing up in El Barrio between 1941 and 1945, the life of the female protagonist paralleling the author's life through her adolescence to a climax marked by her mother's death. The stepfather in the novel is a left-wing Gallego, a refugee of the Spanish Civil War, not unlike Pedro Golpe, a Communist anticlerical Spaniard. Jimmy in *Nilda* is a heroin addict, as was Mohr's older brother.

The initial setting of this novel of the 1940s reflects the tensions of ethnic groups in New York, particularly in those neighborhoods where minimal communication existed between the Puerto Ricans and the police. A walk with her mother and brother through the neighborhood provides portraits of urban violence that are signposts in the book. While trying to find information about her missing "tecato" (drug-addicted) brother, Nilda, her mother, and her brother cross streets marked by a stabbing and a row of young prostitutes who solicit her brother. Jimmy, the drug abuser, has flashy clothes, new cars, and a pregnant girlfriend. Nilda escapes the conflicts of her home – a sick, hospitalized father; many siblings; a room shared with a brother's girlfriend – through her art:

> Nilda loved to draw; it was the thing that gave her the most pleasure. She sat looking at her cardboard box affectionately. Carefully she began to stack her card-

board cutouts. Her stepfather would give her the light grey cardboard that was in his shirts whenever they came back from the Chinese laundry. She cut these into different shapes making people dolls, animals, cars, buildings or whatever she fancied. Then she would draw on them, filling in the form and color of whatever she wanted. She had no more cardboard but she had some white lined paper that Victor had given her. Drawing a line, and then another, she had a sense of happiness. Slowly working, she began to divide the space and she lost herself in a world of magic achieved with some forms, lines and color.

The novel, reflecting the inhospitable and often-hostile environment of the Anglo world, highlights numerous cultural conflicts recognized and acknowledged in today's multicultural world. The schools promote Anglo-American values. Students have their hands rapped with a ruler if they speak Spanish; for more serious infractions they are placed in a corner dunce chair. Notes from parents who are functionally illiterate are challenged for their meaning or validity, as is the X of a parent's signature. Three teachers are profiled in the book: Miss Heinz with anecdotes of her working-class family and middle-class aspirations; Miss Fortinash, with no understanding of Hispanic mourning customs; and Miss Reilly, a Spanish teacher, who demands Castilian accents of Puerto Rican children.

Social-service organizations are also fearsome institutions in *Nilda*. Because of the father's heart attacks and eventual death, the family is forced into the welfare system. The traditional Fresh Air camp experience for city children is divided into two camps, a regimented Catholic camp with obligatory evening milk-of-magnesia rituals and a more socially aware camp in a setting that permits Nilda to find her secret garden, a place of refuge whenever strife appears:

> Breathless, she stared at the flowers, almost unbelieving for a moment, thinking that she might be in a movie theater waiting for the hard, flat, blank screen to appear, putting an end to a manufactured fantasy which had engrossed and possessed her so completely. Nilda walked over to the flowers and touched them, inhaling the sweet fragrance, she felt slightly dizzy, almost reeling. She sat down on the dark earth and felt the sun on her face, slipping down her body and over to the shrubs covered with roses. The bright sash of warm sunlight enveloped her and the flowers; she was part of them; they were part of her.

This happiness sustains the protagonist through Barrio and family problems. Gangs and police beat up innocent youths. Petra, a friend, gets pregnant in junior high school. The neighborhood

is wrapped in World War II politics as effigies of Adolf Hitler, Hideki Tojo, and Benito Mussolini are burned near a sales booth for war stamps and war bonds. American flags, each symbolizing a loved one in the service, appear in apartment windows. Brothers grow up and disappear from the family.

Ethnic events and phenomena are integrated into the Nuyorican experience. Aunt Delia's adventures with *la bolita* (an illegal numbers game), the food prepared at home, and the spiritualist Doña Tiofila, who does a purification of the house, are blended into the Hispanic quilt of Spanish Harlem life. Nilda continues her art and her creative development. Even when family crises are at their worst, fantasy provides an escape from harsh reality:

> Turning away, she lay back on the cot and looked up at the ceiling. Very carefully, she started to search in between and around the cracks, discolorations and peeling paint, that took on different shapes and dimensions for her favorite scenes. This was a game she loved to play. By using her eyes she discovered that, if she concentrated carefully, she actually began to see all kinds of different shapes and forms and exciting events taking place on the ceiling.

Nilda's life is marked by loss and death. In 1943 her stepfather Emilio dies. Jimmy, her brother, is lost to the world of drugs. Leo, another brother, moves away with his girlfriend. But the singular crisis of Nilda's life occurs when her mother becomes ill and dies and the remaining family is dispersed — she to her aunt in the Bronx, Frankie to military service, Aunt Delia to the nursing home. In her last visits to her mother Nilda receives advice that guides her life. Her mother advises her not to "have a bunch of babies and thus lose (waste) her life" and underscores the importance of her identity. As Nilda contemplates her future, she remembers her secret garden.

In *Nilda* Mohr uses realistic and at times coarse street language and integrates popular Puerto Rican Spanish terms, such as *la jara* (police), in the text. An easily accessible work of fiction, it reflects life in the Barrio in the early 1940s.

Her next work, *El Bronx Remembered* (1975), consists of eleven short stories and a novella, "Herman and Alice." The time frame spans the postwar years from 1946 to 1956. Themes change as individual and familial situations are explored, but the malaise of rural Puerto Ricans adapting to the city permeates the collection. Point of view passes from the single narrative voice in *Nilda* to the multicultural perspective of the changing urban neighborhood. Psychological conflicts are explored, and individual character development becomes more significant. The introduction states clearly the nature of the stories: "These migrants and their children, strangers in their own country, brought with them a different language, culture and racial mixture. Like so many before them they hoped for a better life, a new future for their children, and a piece of that good life known as the 'American dream.'"

Dreams and disillusionments characterize the stories. "Once upon a time . . . " describes the discovery by young girls of a body in a semiabandoned building, and "Tell the Truth" depicts the repressive legalistic environment that the drug trade brings to the childhood experience. "Love with Aleluya" returns the reader to the Pentecostal setting of *Nilda*. Two young males pursue a young, attractive "aleluya" and attend the service of "La salvación de Adam [*sic*] y Eva" (The Salvation of Adam and Eve). Mohr satirizes emergent machismo and affectionately indulges adolescent attractions.

Cultures are in transition as the Puerto Rican migration to the Bronx increases. Based on the author's experience, in "Mr. Mendelsohn" a family adopts an aging Jewish gentleman who has raised his six sisters and is left alone in a changing Hispanic neighborhood. Only the high holidays or a family event prevents his Sunday visit next door. The decaying nature of the environment ultimately forces his sisters to relocate him in a nursing home–residential hotel. But Mr. Mendelsohn is not abandoned by his adopted Puerto Rican family.

"A Lesson in Fortune Telling" examines the interethnic fantasy of children when an exotic Gypsy child who tells fortunes and reads palms appears in their classes. Jasmine, mysteriously dressed and living in a storefront apartment, depicts the world beyond the botanica and the *espiritista* (spiritualist) of *Nilda*. Teachers and authority figures represent the majority community as Ms. Braun, the teacher, and Mrs. Gevertz, the vice principal, maintain the school transitions. "The Wrong Lunch Line" also reflects the changing ethnic composition of the Bronx. The teacher and lunch monitor refuse to permit Yvette, a young Puerto Rican child, to join her friend Mildred in the Passover lunch line. The vice principal instructs Yvette not to go where she does not belong. However, the friends laugh at the incident while sharing some matzo.

While some of Mohr's stories focus on ethnic change and diversity, others narrate the Nuyorican experience. "A Very Special Pet" pertains to the rural memories of Graciela that are symbolized by Joncrofo, a skinny white hen that lives in their small

Cover by Mohr for her first book, a novel about a family in a New York barrio

five-room apartment. "Shoes for Hector" presents a familiar tale of family fortunes and hard times when Hector is forced to borrow a pair of orange shoes from his uncle for graduation from high school. He receives several prizes at graduation, including a watch and a twenty-five-dollar check that permits him to buy new shoes.

Perspective changes and the narrative voice constantly shifts in *El Bronx Remembered*. "A New Window Display" depicts a child's reaction to death and funeral rituals, while "Princess" and "Uncle Claudio" examine adult perspectives of class structure and social mores.

The novella "Herman and Alice" is one of the earliest U.S. Hispanic works to confront the topic of homosexuality, portraying a pregnant teenager in an arranged marriage of convenience with a "sensitive" neighbor, Herman Aviles. After the child is born the "Madonna de mis sueños" (Madonna of My Dreams) becomes a typical sixteen year old, and Herman's thoughts return to his lost love Daniel.

Part 4 of the forty-six-page novella reflects the aftermath of this doomed relationship. Herman, back in Puerto Rico, reestablishes his professional life, and Alice, abandoned by a subsequent boyfriend, gives birth to a second child and fantasizes about the once-pleasant relationship with Herman. This bittersweet narrative blends the two perspectives from El Bronx and from the island.

This concern for the marginalized homosexual also appears in *In Nueva York* (1977). In it "The Perfect Little Flower Girl" describes the arranged marriage of Johnny, a partner in a gay couple, when he must enter the military with a lesbian friend in order to provide income and support for his sickly partner Sebastian. This story, set in the Vietnam period, describes their relationship with Raquel Martínez, the next-door neighbor. Throughout the story extended families appear, and the reader learns of the New York City foster-care system, racial and ethnic prejudices, and the love and affection of different family structures. Elements of earlier stories are integrated as Rudi, the store owner around whose business neighborhood life centers, lends Raquel Martínez the meat slicer for the cold cuts for the reception as well as a large coffee urn – his present to his regular customers. As in much of Mohr's writings, the theme of a community overcoming prejudice – ethnic, racial, sexist, or heterosexist – emerges from the text.

*El Bronx Remembered* expands Mohr's narrative from a single speaker to many as the circumstances and values of an emerging Nuyorican culture, different from that of the mainland, emerge. The characters deal with their problems as external forces disappear, and individual destinies are defined in the Bronx of this period. The work also moves from descriptive prose to vivid use of dialogue and to a variety of registers as the diversity within the neighborhood expands. There are fewer expressions in Spanish as the Nuyorican evolves and uses English more. The linguistic shift suggests that Nuyoricans have become permanent members of the North American community and that Mohr has attempted to reach a wider audience.

Mohr's third book, *In Nueva York* (1977), takes the reader to a different New York setting, Losaida on the lower East Side, where the author worked with community-based arts groups in visual and media productions. This series of short stories depicts a neighborhood, centered in a restaurant, where characters appear and reappear in an established setting. They own stores, attend English class, and climb the social ladder, but island values permeate their lives.

"The Operation" shows the diversity of the population with one protagonist, a young Puerto Rican girl named Jennie, and Nate Abrahamson, a retired, sympathetic, aging tugboat captain with no friends. Set against the neighborhood's concern with violence and child molestation, Anglo and Nuyorican mothers express their concerns. In the 1960s change comes to the neighborhood as the Lower East Side becomes gentrified with liberals seeking diversity.

Rudi's restaurant is the central location for a series of stories whose characters gather there. "Lali" reflects the attempt of Rudi to import an "old-fashioned" girl from Puerto Rico as a bride. She falls in love with another worker in the restaurant, Chiquitín's brother Federico. The romance is doomed, the opportunist Federico escapes with stolen funds, and Chiquitín, her coworker, comforts the abandoned lover. Chiquitín himself is the long-lost son of the title character of "Old Mary" and returns to her on the Lower East Side. Her memory of the beautiful, blond, angelic son is somewhat shattered by his surprising appearance. Chiquitín begins working in Rudi's store, and he takes English lessons with Lali in another story called "The English Lesson." And all three are working in the restaurant when "The Robbery" takes place. Chiquitín is injured and Rudi shoots and kills one of the youths who commit the robbery. The thief's mother camps outside the restaurant demanding restitution, a grave marker for her son.

Rudi's luncheonette is also the setting for the conversation of Lillian and Yolanda in "I Never Even Seen My Father." Lillian's explanation of the Freudian interpretation of the Greek myth of Oedipus brings popular culture to comic center stage. Freudian psychology is countered by Lillian's account of the *espiritista* Doña Digna and her successful psychotherapy.

Yolanda's explanation of why individuals turn to drugs is clean and rational, presenting a logical, common-sense approach new to Lillian. Luncheon trade takes the reader back to the neighborhood as Lali, Chiquitín, and others do their work. The girls say goodbye, realizing both that their worlds are different and that they may never see each other again but swearing eternal friendship. Lillian retreats to her building, somewhat relieved that her "ace buddy" will probably never call again.

*In Nueva York* expands the fictional cosmos of Nicholasa Mohr by integrating the people in a neighborhood while expanding character development and diversifying point of view. Language continues to reflect the textures of English, English as a second language, and phrases maintained by second- and third-generation Nuyoricans born and raised in the city. Community building is a theme, and while the occasional robbery or theft may occur, the Barrio or Losaida is a total society, an environment that includes good and bad, right and wrong. A scroungy alley cat serves as continuity, a survivor appearing and reappearing throughout the stories that form the microcosm of the greater society.

*Felita* (1979) details the everyday experiences of an eight year old growing up in an urban community, and *Going Home* (1986) takes the same protagonist at age twelve back to Puerto Rico, her grandmother's paradise, where she must confront island prejudice against Nuyoricans. Written for younger readers, these novellas continue to reflect the changing urban experience, taking place during the 1970s and 1980s.

In *Felita* the first-person narrative voice is childlike, becoming more pensive as the protagonist becomes a young adolescent in *Going Home*. Nevertheless, the conflicts are less autobiographical and more cultural than in *Nilda*. Felita has two older brothers: Johnny, who looks like his mother with light brown skin and short black curly hair, and Tito, who is blond and pale like his father. Felita's initial welcome by the girls in a new neighborhood is friendly, but when the adults intervene, prejudice emerges.

In her first violent encounter with her neighbors Felita is scared, hurt, and angry. She visits her old neighborhood and is afraid to share her experience with her best friend Gigi. Older adolescents beat up Johnny, "the spick." When the landlord recommends they move, the parents are indecisive, wanting their children to have better opportunities. The family moves back to the old neighborhood after their mailbox is broken into and bags of water are thrown on the mother from the rooftop.

Abuelita, who lives in the old neighborhood, represents knowledge and wisdom and is the model of patience and love for her granddaughter. When Felita stays overnight, she shares with her grandmother her fears and concerns about the mean people in the world. Her grandmother educates her beyond race and ethnicity by inspiring Felita with pride in her origins: "We Puerto Ricans are a rainbow of earth colors! Just like the many flowers of one garden. And that garden is the island of Puerto Rico. Although sometimes, we grow pretty flowers right here, just like you." Abuelita resolves Felita's conflict by dealing openly with issues of trust and jealousy. The grandmother's illness provides a last opportunity for a discussion and the transfer of

knowledge; her last conversation is marked by memories of a trip to Puerto Rico planned together with Felita to pick wildflowers in the countryside. Felita plans a visit there and promises her dead Abuelita that she will gather a big bouquet just for her.

In *Going Home*, the sequel to *Felita*, Tio Jorge is retiring to Barrio Antulio, the family village in the country in Puerto Rico. The family will go for two weeks, but Felita will spend the whole summer. Felita is eleven years old, and her brothers, much to her dismay and theirs, now have the responsibility of protecting her. Her brothers are maturing, and Tio Jorge has moved in with them, setting new cultural values for a "señorita." Felita's girlfriends are still the same, but their interests are now focused on boys. New immigrants appear from South America with more-traditional values.

In this novel Mohr addresses important tensions within the Puerto Rican community. The island visit provokes the expected commentaries that suggest that Nuyoricans are at best merely tolerated there. The children from the mainland speak little or poor Spanish and have accepted North American culture. Fights between cousins occur over the use of English and/or Spanish. Differences between mainland and island cultures are clearly delineated. Tito says it best: "And I told them, 'Look, if I'm a Nuyorican from New York, then what happens if somebody comes from Chicago, or Boston or Philadelphia? Are they Chicagoricans or Bostonricans or Phillyricans, or what. Because if so, you're all nothing but a bunch of dumbricans born in P.R.'"

Barrio Antulio is a rural mountain setting too isolated for someone used to busy city life. Drawing permits escape from the routine for Felita, a familiar theme. Religious settings have changed as small Pentecostal, Seventh-Day Adventist, and Baptist churches dot the landscape. Children's games are different, particularly rhymes for jumping rope. Felita feels different and unaccepted by other children. At home she gets called a "spick," and here she is a Nuyorican.

The church youth group celebrates Taino history, and Felita volunteers to do the backdrop for the project. Problems occur as island jealousies emerge, and the finished set is marked with a graphic "Gringita Go Home!" With a quickly repaired set the Taino play goes forward with rave reviews. Felita completes her promise to Abuelita, gathering a bouquet of wildflowers and setting it down at the foot of a flamboyán tree. Felita has completed her mission, learned about her Taino roots, and experienced the prejudice of the island.

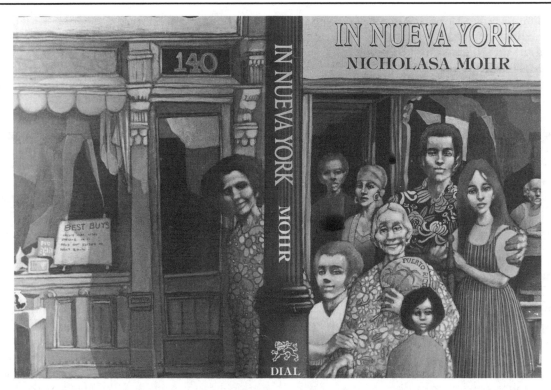

*Dust jacket by Leo and Diane Dillon for Mohr's 1977 book, a collection of stories about the blending of Puerto Rican and New York lifestyles*

In *Going Home* Mohr completes her young-adult novel cycle begun in *Felita*. These two works describe the growth and distancing of two distinctive Hispanic communities, Nuyorican and Puerto Rican, which cling to similar sociocultural roots. Felita and her siblings as well as the reader discover that two separate and different homes exist, Puerto Rico and New York. *Going Home,* in its prejudicial encounters, depicts cultural values in conflict as well as adolescent self-discovery. These two simple novels, with limited psychological character development, provide the contemporary reader with the two contrasting experiences, the island and the mainland.

*Rituals of Survival: A Woman's Portfolio* (1985) is a testimony of women in an urban setting, a series of six stories reflecting the variety of ways in which women live, die, succeed, and fail within the Nuyorican cultural setting. Each story bears a name in its title, thus focusing on the worth of the individual and the literary conceit. The collection represents Mohr's strongest work since *In Nueva York.* Developed over years and tested in public readings, the stories develop plot, characterization, and narrative perspective in mature and realistic prose. The themes are universal, the protagonists real. There is no complicated symbolism or metaphoric imagery.

"Aunt Rosana's Rocker (Zoraida)" depicts a family crisis precipitated by sexual fantasies. In "Time with a Future (Carmela)" generational approaches to aging are explored. Freedom and self-expression, mutually defining concepts, mark each story. In "Brief Miracle (Virginia)" a lesbian attempts to reintegrate herself into the traditional maternal role with a man and his two abandoned children. Zoraida symbolizes spring, Carmela winter, and Virginia autumn. Summer is Lucia in the short story "Happy Birthday (Lucia)." A tubercular young woman seduced into prostitution by an ambitious pimp is hospitalized and awaits visitors on Welfare Island on her birthday. In another seasonal mode, in "A Thanksgiving Celebration (Amy)" a welfare mother with limited income uses her imagination and fantasizes a spectacular meal for her children.

The novella "The Artist (Inez)," which ends the collection, reflects the continuation of a dominant theme — the freedom of the female artist and the projection of the author, alter egos of Nilda and Felita. Mohr confronts the question of how the female protagonist can be complete, creative, and alive in a male world of machos bound to traditional Hispanic roles. Autobiographical elements appear in experiences at the Art Students League as well as in certain family structures.

Inés, the protagonist, sees Joe Batista, a thirty-eight-year-old divorced man and the first man she has ever kissed, as her escape from a repressive stepfamily. The desire to continue her art forces her into deception. While Joe is at law school she secretly attends Art Students League classes, paying for supplies and classes through work as a nude model. Batista discovers her secret and forces her to flee from him and the marriage. The novella dramatizes an encounter two years later when, on the pretext of discussing final divorce papers, Batista attempts to seduce her again and after being rejected attacks her verbally. Freedom is liberation from abusive male pressure – both psychological and physical. The women of *Rituals of Survival: A Woman's Portfolio* find completeness and satisfaction when they escape the psychosocial effects of machismo.

Mohr's work has developed from the autobiographical fiction of her youth in El Barrio to an affirmation of freedom for all women in Hispanic society. Her sense of fantasy and legend continues in *Old Letivia and the Mountain of Sorrows* (1993), a Puerto Rican folktale. Her future projects reflect the elements that have emerged in her publications: myths from Puerto Rico, a new book about love and relationships, and the experience of a new emigrant group from the Dominican Republic in New York. A novel of the Puerto Rican community in the 1920s also awaits her attention.

As a Hispanic-Latina writer, Mohr is marginalized from the traditional sociocultural discourse of other Hispanic-American writers. Her work arises from the concrete experience of the mainland woman, daughter of Puerto Rican immigrants, who chooses to identify herself with the racial and social context of U.S. women writers of color. Mohr distinguishes herself as a product of the Puerto Rican diaspora whose language is English, and as a feminist with urban interests, distanced from the Latin-American canon and separate from Puerto Rican writing. Some of the authors she admires and identifies with include Alice Walker, Tillie Olsen, Raymond Carver, and Víctor Hernández Cruz. By her own statement she finds some island writers, obsessed with race and class, regional and provincial in focus. Her divergence from Puerto Rican writing, therefore, goes beyond ideology and style.

Nuyorican author Nicholasa Mohr reflects in her works more than forty years of Puerto Rican urban experience. Her perspective is female, and her characters from El Barrio, the Bronx, the Lower East Side, and Brooklyn are believable. Her strategic consciousness of the woman's voice and her repressed world determine the singularity of Mohr's position in the Hispanic-Latino literary context. Her work depicts an authentic and aesthetically sophisticated portrayal of the Puerto Rican experience in New York.

**Interviews:**

Roni Natov and Geraldine DeLuca, "An Interview with Nicholasa Mohr," *The Lion and the Unicorn: A Critical Journal of Children's Literature,* 11 (April 1987): 116–121;

Myra Zarnowski, "An Interview with Author Nicholasa Mohr," *The Reading Teacher,* 45 (October 1991): 100–105.

**References:**

Edith Blicksilver, *The Ethnic American Woman: Problems, Protests and Lifestyles* (Dubuque, Iowa: Kendall Hunt, 1978);

John C. Miller, "Nicholasa Mohr: Neorican Writing in Process," *Revista Interamericana,* 9 (Winter 1980): 543–549;

Miller, "The Emigrant and New York City: A Consideration of Four Puerto Rican Writers," *MELUS,* 5 (October 1978);

Eugene Mohr, *The Nuyorican Experience: Literature of Puerto Rican Minorities* (Westport, Conn.: Greenwood Press, 1982);

Sonia Nieto, "Self Affirmation or Self Destruction," in *Images and Identities: The Puerto Rican in Two World Cultures,* edited by Asela Rodríguez de Laguna (New Brunswick, N. J.: Transaction, 1985), pp. 211–226;

Graciela Parral, "Nicholasa Mohr brilla en las letras," *Imagen* (July 1991): 84–86;

Faythe E. Turner, ed., *Puerto Rican Writers at Home in the USA: An Anthology* (Seattle: Open Hand, 1991), pp. 138–156.

# Augusto Monterroso

*(21 December 1921– )*

## Dante Liano
*Università degli Studi de Milano*

## Translated and expanded by Ann González

BOOKS: *El concierto y El eclipse* (Mexico City: Epígrafes, 1952);

*Uno de cada tres y El centenario* (Mexico City: Los Presentes, 1953);

*Obras completas y otros cuentos* (Mexico City: Universitaria, 1959);

*La oveja negra y demás fábulas* (Mexico City: Joaquín Mortiz, 1969); translated by Walter I. Bradbury as *The Black Sheep, and Other Fables* (Garden City, N.Y.: Doubleday, 1971);

*Animales y hombres* (San José, Costa Rica: Editorial Universitaria Centroamericana, 1972);

*Movimiento perpetuoso* (Mexico City: Joaquín Mortiz, 1972);

*Antología personal* (Mexico City: Fondo de Cultura Económica, 1975);

*Lo demás es silencio: La vida y la obra de Eduardo Torres* (Mexico City: Joaquín Mortiz, 1978);

*Mr. Taylor & Co.* (Havana: Casa de las Américas, 1982);

*Viaje al centro de la fábula* (Mexico City: Casillas, 1982);

*La palabra mágica* (Mexico City: Era, 1983);

*Las ilusiones perdidas* (Mexico City: Fondo de Cultura Económica, 1985);

*La letra e: Fragmentos de un diario* (Mexico City: Era, 1987);

*Esa fauna* (Mexico City: Era, 1992);

*Los buscadores de oro* (Mexico City: Alfaguara, 1993).

Augusto Monterroso is one of the best writers of Guatemala. His rigorous style and demanding literary quality stand not only as a lesson but as an awesome goal for writers of the younger generation. Monterroso's literary production, although small, has had an enormous impact on fiction in Latin America. His trademark brevity emerges in marked contrast to the flowery prose of the first half of the twentieth century as well as to the baroque linguistic experimentations of the Boom period. Along with Horacio Quiroga, Jorge Luis Borges, and Julio Cortázar, Monterroso cannot be omitted in any serious discussion of the development of Latin-American short fiction.

Augusto (Tito) Monterroso's first fifteen years were divided between two countries: Honduras, his mother's home, where he was born on 21 December 1921; and Guatemala, his father's birthplace. His middle-class family's frequent moves between the two capitals, Tegucigalpa and Guatemala City, interrupted Monterroso's formal schooling so that he never finished primary school, a lack he still feels. He is almost totally self-educated. After his family finally settled permanently in Guatemala City in 1936, at about the age of sixteen he began copious reading on his own at the Guatemalan National Library, where he also attended night classes, studying foreign languages as well as devouring the Spanish classics. In addition to his personal drive to study during this period, the early death of his father compelled him to go to work to support himself, his mother, and three siblings. Despite this economic hardship he continued to devote his time and energy to literature and, like so many Latin-American writers, to politics.

Monterroso's life is inextricably intertwined with the Guatemalan revolution of 1944. He participated in the literary groups that had been organized in the last years of Jorge Ubico's dictatorship (1931–1944), particularly the Association of Young Artists composed of the so-called 1940s Generation. His first short story was published in 1941 in *El Imparcial*, a Guatemalan newspaper. He also founded and coedited the magazine *Acento*, where he continued to publish his early work. In addition to his literary affiliations, he conspired and participated in efforts to overthrow Ubico. In June 1944 he started a strike among his coworkers that cost him his job. He also participated in the popular antigovernment uprisings and signed a well-known petition demanding Ubico's resignation, "Manifiesto de los 311"

*Augusto Monterroso, circa 1978 (photograph by Efrén Figueredo)*

(Manifesto of the 311). After the fall of Ubico, Monterroso and his friends protested against Col. Ponce Vaides's, whom Ubico had left in his place. As part of his political commitment he founded an opposition newspaper, *El Espectador,* which the government swiftly suppressed after the third issue. Vaides's violent response to all those associated with the paper left Monterroso with no choice but to go into exile. In September 1944 he left for Mexico, where he lived until 1953, working at the Guatemalan embassy and becoming acquainted with a literary group there composed of Mexicans and other Central American expatriates – Rubén Bonifaz Nuño, Ernesto Mejía Sánchez, Rosario Castellanos, and Ernesto Cardenal among others – who were to have an immeasurable impact on the next generation of Latin-American writers. Monterroso continued to contribute to literary magazines in Mexico and Guatemala during these years.

His intelligence and culture were highly esteemed among Guatemalan literary circles. For this reason, when the revolutionary government of Jacobo Arbenz decided to choose its best intellectuals for diplomatic posts, Monterroso was named first secretary to the Guatemalan embassy in Bolivia in 1953. From there he collaborated on the *Revista de Guatemala,* founded by Luis Cardoza y Aragón, an unparalleled example of quality and effort. At the same time he continued his literary work. The overthrow of Arbenz in 1954 meant for him the shared fate of Guatemalan intellectuals: exile. The coup d'état caught him during his stay in Bolivia, after which he went to Chile for two years, where he worked as a proofreader. There he met Manuel Rojas, José Santos González Vera, Luis Enrique Délano, and, more important, Pablo Neruda, whom he helped on the recently founded magazine *La Gaceta de Chile.* In 1956 Monterroso returned to Mexico, where he still lives. He has worked at the Universidad Nacional Autónoma de México, run literary workshops, and continued to publish, mainly in newspapers and magazines. His wife is the Mexican writer Barbara Jacobs.

Monterroso has not returned to Guatemala since 1956 and has published most of his books in Mexico. The Mexican establishment would like to claim him as a Mexican writer, and it officially recognized him in 1975 with the Xavier Villaurrutia Prize, Mexico's most prestigious literary award. Nevertheless, Monterroso considers himself Guatemalan, and Guatemala continues to claim him. Certainly he is one of Central America's most outstanding writers. With other famous authors from Guatemala such as Rafael Landívar, Miguel Angel Asturias, and Luis Cardoza he shares the experience of exile, and like them he follows in the Guatemalan tradition of writing high-quality prose.

179

It is no accident that one of his first short stories, "El eclipse" (The Eclipse, 1952) – later collected in *Obras completas y otros cuentos* (Complete Works and Other Stories, 1959) – centers around an indigenous theme, a common issue in the regional literature of the period. Monterroso approaches the topic with his characteristic minimalist style. The story of a Spanish missionary intent on fooling the Indians with "su arduo conocimiento de Aristoteles" (his arduous knowledge of Aristotle) is a tribute to the intelligence and culture of the Indians without the author's wasting a single word to say so. He merely winks, almost imperceptibly, at his readers. In the complicity between author and reader that Monterroso creates lies the greatness in this seemingly simple story.

In less than two pages, an example of what critic Dolores M. Koch calls "el micro-relato" (the microtale), Monterroso tells the story of a Spanish colonial priest lost in the jungle and discovered by Indians who are about to sacrifice him. In a last attempt to save himself and remembering that an eclipse is predicted for that day, he threatens to make the sun disappear if he is killed. The Indians sacrifice him anyway, reciting all of the dates from the Mayan calendar for which eclipses are predicted.

The three years that the priest has been in the New World, according to the narrator, have been long enough for him to learn a little of the Indians' language, yet with typical colonial superiority and missionary zeal that intends to teach, not learn, the priest has remained ignorant of the Mayans' long-standing culture and centuries of accumulated knowledge, certainly equivalent if not in many ways superior to the priest's Western heritage. Monterroso in this classic story not only satirizes stereotypes and colonial attitudes but offers the readers an interesting reversal of the standard indigenous theme that pervades Guatemalan literature – the Indians in this tale are victors, not victims.

The defeat of the democratic experience in Guatemala was still fresh during the 1950s, and most exiled Guatemalan authors published fervent works against the new regime. Monterroso tackled social problems. One of his most frequently anthologized stories from this period, for example, is "Mr. Taylor" (in *Obras completas y otros cuentos*), an allegory of the presence of multinational corporations in Latin America. Just as has happened innumerable times in the past, a product is discovered by a North American that is valued within his society to the point that it becomes an object of consumption. The irony in Monterroso's story lies in the nature of the product itself: rather than fruit, coffee, or some

other natural resource, the product consists of shrunken human heads. The object could be anything, since any object can be made to seem necessary in a society that creates artificial needs. There is no essential difference between a banana and a shrunken head in terms of export.

Monterroso ironically shows how Mr. Taylor's "company," an obvious reference to the multinational banana companies such as United Fruit, while at first appearing to help the country's economy by providing jobs and generous benefits for workers, actually depletes the country's natural resources, ultimately leaving its workers worse off than before. The effects of such economic exploitation have ramifications in every area of human life. Subsidiary industries boom (in this case the coffin industry); the judicial system of the country is overhauled to facilitate the company with more resources, namely human heads (the death penalty is imposed even for minor offenses); the health-care system is revamped (doctors are rewarded for not curing anyone); foreign policy is affected (war is declared against neighboring tribes to provide more human heads); and the effects of cultural imperialism and arbitrary standards of art are overtly satirized (to own seventeen shrunken heads indicates bad taste, while owning eleven is laudable). Congruent with the intermittent recessions and depressions of capitalism, the scarcity of human heads ultimately leads to the company's collapse, epitomized by the shrunken head of Mr. Taylor himself.

Often missed in discussions of this story is Monterroso's most ingenious satire – the story's frame. Apparently the reader overhears a conversation between two individuals swapping incredible stories or histories. The speaker bills his story of Mr. Taylor as "menos rara" (less strange) and "más ejemplar" (more representative), indicating without explaining the nature of the comparison that a previous story with perhaps a similar theme – cultural or economic imperialism and exploitation – has just been told that is even more unthinkable than that of selling shrunken heads. This technique, similar to Jorge Luis Borges, whom Monterroso greatly admires, of commenting on a story that does not exist or has not been told, inspires the reader to imagine even stranger tales and encourages reflections on Latin-American history itself. One is reminded in Central American history, for example, of such recent examples as Nicaraguan dictator Anastacio Somoza's "Operation Vampire," in which he sold donated blood plasma for a profit to the United States. Such actual historical events make Monterroso's fabrication of the shrunken-head business seem much less far-fetched.

Irony also underlies the parody and caricature in "Primera dama" (First Lady), another well-known story from *Obras completas,* about a Guatemalan president's wife who loves to recite poetry and brutally takes advantage of a children's benefit to recite Rubén Darío's "Los motivos del lobo" (The Wolf's Reasons). The ignorance and lack of culture in the dominant classes can be seen through the clumsy attempts of this presidential pair to appear cultured. Everything they touch becomes vulgar; there is no sentiment that does not become saccharine or absurd.

This theme of the pseudocultured or pseudoartist reappears in "El concierto" (The Concert), where a father must suffer through his daughter's piano concerts, and becomes the foundation for Monterroso's book *Lo demás es silencio: La vida y la obra de Eduardo Torres* (The Rest Is Silence: The Life and Work of Eduardo Torres, 1978). In "Obras completas" (Complete Works), the story that gives the collection its title, Monterroso once again satirizes false culture, but this time within academia. The intellectual castration of a boy by a supposed academic, the details, the seriousness, the futility of the rhetorical exercise of academia – all find an apt picture in the description of the little group of followers who idolize Professor Fombona. The crowning frustration in the narrative centers on the ending of the story, when the young poet becomes instead the young academic specialist on Miguel de Unamuno.

In *Obras completas* Monterroso also offers brief glimpses of the fable, a genre whose use he perfects in *La oveja negra y demás fábulas* (1969; translated as *The Black Sheep, and Other Fables,* 1971). For example, his story "Vaca" (Cow), only a paragraph long, reverberates with significance as the narrator observes a dead cow and subtly criticizes the inability to recognize and reward the work of others, such as the milk the cow has produced for so many years. The cow becomes synonymous with the unappreciated author as the narrator laments that there is no one around to bury the cow, much less to edit his complete works. Probably Monterroso's most well known and certainly his shortest fable is the one-line "El dinosaurio" (The Dinosaur): "Cuando despertó, el dinosaurio todavía estaba allí" (When he awoke, the dinosaur was still there). The ambiguity of the subject (he), the place (there), the time (still), and the many connotations of the word *dinosaur* open this story/sentence to a multitude of interpretations.

The fable is a natural continuation of Monterroso's cultivation of brevity. Certainly Monterroso's

Cover for the 1983 edition of Monterroso's 1969 collection of fablelike stories, some as short as a paragraph or a sentence

fables bear relationships to Greek and Roman mythology and to Spanish neoclassical literature. Closer to home, however, the influence of three Guatemalan neoclassic writers is evident, authors perhaps less well known but certainly known to Monterroso: Rafael García Goyena, Fray Matías de Córdova, and Simón Bergaño y Villegas. Bergaño y Villegas was a passionate defender of scientific progress as well as the ideas of the Enlightenment. Fr. Matías de Córdova, in his apology "La tentativa del león y el éxito de su empresa" (The Lion's Attempt and the Success of His Effort), lists the virtues of humanity in comparison to the animal kingdom, which he sees as decidedly inferior. The fact that these writers also are fabulists does not make them direct sources for Monterroso; for one thing, the quality of Monterroso's work is by far superior. Still, within Guatemalan literary tradition they constitute antecedents that, according to Borges's paradox, have value precisely because of their successor.

Actually, the fact that Monterroso turns to the fable may be more closely related to his contemporaries' widespread tendency in modern Latin-American literature of focusing on language: a linguistic and structural baroque, an elaboration of excess, of experimentation, of an uncontainable torrent of invention and fantasy. The ingenuity of Monterroso is not his rejection of this baroque style but rather his exploration of the other side of the coin. Monterroso's linguistic density is conceptually complementary to, not opposite, the reigning linguistic orgy of the Boom. There is no less effort in the compression of meanings and in the condensation of implied significances, the overriding characteristics of Monterroso's famous brevity. Monterroso does not say more, not because he cannot or does not wish to say more but because he has already said it.

One of Monterroso's phrases contains more information and significance than numerous pages by a lesser writer, requiring various readings and rereadings that successively reveal new and varied implications of the text. Monterroso can be said to create generators of meaning; each little story is the equivalent of a little machine that produces significance. His innovation in narrative technique derives from exaggeration, synopsis taken to the extreme. Many fiction writers count on a notebook in which they write the synopses for what will become longer novels. Monterroso converts the *Aeneid* or Ovid's *Metamorphosis* into a half-page reflection. It is not surprising, then, that he has taken this innovation to its ultimate consequences: "Hoy me siento bien, un Balzac; estoy terminando esta línea" (Today I feel good, a Balzac; I'm finishing this line). The impression he gives is one of a great genius whose timidity prevents him from the exhibition or elaboration of what are often solemnly called great ideas.

Latin-American literature during the 1970s gives the impression of an exuberant positiveness, of great faith in the progress of history. Within this context a book such as *La oveja negra* offers less security. Monterroso's mixture of apocryphal quotations with erudite allusions shakes the foundations of culture itself. His insistence on the relativity of knowledge, the supremacy of appearance over substance, the continual survival of human defects, and the insight that cuts mercilessly through passion make reality appear unattainable and, in any case, bitter, unstable, and painful. Monterroso's cynical humor pervades each story. The title story, for ex-

ample, in a half page outlines inhumanity and hypocritical remorse throughout history, symbolized by the herd that executes the black sheep only to feel guilty later and erect a statue in his honor. The curve that Monterroso throws at the end, however, is to remind the reader of humanity's insistence on learning the wrong lessons from history. The herd continues to execute all the black sheep so that future generations can practice the art of sculpture.

Monterroso's literary development from the fable leads to his creation of another narrative genre, the texts of *Movimiento perpetuoso* (Perpetual Motion, 1972). The next logical step for Monterroso is the elimination of the anecdote and the reduction of the narrative mechanism to the sequence of language itself within the density that has become his trademark style. In this way no theme exists that cannot be literary, or, paradoxically, no specific literary themes exist. Flies, maids, and the stature of a poet all become the subjects of his reflections, which sustain the reader's attention because of genius and linguistic virtuosity in addition to the provocation that such subjects imply in regard to the centrality of the quotidian in a person's life. People do not live thinking about being and time, but of ambitions and defects or of flies, maids, and their own stature. The crystalline rigor of language may be imposed on any theme. In these texts Monterroso perfects his rhetorical arsenal: paradox, allusion, irony, wordplay, parody, the apocryphal quotation, and the long and abrupt phrase. Together they form a style that transmits Monterroso's contagious paradoxical way of thinking and his fundamental skepticism in the face of any subject, linguistic or philosophical. Before a fleeting referent, the only reality is that of the text; the only faith that once in a while moves mountains is literature.

In *Lo demás es silencio* Monterroso emphasizes his mastery of parody. The book recounts the life of Eduardo Torres, a provincial writer, through the testimonies of his friends and a varied anthology of writings, aphorisms, and sayings supposedly by Torres himself, who, to judge by the anthology, is a terrible author surrounded by mediocre friends who tease him a little and play with literature. San Blas needs a town writer, and so Monterroso creates a local myth in the figure of Eduardo Torres. The provincial world in which Torres moves could be reproduced in any city, big or small, of the First or Third World. Monterroso touches one of the secret pulses of any writer in this book: the nightmare that everything is a farce, the terror that everyone, without realizing it, is like Eduardo Torres, the ghost that haunts every writer.

Monterroso's literary techniques are similar to those in *Movimiento perpetuoso,* only here his virtuosity for moving easily from one style to another is centered on the absence of his own authorial voice. Unlike in his previous books, the author does not appear but rather yields his narrative voice to different (false) authors, each with a specific voice. This is reminiscent of the parodies in *Obras completas,* "Primera dama" and "No quiero engañarlos" (I Don't Want to Fool You), for example, in which the embarrassing, interminable speeches of the protagonists reveal them to be idiots. The unity of style lies in what is not said, in the invisible presence of the manipulator of the texts who winks at the reader each time the banality and the pathetic hilariousness of his created world are perceived.

In 1982 an interesting cross between a book about and a book by Monterroso was published: *Viaje al centro de la fábula* (Voyage to the Center of the Fable) is a collection of interviews that came out under Monterroso's own name rather than the names of any of his interviewers. According to critic Juan A. Masoliver, these texts indicate Monterroso's exploration of a new literary genre (the interview) and can be considered more of Monterreso's creative works. Monterroso finds it difficult to respond to interviewers' queries with answers that will be put in print without joking, he says, and thereby sounding frivolous, and he is concerned with becoming overly serious and sounding stupid. According to Masoliver, however, this paradoxical character of Monterroso's interviews permits him to explore new areas of expression and to plumb the depths of his opinions on literature and about his own life.

*La palabra mágica* (The Magic Word, 1983) introduces longer texts that verge on authentic literary essays. If in the previous books there were brief reflections on some everyday themes, in *La palabra mágica* Monterroso reflects at greater length on his reading, his writing, and his life. Longer selections – long being between five and ten pages – such as "Llorar orillas del río Mapocho" (Crying on the Bank of the Mapocho River), which humorously recounts Monterroso's failed attempt to become a literary translator, are interspersed with briefer reflections (one page) such as "Como acercarse a las fábulas" (How to Approach Fables), in which Monterroso offers cynical advice on how to write a fable. The largest part of the volume, however, is concerned with literary themes. What in previous books was only insinuated comes to the surface here: Monterroso's erudition. A privileged memory and a profound culture create a space in which he

*Cover for Monterroso's 1983 collection of essays and reflections*

associates naturally with authors such as Francisco Gómez de Quevedo, Samuel Johnson, and Horace, a space in which he can discuss without snobbishness or stuffiness the significance of a verse by Luis de Góngora, a space in which he sustains a long-distance conversation with Asturias, a space in which Borges and William Shakespeare intermingle – all in the voice of someone who for years, in the solitude of reading, has repeatedly visited them with attentive devotion and the pure joy of reading and who now in this given moment communicates that pleasure. *La palabra mágica* is one of those rare literary books on literature in which the word *critical* is insufficient to explain the substance of its composition.

In 1987 Monterroso published *La letra e* (The Letter E), a diary in which he collects texts written since 1983. In this work Monterroso's erudition emerges in a less systematic way than in *La palabra mágica.* Often his desire to shed the solemnity of his remarks makes him mine the text with explosive wit; at other times his sarcasm resolutely dissolves any suspicion of seriousness. As in all of Monterroso's books, his linguistic virtuosity parallels his conceptual achievement. Yet both are invisible. It is as though one were reading a mysterious old book whose knowledge had long since been forgotten prior to the very act of reading. This invisibility is paradoxically the clearest sign of his style, since the reader is unaware of Monterroso's careful manipulation until much later, when the author obliges the reader to think as he does. In fact, one of Monterroso's characteristics comes from the fact that he teaches the reader to see the world with different eyes, with his own disenchanted and pitying eyes: a world without drama and largely ridiculous when all is said and done.

Monterroso's world becomes lifelike because, despite the literary tapestry, one recognizes it and one recognizes oneself in it. Furthermore, upon this recognition, one subjects it to the critical view proposed by Monterroso himself. The sarcasm that Monterroso applies to the facts of life begins with himself in different episodes in this book, in which he is surprised by human errors; he does not hesitate to make fun of himself or of anyone else for that matter. "Un paso en falso" (A False Step), for example, tells of the writer's own frigid reception by an editor who had never heard of him. Such a story could have been pathetic or angry or melodramatic. Instead, it is full of melancholic humor. The strangeness with which he observes the endless work by humanity that seems to achieve nothing – "Nuestros libros son los rios que van a dar en la mar que es el olvido" (Our books are the rivers that will flow into the sea of forgetfulness), he says at the beginning – is impregnated with compassion. There is a clear consciousness that humanity is full of defects and that those failings are unavoidable, even essential.

Literature for Monterroso converts itself into any activity that aids the understanding of what is real, which forms a substantial part of human be- havior. Monterroso has dedicated his life to literature, and it is that dedication that his work reflects. His characteristic aesthetic and ethical rigor and inflexibility become even more severe as his judgment of humanity becomes more elastic and forgiving. In few writers can one find such profound compassion for human weaknesses and flaws juxtaposed with such biting satire, parody, and humor. Clearly Monterroso deserves attention within any study of Latin-American fiction for his refusal to follow the literary crowd, his willingness to explore a variety of narrative modes, and his constantly critical yet humorous stance in regard to every facet of human existence.

**Interview:**

Rafael Humberto Moreno-Duran, "El lector como animal de presa: Entrevista con Augusto Monterroso," *Quimera,* 26 (December 1982): 66–71.

**References:**

M. A. Campos and others, *La literatura de Augusto Monterroso* (Mexico City: Universidad Autónoma Metropolitana, 1988);

Wilfrido H. Corral, *Lector, sociedad y género en Monterroso* (Jalapa, Mexico: Universidad Veracruzana, 1985);

Dolores M. Koch, "El micro-relato en México: Torri, Arreola, Monterroso y Aviles Fabila," *Hispamérica: Revista de Literatura,* 10 (December 1981): 123–130;

Juan A. Masoliver, "Augusto Monterroso o la tradición subversiva," *Cuadernos Hispanoamericanos,* 408 (June 1984): 146–154;

Silvana Serafin, "L'elemento ludico nella narrativa di Augusto Monterroso," *Rassegna Iberistica,* 35 (September 1989): 3–16;

Saul Sosnowski, "Augusto Monterroso: La sátira del poder," *Zona Franca,* 3 (July–August 1980): 53–57.

# Mario Roberto Morales

*(5 September 1947 –    )*

Ann González
*University of North Carolina at Charlotte*

BOOKS: *La debacle* (Guatemala: Istmo, 1969);
*Manual del guía de turistas, República de Guatemala* (Guatemala: Secretaría de Integración Turística Centroamericana, 1971);
*Obraje* (Quezaltenango, Guatemala, 1971);
*Los demonios salvajes* (Guatemala: Departamento de Actividades Literarias de la Dirección General de Cultura y Bellas Artes de Guatemala, 1978; revised edition, Guatemala: Oscar de León Palacios, 1993); "Yo para estas cosas me llamo René" translated by Asa Zatz as "For These Things My Name Is René," in *And We Sold the Rain: Contemporary Fiction from Central America,* edited by Rosario Santos (New York: Four Walls Eight Windows, 1988), pp. 61–73; "Un peso de encima" translated by Tina Alvarez Robles as "Dead Weight," in *Clamor of Innocence: Central American Short Stories,* edited by Barbara Paschke and David Volpendesta (San Francisco: City Lights Books, 1988), pp. 127–130;
*Epigramas para interrogar a Patricia* (Guatemala: Editorial Universitaria, Universidad de San Carlos, 1982); translated by Ann González as "Epigrams to Interrogate Patricia," *Latin American Literary Review,* 18 (July–December 1990): 87–103;
*El esplendor de la pirámide* (San José, Costa Rica: Editorial Universitaria Centroamericana, 1985);
*Roberto Obregón: Alcanzar la altura de la estrella hundiendo la mano en el charco que la refleja* (San José, Costa Rica: Confederación Universitaria Centroamericana, 1987);
*Epigramas* (Guatemala: Ministerio de Cultura y Deportes, 1990);
*Transfiguración del pájaro serpiente* (Guatemala: Universitaria, 1992).

OTHER: "La nueva novela guatemalteca y sus funciones de clase: La política y la ideología," in Ileana Rodríguez, Ramón Luis Acevedo, and Morales, *Literatura y crisis en Centroamérica:*

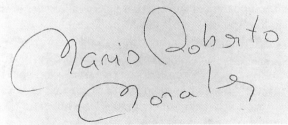

*Ponencias* (San José, Costa Rica: Instituto Centroamericano de Documentación e Investigación Social, 1986), pp. 81–94;

Guatemalan novelist, poet, and critic Mario Roberto Morales is one of the leading representatives of the *nueva novela* (New Novel) in Central

American fiction. He combines the linguistic, temporal, and structural experimentation of the Latin-American Boom fiction of the 1960s with testimonial/autobiographical accounts of the political and social turmoil of the region. His prize-winning novels have attracted national and international critical attention, and some of his work has already been translated into English, a sure sign of his growing importance in Central American letters.

His book of short poems *Epigramas para interrogar a Patricia* (1982) was published in English as "Epigrams to Interrogate Patricia" in 1990 in the *Latin American Literary Review.* Asa Zatz published an English version of one of his short stories in *And We Sold the Rain: Contemporary Fiction from Central America* (1988). In addition, a chapter from his early novel *Los demonios salvajes* (The Wild Devils, 1978) was translated by Tina Alvarez Robles and included as a short story in a recent anthology of Central American writers, *Clamor of Innocence: Stories from Central America* (1988).

Morales has also begun to attract critical attention outside Central America. Noted Latin-American critic Seymour Menton includes extensive coverage of Morales's early work in his most recent edition (1985) of *Historia crítica de la novela guatemalteca,* as do John Beverley and Marc Zimmerman in their seminal work, *Literature and Politics in the Central American Revolutions* (1990). In addition, Morales was invited to speak and read from his work at a literary conference in Boulder, Colorado, in 1991. His novel *El ángel de la retaguardia* (Rear Guardian Angel), which tied for first place in the 1990 Nicaraguan Nueva Novela prize, will be published by Monte Avila of Venezuela and will surely add to his growing international esteem. In the fall of 1993 he was invited to participate in the International Writing Program at the University of Iowa, where he was able to finish his latest novel, a testimonial compilation of Guatemalan voices called "Señores bajo los árboles" (Lords under the Trees).

As is often the case with Latin-American writers, Morales's life has become inextricably fused with his literary production. His novels and short stories are heavily autobiographical, so that to read his fiction is to begin to understand the man and the political context in which he moves. One of the persistent questions in his fiction, for example, is how and why a person acquires a social conscience. Clearly the underlying issue for Morales is why he personally has been plagued or blessed with such sensitivity. In order to understand this phenomenon he repeatedly plumbs the depths of his earliest memories of himself, his family, and his friends.

Mario Roberto Morales was born on 5 September 1947 in the capital city of Guatemala. After his first year his parents moved to Santa Lucía Cotzumalguapa on the southern coast, where his father owned a pharmacy. Ricardo Morales Hernández, a well-to-do businessman, died at fifty-nine in an automobile accident when Morales was only nineteen. He had been his son's best friend and "accomplice," in Morales's words, and although uneducated he was a profound, wise, and good man. His sudden death seems to have been the impetus behind Morales's decision to write.

His mother, Magda Alvarez de Morales, was the daughter of a Spanish immigrant and a Mexican woman from Chiapas. Morales's maternal grandmother was apparently a difficult woman, but for him as a child she was especially supportive, providing a fundamental loving and understanding feminine presence during his early years and forming the basis for an authority figure who appears several times in Morales's early narratives. Morales's maternal grandfather, Camilo Alvarez Fanjul, was a spiritualist-Communist of the Martí and Sandino school called the "Escuela Magnético-Espiritual de la Comuna Universal" (The Magnetic-Spiritual School of the Universal Commune). He and his wife moved to Guatemala at the outbreak of the Mexican Revolution and finally settled in Santa Lucía, where he worked as an accountant and taught spiritism on the side. He was arrested and held prisoner as a Communist during the Ubico dictatorship (1931–1944).

Morales's mother inherited her liberal ideas about social justice and communism in the abstract from her father, notions that became linked in her mind to the situation of the Guatemalan Indians who arrived daily in Santa Lucía. She constantly urged her son to fight for the poor, and it is undoubtedly from this background that Morales's "social conscience," his susceptibility to exotic ideas from his university friends, and his youthful disposition for martyrdom "a la Guevara" emerged.

In the fourth grade Morales returned to the capital to continue his schooling. As an adolescent he attended a bourgeois high school, the English American School, and remained relatively insulated from any understanding of social problems or knowledge of revolutionary activity in his country. His 1978 novel, *Los demonios salvajes,* is based on this period of teenage irresponsibility and political innocence. Once Morales entered Universidad Rafael Landivar, a private bourgeois college run by Jesuit priests where he later graduated with a degree in arts and letters, he was recruited by the Fuerzas Armadas Rebeldes (FAR – Armed Rebel Forces).

He was eighteen years old at the time and already involved in literary circles enamored of the linguistic and structural possibilities of the "new" Latin-American novel, later to be termed the Boom. In 1970 he and some of his literary friends, influenced by the "open" novels of Julio Cortázar, especially *62: Modelos para armar* (1968; translated as *62: A Model Kit*, 1972) and *Rayuela* (1963; translated as *Hopscotch*, 1966), set themselves the task of writing a work in which nothing happened, where the plot was not to be the center of the narrative but where the message would be expressed through the form of the novel. They proposed a spherical structure from which they deduced the center of the novel could be reached from any of its points; the reader would be left with the task of forming connections and patterns. The result of this effort was Morales's first novel, *Obraje* (Work, 1971), which won the Juegos Florales Centroamericanos competition in Quetzaltenango. Until recently Morales believed there were no extant copies of the manuscript since all of his books and papers, which had been left in a safe house in Guatemala when he went to Mexico in 1982, ultimately fell into the hands of the Guatemalan military. Recently, however, a copy he had sent to a professor at the University of Bristol has apparently surfaced and is being sent to him.

Morales remained an active militant in Guatemala until 1973, when he was sent to Italy on an Italian government scholarship to study art history. During his time abroad he retained his connections with the guerrilla movement. This confusing period of his life as an expatriate trying to determine his future in relation to his politics and his art is recounted in his fourth novel, *El ángel de la retaguardia*.

In 1970 he began living as a bohemian in a common-law union that produced two daughters, Mayarí and Anaís; the latter gave him a granddaughter in 1992. During the 1970s, after his return from Europe, Morales's increasing militancy deteriorated his relationship with the mother of his children, and they separated in 1980.

In 1982 he was sent by a revolutionary group with which he had maintained connections since his return from Italy on what was supposed to be a two-week mission to Mexico. He was captured by Mexican authorities, briefly jailed, and subsequently sent to Costa Rica – all recounted in his second novel, *El esplendor de la pirámide*. Since he could no longer return to Guatemala, his revolutionary group, Movimiento Revolucionario del Pueblo (MRP) – IXIM, of which he had been a member

since 1981, gave him the task of forming an international front to support the Guatemalan armed struggle from Managua, Nicaragua. (*Ixim* means corn [*maíz*], food, and life in the four major Mayan languages: Kicché, Kackchiquel, Kekchi, and Mam.)

While he was in Nicaragua, his revolutionary group had serious confrontations and disagreements with the Sandinistas, the Soviets, and the more powerful Guatemalan leftist group Unidad Revolucionaria Nacional Guatemalteca (URNG – National Guatemalan Revolutionary Unit), which had been formed under Cuban pressure and ultimately managed to destroy the MRP. During this conflictive period the representative of the URNG in Managua accused Morales and several others before the Nicaraguan government of trafficking in gold for the Contras, an extremely serious charge at the time implying treason and possibly leading to execution. He and four others were imprisoned in La Loma at the top of the Hotel Intercontinental (Somoza's former bunker) for two months and four days, an experience for Morales far worse than his imprisonment in Mexico. There he had been tortured physically, but since the blows came from the enemy he felt ideologically strong enough to withstand the punishment.

His imprisonment in Nicaragua by the Sandinistas, whom he had considered his friends, was particularly devastating and demoralizing. Morales and his companions speculate that it took only about five or six days to prove their innocence, yet they were detained for two more months and subjected to various forms of psychological torture: silence, darkness, a loss of the sense of time, lies about what was happening on the outside, and threats that they would be executed at any time. They were given little food or water and were detained with other political prisoners. Morales shared a cell with a Somocista colonel and a Contra assassin. The fact that Morales and his friends were detained for two months after the Sandinistas were clearly aware of their innocence indicates for Morales that the Nicaraguan Ministry of the Interior specifically intended to pressure them into leaving Nicaragua. After his release Morales stayed in Nicaragua for approximately two more months; then he left to see his daughters, who were then living in Costa Rica, where he ultimately decided to live.

Morales, who for years did not talk about this traumatic episode in his life, is now trying to write about it. He insists that this injustice is only symptomatic of the internal corruption that has progressively deteriorated the moral authority of the left. He still retains many friends among the Sandinistas,

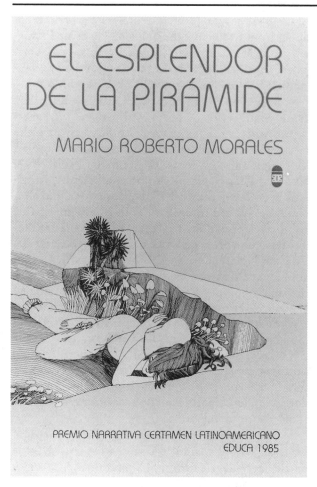

*Cover for Morales's 1985 novel, about an affair between a
Mexican girl and a Guatemalan guerrilla*

entitled "Con tinta sangre" (With Blood Ink). Because of his outspoken political views he appeared in March 1993 on a hit list among twenty-four prominent Guatemalans labeled as "subversives" and was threatened with assassination. The public outcry denouncing this reactionary response to free speech in the new democratic environment was indicative, however, of the changing political climate in Guatemala.

In his early experiments with short narrative in *La debacle* (The Debacle, 1969) and "Aquellos días sin tregua" (Those Days without Truce, circa 1970), a collection of mostly unpublished short stories, Morales retells bits and pieces of his years growing up. The narratives are often short short stories of no more than a paragraph or a page that encapsulate traumatic moments or sharp memories and that as a whole represent decisive instances that collectively have determined the path of Morales's life. One of the still unpublished stories from "Aquellos días sin tregua," "Pirotecnia" (Fireworks), is a brief memory of Morales around age five in the arms of his grandmother as they witnessed a fire that burned down a nearby insane asylum. What marks the story is not the often-recurring theme of social injustice represented by the cries of the insane trapped in the fire and of those who have been saved only to be tied to the lampposts outside the burning building, but rather the narrative strategy that allows both Morales and the reader to perceive the events indirectly. Neither Morales nor the reader actually watches the fire firsthand, but sees it instead reflected in the grandmother's glasses. This metaphor of mirrored reality repeats throughout Morales's fiction as he experiments with the different distortions rendered through the process of reflection. Similarly, Roberto the child never speaks in this short story; it is the grandmother's voice that laments "pobrecitos" (poor things). Morales at five can neither make sense of his world nor experience it unmediated by external factors such as social class and environment – themes that are central concerns throughout Morales's work.

After his initial short stories and first experimental novel *Obraje* in 1971, he wrote *Los demonios salvajes,* which won the Premio Unico Centroamericano de Novela de la Dirección General de Cultura y Bellas Artes in 1977 and was published in a poorly edited form in 1978. (It has recently been reedited and published in a second edition by Oscar de León Palacios, 1993.) The historical period covered in the narrative is the armed resistance in Guatemala beginning with the attempted coup on 13

who with Morales agree that this persecution of its own supporters by the Left has been a crucial mistake in the movement. In 1987, therefore, with the complete defeat and destruction of Morales's revolutionary organization, he moved to Costa Rica and began a master's degree in sociology at the Universidad de Costa Rica, simultaneously working as a translator to earn a meager living. In October 1992 his mother and sister left Guatemala, where they were under constant surveillance, and moved to Tampa, Florida.

After he finished his master's degree, and with improved political conditions in Guatemala, Morales was finally able in 1992 to return and contribute to the process of democratization. At present he is the cultural adviser to the Dirección General de Extensión Universitaria de la Universidad de San Carlos. He also writes a column for the newspaper *Prensa Libre* called "A fuego lento" (Simmering) and is a member of the editorial board and a columnist for the *Revista Crónica.* He writes a regular column

*Morales, circa 1993*

November 1960 by a group of officials in the Guatemalan military and ending after a decade of struggle with the virtual extermination of the rebels. The plot revolves around the author and his group of adolescent friends — all from respectable, middle-class families in Guatemala — and represents a rite of passage for Morales, the first-person narrator, who like the little boy in "Pirotecnia" observes but as yet cannot interpret the political significance of contemporary events. His middle-class background permits him to move through the novel without knowing where he is going. His contact with the outside world of social, economic, and political realities is constantly mediated by the schoolyard wall, his car windows, the rearview mirror, his glasses, his alcoholic stupors, his gang, his girlfriends — indeed by all of the elements his bourgeois urban surroundings provide.

Structurally the novel is complex, divided into the three parts of a soccer match, first half, second half, and overtime, with flash-forwards and flashbacks that permit the reader to understand the narrator's increasing maturity and sense of social responsibility despite his evasion of the political/military issues confronting the country and his participation in the reckless, nonsensical escapades of youth. The story is told through different voices and different print formats (bold, italic, and regular

text), often omitting prepositions to reflect the telegramlike quality of the fiction and including numerous references to the rock and roll music popular at the time.

Essentially *Los demonios salvajes* is two novels in one. The first, "La montaña plana" (The Flat Mountain), is composed of episodes from the narrator's university career, epistolary chapters he sends to his friend El Canche and interweaves with the novel the autobiographical protagonist claims to be writing. That novel, "The Wild Devils," whose title is taken from the name of the narrator's adolescent gang, recounts the protagonist's high-school experiences. The question underlying the novel, which combines the two periods of time, that underpins much of Morales's later fiction is how a person acquires a social conscience, particularly an individual who because of his social status need not be aware of social inequity. Even more problematic, however, is how a person with such awareness handles the guilt of doing nothing to change the social context in which he lives.

Young Roberto owns an Opel, and he and his well-to-do friends tour the country while drinking and carousing; yet there is always the sense of the underprivileged outside the car window. Inserted into the narrative line are chapters that can stand on their own as short stories and that deal with David, a romanticized guerrilla who stands outside the narrator's experience as the unattainable model of heroism. David's presence provides the underlying tension in the novel between the bourgeois alienation of the narrator's friends and the increasing social conscience of Roberto, the clearly autobiographical writer of this tale/testimony. As Morales explores the memories of his high school and college years he directs attention toward his best friend, El Canche, a medical student who has growing doubts about his goals and his place in the social order. Out of the entire group of boys, however, only two, the narrator and El Canche, are affected by such doubts: only they have contact with David; only they feel the terror of clandestine action.

The crucial questions in this novel therefore center on how and why a social conscience forms in a given individual. There are no clear reasons why any of these characters should risk the security of their bourgeois lives to become involved in social revolution. The narrator, by delving into his past and by probing into the motivations of his friend El Canche, seeks answers to these same questions.

This novel – along with *El tiempo principia en Xibalbá* (The Beginning of Time in Xibalbá, 1972), by Luis de Lión (the only Guatemalan Indian novelist, who was kidnapped and "disappeared" in 1984) and Marco Antonio Flores's *Los compañeros* (The Buddies) – initiates what has come to be known in critical circles as the "new Central-American novel." These narratives were not only influenced by the Latin-American Boom emphasis on language and structure but also by "la onda" (the wave) of Mexican novels popular in the 1960s that emphasized the sentiments of the new urban middle-class adolescent and the influence of United States culture, rock music, the generation gap, and the hippie movement. This "Guatemalization" of the New Novel, which added the regional particularities of political testimony, represented for Morales and his literary friends the "death" of Miguel Angel Asturias, Guatemala's Nobel laureate, who by his international recognition had inevitably set the national and regional standards for the writing of fiction. The result in Guatemalan narrative was an unhappy series of attempts to imitate the master. Morales's essay "Matemos a Miguel Asturias" (Let's Kill Miguel Asturias), which attempted to explain the New Novel's simultaneous respect for yet rupture with tradition, still provokes the ire of Guatemalan literary purists.

Morales's third novel, *El esplendor de la pirámide*, which won the Premio EDUCA de la Novela in 1985, is also two stories in one – or more pre-

cisely one story: the love affair between a Mexican girl and a young Guatemalan guerrilla sent to Mexico, and the problem of how to tell a story, how to focus the events. Given Morales's pervasive theme that reality is inevitably mediated by environment and class, his concern in this novel seems to focus instead on how the artist establishes control over these mediating factors. The underlying political reality is the crisis of the armed opposition in the 1980s that was virtually wiped out by the Guatemalan military. The action is broken down into scenes for a movie script. The narrative concern is over how to position the camera, from what angle to shoot the scene. The story is told from second-person point of view as the guerrilla narrates to and through his Mexican girlfriend, as he supposes what her feelings and thoughts must be, as he advises her on where to place the camera and when to zoom in or fade out. The formal concerns give way finally to understated terror when they are both arrested – the fear of torture by Mexican officials, the fear that he will be turned over to Guatemalan authorities, and the despair that Pyramid, the guerrilla's girlfriend, will be hurt or, worse, that she will hate him for having kept his politics secret, because not having warned her is worse than the reality of confinement. The final blow is the girlfriend's agreement not to see him again or to contact him in exchange for her release. From Costa Rica, where the Mexican authorities send the guerrilla, he writes to Pyramid, his lover, and the reader understands that she will not answer. She prefers the memory of the past without danger or commitment and the superficial concerns of acting and filming surfaces. She will not give up her present life, the comfort of the status quo, for political engagement she does not feel.

Morales's fourth novel, *El ángel de la retaguardia*, is also autobiographical and occurs before the action in *El esplendor de la pirámide*. After Morales's adolescence recounted in *Los demonios salvajes* he studies in Europe, the setting of *El ángel de la retaguardia*, before returning to Guatemala to form part of the armed resistance that leads to the action in Mexico and the basis for *El esplendor de la pirámide*. Actually *El ángel de la retaguardia* is four or five simultaneously presented novels in one, making its narrative composition a tour de force. The central story, if there is a center to this novel, is that of Morales's studies in Italy, his work in Switzerland, and his conversations with a leftist friend who is supposed to return to Guatemala to become part of the political opposition but who instead marries and decides to stay in Italy. His revolutionary talk is just talk, no action, and his character emphasizes the difficulty of political engagement and the extent of the possibilities for loss.

Inserted literally into the margins of this story are conversations with Barbara, a hostile dialogue that revolves around the issues of freedom and commitment in love but mirrors the same themes on a political level. These two stories are interrupted, often in midsentence or midword by annotated political inserts, actual excerpts from political doctrine by Guatemalan leaders that indicate the theoretical logic providing direction for the armed struggle. Offsetting this theoretical consistency and logic are the inserts of actual armed confrontations in the 1960s – the guerrilla episodes – in which the fragmentation of the political groups and the impossibility of monitoring guerrilla activity are visible. In practice, the left hand does not know what the right hand is doing; confusion dominates guerrilla activity despite the rebels' apparent clarity of purpose.

Finally, a metafictional thread runs throughout, the novelist's attempt to write a narrative indicated by the subtitle "La casa de las letanías del tango azul" (The House of the Blue Tango Litanies). The would-be novelist goes round and round, running through one critical theory after another, shifting interpretive responsibility from writer to reader to critic, unable to write the book he should – the book about Guatemala, the book he lives in – and unable to escape the Italian villa he rents, the house that is the book, the chapters that are the bricks.

Morales's final version of *El ángel de la retaguardia* adds one more narrative thread, the testimony of a female guerrilla, based on the real case of Rogelia Cruz, a former Miss Guatemala in the Miss Universe contest who was caught by the Guatemalan military and tortured to death. Her voice from beyond the grave testifies to the horror of oppression as she is raped before and after her death, a voice that offers the single female perspective the novel had been lacking.

These various narrative threads form the fragmentary structural basis of the novel, a centrifugal structure that Morales himself pictures as a grenade exploding outward. Despite this splintering effect of stories breaking in on each other, however, there is a sense of the whole in motion, like the dissonance of a contemporary symphony. In fact, the fiction begins as a technician tests his recording instruments, and the story itself becomes a cassette recording, sides A and B, with instructions for playing (or reading). Side A (*Adagio brillante*) indicates the forcefulness of the first part of the symphony, the many

*Corrected page from the typescript for Morales's story "Pirotecnica," scheduled for the forthcoming collection "Aquellos días sin tregua"*

parts playing at odds, flying apart yet making the whole. Morales's humor is continually offset by the horror of political struggle and the existential difficulty of deciding to take action, whether it is political action or the personal struggle of the novelist to write. Side B (*Allegro ma non troppo*) indicates that one may laugh but that one should proceed with caution; the undercurrent of struggle is always present and belies the humor.

The key story from which the title itself is taken is not only indicative of Morales's ability to capture the ludicrous amid crisis but also symbolic of the divergence between theory and practice in the Guatemalan armed insurrection of the 1960s. A guerrilla backs away as gunfire breaks out only to feel himself jabbed from behind as he literally rams himself onto the outstretched finger of a statue of an angel, guarding his rear flank and pointing him forward, protecting him and wounding him simultaneously.

Morales's latest book, "Señores bajo los árboles," is a conscious effort to "trabajar las hablas," that is, to work with distinct voices, and falls within the recent group of testimonial novels emerging from Latin America following the Boom in Latin-American fiction of the 1960s and 1970s. The book is an effort to counter the Guatemalan army's largely successful plan to eradicate the cultural nuclei of the Indian communities by assassinating their oldest members, the keepers of tradition, and thereby destroying the cohesion of the indigenous groups. Rather than considering himself to be the author of a novel, Morales sees his task in this book as that of an artisan in organizing the various voices of the elderly, the children, and the men and women whose testimonies he has been collecting for years. He has attempted to deemphasize overt denunciation, to eschew gratuitous emotionalism, and to avoid the overuse of fictional techniques. In his latest work he searches for balance, avoiding the one-sided romantic version of the revolutionary. The guerrillas, he claims, were also involved in massacres and committed atrocities of their own. "Señores bajo los árboles" represents the voices of victims from all sides of the political crisis of the 1980s and as such has a credence and a power that surpass the single first-person accounts that predominate in the contemporary Central American testimonial novel.

Morales admits his indebtedness to Asturias, for both his willingness to experiment with language and to engage political themes. He also feels a debt to American writers, specifically John Steinbeck, John Dos Passos, Jack Kerouac, J. D. Salinger, and William Faulkner. Yet his fiction is not imitative but part of a new current of highly creative and experimental fiction (new novels) coming out of Latin America and especially Central America during the last thirty years. It is also the product of specific historical events in Guatemala influenced by the revolutionary tracts of rebel leaders, testimonies from the witnesses and victims of governmental and military repression, and Morales's own experiences with both the Right and the Left. What separates Morales's fiction from the stream of political and social denunciations pouring out of Latin America, however, is his creative genius, his sophisticated manipulation of language and narrative strategies, his ideological commitment to the revolutionary struggle in Guatemala, and his ability to capture the pervasive humor of daily life amid an overwhelming sense of frustration and defeat.

### References:

John Beverley and Marc Zimmerman, *Literature and Politics in the Central American Revolutions* (Austin: University of Texas Press, 1990);

Ann González, "La formación de la conciencia social en *Los demonios salvajes* de Mario Roberto Morales," in *La literatura centroamericana,* edited by Jorge Román Lagunas (New York: Edwin Mellen, 1994), pp. 343–350;

Seymour Menton, *Historia crítica de la novela guatemalteca,* second edition (Guatemala: Editorial Universitaria de Guatemala, 1985);

Zimmerman, Raúl Rojas, and Patricio Navia, eds., *Guatemala: Voces desde el silencio: Un collage épico* (Guatemala: Oscar de León Palacios, 1993).

# Carmen Naranjo

*(30 January 1930 –  )*

Ardis L. Nelson
*East Tennessee State University*

BOOKS: *Canción de la ternura* (San José: Elite, 1964);
*Hacia tu isla* (San José: Artes Gráficas, 1966);
*Los perros no ladraron* (San José: Costa Rica, 1966);
*Misa a oscuras* (San José: Costa Rica, 1967);
*Memorias de un hombre palabra* (San José: Costa Rica, 1968);
*Camino al mediodía* (San José: Lehmann, 1968);
*Responso por el niño Juan Manuel* (San José: Conciencia Nueva, 1971);
*Idioma del invierno* (San José: Conciencia Nueva, 1971);
*Hoy es un largo día* (San José: Costa Rica, 1972);
*Diario de una multitud* (San José: Editorial Universitaria Centroamericana, 1974);
*Por Israel y por las páginas de la Biblia* (San José: Fotorama de Centro América, 1976);
*Cinco temas en busca de un pensador* (San José: Ministerio de Cultura, Juventud y Deportes, 1977);
*Las relaciones públicas en las instituciones de seguridad social* (San José: Instituto Centroamericano de Administración Pública, 1977);
*Mi guerrilla* (San José: Editorial Universitaria Centroamericana, 1977);
*Cultura: 1. La acción cultural en Latinoamérica. 2. Estudio sobre la planificación cultural* (San José: Instituto Centroamericano de Administración Pública, 1978);
*Ejercicios y juegos para mi niño (de 0 a 3 años)* (Guatemala City: UNICEF, 1981);
*La mujer y el desarrollo* (Mexico City: Sep Diana, 1981);
*Homenaje a don Nadie* (San José: Costa Rica, 1981);
*Mi niño de 0 a 6 años* (Guatemala City: UNICEF, 1982);
*Ondina* (San José: Editorial Universitaria Centroamericana, 1983);
*Nunca hubo alguna vez* (San José: Universidad Estatal a Distancia, 1984); translated by Linda Britt as *There Never Was a Once Upon a Time* (Pittsburgh: Latin American Literary Review Press, 1989);

*Carmen Naranjo, 1992 (photograph by Ardis L. Nelson)*

*Estancias y días,* with Graciela Moreno (San José: Costa Rica, 1985);
*Sobrepunto* (San José: Editorial Universitaria Centroamericana, 1985);
*El caso 117.720* (San José: Costa Rica, 1987);
*Otro rumbo para la rumba* (San José: Editorial Universitaria Centroamericana, 1989);
*Mujer y cultura* (San José: Editorial Universitaria Centroamericana, 1989);
*Ventanas y asombros* (San José: Editorial Universitaria Centroamericana, 1990).

PLAY PRODUCTIONS: *¡Y así empezó!*, Panama City, Teatro Nacional de Panamá, 24 February 1969;

*Adivíneme usted*, San José, Teatro Nacional, September 1980.

OTHER: *La voz*, in *Obras breves del teatro costarricense*, volume 2, edited by Carlos Franck (San José: Costa Rica, 1971), pp. 85–121;

"El truco florido," translated by Corina Mathieu as "The Flowery Trick" in *Five Women Writers of Costa Rica*, edited by Victoria Urbano (Beaumont, Tex.: Lamar University, 1978), pp. 3–5;

"Inventario de un recluso," translated by Mary Sue Listerman as "Inventory of a Recluse" in *Five Women Writers of Costa Rica*, pp. 13–16;

"El viaje y los viajes," translated by Marie J. Panico as "The Journey and the Journeys" in *Five Women Writers of Costa Rica*, pp. 6–12;

"Y vendimos la lluvia," translated by Jo Anne Engelbert as "And We Sold the Rain" in *And We Sold the Rain: Contemporary Fiction from Central America*, edited by Rosario Santos (New York: Four Walls Eight Windows, 1988), pp. 149–156;

"Los dos santos medievales de mi abuela bizantina" and "Cuando floreció lo marchito," translated by Linda Britt as "My Byzantine Grandmother's Two Medieval Saints" and "When New Flowers Bloomed," in *When New Flowers Bloomed: Short Stories by Women Writers from Costa Rica and Panama*, edited by Enrique Jaramillo Levi (Pittsburgh: Latin American Literary Review Press, 1991), pp. 59–67;

"Ondina," in *Latinos: Narrativa contemporánea desde catorce países*, edited by Poli Delano (Buenos Aires: Instituto Movilizador de Fondos Cooperativos C.L., 1992), pp. 47–54;

"Dulce violencia" and "Infinitas partes de un temperamento," in *Relatos de mujeres: Antología de narradoras de Costa Rica*, edited by Linda Berrón (San José: Mujeres, 1993), pp. 41–48;

"¿A qué no me van a creer?," translated by Barbara Paschke as "Believe It or Not" in *Costa Rica: A Traveler's Literary Companion*, edited by Barbara Ras (San Francisco: Whereabouts Press, 1994), pp. 1–9.

SELECTED PERIODICAL PUBLICATIONS – UNCOLLECTED: "Manuela siempre," *Escena*, 5, no. 12 (1984): 23–31;

"Los Quijotes modernos: Ensayo de incorporación a la Academia Costarricense de la Lengua," *Alba de América*, 8 (July 1990): 289–304.

Carmen Naranjo is one of the most important literary figures in Costa Rica today. She has published seven volumes of poetry, seven novels, four books of short stories, and four books of essays. A creative and visionary writer, Naranjo incorporates a variety of innovative techniques in her works of fiction, several of which have won literary awards throughout Central America. She is read widely in Latin America but has become known only recently in the United States, mostly through translations of her short stories.

Carmen Naranjo Coto was born on 30 January 1930 in Cartago, the original capital of Costa Rica, some twenty kilometers from San José. Her father, Sebastián Naranjo Prida, was from Santa Cruz de Tenerife in the Canary Islands. Her mother, Caridad Coto Troyo, was from a family of Sephardic origin who immigrated to Costa Rica in the sixteenth century. Her father had a fabric store in Cartago for a while but was not much of a businessman. When Carmen was three years old the business failed and the family moved to San José, where Sebastián joined a family business. Carmen was the third of four children and the only daughter. Since the family's economic situation was somewhat precarious, they lived an austere life in the outskirts of San José. Carmen and her brothers Manuel, Mario, and Alfonso learned how to work at an early age to help the family.

At age seven Carmen suffered a severe case of polio, resulting in an atrophied arm. During her convalescence she did her first year of schooling with a tutor and read copiously from the large collection of books in the family library. Her favorite books were Plato and Aristotle and other Greek works such as *Daphnis and Chloë*, a reading level well beyond her years. Between eight and twelve she read Fyodor Dostoyevsky and Leo Tolstoy. At fifteen her father gave her the Royal Spanish Academy edition of *El siglo de oro español* (The Golden Age of Spanish Literature), which had a marked influence on her career as a writer.

Naranjo went to primary school at the Escuela República del Perú (Republic of Peru School), and she graduated from the Escuela Superior de Señoritas (High School for Young Women) in San José. In her late teens she read William Faulkner, Walt Whitman, Emily Dickinson, Jules Verne, and Carson McCullers. It was not until the mid 1960s, after publishing her first novel, that Naranjo began reading Latin-American authors such as Juan Rulfo, Carlos Fuentes, Octavio Paz, Julio Cortázar, and Jorge Luis Borges.

Having grown up with three brothers, Carmen was rebellious and aspired to be a doctor. Medical school was out of the question financially since it meant study abroad, so she resigned herself to studying liberal arts at the University of Costa Rica. By this time Naranjo already knew she had a vocation for writing. She read voluminously, kept a diary, and wrote speeches on themes of solidarity and charity for her father to present at the Spanish Society, of which he was a member.

Upon her graduation from the university with a licentiate degree in 1953 Naranjo worked as a clerk in the Caja Costarricense del Seguro Social (Bureau of Social Security), beginning what was to become a full and illustrious career in the public sector. Shortly thereafter she took a job with the United Nations in Venezuela, where she wrote her first book of poetry, *Canción de la ternura* (A Tender Song, 1964), inspired by the nostalgia she felt for her family and by her first encounter with the magic and art of the written word. Due to an elevated sense of discretion and loyalty to her family, however, she did not seek to publish the book at that time. Although she got along well with her father, who admired her capacity for writing, Naranjo's modesty did not allow her to show him her poetry.

Her mother still does not understand or appreciate Naranjo's preference for writing and a public life over having a husband and children. Naranjo was married briefly in her twenties, but her sense of cultural responsibility and her obsession for writing left no room for the constraints of a conventional marriage, and her critical view of reality left her with no desire to bring children into a troubled world.

Returning to Costa Rica in 1964, Naranjo resumed work in the public sector, first as an assistant manager of the Costa Rican Electric Company, then as an assistant manager of La Caja, where she eventually became secretary general. By 1964 Naranjo's literary career began to take off. In a literary workshop led by Costa Rican essayist Lilia Ramos, Naranjo received the recognition and encouragement she needed to publish her first work. Naranjo published two more books of poetry, one dedicated to her father, who died in 1962 – *Hacia tu isla* (Toward Your Island, 1966) – and another dedicated to uncovering religious hypocrisy, *Misa a oscuras* (Mass in the Darkness, 1967). The latter represents the culmination of a long-term crisis in her religious beliefs, which had been dealt a serious blow

*Naranjo at age fifteen*

as early as her first communion. It was not until her research into Judaism while serving as Costa Rican ambassador to Israel (1972–1974) that she rediscovered her Catholicism.

An overview of Naranjo's novels and short stories reveals that one of her major themes is the portrayal of the contemporary Costa Rican on all levels of urban life. In effect, her fictional works provide an intuitive documentation, analysis, and critique of the situations in which a myriad of people find themselves and the attitudes, experiences, and actions or lack thereof that are the responses to those situations. As with most new Latin-American fiction writers, Naranjo integrates narrative technique with thematic concerns in her prose. One of the most important characteristics of the new Latin-American narrative as exemplified in Naranjo's prose is a search for authenticity in language and national identity, resulting in a high priority given to the representation of the spoken word in the literary work. In general there is also a rupture with the main features of the traditional novel, such as plot line, chronological sequence, and character development, all of which are minimized if not absent in Naranjo's fiction. In their place is a fragmented, more true-to-life representation of lived experience, which requires the active participation of the reader in order to complete the meaning of the text.

Naranjo's first three novels make up what might be considered a trilogy dedicated to the *don Nadies* (Mr. Nobodies) of this world, the anonymous men of the middle class, a relatively recent phenomenon in Costa Rica. Massive social reform instigated during the epoch of social democracy beginning in 1948 and solidified under the aegis of the National Liberation party, founded in 1952, led to the creation of numerous state agencies and many jobs for white-collar workers. Naranjo belonged to this generation and was an activist for social change and a leader in the cultural development of the country. Idealism slowly changed to disillusionment when plans were distorted more often than fulfilled as newly formed agencies became bureaucratic monsters, dehumanizing and alienating the common man rather than uplifting him, as was the initial goal.

Naranjo's narratives break with the rural *costumbrista* (novel of manners) tradition of the Costa Rican novel. Her works focus, rather, on urban life, especially that of the middle-class bureaucrat, depicted in an environment dominated by men and inspired by her firsthand experience at La Caja. Her fiction is unique in her avant-garde writing techniques, her comprehensive and profound vision of Costa Rican social reality, and her intimate understanding of the world of men from a thinking woman's perspective. Reflecting on her early works and her discovery of the art of writing, Naranjo said in a 1993 interview with Ardis L. Nelson, "Como con un lápiz podés encontrar la sangre. Como con un afán de buscarte a ti mismo podés encontrar a toda la humanidad" (It is as if with a pencil you can draw blood. As if in your desire to find yourself you find all humanity).

Her first novel, *Los perros no ladraron* (The Dogs Did Not Bark, 1966), recounts twenty-four hours in the life of a petty bourgeois who works in a state agency, ever at the mercy of an egocentric, manipulative boss. The protagonist, his colleagues, his wife, and his lover are all anonymous characters in a narrative made up completely of dialogue that chronicles the drab existence of the worker as he goes from home to the bus, to the café, to work, to the hospital, to his lover's apartment, to the bars, and back home again in thirty-two brief chapters. The theme revolves around the effects of the office hierarchy on the worker, who is just a cog in the wheel of the state bureaucracy and whose very existence hinges on the whims of his superiors. He leads an unfulfilling life, frustrated at every turn by a lack of appreciation for what he does and with no hope for any improvement of his lot. The dialogical structure of the work allows for multiple perspectives on the subject and requires active participation on the part of the reader, who must complete the mosaic of the mostly unnamed characters' interactions. Death is seen as the only escape from a futile and miserable life. The book was awarded the 1966 Aquileo Echeverría Prize for the Novel in Costa Rica and launched Naranjo's career as a fiction writer. It represents the successful use of language to express authenticity, an investigation into a national concern, and the involvement of the reader to create the meaning of the work, all characteristics of the new Latin-American narrative.

*Memorias de un hombre palabra* (Memories of a Word Man, 1968) charts the life of a lower-middle-class male from his early years to middle age. Once again the protagonist is anonymous, but the reader gets to know him intimately as he suffers rejection after rejection, beginning with his parents. His father left his mother before he was born, and his mother never shows any affection for the child. Indeed, she warns him that once she has fulfilled her obligations to him he would be on his own. She literally kicks him out of the house when he lands his first job, sending the disoriented, miserable boy into the world to make it as best he can. He manages to keep his job as a clerk in a store for many years, although he leads a drab, lonely existence marked by extreme introspection and anguish. The only highlights in his life are the occasional times he reaches out to another, only to be misunderstood and rejected, or when another, such as Elisa, reaches out to him. But his lack of trust spells doom for the relationship, and his honesty lands him in the hospital. He turns to thievery to maintain a newfound thrill in the possession of material goods. When he is discovered, he loses his job and becomes a philosophizing vagrant who finally finds happiness in the arms of a childhood friend, Adelilla, who gives him a child.

*Memorias de un hombre palabra* is about the desperation of a child who is neither wanted nor loved and who grows up to become a social misfit with no sense of self-worth. As a work in Naranjo's trilogy it represents the frustrations of the anonymous near-poverty-level individual who has no hopes for the future and is driven to dangerous pastimes for a thrill. The book is written in an innovative style in which the protagonist's thoughts and words are presented in a narrated interior monologue in which his exact spoken words are not indicated while the

*Mayor Rotchild of Bat-Yam and Naranjo in 1973, when she was Costa Rican ambassador to Israel*

words of others are presented clearly as dialogue lines. The work is an intense examination of the innate creativity and optimism that persists even within the most unfortunate of society's children.

*Camino al mediodía* (The Road at Midday, 1968) completes the trilogy with the first-person account of a man who reads about his best friend's death in the newspaper at 7:30 A.M. and proceeds to the funeral home, eventually joining the cortege to the cemetery. During the five hours in which the action of the novel takes place, the protagonist suffers a severe headache and becomes aware that his friend, an upper-middle-class bureaucrat named Eduardo Campos Argüello, committed suicide. In his search for the funeral parlor he realizes that he seems to be invisible to others, and he has the uncanny experience of coming upon phantoms from the past of his deceased friend and revisiting scenes of funerals involving close family and friends. On the way to the cemetery the protagonist overhears all the gossip about the deceased's private and public life, with which he seems to be intimately acquainted. When Eduardo's colleagues give eulogies at the gravesite, the protagonist directs his commentary to the de-

ceased, contradicting the flowery speeches with the truth about his life. The deceased was an ambitious man from an upper-middle-class family who sacrificed his true self for the pursuit of wealth and status. Driven by self-interest and greed, he became the president of a bank and achieved the high profile he sought. The lies, deceit, and hypocrisy that maintained the precarious balance of his folly led to his financial demise. The novel exposes the vacuousness of a life based on false materialistic values.

Naranjo's style in *Camino al mediodía* is unique, with ninety pages of uninterrupted text presented variously by an omniscient third-person narrator, an unnamed first-person protagonist whose interior monologue is set off in quotation marks, and numerous other characters whose dialogue lines are also set off in quotations. For the first time in Naranjo's fiction the fantastic element predominates. The invisible protagonist realizes that he is the deceased Eduardo Campos Argüello, or at least an integral part of him. Perhaps he is Eduardo's soul or conscience, which had separated from him long ago, when his ambition overcame his youthful goodness. Even this character, who may be seen as despicable, is treated with compassion by Naranjo as she shows the way out through truth and sincerity as personified in the conscience. The book won second prize for the novel in Los Juegos Florales Centroamericanos y de Panamá (The Central American and Panamanian Floral Games) celebrated in Quezaltenango, Guatemala, in 1967.

In 1970 Naranjo began teaching writers' workshops, the perfect environment for sharing her gift of self-expression and for mentoring aspiring writers. Her next novel, *Responso por el niño Juan Manuel* (Funeral for the Child Juan Manuel, 1971), is a direct result of those workshops. The story takes place the night of the wake being held for the fifteen-year-old Juan Manuel, a friend who at the same time is the invention of Luis, Oquendo, Ernesto, and Jorge, youths seeking a common goal to solidify their friendship and create meaning in their lives. Luis is the most sensitive and creative, Oquendo is the artist who draws the physical portrait of Juan Manuel, Ernesto is the cynic, and Jorge is skeptical but has the best understanding of the others. The friends tell stories about Juan Manuel, an orphan who in turn invented a friend named Carlitos to keep him company. The unsatisfied curiosity of two strangers invited to the wake heightens the enigma of Juan Manuel and the cause of his death.

There are multiple themes and levels of fiction in *Responso,* which includes "passages . . . where as many as six metafictional levels operate simultaneously," according to Raymond D. Souza. While the search for authenticity and its resultant existential anguish are important themes, literary creativity is by far the predominant concern. "De la misma experiencia de los talleres, come se reúne un grupo de gente y van creando personajes, esos personajes a su vez creando otros personajes. Y como los primeros se van dando cuenta de que para que tengan validez, los personajes creados hay que matarlos" (Just as in a writers' workshop where people meet and create characters for their stories, Luis, Oquendo, Ernesto, those characters in turn create other characters. Then the first ones come to realize that the characters they have created must die in order to be real), Naranjo says in the 1993 interview. *Responso* is narrated first by an omniscient third person, but then each of the characters narrates different sections as each delves into his inner dilemma and his relationship to Juan Manuel. The book received the Aquileo Echeverría Prize for the Novel in Costa Rica in 1971 and second prize for the novel in Los Juegos Florales de Guatemala in 1968.

In 1971 Naranjo was named as one of the top administrators of La Caja, a position never before held by a woman in Costa Rica; she held it for six years. During these years she also held other political posts and traveled widely in various capacities. From 1972 to 1974 she was the Costa Rican ambassador to Israel, where she wrote the essays later published as *Por Israel y por las páginas de la Biblia* (Passing through Israel and the Pages of the Bible, 1976), the short stories *Hoy es un largo día* (Today Is a Very Long Day, 1972), and the book-length poem *Mi guerrilla* (My Own War, 1977).

*Hoy es un largo día* provides vignettes of the lives of ordinary people in a variety of situations, tinged now and again with irony and sarcasm, mystery and mysticism, fantasy and the fantastic. Each story provides an insight into Naranjo's philosophical outlook. The title story sketches a few disparate characters in a provincial town whose lives are more intertwined than they would like the neighbors to know. An omniscient narrator alternates between a meeting in the town hall and the intimacy of a private home, offering just enough information to allow the reader's imagination to fill in the gaps of the love triangles. The interplay of passions and appearances leads to all the characters getting what they want in the end.

The stories in this collection represent the recognition that everyone's attitudes and actions, whether political or personal, are but repetitions of what has gone before in the comedy of errors that humanity encompasses. For Naranjo, this book is "una conversación mía con el público" (a conversation I am having with the public), in which she integrates technical skill with profound insights and observations on the human condition. The book was well received critically and awarded the Editorial Costa Rica Prize for the Short Story in 1973.

During 1969–1970 Naranjo was invited to participate in a writers' workshop at the University of Iowa, where she taught a course on Latin-American literature and wrote her next novel, *Diario de una multitud* (Diary of a Multitude, 1974), based on her remembrances of San José. The first title that came to her when she began to write was *San José el insoportable* (Unbearable San José), for she would be writing from a critical perspective. Although Naranjo has lived almost her whole life in the city, she finds that the Costa Rican countryside is the truly lovely part of the country while the capital is ugly.

Due to the experimental nature of this novel it is impossible to discuss the characters and describe the story separately from the style and narrative techniques of the work. Instead of character and plot development, the novel consists of innumerable anonymous voices in fragments of dialogue and interior monologue that take place in San José. The book is divided into three chapters: "Hilos" (Threads), "Claves" (Clues), and "Tejidos" (Knitting). "Hilos" is a collage of voices that speak simultaneously one morning. It consists of more than twenty dialogues, several brief descriptive fragments of trivialities and one-sided conversations such as telephone calls, and segments that may be letters or postcards. Frequently there are paragraphs with several voices, each presenting his or her viewpoint in a run-on style, without dialogue indicators. Except for three fragments in which two women discuss a department-store sale, none of the segments seems to be directly interrelated. The socio-economic level of the speakers runs the gamut from the homeless to the well-to-do, and every possible everyday topic seems to be on the agenda of this collective personality, from a street vendor's activities to old family vengeances, from greetings and gossip to a critique of the country, a letter to the president, and a veterinarian's advice.

"Claves" contains meditations by an omniscient narrator who philosophizes and offers contradictory possibilities that may be keys to understanding the novel. It also includes sparse dialogue lines between two lovers as they go through different stages of their relationship. The emphasis on orality that so dominates the first and largest section of the book is here replaced by metaphoric language in the form of a monologue by the principal narrator. "Tejidos" brings together the loose threads of "Hilos," and a basic story line can be found here as a group of rebellious youths confront and threaten an old man and later become confused and excited by a shotlike sound. There is a blending of anonymous voices: the young radicals, who express their desire for freedom by throwing stones through windows; the poor, who spontaneously join in the looting and burning of stores; the store owners as they desperately try to save their merchandise; and the upper-middle-class folks who take refuge in their homes. The lovers from "Claves" return to find the city in ruins and the politicians thinking that tomorrow will be another day.

*Diario de una multitud* is Naranjo's most critically acclaimed novel. For Raymond D. Souza it is "a portrait of the frustrations, mediocrity, and sheer boredom of urban life . . . an ironical and satirical apprehension of reality." He sees Naranjo's ideology as "decidedly liberal and her epistemological stance contextualistic." Alicia Miranda Hevia discusses the affinity of the novel with other Latin-

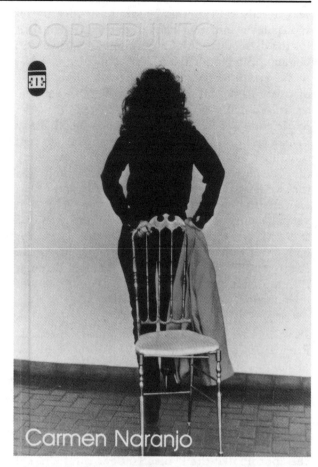

*Cover for Naranjo's 1985 novel, about a rebellious young woman in search of her identity*

American novels of the Boom. Luz Ivette Martínez analyzes *Diario de una multitud* as an antinovel and compares it with Julio Cortázar's *Rayuela* (1963; translated as *Hopscotch,* 1967) in its rupture with traditional structure, lack of conventional characters, use of language to demonstrate the lack of communication, freedom of narrative techniques, lack of an external narrator, and active participation of the reader. *Diario de una multitud* was awarded the Prize for the Novel by the Superior Council of Central American Universities.

Naranjo's experience as ambassador to Israel was a turning point in her multifaceted career. The recognition she received from serving in this prestigious post, as well as from the weekly essays she published in Costa Rican newspapers during her time in Israel, made her a popular figure. She was asked by the administration of Daniel Oduber Quirós to serve as minister of culture, youth, and sports in 1974. This was a time of great enthusiasm for the recently formed Ministry of Culture, which sought to unite the educated and illiterate in a process of cultural training. Naranjo was directly responsible for initiating many institutions established for the dissemination of culture: the Department of Cinema, the National Theater Company, the National Symphonic Orchestra, the publishing house of Costa Rica, and the College of Costa Rica. She organized many events that encouraged the active participation of the citizens. Her book-length essay *Cultura* (1978) is dedicated to clarifying the concept of culture and how it manifests itself in everyday life. Concurrent with this assignment, Naranjo was the administrative coordinator of the Central American Institute of Public Administration. After two years as minister of culture, Naranjo resigned due to a lack of support for some of her projects. She had been called subversive for exposing Costa Rican society to the ills of their country through filmed programs about issues such as deforestation, malnutrition, poverty, and alcoholism.

Even after her resignation, she continued to serve in various cultural and political capacities. From 1976 to 1978 she was vice-president of the Association of Caribbean and Central American Writers and vice-president of the Worldwide Association of Writers and Journalists. She served as advisor for the Organization of American States (OAS), directing the installation of social security systems in El Salvador and the Dominican Republic; and she coordinated the United Nations International Children's Emergency Fund (UNICEF) Early Childhood Education Program for Central America and Panama, working in Guatemala (1976–1978) and Mexico (1978–1980). In 1977 the Spanish government awarded Naranjo membership in the Order of Alfonso X El Sabio. Returning to Costa Rica in 1980, Naranjo became director of the Costa Rica Museum of Art (1980–82), then Director of EDUCA (Editorial Universitaria Centroamericana [Central America Universities Publishing House], 1982–1992).

Experiences she had during the times spent working with the OAS and with UNICEF in the Caribbean and in Guatemala led to the themes of the stories published in *Ondina* (1983). Two representative stories of *Ondina* are "Simbiosis del encuentro" (Symbiosis of a Couple) and "Los señores matosos de la casa alta" (The Maniacal Señores at the Top of the Hill). In "Simbiosis del encuentro" Ana and Manuel are told by friends they would be perfect for each other, and they meet at a party arranged partly for this purpose. They fall madly in love and are inseparable for a time, but during a cooling-off period arguments begin. After a weeklong separation Manuel returns feeling sick and

needy, so he stays on with Ana. They finally go to a doctor and, to their consternation, discover that Manuel is pregnant. This unheard-of situation leads them to do research, to no avail, and to travel to a neighboring country to have their child. Ana's disgust with Manuel's condition prompts her to drop him off alone at the hospital door. When she returns the following day he is nowhere to be found. During her desperate search for Manuel and her child, Ana gradually turns into a man. The story presents that aspect of relationships whereby people lose their individuality and become increasingly like the significant other. It is also a feminist statement on male lack of compassion for the suffering of childbearing.

"Los señores matosos de la casa alta" is also about a couple, but in this case they marry, have a child, and remain together for many years, not so much for love but due to the fact that the husband is an absolute tyrant and the wife is submissive and servile. When the couple first met, he laid down the conditions of the marriage, making it clear that it is a serious matter to marry when a man has ambition and seeks power. She vowed to please him in all respects and never to complain. Although it was rumored they were happy, the wife had no will or voice of her own. She helped her husband run the businesses, which he did in a heartless and dictatorial manner.

The story is told by a third-person omniscient narrator about the rise to power of an egocentric man whose every act is openly dictatorial. The story may be a metaphor for Central American politics, but it is certainly a variation on the French proverb *plus ça change, plus c'est la même chose* (the more things change, the more they remain the same). *Ondina* won the EDUCA prize for Latin-American narrative in 1982 and is one of Naranjo's most provocative works.

*Nunca hubo alguna vez* (1984; translated as *There Never Was a Once Upon a Time,* 1989) is a book of short stories based on Naranjo's experiences with young people. It is written particularly for children from twelve to nineteen. The title story is a sensitive first-person account of the hurt and disillusionment of ending a friendship. Written in the form of a letter, it reviews the events leading up to the estrangement and includes the narrator's own feelings and observations. Her friend had insisted that she ride her new bicycle one day. Unfortunately she had an accident and ran into a truck, ruining the bike and the friendship.

"Dieciocho formas de hacer un cuadrado" (Eighteen Ways to Make a Square), also narrated in

*Naranjo with students and teachers, at a writing workshop in San José, August 1992 (photograph by Ardis L. Nelson)*

the first-person, describes the contest invented by the narrator's friend Pepe to entertain his friends when they are all home in bed with the flu. He responds first by drawing a square in twenty-three different ways, graphically represented in the text, but later decides it is a question of mental squares and comes up with nineteen examples, such as "Cuando elogiás algo que no te gusta y te lo regalan" (When you fawn over something you do not like and then they give it to you) and "Cuando te creés alguien por querer parecerte a otro" (When you believe you are somebody for wanting to be like someone else). This book is popular with young people, who find it easy to identify with the characters.

*Estancias y días* (Places and Days, 1985) is a book of story-essays written with Graciela Moreno in which the chapters alternate between those written by Moreno – "Estancias" – and those written by Naranjo – "Días." Both write in the first-person singular voice, thus creating an interior monologue, but one in which each author attempts to speak with her representative demons. For Moreno it is death, for Naranjo existential anguish. "Estancias" is a coming to terms with death in a strictly poetic way, where death is a constant companion and even a

lover. Naranjo's "Días" have a chronology, dating from 1963 to 1981, a trajectory of searching for self-understanding, acceptance, and authenticity with others. The whole book is pessimistic in tone and suggests a time of physical and emotional crisis.

*Sobrepunto* (Point Over Point, 1985) is the story of Olga, an intimate study of a confused and rebellious young woman as told by her friend, admirer, and confidant, the solitary hijo del pulpero (son of the grocer) through his diary and memories. This male narrator is the only person in Olga's life who accepts her as she is. Her own mother, a prostitute, sold her to her grandparents, who brought her up in physical comfort but without love. Olga's search for her own identity leads her on a tortuous path that always ends in frustration. She is thrown out of school for improper conduct. Her boyfriend's family rejects her because of her lineage. She is always considered an outsider, in part because her parents were not born in Costa Rica and in part due to her mother's disgraceful lifestyle. Olga marries Miguel and has children, but there is no love in the relationship. By mutual accord they divorce and celebrate with a large party to announce their change in status. Miguel marries his lover, but Olga's relationship with Juan falls apart when he decides to stay with his wife.

After her well-intentioned efforts at marriage and motherhood Olga succumbs to a degenerate existence following a self-styled philosophy of liberation she calls *sport*. She has a series of lovers and becomes a drug addict, losing her children to Miguel as a result. El hijo del pulpero, a friend of Olga's since childhood, provides the only point of view available to the reader. He is obsessed with Olga, is a good listener, is at her bid and call, never judges or criticizes her, and supports her emotionally to the very end. Although he makes numerous attempts to intercede on Olga's behalf with her family and friends, el hijo del pulpero is also frustrated in his efforts since he too is an outsider – his family is of German descent. While it seems that he loves her, the narrator's platonic relationship with Olga is essentially passive, his perspective that of a sympathetic observer as he befriends this capricious, self-indulgent creature who is at the same time a victim of social stigmas.

This novel, actually written in the 1960s, was kept in a drawer for twenty years and published subsequently without any changes to the manuscript. It is impressive that such a timely novel for the 1980s was written twenty years earlier. The narrative style is experimental, an attempt to write according to the French style of painting called pointillism ( *puntillismo*), thus the title *Sobrepunto*. Translated from the realm of the pictoral to that of the verbal, *puntillismo* can be seen to express an eternal present, that of Olga entering the room where el hijo del pulpero writes and meets with her. Although he has not seen her in a long time, there is no chronology in the telling. Her presence is eternal in his memory and his diary, which make up the bulk of the story. As is typical in Naranjo's works, *Sobrepunto* makes a sociopolitical statement, in this case expressing disillusionment with the revolution of 1948 and the counterrevolution of 1955 as well as a critique of a closed and hypocritical society. This important work awaits serious critical attention.

*El caso 117.720* (Case Number 117. 720, 1987) is the story of Antonio, a man from a good upper-middle-class family who has had a respectable career in the public sector but who seemingly has become schizophrenic in midlife and is kept in a room in his mother's house. The personal side of the story is framed by a scientific discourse at the beginning and end of the novel. As the medical specialist delineates the particulars of case 117. 720, he also waxes philosophical, discussing the illness in meta-

phorical terms. The scientific exams have yielded no answers, and the teacher admits that it is a mystery that may be solved only in the future. Antonio is the narrator of most of the book, his interior monologue interspersed with dialogue from the people who have been part of his life: his mother doña Amalia, his sisters Lucrecia and Margarita, his ex-wife Marta and her lover Juan, and two maids who take care of him in his isolated room.

In his demented state Antonio believes himself to be a pine tree that grows beets that he can pick from his body and throw at the spider that threatens him. He can no longer communicate verbally with others, a condition made evident in the text by the lack of dialogue lines preceding the words he wishes to express. Antonio's activities are severely restricted, for he finds it nearly impossible to move. His monologue describing the difficulty he has in retrieving a pencil from the floor suggests a catatonic state. Despite these limitations, his thoughts are lucid at times, such as his understanding that life is "un hueco en el vacío" (a hole in the void). He realizes that he can enter one hole and come out in another, an apt poetic depiction of a schizophrenic state. He also has vivid recollections of his past life, so vivid that they color his perception of people in the present. He cannot see the people who enter his room except as shadows, and he cannot believe that a shadow resembling his mother actually could be she because she never had time for him in the past. Antonio's reaction to his mother's presence in the room suggests that he grew up feeling unloved and distant from her, possibly providing an early source of distress that led to his illness.

The final discourse declares that case 117. 720 has been resolved. Antonio's illness is attributed to unstable blood pressure over the period of a lifetime, and a list of physical and psychological symptoms is provided. Stylistically, however, this final portion of the book becomes a pessimistic commentary on life, human relationships, and justice. Each and every phrase of the scientific speech is followed by a rebuttal, a question, or a contradictory remark in parentheses, indicating that the logic of the discourse is riddled with error. This is the story of a sensitive, introspective man who goes crazy because of the degeneration of social values. Antonio may also be seen as a metaphor for Costa Rica, a country that no longer exists, according to Naranjo in a 1993 interview with Nelson: "Es decir que Costa Rica ya no es nada. Nos manda el fondo económico mundial. Ya no existimos como un país, ya no tomamos decisiones" (Costa Rica no longer has an identity. The World Bank controls us. We no longer exist as a country, we no longer make decisions).

*Otro rumbo para la rumba* (Another Rhythm for the Rumba, 1989) includes a clever story called "En todas partes se puede" (Anywhere It Is Possible). A poor Latin-American woman saves up money for a passage to the United States by selling everything she owns and finds herself struggling for survival in New York. She resorts to selling her body, but it makes her nauseous, so she seeks refuge in Bloomingdale's, a store big enough to be a city unto itself. She sleeps in a display waterbed as a model and steals from the store to set up her own business. Her success story gets around and other Latin Americans take up residence in the store, driving the unnamed protagonist to head for Macy's. The story is a humorous tale of a silent invasion of the United States by Latin-American rogues.

"Y vendimos la lluvia" (translated as "And We Sold the Rain," 1988) is a masterful tale of how a small country, presumably Costa Rica, meets its economic crisis by selling its most abundant natural resource, the rain, to an Arab nation. Their recovery is short-lived, for the water that turns the desert into an oasis is now scarce in the homeland and life is no longer possible. The story is chillingly accurate in terms of what may happen when the rain forests have all been sold to pay the foreign debt. The story has received no critical attention, although it is the title story of a collection of Central American fiction translated into English. *Otro rumbo para la rumba* is a book of maturity in which a myriad of topics are handled with insight and irony. Along with most of her works, it has yet to receive serious critical attention.

Costa Rica has recognized Naranjo's contributions to its culture by giving her several prestigious awards. She received the Premio Magón de Cultura (Magón Prize for Culture) in 1986; in 1988 she became a member of the Academia Costarricense de la Lengua (Costa Rican Academy of Language), the acceptance speech for which was published as "Los Quijotes modernos" (1990); and a cultural week was held in her honor in 1989 at the Universidad de Costa Rica, IV Semana Cultural en Homenaje de Carmen Naranjo. In that same year she became a leader for women's rights in Costa Rica when she drafted and promoted the controversial Ley de la Igualdad Real (Law for Social Equality of Women). Naranjo has used every possible outlet at her disposal to educate the Costa Rican public and to work for change in laws, attitudes, and customs. Another example of this effort is her collection of forty brief essays addressed to the Costa Rican woman, *Mujer y cultura* (Woman and Culture, 1989).

Carmen Naranjo is an exceptional person in many ways. Despite the fact that her life has been more public than private, she has written and published extensively and is held in the highest esteem by all those who have known her: students, friends, politicians, academics, family members, and other writers. She conducts weekly *talleres* (workshops) for aspiring writers and occasional art workshops to teach drawing in her modest library on the patio of the family home on the congested Avenida Central. She has published one book of her art, *Ventanas y asombros* (Windows and Surprises, 1990), which are ink line drawings, and her work continues to incorporate more and more color. Since October 1993 she has been writing a daily column in *El Día,* one of the popular daily newspapers in San José, on topics ranging from indigenous groups in Panama to music, poetry, and popular expressions in Costa Rica.

At present she has seven works ready to be published and one major work in progress. The two volumes of poetry are *En el círculo de los pronombres* (In the Circle of Pronouns) and *En esta tierra redonda y plana* (On This Round and Flat Earth). The five volumes of short stories are *Los girasoles perdidos* (The Lost Sunflowers); *Pasaporte de palabras* (A Passport of Words); *Fugaz y eterno* (Fugacious and Eternal); *Los poetas también se mueren* (Poets Also Die); and *En partes* (In Parts). An ongoing autobiographical novel is entitled *Insomnios de una adolescente que nació vieja* (Sleepless Nights of an Adolescent Who Was Born Old).

Naranjo's only retreat from the hectic pace of San José is an occasional weekend trip to an austere cabin in the country near Alajuela on a small coffee farm she purchased after her trip to Israel. In the city she lives in a supportive environment of family members and spends most of her waking hours teaching and writing.

## Interviews:

Evelyn Picón Garfield, *Letras,* 11–12 (January–December 1983): 215–226;

Rose S. Minc and Teresa Méndez-Faith, "Conversando con Carmen Naranjo," *Revista Iberoamericana,* 51, nos. 132–133 (July–December 1985): 507–510;

Juana A. Arancibia, "Entrevista con Carmen Naranjo," *Alba de América: Revista Literaria,* 9, nos. 16–17 (1991): 403–405;

Lourdes Arizpe, "An Interview with Carmen Naranjo: Women and Latin American Literature," in *Revising the Word and the World: Essays in Feminist Literary Criticism,* edited by Veve A. Clark, Ruth-Ellen B. Joeres, and Madelon Sprengnether (Chicago: University of Chicago Press, 1993), pp. 51–63.

**Bibliography:**

María Eugenia Acuña, *Bibliografía comentada de Carmen Naranjo,* special issue of *Letras,* 22 (January–June 1990): 1–193.

**References:**

Linda Britt, "A Transparent Lens? Narrative Technique in Carmen Naranjo's *Nunca hubo alguna vez,*" *Monographic Review/Revista Monográfica,* 4 (1988): 127–135;

Richard J. Callan, "Archetypal Symbolism in Two Novels of the Costa Rican, Carmen Naranjo," in *Ensayos de literatura europea e hispanoamericana,* edited by Felix Menchacatorre (San Sebastián, Spain: Universidad del País Vasco, 1990), pp. 61–65;

Alicia Miranda Hevia, "Introducción a la obra novelesca de Carmen Naranjo," *Cahiers du monde hispanique et luso-bresilien/Caravelle,* 36 (1981): 121–129;

Hevia, *Novela, discurso y sociedad: "Diario de una multitud"* (Desamparados, Costa Rica: Mesén, 1985);

Hevia, "La prosodia de *Diario de una multitud,*" *Káñina: Revista de Artes y Letras de la Universidad de Costa Rica,* 7, (January–July 1983): 9–12;

Luz Ivette Martínez Santiago, *Carmen Naranjo y la narrativa femenina en Costa Rica* (San José: Editorial Universitaria Centroamericana, 1987);

Martínez Santiago, "Trayectoria de la obra de Carmen Naranjo," *Alba de América: Revista Literaria,* 9, nos. 16–17 (1991): 153–162;

Sonia Marta Mora Escalante, "*Diario de una multitud* de la crítica al desengaño," in *Evaluación de la literatura femenina de Latinoamérica, Siglo XX: II Simposio Internacional de Literatura: Tomo II,* edited by Juana Alcira Arancibia (San José: Editorial Universitaria Centroamericana, 1986), pp. 51–65;

Ardis L. Nelson, "Carmen Naranjo and Costa Rican Culture," in *Reinterpreting the Spanish American Essay: Studies of Nineteenth and Twentieth Century Women's Essays,* edited by Doris Meyer (Austin: University of Texas Press, 1994), pp. 289–306;

Evelyn Picón Garfield, "La luminosa ceguera de sus días: Los cuentos 'humanos' de Carmen Naranjo," *Revista Iberoamericana,* 53 (January–June 1987): 287–301;

Patricia Rubio, "Carmen Naranjo (Costa Rica)," in *Spanish American Women Writers: A Bio-Bibliographical Source Book,* edited by Diane E. Marting (New York: Greenwood Press, 1990), pp. 350–359;

Raymond D. Souza, "Novel and Context in Costa Rica and Nicaragua," *Romance Quarterly,* 33 (November 1986): 453–462;

Jorge Valdeperas, *Para una nueva interpretación de la literatura costarricense* (San José: Costa Rica, 1979), pp. 111–121;

Aura Rosa Vargas, "*Los perros no ladraron:* Una novedad técnica en la novelística costarricense," *Káñina,* 1 (July–December 1977): 33–36.

# Lino Novás Calvo

*(24 September 1903 – 23 March 1983)*

Lorraine Elena Roses
*Wellesley College*

BOOKS: *El negrero: Vida novelada de Pedro Blanco Fernández de Trava* (Madrid: Espasa-Calpe, 1933);

*Un experimento en el barrio chino* (Madrid: Reunidos, 1936);

*La luna nona y otros cuentos* (Buenos Aires: Nuevo Romance, 1942);

*No sé quién soy* (Mexico City: Viñetas de Rigol, 1945);

*Cayo Canas* (Buenos Aires: Espasa-Calpe Argentina, 1946);

*En los traspatios* (Havana: Páginas, 1946);

*El otro cayo* (Mexico: Nuevo Mundo, 1959);

*Maneras de contar* (New York: Las Américas, 1970);

*Lino Novás Calvo: Obra narrativa,* edited by Jesús Díaz (Havana: Letras Cubanas, 1990).

SELECTED TRANSLATIONS: William Faulkner, *Santuario* (Madrid: Espasa-Calpe, 1934);

Aldous Huxley, *Contrapunto* (Buenos Aires: Sudamericana, 1942);

Ernest Hemingway, *El viejo y el mar* (Buenos Aires: Guillermo Kraft, 1954).

SELECTED PERIODICAL PUBLICATIONS –
UNCOLLECTED: "El camarada," *Revista de Avance,* 2, no. 21 (15 April 1928): 8;

"Proletario," *Revista de Avance,* 3, no. 23 (15 June 1928): 146;

"Daisy Tornasol," *Revista de Avance,* 4, no. 32 (15 March 1929): 77;

"Un hombre arruinado," *Revista de Avance,* 4, no. 40 (15 November 1929): 335, 336, 348;

"Vida y muerte de Pablo Triste," *Social,* 15, no. 9 (September 1930): 51, 106;

"La cabeza pensante," *Orbe,* 1, no. 11 (22 May 1931): 25;

"¡Arre! Mula: Confesiones de un carrero," *Orbe,* 1, no. 15 (19 June 1931): 12–13;

"Un encuentro singular," *Gaceta Literaria,* 5, no. 113 (1 September 1931): 6–7;

"El flautista," *Social,* 14, no. 7 (July 1937): 36;

*Lino Novás Calvo*

¡Trínquenme ahí bien a ese hombre!," *Orígenes,* 1, no. 1 (Spring 1944): 26–30;

"El cuarto de morir," *Orígenes,* 5, no. 18 (Summer 1948): 3–13;

"Esto también es gritar," *Cuadernos Americanos,* 7 (July–August 1948): 261–282;

"A ese lugar dónde me llaman," *Orígenes,* 8, no. 27 (1951): 18–24;

"Elsa Colina y los tantos millones," *Bohemia,* 31 (August 1952): 4–6, 8, 129–131, 137–139;

"La gripe española," *Papeles de Son Armadans,* 182 (May 1971): 179–188;

"Granitos de maiz," *Exilio,* 6, no. 1 (Spring 1972): 83–94;

"La vaca en la azotea," *Papeles de Son Armadans,* 204 (March 1973): 281–292;

"Hacia dónde se acuesta el sol," *Papeles de Son Armadans,* 213 (December 1973): 171–188.

A recognized master of the Spanish-American short story, Lino Novás Calvo is noted for his finely honed portraits of marginalized and alienated characters who struggle to survive against formidable odds. Stylistically, Novás Calvo's rendering of quintessentially Cuban popular speech, rhythms, syntax, and forms of expression has exerted strong influence on younger writers. His only novel, *El negrero* (The Slave Trader, 1933), has also held extraordinary interest for critics who admire the subtlety of its historical re-creation of a Spanish-born slave trader.

The first prominent Cuban writer exiled in the wake of the revolution of 1959, Novás Calvo continued to write in the United States, where he lived until his death. It is difficult to describe his reputation or the reception of his work without taking into account the profoundly pernicious schism that divides "the two Cubas," that is, writers in Cuba versus those living in exile. The critic's task is all the more arduous because after 1960 Novás Calvo turned his fiction into a symbolic weapon to wield against a revolution that he believed had betrayed its own ideals. Meanwhile, Cuban critics at home, when not completely ignoring writers in exile, cast aspersions on them as foes of the people's revolution.

Nevertheless Novás Calvo's books transcend these divisions and continue to attract readers both inside Cuba and abroad. Jesús Díaz, editor of the first collection of Novás Calvo's writing to be published in Cuba after his defection, celebrates two aspects: his remarkable descriptions of natural forces in the Caribbean and his role in narrowing the enormous gap between spoken and written language. Novás Calvo is unquestionably one of the foremost writers of Cuba's "first republican period," the early decades of the twentieth century following independence from Spain and from U.S. military occupation.

Nourished by his readings in European and North American literature – especially Louis-Ferdinand Céline, Pío Baroja, Sherwood Anderson, Erskine Caldwell, John Steinbeck, and Ernest Hemingway – his concern with form impelled him to experiment with cinematic techniques, suggesting emotion rather than describing it, and presenting a succession of situations that evoke the desired mood.

Documents discovered after his death by Lorraine Elena Roses in Novás Calvo's native village of Grañas del Sor (Galicia, Spain) indicate that a child named Lino Gonzalo was born on 24 September 1903 to María Calvo Rego. The child is described as an "hijo natural, no reconocido" (illegitimate child, not recognized). A colophon on the same document states that on 2 January 1909 Lorenzo Novás recognized the boy as his son; thus Lino Gonzalo Calvo became Lino Gonzalo Novás Calvo. The testimony of villagers indicates that as a boy he attended school, plowed the land, and tended cows until he immigrated to Cuba in 1919 or 1920, accompanied by a maternal uncle.

Many years later, when interviewed by literary critics, Novás Calvo rearranged the dates and intimated that he was born not in 1903 but in 1905 and was only about seven when he arrived in Havana. This alteration has the effect of substituting a Cuban childhood for the one he actually lived in Spain. Critics did not discover the invention until recently and not only accepted but also perpetuated the idea of a completely self-educated Novás Calvo who was hardly Spanish at all but whose formative experiences occurred in Cuba. In contrast, his relatives and contemporaries in Grañas del Sor, when interviewed in 1986, recalled him attending grade school in the village and departing as a young man of sixteen or seventeen. The notion of a small child cast away on distant shores to fend for himself, later to become an author, matches the sympathetic persona drawn in certain of his stories such as "En el cayo" (On the Key, 1932), "A ese lugar dónde me llaman" (To the Place Where I'm Called, 1951), and "La primera lección" (First Lesson).

It is unclear why Novás Calvo would wish to shift critical attention from the details of his early life in Spain to a fictitious Cuban boyhood. One reason could be the bitter memory, cited by him in a 1976 interview, of enmity between the Novás and Calvo family lines which is consistent with his repudiation of the father who later sought him out in Havana. Another, suggested to Roses by his daughter Himilce, could be a deep-seated need not to be perceived as a "gallego" (Galician) at a time when Galician immigrants were looked down upon. In any case the partial disavowal of his Spanish past resulted in his becoming universally recognized until recently as a Cuban, not a Hispano-Cuban, writer.

There is no reason to doubt Novás Calvo's oft-quoted assertion that in Cuba he supported himself at menial jobs that exposed him to harsh conditions in the factories and fields: he cut cloth in a hat factory, shucked oysters in a restaurant, harvested sugarcane, and became a stevedore producing charcoal on an island. In a 1977 interview with Roses he

Cover for Novás Calvo's 1970 collection of short stories written
from the 1930s to the 1960s

referred to himself as a "poor white" living among black, Creole, and biracial Cubans, a kind of Faulknerian character. This ethnic and cultural mix of the island became thematically central to his writing. His interest in literature and in learning foreign languages (English and French) probably developed in night classes or correspondence courses rather than formal education, which he could not afford.

Entry to the literary world came unexpectedly when a poem, "El camarada" (Comrade), was accepted for publication in the avant-garde Havana journal *Revista de Avance* in 1928. The poem was followed by another; his first effort in the short-story genre, "Un hombre arruinado" (A Ruined Man, 1929); and numerous review articles. Novás Calvo was embraced by members of the literary elite, who had come to realize that the "masses" – peasants, blacks, and workers – must be included in political

agendas and who saw in him an emergent writer of the people. Novás Calvo's mentors found him his first white-collar job in a bookstore and introduced him to leading intellectuals, journalists, and writers, including Jorge Mañach, Juan Marinello, Alejo Carpentier, Fernando Ortiz, and Martí Casanovas. Surrounded by intellectuals and afforded access to books and journals, Novás Calvo rapidly acquired a sophistication and breadth of knowledge that placed him within the premier literary circles of Havana in the 1920s.

Around this time he began to publish quasi-autobiographical stories in the voice of a Havana hack driver. The first of these, "La cabeza pensante" (The Thinking Head, 1931), was a story told in a stylized colloquial Cuban idiom. Its protagonist, Jacobo, a lonely taxi driver obsessed with the occult, descends into despair and ruin. This signature piece sets the course of Novás Calvo's later work. Internal, psychological realities crystallize into metaphor, and colloquial voices take on the flavor of poetry. Novás Calvo struck a new and original literary note for Cuban narrative, long bogged down in *criollismo,* or localist realism. The stories that follow also draw on Novás Calvo's experiences as a cab driver in Havana and continue in the same colloquial yet poetic vein as "La cabeza pensante." They always center on outsiders, the forgotten of Cuban society – usually factory workers, servants, and street vendors whose voices he brings to the fore.

By the middle of 1931 Novás Calvo had become a regular contributor to various magazines – *Revista de Avance, Orbe, Revista de la Habana,* and *Social* – but the political and economic situation in Cuba had deteriorated. Gen. Gerardo Machado, elected president in 1924, assumed dictatorial powers in 1927, instigating a wave of repression and persecution. Many of Novás Calvo's associates had been either jailed or exiled; close to members of the resistance, he felt hard-pressed.

A foreign assignment for *Orbe* gave him an opportunity to return to Spain. The assignment positioned him in his native country at an exhilarating time: the Spanish republic had been proclaimed, and Novás Calvo was assigned to report on the changes in intellectual, cultural, and political life. He accepted the job and traveled by ship to La Coruña, not far from his native village, where his mother still resided. Thus his first dispatches were descriptions of pastoral life in Galicia as well as an opportunity for experimentation with new autobiographical material. The chronicles of his transatlantic voyage and arrival in Grañas del Sor were published in the summer of 1931. One of his articles caused a controversy in Grañas because some villagers disputed Novás Calvo's description of women pushing the plow, saying that only men did this work. Novás Calvo is said to have replied with his characteristically noncombative candor, "Tengo que escribir lo que veo" (I must write what I see). Two short stories, "Un encuentro singular" (A Singular Encounter, 1931) and "La primera lección," were inspired by Novás Calvo's brief interlude in Galicia.

He moved on to Madrid and began his interviews in earnest while seeking other ways to supplement his meager income as a stringer. Perhaps the most important event of his career in Madrid was the publication, in the prestigious *Revista de Occidente,* edited by José Ortega y Gasset, of three stories: "La luna de los ñáñigos" (The Moon Ceremony), "En el cayo," and "Aquella noche salieron los muertos" (The Night the Dead Rose from the Grave). Their publication in 1932 marks his acceptance by the Spanish intellectual elite and his debut on the international scene. All three stories narrate adventures in Cuba and its outlying keys, opening up a world at once strange and seductive to Spanish and Latin-American readers. All three stories were included in significantly altered form in his 1942 collection *La luna nona y otros cuentos* (The Ninth Moon and Other Stories).

The three stories can be seen as a trilogy of Caribbean exotica. Transcending the distance that separates social literature from pure poetry, Novás Calvo forged a literary mode that anticipates and predates the much-vaunted magic realism now identified with Latin-American writers such as Juan Rulfo, Gabriel García Márquez, and Carpentier. For example, "La luna de los ñáñigos," set in a shantytown inhabited by Afro-Cubans on the outskirts of Havana, tells about eerie events that took place in a now-deserted area. When a black woman kills herself out of despair and unrequited love for a white man, her enraged mother turns to the *ñáñigos,* a secret Afro-Cuban religious sect, for vengeance. She targets a white woman named Garrida, a Galician immigrant who intensely wants to belong to the black community. As the participants begin celebrating their rites, the white woman becomes transfigured, speaking and moving like the blacks, thus narrowly escaping impending violence. The authenticity of the material, based on research on the *ñáñigo* sect by Cuban ethnologist Fernando Ortiz, melds with the magical dimensions of the now-abandoned spot where the transfiguration took place. This fusion of the real and the magical in narrative discourse, accomplished in 1932, is an early display of magic realism, but critics and publicists have tended to overlook Novás Calvo's contribution to this mode. Significantly, in the 1942 version of the same story, renamed "En las afueras" (On the Outskirts), there is no question of magic or metamorphosis; rather, Garrida's transformation is an outward manifestation of her own perception of herself as black and her intense need to belong.

*Orbe* ceased publication in March 1938, and Novás Calvo found a way to support himself with literary translations. He made his debut as a translator from English into Spanish of Faulkner, with *Santuario* in 1934 (*Sanctuary,* 1932), the first translation of Faulkner into another language. D. H. Lawrence's *Kangaroo* (1925) and Aldous Huxley's *Point Counter Point* (1928) were other translation projects that he completed in the 1930s. Later he translated Hemingway's *The Old Man and the Sea* (1952)

*Novás Calvo in 1973*

as *El viejo y el mar,* and was thus influential in introducing a North American author to Spanish and Latin-American readers.

In addition to the short stories and translations Novás Calvo published in Spain before the civil war, he wrote a historical novel, *El negrero.* Secluded in the dimly lit reading room of the Atheneum in Madrid, Novás Calvo completed in three months the research and writing of *El negrero,* a blend of history and invention (or "biografía novelada") continuously in print since 1933. Inspired by his reading of Pío Baroja's *Paradox, rey* (1906; translated as *Paradox, King,* 1937) and based on earlier slavery literature, the novel explores the dark psychological roots of a depraved man with a surname *Blanco* (white) appropriately suggesting exploitation of one race by another. *El negrero* explores the moral ambiguities of the relationship between Europe, Africa, and the Caribbean and examines the contradictions that attend the birth of a unique society. This novel is the precursor of other Cuban novels in the same vein by Carpentier — *El reino de este mundo* (1949; translated as *The Kingdom of This World,* 1957) — and Antonio Benítez-Rojo — *El mar de las lentejas* (1979; translated as *Sea of Lentils,* 1990). In some ways similar to the nineteenth-century abolitionist novels written to influence public opinion against slavery, *El negrero* depicts the horrors of the Middle Passage and the sufferings of African slaves, describing mulatto or black characters who are themselves involved in this reprehensible commerce. In its poetic discourse and incorporation of Afro-Cuban forms, colors, and textures, the novel also manifests its links to the *poesía negrista* movement that flourished at this time, the Cuban version of Spanish-American *indigenismo* and literary populism.

In narrating the life of a Spaniard who enriched himself on the transatlantic slave trade during the early to mid nineteenth century, Novás Calvo engages with several issues of intense political, intellectual, and ethical import to his contemporaries. As William Luis has shown, *El negrero: Biografía novelada,* written when General Machado was deposed, may be read as a Cuban political allegory about despotism; as a response to Western intellectual interest in Africa and the concept of negritude; and finally as a commentary on Oswald Spengler's thesis on the decline of Western civilization.

Luis also demonstrates that Novás Calvo drew on various factual accounts of Blanco and the slave trafficking era as well as earlier biographies of other slavers — especially Brantz Mayer's life of Theodore Canot, *Adventures of an African Slaver* (1854) — to create his nefarious protagonist. However, Novás

Calvo also took liberties with the character, rearranging some biographical data and ascribing to him an incestuous alliance with a sister in order to enhance the villainy of Blanco's career. According to Luis's provocative reading of this important novel, Blanco's pathology reflects on Western culture, implying that the moral collapse of Europe did not begin with World War I but much earlier, with European corruption of Africa and the slave trade.

Novás Calvo's promising career in Spain was interrupted by the outbreak of the Spanish Civil War in 1936. Like Hemingway, he served as front-line correspondent and witnessed some of the bloodiest and most harrowing moments of the Spanish conflagration. It was a baptism of fire. First, according to Salvador Bueno, Novás Calvo almost created a riot in Santander in one of the prisons because when on assignment he took photographs showing prisoners' faces. Then an article he wrote about the Asturian miners' revolt led to his being accused of Fascist sympathies. He was condemned to death and narrowly escaped execution. Disillusioned by the betrayal of his former heroes, Novás Calvo fled the war zone and was among hundreds who crossed the Pyrenees on foot. On the French side he waited in a refugee camp until friends sent the necessary funds for him to return to Cuba. He left Europe never to return, with the conviction that revolutions were a facade for hypocrisy and a haven for opportunists.

Once again in Havana and determined to remain aloof from politics, Novás Calvo began work as a translator for the journal *Ultra,* edited by Fernando Ortiz, the leading scholar of Cuba's African roots and a true discoverer of the importance of the African contribution to Cuban culture. Novás Calvo also joined the staff of the weekly *Bohemia,* which was critical of the Fulgencio Batista regime. Now an assistant editor, he narrowly avoided a clash with government officials when one of his editorials referred to Batista as a dictator. Confronted by an irate Batista subordinate, he avoided retaliation by saying, somewhat disingenuously, "No soy yo él que le dice dictador. Lo dice todo el mundo" (It's not I who's calling him a dictator. Everyone is saying it).

In 1940 he met journalist Herminia del Portal, and after what was known as a "trial marriage" among freethinkers of the time, they married in a civil ceremony. Their lasting union produced one daughter, Himilce, in 1944; she became a writer many years later in the United States.

During the 1940s Novás Calvo published two of his most important collections of short stories, *La luna nona* and *Cayo Canas* (1946). *La luna nona* marks

a departure from the intensely lyrical idiom and the animistic vision of the short stories written in Spain and introduces a more analytical, even behavioristic approach to character delineation. The narrative voice is no longer that of a protagonist or participant in harrowing adventures but a distant and omniscient narrator. One of the most remarkable stories in the collection is "La noche de Ramón Yendía" (Ramón Yendía's Night), written in 1933 and inspired by the revolution that overthrew Machado. Yendía is a cab driver who once helped the resistance and has unwittingly become implicated with the counterinsurgency. Yendía, the ultimate innocent victim, is killed in a car chase that occurs because he imagines he is being pursued.

As a volume *Cayo Canas* has more cohesiveness than *La luna nona* in that it encompasses a total Cuban and Caribbean reality with rich geographical and historical texture. The continuity of themes and settings produces a panoramic effect enhanced by the sweep of the poetic idiom and the majesty of the descriptions. The title story – elsewhere entitled "El cayo incendiado" (The Burning Island) – recounts the horrific end of a man stranded on a lonely offshore island. Other stories in the collection describe coming-of-age in the Havana streets. In addition to these stories, Novás Calvo also published stories in the influential journal *Orígenes,* published by José Lezama Lima, including "El cuarto de morir" (Death Room, 1948) and "A ese lugar dónde me llaman."

In contrast, the next decade was one of absorption in journalism and scant literary production – ephemeral pieces in *Bohemia* and many short stories of which the author did not even keep copies and that have yet to be unearthed in Cuba. His mood was despondent, and he ceased to write novels or art stories. Cuban critic Jesús Díaz concludes that this silence led to "literary suicide" and can be interpreted as an expression of profound pessimism. Novás Calvo became increasingly reclusive and skeptical of the role that literature could play in stimulating awareness of social injustice or exploitation. Once, when asked by César Leante, a younger writer, about his creative work, he retorted, "¿Y Vd.? ¿Por qué escribe literatura todavía?" (And you? Why are you still writing?).

The date 1 January 1959 marks the beginning of the Cuban revolution led by Fidel Castro. Novás Calvo, who knew Castro personally and had even edited some articles by him for *Bohemia,* was skeptical and felt personally threatened by Castro supporters at *Bohemia.* In August 1960 he abruptly left his home, the television blaring to avert suspicion, and sought asylum from the Colombian ambassador. After some days in the Colombian embassy he was allowed to leave for Miami, where he joined Herminia and Himilce. First in Miami and then in New York City, he continued writing for *Bohemia Libre* and *Vanidades,* edited by Herminia. His own creative work suffered. Like a tree unable to survive the shock of transplantation, Novás Calvo, cut off from his earlier sources of inspiration in Cuba, did not develop a sustained literary response to his new surroundings. He lived with his family on Seventy-second Street on the East Side of Manhattan until 1967, when he became visiting professor at Syracuse University. It was not the first time he had taught, for he had been a French professor at the Escuela Normal in Havana. Novás Calvo loved Syracuse University and considered his years there the happiest in his life. After a stroke in 1973 he retired and moved back to New York City, where he died in 1983. His remains are interred, at his request, at Syracuse University.

One last collection of his late writings was published under the title *Maneras de contar* (Ways of Telling) in 1970. An extremely uneven and heterogeneous collection, it includes stories from the 1930s and 1940s as well as new ones that focus on dramatic moments of the Cuban revolution viewed from an antirevolutionary perspective, exploring the tensions between political commitment and personal loyalty. Often the theme of retribution is overemphasized, and aesthetic effects are sacrificed to the external mechanics of plot, such as reversals and surprise endings. In a future anthology of selected works by Novás Calvo, nevertheless, one would want to include such stories as "La abuela Reina y el sobrino Delfín" (Our Grandmother Reina and Her Nephew Delfín), "Mi tío Antón Luna" (My Uncle Antón Luna), "Una cita en Mayanima" (A Rendezvous at Mayanima), and "El secreto de Narciso Campana," (Narciso Campana's Secret), all of which evince a renewal of his creative energies.

In "La abuela Reina y el sobrino Delfín" political upheaval furnishes the backdrop for the tale, cast in the form of a letter from one sister to another, of an old woman who has lost most of her family in the early days of the revolution. After her house is expropriated, she begins to obsess about a nephew, Delfín, believed by others to be dead, who will avenge her for her suffering. Though María, the letter writer, has heard of a cousin named Delfín from an illustrious and patriotic family, she cannot tell where fact ends and Reina's imagination begins. Meanwhile, as the revolution continues house ex-

propriations, Reina tells of acts of revenge that have been carried out by Delfín, and the servants begin to ridicule her. Only one of them, Lázara, prevents the eviction of Reina because she believes the old woman has occult powers and fears harm will come if she provokes her. This situation sets the stage for Reina to bring about the extraordinary events that transpire when a band of three armed men and one old woman descend to slaughter the family's persecutors. The reader is left to decide whether this is a realistic tale of a counterrevolutionary plot or a fantastic one about supernatural events that bring an imagined revenge into actual being.

It is possible to speculate on Novás Calvo's fate if he had not fled Cuba. Jesús Díaz suggests he would have thrived under a new revolutionary policy elevating the status of writers and artists. Novás Calvo himself believed otherwise – that he would have suffered persecution and his life would have been endangered. Be that as it may, once he left Cuba nothing by him or about him was published in that country until 1990, when Letras Cubanas brought out *Lino Novás Calvo: Obra narrativa,* a selection of his works, with a foreword by Díaz.

Novás Calvo broke with the prevailing literary trends of his time and paved the way for the continued evolution of colloquial and poetic language in narrative discourse, making possible the even-more-daring experiments of Guillermo Cabrera Infante, who acknowledges his influence. Novás Calvo's ceaseless elaboration of the themes of persecution, resistance to tyranny, and the quest for freedom continues to set a benchmark and spark the imagination of writers today.

In Cuba, Lino Novás Calvo excelled at portraying the lives of the poor and creating a place for them in literature but resisted pressure to champion political ideas in his writing even as he rejected art for art's sake. A sophisticate disguised by an ingenuous air, he chose a middle course between aestheticism and social engagement that injected new vitality into the venerable Latin-American tradition of protest literature. Nevertheless, he disappointed the expectations of Cuban intellectuals and writers at the time of the 1959 revolution. Novás Calvo became the first of many writers to go into exile, a paradigm of the writer torn from his roots and struggling to endure as an artist without an audience.

His exile also deprived him of colleagues who might have furthered his career. No one in Cuba could write about a "gusano" (defector), and outside Cuba and the Spanish-speaking world he was little known since hardly any of his work had been translated. No self-promoter, Novás Calvo kept a low profile in the United States even after he became a citizen. After 1973 ill health limited his possibilities for public appearance and ultimately for artistic creation; his speech faltered, his hand trembled, and his handwriting became illegible. His importance to literary history, however, is attested by his inclusion in literary anthologies, articles in academic journals, and individual translations of his stories. Novás Calvo's reputation is likely to soar with any political change in Cuba that will usher in acceptance of Cuban literature of the diaspora.

**Interview:**

Lorraine (Ben-Ur) Roses, "Conversación con Lino Novás Calvo," *Linden Lane Magazine,* 2, no. 2 (April–June 1983): 3.

**References:**

Enrique Anderson-Imbert, "La originalidad de Lino Novás Calvo," *Symposium,* 29, no. 3 (Fall 1975): 212–219;

Salvador Bueno, "A Cuban Storyteller," *Americas,* 3, no. 2 (February 1951): 10–12, 41, 44–45;

Agustín del Saz, "Lino Novás Calvo y la novela de protesta social," *Revista Cubana,* 26 (June 1950): 320–323;

Sergio Fernández, "Lino Novás Calvo, hechizador de negros," *Universidad* (Universidad de Nuevo León, Monterrey, Mexico), nos. 14–15 (April 1957): 47–55;

Alberto Gutiérrez de la Solana, *Maneras de narrar: Contraste de Lino Novás Calvo y Alfonso Hernández-Catá* (New York: Torres, 1972);

Luis Leal, "The Pursued Hero: 'La noche de Ramón Yendía,' " *Symposium,* 29, no. 3 (Fall 1975): 255–260;

Myron I. Lichtblau, "Reality and Unreality in 'La vaca en la azotea,' " *Symposium,* 29, no. 3 (Fall 1975): 261–265;

William Luis, *Literary Bondage: Slavery in Cuban Narrative* (Austin: University of Texas Press, 1990);

Hector Romero, "El realismo mágico y lo fantástico: Un acercamiento a Lino Novás Calvo," *Iris,* 2 (1988): 101–108;

Lorraine Elena Roses, "La doble identidad de Lino Novás Calvo," *Linden Lane Magazine,* 5, no. 3 (July–September 1986): 3–4;

Roses, "La época española de Lino Novás Calvo," *Chasqui,* 6, no. 3 (May 1977): 69–76;

Roses, *Voices of the Storyteller: Cuba's Lino Novás Calvo* (Westport, Conn.: Greenwood Press, 1986);

Raymond D. Souza, "La imaginación y la magia en la narrativa cubana (1932–33)," *Caribe,* 2, no. 2 (Fall 1977): 87–96;

Souza, *Lino Novás Calvo* (Boston: Twayne, 1981).

# Miguel Otero Silva

*(26 October 1908 – 27 August 1985)*

Rick McCallister

*University of South Carolina at Spartanburg*

BOOKS: *12 poemas rojos* (N.p.: Caribe, 1933);

*Agua y cauce* (Mexico City: México Nuevo, 1937);

*Fiebre* (Caracas: Elite, 1939);

*25 poemas* (Caracas: Elite, 1942);

*Casas muertas* (Buenos Aires: Losada, 1955);

*Polémica sobre arte abstracta,* by Otero Silva and Alejandro Otero Rodríguez (Caracas: Ministerio de Educación, 1957);

*Elegía coral a Andrés Eloy Blanco* (Caracas: Vargas, 1958);

*El cercado ajeno: Opiniones sobre arte y política* (Caracas: Pensamiento Vivo, 1961);

*Oficina no. 1* (Buenos Aires: Losada, 1961);

*Sinfonías tontas* (Caracas: Casa del Escritor, 1962);

*La muerte de Honorio* (Buenos Aires: Losada, 1963);

*Discurso de orden pronunciado en la sesión solemne del 23 de enero de 1965* (Caracas: Dirección de Relaciones Públicas del Concejo Municipal, 1965);

*DMOS: Exposición donación* (Caracas: Museo de Bellas Artes, 1965);

*La mar que es el morir* (Caracas: Arte, 1965);

*25 cuadros de pintores venezolanos* (Caracas: Shell de Venezuela, 1965);

*Poesía hasta 1966,* edited by José Ramón Medina (Caracas: Arte, 1966);

*Umbral* (Caracas: Ateneo, 1966);

*México y la revolución mexicana: Un escritor venezolano en la Unión Soviética* (Caracas: Universidad Central de Venezuela, 1966);

*Cuando quiero llorar no lloro* (Caracas: Tiempo Nuevo, 1970; revised edition, Caracas: Tiempo Nuevo, 1971; revised edition, Caracas: Tiempo Nuevo, 1972);

*Discurso de incorporación como individuo de número* (Caracas: Academia Venezolana de la Lengua, 1972);

*Poesía completa* (Caracas: Monte Avila, 1972);

*Un morrocoy en el cielo* (Caracas: Tiempo Nuevo, 1972);

*Miguel Otero Silva*

*Andrés Eloy Blanco: Homenaje en el LXXVIII aniversario de su natalicio,* with Manuel Alfredo Rodríguez (Caracas: Congreso de la República, 1974);

*Florencia, ciudad del hombre* (Caracas: Arte, 1974);

*Ocho palabreos* (Caracas: Tiempo Nuevo, 1974);

*Mitología de una generación frustrada* (Caracas: Universidad Central de Venezuela, 1975);

*Romeo y Julieta* (Caracas: Fuentes, 1975);

*¿Quién fue Andrés Eloy Blanco?* (Caracas: Ministerio de Educación, 1975);

*Obra humorística completa* (Barcelona: Seix Barral, 1976);

*Obra poética* (Barcelona: Seix Barral, 1977);

*Prosa completa: Opiniones sobre arte y política* (Barcelona: Seix Barral, 1977);

*Lope de Aguirre, príncipe de la libertad* (Barcelona: Seix Barral, 1979);

*Ahora que entre nosotros sólo puede haber palabras* (Montevideo: Aula, 1982);

*Obra escogida* (N.p.: Progreso, 1982);

*Un morrocoy en el infierno* (Caracas: Ateneo, 1982);

*Tiempo de hablar* (Caracas: Academia Nacional de Historia, 1983);

*Discurso de incorporación* (Caracas: Academia Venezolana, 1984);

*La piedra que era Cristo* (Bogotá: Oveja Negra, 1984);

*Casas muertas, Lope de Aguirre* (Caracas: Ayacucho, 1985);

*La poesía social de Miguel Otero Silva* (Caracas: Ateneo, 1985);

*Semblanza de un hombre y de un camino* (Caracas: Centauro, 1985).

OTHER: Pablo Neruda, *Para nacer he nacido,* edited by Matilde Neruda and Otero Silva (Barcelona: Seix Barral, 1981); translated by Margaret Sayers Peden as *Passions and Impressions* (New York: Farrar Strauss Giroux, 1983).

Venezuelan cultural expression of the twentieth century has mirrored the liberal origin of its Creole elite, which evolved from a *comprador* (consumer) class and saw itself as part of a potentially great liberal metropolis capable of modernizing the country. The classic liberal free market had been discredited by the actions of Venezuelan dictator Juan Vicente Gómez and others who handed over the national wealth for luxury products for the elite. An alternative based on economic reform – import substitution – was promoted by the new generation of writers and the populist Acción Democrática party, inspired by Rómulo Gallegos's great novel *Doña Bárbara* (1929), whose message was that civilization conquers barbarism.

Miguel Otero Silva's novels parallel the rise and fall of the modern novel in Venezuela with the rise and climax of bourgeois democracy, beginning with *Fiebre* (Fever, 1939), the first avant-garde novel in Venezuela. His next four novels chronicle modern Venezuelan sociopolitical history in avant-garde fashion, ending with *Cuando quiero llorar no lloro* (When I Wish to Cry I Cannot, 1970), which took Boom structures to their limits, creating an almost-baroque text and nearly resulting in self-parody. After a hiatus of nearly ten years, he abandoned Boom techniques for postmodern historical novels

that diagnosed the roots of Venezuelan culture, such as *Lope de Aguirre, príncipe de la libertad* (Lope de Aguirre, Prince of Liberty, 1979) and *La piedra que era Cristo* (The Rock That Was Christ, 1984).

Otero Silva was born 26 October 1908 in Barcelona, the capital of the Venezuelan state of Anzoátegui, to Henrique Otero Vizcarrondo and Mercedes Silva Pérez. When he was six years old, his family moved to Caracas, where he attended high school at the Liceo Caracas. He then studied engineering for four years at the Universidad Central de Venezuela. He failed to graduate, however, due to his increasing interest in righting the social and economic conditions produced by the absolutist dictatorship of the infamous Gómez.

His literary and journalistic career began at a relatively early age. His first poem, "Estampa" (Stamp), written in modernist style, was published in 1925. In the same year he published a collection of humorous sketches in national magazines. His increasing radicalism, however, led him to a more militant literary bent, hence his conversion to *vanguardismo* (the avant-garde). His absorption in ideological concerns carried him toward a career in politics, journalism, and literature – all of which fed each other in a creative sense.

In 1928, as an engineering student at the Central University of Venezuela, Otero Silva associated himself with *Válvula,* a formerly manifestolike magazine of the avant-garde. The literary meetings of the participants soon developed a political orientation, especially with the arrival of Rómulo Betancourt, who at that time held leftist views. The second week of February 1928 was designated as Student Week by the literary group. Although the more immediate purpose of the festivities was to establish a student cultural center, they developed into political protest. The literary movement born of the events of 1928, also known as *criollismo,* was rooted in a celebration of agrarian development and national pride and had antecedents in Venezuelan positivism and modernism and in the satire of José Rafael Pocaterra and Teresa de la Parra. Like those of Andrés Eloy Blanco, who headed a parallel movement in poetry, their works included social description and protest designed to eradicate rural apathy, criticize American imperialism, integrate the peasantry, represent the labor movement, and incite social revolution or at the least fundamental reform. Most of this group oscillated between nationalism and communism.

Rómulo Gallegos was by and large the inspiration of the "Generation of '28"; his former students rebelled against Juan "Bisonte" Gómez, reciting verses against him and stoning him in effigy during the carnival. When about thirty students were arrested, the rest sent the dictator a telegram demanding to be arrested. About two hundred signees were arrested and jailed for two weeks and received as heroes upon their release. On 7 April a military revolt was crushed; a few hundred students were arrested and spent six months building roads. Among those arrested was Otero Silva.

The immediate upshot of crushing the "Revolution of 1928" was a diaspora of students sent or encouraged to go overseas, where they came into contact with revolutionary modes of thought as well as the philosophies that formed the bases of new trends in art, science, literature, politics, and economics. The ultimate result was a complete renewal of Venezuelan culture. A secondary result of the uprising was *Fiebre,* Otero Silva's first book of prose, which began as a simultaneous record of the events with the final touches written in 1932. Due to the vicissitudes of exile and imprisonment, it was not published until 1939.

In 1929 Otero Silva was involved in a conspiracy to capture Curaçao and use it as a base of operations against the Gómez government. Upon landing in Venezuela the group was defeated, and Otero Silva was forced to flee to Catalonia, Spain. In 1936, a year after the death of Gómez, Otero Silva returned to Venezuela and dedicated himself to poetry and journalism. The next year, however, due to his political agitation, he was exiled by the new tyrant, Gen. Eleazar López Contreras. Otero Silva traveled through Mexico, the United States, and Cuba. In Mexico he published *Agua y cauce* (Water and Channel, 1937), his second book of poems. After the publication of *Fiebre* in 1939 Otero Silva spent the next fifteen years almost exclusively devoted to journalism, publishing serious articles and satires on Venezuelan culture and politics.

*Agua y cauce* is a record of the writer's years of exile and political struggle. Rather strident in its political theme and avant-garde structure as well as its focus on Venezuela, it broke with the past in its use of popular forms and everyday speech. José Ramón Medina sees the vanguard quality of the poems as rooted more in visual description and bold language than in a baroque overreliance on metaphor.

*Fiebre,* Venezuela's first vanguard novel, is a testimonial work principally from Otero Silva's own point of view as narrated by the protagonist Vidal Rojas. The ending in Palenque prison camp, however, is from the perspective of his friends, since Otero Silva had managed to escape into exile. In many ways, although it is narrative, the work displays the writer's poetic talents to a great degree due to its uninhibited, forceful use of language.

The narrative begins with an enigmatic slogan, allegedly taken from a Jewish funeral, which becomes the watchword of the "revolution." It is followed by Vidal Rojas's skeptical, almost cynical observations and demonstrations: that although Venezuela's upper class is theoretically descended from highborn Spanish conquistadores, he personally does not know of a family that does not carry African or Indian blood, that does not have an illegitimate grandparent, or that did not make its money illegally. The vapid lack of culture is highlighted in the following exchange between a student and a young woman of the oligarchy whom he ridicules using the following line from *Don Quixote,* "¿Maritornes, quieres folgar conmigo?" ("Maritornes, do you want to 'have fun' with me?"), to which she replies, "No, Oyarzábal. Este Fox-Trot lo tengo comprometido" (No, Oyarzábal. I've already promised this fox-trot to someone else).

The most salient aspect of the novel is the chasm between verisimilitude – the popular perception of reality as seen or received by society – on one hand and objective reality on the other. As testimony the book chronicles the folly of those who put their faith in verisimilitude as expressed in popular opinion, adherence to authority, and so on only to face the consequences of objective reality. In this way the "revolution" rapidly becomes a comedy of errors in which the wrong voices are heeded and the wrong decisions are taken. One example is the argument between Figueras, the most conscientious worker-leader, and Saldaña, the law student. Saldaña is extremely vociferous in urging an armed attack even though, as Figueras points out, he is the son of the owner of the factory where Figueras works. Figueras, on the other hand, is against the coup. The students follow Saldaña, who eventually deserts them.

The most egregious error of reliance on verisimilitude is committed by Rojas, so skeptical in everything else, whose trust in his girlfriend leads to his capture and imprisonment. The revelation of so many layers of contradictions makes the work an excellent guide to Venezuelan realities of the era. The description of the university campus and environs makes it a geography of power. The university was once a convent and is now surrounded by the headquarters of the Jesuits, the National Library, the Congress building, the police barracks, a gambling casino, and the Academy of History. It is an architectural expression of the seven liberal arts.

MIGUEL OTERO SILVA

CUANDO QUIERO LLORAR
NO LLORO

BIBLIOTECA BREVE
EDITORIAL SEIX BARRAL, S. A.
BARCELONA

Cover for Otero Silva's 1970 novel, about three boys from
different social environments

The use of symbolic names is transparent and is relatively constant in Otero Silva's work: Vidal Rojas the skeptic (*vital,* [vital]; *rojo,* [red]), Cecilia the girlfriend (*ciega,* [blind]), Saldaña the agent provocateur (*salado,* [unlucky]; *dañino,* [harmful]), Figueras the labor leader (Figaro, the servant-critic of the aristocracy in two comedies by Pierre-Augustin Carou de Beaumarchais), and so on until Palenque (stockade), an indigenous site of human sacrifice. This transparency, though a bit ingenuous, adds to the sincerity of the work although it creates a new layer between the raw testimony and the final work by imbuing the characters with an archetypal dimension.

Upon Gen. Isaías Medina Angarita's assumption of power in 1941, Otero Silva returned to Venezuela. He then began the weekly humor publication *El Morrocoy Azul,* (The Blue Morrocoy), which showed a decidedly satirical perspective. His next

book was the collection *25 poemas* (25 Poems, 1942). He did not publish another book until 1955 with *Casas muertas* (Dead Houses). In 1943 he founded *El Nacional,* a daily newspaper, in Caracas, and in 1946 he ended his relationship with *El Morrocoy Azul* in order to build up *El Nacional.* His article "La chusma de Jorge Eliécer Gaitan" (Jorge Eliécer Gaitan's Riffraff), published 5 May 1948, caused a great stir in Colombia and Venezuela for its defense of the mob reaction to the assassination of the only politician who had ever served the interests of the masses. Soon afterward Venezuela's first democratic government was overthrown, occasioning a poem of solidarity from Chilean poet Pablo Neruda, "Carta a Miguel Otero Silva, en Caracas" (Letter to Miguel Otero Silva, in Caracas, 1948). The next year Otero Silva obtained a licentiate in journalism and was elected president of the Venezuelan Association of Journalists.

*Casas muertas,* generally considered Otero Silva's most acclaimed novel, describes the effect of a turn-of-the-century malaria epidemic on a small town. *Casas muertas* is an influential text for later novelists but also draws on examples common to its generation such as epic and foreign models. The town of Ortiz, Neruda adds, also mirrors the chaotic reality of Latin America in its mixture of vitality and desolation. Malaria is a metaphor for the social destruction and misery wrought by Gómez and others of his ilk. Yet the desolation is part of a national transformation from a rural parochial society to a modern society rooted in industry and petroleum. Otero Silva avoids *tremendismo,* the gratuitous use of violence as seen in the novels of José Camilo Cela and others, by narrating in a lyrical realism that names and describes the things and actions of his country from the heartless to the tender and merciful.

Characterization is not complex, yet Otero Silva establishes relationships before the sociopolitical nature of the novel becomes apparent, which makes the novel more convincing than most such works. The reader comes to know the people and then condemn injustice through their eyes. Stylistic devices are subtle but effective; for example, repetition is utilized to emphasize personality traits but does not dominate the narrative. Carmen Rosa is highlighted by the contrast between her victory and Sebastián's defeat, between her persistence and Celestino's resignation.

The novel begins with the funeral of Sebastián, a symbol of virility in a sterile landscape of death. He is mourned by Carmen Rosa, a second symbol of vitality. Her garden in the dying town functions as an oasis of life, reflecting the town's former prosperity, seen through flashbacks centering on her and her family. In the epilogue she persuades her mother and their servant to go to the oil fields of Oriente. Carmen Rosa's grit and determination in many ways establish her as an opposite of Gallegos's Doña Bárbara.

Many critics have suggested that the true protagonist of the novel is the town and its slow agony. This idea is reflected in the title and in the many contrasts between the town's opulent past and desolate present, which is compared to acts of siege and pillaging. Orlando Araujo explains that the novel was conceived as a chronicle of structural economic change. This multidimensionality saves the work from falling into a flat socialist realism common to the era. As Guillermo de Torre points out, its verisimilitude is supported by a largely judicious use of local color, popular language, and symbols.

*Polémica sobre arte abstracta* (Polemic on Abstract Art), which appeared in March 1957, established Otero Silva as a defender of avant-garde modes of expression in all arts. The work was occasioned by an official rejection of abstract art mirroring the Nazi eradication of so-called degenerate art, exposing the petty, vicious nature of the regime. After the fall of Gen. Marcos Pérez Jiménez in 1958 Otero Silva was elected senator from the state of Aragua, and he demonstrated great efforts on behalf of art, culture, and folklore. His great accomplishment of that year, however, was *Elegía coral a Andrés Eloy Blanco* (Choral Elegy for Andrés Eloy Blanco), lamenting the death in exile of the great national poet and activist. A distinct poetic voice from nature is used in each poem with efficacious sparseness and certainty. The identification of the people with the most characteristic elements of Venezuelan geography raises the elegy to the level of national expression, transcending the feelings of the individual. The collective nature of the elegy served as a national eulogy for this martyr for democracy.

In 1960 Otero Silva was awarded the Premio Nacional de Periodismo and named a corresponding member of the Academia Nacional de Letras de Uruguay. Fueled by a desire to democratize not only the political process but the entire society, he asked himself what were the socioeconomic errors of the military dictatorship. Propelled by these questions, Otero Silva went to El Tigre, an oil town, investigated conditions, and interviewed residents. This testimony formed the basis of *Oficina no. 1* (Office No. 1, 1961).

*Oficina no. 1* is a sequel to *Casas muertas* temporally, picking up the life of Carmen Rosa where the previous novel leaves off to mix it into the lives of others: those who are totally unlike her – Francis J. Taylor, Charles Reynolds – and those who are like her – Tony Roberts, Graciela Alcalá, and Nelly. Otherwise it is a totally different work; according to de Torre it is an "antinovel," to employ an overused term from the 1960s. Today it would be called a novel of the Boom period. It moves away from personal characterization by assigning a chapter to each "witness" – including "Electric Light" and "Petroleum" – the point of the work being the assault by the capitalist petroleum industry upon human destiny.

*Oficina no. 1* begins with the forgotten people who arrive on Rupert's bus from dead towns. Far from her home, Carmen Rosa has to defend herself against one-eyed Montero and Avelino the Turk. Finally she yields herself to Matías Carvajal, who resembles her lost Sebastián, even though he is married and has a daughter. Transitory love, she rationalizes, is better than nothing. Although she is not the only protagonist of the novel, which centers on the oilfields, her presence is everywhere and everything is done so that her destiny will be carried out.

If *Casas muertas* is a novel of individual ambition, then *Oficina no. 1* is a novel of objective reality. Alone in El Tigre, Carmen Rosa is obligated to dispose of her previous notions of moral behavior. Though in Ortiz she was seen as an example of virtue, in El Tigre she gives herself up to a married schoolteacher. In the new society such niceties as virtue have little meaning; survival is what counts. Once again the reader sees the conquest of dreams and popular notions of reality by objective reality. If *Casa muertas* stands for "dead houses," then *Oficina no. 1* stands for "ill-born houses," suggests Araujo. The death of an agricultural center is followed by the rise of an oil town. Even the names suggest the differences: Santa Rosa de Ortiz, rooted in a colonial Christian tradition yet reduced to barrenness (and similar to *ortiga,* [nettle, poison ivy]), and El Tigre, echoing the savagery of foreign economic exploitation. Despite its stark contrasts, the work is Otero Silva's most effective political novel in that the characters are credible. Together they offer a litany against the destruction of human potential wrought by the petroleum industry.

*La muerte de Honorio* (The Death of Honorio, 1963) deals with the dictatorship of Pérez Jiménez and is interesting as a social document, although its modern techniques and resources are not always effective. It is an artificial novel formed from individual tales joined by common circumstances: five men of ordinary intelligence who are known by their occupations rather than their names. When a prison trusty calls them by their real names for mail call, their own names sound strange to their ears. There is no main character, for all the characters are equal. In this sense the novel is a rewriting of Lope de Vega's play *Fuenteovejuna* (circa 1619), for the military dictatorship is overthrown by a multitude of individual acts rather than a singular blow.

Structurally the novel consists of two sections titled *cuadernos* (notebooks): "Cinco que no hablaron" (Five Who Did Not Speak) and "Honorio y su muerte" (Honorio and His Death). The first *cuaderno* is divided into six chapters. The first, "El YVC-ALI," narrates the prisoners' flight to the prison camp aboard a plane whose identification letters seem to spell out the name of some exotic bird. The remaining five chapters of the *cuaderno* contain the testimony of the individuals in the cell: "El Te-

nedor de Libros" (The Bookkeeper), "El Periodista" (The Journalist), "El Médico" (The Physician), "El Capitán" (The Captain), and "El Barbero" (The Barber). "Honorio y su muerte" serves as an epilogue that highlights the coming of democracy, in which false honor/Honorio is no longer necessary, for truth and justice will prevail.

Although *La muerte de Honorio* portrays the triumphal birth of democracy in modern Venezuela, Otero Silva is frustrated by real events. The military officers, it seems, were only replaced by the "betancures," the new governing caste who applied the dictates of the oil companies to the country. With the triumph of Acción Democrática came the complete destruction of rural life as peasants were drawn to the city to form labor pools in the shantytowns. Progressive forces perceived that one type of class domination was substituted for another. Sadly, by the time the novel came to press, events had overtaken the initial euphoria of liberation. This time Otero Silva himself was the victim of false popular perception.

The collection of poems *La mar que es el morir* (The Sea Which Is Death, 1965) includes *glosas* (referential or commentary verses), and the title itself is a *glosa* of Jorge Manrique's *Coplas por la muerte de su padre* (Verses on the Death of His Father, 1476), the great Spanish Renaissance elegy focusing on the interaction between life and death. The same year Otero Silva traveled to Russia and Poland, where he was well received. In 1966 *Umbral* (Threshold), a book of poems on the horror of war and other sociopolitical themes, appeared.

*Cuando quiero llorar no lloro* is the product of years of frustration with the lack of social justice under bourgeois democratic rule. The title is from Rubén Darío's "Canción de otoño en primavera" (Song of Autumn in Springtime), in which the poet mourns the disappearance of youth: "Cuando quiero llorar no lloro / y a veces lloro sin querer" (When I wish to cry I cannot / and sometimes I cry without wishing to). John S. Brushwood sees the novel as "an effective use of innovative narrative techniques by an author who insists on social relevance and thereby carries the message through the structure." The book was very much a product of its time and seems rather hackneyed in its overuse of Boom literary accoutrements such as the interweaving of narrative levels. The anachronistic introduction, set in the reign of Diocletian, is overblown and at times gives a "boys will be boys" quality to the martyrs' youthful spirit of defiance. To add to the confusion, the "four crowned martyrs" referred to are completely legendary. This item is important in that all proper names are symbolic or referential.

The novel is set in context by a chronicle of the year 1948, when the three protagonists were born, Venezuela's first democratic government was overthrown, and the cold war began. The three boys in question, born on the feast day of the Crowned Martyrs, were given the same first name, Victorino ("little victor") – the other martyrs' names are antiquated – and have variations of the same surname. Pérez, from the dispossessed poor, is as common a surname as Jones, is also the name of the last dictator, and is suggestive of the "rock" pun in Pedro (piedra); Perdomo, from the working-class majority, has Dantesque connotations of the *perduto uomo* (lost man) in the Venezuelan *inferno*; and Peralta, from the oligarchy, echoes its aristocratic suffix, *alta* (high).

Idealistic youth struggle against a liberal democratic means of class domination, each according to his class experience. Pérez, as an outcast, has no class consciousness and therefore acts like a wild animal in a struggle for survival. Perdomo rejects the old Marxism of his father and attempts to apply revolutionary praxis through armed force. Peralta is a spoiled playboy who perceives his class background as an aura of invulnerability. His genealogy, nevertheless, is revealing, for though he is the son of the high-sounding Argimiro Peralta Heredia, whose name alludes to money and good breeding, he is also the grandson of Argimiro Peralta Dahomey, whose maternal last name reveals West African ancestry.

All three Victorinos meet their destiny on the same day, giving the impression that Otero Silva equates the three. R. J. Lovera de Sola, however, sees Perdomo as a victim of the establishment and believes that the author does not understand his own character. Perdomo seems to stand out as the only unselfish member of the trio. He is the only one to sacrifice himself willingly for a cause. Unlike the other protagonists, Victorino Perdomo is a member of an economically active society, yet he is a militant of the Unidad Táctica de Combate (Tactical Combat Unit), for he feels he has no stake in society. The author's apparent lack of sympathy for the character may result from generational differences; once again verisimilitude seems to get in the way of objective reality.

In 1978 Otero Silva coedited Pablo Neruda's book of personal anecdotes *Para nacer he nacido* (I Was Born to Be Born). The same year he declined an offer from the Left to serve as a unification candidate for the presidency. Instead, he went to Isla Margarita to research his next novel, *Lope de Aguirre, príncipe de la libertad* (1979). As the title suggests, the novel reaches back to the founding of the nation, yet the tyrannies and longing for freedom expressed by the schizophrenic leader echo throughout the entire history of Latin America. There is an almost-chaotic use of cinematic technique as Lope de Aguirre is seen from every possible perspective. Although the reader is treated to an in-depth analysis of the protagonist, the author also puts words in his mouth, as when he has Aguirre mouth the anachronistic discourse of Simón Bolívar on the fall of the first Republic of Venezuela. In this sense Otero Silva presents tyranny and bourgeois democracy as two sides of the same coin with a common history.

In 1983 he went to Italy to work on his last novel, *La piedra que era Cristo,* based on the life of Jesus. The novel appeared in 1984 and emphasized the role of Jesus as a loving and merciful being who sought justice for humanity. Structurally the novel reads like a screenplay in its reliance on direct mimesis. Jesus' words are appropriated in support of socialism, thereby deconstructing the traditional alliance between the church and business. The importance of Otero Silva's last two novels lies in taking back history in the name of the people by stripping it to its essentials, defeating verisimilitude and ideology by confronting them with objective reality.

In his later years Otero Silva received many awards for his literary talent. In 1967 he was named to the Venezuelan Academy of the Language, and the government honored him with the Order of Andrés Bello and the Order of Francisco Miranda. In 1980 Otero Silva won the Lenin Prize for Literature. He dedicated the prize money to build a statue of anti-imperialist Gen. Augusto Sandino in Caracas. In 1982 Otero Silva was named to the Order of Gen. Joaquín Crespo and in 1985 was named doctor honoris causa by the Universidad de Mérida. The same year, he received the Félix Varela Award from Cuba. Otero Silva died in Caracas on 27 August 1985 of a heart ailment at age seventy-six. He was survived by his wife, Mercedes Baumester de Otero, and by two children from a previous marriage.

Miguel Otero Silva's legacy to Venezuela lies not only in his own literary work but also in his generous actions as patron of progressive literature and art. He tirelessly promoted young writers in his efforts to create a genuine national culture rooted in sociopolitical realities and dedicated to change. For his labors he was universally recognized as the "grand old man of the left." His greatness stems in part from the sincerity of his partisan beliefs, which he used as a yardstick to measure the progress of his society. Taking risks he was not always correct in his observations, yet he was courageous in asking difficult questions to the end of his life. Together with Rómulo Gallegos and Eloy Blanco, Otero Silva stands as one of the great creators of modern Venezuelan literary expression.

**References:**

Orlando Araujo, *Narrativa venezolana contemporánea* (Caracas: Nuevo, 1972);

John Beverley, "Venezuela," in *Handbook of Latin American Literature,* edited by David Foster (New York: Garland, 1987), pp. 559–577;

John S. Brushwood, *The Spanish American Novel* (Austin: University of Texas Press, 1975);

Joaquín Gabaldón Márquez, *Memoria y cuento de la generación del 28* (Caracas, 1958);

William Krehm, *Democracies and Tyrannies of the Caribbean* (Westport, Conn.: Lawrence Hill, 1984);

R. J. Lovera de Sola, "*Cuando quiero llorar no lloro:* Tres vidas paralelas de jóvenes venezolanos vistas por un novelista pesimista," *Letras Nuevas,* 5 (August–September 1970): 32–33;

Angel Mancera Galleti, *Quienes narran y cuentan en Venezuela* (Caracas: Caribe, 1958);

José Ramón Medina, Introduction to *Obra poética* (Barcelona: Seix Barral, 1975), pp. 9–43;

Medina, "Vida y trayectoria literaria de Miguel Otero Silva," introduction to *Casas muertas, Lope de Vega: Príncipe de la libertad* (Caracas: Ayacucho, 1985), pp. ix–xxvii;

Domingo Miliani, *Tríptico venezolano* (Caracas: FPC, 1985);

Nelson Osorio, *La formación de la vanguardia literaria en Venezuela* (Caracas: Academia Nacional de la Historia, 1985);

Fernando Paz Castillo, *Miguel Otero Silva: Su obra literaria* (Caracas: Universidad Central de Venezuela, 1975);

Emir Rodríguez Monegal, "Tradition and Renewal," in *Latin America in Its Literature,* edited by César Fernández Moreno (New York: Holmes, 1980), pp. 87–114;

Efraín Subero, *Cercanía de Miguel Otero Silva* (Caracas: Oficina Central de Información, 1975);

Guillermo de Torre, *Tres conceptos de la literatura hispanoamericana* (Buenos Aires: Losada, 1963).

# Alfredo Pareja Diezcanseco

## (12 October 1908 – 3 May 1993)

### Michael Handelsman
*University of Tennessee at Knoxville*

BOOKS: *La casa de los locos* (Guayaquil, Ecuador: Artes Gráficas, 1929);

*La señorita Ecuador* (Guayaquil, Ecuador: Jouvin, 1930);

*Río arriba* (Guayaquil, Ecuador: Talleres Gráficos, 1931);

*El muelle* (Quito, Ecuador: Bolívar, 1933);

*La Beldaca* (Santiago, Chile: Ercilla, 1935);

*La dialéctica en el arte: El sentido de la pintura* (Portugal, 1936);

*Baldomera* (Santiago, Chile: Ercilla, 1938);

*Hechos y hazañas de don Balón de Baba y su amigo Inocente Cruz* (Buenos Aires: Club del Libro, 1939);

*Hombres sin tiempo* (Buenos Aires: Losada, 1941);

*Las tres ratas* (Buenos Aires: Losada, 1944);

*La hoguera bárbara: Vida de Eloy Alfaro* (Mexico City: Compañía General Editora, 1944);

*Breve historia del Ecuador* (Mexico City: Secretaría de Educación Pública, 1946); revised and augmented as *Historia del Ecuador,* 4 volumes (Quito, Ecuador: Casa de la Cultura Ecuatoriana, 1954); revised and enlarged edition, 2 volumes (Quito, Ecuador: Casa de la Cultura Ecuatoriana, 1958);

*Consideraciones sobre el hecho literario ecuatoriano* (Quito, Ecuador: Casa de la Cultura Ecuatoriana, 1948);

*Vida y leyenda de Miguel de Santiago* (Mexico City: Fondo de Cultura Económica, 1952);

*La advertencia* (Buenos Aires: Losada, 1956);

*La lucha por la democracia en el Ecuador* (Quito, Ecuador: Rumiñahui, 1956);

*Thomas Mann y el nuevo humanismo* (Quito, Ecuador: Casa de la Cultura Ecuatoriana, 1956);

*El aire y los recuerdos* (Buenos Aires: Losada, 1959);

*Temario para el curso de historia política de América Latina* (San Juan, P.R.: Departamento de Hacienda, Servicio de Compra y Suministro, 1963);

*Los poderes omnímodos* (Buenos Aires: Losada, 1964);

*El Ecuador de Eloy Alfaro* (Mexico City: Secretaría de Educación, 1966);

*Las pequeñas estaturas* (Madrid: Revista de Occidente, 1970);

*Historia de la República* (Quito, Ecuador: Ariel, 1974);

*La manticora* (Buenos Aires: Losada, 1974);

*Las instituciones y la administración de la Real Audiencia de Quito* (Quito, Ecuador: Universitaria, 1975);

*Ecuador, de la prehistoria a la conquista española* (Quito, Ecuador: Universitaria, 1979);

*Ecuador la República de 1830 a nuestros días* (Quito, Ecuador: Universitaria, 1979);

*Ensayos de ensayos: Una selección de los aparecidos en diversas publicaciones periódicas de varios países* (Quito, Ecuador: Casa de la Cultura Ecuatoriana, 1981);

*Notas de un viaje a China* (Quito, Ecuador: Casa de la Cultura Ecuatoriana, 1986);

*El entenao* (Guayaquil, Ecuador: Universidad de Guayaquil, 1988);

*El Populismo en el Ecuador* (Quito, Ecuador: ILDIS, 1989);

*Baldomera; Las pequeñas estaturas* (Caracas: Ayacucho, 1991).

The 1930s marked the beginning of modern Ecuadoran literature. Unlike their predecessors, who viewed literature as a pastime of cultural refinement detached from everyday reality, Ecuador's writers of the Generation of 1930, and in particular those who formed the Grupo de Guayaquil (Joaquín Gallegos Lara, José de la Cuadra, Demetrio Aguilera Malta, and Alfredo Pareja Diezcanseco), created a literature of social realism in which the world of the exploited and impoverished masses of Ecuador became the centerpiece of the most important literary works of the period. By abandoning a literary tradition of exotic places and European fashion, the new writers aspired to create a genuinely Ecuadoran literature in its language, themes, and characters. From the time of his emergence as one of the original members of the Grupo de Guayaquil, Alfredo Pareja Diez-

*Alfredo Pareja Diezcanseco*

canseco was among the most influential writers of Ecuador's modern period. For more than sixty years he distinguished himself as a productive novelist and historian. Few writers in Ecuador have demonstrated the same level of continuity and commitment to evolve as a novelist as Pareja Diezcanseco. Jorge Enrique Adoum, one of Ecuador's foremost writers of the twentieth century, has claimed that Pareja Diezcanseco is Ecuador's only professional novelist.

Despite the European roots of his ancestry, which might suggest a social position of privilege, Pareja Diezcanseco was the product of an urban middle-class background characterized by hard work and sacrifice. The youngest of twelve children, Pareja Diezcanseco was born on 12 October 1908 in Guayaquil, Ecuador, and was his family's principal provider by the time he was sixteen. Although his formal education ended at an early age due to his family responsibilities, Pareja Diezcanseco's entire life has been one of self-education and teaching. Moreover, the broad range of jobs that he held throughout his lifetime deepened his understanding of Ecuador's pluralistic society. Businessman, bookseller, pharmaceutical salesman,

journalist, accountant, teacher, diplomat, and banker are just some of the jobs he held. At every step of the way, however, Pareja Diezcanseco's life was marked by a struggle to maintain a balance between the need to provide for his family and his deep desire to study and write. "En verdad he ejercido ... todos los oficios honestos que ... se puede imaginar. Pero mi insatisfacción tremenda ha sido la de no tener tiempo para escribir" (In truth I have worked at all the honest jobs imaginable. But my greatest dissatisfaction is not having had time to write). In 1934 Pareja Diezcanseco married Mercedes Cucalón Concha, with whom he had three children: Cecilia, Jorge, and Francisco.

Pareja Diezcanseco's accomplishments include his appointments as chief officer of the United Nations Relief and Rehabilitation Administration for Mexico, Central America, Argentina, Uruguay, and Paraguay (1945–1948) and as Ecuadoran ambassador to France (1983–1984). He received Ecuador's highest award for literature and cultural achievements, the Premio Nacional de Cultura Eugenio Espejo, for 1979–1980.

Faithful to his urban middle-class upbringing, Pareja Diezcanseco devoted almost all of his fiction to depicting life in the two principal cities of Ecuador, Guayaquil and Quito. Consistent with the social realism prevalent in much of Ecuadoran modern literature, Pareja Diezcanseco utilized his literary works to uncover the corruption and degradation that continue to beset Ecuadoran society. Although his works are anchored in an identifiable social context, he was careful to avoid writing propagandistic and tendentious literature: "la política tiene tareas inmediatas y la inmediatez perjudica la visión artística y la de la sociedad humana en general" (Politics has immediate tasks, and immediacy harms the artistic vision and that of human society in general). While disavowing any connection with communism or party politics, Pareja Diezcanseco insisted that he was an open-minded individual of the Left who believed strongly that the world would one day be Socialist.

In addition to Pareja Diezcanseco's commitment to uncover the many social ills of Ecuador while writing works of artistic merit, all of his fiction is deeply grounded in contemporary Ecuadoran history. Major events and people of twentieth-century Ecuador fill Pareja Diezcanseco's novels, which thus constitute an important source for understanding the country. It has often been said that the most authentic written record of Latin-American history can be found in its novels. Pareja Diezcanseco's works corroborate this notion.

Pareja Diezcanseco's development as a novelist can be traced through four stages: an early period of gestation (1929–1931); a period of literary maturity in which he succeeded in establishing himself as one of the principal novelists of Ecuador (1933–1944); the period in which he wrote the first three novels of his ambitious literary project titled *Los nuevos años* (The New Years), in which he attempts to re-create much of twentieth-century Ecuadoran history and its social milieu (1956–1964); and a period of experimentation in which he completed the final two novels of *Los nuevos años* (1970–1974).

Most critics agree that Pareja Diezcanseco's earliest novels are of little literary value. However, *La casa de los locos* (The Insane Asylum, 1929), *La señorita Ecuador* (Miss Ecuador, 1930), and *Río arriba* (Up the River, 1931) are important in preparing the way for his later novels. Some of the major concerns that characterize Pareja Diezcanseco's work as a novelist are already evident in these "esfuerzos primitivos" (primitive attempts), according to Karl H. Heise. *La casa de los locos* is a political novel in which Pareja Diezcanseco's protests and critical perspective of the times incurred the wrath

of many readers unaccustomed to such frankness and daring. In *La señorita Ecuador* he revealed himself as a champion of the middle and working classes whose progress traditionally had been stifled by Ecuadoran oligarchy. The novel is based on an actual beauty contest in which a young woman of modest socio-economic means defeated the contestant favored by the local aristocracy. Pareja Diezcanseco saw in this event a kind of symbolic struggle of what was happening in Ecuadoran society at large. With *Río arriba* he offered a psychological novel heavily influenced by Freudian theories of abnormality and characterized by lengthy philosophical discourses. Despite its excesses, however, the novel constitutes a step forward in his use of narrative technique.

Pareja Diezcanseco's first novel to receive critical acclaim in Ecuador and abroad was *El muelle* (The Wharf, 1933). Several writers from the Grupo de Guayaquil and Ecuador's sierra region who formed the nucleus of the Generation of 1930 had already launched their literary project of social realism, captivating readers throughout Latin America and setting the stage for Pareja Diezcanseco to add an urban dimension to a body of literature that until then had focused primarily on rural Ecuador. The general appeal of *El muelle* was also due to his globalization of Ecuadoran social problems, linking them to the Great Depression.

The novel takes place in New York City and Guayaquil and in part is based on the experiences Pareja Diezcanseco had while living in New York in 1930. As Ecuador sees its cacao boom come to an end, Juan Hidrovo leaves for New York in search of work and economic opportunity. While in New York, however, his dreams of progress are destroyed by poverty, racism, and a longing for his roots. He returns to Guayaquil, and his dreams for a better life again are smashed by an inherently unjust and exploitative socio-economic system. As Pareja Diezcanseco champions the causes of the urban poor, he makes it clear that his characters have the will and talent to be productive citizens. Unfortunately, those in control of society never give the poor a legitimate chance to grow and prosper.

Despite its favorable critical reception and its historical importance in the development of the urban novel in Ecuador, *El muelle* is still a long way from offering readers complex and provocative characters. Its structure is basically dualistic – good versus evil – and although Pareja Diezcanseco avoids overt preaching, his intentions to use the novel to right social wrongs tend to be simplistic.

*Pareja Diezcanseco in 1958*

Many of the same concerns and approaches to dealing with Ecuadoran society evident in *El muelle* are also present in *La Beldaca,* a novel published in 1935 while Pareja Diezcanseco was living in political exile in Chile. The dualistic structure of good against evil continues to be the framework in which he denounces the exploitation suffered by the poor, humble masses of the Ecuadoran coast. The victims of the novel are from the Santa Elena Peninsula located about one hundred miles northwest of Guayaquil. Jesús Parrales, the protagonist, is a hardworking fisherman who sacrifices everything to own his own fishing boat, *La Beldaca*. Eventually Parrales loses the boat along with the business he had developed to a corrupt entrepreneur who had originally loaned him the money to buy *La Beldaca* at high interest rates and with legal obligations that guaranteed financial disaster.

*La Beldaca* is full of descriptions of the customs and traditions of the Ecuadoran coastal *cholo* (mixed blood). In his zeal to denounce injustice, however, Pareja Diezcanseco creates characters who are too naive in the ways of the world. Ecuadoran literary critic Edmundo Ribadeneira has not only complained about Pareja Diezcanseco's tendency to be superficial when dealing with Ecuadoran social ills but also has argued that his early characters are too passive and not truly representative of the Ecuadoran masses.

Nonetheless, an aspect that begins to take on vital importance in *La Beldaca* and that became Pareja Diezcanseco's trademark in his later works is the integration of fiction and twentieth-century Ecuadoran history. Jesús Parrales's tragedy unfolds during the turbulent years surrounding the rise and fall of Ecuadoran liberalism (1885–1935). The contrast between the noble ideals of the Liberal Revolution of 1895 and the stark living conditions of the coastal peoples of the Santa Elena Peninsula heightens the sense of failure and desperation that Pareja Diezcanseco describes.

The first organized-labor strike in Guayaquil and the massacre of more than one thousand protesters on 15 November 1922 make up the historical frame in the novel *Baldomera* (1938). According to Pareja Diezcanseco, his female protagonist was based on a real person from the slums of Guayaquil, and unlike his previous passive characters Baldomera captures the reader's imagination because of her indomitable spirit and her penchant for attacking anyone and everyone who might threaten her freedom and sense of dignity.

As Pareja Diezcanseco leads Baldomera and the other characters through the streets of Guayaquil, the city becomes more than a simple setting or background and takes on a life of its own. The direct references to well-known places in Guayaquil and the exactness with which Pareja Diezcanseco describes them help blur many distinctions traditionally made between fiction and reality. The result is that he challenges his readers' complacency and forces them to confront many of the social complexities and contradictions of Guayaquil.

Although Pareja Diezcanseco focuses on the so-called urban underworld of prostitutes, thieves, prisoners, and broken families, *Baldomera* does not present only the bad and ugly aspects of city life. The struggle to survive and the search for a better life permeate the entire novel, and unlike the Manichaean structure of his earlier novels, *Baldomera* is enriched by his ability to avoid stereotypes and easy solutions to complex social problems.

The most important aspect of *Baldomera,* however, is Pareja Diezcanseco's portrayal of Baldomera herself. The characterization of the female protagonist is a daring departure from traditional women characters in Ecuadoran literature. Neither virgin nor femme fatale, Baldomera is a woman who fights for her right to be actively responsible for her own actions, regardless of the consequences. Although married and the mother of several children, Baldomera does not hide in the shadows of a husband or a lover. She is strong willed and independently courageous yet not devoid of weaknesses and human vices. Baldomera is a composite of many of the urban working women found throughout Ecuador and the rest of the world; she is also one of the most memorable characters in Ecuadoran literature.

*Hechos y hazañas de don Balón de Baba y su amigo Inocente Cruz* (Facts and Deeds from don Balón de Baba and His Friend Inocente Cruz, 1939) was a commercial success, selling all ten thousand copies of the original printing. In this novel Pareja Diezcanseco temporarily abandons his serious tone and creates a humorous text reminiscent of Miguel de Cervantes's *Don Quixote* (1605–1615). While don Balón ridicules Ecuadoran society and its shortcomings, he is accompanied by his country-bumpkin friend Don Inocente. Despite its humor and com-

mercial success, however, *Hechos y hazañas de don Balón de Baba y su amigo Inocente Cruz* has not been well received by literary critics. The obvious models of Don Quixote and Sancho Panza seem to have led most critics to conclude that Pareja Diezcanseco's novel lacks originality and vitality.

In 1938, during a period of political unrest in Ecuador, Pareja Diezcanseco was imprisoned for the political positions he adopted while serving briefly as a member of congress. The experience in prison provided him with the necessary inspiration to write *Hombres sin tiempo* (Men without Time, 1941). The protagonist, Nicolás Ramírez, who narrates the novel, is convicted of attempted rape and murder and sentenced to sixteen years in the infamous García Moreno Penitentiary. Pareja Diezcanseco's experiments with several literary techniques, such as interior monologue and flashbacks, make *Hombres sin tiempo* unlike his previous works of fiction. Rather than focusing on broad social problems with a large gallery of characters, he explores the mind of a lonely man who appears to find some degree of worth and meaning in prison. In this novel Pareja Diezcanseco gives readers a realistic view of prison conditions, dealing frankly and openly with such themes as homosexuality, arbitrary punishment, human isolation, and the need for meaningful prison reform.

*Las tres ratas* (The Three Rats, 1944) marks both a return to the urban-kaleidoscopic novel form that Pareja Diezcanseco had been cultivating since the 1930s and the end of this second period of development as a novelist. Once again Guayaquil is the stage from which Pareja Diezcanseco denounces Ecuadoran social ills. But instead of addressing the needs and problems of the working class, in *Las tres ratas* he examines the decline of a middle-class family with strong ties to the Liberal Revolution of 1895.

The novel follows the tribulations of three unmarried sisters who lose their property in the country and are forced to immigrate to Guayaquil. The narrative is characterized by multiple conflicts and struggles that move the reader from the internal world of each character to the world at large. Throughout the work the principal characters struggle with their own personal demons and against one another. Moreover, both individually and collectively they fight a social system that has little interest in three single women who must provide for themselves.

Literary critics often have noted the important presence of women characters in Pareja Diezcanseco's novels. Angel F. Rojas observes that no other

ALFREDO
PAREJA
DIEZCANSECO
LAS
PEQUEÑAS
ESTATURAS

CIMAS DE AMERICA 🦉 REVISTA DE OCCIDENTE

*Cover for Pareja Diezcanseco's 1970 novel, which was
influenced by the Latin-American Boom*

novel. During this interlude he actively cultivated other interests and wrote history, biography, and essays. Important works of this period are Pareja Diezcanseco's biographies of Eloy Alfaro, the father of Ecuador's Liberal Revolution of 1895 (*La hoguera bárbara: Vida de Eloy Alfaro* [The Barbarous Bonfire: A Life of Eloy Alfaro, 1944]) and the seventeenth-century Quito painter Miguel de Santiago (*Vida y leyenda de Miguel de Santiago* [The Life and Legend of Miguel de Santiago, 1952]). Also of special importance, at least with regard to Pareja Diezcanseco's next series of novels, is his *Breve historia del Ecuador* (Brief History of Ecuador, 1946), later revised and augmented as *Historia del Ecuador* (History of Ecuador, 1954).

Pareja Diezcanseco made it clear that his way of writing history is very much an interpretation. In many ways his work confirms the close relationship that exists between writing history and narrative fiction. According to Pareja Diezcanseco in *El duro oficio* (The Hard Task), edited by Francisco Febres Cordero, "No soy un historiador imparcial. Creo que hasta en la investigación histórica hay una carga subjetiva, quizá subconsciente hasta en el hecho de seleccionar los documentos" (I am not an impartial historian. I believe that even in historical research there is subjectivity, perhaps unconscious, even in the selection of documents).

The presence of historical events in Pareja Diezcanseco's earlier novels has been noted. But it was only after his extensive work as a historian that he created a narrative project in which he truly integrated his interests in history and fiction. Rather than serving merely as background or setting, twentieth-century Ecuadoran history became the core of his series of novels published between 1956 and 1974.

Mainly because of radical differences in style and narrative technique, this period appears to be the result of two distinct phases in Pareja Diezcanseco's development as a novelist. The first three novels – *La advertencia* (The Warning, 1956), *El aire y los recuerdos* (The Air and Memories, 1959), and *Los poderes omnímodos* (All-Embracing Powers, 1964) – are consistent with his earlier fiction, which is characterized by its uncomplicated, straightforward narrative structure. However, in the 1970s his work turns inward and becomes notably more obscure and oblique.

Pareja referred to these novels, the first in the series *Los nuevos años,* as a kind of roman-fleuve in which readers follow the lives of a group of characters in more than one work. Since Pareja seeks to recreate the spirit of the age he writes about and

Ecuadoran writer has created as many female characters as Pareja Diezcanseco. Moreover, his characterization of Eugenia, the second oldest of the three sisters in *Las tres ratas,* is an important attempt to depict women and their lifestyles with complexity and depth. Unlike the mythical qualities of Baldomera, the reader's fascination with Eugenia is based on her not being a larger-than-life figure. Because of this absence of hyperbole and exaggeration, Eugenia is probably his most convincing female character.

Although *Las tres ratas* won second prize among Ecuadoran entries to the 1941 Farrar Rinehart international novel contest and despite its having been the basis for an Argentine film in 1946 also titled *Las tres ratas,* Pareja Diezcanseco has expressed deep dissatisfaction with the work because of the haste with which he wrote it.

After completing *Las tres ratas,* it was almost ten years before Pareja Diezcanseco returned to the since he pays great attention to historical accuracy, *Los nuevos años* can properly be regarded as a historical novel as well. . . ." Regardless of how one classifies this narrative project, each novel records historical events that Pareja Diezcanseco himself experienced, and thus the testimonial nature of the novels – particularly in the first three novels – is especially prevalent.

In *La advertencia,* the first novel of the series, Pareja Diezcanseco focuses his attention on the Revolución Juliana, the military coup of 1925 that sought to correct the abuses of a government that had abandoned the liberal principles of Eloy Alfaro and the Liberal Revolution of 1895. The Revolución Juliana was carried out by a group of young officers whose socialistic ideas promised to move Ecuador into a new era of modernity. Many factors contributed to the failure of the coup, and in *La advertencia* Pareja Diezcanseco dissects the period with all of its confusion and contradictions. By means of multiple characters and continuous dialogue among them he vividly re-creates the lack of ideological consensus during the period. Despite the disappointments and failures associated with the Revolución Juliana, Pareja Diezcanseco leaves his readers with a sense of optimism while insisting that 1925 marks a new beginning in Ecuadoran history:

> Una nueva etapa ha comenzado. . . . Así . . . a partir de 1920, y avanzada ya la conquista ideológica liberal, su acción, muchas veces a su pesar, por los hombres más que por las ideas, deja libre paso a las ideas socialistas, de las que la revolución juliana es una expresión imperfecta, débil y sin fundamentos prácticos o científicos, pero de todos modos clarificadora. Estos son los nuevos años.

> (A new age has begun. . . . And so . . . beginning in 1920, and with the ideological victory of liberalism well under way, many times despite itself, because of people rather than ideas, it opens the way to socialist ideas, of which the July Revolution is an imperfect expression, weak and without practical or scientific bases, but nevertheless illuminating. These are the new years.)

In 1959 Pareja Diezcanseco followed *La advertencia* with *El aire y los recuerdos,* a novel anchored in the civil strife of 1932 that ended in four days of violent street fighting between conservatives and liberals. Once again the author blends history and fiction. As many well-known historical figures of the period debate their highly documented ideas with purely fictional characters, Pareja Diezcanseco inspires his readers to expand upon the eyewitness accounts of the novel and interpretations of the events of the period. Readers familiar with the his-

torical references are expected to be critical and judgmental. Indeed, Pareja Diezcanseco's extensive use of this kind of open dialogue in the novel appears to be an early attempt in Ecuadoran literature to break down the traditional barriers that have separated the reader from the text and have insisted on the reader's passivity. Curiously, one of the characters of the novel argues that Ecuadoran literature needs to be polyphonic if it is to capture reality in its totality. In anticipation of later theories that deal with reader response and reception, in *El aire y los recuerdos* Pareja Diezcanseco opens the way for the reader's voice to be an integral part of that polyphonic experience.

*Los poderes omnímodos* takes up where the previous novel ends, covering the period between 1933 and 1944. During that time Ecuador continued to suffer from political chaos and instability and saw the rise of one of its most controversial politicians of the twentieth century, Dr. José María Velasco Ibarra. Much of *Los poderes omnímodos* revolves around Velasco Ibarra's populist politics and the ensuing manipulation of the hopes and dreams of the masses. With basically the same cast of characters encountered in the previous two novels, Pareja Diezcanseco delves even deeper into the growing sense of frustration of those who find it increasingly difficult to hold on to their belief that Ecuador is on its way to better times. The moral and spiritual decay so obvious in this novel, and in Ecuadoran politics of this period, move Pareja Diezcanseco and his narrative fiction to a final stage of development marked by a language of irony, parody, and satire.

It is difficult to read *Las pequeñas estaturas* (Small Statures, 1970) and *La manticora* (The Manticora Monster, 1974) without giving some thought to the possible influences of several successful Latin-American Boom writers of the 1960s on Pareja Diezcanseco. While the narrative technique and structure employed in these last two novels represent a drastic departure from the rest of his fiction, they do not necessarily contribute to a higher quality of writing. Much of *Las pequeñas estaturas* and *La manticora* seems artificial and lacks spontaneity. Nonetheless, Pareja Diezcanseco was seeking more appropriate ways to express his evolving view of Ecuador. By the time he published *Las pequeñas estaturas* he seemed to have exhausted his descriptive approach to telling the story of his generation. After some fifty years of broken promises and crushed dreams, he assumed a position of skepticism about past, present, and future leaders.

*Las pequeñas estaturas* is a product of the revolutionary, iconoclastic 1960s, and especially of the brief period of military rule in Ecuador that began in 1963. Pareja Diezcanseco re-creates an atmosphere of fear, persecution, violence, and irrationality through distortion and ambiguity. At each step of the way he ridicules and mocks his characters' inability to understand their most urgent social problems and condemns their failure to create imaginative and effective solutions.

Unlike his previous novels, which were dependent upon particular circumstances in Ecuador, *Las pequeñas estaturas* offers a more Latin-American focus. During the 1960s progressive groups from throughout the continent were in close contact and were committed to creating a unified Latin-American front against common enemies and threats; Pareja Diezcanseco's attempt to transcend national boundaries in this novel is consistent with the times.

*La manticora* is Pareja Diezcanseco's final novel and undoubtedly his most ambitious. Shortly after completing it he suffered a serious heart attack, which in no small measure was due to the strain of finishing the work. According to him, *La manticora* is an expression of the horrible dream shared by many countries that speaks of a mythical monster that preys upon human flesh. Naturally, in its symbolic sense the manticore represents any threat to Latin-American freedom and development.

In this novel Pareja Diezcanseco uses metafiction, intertextuality, and a dialogical structure akin to drama. Throughout the novel Pablo Canelos, the principal character of *Los nuevos años,* and the narrator – supposedly Pareja Diezcanseco – discuss and debate the relationship between author and text. Just as Don Quixote sought his autonomy from Cervantes, so Pablo Canelos challenges Pareja Diezcanseco's authority. In fact, Pablo thinks he is writing *La manticora* as he tries to spring free from his creator, Pareja Diezcanseco. The entire conflict between author and character encountered in *La manticora* symbolizes the creative process and the extent to which each author struggles with and agonizes over his text.

*La manticora* is a novel of intense anguish in which many characters discuss their opinions about everything from philosophy and religion to social justice and peace. Because everything appears to be relative and highly subjective, Pareja Diezcanseco's characters are lost in a postmodern world devoid of any concrete sense of truth and stability.

Yet *La manticora* ends on an optimistic note. True to his beginnings as a novelist of the 1930s, when social realism was founded on the quest for change and the belief that such change was possible, Pareja Diezcanseco seems to come full circle as he rediscovers society's forgotten and exploited masses and their potential to create a world of justice. His message is clear as he concludes that there are no manticores or mythical monsters to fear – or to use as an excuse for inaction. At some point since the 1925 Revolución Juliana that Pareja Diezcanseco treated in the first novel of *Los nuevos años,* the ideals of a more just society were lost in a quagmire of ineffective, unimaginative leadership that actually abandoned the very people whose causes it claimed to champion. Pareja Diezcanseco closed out his career as a novelist by trying to rekindle that lost spirit of democratic change.

Alfredo Pareja Diezcanseco was the last survivor of the original group of Ecuadoran writers identified as the Generation of 1930. After the publication of his last novel in 1974, he continued to be an active scholar and contributor to Ecuadoran arts and politics. While his ideas and interpretations have stimulated critical debate, there is little doubt that the quantity and breadth of his work constitute a standard against which future generations of Ecuadoran writers will be judged.

**References:**

Jorge Enrique Adoum and Pedro Jorge Vera, eds., *Narradores ecuatorianos del 30* (Caracas: Biblioteca Ayacucho, 1980);

Francisco Febres Cordero, ed., *El duro oficio* (Quito, Ecuador: Municipio de Quito, 1989);

Karl H. Heise, *La evolución novelística de Alfredo Pareja Diezcanseco* (New York: La Librería, 1973);

Alberto Rengifo, *La narrativa de Alfredo Pareja Diezcanseco* (Quito, Ecuador: Banco Central del Ecuador, 1990);

Edmundo Ribadeneira, *La moderna novela ecuatoriana,* second edition (Quito, Ecuador: Editorial Universitaria, 1981);

Angel F. Rojas, *La novela ecuatoriana* (Mexico City: Fondo de Cultura Económica, 1948);

Barbara Schlüter, *Literatura y praxis social en el Ecuador: La novela La advertencia de Alfredo Pareja Diezcanseco* (Guayaquil, Ecuador: Universidad de Guayaquil, 1987).

# Cristina Peri Rossi

*(12 November 1941 –  )*

Hugo J. Verani
*University of California, Davis*

Translated by Fred de Ráfols

BOOKS: *Viviendo* (Montevideo: Alfa, 1963);
*El libro de mis primos* (Montevideo: Marcha, 1969);
*Los museos abandonados* (Montevideo: Arca, 1969);
*Indicios pánicos* (Montevideo: Nuestra América, 1970);
*Evohé: Poemas eróticos* (Montevideo: Girón, 1971);
*Descripción de un naufragio* (Barcelona: Lumen, 1975);
*Diáspora* (Barcelona: Lumen, 1976);
*La tarde del dinosaurio* (Barcelona: Planeta, 1976);
*Lingüística general* (Valencia: Prometeo, 1979);
*La rebelión de los niños* (Caracas: Monte Avila, 1980);
*El museo de los esfuerzos inútiles* (Barcelona: Seix Barral, 1983);
*La nave de los locos* (Barcelona: Seix Barral, 1984); translated by Psiche Hughes as *The Ship of Fools* (London: Readers International, 1989);
*Una pasión prohibida* (Barcelona: Seix Barral, 1986); translated by Mary Jane Treacy as *A Forbidden Passion* (Pittsburgh: Cleis, 1993);
*Europa después de la lluvia* (Madrid: Fundación Banco Exterior, 1987);
*Solitario de amor* (Barcelona: Grijalbo, 1988);
*Cosmoagonías* (Barcelona: Laia, 1988);
*Fantasías eróticas* (Madrid: Temas de Hoy, 1991);
*Babel bárbara* (Barcelona: Lumen, 1991); translated by Diana P. Decker in *Quarterly Review of Literature,* 31 (1992): 2–52;
*La última noche de Dostoievski* (Madrid: Grijalbo/Mondadori, 1992).

Cristina Peri Rossi is an established writer. She has amassed a substantial body of work that amounts to twelve books of fiction, six of poetry, and one of essays. Yet generic classifications of her work on the basis of standard terminology prove to be unsatisfactory if not futile. The disappearance of generic boundaries is due mainly to a confluence of languages and to a unified artistic perception that does not heed the call of discursive thought, responding instead to a poetic attitude, a lyrical vision. Her tales break down the logical interrelation of their parts and renounce all novelistic development and anecdotal mimesis in favor of the presentation of states of consciousness as images. The lyrical attitude, playful exploration of reality, metaphorical profusion, and digressive and cumulative forms are all signs of a poetic reality, a total experience intolerant of boundaries.

Born on 12 November 1941 in Montevideo, Peri Rossi has lived in Barcelona since 1972. To avoid the political repression that resulted in a massive exodus of intellectuals, she fled her native Uruguay shortly before the military coup d'état. Before her exile she was a professor of literature and already an established writer with five books to her name. In Spain she has worked primarily as a journalist and translator. She was recently professor of Latin-American literature at the Universidad Autónoma de Barcelona and has directed the literary series of a publishing house in that city.

Peri Rossi's preexile fiction reveals a deep dialectic connection with a Uruguayan society shaken by violence, tending to transfigure concrete historical facts, the "panic signs" of individual and institutional insecurity, into allegorical tales charged with dazzling imaginative freedom. Before 1972 each of her books of fiction – *Viviendo* (Living, 1963), *Los museos abandonados* (The Abandoned Museums, 1969), *El libro de mis primos* (My Cousins' Book, 1969), and *Indicios pánicos* (Panic Signs, 1970) – reiterates the vision of a disintegrating world. Still, the dominant features of her work – playfulness, eroticism, the world of children, satire, the theme of liberation – are freely woven into stories that elicit fundamental questions about the nature of contemporary narrative. Certain aspects may stand out in one book or in another – the allegorical transfiguration of reality in *Los museos abandonados,* the world of children in *La rebelión de los niños* (The Children's Rebellion, 1980) – but all her stories maintain a het-

*Cristina Peri Rossi, circa 1988 (photograph by Guillermina Puig)*

erogeneous sense of invention as they alternate spontaneously between diverse motifs, never letting any one feature dominate – a creative propensity that rules out the possibility of reducing Peri Rossi's work to mere isolated components cut off from its diverse and complex context. Peri Rossi's tales tend to disperse and fragment. The story is held in check by a metaphorical exploration of the senses, resorting to a lyrical expansion of overlapping events without causality. Peri Rossi delivers an unharmonious and unfinished universe in which digression is the essence of her narrative art.

An irreverent disposition motivates her preexile fiction; allegory or satire prevails in the presentation of alienated lifestyles. By overcoming the objective relationship between language and its referent Peri Rossi takes the reader beyond the expected and establishes a critical distance that stimulates thought and comprehension of the desolate reality she recreates.

For instance, the stories in *Los museos abandonados* distinguish themselves by the demythification of what is ordained, by the allegorical transfiguration of a sterile order that produces only alienation and estrangement in people. Three of the four stories are presented as an inseparable totality in which a couple witnesses the destruction of the world, of a civilization, of a civil order, and of a special way of conceiving love, art, and society. The process of producing meaning is similar in all three, based on the incessantly renewed games to which an idle couple of survivors from the past cling, a couple that turn in upon themselves and shun social commitment. In "Los juegos" (The Games), the high point of the book, the growing frenzy of the erotic games invented by the couple snuffs out the boredom of endless nights in the dark and dusty halls of an enormous abandoned museum. The couple shelter their desolation by pursuing physical pleasure, indifferent to the ruins they leave behind and unconcerned about the destruction caused by their fury of love. The erotic relationship evolves into a lewd ceremony in which neither compromise nor true communication is possible, an aesthetic ritual with little sense beyond the value of its own lavishness. Reality bursts in a blossoming of images until it disintegrates into a game of false appearances, a vertiginous hall of mirrors. In the world of old myths and discarded cultural traditions of another tale, "Un cuento para Eurídice" (A Story for Eurydice), the couple take refuge by inventing stories that would recover the vanishing outlines of the past. In "Los refugios" (The Refuges), the last story of the book, the couple latch onto the memory of a corrupt world, unable to participate in the establishment of a new order. The stories of *Los museos abandonados* denaturalize the very elements of reality that nourish them. The narrative makes its presence felt without direct references to the sociohistorical context of Uruguay – a kind of narrative by omission but also a narrative that reveals an acute critical conscience. A sense of allegory permeates the exploration of abandoned museums: the sterility of human coexistence in a decadent world is thus corroborated.

*El libro de mis primos* brings together the salient features of Peri Rossi's fiction. Bereft of plot and unparaphrasable, it moves freely from prose to verse. The story is disseminated as a proliferation of sequences, valid in themselves but which relegate any possible novelistic coherence to the background. The logic of the sequences is neither causal nor psychological; there is no concatenation of events or thematic units. New motifs appear, and the story of a family's life develops in multiple directions without adhering to any plot that would steer it toward a resolution of the tensions it generates, thus ushering in the apprehension of the instantaneous, of the fragment that refuses to condition its parts. Such discontinuity is characteristic of Peri Rossi's fiction.

*El libro de mis primos* captures the progressive disintegration of a patriarchal family conditioned by the conventions of a corrupt order and fettered by the alienating power of the past. The women are condemned to routine tasks such as housecleaning and are revered solely for their fertility; the men remain aloof from social obligations, immobilized by atrophied remembrances that close them off from the outside world. The result is total paralysis and affective debilitation, as Mario Benedetti has said. This static world, condemned to fail to understand the vertiginous changes of society, finds its counterweight in the dynamism of children, the cousins mentioned in the title of the novel. Initiative, action, and the future belong to the generation of Oliverio, the child narrator whose insight uncovers the breakdown of an aging social state.

The story converges into two endings that respond to the need of arriving at a total demythification of the past and at a new ethic. In one ending the game of soldiers and guerrillas metaphorically illuminates the sense of the represented world; the game ends when a stone from Oliverio's slingshot destroys the patriarchal house before the cousins' din. The novel comes to a close awaiting the coming

of a new social order. The last chapters gather the shreds of the life of the elder cousin, Federico, who abandons the familiar cloister and freely chooses a possibility of change: he enlists with the urban guerrillas with the uncertain task of building a more humane society.

The effort to recover the outlook of children is a way of indicting the world of adults. In his prologue to Peri Rossi's *La tarde del dinosaurio* (The Afternoon of the Dinosaur, 1976), Julio Cortázar states that in her stories children are witnesses, victims, and judges of those who sacrifice them in creating, educating, loving, and dressing them. In *El libro de mis primos* as well as in *La tarde del dinosaurio* and *La rebelión de los niños* the intentional reduction of the world as seen through the innocent yet lucid and satiric eyes of a child reveals the nostalgia of a free existence, of a lost elemental order. In these two collections of stories the world of children persistently reappears. As in surrealism, Peri Rossi's proclivity to build stories around children responds to the need for replacing the control of logic with a space free from the exigencies of social life. Indifferent to verisimilitude and to social conventions, a child's arbitrary combinations, innocent distortion of events, and extraordinary resourcefulness are all telling means of showing amazement at the vulnerability and paradoxes of life. Children have the power to dispose of language with complete freedom and to project themselves toward the realm of the possible, affirming finally that playful will that runs throughout her literary work.

In *El libro de mis primos* Peri Rossi resorts to satire as an efficient means to ridicule social hierarchies and subvert the implicit notion of normalcy. The daily activities of a family are distorted by means of hyperbolic inventiveness reminiscent of Gabriel García Marquez's *Cien años de soledad* (1967; translated as *One Hundred Years of Solitude,* 1970). The purpose is to desacrilize prestigious standards and to demythify images valued by bourgeois tradition and accepted by society without question. The satiric impulse reduces routine acts of human coexistence to absurd and grotesque situations, to patterns of life degraded by mechanical repetition, in order to attract attention to the conventions that a fossilized social order imposes and that custom either hides or denies. Human confinement to an opulent mansion and submission to routines typical of a patriarchal regime unable to renew itself unleash the satiric catharsis.

The inordinate distortion of life in the patriarchal mansion takes several directions: the typical aspects of capitalist ideology (accumulation of wealth)

## CRISTINA PERI ROSSI

### El museo de los esfuerzos inútiles

**SEIX BARRAL**

*Cover for Peri Rossi's 1983 book, a collection of stories*

and of traditional institutions (marriage, maternity) as well as the condition of the individual in bourgeois society receive the brunt of the author's corrosive irony. Women, devitalized survivors of an inhibiting order, move like clucking hens or mechanical marionettes. The servility of women, always immersed in domestic chores, opens the novel to hyperbolic forms of expression; the irony of the situation emanates from the exaggeration of Oliverio's mother's and aunts' actions.

The pleasure and necessity of writing and the search for a malleable and sensible expression are also characteristic traits of Peri Rossi's work. Her idiomatic sensibility is evident in her baroque style, in her delight with language, and in her pleasure in detaining the narrative impulse. The syntactic convolutions, the free and imaginative unfolding of the language, and the proliferation of enumerative series all give her writing a self-referring, enveloping rhythm that places the reader at its center. Thus a

constant in her work – if less developed in her postexile works – is the hedonistic game of indulging in the pleasure of language itself.

The desire to break with all that limits human freedom and to strip away conventionalities and hypocrisies is common to both language and eroticism; as the well-known French critic Roland Barthes has affirmed, eroticism and language are similar pleasures. To Peri Rossi language is not just a vehicle of thought or an instrument of communication; it is erotic material to be metamorphosed into an object of pleasure that shares in the same space as human beings. Faced with a new word, Oliverio says in *El libro de mis primos* that she enjoyed playing with new words.

The exaltation of love in her work is an attempt at making instinctual powers acceptable and uncovering sensual desires. The positive is always associated with natural values free from all prejudice, whether or not they transgress society's mores. Lesbianism, an obsessive theme in *Evohé* (1971) and a recurring one in *Diáspora* (1976); the incestuous implications of the brothers in love with their own image in "De hermano a hermana" (From Brother to Sister) in *La tarde del dinosaurio;* Federico's incestuous relations with Alejandra and Aurelia, blind to guilt or taboo, in *El libro de mis primos* – all exemplify Peri Rossi's love of converting writing into an enterprise of complete liberation. The attraction of incest is another expression of nostalgia, a natural impulse denied by the Christian notion of sin, as if a love uncontaminated by foreign elements was sought, a love that would revert to an original order and identify with extensions of the self. Eroticism establishes a gratifying bond of a playful nature that involves the totality of being, a means of recapturing the natural state. In Peri Rossi's fiction eroticism and satire are instruments of the demythification of the established and prescribed that transmute desires and needs into a celebration of the creative act and the pleasure of the text.

Exile constitutes a determining factor in the change of her literary work. Beginning with *Descripción de un naufragio* (Description of a Shipwreck, 1975), the themes of exile, uprooting, diaspora, reflections on an unforeseen voyage, and life as "a useless passion" – Jean-Paul Sartre's phrase and a recurring theme in *Una pasión prohibida* (1986; translated as *A Forbidden Passion,* 1993) – are deeply imprinted in her recent literary work. These themes gradually begin to be built around a European cultural tradition. In *La nave de los locos* (1984; translated as *The Ship of Fools,* 1989), Peri Rossi uses a medieval topic associated with the involuntary voyage and with exile and condenses a sentiment felt throughout history: the misfortunes of someone banished from any form of hope or bond with society. The image of estrangement and of the one-way crossing is tied to "El viaje inconcluso" (The Unfinished Voyage), a story in *El museo de los esfuerzos inútiles* (The Museum of Useless Efforts, 1983), and to a poem in *Europa después de la lluvia* (Europe after the Rain, 1987), titled "La nave de los locos," which establishes an intertextual dialogue with a chapter in her novel of the same title.

*La nave de los locos* is a lucid reflection on uprooting and displacement: in a troubled era, modern society subsists only fragmented and deprived of finality. Around the image of the voyage the novel presents successive stories of outcasts bereft of belongings and companions, symbolic figures in perpetual flight conscious of traveling without a fixed destination and alienated from society. The twenty-one chapters entitled "El viaje" (The Voyage) alternate in counterpoint with the description of *El tapiz de la creación* (The Tapestry of Creation), a tapestry woven in the late eleventh century and preserved at the cathedral of Gerona which is worn and mutilated but so geometric that it is possible to reconstruct the missing half in the easel of the mind. Medieval theology built a world with one sole ideology. The tapestry is a metaphor for a redeeming, unmodifiable object that reproduces a harmonic order counterposed to the chaos of the contemporary world, the world of "the ship of fools." In the manner of an inconclusive and fragmented tapestry that reflects reality, Peri Rossi's novel sets forth a reflexive mode of representation that duplicates the experience of disorder.

The protagonist Equis — literally the letter X, as in exile, exclusion, expatriation, expellee, expulsion — sets out on an inconclusive tour of various cities. Within the geographic voyage is a historical one, which gives the reader a multidimensional reflection on the precarious position of the exile. Condemned to temporariness and wandering, Equis accepts precariousness as a form of survival. The other characters are also blurred and interchangeable; they are denied apparent individuality and psychological development. Exiled from themselves and from the world, they surpass geographic, political, and temporal barriers. Aboard a transatlantic tourist liner, La Bella Pasajera (The Beautiful Passenger), is a mere instrument of pleasure; Vercingetórix, who shares his name with the leader of the Gauls in a revolt against Rome in 52 B.C., is a former political prisoner and a survivor estranged

from his past; Gordon, an astronaut who went to the moon, is now preoccupied with reconstructing and evoking his memories; a deluded and eccentric Morris dedicates himself to collecting pipes, maps, and other objects; Graciela, the natural woman liberated from all inhibitions and social norms, awakens masculine fears; Percival and Eva are like reflections of the nostalgia for a lost paradise; and Lucía is the light that guides humanity into reconciling differences and overcoming inherited conventionalities. The characters are drawn from readings of voyages that allegorize exile as a permanent condition.

Art is by nature a means of breaking the automatism of our perceptions. The unexpected provokes a defamiliarization evident in perverse sexual relations, transgressions that mend the nostalgia for an instinctive, nonrepressive order, a utopian return to lost curiosity or harmony. The characters destroy the reader's horizon of expectations with relationships that elicit strangeness, in which the humor of incongruence and the unforeseen cannot be discounted. Vercingetórix is incurably attracted to little girls or midgets. Equis is more inclined toward elderly ladies; on a tropical island surrounded by provocative women he seduces a Swedish lady of at least sixty-eight whose voluminous body prevents her from moving without difficulty. Her corpulence, flabbiness, and wrinkles provoke in him a perverse erotic excitement. Morris, who awakens public distrust with his artificially elaborate way of speaking, falls hopelessly in love with a nine-year-old boy, Percival.

Peri Rossi ironically rewrites the search for the Holy Grail — emblem of divine grace or moral purity — and explores the irreversible process of the degradation of life. The fable is introduced in the novel in an anti-idyllic setting: a contaminated lake so rank with waste that it poisons the ducks. The lucid eyes of the child perceive elemental truths and hark back to a past gone forever. Percival resists accepting the contamination of the lake, and his fusion with nature transports him to a harmonious region, while the loss of this primordial state causes the withering of spiritual life. His mother, Eva, the first transgressor who dared question divine law, accepts that Morris falls in love with her son, since nonconformity is at the very root of Christian civilization. When Morris tells Equis of his love for Percival, Equis responds that hell is not being able to love. To love without restrictions, to naturalize the power of instincts, and to reconcile the primitive freedom of love with the repression of reason are the central preoccupations in Peri Rossi's work.

*Peri Rossi, circa 1983 ( photograph by Rosa Marqueta)*

In tune with the aesthetics of discontinuity and fragmentation that proliferate in twentieth-century art, *La nave de los locos* subscribes to a narrative mode that is both digressive and capricious. The multiplicity of stories that incessantly begin, never to end, coexist by a logic of heterogeneity. The tales tend toward stasis and dispersion. The compilation of stories of diverse natures breaks the novelistic mold and replaces it with a pluralistic writing that tends to blur the frontiers between genres. Disconnectedness and formlessness provoke the fragmentation of discourse and the deconstruction of the concept of story as a coherent whole. The novel includes poems, songs, children's compositions to Adam and Eve, an onboard diary, rewrites of newspaper articles, comments on or parodies of books, descriptions of *El tapiz de la creación,* and footnotes – lists of Equis's possible names, edicts on hospitality to foreigners, reflections on the precarious condition of the exiles, games to determine the true names of cities evoked in the book, and so on. Such textual multiplicity alters reading habits: all attempts at holding onto the thread of the story are repeatedly interrupted by displacements, long digressions, and incongruent jumps in a story that is infinitely transformed and inconclusive. The heterogeneous interweaving of disconnected narratives produces a polyphonic discourse whose most distinctive features are a dissonant montage and a playful attitude.

Seriousness and humor are found naturally imbedded in Peri Rossi's fiction. Humor springs from unexpected changes in direction, which playfully destroy the reader's expectations. Irreverent remarks are projected beyond the merely comical and give rise to a reflexive bond between statements. The questioning of human misfortunes through a playful distancing destabilizes oppressive and insidious practices that society has naturalized. As in Cortázar, humor and play are fruitful components that emerge at critical moments to mitigate the tragic undercurrent of the narrative and at the same time to erode the reader's mental conditioning. The humor is introduced by breaking from the story line of the narrative and hurling the reader toward a logic of unexpected relationships. The playful digressions function as an anticlimax and ease the terror of misfortune. For example, as we learn of Vercingetórix's painful past – incarcerated in a ghost town covered with dust from a cement factory and surrounded by prisoners who die violently without leaving a trace – the story is interrupted with a footnote about the armed forces' interest in poetry, a pastime that requires the prisoners' participation. Lightheartedness operates as a means to establish a distance from the pathos of the uncertain destiny that reality has prepared for the exiles. Humor is thus converted into an essential component of Peri Rossi's fiction, a feature that tears down established norms and oppressive hegemonies.

*La nave de los locos,* a metaphor for humanity's perennial uprooting and estrangement, bases its coherence on a subversive and demythifying attitude that transgresses all boundaries. Playfulness and existential abandonment, veracity and fantasy, and tenderness and cruelty all coexist admirably in a protean text. It is not by chance that the recuperation of a medieval topic is proposed as a bitterly critical allegory of a splintered humanity's evolution and as a text that reestablishes a connection between completely free writing and the knowledge that people are aliens in the world.

Peri Rossi's most recent books of fiction might properly be considered examples of her mastery to handle and develop the familiar repertoire of procedures and attitudes found throughout her work. If the experiences of exile and all forms of oppression are persistent images that she rewrites again and again, there is no doubt that erotic love and powerfully inventive fiction are also recurrent motifs. In *Solitario de amor* (Lonely Love, 1988), a lyrical novel, a man reconstructs a story of boundless, obsessive, and solitary passion, questioning the limits of sexual identity as well as the nature of subjectivity. The subversive potential of humor, irony, parody, and the absurd, distinctive traits of her literary practice, reaches a radical antimimetic and highly imaginative treatment in *Cosmoagonías* (Cosmic Agonies, 1988) and *La última noche de Dostoievski* (Dostoyevsky's Last Night, 1992). The awareness of living at the end of a historical period – the "cosmic agonies" of the first title – with its crumbling cities, unconscious fears and desires, and displaced and defamiliarized fantasies (for instance, clubs for suicidal, amnesiac, or indecisive persons), moves in her fourth novel toward a playful and flippant takeoff on Fyodor Dostoyevsky's fascination with gambling that generates a relentlessly ironic, postmodern vision of humanity reduced to absurdity and undermines once again the very notion of representation and the reading experience.

From its beginning, the genuine excellence of Cristina Peri Rossi's fiction and poetry illustrates the range and inventiveness of contemporary Latin-American literature.

**Interviews:**

John F. Deredita, "Desde la diáspora: Una entrevista a Cristina Peri Rossi," *Texto Crítico,* 4, no. 9 (May 1978): 131–142;

Susanna Ragazzoni, "La escritura como identidad: Una entrevista con Cristina Peri Rossi," *Studi di Letteratura Ispano-americana,* 15–16 (1983): 227–241;

Susana Camps, "La pasión desde la pasión: Entrevista con Cristina Peri Rossi," *Quimera,* 81 (September 1988): 40–49.

**References:**

Elena Araújo, *La Scherezada criolla* (Bogotá: Universidad Nacional de Colombia, 1989), pp. 61–70, 161–166;

Mario Benedetti, "Cristina Peri Rossi: Vino nuevo en odres nuevos," in his *Literatura uruguaya siglo XX,* second edition (Montevideo: Alfa, 1969), pp. 321–327;

Gina Cánepa, "Claves para una lectura de una novela de exilio: *La nave de los locos* de Cristina Peri Rossi," *Anales* (Göteborg, Sweden), 1 (1989): 117–130;

Debra Castillo, "(De)ciphering Reality in 'Los extraños objetos voladores,'" *Letras Femeninas,* 13, nos. 1–2 (1987): 31–41;

Cover for Peri Rossi's 1984 novel, which unites life and writing as types of voyages

Amaryll B. Chanady, "Cristina Peri Rossi and the Other Side of Reality," *Antigonish Review,* 54 (Summer 1983): 44–48;

Julio Cortázar, "Invitación a entrar en una casa," prologue to Peri Rossi's *La tarde del dinosaurio* (Barcelona: Planeta, 1976), pp. 7–9;

Lucía Guerra Cunningham, "La referencialidad como negación del paraíso: Exilio y excentrismo en *La nave de los locos* de Cristina Peri Rossi," *Revista de Estudios Hispánicos,* 23 (May 1989): 63–74;

Lucía Invernizzi Santa Cruz, "Entre el tapiz de la expulsión del paraíso y el tapiz de la creación: Múltiples sentidos del viaje a bordo de *La nave de los locos* de Cristina Peri Rossi," *Revista Chilena de Literatura,* 30 (November 1987): 29–53;

Amy Kaminsky, "Gender and Exile in Cristina Peri Rossi," in *Continental Latin-American and Francophone Women Writers,* edited by Eunice Myers and Ginette Adamson (Lanham, Md.: University Press of America, 1987), pp. 149–159;

Elia Kantaris, "The Politics of Desire: Alienation and Identity in the Works of Marta Traba and Cristina Peri Rossi," *Forum for Modern Language Studies,* 25 (July 1989): 248–264;

Gabriela Mora, "El mito degradado de la familia en *El libro de mis primos* de Cristina Peri Rossi," in *The Analysis of Literary Texts,* edited by Randolph D. Pope (Ypsilanti, Mich.: Bilingual Press, 1980), pp. 66–77;

Mora, "*La nave de los locos* y la búsqueda de la armonía," *Nuevo Texto Crítico,* 1, no. 2 (1988): 343–352;

Mabel Moraña, "Hacia una crítica de la nueva narrativa hispanoamericana: Alegoría y realismo en Cristina Peri Rossi," *Revista de Estudios Hispánicos,* 21 (October 1987): 33–48;

Moraña, "*La nave de los locos* de Cristina Peri Rossi," *Texto Crítico,* 12, nos. 34–35 (1986): 204–213;

Marta Morello-Fosch, "Entre primos y dinosaurios con Cristina Peri Rossi," in *Mujer y sociedad en América Latina,* edited by Guerra-Cunningham (Santiago: Del Pacífico, 1980), pp. 193–201;

Carlos Raúl Narváez, *La escritura plural e infinita: El libro de mis primos de Cristina Peri Rossi* (Valencia: Albatros, 1991);

Narváez, "La poética del texto sin fronteras," *Inti,* 28 (Fall 1988): 75–88;

María Rosa Olivera-Williams, "*La nave de los locos* de Cristina Peri Rossi," *Revista de Crítica Literaria Latinoamericana,* 12, no. 23 (1986): 81–89;

Montserrat Ordóñez, "Cristina Peri Rossi: Asociaciones," *Eco,* no. 248 (June 1982): 196–205;

Elide Pittarello, "Cristina Peri Rossi: 'Los extraños objetos voladores' o la disfatta del soggetto," *Studi di Letteratura Ispano-americana,* 13–14 (1983): 259–287;

Mercedes M. de Rodríguez, "Oneiric Riddles in Peri Rossi's *La nave de los locos,*" *Romance Languages Annual,* 1 (1989): 521–527;

Gustavo San-Ramón, "Fantastic Political Allegory in the Early Work of Cristina Peri Rossi," *Bulletin of Hispanic Studies,* 67, no. 2 (1990): 151–164;

Cynthia A. Schmidt, "A Satiric Perspective on the Experience of Exile in the Short Fiction of Cristina Peri Rossi," *Americas Review,* 18 (Fall-Winter 1990): 218–226;

Saúl Sosnowski, "*Los museos abandonados,*" *Sur,* 349 (July–December 1981): 147–155;

Mavel Velasco, "Cristina Peri Rossi y la ansiedad de la influencia," *Monographic Review,* 4 (1988): 207–220;

Hugo J. Verani, "Una experiencia de límites: La narrativa de Cristina Peri Rossi," *Revista Iberoamericana,* 118–119 (January–June 1982): 303–316;

Verani, "La historia como metáfora: *La nave de los locos* de Cristina Peri Rossi," *La Torre,* new series 4, no. 13 (1990): 79–92;

Verani, "La rebelión del cuerpo y el lenguaje (a propósito de Cristina Peri Rossi)," *Revista de la Universidad de México,* 37 (January–March 1982): 19–22.

# Nélida Piñon

*(3 May 1935 –   )*

Regina Igel
*University of Maryland at College Park*

BOOKS: *Guia-mapa de Gabriel Arcanjo* (Rio de Janeiro: G.R.D., 1961);

*Madeira feita cruz* (Rio de Janeiro: G.R.D., 1963);

*Tempo das frutas: Contos* (Rio de Janeiro: José Álvaro, 1966);

*Fundador* (Rio de Janeiro: José Álvaro, 1969; revised edition, Rio de Janeiro: Labor do Brasil, 1976);

*A casa da paixão* (Rio de Janeiro: Sabiá, 1972);

*Sala de armas: Contos* (Rio de Janeiro: Sabiá, 1973);

*Tebas do meu coração* (Rio de Janeiro: José Olympio, 1974);

*A força do destino* (Rio de Janeiro: Record, 1977);

*O calor das coisas: Contos* (Rio de Janeiro: Nova Fronteira, 1980);

*A república dos sonhos* (Rio de Janeiro: Francisco Alves, 1984); translated by Helen Lane as *The Republic of Dreams* (New York: Knopf, 1989);

*A doce canção de Caetana* (Rio de Janeiro: Guanabara, 1987); translated by Lane as *Caetana's Sweet Song* (New York: Knopf, 1992).

OTHER: "Cortejo do Divino," in *Os melhores contos brasileiros de 1973* (Pôrto Alegre, Brazil: Globo, 1974), pp. 159–166;

"Missa do Galo," in *Missa do Galo: Variações sobre o mesmo tema,* edited by Osman Lins (São Paulo: Summus, 1977), pp. 23–44;

"A sagrada família," in *O conto da mulher brasileira,* edited by Edla Van Steen (São Paulo: Vertente, 1978), pp. 183–190;

"Ave do paraíso" and "I Love My Husband," in *Mulheres e mulheres,* edited by Rachel Jardim (Rio de Janeiro: Nova Fronteira, 1978);

"A sombra da caça," in *O papel do amor* (São Paulo: Indústria de Papel Simão, 1979), pp. 99–107;

"Bravura," in *O novo conto brasileiro,* edited by Malcolm Silverman (Rio de Janeiro: Nova Fronteira, 1985), pp. 313–318;

"Bird of Paradise" and "The New Kingdom," translated by Evelyn Picon Garfield in *Women's Fic-*

*Nélida Piñon*

*tion from Latin America,* edited by Garfield (Detroit: Wayne State University Press, 1988).

Nélida Cuiñas Piñon figures as one of the major contemporary writers of fiction in Brazilian literature. Her foremost contributions are novels and short stories. She holds a degree in journalism and has brought many literary topics into focus in the leading Brazilian newspapers. Though the author resides in Rio de Janeiro, she is a world traveler by avocation and spends periods of time living in Brazil, Europe, and the United States. An articulate and knowledgeable lecturer, she is continually invited to address university communities throughout the world on subjects ranging from her own fictional works to Brazilian topics to Latin-American literature. Since January 1991 Piñon has spent four months every year as the incumbent professor of the Dr. Henry King Stanford Chair in Humanities at the University of Miami in Coral Gables, Florida. When in Rio de Janeiro she assumes various professional duties, among them attending the weekly meetings of the respected Brazilian Academy of Letters, to which she was elected in 1989.

Piñon's fiction embodies a convergence of cultural traditions rooted in Spain and imparted to her through her Brazilian upbringing among devoted family members of Spanish Galician descent. The author's deep insight into the artistic potential of the Portuguese language is accompanied by a nonconformist regard for conventional fiction. Yet nothing in Piñon's work is ever improvised: her books are produced through a self-imposed discipline that includes at least eight hours of daily writing followed by revisions and further refinement of selected passages. In almost three decades she has created eight novels and three volumes of short stories. Many of her short stories have been included in significant anthologies. The author has occasionally stated that her favorite means of literary expression, however, lies in the novel because of its pluralistic dimensions. In her career as a novelist she has received several prizes, among them the 1972 Mário de Andrade Prize by the Association of Art Critics of São Paulo, the P.E.N. Club of Brazil Prize, and the Association of Art Critics of São Paulo Prize for the best fictional work in 1984 – the last two for the novel *A república dos sonhos* (1984; translated as *The Republic of Dreams,* 1989).

Nélida Piñon was born on 3 May 1935 in Rio de Janeiro, the only daughter of Lino Piñon Muiños and Olivia Carmen Cuiñas. Her mother was born in Brazil, but her father and both sets of grandparents were from Galicia, Spain, a region that had a strong influence in her formative years. Piñon was first introduced to her heritage through narratives told by her elders. Before she was twelve, her parents granted her the opportunity to travel to a rural village in her ancestral land. During the two years they allowed her to stay, she became intimately acquainted with the heritage of her people and the landscape of Galicia.

Piñon is fond of stating in interviews that many of the personal traits of her predecessors as bearers of the Galician culture played a prominent role in both her character and her literary development. Once, in a meeting with journalist Luís González Tosar, she was asked about the importance of her origins in the unfolding of her career, and she replied in Galician:

> Eu considérome unha escritora brasileira ... Ser do trópico é vivir unha realidade tan orixinal, tan diferente ... Pero no meu caso isto está mesturado coa tradición europea.... Veño duns ancestros que son heroes cotiáns. Eu herdo a obriga, o deber e o pracer de vivir con intensidade, de non permitirme preguizas, renuncias inútiles, herdo unha ilusión polo traballo. A pesar de que fun educada cun determinado grao de confort e de benestar económico, nunca renunciei ó trabalho, mesmo no meu oficio de escritora os meus libros son producto dun intenso traballo.... sendo nena, eu sabia que nacera nunha casa diferente ás dos outros nenos brasileiros, porque eu arrastraba as lendas doutro país, a cultura doutro país, outra comida, outros cheiros, outra imaxinación. Cando chego a Galicia, fundo esas dúas culturas, cristalizo naquilo que vai ser Nélida Piñon no futuro.

> ( I see myself as a Brazilian writer ... Being from the tropics is to live an original and different reality ... But my upbringing is mixed with the European culture.... I descend from people who were everyday heroes. I inherited their sense of responsibility and duty, their pleasure of living life intensively, and their lack of a self-indulged laziness or attitude of easy resignation; I inherited their commitment toward work. In spite of having been raised surrounded by comfort and a good level of economical well-being, I never refrained from work, including my writing, for my books are a product of intense work.... I was still a girl when I realized that I was born in a house that was different from the homes of other Brazilian children, since I carried with me the legends and the culture of another country, with its different kind of food and aromas and a distinct imagination. When I arrived in Galicia, I melded those two cultures, converging both of them in what would become the future Nélida Piñon.)

The author dedicated her first three novels to her father, mother, and grandparents respectively.

Piñon's Catholic upbringing at home and in her high school, directed by German nuns, continued through the years as she attended the School of Journalism at the Catholic University of Rio de Janeiro, under the direction of Jesuit priests. As a counterpart to her rigid formal education, however, her father granted her unrestricted access to books, even opening an account in her name at one of the most complete, up-to-date bookstores in Rio de Janeiro while she was an adolescent. Another activity she passionately cultivated was almost-daily attendance at ballets and operas, the latter the focus of an obsessive worship on her part. She said to an interviewer in 1986, "Quanto à ópera . . . tudo é possível. Não carece de verossimilhança para comover e despertar credibilidade. . . . desde cedo, eu me habituei aos absurdos, aos paradoxos, e isto porque, além da própria vida, tinha a ópera como referência" (In opera . . . everything is possible. It does not depend on verisimilitude to generate emotion and credibility. . . . From an early age I became used to the absurd and to the paradoxical, because beyond life itself, opera served as another point of reference for me). The years of disciplined religious schooling, the freedom of selecting her own reading matter and attending artistic programs of her own choice, were influential in Piñon's view of the world. Her first two novels, *Guia-Mapa de Gabriel Arcanjo* (Guide-Map of Archangel Gabriel, 1961) and *Madeira feita cruz* (Wooden Cross, 1963), more than any of her later fiction, bear marks of these peculiar circumstances in her upbringing, merging the dogmatic rules instilled by her austere teachers with the cultivation of an independent mind by her own parents.

Those first novels also reveal Piñon's immersion in the Portuguese language, where she explores its possibilities, harvesting the most elaborate, intricate, and challenging forms of literary communication. All of her novels and most of her short stories can be read as innovative contributions to Brazilian literature in more than one aspect. Some of the several dimensions of the author's experimental features include semantics, plot originality, and unconventional graphic representations such as the suspension of sentences in the middle of a thought and the incorporation of paragraphs or chapters in a distinctive type.

*Guia-mapa de Gabriel Arcanjo* and *Madeira feita cruz* introduced a unique way of writing fiction and of reading it in Brazil. Each is equally representative of her complex manipulation of language marked by excessive elaboration in dialogue. Twisting a unique sentence, for example, into a prismatic interplay of significances renders both the conversations and the narrative text artificial and obscure. As a result, her first two novels require some forbearance on the part of the reader, who might see in their multifaceted meaning an obstacle to understanding. A common argument among critics at the time was that, because her writing was filled with simultaneous and ambiguous meanings, one had to search for the implicit connotations embedded in the stories. General readers tended to see this quest as an unusually difficult task. In retrospect, however, these novels are good indicators of Piñon's development in terms of the continuity and the abandon-

ment of some of the devices she used in them. The embryonic elements that are found further evolved in most of her later novels and short stories include three dimensions of writing: the textual, characterization, and the author's worldview.

The primary aspect of the textual dimension is her archetypal discourse, which finds its sources in the Bible, pagan beliefs, or Greek antiquity or some other historical period. Plots are usually set in or at the fringes of forests and are allegorical, with animistic characters who exist in a mystical atmosphere. Also in the textual dimension is her scrutiny of the semantic possibilities of a particular word and the ramifications of its bonding and interactions within a sentence.

Piñon's treatment of character is another signature trait of her work. Her finely detailed descriptions of her characters' instincts, attitudes, behavior, and relationships are skillful, as is her use of parody or mimicry of time-honored figures in the religious or secular history of civilization. Foremost, however, is her probing of ethical values and her penetrating insight into people's deep yearning for freedom, either as a release from each other's manipulative actions or as a struggle for emancipation from political and social oppressors.

These textual innovations and the sensitive treatment of her characters reflect Piñon's worldview. It seems to be her aspiration to complement or fuse humanity and nature as if to imply that they should never have separated. She searches for a balance in her fiction between empirical reality and the intangible world. Her relentless experiment with texts, words, and subjects, resulting in a narrative enriched by a diversity of configurations, metaphors, and allegorical meaning, may stem from her respect for oral traditions.

Other facets of Piñon's earliest novels are anchored largely in her use of lengthy sentences reminiscent of a mannered, pompous style, techniques she eventually abandoned. This early style led to a certain opacity in the exchanges among characters, which tended to deflect the reader's comprehension, as if the understanding and accessibility of the text were reserved for sophisticated linguists only. Piñon's controversial reputation for the ability to coil, turn, and twist sentences derives primarily from these two novels. A sign, however, that her writing was to become less enigmatic and more articulated appeared not long after the publication of the second novel – the book of short stories *Tempo das frutas* (The Season of Fruits, 1966). After that her works increasingly use more straightforward and explicit language. Although still employing elabo-

*Piñon in the mid 1980s*

rate artistry, Piñon began to turn out texts devoid of their formerly cryptic character, all the more accessible for their verbal economy and unique plot arrangements.

*Guia-mapa de Gabriel Arcanjo* introduced her to readers and critics and introduced them to her deeply rooted religiousness, her initial taste for twisted phraseologies, and her challenging mind. These traits are conspicuous in the long dialogue between Mariella, a young woman, and the Archangel Gabriel, a biblical figure close to God in the Hebrew and Christian scriptures. Their exchanges are a metaphorical chart of thoughts and advice on human behavior combined or contrasted with philosophical and theological precepts and alternately reflected and deflected by the heavenly being and the human. As her confidant and spiritual guide adept at material affairs as well, the angel functions in the novel as a literary device to unfold Mariella's musings on subjects important to her daily life as a woman, ranging from sin to solitude to the existence of God. Making an effort to understand her viewpoint on life, the specter even samples some of her worldly practices through becoming intimate with her.

Given Piñon's upbringing, reflections of her religious involvement can be discerned in both the title and the text of the novel. It hardly seems coincidental that her first book extensively displays Mariella's emerging sense of freedom from the dogmas of a religious education and the nonreligious, informal directions that she enjoyed in her formative years. As a result, the mystical atmosphere in which the characters' dialogues unfold complements the main topic of the novel, Mariella's development of her own mind, especially on the subject of sin, its role in human lives, and its part in the divine order. The message conveyed from the arguments presented between the woman and the angel is that even what is called sin in the Christian scripture — subtly indicated as sexual intercourse — is a force able to bring humanity closer to God, for it is part of his order and therefore a component of nature. It would be simplistic to see Mariella and Gabriel as opposing gladiators in such a vast arena of reflections. On the contrary, they appear to be amicably explaining their positions on philosophical and religious matters, trying to persuade the other to accept their differences. On both counts they fail. Unable to reconcile their distinct views, they part at the end.

In addition to the exchange of information among the characters — human, angelic, and some less significant mythological ones — the text is intertwined with theatrical scenes, surrealistic descriptions, and fragments of poems. These elements not only extricate the novel from traditional novelistic practices in Brazil but also from the circle of innovative fiction emerging among Piñon's contemporaries. Her unique creativity thrust her into a web of conflicting criticism, for reactions to it were mixed. With its highly charged innovative language and seemingly endless conversations on polemical subjects, the novel was not well received by some critics and even less welcomed by a public hardly able to understand the literary novelties she introduced. However, neither the negative critics nor the scant readership discouraged Piñon. She pursued in the novel that soon followed her own pragmatic approach to literature, cultivated by her poignant and analytical perception of life's contingencies.

The use of mysticism continued in *Madeira feita cruz*. A literary exposition on human passions, it employs a resourceful style again based on extracting the atypical and unusual from the language. It depicts the coexistence of a couple and their domestic helper, who live at the edge of a thick forest. The esoteric is presented by the mystical man Pedro, who is confronted with the acquiescence of his wife Maria and confounded by Ana, an instinctive, compulsive young woman. Within the all-encompassing presence of a forest, the narrative is pervaded by a passionate, mystical atmosphere emanating from these three characters. This massive greenery either blends or contrasts with Pedro's invocation of mysterious deeds and Ana's physical cravings. The man's aloofness in the presence of the girl and indifference to her impulsive moves imply an ironic distance between religious fanaticism and nature in spite of the closeness in the living conditions of these two people. The forest, a majestic mother-figure nurturing the self-restrained Pedro and the impulsive Ana, also provides the means for a spiritual death and rebirth of these characters. A metamorphosis taking place within Ana goes unnoticed by Pedro in his self-proclaimed lofty vision. The forest, a silent but eloquent companion of both characters, engulfs them all in the highly symbolic end of the novel.

The title of the novel, an elliptical sequence of the terms *madeira* (wood), *feita* (made), and *cruz* (cross), indicates in Portuguese the transmutation of wood into a cross. It acquires a clearer meaning in the reading of the novel, in which the wood, as a leitmotiv, is depicted in a variety of ways: a thick door at Pedro and Maria's hut, the trees downed by Ana's father and brother, a bridge built by her brother, part of an oven where Ana prepares cornbread, the forest where she goes to find solace and the companionship of nature, logs burning in a fireplace, and the material for an icon representing Jesus on the cross.

While the narrative resounds with ecclesiastical formality, the characters' names are related to biblical archetypes. A few of them have preserved some of their namesakes' traits: Maria remains faithful, though frustrated, for the duration of her marriage to Pedro (Peter), a religious fanatic unswervingly devoted to prayer sessions who as a husband has decided not to interfere with Maria's virginity in order that both be bestowed with divine grace. Like the first apostles, Pedro, although not a fisherman but a tavern owner, is devoted to an ascetic life and to proselytism. Ana, brought to their house by her impoverished father, works as a maid whose wages go to her family. She does so, silently observing the fanatic immersion of Pedro into religious rituals, thus suggesting the prophetess Anna of Jerusalem, who quietly witnessed the arrival of Jesus as a child to the temple but who was hardly seen (Luke 2:36). Piñon proceeds to draw her characters from a reservoir of archetypes. She vests Isaías, Ana's brother, with a metaphorical robe befitting the prophet Isaiah, who bestowed upon his emulator the gift of foreshadowing events.

The woodsman's enigmatic words "quem usa o machado pretende múltiplas brincadeiras na finalidade de atingir o enredo" (whoever uses the ax intends many games within the scope of reaching the subject matter) gain a multifaceted interpretation in the unfolding of the novel. Within a broad range of meaning, they may represent a writer's attempts to reach the heart of fictional matter, while from a specific perspective they may express the attempts undertaken by these particular characters in the forest, struggling to come to an understanding either of themselves or of a world beyond their reach. The use of such allegory even by a less important character such as Isaías typifies Piñon's attempts to understand the craft of writing, an endeavor that is both an enigmatic and a challenging proposition at this early phase of her career. The trope lurks along the concise chapters of the novel as if plotting an invisible trajectory that Ana, Pedro, and Maria are cast to follow, predetermined to do what they do. The mesh of conflicts among these and other characters is stressed by a solemn style, supported by a slow narrative pace that tends to render the discourse artificial. Nevertheless, Piñon's characteristic departure from orderly, aligned sentences and clear meanings for scenes was reviewed by critics as original and resourceful although somewhat confusing.

In Piñon's first two novels innovation paralleled hermeticism, and much of the criticism she received was for the latter. However, with the unyielding sense of freedom that has characterized her personal actions from an early age, she was not discouraged by antagonistic reviewers, as revealed in an interview with Isa Cambará: "É verdade que, atualmente, a crítica me aceita. Mas, não fiz concessão alguma. . . . Em 1961, quando estreei, ganhei o estigma de ser uma escritora difícil, uma escritora de elite, quando, naquele momento, eu estava iniciando minha campanha pessoal, minha campanha de artista em relação a uma linguagem . . . eu não creio em textos difíceis. Creio em textos bem escritos" (It is true that today the critics accept me. However, I did not make any concessions to them. . . . In 1961, when I first started my career, I was marred with the label of difficult writer, as an author who writes for the elite, but then I was starting my personal journey as an artist concerned with the language . . . I do not believe in difficult texts. I believe in well-written texts). Eventually Piñon relinquished the exercise of overexploring wordplay and meanings, liberating the narrative from its impenetrable texture. The progression toward making the discourse less convoluted is first evident in the short stories gathered in *Tempo das frutas*.

Published within the same five years that included the two previous publications, the eighteen stories in *Tempo das frutas* stand out for their conciseness of plot, unconventional delineation of characters, and unique topics. Piñon retains a sophisticated way of transposing tangible reality into fictional representation and continues to delve into the characters' thoughts, feelings, and passions. Moreover, besides fostering her inclination for embroidering plots around archetypes, she appends to them such elements as the absurd, the ironic, the humorous, the grotesque, the cynical, and the erotic, all components of a new development in her work. Although not limited to these stories, these devices are easily apparent in her fiction after *Tempo das frutas*.

The absurd can be found in the title story, in which the reflections of a contemporary woman about to give birth at age seventy are articulated along with the biblical archetype of Sara's late childbirth (Genesis 15). A humorous interlude appears in "Passeio no amor" (A Promenade of Love) in which the protagonist's identity is concealed throughout the narrative only to be revealed in an unexpected twist in its last line. An ironic succession of events slowly unfolds in "Fraternidade" (Fraternity) as a woman's sisterly devotion is portrayed as a sentiment that escalates from incestuous love to sexual passion for a stranger and culminates in fratricide, a word whose first syllable grotesquely echoes the title. A cynical shift is devised in "Os selvagens da terra" (The Savages), a story about a religious man and his passive female companion who alternate between an apparently formal relationship and a sexually unbridled experience in communion with the wilderness of nature. The erotic again emerges in "Aventura de saber" (Adventure in Knowledge), a story about the sensual obsession of a teacher for a young boy.

Whereas Piñon's earlier works of fiction show a strong tendency to rewrite accumulated experiences, in *Tempo das frutas* she disrupts her own customary practice. Liberated from its strict, metaphorical dependency, the language of her new writing is somehow less challenging. She shifts to a narrow strip of time and space allowed by the short story and therein expresses empirical reality in the terminology of her characters' ruminations on changes in their lives. This collection of short fiction was the gate through which Piñon's career bolted into recognition by influential critics and a much more favorable readership. From a formerly tight discourse in which words and sentences were like complex tapestries of thought and feeling, she moved to a more flexible way of narrating, even dabbling in some passages in the oral tradition of telling stories she had captured through the years from her elders. Without yielding to the pressures of the critics who wished that she were an easier writer, she developed her fiction through her own literary maturity. Along the way she cultivated a narrative technique still wrought with care and consciousness, yet without sacrificing its pluralistic meanings and the many other layers of attributes inherent to the richness of her style.

In 1969 Piñon was invited by Prof. Afrânio Coutinho, then chair of the Department of Letters at the Federal University of Rio de Janeiro, to conduct its first workshop on literary creativity. That same year her novel *Fundador* (Founder) was published. Translated into three languages, it was issued seven years after its first publication in a second edition reviewed by the author. A type of Gothic romance, it revives devices used in her earlier narratives – including symbolic meanings given to objects, descriptions of erotic activities among a confined cluster of people, archetypal namings of characters, and an intense scrutiny of characters' intentions, thoughts, and moods – all under an enveloping and formidable forest. *Fundador* offers a perspective of Latin America in one of its phases of struggle against oppressive regimes, evoking adventures typical of medieval tales couched in modern revolutionary jargon. It combines the attributes of an adventure narrative in the tradition of the Arthurian tales with an idealistic text calling for social change and probing ethical values in times of war and peace.

This epic novel gives a new focus on Piñon's career. The narrative dispenses political messages combined with the heroic deeds of a man who becomes the founder of a village carved out of the middle of a dense forest. Leading its small population of radicals in their preparation to challenge their powerful social oppressors, the self-professed founder of a new religion demystifies idols, turning them into mere men and women with attributes and flaws, and explores the concept of the duality of eternity and the transience of time. Furthermore, echoing earlier motifs found in her fiction, a maternal animistic characteristic is represented in the forest in its nurturing and protection of the characters. An underlying sense of humanity irrevocably united to nature comes from the episodes in the founder's narrative. As a vessel for experiments with time, space, and action, the novel can be characterized as reflecting some postmodernist trends for its challenging displacement of the classical concepts of order and truth and techniques that further advanced Piñon in innovative fiction.

In 1972 another absorbing novel, *A casa da paixão* (The House of Passions), was published. As the title indicates, the setting is a house, a space with openings and closures, but is also to be understood as an allegorical body where dramatic events are bred between men and women. Signs and metaphors refer to a sweeping display of passions encompassing potential incest, heterosexual intercourse, and the bizarre desires of the four characters who inhabit the house. The narrator tells about Marta, the main character – her puberty, maturity, and sun-worshiping habits, and her father's love, bordering on incest in his practice of voyeurism. Antonia, the maid, is satisfied to be among animals, and Jerônimo is brought up by Marta's father to be her sexual partner. The house of passions resembles a furnace. Illuminated and fed by the sun, it retains love and unleashes ardor, as if these sensations were both holy and profane, venerated and scorned, with no clear distinction between them. In the midst of this ambiguity these four characters who cohabit the house (and its multiple meanings) accept and deliver offerings to an invisible but omnipotent pagan god of love, who is intrinsically revered and represented by the heat of the sun's rays upon the earth. The characters are surrounded by a mighty forest,

Cover for Piñon's 1987 novel, about the residents of a small Brazilian town

which complements the individuals in their encounters with unleashed human passions. From an early age Marta finds in the forest a nurturing mother, learns of sexual stimulation by playing with the sun's rays, and perceives stones as her warm confidants. Feeling herself a part of nature, she also feels that she has a right to claim equal partnership in the uninhibited sexual act that brings the narrative to its end. The story follows the archetype of Adam and Lilith, conveying a feminist literary stance by the author already evident in Mariella, who first questioned freedom of the will and practices of love, and in several female characters in *Fundador*.

Piñon's feminist views are also revealed in meetings with the press. Her pursuit of equality for the sexes not only includes harmony with man, as upheld in her fiction, but denounces a still-current arbitrary bigotry against writing by women.

One conspicuous trait of *Tebas do meu coração* (Thebes of My Heart, 1974) is advanced without reservation: it is exempt of chapters or any other division or section. In her successful attempt to break with the conventional linear nature of events, Piñon's mode of narrating is a subversive tool against traditional syntax, both in language and in fiction. This original deviation from common discourse in the novel is evident in its intricate composite of reality and dream, action and inaction. Characters' garrulous exchanges alternate with silence charged with meaning, direct statements with sagacious innuendos. It also includes love and sex and a range of sentiments connecting them, humor and drama, the joy of life and astonishment concerning death. The city of Santíssimo is the setting for characters involved in a dialectical argument and a place where many strange things seem to happen, including the theft of the bells of the city church and a humorous war in which cookies are substituted for bullets.

The idea of Thebes, the Greek model of passion and the heart of the novel, conspicuously suggests a surrealistic atmosphere in its mythological background and bellicose history. Santíssimo, fictionally located in Brazil, is timeless since there is no allusion to past, present, or future. Its inhabitants, busy in their daily occupations and jealous of the progress of the neighboring town of Assunção, are alert in their preparations for war. The novel suffers from an abundance of characters, all involved in labyrinthine actions including conflicts among themselves, introspection, and surrender to outside forces, imaginary and real. Many of the archetypal characters are named after religious symbols (Eucharistic, Pilgrim), historical and literary figures (Attila, Héloïse), and scatological suggestions (Próstatis, Rectus). In jest the author contrives the convergence of disparate emblems of history, such as Vikings and baroque angels for example, deriving amusement from the playful puzzle of their juxtapositions in the text. Comic situations scattered throughout the web of adventures permeate the story of Santíssimo, foreshadowing her next novel, *A força do destino* (The Strength of Destiny, 1977).

This novel, with a title similar to Giuseppe Verdi's opera *La forza del destino* (1862), is a parody of this tragic story. The narrative fits within the frame of postmodern discourse for its obvious rupture with the conventional truth of a text. By breaking away from convention, the narrative includes a displacement of the center of interest. The libretto of a young couple's unfortunate love was based on the Romantic novel *Don Alvaro o La fuerza del sino* (Don Alvaro, or the Force of Destiny, 1835), by

Angel de Saavedra, Duke of Rivas. The story unfolds in Spain and Italy at the end of the seventeenth century, when the heinous Marquis of Calatrava becomes adamantly opposed to the marriage of his daughter Leonora to the lesser noble Don Alvaro. The couple is confronted by the Marquis when a weapon belonging to Alvaro accidentally discharges, killing the father. Overwhelmed by the tragedy, the couple separates. She enters a convent; he goes to war. During this period Alvaro starts a friendship with Carlos, a fellow soldier who, unbeknownst to them, is Leonora's brother, who has sworn vengeance for the assassination of his father. This mutual discovery precipitates a duel in which the brother dies, but not before killing Leonora. The tragedy leaves Alvaro alone, filled with guilt, nostalgia, and suffering for the rest of his life.

This melodrama is the focus of Piñon's derision, conveying her ability to re-create a new dimension for a time-honored opera she had revered since childhood. She is able to manipulate the preexisting elements of characters, plot, and scenario by inserting herself into the narration as a chronicler and a narrator and by becoming part of the action she re-creates. Furthermore, she dares to have her presence acknowledged by the characters, including Alvaro and Leonora, who consult with the chronicler before taking new steps in their lives. She reasons with them, laughs at their excesses and at Leonora's naiveté, ponders the maid's purposes for helping the lovers, reflects on a friar's objectives for trying to save their bodies and souls, and so on. The tragedy is transformed into a humorous piece through Piñon's ironic gaze and the insertion of language reflecting contemporary slang and prosaic usage of Brazilian Portuguese. These traits represent a break with her unequivocal respect for the cultivated facet of the written language. They also represent a detachment from traditional parody by creating a new narrative from the heart of the canonized text, by uncovering the making of a novel, and by unmasking the narrator's strategies in the manipulation of characters and events. The reconstruction that results in the text depends on the deconstruction of the original text, which she accomplishes without deviating from the original design. Thus, in order to appreciate the contrast, the reader must have a previous acquaintance with the original text.

As Piñon honored her devotion to the opera by rewriting *La forza del destino*, her next novel, *A república dos sonhos,* is a tribute to her Spanish Galician ancestors. Like the author's father, Madruga is a young boy who sets out as an emigrant from Spanish Galicia to Brazil. During the crossing he meets

Venâncio, a Gypsy of uncertain origin also on his way to a mythical country that fills their imaginations with dreams. Both characters, the firm and determined Madruga and the bohemian wanderer Venâncio, are the two faces of any emigrant's purpose, to conquer the new land and be conquered by it. Success in *A república dos sonhos* is measured on a sliding scale by which both characters become winners on their own terms.

The novel can be perceived through at least two dimensions: as a portrayal of the emigrants' hardship throughout their contribution to the formation of Brazilian culture and as a self-reflective discourse characterized for the most part by its oral nature. The telling of stories is the emigrants' ethnic legacy, something Piñon extrapolated as a common denominator for the merging of oral literature into written discourse. Some of the characteristics of the work have appeared in previous novels; others are new to this novel, such as the significance imparted to names, as in Madruga, a shortened version of the Portuguese word *madrugada* (dawn), appropriate for the man who starts a new life in Brazil, and in Esperança (hope) for his daughter who dares to break away from patriarchal structures, whose own daughter Breta eventually gathers the stories bestowed on her and transforms them into a book. Another common trait found in Piñon's work is the presence of archetypes, represented here by Spanish Galician legends and superstitions juxtaposed with the tangible realities of Brazilian political encounters and conflicts — the former a legacy imparted by three generations of Galician peasants, the latter experienced in contemporary Brazil by Madruga and his descendents. His granddaughter Breta is the last link between the family's saga within the political and social fabric that envelops their lives in Brazil for a period of almost eighty years, from 1913, the date of Madruga's arrival, until the 1980s.

The narrative is engaged artistically, socially, and politically. Its artistry discloses an introspective mood that reveals the making of a novel through the voices of Madruga, Breta, and Eulália, the grandmother. In the course of their stories, the land of Galicia is subtly compared to Brazil, for both were colonized by Portugal and Spain respectively and therefore equally devoid of the opportunity to develop their own unique attributes. Socially the novel can be read as a praise of free enterprise, among other possible interpretations, because Madruga climbs the ladder of financial success from peasant to industrialist in Brazil. Though he is grateful to his "republic of dreams," his stories also tell of unfairness and unpleasantries suffered by his

generation of expatriates. He and Breta, his favorite listener, combine their viewpoints of the same story, to some extent including the Africans in the formation of Brazilian culture along with the Europeans and the native born, all elements that enter into the composition of the inspiring new republic. Politically the history of Brazil is exposed primarily through the scrutiny of Venâncio, the former gypsy who tries to forget his loneliness by conducting historical research at the National Library of Rio de Janeiro. Through Venâncio, the oppressed but dignified wanderer, Piñon creates an opportunity to reiterate her aversion toward autocracy as practiced in Brazil. The novel becomes an intellectual voice against the dictatorship of Getúlio Vargas in the 1940s, the settling of the dictatorship in the 1960s, and the unfolding of censorship, persecution, and exiles in the 1970s, which brought the dream republic to a close.

*A república dos sonhos* is a massive, carefully crafted work of imagination profusely populated by allusions, panoramic history, and characters who anonymously make history. To the women Piñon gives an extensive voice, consistent with all of her work. Eulália is the one who holds the line of remembrances; Esperança, her daughter, dares to infringe upon the system; and Breta, the inheritor of this ancestry of courage, assimilates, transforms, and retells their legacy. From this perspective the novel can be said to embrace a feminist point of view. Politically, by encompassing a large period in Brazilian history and the extended historical dimension of Galicia as well, the novel denounces the colonial system that engulfed their peoples in similar traps of repression. Brazilian literature has seldom been represented by such a dense work of fiction, much less with such a unique quest for integrating social, political, historical, and personal portraits of the country and the people attracted to its legendary exuberance.

Piñon's latest book, *A doce canção de Caetana* (1987; translated as *Caetana's Sweet Song*, 1992), was written in Barcelona, Spain. This city contrasts in every aspect with Trindade (Trinity), the tiny town where most of the action of the novel takes place. Unlike other small towns in Piñon's work, Trindade retains a definite similarity with the villages scattered throughout the Brazilian hinterland. Besides a conspicuous main street, it has a theater, a hotel, a train station, and a brothel; but what concerns its people is that it is well represented by a sheriff and a powerful local man, Polidoro, who has kept his love for Caetana, an aspiring opera singer, for twenty years. Surrounded by the entire town, she will have to resign herself to finding in its dusty theater the glory she dreamed of achieving in the prestigious Municipal Theater of Rio de Janeiro.

In *A doce canção de Caetana,* Piñon relives her passion for opera, unfolding events and circumstances appropriate to lines, songs, and scenes. Moreover, the novel is like a village feuilleton that latches onto the rumors, gossip, passions, dreams, and frustrations of a large sector of its population. She treats the characters with a mixture of irony and tenderness, letting them emerge with traits true to common life with their extended range of passions and idiosyncrasies and their basic humanity. Although Piñon maintains respect for her characters' independence, she nevertheless retains control of their whereabouts, calling them back to the scene or to the text. An atmosphere of ironic humor pervades the entire novel, oscillating between the extravanganzas of an opéra bouffe or light entertainment and an allegorical play with a flexible though meticulous script. Features such as archetypal names are present in this novel as well. Another tie to her other works is a deliberate political statement in the narrative, suggestive of the author's continuous abhorrence of autocratic regimes such as the one in Brazil when the novel was written.

Nélida Piñon has redefined fiction by writing in her native idiom. On a larger scale, she may have changed forever her contemporaries' view of the literary imagination itself, for even as she addressed time-honored themes she met them with an entirely new language. Between her first book and her latest, she has crossed a vast distance in her treatment of narrative. Such work inspires confidence in the future of literary fiction as a craft that still demands, and finds in authors such as Piñon, an artistic explorer who is at the same time a writer faithful to her literary inheritance.

## Interviews:

Farida Issa, "Entrevista con Nélida Piñon," *Nueva Narrativa Hispanoamericana,* 3, no. 1 (1973): 133–140;

Isa Cambará, "O sorriso sem medo de Nélida," *Folha de S. Paulo, Ilustrada* (15 April 1978): 29;

Luís González Tosar, "Nélida Piñon ou a paixon de contar," *Grial: Revista Galega de Cultura,* 105 (January–March 1990): 39–55;

Vasda B. Landers, "Interview with Nélida Piñon," *Belles Lettres,* 6 (Winter 1991): 24–25.

## Bibliography:

Ana Rosa Núñez and Lesbia O. Varona, *The World of Nélida Piñon, Partial Bibliography* (Miami: Otto G. Richter Library, University of Miami, 1992).

## References:

Vilma Areas, "Do adamastor camoniano a 'Sala de Armas' de Nélida Piñon," *Coloquio,* 27 (1974): 32–39;

Nelly Novaes Coelho, "A casa da paixão e as forças primordiais da natureza," *Convivium,* 16 (May–June 1973): 216–228;

Coelho, "*A República dos Sonhos*: Prémio ficção/84 APCA: Memória, historicidade, imaginário," *Convivium,* 28 (May–June 1985): 257–265;

Horácio Costa, "À margem de 'A República dos sonhos' de Nélida Piñon," *Luso-Brazilian Review,* 24 (Summer 1987): 1–15;

Denise A. D. Guimarães, "Uma poética de autor: Leitura de um texto de Nélida Piñon," *Estudios Brasileños,* 5, no. 9 (1980): 39–55;

Cecilia de Lara, "O 'indevassável casulo': Uma leitura de 'A República dos sonhos' de Nélida Piñon," *Revista do Instituto de Estudos Brasileiros,* 27 (1987): 27–36;

Gregory McNab, "Abordando a história em *A República dos sonhos,*" *Brasil/Brazil: Revista de Literatura Brasileira,* 1 (1988): 41–53;

Naomi Hoki Moniz, "A casa da paixão: Ética, estética e a condição feminina," *Revista Iberoamericana,* 126 (January–March 1984): 129–140;

Maria Luiza Nunes, "*A força do destino* by Nélida Piñon," *Revista Iberoamericana,* 108–109 (January–December 1979): 712–716;

José Ornellas, "El mundo simbólico y filosófico de *Madeira feita cruz* de Nélida Piñon," *Nueva Narrativa Hispanoamericana,* 3, no. 1 (1973): 95–102;

Teresinha Alves Pereira, "Sobre un cuento de Nélida Piñon: 'Sala de Armas,' " *Revista de Cultura Brasileña,* 49 (July 1979): 118–120;

Giovanni Pontiero, "Notes on the Fiction of Nélida Piñon," *Review,* 76, no. 19 (1976): 67–71;

Ellen Spielmann, "*A Força do Destino,*" *Revista de Crítica Literaria Latinoamericana,* 15, no. 30 (1989): 209–219;

Mario Vargas Llosa, "Presentación de un libro de Nélida Piñon," *Revista de Cultura Brasileña,* 48 (January 1979): 81–91.

# Sergio Ramírez
## (5 August 1942 – )

### Nicasio Urbina
*Tulane University*

BOOKS: *Cuentos* (Managua: Nicaragüense, 1963);

*Nuevos cuentos* (León, Nicaragua: Universitaria, 1969);

*La narrativa centroamericana* (San Salvador: Universitaria, 1970);

*Tiempo de fulgor* (Guatemala: Universitaria, 1970);

*Mariano Fiallos: Biografía* (León, Nicaragua: Universitaria, 1971);

*De tropeles y tropelías* (San Salvador: Universitaria de El Salvador, 1972);

*Charles Atlas también muere* (Mexico City: Joaquín Mortiz, 1976); translated by Nick Caistor as *Stories* (New York: Readers International, 1988);

*¿Te dió miedo la sangre?* (Caracas: Monte Avila, 1977); translated by Caistor as *To Bury Our Fathers* (New York: Readers International, 1979);

*Biografía de Sandino* (Managua: Ministerio de Educación, 1979);

*Sandino siempre* (León, Nicaragua: Universitaria, 1980); translated by R. E. Conrad as *Sandino, the Testimony of a Nicaraguan Patriot* (Princeton: Princeton University Press, 1990);

*El muchacho de Niquinohomo* (Managua: Departamento de Propaganda y Educación Política de F.S.L.N., 1981); republished as *Sandino, el muchacho de Niquinohomo* (Buenos Aires: Cartago, 1986);

*El alba de oro: La historia viva de Nicaragua* (Mexico City: Siglo XXI, 1983);

*Balcanes y volcanes y otros ensayos y trabajos* (Managua: Nueva Nicaragua, 1983);

*Sandino es indohispano y no tiene fronteras en América Latina* (Managua: Departamento de Agitación y Propaganda del F.S.L.N., 1984);

*Seguimos de frente: Escritos sobre la revolución* (Caracas: Centauro, 1985);

*Estás en Nicaragua* (Barcelona: Muchnik, 1985); republished as *Julio, estás en Nicaragua* (Buenos Aires: Nueva América, 1986); translated by Darwin J. Flakoll as *You Are in Nicaragua* (Willmantic, Conn.: Curbstone Press, 1990);

*Sergio Ramírez (photograph © Piers Cavendish)*

*Charles Atlas también muere, De tropeles y tropelías y otros cuentos* (Managua: Nueva América, 1986);

*Las armas del futuro,* edited by Reynaldo González (Havana: Ciencias Sociales, 1987);

*Castigo divino* (Madrid: Mondadori, 1988);

*La marca del zorro: Hazañas del Comandante Francisco Rivera Quintero contadas a Sergio Ramírez* (Managua: Nueva Nicaragua, 1989);

*Confesión de amor* (Managua: Nicarao, 1991);

*Clave de sol* (Managua: Nueva Nicaragua, 1992).

OTHER: *Cuento nicaragüense,* edited by Ramírez (San José, Costa Rica: Editorial Universitaria Centroamericana, 1969);

*Antología del cuento centroamericano,* edited by Ramírez (San José, Costa Rica: Editorial Universitaria Centroamericana, 1971);

*El pensamiento vivo de Sandino,* edited by Ramírez (San José, Costa Rica: Editorial Universitaria Centroamericana, 1974); revised and enlarged as *El pensamiento vivo de Augusto C. Sandino,* two volumes (Managua: Nueva Nicaragua, 1984).

Sergio Ramírez is currently the most important fiction writer of Nicaragua, for the quality of his prose as well as for his political visibility. His three published novels are examples of his ability to construct highly structured plots with interesting, well-rounded characters that are both entertaining and significant. Polyphonic and fragmentary, his novels are not easy to read, demanding an attentive and active reader. His short stories are compact, tightly structured, elegantly written, and effective, making him one of the best practitioners of the genre in Nicaragua. While his narratives often deal with everyday life and events, he manages to give them literary quality and aesthetic value.

Sergio Ramírez Mercado was born in Masatepe, a small town in the province of Masaya, Nicaragua. His father, Pedro Ramírez Gutiérrez, was a small farmer and local politician, and his mother, Luisa Mercado Gutiérrez, was a schoolteacher. He attended elementary and high school at the Instituto Anastasio Somoza García, where his mother was the principal for many years, although in his interview with Margaret Randall he claims to have studied with the Christian Brothers in Diriamba and Managua. Nydia Palacios, one of the most reliable sources available on Ramírez, confirms that he attended high school at the National Institute in Masatepe and was first in his class. Coming from a family of liberal traditions with many ties to the Somozas, Ramírez grew up under the protection of the regime. From childhood he was a good writer, a skillful editor, and an eloquent speaker. He was director of the school newspaper *La Voz,* where he published several articles and poems – some of them praising the dictator – and founded the magazine *Poliedro,* for which he did most of the work.

After his high-school graduation he went to León and entered the national university with a scholarship from Luis Somoza Debayle. There his political views started to change. In an interview with Steven White he explains about those years:

I came to León to study law in May of 1959, and it was one of the turning points of my life. I came from a provincial background that was quite poor – I am referring to the village where I was born – with a very limited knowledge of literature that I acquired in high school. I was also distant from the fight against the dictator, which has an intense center in León, a university city. Somoza García, the founder of the dictatorship, was executed here [in] 1956 by a poet named Rigoberto López Pérez and professors and students had been shaken by the repression that followed the death of the tyrant. Among these people were Carlos Fonseca and Tomás Borge. Just a few months before my arrival in León, Tomás had fled to Honduras after being released from jail owing to student pressure. Carlos Fonseca had returned from Moscow in December of 1957 and suffered imprisonment just for having taken that trip and writing his book, *Un nicaragüense en Moscú* (A Nicaraguan in Moscow), which the students read clandestinely. He was also persecuted and sent into exile to Guatemala in April of 1959.

This was the political climate when Ramírez arrived in León. Just a month after his arrival classes were suspended due to the failed invasion of Olama y Mollejones, and shortly thereafter the massacre of El Chaparral took place. The National Guard responded to a massive protest in the streets of León with violence and bullets. "Four students were killed and more than seventy wounded," Ramírez continues. "The massacre had an intense effect on the city and on the country. For me, and many others from my generation, it was the point of no return. We were deeply and decidedly shaken."

Ramírez and Fernando Gordillo then published a literary magazine called *Ventana* (Window), where he published several of his short stories and some poems. Ramírez commented about the ideology of the group in his interview with White: "The magazine and the group were born with the wounds of the massacre. We were repulsed by the dictatorship and had a militant conception of literature – not socialist realism or anything like that. But from the beginning we did reject the position that had reigned in Nicaragua up to that time in terms of artistic labor: the famous story of art for art's sake; the artist's sworn aversion to political contamination." In four years nineteen issues of *Ventana* were published. Although some of the pieces included were overtly political, in general the magazine stayed away from political debate and maintained a high literary quality, serving as a space for artistic achievement and literary development.

By the time Ramírez graduated from law school and *Ventana* slipped into extinction, he had published his first book, a collection of ten short stories titled simply *Cuentos* (Short Stories, 1963). It was published with a prologue by Mariano Fiallos Gil, then president of the Universidad Nacional Autónoma de Nicaragua in León, whose biography Ramírez wrote a few years later. Although the style is rough and the stories are deceitfully simple – his first short stories are rudimentary and linear in their structure – their prose already reveals a canny storyteller and political thinker.

"El cobarde" (The Coward) is an example of the uses of colloquial Nicaraguan language, an aesthetic concept from which the author soon departed. In "El estudiante" (The Student), the most autobiographical of these stories, the reader witnesses the arrival in León of a young high-school graduate, his discovery of university life, and the economic difficulties he suffers. As one reads this volume, the stories become richer and more interesting, with multiple meanings and levels of reading. "El hallazgo" (The Finding) explores the mysteries of identity and personality as the customers of a bar find some resemblance between the bartender and movie actor Gregory Peck. The character, unaware at the beginning of this resemblance, takes full control of his new role during the course of the narrative. At the end everybody has forgotten the apparent resemblance except the character, who will spend the rest of his life as a double for the famous actor. "La banda del Presidente" (The President's Band) narrates the slow but irreversible process by which the population loses all interest in politics. The desperate president arranges for a military coup d'état in order to restore some level of concern among the population for the national political life. As a result the military takes control of the country and never returns it to the rightful president. In the last story, "El poder" (The Power), an obscure legal secretary experiences what it is like to be in charge, to have political power. This book is representative of the first stage in the author's evolution. While the first stories are more realistic and autobiographical, the later ones are more allegorical, exploring what will become one of Ramírez's most important themes: power and political life. These stories reflect the political evolution of the young law student who arrives in León in 1959 as he develops into a political activist and the organizer and editor of the literary magazine *Ventana* and who later becomes a politician himself.

After León, Ramírez did not return to Masatepe to open a law office as his father had dreamed. He married Gertrúdiz Guerrero Mayorga and went instead to San José, Costa Rica, in 1964, where he was offered a position with the Central

*Ramírez in the early 1980s*

American University Council. "By that time," he told Randall, "I wanted to be a writer, no matter what it took." Ramírez started to write *Tiempo de fulgor* (Time of Brilliance, 1970), his first novel, and some short stories he later published. In 1967 Ramírez and a group of intellectuals from Central America founded the publishing house Editorial Universitaria Centroamericana (EDUCA) under the sponsorship of the Central American University Council. EDUCA was for many years the most important publisher in Central America. The importance of this enterprise was tantamount to the development of a literary consciousness in Central America since it published important works by traditional as well as new Central American authors. The following year Ramírez was appointed secretary-general of the Central American University Council, a post he held until 1973.

*Nuevos cuentos* (New Short Stories) appeared in 1969. The five collected stories represent a qualitative leap in the development of Ramírez's craftsmanship as a writer. Much more complex in their narrative structure and loaded with psychological insight and well-structured plots, these stories represent a more mature and gifted creator. "Benditoescondido" (Holy-Hidden), the first, a story of destiny, willpower, and the irony of life, narrates in parallel form the friendship of two boys and their meeting many years later when one of them has become a thief. In "Un lecho de bauxita en Weipa" (A Bed of Bauxite in Weipa) Ramírez portrays a complex vision of love and human faithfulness told through complex narrative levels foreshadowing the gifted narrator of his first novel. In the next story, "Nicaragua es blanca" (Nicaragua Is White), the narrator tells of an unbelievable night when it snowed in Nicaragua and the president's political manipulation of that event to make the natural phenomenon a celebration of his regime. Well narrated, with an excellent handling of meteorological jargon, this short story has become a classic of Nicaraguan literature.

"El centerfielder" (The Centerfielder) is perhaps his best short story. Brief and constructed with a great sense of proportion and equilibrium, it narrates the story of an old baseball player imprisoned because his son has joined the guerrilla movement. Through temporal leaps the old man recounts scenes from his life as a baseball player, and through interior monologue the reader learns about his plan to escape from prison. At the end of the story the captain gives the order to kill the old man, using the same scheme the old man had planned for his escape. In "El centerfielder" Ramírez has become a mature and experienced short-story writer using the skills and resources of the genre at its best.

Ramírez finished *Tiempo de fulgor* in 1968; it was published in 1970. Extremely complex in its structure, it presents in a fragmentary way the life of Glauco María Mendiola Sepúlveda, a nineteenth-century Nicaraguan. Although relatively short it is not an easy novel to read, divided into twelve chapters, some composed of several sections, so that the reader must constantly look for clues and markers to be able to situate the text within the story. In this respect *Tiempo de fulgor* partakes of the chaotic structure of the postmodern novel, although its language and its treatment of the world it portrays can better be described as magic realism. The narrator's point of view is unstable, changing continuously from an omniscient third-person perspective to second person and to first person with interior monologue, thus contributing to the polyphonic, chaotic nature

of the text. In this novel Ramírez examines the Contreras, a petit bourgeois family in León reminiscent of the Contreras who ruled Nicaragua in the sixteenth century and revolted against the Spanish crown. The family claims to be related to the Virgin Mary through the Mendiola side of the family, and in their prayers they invoke her as an old dead relative. In this sense the novel studies the social structure of the country – its contradictions and vices, its weaknesses and its system of values.

The text of *Tiempo de fulgor* revolves around the image of an old yellowish picture that recurs repeatedly in the narrative. The picture, whose subjects are never explicitly identified but whose identities the reader must decipher, is a symbol of the inexorable passing of time and its retention in the fixed image registered in the picture. Whenever the picture enters the scene, the narration switches to second person, as if the text of the picture were imposed by somebody else. There is a mysterious, almost-magical aura to the picture, which stands for a form of memory in which the history of the family is inscribed. Thus while the novel tells the story of the family, the picture tells the story of a moment, probably the only moment of happiness for Aurora Contreras, around which the rest of the novel revolves.

If in his short stories Ramírez demonstrates his ability to construct well-developed plots, in *Tiempo de fulgor* he proves his capacity for orchestrating various narrative levels and for maintaining a level of indeterminacy in the narrative that contributes to the ambiguity of the text. Although the novel is at times dull and melancholic, Ramírez comes across as a skillful and brilliant young writer.

In 1971, while working as secretary-general of the Central American University Council, Ramírez wrote and published two other books. One is a 1971 biographical essay of Fiallos, his mentor and protector. Well researched and written in a conversational but proper style, Ramírez's portrait is positive. *Mariano Fiallos: Biografía* saves for posterity an important phase of the national university in Nicaragua: its fight for autonomy and the story of one of its most distinguished presidents.

The other book, *De tropeles y tropelías* (Rush and Mad Rush, 1972), is a collection of fables whose main character is S. E. (Su Excelencia [Your Excellency]). It won first prize in a literary contest sponsored by *Revista Imagen* in Caracas, Venezuela. Although ingenious and humorous, Ramírez lacks the sarcastic genius necessary to write good political satire. Many of the stories are interesting and well conceived, but the endings are often dull and somber, destroying the satiric effect. Some remarkable exceptions are "De los juegos de azar" (About Games of Chance) and "Del olvido eterno" (About Eternal Oblivion).

Along with his creative writing during those years Ramírez was involved in editorial work, organizing an anthology of Central American short stories that would be a major contribution to the organized study of the genre in Central America. The second project was a compilation of Augusto Cesár Sandino's writings and letters under the title *El pensamiento vivo de Sandino* (The Living Thought of Sandino, 1974). This first edition and the subsequent revisions and enlargements became the official bible of the Sandinista movement. Although there were other compilations and anthologies, Ramírez's edition became required reading for the militants of the Frente Sandinista de Liberación Nacional (FSLN) and those interested in the life and thought of the Nicaraguan hero.

In 1973 Ramírez left Costa Rica for Berlin to fulfill a lifelong dream of being a full-time writer. In 1967 he had met Peter Achults-Kraft, a German who worked for the United Nations in El Salvador, and through him Ramírez was able to obtain a scholarship in 1973 from the Berlin academic exchange program. There he finished *¿Te dió miedo la sangre?* (Did the Blood Scare You?, 1977; translated as *To Bury Our Fathers,* 1979); wrote "El muchacho de Niquinohomo" (The Boy From Niquinohomo), originally the prologue to the German edition of *El pensamiento vivo de Sandino;* and completed the essay *Balcanes y volcanes y otros ensayos y trabajos* (Balkans and Volcanoes and Other Essays and Works, 1983), an interpretation of the cultural history of Central America. In addition, he wrote "Ventana," a weekly column for *La Prensa Literaria* about cultural information.

Two years later, in 1975, Ramírez went back to Costa Rica. Apparently for him the decisive point in his political and literary career was the abduction of a group of politicians close to Somoza at the house of José María Castillo by a commando of the FSLN in December 1974. Ramírez formally joined the FSLN in September 1975, working from Costa Rica in propaganda and international information, denouncing violations of human rights in Nicaragua, working with a network of solidarity committees around the world, and organizing the Group of Twelve, which gained support for the FSLN from the private sector and many political organizations. In 1976 he was again elected secretary-general of the Central American University Council, but as he confessed in his interview with Randall, "it was just

Cover for the 1990 Madrid edition of Ramírez's 1989 book, a testimonial account of Francisco Rivera Quintero's involvement with the Sandinistas

a cover – I never really worked in that post again. The cover was useful for all sorts of political tasks, because CSUCA [the Central American University Council] had diplomatic status in Costa Rica."

His collection of short stories *Charles Atlas también muere* (Charles Atlas Also Dies, 1976; translated as *Stories,* 1988), which was in the hands of its publisher for several years, was released. Only two of the six stories are new; the other four had been published in *Nuevos cuentos.* The title story is a demythification of the American idol. A poor Nicaraguan telegraph operator develops his body with the Charles Atlas dynamic-tension method and is invited to visit Atlas in New York. He is disillusioned when he meets Atlas, an immense deformed body prostrate in his deathbed. The narrator turns out to be a sort of double of Charles Atlas, reliving many of the scenes of his life. The fascinating, well-written story deconstructs one of the better-known North American myths in Latin America.

The last story, "A Jackie, con nuestro co-razón," (To Jackie, with Our Heart) takes on another icon of American culture: Jacqueline Kennedy and her projected visit to Nicaragua. Upon the news of her visit Nicaraguan high society goes crazy. The members of the Virginia Country Club go through an incredible ordeal in order to be the exclusive hosts of the first lady. They buy the *Queen Elizabeth* to receive Jackie, who is coming by yacht, but at the end she never arrives. In this story Ramírez ridicules the dreams and aspirations of the Creole bourgeoisie, showing the mechanisms of dependency and colonialism prevalent among the upper classes. Although openly critical of the political situation, Ramírez succeeds in keeping both of his narratives away from political propaganda and pamphleteering discourse, creating two stories of indisputable literary value and political significance.

Amid the struggle to overthrow the Somoza dictatorship, *¿Te dió miedo la sangre?* was published in Caracas. It was not only timely but also significant, for even people who did not read the novel were attracted by the title when the country was immersed in an enormous bloodbath. The novel is divided into ten chapters covering 1930 to 1961, just before the foundation of the FSLN, and smoothly intertwines five story lines. "El hombre" (the man) and "los hijos del hombre" (the sons of the man) allegorically represent the Somoza dynasty; although their presence is not central to the story, each one of the actions portrayed is somehow related to their regime and their power. Santiago Taleno, better known as el Turco (the Turk), has had an impoverished childhood with his father selling monkeys, looking for gold, and selling hats, pocket mirrors, and soap. His brother is killed by a bull, and his father meets a new woman, moves to Managua, and starts working for el hombre. El Turco enters the military academy and serves the regime until one day he falls in disgrace and flees for Honduras. El Indio Larios (Larios the Indian) is a private in Somoza's National Guard. He is a hero in the fight against Sandino and an effective host to Americans in Managua until one day he leads a revolt against el hombre. He is imprisoned but finally escapes and goes to Guatemala. Another story line involves el Jilguero (the Goldfinch), whose grandfather was a presidential candidate running against el hombre. He wins the elections but el hombre is declared victorious. In another fraudulent election his sister loses a beauty contest to Col. Catalino López's daughter, and his brother is executed. El Jilguero is

also forced to seek refuge in Honduras. Another of the narrative lines is that of *Trío los caballeros* formed by Lázaro, who is killed in Managua; Pastorita; and Raúl, who also is exiled in Honduras.

The narrative structure of the novel is systematic but complex, demanding a meticulous reading. It starts in Guatemala, when Colonel López is sent there to attend the funeral of another dictator, Castillo de Armas. El Turco, el Indio Larios, and el Jilguero take him to a brothel and make him pay for all he has done. From there the novel goes back in time, taking up different threads of the stories, jumping from one story line to another, and slowly putting together the whole narrative structure. Notwithstanding the difficulties and complexity of the text, it is Ramírez's most popular novel so far and has been translated into five languages. Its success is due partly to its political implications and the role of Ramírez within the Sandinista revolution, but the novel reflects his outstanding literary abilities and deserves more critical attention than it has received.

By the time *¿Te dió miedo la sangre?* was published, creative writing was far from Ramírez's mind: he was actively involved in the final offensive against one of the longest dictatorial dynasties in modern history. The offensive stage of the revolution was put in motion by the Tercerista faction, whose main representatives were the Ortega brothers. The Group of Twelve was instrumental in gaining international recognition for the FSLN, giving it serious credibility. They formed a provisional government in Costa Rica and were ready to take political control of Nicaragua, but the final military offensive did not come as soon as they expected. Thus on 17 October 1977 they published a manifesto in which they publicly supported the FSLN and its struggle. As Ramírez said to Randall, "The political impact was tremendous. For the first time in the history of Nicaragua a group of priests, businessmen, intellectuals, and professionals came in support of the FSLN's armed struggle." Soon thereafter Pedro Joaquín Chamorro was killed, and the insurrection gained momentum. When in 1979 Somoza left Nicaragua, taking the bodies of his father and brother, Ramírez was one of the five members of the Junta of National Reconstruction.

In the following years he mainly published political essays. In 1979, right after the revolution, he published *Biografía de Sandino* (Sandino's Biography); the following year, *Sandino siempre* (Sandino Always; translated as *Sandino, the Testimony of a Nicaraguan Patriot*, 1990); and in 1981 *El muchacho de Niquinohomo*. In 1983 two important books of essays were released: *Balcanes y volcanes y otros ensayos y trabajos* gathers seven essays about Central American cultural history. The first, "Balcanes y volcanes," is a serious attempt to understand the history and social organization of Central America. The other essays deal with literary and political matters, some of them dating from his times in Berlin and San José, others more recently written as part of his work as a member of the junta. The other collection, *El alba de oro* (The Golden Dawn), gathers political speeches and articles of a more propagandistic, pamphleteering nature. The same can be said of *Seguimos de frente: Escritos sobre la revolución* (Moving Forward: Writings on the Revolution) and *Estás en Nicaragua* (translated as *You Are in Nicaragua,* 1990), both published in 1985. *Las armas del futuro* (The Arms of the Future, 1987) is another volume of essays.

In 1984 Ramírez was elected to the vice-presidency with Daniel Ortega at the top of the ticket in an election critics claimed was as fraudulent as the ones staged by Somoza. At that time the contra war, the embargo by the United States, the inability to manage and run businesses, widespread corruption, and the virtual looting of the national treasury had the economy of Nicaragua in shambles. There was no apparent justification for the revolution at that point. Opponents claimed it had turned into a repressive, destructive military dictatorship lacking the popular support that it once had, to the point that even the international Left was beginning to turn its back on the Sandinistas. Nevertheless, Ramírez continued to defend the regime and to profit from his political position.

In 1988, while vice-president of Nicaragua, Ramírez published his novel *Castigo divino* (Divine Punishment), a narrative that combines history and fiction. The story is based on the well-known scandal that shook the city of León in 1933. Oliverio Castañeda, a Guatemalan, went to León to study law, bringing with him his new spouse, Marta, who died shortly after their arrival. After her tragic death Don Enrique Gurdián Castro took Castañeda to live with him. Ena Gurdián, his only daughter, died on 3 October, and on the ninth of the same month Don Enrique died in similar circumstances. Ramírez took the main facts of the case and developed his novel by changing a few names and circumstances, adding many details, and involving several people and writers, some of them contemporaries of the crime but many of them young contemporary writers who could not have been participants in the case. The narrative is based on letters, legal documents, testimonies, sworn affidavits, journalistic articles, and conversations, creating a polyphonic narrative texture that, although

Cover for the 1992 Madrid edition of Ramírez's 1991 novel

not new, represents an enormous effort on the part of the author.

Due to its theme *Castigo divino* belongs to the tradition of the detective story. Atanasio Salmerón fulfills the role of the investigator surrounded by helpers too blind to see the truth. Capt. Anastacio Ortiz represents the police, uncomfortable in his role and ready to do whatever is necessary to punish the criminal. The judge is Fiallos, Ramírez's mentor and friend, a faithful and straight lawman who wants to see justice served. Due to the nature of the story *Castigo divino* also has some similarities with the *folletines,* popular sensational novels produced for mass consumption in Latin America. An interesting factor in Ramírez's novel is the parallel drawn between the case and *Castigo divino,* a Spanish-language version of an American film featuring Charles Laughton and Maureen O'Sullivan.

By establishing this parallel the author introduces another element of great interest for modern literary criticism. Through the film, whose title in Spanish alludes to the novel being read, a connection is made among the fiction of the film, the actual case, and the representation of the case in the novel. A similar effect is presented in reference to the report of journalist Rosalío Usulutlán published in *El Cronista* on 25 October 1933, where the journalist reported the facts of the case; Ramírez changes the names of the persons involved and the text of the novel where the original names had been changed as well. Another dimension of this effect is the self-reflexiveness present at the end of the novel when poet Alí Vanegas and Judge Fiallos are talking about the novel: "algún día van a querer hacer de todo esto" (one day somebody will want to write about all this). This play of referential doubling is a fascinating feature, one of the many critical values of the novel.

Also of great importance is the function of the narrator, who at the end of the novel reveals himself as the author, mentioned by his first name. All through the novel the narrator hides behind his sources, manipulating the narrative material in a deliberate way, but the attitude of the narrator is far from traditional as he departs from historical veracity and incorporates many imaginary elements, creating a game of identities and a series of private jokes. Thus Dr. Salmerón in his rejoinder to Dr. Darbishire's article mentions contemporary writers such as Alfredo Bryce Echenique, Antonio Skármeta, and Carlos Monsiváis as medical authorities, and Omar Cabezas Lacayo, the author of *La montaña es algo más que una inmensa estepa verde* (1982; translated as *Fire from the Mountain: The Making of a Sandinista,* 1985), turns out to be the keeper of the cemetery. Thanks to these games the novel, which otherwise would be boring and excessively long, becomes more readable. This change in the position of the narrator is best seen in the way he enters the story to become another character of the plot, talking to Judge Fiallos and Captain Prío, whose conversation the narrator records and later transcribes into the novel. Toward the end the text starts to lose its documentary tone and suffers from accidents of memory and recollection. It becomes more humanized, opening new avenues of interpretation and meaning. *Castigo divino* is one of the most ambitious novels written by a Nicaraguan. Ramírez managed to write a monumental work of fiction while serving as vice-president of Nicaragua.

His next book, *La marca del Zorro* (The Mark of Zorro, 1989), is the testimonial narrative of Francisco Rivera Quintero, who told his story to Ramírez in a sixteen-hour videotaped interview. Although Ramírez thinks that the *testimonio* "es un género que tiene una vida efímera" (is a genre with an ephemeral life), according to an interview with Ed Hood, he acknowledges in the prologue the importance of Rivera Quintero's account for the history of the revolutionary movement as well as for the exceptional nature of the story. Including many collaborators in different capacities, the book is a collective enterprise. One of the several *testimonios* given by members of the FSLN, *La marca del Zorro* is a voluminous, informative text illustrating the long and bloody road to overthrow the Somoza regime.

In the 1990 elections Ramírez and Ortega ran again as candidates for the Sandinista party for the presidency and vice-presidency of Nicaragua. In the most honest and supervised elections in the history of Nicaragua, they lost to the Unión Nicaragüense Opositora (UNO), headed by Violeta Chamorro. Appointed to the National Assembly, the unicameral congress of the country, Ramírez acted as minority leader heading the Sandinista side. He also was appointed to the National Directorate of FSLN in the restructuring that followed the electoral defeat, the first civilian appointed to the military leadership of the FSLN. From his position in the National Assembly Ramírez with his group has boycotted the agenda of the legislative branch of government, which is trying to reverse the appropriation of hundreds of parcels of land and pieces of real estate by Sandinista leaders in the last three months of their administration. In August 1992, for example, the assembly came to a standstill when the minority group simply stopped attending the work sessions and the assembly could not legislate for lack of a quorum. In November 1992 the Supreme Court ruled the move of the president of the National Assembly to elect a new secretary and resume business unconstitutional, and on 29 December 1993 President Violeta Chamorro – who has apparently rejected the coalition originally supporting her and has been governing with the Sandinistas – discharged by decree the leadership of the assembly and called for a new election. Nicaragua seems once again to be on the brink of civil war.

Amid this political upheaval Ramírez continues his work as a writer. In 1992 he published his latest collection of short stories, *Clave de sol* (Key of G), nine stories whose quality and literary value reaffirm his position as Nicaragua's best fiction writer. The book is conceived as an homage to the many musicians in his family, thus the title. "Juego perfecto" (Perfect Game) and "Tardes de sol"

(Sunny Afternoons) deal with baseball, one of the author's passions and Nicaragua's national sport. "Juego perfecto" narrates the pride of a father whose son is pitching a perfect game; "Tardes de sol" deals with a famous Cuban pitcher, Silverio Pérez, and his secret love affair with Michi, the daughter of the team's president, Chelú. The narrator of the story is Carmelita, a mature woman who is a bar owner and Chelú's lover. The protagonist is Silverio Pérez, the illegitimate son of the original baseball player, who is about to pitch his first game for Granada's baseball team. Both of these stories capitalize on Nicaragua's passion for baseball, but they manage to go beyond the limitations of the game and deal with matters of pride and human behavior.

"Volver" (To Return) is the story of a man who returns to his hometown of Masatepe (Ramírez's hometown) after many years away. The protagonist returns on 5 August 1942, Ramírez's birthday. He walks through the desolate streets and visits his old house, lost by his father at the dice table. Nothing really happens in this story; it is the reminiscence of the man — sitting in the living room of his former house, now turned into a brothel — of the time when his father came home and told them that he had lost the house, took his gun, went into the bathroom, and killed himself.

Better in the composition of its plot is "Heiliger Nikolaus" (Saint Nikolaus), set in 1984 in Managua, where a Venezuelan from Maracaibo who has been living in Berlin for many years gets a Christmas job as Santa Claus. He goes to a house and does his job, and when he is almost ready to go the lady of the house, Frau Schleting, shows up in the living room drinking and dancing. After many glasses of champagne they are both dancing when Herr Schleting, armed with his shotgun, starts firing indiscriminately. The Latin Santa is of course the one who pays for the scandal.

"Ilusión perdida" (Lost Hope) most closely deals with music. It is the story of Lisandro Ramírez, who married Migdalia Laguna and had fourteen sons but at the same time had innumerable affairs and composed one song for each of his occasional girlfriends. Migdalia comes out a winner in this story, although it is typical of Nicaraguan machismo and gender differences in which the male is expected to act as a Don Juan while his wife suffers in silence, faithful and devoted.

A humorous, entertaining story is "La mucura que está en el suelo" (The Pitcher that's on the Floor). It combines music, dancing, the university years of struggle against the regime, and love but is

also a story about growing up and settling down within the establishment, evidenced by the two young revolutionaries working for the regime at the end of the story. More interesting are the point of view and the manner in which the story is told than the story itself.

"Pero no lloraré" (But I Will Not Cry), dated January 1991, is the story of a young schoolteacher who sees and loves two men on their way to war and then sees them coming back in plastic bags. It is not the fact in itself that makes the tragedy but rather it is the second time that it happens to her, in exactly the same manner. As is the case with other Ramírez stories, repetition and doubling are at the center of the plot.

"Kalimán el Magnífico y la pérfida Mesalina" (The Wonderful Kalimán and the Treacherous Mesalina) is the story of a young man who hears voices telling him who is cheating on whom and whose love is being betrayed, but what the voices fail to tell him is the news of his own deception. The last story, "La suerte es como el viento" (Luck Is Like the Wind), dated May 1992, is about the newly organized scratch lottery popularly called *la raspadita*. In this story Ramírez explores the dark sides of ambition and greed. Although none of the pieces in *Clave de sol* are truly exceptional, they all have unquestionable literary value. With this collection Ramírez reaffirms his place as the most talented writer of fiction in Nicaragua.

Sergio Ramírez continues to live in Managua. A poor man in 1979, when he first took office, he is wealthy today, the owner of houses, real estate, land, and bank accounts. He has managed, however, to maintain a separation between his role as politician and political writer and his role as an author of fiction. Although the subject matter of his novels and short stories almost always deals with political issues, he is careful not to use his work for political speeches and propaganda. As he said to Jorge Ruffinelli and Wilfrido H. Corral in an interview:

> Tratar de que la creación literaria no se vea afectada por prejuicios políticos o por la necesidad que yo podría tener de plasmar en mi obra literaria un discurso político que le sume adeptos a la causa revolucionaria. En este sentido yo he tratado de hacer como si no hubiera estado en el gobierno o no hubiera estado en la política, para poder crear una obra literaria que tenga calidad profesional y que brinde también por sí misma nuevas rupturas, nuevas perspectivas hacia el futuro.
>
> (I endeavor not to let my literary creation be affected by political judgments or by the need that I might have to

inscribe in my literary work a political discourse aimed at bringing supporters to the revolutionary cause. In this sense I have tried to think as if I had never been in government or in politics in order to create a literary work of professional quality, so that it will by itself bring forth new breakthroughs, new perspectives for the future.)

This attitude is a rare quality for a man who has been an instrumental part of one of the most controversial regimes in the history of Nicaragua, but it is a quality that has gained him an outstanding position in Nicaraguan literary history and an important place in Latin-American literature as well.

## Interviews:

Margaret Randall, *Risking a Somersault in the Air: Conversations with Nicaraguan Writers* (San Francisco: Solidarity, 1984), pp. 21–40;

Steven White, *Culture and Politics: Testimonies of Poets and Writers* (New York: Lumen Press, 1986), pp. 75–84;

William Frank Gentile, "An Interview with Sergio Ramírez Mercado," in his *Nicaragua* (New York: Norton, 1989), pp. 123–131;

Jorge Ruffinelli and Wilfrido H. Corral, "Un diálogo con Sergio Ramírez Mercado: Política y literatura en una época de cambios," *Nuevo Texto Crítico,* 4, no. 8 (1991): 3–13;

Ed Hood, "Entrevista con Sergio Ramírez," *Revista de Estudios Colombianos y Latinoamericanos* (1993).

## References:

Nydia Palacios, "La técnica narrativa en Sergio Ramírez," Ph.D. dissertation, Universidad Nacional Autónoma de Nicaragua, 1971;

Claudia Schaefer, "La recuperación del realismo: *¿Te dió miedo la sangre?,*" *Texto Crítico,* 13, nos. 36–37 (1987): 145–152;

Nicasio Urbina, "Un hito en la narrativa nicaragüense," *Revista Nicaragüense,* 1 (April 1992): 101–105.

# Julio Ramón Ribeyro

*(31 August 1929 –   )*

Efraín S. Kristal
*University of California, Los Angeles*

BOOKS: *Los gallinazos sin plumas* (Lima: Círculo de Novelistas Peruanos, 1955);
*Cuentos de circunstancias* (Lima: Nuevos Rumbos, 1958);
*Crónica de San Gabriel* (Lima: Tawantinsuyu, 1960);
*Tres historias sublevantes* (Lima: Mejía Baca, 1964);
*Las botellas y los hombres* (Lima: Populibros Peruanos, 1964);
*Los geniecillos dominicales* (Lima: Populibros Peruanos, 1965);
*El último cliente* (Lima: Teatro Universitario de San Marcos, 1966);
*Vida y pasión de Santiago el Pajarero* (Lima: Universidad Nacional Mayor de San Marcos, 1966);
*La palabra del mudo: Cuentos 52/72,* 2 volumes (Lima: Milla Batres, 1973); enlarged as *La palabra del mudo: Cuentos 52/77,* three volumes (Lima: Milla Batres, 1977); partially translated by María Rosa Fort and Frank Graziano as *Silvio in the Rose Garden* (Gettysburg-Logbridge: Rhodes, 1989); expanded as *La palabra del mudo: Cuentos 52/92,* four volumes (Lima: Milla Batres, 1992);
*J. R. Ribeyro: Antología* (Lima: Peísa, 1973); republished as *Antología* (Lima: Inca, 1973);
*La juventud en la otra ribera* (Lima: Mosca Azul, 1973);
*Dos soledades,* by Ribeyro and Emilio Adolfo Westphalen (Lima: Instituto Nacional de Cultura, 1974);
*Cuentos,* edited by Pedro Simón (Havana: Casa de las Américas, 1975);
*Teatro* (Lima: Instituto Nacional de Cultura, 1975);
*Prosas apátridas* (Barcelona: Tusquets, 1975); revised and enlarged as *Prosas apátridas/Aumentadas,* edited by Carlos Milla Batres (Lima: Milla Batres, 1978); revised and enlarged as *Prosas apátridas (completas)* (Barcelona: Tusquets, 1986);
*La caza sutil: Ensayos y artículos de crítica literaria,* edited by Milla Batres (Lima: Milla Batres, 1975);

*Julio Ramón Ribeyro, circa 1989*

*Cambio de guardia* (Lima: Milla Batres, 1976);
*Atusparia* (Lima: Rikchay Perú, 1981);
*Sólo para fumadores* (Lima: El Barranco, 1987);
*Dichos de Luder* (Lima: Jaime Campodónico, 1989);
*Silvio en el rosedal* (Barcelona: Tusquets, 1989);
*La tentación del Fracaso I: Diario personal 1950–1960* (Lima: Jaime Campodónico, 1992);
*La tentación del Fracaso II: Diário personal 1960–1974* (Lima: Jaime Campodónico, 1993).

Julio Ramón Ribeyro, a major figure in Peruvian letters, has not yet been adequately recognized outside his native country. Ribeyro has never thought of himself as a professional writer, yet his literary career, spanning more than four decades, has been as prolific as that of any twentieth-century Peruvian with the exception of Mario Vargas Llosa. Ribeyro has published some twenty books of short novels, literary essays, and plays. He is a pioneer in the literary exploration of Peruvian urban life and the creator of a personal blend of essays, autobiography, and fiction called the *Prosas apátridas* (Prose of a Man without a Country, 1975), short texts of intimate thoughts and literary sketches.

Julio Ramón Ribeyro was born in Lima on 31 August 1929 into a middle-class family with illustrious ancestors. He spent his youth in the Peruvian capital and some of his vacations in his family's hacienda some eight hours by horse from Santiago de Chuco, the city made famous in the Spanish-speaking world by its native son César Vallejo, Peru's greatest poet. Ribeyro studied law at the Catholic University of Lima. In 1952 he traveled to Spain to study journalism. Thereafter he held odd jobs in France, Belgium, and Germany as he wrote and published his first books. In 1958 he returned to Peru, and his youthful idealism led him to the central Andes to a post as director of cultural affairs in the peripheral University of Huamanga. In 1960 he returned to France, where he married, had a son, and took up permanent residence. He survived a life-threatening disease, but this did not dissuade him from smoking. He worked as a journalist for the France-Presse agency from 1960 until 1970, when he began his diplomatic career first as cultural attaché of the Peruvian embassy (1970–1980), then as Peru's ambassador at UNESCO.

From the publication of *Los gallinazos sin plumas* (The Featherless Buzzards, 1955) to the recent "La casa es la playa" (The House Is the Beach), included in *La palabra del mudo: Cuentos 52/92* (The Word of the Mute: Stories 52/92, 1992), Ribeyro has been considered by many critics the Peruvian master of the short story. His eight books of short stories generally are not organized thematically. An exception is *Tres historias sublevantes* (Three Rebellious Stories, 1964), a collection of three stories set in the three distinct geographical regions of Peru: the coast, the Andes, and the jungle. He has practiced both the urban-realist and fantastic modes in stories set almost without exception from the 1940s to the 1970s. Most of his eighty stories occur in Peru, but Europe is the backdrop of some. His Peruvian stories show a wide thematic and geographic diversity: he has written tales about traveling circuses in the cities of the jungle, military skirmishes on the border between Peru and Ecuador, Indian oppression in the Andes, and the justice system in

military outposts. He made his first impact on the Peruvian literary scene in the 1950s with his stories about the city and in particular about the muted, tragic lives of marginalized or pauperized urban dwellers in the midst and on the fringes of self-complacent, well-to-do urban society. This aspect of his literary production is captured in the title of his most important work, *La palabra del mudo* (volumes one and two, 1973; volume three, 1977; volume four, 1992), which includes most of his published short stories. Ribeyro became the chronicler rather than the spokesman of inarticulate people whose predicaments seem more poignant because they cannot express themselves. He wrote about characters previously unrepresented in Peruvian literature: children who scavenge in garbage dumps and dwellers of the escarpments, flat roofs, shantytowns, and other makeshift communities. He has written about the frustrations of petty bureaucrats, the humiliations of servants, the violence of the Peruvian ports, and the sexual tensions and frustrations observed in insignificant jobs and low-life bars.

His contribution to the short story is not in his technical innovations, although he has experimented with literary form in stories such as "El Carrusel" (Carousel, 1977), whose title alludes to the structure of the story rather than its content. In it he creates a series of self-contained but interrelated short narratives in a circular construction in which the first narrative is the conclusion of the last one. In general, however, he has been faithful to the great nineteenth-century tradition of the narrative succinctness of writers such as Edgar Allan Poe and Anton Chekhov and to the twentieth-century Joycean or Kafkaesque short story that establishes a particular mood or atmosphere.

Ribeyro's most characteristic stories occur in a fatalistic atmosphere in which the narrator describes a world he cannot explain and the characters are invariably involved in situations that lead to calamity, failure, or incomprehension. The phrase Ribeyro uses for one of his characters, a man "excluido del festín de la vida" (excluded from life's banquet), applies to his most memorable protagonists. His characters tend to enter into frustrating situations in which things go wrong. Some become entrapped by circumstances beyond their control; others delude themselves into believing they can succeed in projects doomed to failure from the start. In Ribeyro's narrative world, self-delusion makes failure and defeat all the more pathetic. The more enlightened of Ribeyro's characters struggle toward a stoic acceptance of a destiny they do not understand. The most memorable of these, Silvio, the lonely violinist from "Silvio en el rosedal" (Silvio in the Rose Garden, 1977), comes to terms with his failed search for understanding with the realization that serenity is a viable response to incomprehension.

Ribeyro has written several short stories worthy of inclusion in anthologies of world literature. "La insignia" (The Badge, 1952) and "Los gallinazos sin plumas" are characteristic examples of his finest fiction in the fantastic and realistic modes. The protagonist of "La insignia" wears a badge he found in a waste dump. He visits a bookstore, whose owner gives him news of a man's death in a remote country. Annoyed by the bookseller's overture, he leaves the bookstore and is accosted by a passing stranger who hands him a bewildering invitation to a gathering. At the meeting he encounters people wearing badges like his own and waiting for a formal address by the president of an organization to which they all belong. He finds the lecture incomprehensible but pretends to understand it. He is invited to join the organization when he repeats the news he heard at the bookstore as though privy to its significance. Twenty years later, still oblivious to its purpose, he becomes the president of the powerful organization with members in all corners of the world. The story can be read as a critique of private organizations, a sinister parody of bureaucratic life, or a Kafkaesque parable about success. The tone of the tale is not moral – the protagonist does not live by ethical standards – yet there is an ethical dimension to this story when one wonders why the fateful badge was once discarded.

In "Los gallinazos sin plumas," one of Ribeyro's best social-realist tales, two young brothers are forced by don Santos, their disabled and cruel grandfather, to scour waste dumps in search of food for a hog intended for sale. The two boys are likened to the gallinazo, a scavenger bird found along the Peruvian coast. Alluding to Eugene O'Neill's play The Hairy Ape (1922), the story makes an allegorical comment on the animalization of the human experience in a pauperized social environment. The abusive grandfather, more concerned about the well-being of his hog than his hungry grandchildren, exhorts the boys to work even when they are ill. In an act of rage one of the boys strikes his grandfather with a rod. As the old man helplessly stumbles into the pigsty, the two brothers abandon him and face the uncertainty of a ruthless urban existence.

Ribeyro is best known for his short stories, but he is also a novelist who has explored, better than anyone else in Peruvian literature, the experience of those members of the old quasi-feudal order who lost their political power and personal influence when their old ways became archaic and obsolete. The protagonists of his first two novels, Crónica de San Gabriel (Chronicle of San Gabriel, 1960) and Los geniecillos dominicales (Geniuses of Sunday, 1965), loosely based on autobiographical experience, are young men from families whose names represent the grandeur of Peru's national past but who have lost their wealth and prestige. The first novel is the story of Lucho, a lazy, disobedient adolescent from Lima sent to San Gabriel, the family hacienda. In a healthy social and physical environment his uncle, the Andean patriarch of the family, is expected to instill in the rebellious young man a sense of discipline. Lucho's experience, however, is neither healthy nor moral. He finds himself in the midst of a strange, incestuous family beset by irreversible financial and moral troubles, and without realizing it he witnesses the dissolution of the Peruvian aristocratic order. His uncle is not inclined to discipline Lucho. A troubled man, he has to cope with his unruly, sensual daughter, the lunacy of other family members, Indian uprisings, and natural catastrophies. It is as though nature, history, and society were acting together to terminate the feudal era. When Lucho is allowed to return to Lima, he is unchanged, undaunted, and oblivious to the fact that he has witnessed the collapse of the family dynasty. The novel ends with Lucho's nostalgia for the empty beaches of the Peruvian coast and with the murmuring sounds of the waves washing ashore, an image of quiet desolation.

Los geniecillos dominicales can be read as a continuation of Crónica de San Gabriel. It is a sort of picaresque novel about the misadventures of Ludo, a young man who wallows in a world of mediocrity. Living off his family's ever-diminishing wealth and unable to hold a job, he wanders through Lima, a city whose streets, public monuments, and history bear the names and portraits of his once-important family. In twenty-four chapters Ludo's hopes are continually raised and relentlessly dashed. The novel tells of his successive mishaps in love, sex, business, and literature. In a poignant chapter Ludo represents his embarrassed branch of the family in the wedding of a distant but well-to-do cousin. At the party he quickly realizes he has been invited out of obligation: he is willfully disregarded by hosts and guests. Humiliated, he escapes to an empty sitting room, where he realizes he has been followed by an aunt who has been keeping an eye on him to protect the valuables of the house. Excluded from respectable society, Ludo associates with the lower strata of Peruvian society, a world of prosti-

Cover for Ribeyro's 1989 collection of short stories

tutes, blackmailers, and delinquents. Eventually he is unwillingly involved in a crime and is led to commit a murder.

Ribeyro's third novel, *Cambio de guardia* (A Change of Guard, 1976), more ambitious and less successful than the first two, depicts the fragmented experience of a nation about to suffer a brutal military coup d'état. The novel is constructed on two narrative levels: the first tells the story of the imminent rise to power of a military dictatorship and tries to suggest that the ominous historical event about to take place is the result of a web of human interconnections in which chance, circumstance, and petty frailties play as much of a role as the evil designs of those hungry for power. The second narrative line centers around a judge whose private life belies his public repute. He orchestrates sordid orgies and depraved erotic encounters. The two narrative lines are loosely connected, but taken together they suggest that sexual degradation thrives

in a climate of social and political corruption and that the responsibility for a deplorable political situation is not restricted to those in the highest spheres of power.

Ribeyro's novels and short stories explore a wide range of themes and settings, but they share a common skeptical tone. Ribeyro's narrators are willing to comment on the world they describe but not to explain or even attempt to understand it. His narrators are able to enter his characters in order to report their thoughts, but they will not judge those characters. Ribeyro's plots are hardly ever told directly by the narrator, who usually displaces himself with a character who in turn becomes a witness to an unfolding story in which he may or may not take part. In some of the stories, such as "Por las azoteas" (On the Rooftops, 1958), the witness, a child who meets a man living on a roof, is unaware of what he has discovered. The narrator does not provide any information about the man the child has befriended, but the reader can deduce that the story is about the dying days of a sensitive but spiritually tortured man of letters.

Ribeyro's narrators observe human beings with the same distance and aloofness with which they observe objects. In some of Ribeyro's most curious stories, including "Los jacarandás" (The Jacarandas, 1970) and "El ropero, los viejos y la muerte" (The Armoire, Old People, and Death, 1972), the protagonist can be a physical object. In "Noche cálida y sin viento" (A Balmy, Windless Night, 1968) a man walks toward a swimming pool as though entering a world of danger and erotic expectation between two human beings. The narrator's inability to understand his world is mirrored in the pathos of many of Ribeyro's characters who are unable to understand or explain their situation. In a sense the skeptical tone of the narrator is illuminated by the meekness of his displaced and disenfranchised protagonists.

Skepticism is a useful label to designate important aspects of Ribeyro's narrators, but it would be misleading to apply it straightforwardly to Ribeyro himself. In *La caza sutil* (The Subtle Hunt, 1975), a collection of literary articles, Ribeyro has called himself an optimistic skeptic, a man able to recognize problems but unable to give solutions he nonetheless hopes exist. In *Prosas apátridas,* in which Ribeyro offers a glimpse of his intimate thoughts, he expresses a nuanced view of his brand of skepticism, saying that it would be terrible if after so much reflection one were to arrive at the conclusion that history is a game without rules or a game whose rules are invented as one plays and in the end imposed by those who win.

*Prosas apátridas* includes short texts in prose combining personal thoughts, literary ideas, aphorisms, and prose poetry. These texts are called "Prose of a Man without a Country" partly because they were written when Ribeyro was in France. The book includes intriguing observations about France and the French, but it is more about his literary and intimate world during his French years than about his experience with France. In these texts Ribeyro expresses his views on art, life, and society, affirms his love of literature despite its inadequacies and affectation, and expresses his distaste for empty erudition and meaningless rhetoric. He gives his views on alcohol, sex, fatherhood, disease, and death as well as his philosophical reflections on the physical limitations of intellectual pursuits, the superiority of friendship over love, and the solitude of the writer. He expresses his perplexity at the trivial events that can change individuals and with certain reserva-

tions affirms his faith in Marxism as the best available attempt to understand human reality. Ribeyro's attitudes toward Marxism seem to go against the grain of the skepticism of his short stories and novels. This political tendency is more clearly underscored in his plays, in which situations tend to be more openly ideological and the skeptical voice of his characteristic narrators is absent.

Ribeyro began writing drama during the 1950s. His complete plays, with the exception of *Atusparia* (1981), are collected in *Teatro* (Theater, 1975). Ribeyro has written several farces about the self-delusion of hypocritical would-be writers and others about military officials reserving their allegiance for whoever gains power in order not to lose their personal privileges; he has written political plays about racism against Indians and about class struggle. For instance, in *Fin de semana* (Weekend), a play based on his short story "La piel de un indio no cuesta caro" (An Indian's Skin Is Cheap), a couple is unmoved by the death of an Indian.

Ribeyro's plays are not as rich from a literary point of view as his prose, in which he depicts a world his skeptical narrators are unable to comprehend. This aspect of his literary world reappears in *Dichos de Luder* (Luder's Sayings, 1989), a collection of short texts in which Ribeyro creates an alter ego, Luder, who makes pithy statements and engages in short dialogues. Luder is the embodiment of the ironic tone of some of the texts in *Prosas apátridas,* where bittersweet reflections about death and literature are intertwined. Not coincidentally, the name Luder is similar to Lucho and Ludo, the protagonists of Ribeyro's first two novels who themselves evoke playful or painful situations colored with irony.

Ribeyro is likely to be remembered for his masterful stories and for his fine and compelling short narrative prose. He stands in the tradition of Latin-American writers as different as Gabriel García Márquez and Octavio Paz, who depict solitude as they hope to overcome it. In his literary world, fraught with suffering, frustration, and incomprehension, a secret desire for human solidarity is invariably though silently affirmed.

### Bibliography:

Fernando Vidal, "Apuntes para una bibliografía de Julio Ramón Ribeyro," in Ribeyro's *La caza sutil* (Lima: Milla Batres, 1975), pp. 157–168.

### References:

Earl M. Aldrich, "Recent Peruvian Fiction: Vargas Llosa, Ribeyro, and Arguedas," *Research Studies,* 35 (1968): 227–283;

Mario Castro Arenas, *De Palma a Vallejo* (Lima: Populibros Peruanos, n.d.), pp. 98–101;

Sara Castro Klarén, "El dictador en el paraíso: Ribeyro, Thorndike y Adolph," *Hispamérica,* 7, no. 21 (1978): 21–36;

Antonio Cornejo Polar, "Los geniecillos dominicales: Sus fortunas y adversidades," in his *La novela peruana: Siete estudios* (Lima: Horizonte, 1977), pp. 145–158;

Graciela Coulson, "Los cuentos de Ribeyro: Primer encuentro," *Cuadernos Americanos,* 195 (July-August 1974): 220–226;

Washington Delgado, "Fantasía y realidad en la obra de Ribeyro," prologue to Ribeyro's *La palabra del mudo,* volume 1 (Lima: Milla Batres, 1973), pp. xii–xvi;

Alberto Escobar, *Patio de letras* (Lima: Caballo de Troya, 1965);

Dick C. Gerdes, "Julio Ramón Ribeyro: Un análisis de sus cuentos," *Kentucky Romance Quarterly,* 26, no. 1 (1979): 51–65;

Efraín Kristal, "El narrador en la obra de Julio Ramón Ribeyro," *Revista de Crítica Literaria Latinoamericana,* 10 (1984): 155–169;

Alejandro Losada, "Julio Ramón Ribeyro: La creación como existencia marginal y el subjetivismo negativo," in his *Creación y praxis: La producción literaria como praxis social en hispanoamérica y el Perú* (Lima: Universidad Nacional Mayor de San Marcos, 1976), pp. 82–94;

Wolfgang Luchting, *Julio Ramón Ribeyro y sus dobles* (Lima: Instituto Nacional de Cultura, 1971);

Abelardo Oquendo, "Alrededor de Ribeyro," prologue to Ribeyro's *Prosas apátridas/Aumentadas* (Lima: Milla Batres, 1978), pp. xix–xx;

Julio Ortega, "Julio Ramón Ribeyro: La naturaleza del código," in his *Crítica de la identidad: La pregunta por el Perú en su literatura* (Mexico City: Fondo de Cultura Económica, 1988), pp. 181–202;

José Miguel Oviedo, "Ribeyro, o el escepticismo como una de las Bellas Artes," prologue to Ribeyro's *Prosas apátridas* (Barcelona: Tusquets, 1975), pp. 7–25;

Mario Vargas Llosa, "Ribeyro y las sirenas," in his *Contra viento y marea, III (1964–1988)* (Barcelona: Seix Barral, 1990), pp. 531–535;

Fernando Vidal, "Ribeyro y los espejos repetidos," *Revista de Crítica Literaria Latinoamericana,* 1 (1975): 73–88.

# Edgardo Rodríguez Juliá

(9 October 1946 –   )

Rubén Ríos Avila
*University of Puerto Rico*

Translated by Gabriela Alfaraz and Renée Dussan

BOOKS: *La renuncia del héroe Baltasar: Conferencias pronunciadas por Alejandro Cadalso en el Ateneo Puertorriqueño, del 4 al 10 de enero de 1938* (San Juan: Antillana, 1974);

*Las tribulaciones de Jonás* (Río Piedras, P.R.: Huracán, 1981);

*El entierro de Cortijo* (Río Piedras, P.R.: Huracán, 1983);

*La noche oscura del niño Avilés* (Río Piedras, P.R.: Huracán, 1984);

*Campeche, o, Los diablejos de la melancolía* (San Juan: Instituto de Cultura Puertorriqueña, 1986);

*Una noche con Iris Chacón* (San Juan: Antillana, 1986);

*Maldonado, Adál Alberto: Galería Luigi Marrozzini presenta Mango mambo* (San Juan: Ilustres Estudios, 1987);

*El cruce de la bahía de Guánica* (Río Piedras, P.R.: Cultural, 1989);

*Puertorriqueños: Album de la sagrada familia puertorriqueña a partir de 1898* (Madrid: Playor, 1989).

SELECTED PERIODICAL PUBLICATION – UNCOLLECTED: "Tradición y utopía en el barroco caribeño," *Extramares: International Magazine of Arts and Letters,* 1, no. 1 (1989): 3.

*Edgardo Rodríguez Juliá, circa 1991*

Edgardo Rodríguez Juliá is one of the most prolific and ambitious Caribbean writers of recent times. Since 1974, when *La renuncia del héroe Baltasar* (The Renunciation of the Hero Baltasar) appeared, he has published eight books: two novels on the eighteenth century, one of them ominously long since it presents itself as the first installment of a still-unfinished trilogy; four collections of short works chronicling modern Puerto Rico from the beginning of the Muñoz era to the Cerro Maravilla murders; a thorough critical study of José Campeche, the first Puerto Rican painter of the colonial era; and *Puertorriqueños: Album de la sagrada familia* *puertorriqueña a partir de 1898* (Puerto Ricans: An Album of the Sacred Puerto Rican Family Since 1898, 1989), a history of the development of the island's petite bourgeoisie based on the snapshots from a photograph album. In addition, Rodríguez Juliá's acute and iconoclastic chronicles appear regularly in the Sunday magazines of the local press, and his more academic essays appear in several university journals in Puerto Rico and abroad. His work follows a narrative plan in which the novels are intimately linked to historical or sociological chronicles to produce a textuality with roots in the traditional genre of the chronicles of conquest and colonization.

Rodríguez Juliá's capacity for production, joined with his indisputable talent for astutely delving into the ways of things Puerto Rican, has lent him an aura of ubiquity that for some makes him an irreverent enfant terrible, while for others he is the conscience of contemporary Puerto Rico, a country concerned with cultural, ethnological, and political identity. What may surprise some readers about Rodríguez Juliá is his citing of so many diverse authorities when supporting his outpourings and investigations. While in his novels he half-tenderly, half-parodically rewrites historical chronicles in order to construct bold, brilliant attempts to portray the beginnings of Puerto Rican culture in the eighteenth century, his modern chronicles take his acute observations on the behavior of the masses in various public rituals — from the official burials of national heroes to the popular public funerals of musicians to religious meetings and cabaret shows — and employ them to capture the multiplicity of codes, the babble of tongues that comprise the mosaic of contemporary Puerto Rico. He has successively taken on the guises of ethnologist, historian, chronicler, literary critic, art critic, photographer, theorist and critic, sports commentator, would-be pornographer, humorist, spiritual advisor, and many others, the possible exception being the mask of political scientist. To him nothing Puerto Rican is foreign, and almost all investigative strategies are familiar to him.

There have been few Puerto Rican writers more ambitious in their literary scope. The only other contemporary writer comparable to Rodríguez Juliá in terms of grandness of ambition is Luis Rafael Sánchez, whose desire to produce writing of jewellike perfection has limited his production. Rodríguez Juliá exhibits an enthusiastic virtuosity that shows no fear of leaving a somewhat untidy muddle in one or another of his texts or of producing an almost-uncontrolled baroque excess, as in the case of *La noche oscura del niño Avilés* (The Dark Night of the Boy Avilés, 1984).

If Puerto Rico finds its great ventriloquist in Sánchez, an author capable of reproducing and mimicking the entire range of Puerto Rican accents, it finds in Rodríguez Juliá the author of the island's most severe indictment, as if his research condemned him to the repeated discovery of renunciations and abdications of responsibility, failures, flaws and weaknesses, duplicities, and pieces of un-

finished business that he finds in all of Puerto Rican history. From René Marqués, the most prominent Puerto Rican writer of the 1950s and 1960s, Rodríguez Juliá inherited an ethical imperative, an awareness of writing as the interpretation of a national soul. In Rodríguez Juliá's texts, the author seems to hold tight to a critical distance that marks the limits of his self-depiction.

The sort of text Rodríguez Juliá writes tends toward openness but remains nostalgic for a center that would give it a finished texture and allow it to stand for that sort of traditional work referring to a perceiving subject creating that work. All of his texts are presented as investigations into an enigma, whether the enigma be Baltasar, the Niño Avilés, Cortijo, Muñoz Marín, Iris Chacón, or the utopian New Venice, but in all of these cases the spotlight is also turned on the portrayer of the enigma, perhaps as the true dark center of the narration.

At the beginning of *La renuncia del héroe Baltasar* Prof. Alejandro Cadalso, principal narrator of the novel, says that Baltasar Montáñez is an enigma that crosses history like a dark cloud and has much to say, from the distance of the centuries, about the human condition. Few words recur more often in these texts than enigma, dark, darkness, and dark night. The predominant gesture of the author is pulling back the curtain, illuminating the dark spaces of what the text calls, half-parodically and half-seriously, "the human condition." In *La renuncia del héroe Baltasar* the figure unveiled is that of an imaginary black man who at the end of the eighteenth century manages to become secretary of state when he marries the white daughter of the former secretary. The Machiavellian bishop Larra manages to bring this situation about through a chain of evil schemes so that he can keep a damper on the revolt he sees coming from the majority black population of the colony. Baltasar is a fiction invented by the state to maintain the balance of power, and the novel is the story of his victimization, his resentment, and his eventual madness.

The enigma of Baltasar springs from his mysterious renunciation of power. First he refuses to be a hero of the black resistance, a role to which he seemed destined as the son of a rebellious runaway slave. Then he resigns from his post in the government after the bishop takes it upon himself to provide the circumstances under which Baltasar's position might have been made even more powerful. In his madness Baltasar devotes himself entirely to the digging of an enormous dry moat meant to protect the fortifications of San Juan, which serves as a hallucinatory utopian space. Poisoned by the rejection of everyone in his life and in his would-be utopia by their seeing him as an imposter and rejected even by his wife, who refuses to go to bed with a black man, he dedicates himself to choreographing the most licentious and refined orgies imaginable. These orgies are in turn drawn by the leprous architect of the court, who illustrates them as meticulously as the prints in the books of the Marquis de Sade.

Even in this first novel one finds the coordinates of the ruling structure of all Rodríguez Juliá's writing. The fundamental motif by which the author attempts to posit Puerto Rico as a cultural entity as early as the eighteenth century, and above all as a subject of literature, is the motif of illegitimacy. Baltasar is a hypocrite to the blacks and to the state, a man condemned to duplicity. He cannot aspire to power because power in Rodríguez Juliá's works emanates from legitimacy, purity, or nature, and Baltasar is hybrid and equivocal, a perversely urban creature. Therefore this meticulous construct, this fictitious hero, this playfully parodic way of imitating the solemn rhetoric of eighteenth-century oratory will not work as the basis for a myth. The construction of the myth is undermined from the beginning by the impotence of its protagonist. If Rodríguez Juliá's journey to the eighteenth century has as its ethical mission the search for a governing principle, the depiction produced by his interweaving of historical horizons serves only to create a monster. Baltasar is a creature of both one species and another, the grotesque embodiment of two opposed and irreconcilable wills, but in this case the monster is not turned into a symbol of dual human nature but rather persists as a monster.

An underling who comes to power and who manages neither to vindicate his social class nor to rise above it, nor to put it out of his mind and govern without guilt, has as the only possible solution to his dilemma the renunciation of power. Nevertheless, Baltasar does not resign his post in order to return to the role of underling but rather to occupy another space, the space of pure imagination alien to reason — the space of madness. The Garden of Misfortunes he builds works as an emblem of the products of the imagination. Likewise, the orgies illustrated by the leprous architect are an attempt to give aesthetic authority to raving desires, as though pure sex were the consolation of the defeated or resentful. It is within that space of wild desire that the writing of this novel transpires, as though the impossibility of resolving itself into a paradigm of power and producing a true hero left the road of perversion as the only possible way out. Baltasar's ravings are an emblem of the realm of art. For the figure of the author as for

Baltasar, entering the space of imagination implies an abdication of power, a renunciation of the possibility of channeling language into the structures of the institutionalized order of politics.

The motif that serves as the ground of this text is not necessarily found in the journey to the eighteenth century or in the identification of the national ethos. It is found rather in the identification of writing and power, and in Latin America the institution of literature has never been conceived of in any other way. A region whose writers have regularly occupied ministerial and diplomatic posts, whose educated men and women are the designers of state educational and cultural policy or who build a model nation that may start a republic on the road to its great destiny, a region in which writers can be presidents, is a region where writing also has been understood as one way of rising to power.

Baltasar has neither the antagonistic force nor the seductive charm that might have allowed him to become an authorial center. Nor is this the case in other authorial depictions, either in *La noche oscura del niño Avilés* or in the modern chronicles. In Rodríguez Juliá's work the characters are always in search of an author — or rather, all the characters are possible authors, and the pivot of their deauthorization is the absence of a tradition, even if the text intended only (or above all) to replace it. Tradition in Rodríguez Juliá is, to use his own expression in "Tradición y utopía en el barroco caribeño" (Tradition and Utopia in the Caribbean Baroque, 1989), a shadow-filled ravine.

In the two funeral chronicles of the Muñoz era, *Las tribulaciones de Jonás* (The Tribulations of Jonás, 1981) and *El entierro de Cortijo* (Cortijo's Burial, 1983), it is as if the text can only narrate Luis Muñoz Marín's absence and his 1980 death. Muñoz Marín is the would-be author condemned to the melancholy contemplation of his own failure. In the politician Rodríguez Juliá finds the alter ego of his writing.

*Las tribulaciones de Jonás* is the chronicle of the Muñoz of the people while *El entierro de Cortijo* is the chronicle of the people of Muñoz. The narrator always appears in these chronicles as an alternate presence — sometimes an observer, sometimes a collaborator, and other times an antagonist to the multitude or to its official representative, Muñoz Marín. In *Las tribulaciones de Jonás* the narrator is Muñoz's partly baffled, partly captive, partly repelled spectator, oscillating between the degraded reflection of the writer as an outcast of power and the writer as indignant, resentful of the little power the state confers upon its keepers and ministers. In *El entierro de*

*Cover of the 1991 edition of Rodríguez Juliá's 1983 novel, which is set in a Puerto Rican housing project*

*Cortijo* the author is the narrator torn between tenderness and delirium standing outraged in the Luis Llorens Torres public-housing project, Muñoz's dystopia, where the name of a modernist dandy poet ironically symbolizes the limited ability of literature to portray the grotesque space of the people. The public-housing project, where a wake is held over Cortijo, the priest of the black and mulatto proletariat, is the unreadable dystopian space that continues to resist codification.

In *La noche oscura del niño Avilés* there is a systematic attempt to found a utopia of Puerto Rican descent. New Venice would be that libertarian, utopian city in which a mythical nation of runaway slaves is founded but which, according to the narrator, has disappeared from the collective memory of the community. The novel is the attempt to recover

that lost memory through the invocation of a transcendental, mythic, and ritual memory able to lead the people back into contact with their lost origins. Nevertheless, the major obstacle the reader encounters at the moment of experiencing this mythical memory is a strategy of inexorable digression imposed on the reading process by a chain of authorial figures. The narrator contends with the chronicles of Gracián, secretary to the repressive Bishop Trespalacios, with the chronicles of Julián Flores, a Creole sympathizer of the black cause who signed his testimonies "The Renegade," and with a series of petty chroniclers who subject events to repeated mediations. There are also apocryphal manuscripts supposedly written by The Renegade and a diary purportedly written by Bishop Trespalacios, and a narrative reader named Alejandro Juliá Marín keeps breaking in to distract the reader with alternate series of footnotes that reinterpret, contradict, or detail the crucial events of the narrative even as they half-parodically, half-sublimely echo the poetic prose of the novel. *La noche oscura del niño Avilés* moves lumberingly, the victim of a suffocating labyrinth of baroque ellipses. Rodríquez Juliá's baroque style seems unable to free itself sufficiently from parody and the awareness of its own falsification.

The grandest moment in the novel occurs when The Renegade, sent as an envoy, descends into the kingdom of the rebel leader Mitume and finds an ineffable paradise of the flesh. This episode achieves an intermittent brilliancy, but it is always too close to the grotesque to produce a mythic epiphany. Even the climax of the novel, the rescue of Niño Avilés (a symbol of liberation from slavery) and the construction of a diabolic legend making him out to be possessed so as to turn the people away from his liberating magnetism, is virtually thrown away at the beginning of the novel, as if in assembling the narrative structure the possibility of suspense or dramatic intensification were not considered, even though these might be perfectly viable rhetorical means toward epiphany. One must run a difficult course of hurdles that interfere with the progression of the narrative, as if some obsessed reader inside it were constantly stopping to ask questions.

The name heard most often for this privileged reader is Alejandro Juliá Marín, who previously appeared in *La renuncia del héroe Baltasar,* where Prof. Alejandro Cadalso, 1930s academic and the principal historian of Baltasar Montáñez, used him as a literary witness of the period by quoting sections from his plays. Alejandro Juliá Marín serves as an analogy to the process of producing and receiving the tale, the telling of the tale, even while it is occurring. His first name, which he shares with Cadalso, alludes to Alejandro Tapia y Rivera, locating the authorial center in colonial times as a means of claiming authority over the period comprised within the myth. The last names, Juliá Marín, on the other hand, allude to Rodríguez Juliá's great uncle Ramón Juliá Marín, author of two novels, *Tierra adentro* (Interior Land, 1911) and *La gleba* (The Clod, 1912), both of which angrily chronicle the agrarian bourgeoisie's displacement after the U.S. invasion of Puerto Rico. Thus in this compound name is a juxtaposition of historical moments crucial to the development of Puerto Rican culture: the consolidation of colonial society in the nineteenth century and the rupture caused by the invasion. Cadalso is another authorial alter ego, representing the 1930s generation, the first generation of Puerto Rican intellectuals to come of age under U.S. domination and the generation whose essays formed the foundation for national identity. Through these compound formulas, in which literary and family lineages are merged, the author creates an image of the stock to which he belongs from the point of view from which he wishes his texts to be read. One of the most captivating moments in *La noche oscura del niño Avilés* is the episode of the great ear, that strange room in the form of a spiral that the evil Bishop Larra has had built to house Niño Avilés, based on the true story of a deformed child the people transform into their most powerful symbol.

In the interior of the huge ear lies a deformed and helpless creature, Niño Avilés, who, more than a figure of the people, serves in the novel as a ruse seized upon by authority in order to fabricate an image. The bishop manages to amplify the sound of the child's crying so greatly that the room becomes an ominous echo chamber, the crying acquires mythic proportions, and rumor spreads that Niño Avilés is possessed. That manipulation of sound, of the voice – in this case of the innocent crying of a child who symbolizes the people – acquires the force of a symbol for all of Rodríguez Juliá's fiction, for the novels and chronicles serve as a kind of hyperbolic ear always ready to amplify not only voices but the registers of speech itself. Hyperbole, which usually borders on parody, caricature, or the grotesque, strips populist rhetoric of all mythicizing possibility. The rhetoric builds its authority on amplification and distortion; the rituals by which a people establishes the image of its identity are always subjected to that demythicizing process, as if as soon as they are portrayed they are forever invalidated as possible instruments of the revelation of the national ethos.

In *Campeche, o, Los diablejos de la melancolía* (Campeche, or The Devils of Melancholy, 1986) the mulatto painter José Campeche of the colonial era is presented as a prefiguration of the Puerto Rican author whom Rodríguez Juliá incarnates. The future that Campeche anticipates is experienced from the present tense of the narrative as the nostalgia for a future into which the past has not been able to lead. Ironically, in the figure of Campeche, Rodríguez Juliá portrays the foretelling of his own fate in the past. The two men mirror each other, there is an unresolved doubleness, and they are seen to be condemned to duplicity, to illegitimacy. Campeche's melancholy, which Rodríguez Juliá perceptively discerns in the equivocal expression of the portrait of Governor Ustáriz and in the pained countenance of his portrait of Niño Avilés, results from the fact that utopia and reality, art and life, are out of phase, as may be seen by the presence in the paintings of emblems employed by the painter to invoke power versus the absence of the painter's mulatto world and its people from those paintings. One might say that Rodríguez Juliá writes in order to fill these voids in Campeche's work, that Rodríguez Juliá's work attempts to restore the symmetry between people and utopia, between the state and the country. The secret of the balance lies in the possibility of shaping a text that manages to identify with the lower ranks of the hierarchy without that text thereby abandoning its connection to power. But in order to do this, a text that is simultaneously authentic and ceremonial, private and official, individual and gestural, utopian and populist, would have to be produced. It is out of that impossibility that the white space that defines the authorial space in all of these texts arises.

In these texts the writer constantly wishes to purify his pose of all the noise and commotion of the amorphous, contradictory Puerto Rican collectivity, forever halfway between tenderness and delirium. In the essay *Una noche con Iris Chacón* (A Night with Iris Chacón, 1986) he describes the complexities of that pose. He wishes to celebrate the people's cerebration yet found his own, without distractions. In the masses the equation that restores his celebrated cerebration to him is confirmed, strictly erotic, an ancient orgiastic ritual. The imminent appearance of the portentous Iris Chacón on the scene is analogous to the descent into Mitume's dark kingdom or the encounter with the boy monster. For in Rodríguez Juliá's works identification with the people is always achieved through unbridled desire.

Like Baltasar, the narrator in *Una noche con Iris Chacón* can only understand intimate commerce with the masses through perversion. The last collection of chronicles, *El cruce de la bahía de Guánica* (The Crossing of the Guánica Bay, 1989), is a reiteration of this principle. With the lecherous eyes of an incurable sensualist who sees in the people only the object of his unbridled desire, a narrator watches the crowds that go to the beach to swim. The masses in *Una noche con Iris Chacón* are always a variant of the mob. Rodríguez Juliá's striking of this pose is constantly threatened by the delirious multitude. One way of describing this dilemma is to say that Rodríguez Juliá is a postmodern author possessed by a premodern nostalgia. His handling of writing as textuality, opening and postponing as distinct from meaning, leads him to view culture in a way that poststructuralist critics have described as the wisdom (or nonwisdom) of the ages. However, what could be called Rodríguez Juliá's Caribbean disposition places him within a world prior to the dissemination of meaning and hungry for a center, governed by a model of the Latin-American author as the man of letters whose true function is to educate the people.

The masses cannot be drawn save by their excesses or their deformities, and the possible author dejectedly withdraws, disassociated from his audience and lost in his own lucubrations as on that night with Iris Chacón when he decided that the celebration of his own cerebration was preferable to the celebration of the performance. The narrator retreats from his fallen hero or from his unsatisfying masses in order to continue seeing himself in them from a distance. Every text restores to a writer his own unrecognized and unfamiliar countenance, as if he were some other, and in Rodríguez Juliá that other is the native land that refuses to be brought together into one manageable model but that imposes itself on him as his most faithful self-portrait. The would-be author of his people writes so as to let himself be written by them and to shrug and say, like Gustave Flaubert said of his Madame Bovary, "Puerto Rico, c'est moi" (I am Puerto Rico).

**References:**

Antonio Benitez Rojo, *La isla que se repite: El Caribe y la postmodernidad* (Hanover, N.H.: Ediciones del Norte, 1989);

Roberto González Echevarría, *The Voice of the Masters: Writing and Authority in Modern Latin American Literature* (Austin: University of Texas Press, 1985);

Rubén Ríos Avila, "El apetito y el asco," *Puerto Rico Ilustrado,* supplement of *El Mundo,* 12 November 1989, pp. 20–23.

# Ernesto Sábato

*(24 June 1911 – )*

Angela B. Dellepiane
*City University of New York*

BOOKS: *Tres glosas* (La Plata, Argentina: Teseo, 1942);

*Uno y el universo* (Buenos Aires: Sudamericana, 1945);

*Elementos de física,* with Alberto P. Maiztegui (Buenos Aires: Espasa-Calpe, 1946);

*El túnel* (Buenos Aires: Sur, 1948; revised edition, Buenos Aires: Universitaria, 1966); revised definitive editon (Barcelona: Seix Barral, 1991); translated by Harriet de Onís as *The Outsider* (New York: Knopf, 1950); translated by Margaret Sayers Peden as *The Tunnel* (New York: Ballantine, 1988);

*Hombres y engranajes: Reflexiones sobre el dinero, la razón y el derrumbe de nuestro tiempo* (Buenos Aires: Emecé, 1951);

*Heterodoxia* (Buenos Aires: Emecé, 1953);

*El otro rostro del peronismo: Carta abierta a Mario Amadeo* (Buenos Aires: López, 1956);

*El caso Sábato: Torturas y libertad de prensa – Carta abierta al General Aramburu* (Buenos Aires, 1956);

*Sobre héroes y tumbas* (Buenos Aires: Fabril, 1961); revised definitive edition (Barcelona: Seix Barral, 1991); part 3 translated by Stuart M. Gross as "Report on the Blind," *TriQuarterly,* 13–14 (Fall-Winter 1968–1969): 95–105; translated by Helen R. Lane as *On Heroes and Tombs* (Boston: Godine, 1981);

*El escritor y sus fantasmas* (Buenos Aires: Aguilar, 1963);

*Tango: Discusión y clave* (Buenos Aires: Losada, 1963);

*Tango, canción de Buenos Aires* (Buenos Aires: Centro Arte, 1964);

*Obras de ficción* (Buenos Aires: Losada, 1966);

*Que es el existencialismo: Conferencia pronunciada en la Escuela No. 38, Camillo y Adriano Olivetti Merlo* (Buenos Aires: Olivetti, 1967);

*Informe sobre ciegos* (Buenos Aires: Centro Editor de América Latina, 1968);

*Tres aproximaciones a la literatura de nuestro tiempo: Robbe-Grillet, Borges, Sartre* (Santiago: Universitaria, 1968);

*La convulsión política y social de nuestro tiempo* (Buenos Aires: Edicom, 1969);

*Itinerario* (Buenos Aires: Sur, 1969);

*Obras: Ensayos* (Buenos Aires: Losada, 1970);

*Ernesto Sábato: Claves políticas* (Buenos Aires: Rodolfo Alonso, 1971);

*La cultura en la encrucijada nacional* (Buenos Aires: Crisis, 1973);

*Eduardo Falú,* with León Benarós (Madrid: Júcar, 1974);

*Abaddón, el exterminador* (Buenos Aires: Sudamericana, 1974); revised definitive edition (Barcelona: Seix Barral, 1991); translated by Andrew Hurley as *The Angel of Darkness* (New York: Ballantine, 1991);

*Páginas vivas,* edited by María Isabel Murtagh (Buenos Aires: Kapelusz, 1974);

*Antología,* edited by Z. Nelly Martínez (Buenos Aires: Librería del Colegio, 1975);

*Diálogos,* with Jorge Luis Borges (Buenos Aires: Emecé, 1976);

*Apologías y rechazos* (Barcelona: Seix Barral, 1979);

*Cuatro hombres del pueblo,* with Antonio Berni (Buenos Aires: La Ciudad, 1979);

*Un dios desconocido: Romance de la muerte de Juan Lavalle (de "Sobre héroes y tumbas")* (Buenos Aires: Dabini, 1980);

*La robotización del hombre y otras páginas de ficción y reflexión* (Buenos Aires: Centro Editorial de América Latina, 1981);

*Narrativa completa* (Barcelona: Seix Barral, 1982);

*Páginas de Ernesto Sábato* (Buenos Aires: Celtia, 1983);

*The Writer in the Catastrophe of Our Time* (Tulsa, Okla.: Council Oak Books/Hecate/University of Tulsa, 1990).

OTHER: Kurt Lipfert, *La televisión: Una breve exposición del estado actual de la técnica de la televisión,* translated by Margarita H. de Bose, revised by

*Ernesto Sábato (photograph by Frederick L. Dodnick)*

Sábato (Buenos Aires & Mexico City: Espasa-Calpe, 1940);

Bertrand Russell, *El A.B.C. de la relatividad,* translated by Sábato (Buenos Aires: Imán, 1943);

*Mitomagia: Los temas del misterio,* edited by Sábato (Buenos Aires: Latinoamericanas, 1969);

*Testimonios: Chile, septiembre, 1973,* introduction by Sábato (Buenos Aires: Crisis, 1974);

*Viaje a los mundos imaginarios,* edited by Sábato and Anneliese von der Lipper (Buenos Aires: Legasa, 1983).

Ernesto Sábato is the most important contemporary intellectual figure of Argentina, not only due to his literary oeuvre but also to the prominent and courageous role he has played as the voice of reason against oppressive military regimes. His political importance was confirmed in 1984 when the democratic government of Raúl Alfonsín nominated him to preside over the National Commission of Disappeared Persons, whose report, *Nunca más* (Never Again, 1984), Sábato wrote. He has achieved international status, lecturing throughout Latin America, Europe, Israel, and at major universities in the United States. He is a Chevalier de l'Ordre des Arts et des Lettres and Chevalier de la Légion d'Honneur of France; he has received the Cervantes award and the Gran Cruz al Mérito Civil in

Spain, the Jerusalem prize in Israel, the Medici award in Italy, the prize of the Stuttgart Institut für Auslansbeziehungen from the former West Germany, and the Gabriela Mistral prize of the Organization of American States. The government of Argentina has bestowed upon him the highest award given to those who have most contributed to the enrichment of its cultural heritage, the Prize of National Consecration, and has declared him an "illustrious citizen."

Ernesto Sábato was born on 24 June 1911 in Rojas, an old village in the province of Buenos Aires, of northern Italian immigrant parents who owned a flour mill. His schooling and university studies were completed in La Plata, the capital of Buenos Aires province, where he received his Ph.D. in physics in 1937. His years at the university (1929–1937) coincided with a crucial time in Argentine politics. Deeply feeling current social problems, Sábato spent five years as a member and speaker for the Communist party, though he was persecuted for his political activism. In 1934 he secretly traveled to the Antifascist Congress in Brussels as a representative of the Communist Argentine Youth Organization. But as his understanding of communism as an absolutist movement began to increase, his allegiance began to crack. He thus suffered a spiritual and ideological crisis that compelled him to refuse the party order to proceed to Moscow for indoctrination, a denial that meant total separation from the party and triggered his first spiritual crisis.

In 1938 he won a fellowship to continue studies in nuclear physics at the Joliot-Curie Laboratory in Paris. A year later he spent several months working on the same subject at the Massachusetts Institute of Technology. During his Paris sojourn Sábato became acquainted with surrealist painters and literary figures; this was a major turning point in his life, for it was then that he had his first glimpse of his real avocation . . . literature. Significantly, in Paris he began his first novel, "La fuente muda" (The Silent Fountain), which was never published in its entirety although some chapters appeared later in the well-known literary magazine *Sur* in the November 1947 issue.

In 1940 he became a professor of theoretical physics at the University of La Plata while also teaching in Buenos Aires at the Instituto del Profesorado Secundario. During that time an illustrious former teacher at the secondary school in La Plata, the well-known Dominican man of letters Pedro Henríquez Ureña, opened doors for Sábato to two prestigious organs of intellectual life in Buenos Aires: the magazine *Sur,* directed by Victoria Ocampo, and the newspaper *La Nación.* Unfortunately, during the first dictatorship of Juan Domingo Perón, Sábato lost both his jobs for being too vocal in his opposition. His economic situation, together with his increasing dissatisfaction with the world of science, precipitated his second spiritual crisis in 1943: he broke with physics and embraced literature with its uncertain future.

In 1936 he eloped with Matilde Kusminsky Richter, his sweetheart from his university days and later had a son, Jorge. For the first ten years of their marriage life was hard. The family lived in poverty with only the income from his articles, conferences, and his poorly paid work as adviser to three publishing houses. For two months in 1947 he was assistant to the executive committee of United Nations Educational, Scientific, and Cultural Organization (UNESCO) in Paris and Rome, but Sábato was uncomfortable with bureaucracy. With the fall of Perón in 1955 he became director of the popular weekly *Mundo Argentino* (Argentine World) but was forced to resign for denouncing irregularities in the de facto military government. Between 1958 and 1959 he was director of cultural relations at the Foreign Ministry.

Sábato has always been a complex, independent personality. His scientific background and his

artistic passion show clearly an Apollonian and a Dionysian side to his personality. In contrast with the boy from the provinces coexisted the Communist from the big city; next to life in the laboratory, the bohemian, nocturnal, surrealistic life; together with the physicist, the writer of fiction; along with the well-organized, methodical man, the sarcastic rebel. Sábato still lives in the proletarian suburb of Santos Lugares near Buenos Aires, devoted, due to eyesight problems, to another of his passions: painting, which he professes has always been his initial vocation. He is presently writing his memoirs, an exposition of his literary career and the personalities he has known during his long and extremely active life, and he still attends seminars and symposia devoted to his work in three continents. He has never, however, given up his position as watchdog of the troubled political life of his country; in fact, it may be said that Sábato *is* its conscience.

There is great coherence between Sábato the writer and Sábato the man. His literary work is an extension of his anxieties just as his life is a crystallization of his ideals. Thus in order to comprehend Sábato's novels, it is first necessary to understand the ideas that sustain his fictional world. Both his essays and novels derive from the same system of obsessive ideas. Sábato, like French writer and philosopher Jean-Paul Sartre, is a thinker who expresses his ideas most fully and easily through fiction.

*Uno y el universo* (The Self and the Universe, 1945) was his first book of essays. It includes seventy-four articles that debate philosophical, scientific, and artistic subjects in simple but forceful prose that both excites the reader and provokes thought. There are also commentaries about historical characters such as Nicolaus Copernicus and Galileo Galilei and about education, common sense, religion, historical facts, and the sexes. Many of the articles display fine satire. Sábato is not limited to discussing or presenting a concept; he fulminates it with satire, bitter humor, and skepticism. This first book presages preoccupations prominent in later essays and novels. Also present are most of the elements of Sábato's particular aphoristic essay style: directness, nakedness, and simplicity. This book signals Sábato's ideological transition from a world of reason to that of existential humanism.

*Hombres y engranajes* (Of Men and Gears, 1951) marks a rupture with Sábato's former convictions. It has been deemed a spiritual autobiography, the diary of a personal yet universal crisis. Carefully organized in five parts, its last part is a sort of recapitulation and a program to confront the crisis of con-

*Sábato in the late 1940s (photograph by Lydia Márquez)*

temporary society. Again these essays are philosophical, sociological, and political, but the fourth part contains Sábato's more obsessive and central notions related to his literary work. Here Sábato divorces himself from the Apollonian world of exact science and submerges himself in the world of letters. He discusses "La esencia del Renacimiento" (The Essence of the Renaissance) with irony and sarcasm that soften the systematic reductio ad absurdum to which he exposes some concepts in order to destroy them. The human creature has become a thing in "El universo abstracto" (The Abstract Universe), devoid of desires or instincts, dominated by machines and science, and reduced to total impersonality. In "La rebelión del hombre" (The Man's Rebellion) he analyzes the Romantic, existential, Marxist, and surrealist rebellions, which culminates in the article "Las artes y las letras en la crisis" (The Arts and Letters in the Crisis). In the last part of the book Sábato develops what ten years later he calls his "Metaphysic of Hope," on the basis of which he will create in his novel *Sobre héroes y tumbas* (1961; translated as *On Heroes and Tombs,* 1981) his character Martín. That metaphysics is a "new synthesis," the recuperation of the human dimension of

science and technology so that human beings will not be lost within its mechanisms as if they were just another bolt. *Heterodoxia* (Heterodoxy, 1953), like his first book, is also written as a diary, diverse articles in which Sábato continues to ruminate around variations of the same subject: art as the most complete expression of humanity's rebellion against a mechanized and abstract universe. Sábato expresses his discomfort with an inhuman and excessively rational world through the antagonistic opposition of the concepts man and woman, which is the point of departure for other antitheses: novel (the nocturnal) versus essay (the diurnal), scientific language versus life language, and art versus science. Some articles in this book discuss the literary principles that are the foundation of his fictional works, which he fully explains in his next book of essays.

*El escritor y sus fantasmas* (The Writer and His Ghosts, 1963) most clearly exposes two of Sábato's obsessions: literary creation in general and the writing of novels in particular. Controversies engendered by his second novel, published in 1961, impelled him to publish notes he had previously compiled. He felt compelled to explain not only the impetus for his writing, but also what he believed constituted a novel and the related phenomenon of artistic creation. His ultimate goal was to tighten some concepts that were lightly used, particularly that of realism in the literature of the 1960s. The book has three parts. The first part encompasses fifty questions about Sábato's work; his scientific career; his problems and attitudes as a writer; his views about Argentine literature; about psychological, nationalistic, *engagé* (politically engaged), and ludicrous literature; and how he sees his own work within the greater framework of Argentine literature.

In the second part, Sábato lucidly expounds the development of Western culture to demonstrate the rebellion of modern humanity against a "technolátrica" (technolatric – Sábato's term) society through contemporary art. Thus Sábato sees literature as a metaphysical phenomenon, not merely as an aesthetic one. For him the novel is a way of perceiving the world. Sábato's defense of the novel as an integral vision of life is to a great extent a defense of a kind of neo-Romanticism, a new attitude in Latin America that fertilized a field many saw previously as sterile. The third part of the book is an intellectual catalogue referenced to literature.

In 1970 Losada published two volumes comprising Sábato's complete works. The volume devoted to his essays includes the four texts analyzed above as well as articles that first appeared in newspapers and magazines or as prologues or parts of volumes devoted to specific subjects, such as "Sobre los dos Borges" (About the Two Borges) and "Sartre contra Sartre" (la misión trascendente de la novela)" (Sartre against Sartre or the Transcendental Mission of the Novel). In these volumes are articles about Argentine culture, Sábato's literary influences (Gustave Flaubert, Ureña, Sartre), and painting. In particular, "Una teoría sobre la predicción del porvenir" (A Theory about the Prediction of the Future) can be used as a tool to decipher his last novel, *Abaddón, el exterminador* (Abaddon, the exterminating Angel, 1974; translated as *The Angel of Darkness,* 1991).

Sábato believes that the novel is the sole form, apart from theater, in which true reality can be seen, a genre closer to metaphysics than to literature. The central, obsessive subjects and ideas of his novels and essays include a deep existential preoccupation with the human being, literary creation, and his beloved country, which he never left even when his personal safety was at stake. Whereas the texts in which Sábato reflects on these obsessions are dispersed among his essays, in his fictional works they are united, forming a tight synthesis. *El túnel* (1948; translated as *The Outsider,* 1950; translated as *The Tunnel,* 1988) is the confessional story of an apparent crime of passion narrated from a jail cell by the criminal – Pablo Castel, a painter. No description of the outside world or of other characters is given. The story, narrated from its denouement backward, constitutes an internal search by Castel, who is trying to understand his crime. The novel dwells on the murky unconscious and its irrational dreams, premonitions, and contradictory certitudes, which Castel reviews with clarity and implacability. Naked language expresses Castel's social alienation, the tunnel of the title: the fact that Castel is living in the hermetic tunnel of his self. The narration of the story by a first-person protagonist with frequent phrases addressing the reader gives the sense of a confession being whispered in the ear. The author becomes nonexistent, the reader occupying the place of the single person for whom Castel is writing and whose understanding he desperately needs. Castel appears to be an arrogant and cynical man who despises remembrances and eulogizes the decency of criminals, who detests himself and his weaknesses, and although capable of humorous sarcasm is endowed with a sick sensibility, which he expresses in his paintings.

Castel's confession goes back to spring 1946, when he exhibited his painting *Maternidad* (Maternity). Only María Iribarne, a spectator, seems to understand a small motif on one side of the painting. His subsequent relationship with and love for María reveals Castel's disorientation and the murky maze of his mind. María is an enigmatic, melancholy, seemingly sensitive young woman whose gaze "parecia venir de atrás" (seemed to come from somewhere in the past). She is married to a blind man and is perhaps promiscuous and evidently unhappy. Castel is irresistibly attracted and develops a possessive, furious passion for her, exacerbated by bouts of jealousy and oedipal fancies. Although his passion is consummated he remains unhappy, searching for an absolute communication he cannot find in their relationship. His crime is not the result of jealousy but rather an aspect of his tunnel of incommunication, like his irrational hatred of groups and of the blind, his scorn for the world at large, his lack of hope, and his fear of women. The novel illustrates one of Sábato's obsessions: the questioning of love as a passage toward the absolute and as an antidote against solitude. Sábato includes in this novel the ideas presented in *Heterodoxia,* particularly the magic, noncausal world of women versus the causal one of men – in this case Castel, who through his artistic intuition can feel another world but cannot reach it. This simple yet suspenseful novel could be viewed as the fictional incarnation of the thesis first explained in *Hombres y engranajes.* Seen as a denunciation of humanity's inability to communicate, *El túnel* belongs to the existential philosophy of the twentieth century and is already a classic within Argentine literature.

*Sobre héroes y tumbas* was Sábato's second and most successful novel, a major, complex fictional work that won him a place at the vanguard of Spanish-American literature and as a master of the twentieth-century novel. With his first novel, it shares Sábato's essential subjects: the necessity of the absolute, solitude, and the need for, as well as the impossibility of, communication among human beings. The subject of blind people now expands to an entire section of the book, which in itself could form a hallucinatory, obsessive, fantastic, surrealistic novel. *Sobre héroes y tumbas* is almost a baroque novel in which, unlike Castel's nihilism, Martín's hope predominates; the reader is not confronted with the tragedy of one man but with that of an entire nation. The novel is enriched not only with human conflicts but with digressions about diverse subjects, such as the manifestation of the soul in the body; artists and their creations and fights with the critics and the public; individuals as lonely beings facing death; Argentine soccer; human destiny; Argentina's former customs and national so-

Cover for Sábato's 1948 novel, narrated by an artist who has
murdered his mistress

cial types; prostitution and pornography; the meaning of nationalism, capitalism, Marxism, and Peronism; jealousy and frivolous women; Argentine class divisions; advertising as science; Miguel de Cervantes's *Don Quixote* (1605–1615); America as a myth; and so on. The approximately forty different topics represent a vast mural of modern Argentina.

*Sobre héroes y tumbas* is carefully organized in four parts narrated from various points of view, which demands active participation by the reader. It appears to be the fictionalized treatment of the ego and the id, an effort to express a neo-Romantic–existential–phenomenological image of the contemporary human condition. Chronologically, the novel begins at the end, presenting a transcription of a newspaper article informing the reader that on 24 June 1955 Alejandra Vidal Olmos, the last descendant of a prominent but impoverished Argentine family, killed her father Fernando and then set everything afire, killing herself also. Fernando has left an "Informe sobre ciegos" (Report on the Blind) suggestive of an evil reason for the sacrifice. A few days before the fire the Argentine navy tried to

overthrow Juan Perón, and Buenos Aires was bombarded. Later a group of impassioned Peronists pillaged and set afire the oldest Buenos Aires churches. This historic plot constitutes a violent, fated counterpoint to the fictional plot depicting the destiny of the father and daughter. But there is more in the novel: a love story about Alejandra and Martín, the chronicle of the patrician family Vidal Olmos, the seemingly incestuous relationship between Alejandra and her father, and the frustrated suicide attempt by Martín and his subsequent, hopeful trip to the future. This melodrama is manipulated in an artistic way, according to Leo Pollmann.

In the first and fourth parts of the novel the heroic, epiclike narrative of the march to exile of Gen. Juan Lavalle's men with his corpse appears. The saga of this hero in a nineteenth-century fight against the dictator Juan Manuel de Rosas constitutes a counterpoint to the narration of contemporary facts. Sábato tries to show not only contemporary Argentina but also its past in searching for the roots of contemporary history. The third part of the novel, "Informe sobre ciegos," is a frenzied narrative in which, as in surrealist philosophy, the incomprehensible states of hallucination and nightmare permit understanding of the irrational forces of the human mind. The descent by Fernando into the sewers of the so-called sect of the blind is both mystical and sacrilegious, a supreme form of self-knowledge and hence the ultimate cognition of the indescribable designs of life.

On another level *Sobre héroes y tumbas* unfolds the entire pattern of Argentine social classes – landowner, Italian immigrant, proletarian, high bourgeoisie, business, middle class, social parasite – each precisely characterized not only through thought and action but also through specific linguistic expression. In this manner Sábato creates a gallery of unforgettable characters, juxtaposing serious, even tragic, personalities with others full of humor, common sense, or cynicism, mixing authentic human beings with false ones. This problematic book is widely considered one of the fundamental texts of contemporary Argentine literature.

Sábato's anguished last novel, *Abaddón, el exterminador,* is not only an attempt to understand the collective unconscious of Argentina and of its history but also a self-reflective text that examines and dramatizes its own creative process. In it the author himself is one of the characters, a mad hero who cohabits with his doppelgängers in order to penetrate the great mystery of life and its artistic creation. Sábato achieves his own analysis while writing the novel. Here Sábato-as-character feels trapped in such a way that the reader becomes witness to Sábato's bloody combat with literary creation. With his own complete name or under the initial "S," Sábato-as-character is in a schizophrenic way his own impotent witness. "S" has the same marks of identity as the real Sábato with his parapsychological interests and constant obsessions. Sábato also appears as the "Maestro," possibly the catalyst for all of these metamorphoses of the literary persona. Another slippery character, "R," appears in certain critical moments of the plot and is perhaps the deepest form assumed by the author. This doppelgänger, though seldom mentioned, presides over the whole novel. The choice of the letter *R* may indicate the place where Sábato was born (Rojas) or the possibility of being born again (*renacer* in Spanish) or a rediscovery or remembrances – words that are significant not only in the context of the novel but in the comprehension of Sábato's obsessive ideas.

*Abaddón, el exterminador* is divided into two parts. The first takes place in Buenos Aires during 5–6 January 1973, the feast of the Epiphany. It narrates the stories of three men: Nacho, a young man with incestuous and existential suicidal tendencies; the madman Natalicio Barragán, witness to an apocalyptic prophecy; and Marcelo, a revolutionary petit bourgeois tortured to death by the police. The three stories, as the reader discovers in the second part, begin in 1972. The real center of the novel is Sábato, the author-as-character(s), observed by Bruno, the impotent witness of that unjust reality. The first part is a preamble. The narration is achieved through two different types of parallel discourses: the fictional stories mentioned above and the metadiscourse of Sábato-as-character(s) of the novel that Bruno is trying to write. In the second part the all-encompassing vision that is the objective of the novel is rendered through 114 confessions, dialogues, dreams, poems (by Sábato and others), journalistic notes, and fragments of letters that perhaps are related to some of the characters and facts of the first part, although this is not made clear unequivocally. In this part the reader returns to Sábato's childhood, adolescence, and youth and to the Paris of the 1930s, especially to the Joliot-Curie Laboratory and to the surrealists. The reader is taken to the fictional city of Capitán Olmos, ancestral birthplace of the Vidal Olmos family and of Bruno Basán, a character that had already appeared in *Sobre héroes y tumbas* and one of the fictional doppelgängers of Sábato's personality. Thus the novel shows a calculated artistic disorder, particularly because each entry is preceded by fragmentary phrases, giving the impression of notes gathered at random. Nevertheless, the puzzle slowly begins to reveal its well-conceived structure, less apparent than that of the previous novels but more complex. If in earlier novels the characters are fleshed out in Sábato's usual dualities, in *Abaddón, el exterminador* the reader is in the domain of the nocturnal and the diurnal, of discursive and metaphoric language, of tragedy and parody, and of the real world and the imaginary. Negative, dark, irrational elements create a disoriented Sábato-as-character, an impotent creature confronted with a contradictory, absurd, and disjointed world. This is precisely what justifies his doppelgängers, his attempts to understand from varying perspectives a perplexing reality. Everything that is positive, clear, and rational is transmitted through theories, analyses, and explanations. There are also chats, interviews, and the lyrical chronicle of the death of Che Guevara, conceived like the episode of Lavalle in *Sobre héroes y tumbas* as a counterpoint to illustrate Sábato's beliefs (in this case, the same utopian ideal) about the New Man that Guevara tried to achieve through armed revolt.

*Sábato receiving the Miguel de Cervantes Prize from King Juan Carlos of Spain, April 1985*

*Abaddón, el exterminador* demonstrates the universe of Sábato's personal interests as explained in his essays, with the addition of the author himself as tormented, satirized, and forgiven by his own character-torturers.

Ernesto Sábato is present in all his texts, fiction and essay. His writings are antidogmatic and testimonial, denouncing the present times. In them an overflowing, tortured imagination, a cognitive and speculative inquiry, an extreme sensibility, and a visceral passion for the development of his subjects are harmoniously blended. His work has therefore justly stimulated a revitalization of both the novel and the essay within Argentine letters and Latin-American literature at large.

**Bibliographies:**

Nicasio Urbina, "Bibliografía crítica completa de Ernesto Sábato, con un índice temático," *Revista de Crítica Literaria Latinoamericana,* 14, no. 27 (1988): 177–221;

Urbina, "Bibliografía crítica comentada sobre Ernesto Sábato, con un índice temático," *Hispania,* 73 (December 1990): 953–977;

Alfredo A. Roggiano, "Crono-bio-bibliografía seleccionada y comentada de Ernesto Sábato: Itinerario del hombre y del escritor," *Revista Iberoamericana,* 58, (January–March 1992): 15–32.

**References:**

Earl M. Aldrich, Jr., "Esthetics, Moral and Philosophic Concerns in *Sobre héroes y tumbas*," in *Romance Literary Studies: Homage to Harvey L.*

*Johnson,* edited by M. A. Wellington and M. O'Nan (Potomac, Md.: Porrúa Turanzas, 1979), pp. 3–14;

Salvador Bacarisse, "*Abaddón, el exterminador:* Sábato's Gnostic Eschatology," in his *Contemporary Latin American Fiction* (Edinburgh: Scottish Academy Press, 1980), pp. 88–109;

Armand F. Baker, "Psychic Integration and the Search of Meaning in Sábato's *El túnel*," *Hispanic Journal,* 5, no. 2 (1984): 113–125;

Trinidad Barrera López, *La estructura de "Abaddón, el exterminador"* (Madrid: CSIC, 1982);

Richard J. Callan, "Sábato's Fiction: A Jungian Interpretation," *Bulletin of Hispanic Studies,* 51 (1974): 48–59;

Carlos Catania, *Genio y figura de Ernesto Sábato* (Buenos Aires: Eudeba, 1987);

María A. Correa, *Genio y figura de Ernesto Sábato* (Buenos Aires: Eudeba, 1971);

*Cuadernos Hispanoamericanos,* special issue on Sábato, 131, nos. 391–393 (1983);

Angela B. Dellepiane, *Ernesto Sábato: El hombre y su obra* (New York: Las Américas, 1968);

Dellepiane, *Sábato: Un análisis de su narrativa* (Buenos Aires: Nova, 1970);

David W. Foster, *Currents in Contemporary Argentine Novel: Arlt, Mallea, Sábato and Cortázar* (Columbia: University of Missouri Press, 1975), pp. 70–97;

Foster, "The Integral Role of 'El informe sobre ciegos' in Sábato's *Sobre héroes y tumbas*," *Romance Notes,* 14 (1972): 44–48;

Helmy F. Giacomán, ed., *Homenaje a Ernesto Sábato* (New York: Las Américas, 1973);

Giacomán, ed., *Los personajes de Sábato* (Buenos Aires: Emecé, 1972);

Luis González del Valle and Catherine Nickel, "Contemporary Poetics to the Rescue: The Enigmatic Narrator in Sábato's *El túnel*," *Rocky Mountain Review*, 40, nos. 1–2 (1986): 5–20;

Z. Nelly Martínez, "El elemento lúdicro en *Sobre héroes y tumbas*," *Kentucky Romance Quarterly*, 23 (1976): 175–183;

Graciela Maturo, ed., *Ernesto Sábato en la crisis de la modernidad* (Buenos Aires: Fernando García Cambeiro, 1985);

Thomas C. Meehan, "Metafísica sexual de Ernesto Sábato: Tema y forma en *El túnel*," *Modern Language Notes*, 83 (1968): 226–252;

Nivia Montenegro, "The Structural and Thematic Elements in *Abaddón, el exterminador*," *Latin American Literary Review*, 12 (1978): 38–56;

William Nelson, "Sábato's *El túnel* and the Existential Novel," *Modern Fiction Studies*, 32, no. 3 (1986): 459–467;

Harley D. Oberhelman, *Ernesto Sábato* (New York: Twayne, 1970);

Mariana D. Petrea, *Ernesto Sábato: La nada y la metafísica de la esperanza* (Madrid: José Porrúa Turanzas, 1986);

Leo Pollmann, *La nueva novela en Francia y en Iberoamérica* (Madrid: Gredos, 1971), pp. 89–95, 264–267, 274–283;

Margaret C. Redd, " 'Report on the Blind': Sábato's Journey into the Fantastic," in *The Scope of the Fantastic: Culture, Biography, Themes, Children's Literature*, edited by Robert A. Collins and Howard D. Pearce (Westport, Conn.: Greenwood Press, 1985), pp. 147–153;

*Revista Iberoamericana*, special issue on Sábato, 58, (January–March 1992);

Henry J. Richards, "The Characterization of the Ontologically Insecure in *El túnel*," *Kentucky Romance Quarterly*, 24 (1977): 151–162;

Richards, "Digression in the Structure of *El túnel*: An Aspect of Sábato's Art," *Kentucky Romance Quarterly*, 29, no. 4 (1982): 405–422;

Gemma Roberts, *Análisis existencial de "Abaddón, el exterminador" de Ernesto Sábato* (Boulder, Colo.: SSSAS, 1990);

Nicolás Shumway, "Sábato vs. Quique: Una colaboración de opositores," *Revista Iberoamericana*, 49, (October–December 1983): 829–838;

Gustav Siebenmann, "Ernesto Sábato y su postulado de una novela metafísica," *Revista Iberoamericana*, 48, (January–June 1982): 289–302;

Nicasio Urbina, "La lectura en la obra de Ernesto Sábato," *Revista Iberoamericana*, 53, (October–December 1987): 823–836;

A. M. Vázquez-Bigi, ed., *Epica dadora de eternidad: Sábato en la crítica americana y europea* (Buenos Aires: Sudamericana/Planeta, 1985).

# Jaime Saenz
## *(8 October 1921 – 13 August 1986)*

Javier Sanjinés C.
*University of Maryland at College Park*

BOOKS: *El escalpelo* (La Paz: El Progreso, 1955);
*Muerte por el tacto* (La Paz: Editora Nacional, 1957);
*Aniversario de una visión* (La Paz: Burillo, 1960);
*Vistante profundo* (La Paz: Burillo, 1964);
*El frío; Muerte por el tacto; Aniversario de una visión* (La Paz: Burillo, 1967);
*Recorrer esta distancia* (La Paz: Burillo, 1973);
*Obra poética* (La Paz: Biblioteca del Sesquicentenario de la República, 1975);
*Bruckner: Las tinieblas* (La Paz: Difusión, 1978);
*Felipe Delgado* (La Paz: Difusión, 1979);
*Imágenes paceñas* (La Paz: Difusión, 1979);
*Al pasar un cometa* (La Paz: Altiplano, 1982);
*La noche* (La Paz: Talleres Escuela de Artes Gráficas del Colegio Don Bosco, 1984);
*Los cuartos* (La Paz: Altiplano, 1985);
*Vidas y muertes* (La Paz: Huayna Potosí, 1986);
*La piedra imán* (La Paz: Huayna Potosí, 1989);
*Los papeles de Narciso Lima-Achá* (La Paz: Instituto Boliviano de Cultura, 1991).

SELECTED PERIODICAL PUBLICATION – UNCOLLECTED: "El aparapita de La Paz," *Mundo Nuevo,* 26–27 (August–September 1968): 4–8.

Jaime Saenz is one of the most complex and interesting writers of modern Bolivia. Irrational and oblivious to the construction of clear and well-defined meanings, his work occupies an exceptional place in Bolivian literature. Like few other authors, his narrative flows from a personal poetic universe that cannot be considered separately from the writer's eccentric life. Made of syntactic twists, paradoxes, and tautologies, Saenz's poetry is connected to his fiction, particularly to *Felipe Delgado* (1979), a novel of the modern grotesque.

Born in La Paz, Bolivia, on 8 October 1921, Saenz devoted his life to the exploration of the dark, gloomy side of the city. His penchant for the study of a magical underworld inhabited by drunken free-loaders led him to a unique, mystic search of the human spirit while at the same time suppressing the real, objective world. Saenz's total submersion in the study of the cadaverous and his frequent visits to the city morgue convinced him that his aesthetics should examine not the life-world, the world as we know it, but the profound death-world. Rejecting the routines of everyday life, Saenz set himself to work in the construction of a poetic universe where the human body plays a decisive, although negative, role.

For Saenz the profound essence of being is completely at odds with the material appearance of things. Separating the apparent and superficial world from the interior and meaningful presence of death, Saenz conceives the corporeal as simply an instrument of life, a surface marked by disintegration. This negation of the sensible world results in a shocking split of the self. Indeed, the phantoms that Saenz invents, multiplies, and brings back to life are symptoms of the troublesome lack of psychic unity. This situation, which leaves the writer to debate with his own self, does not open up a dialogue with the world. Consequently, without dialogue and symbolization, communication between human beings cannot take place.

Narcissistic because it is constantly talking to an absent presence of its own self, the poetic voice searches for a "you" that has no corporeal reality. This "you" manifests itself through hallucinations and delusions that betray a morbid preoccupation of the individual with his own essence. In Saenz's poetic universe this "you," this eternal wait — "un estarse" (just being there) he calls it — for the unknown is the indefinite postponement of identity, an avowal of the death drive that leads to annihilation and corporeal self-destruction.

*Aniversario de una visión* (Anniversary of a Vision, 1960), one of Saenz's most revealing works of poetry, is marked by the division between the "I" and the "you." Emerging from the bottom of the

*Jaime Saenz*

corporeal self, the "you" splits the ego as it invades the mind and produces a chaotic sense of euphoria:

> — mas, estoy solo y deslumbrado y necesito
> socorro frente a este paroxismo de exageraciones,
> las que anuncian algún júbilo caótico
> — y no sé si tú eres o si es el demonio quién me
> deslumbra y me hace ver lo que no se ve.

> ( – but, I am alone and dazzled, and I need
> help in front of this paroxysm of exaggerations,
> which announce some chaotic euphoria
> — and I don't know if it is you or the devil that
> dazzles me and makes me see what cannot be seen.)

The split of the self and the ungraspable demonic essence of the "you" are also at the core of the poems of *El frío* (The Cold, 1967):

> dudo que seas tú una realidad bajo la luz del sol,
> con ese fugitivo paso en la espesura de las sombras
>     atravesando el cristal del frío,

> perdiéndote en lo profundo de la ciudad mientras yo te
> busco,
> ocultándote de mi vista y alejándote del infierno en el que
> noche tras noche creo poder encontrarte . . .

> (I doubt that you may be a reality under the sun,
> with that brief step in the density of the shadows cross-
>     ing the crystal glass of the cold,
> losing you in the depths of the city while I search for
>     you,
> hiding from my sight and withdrawing from the in-
> ferno in
>     which I think I can find you night after night . . . )

In Saenz's fiction there is a relation between this fractured ego and the constant distortions of reality – the apparitions that haunt the fictional characters – that may be described as stances of the mind toward the fearsome, the grotesque, the uncanny. But as an artist of the grotesque, Saenz does not merely distort surfaces: he creates a more meaningful context – what he calls the "mundo interno" (interior world) – in which such distortions are possible, an implied world of cellars, morgues, and caves where the surface of reality is metamorphosed in order to tell a deep, qualitative truth. In so doing Saenz does not address the rationalist or the scientist in the reader but the child or the potential psychotic.

*El escalpelo* (The Scalpel, 1955), his first collection of poetic prose, is an appropriate metaphor for the surgical incision that Saenz introduces in the corporeal self. Obsessed with sickness and childhood, he explores throughout the book different instances of bodily decay. Short stories about children with epilepsy and physical abnormalities are combined with extreme situations in which childhood is dominated by insecurity, solitude, and the ambiguous presence of the revered and rejected "you."

The central theme of *El escalpelo* is the dialogue between the "I" and the "you." "Horrible en mi presencia, tú" (Horrible in my presence, beloved you), writes Saenz to indicate the ambivalent feeling of the divided self. Hated and loved, this "you" to which the "I" is attracted is both a menace and an obstacle. In this intense and constant dialogue Saenz seems fascinated with the physical extremes of the infantile, neurotic, and psychotic subject. These extremes are significant because through them *El escalpelo* studies the role of the body and physicalness in the destabilization of the subject. This exploration is fully developed years later in *Felipe Delgado*, Saenz's most important novel and a masterwork on the grotesque.

*Felipe Delgado* is a challenging study of the city of La Paz. As with Saenz's poetry, its reception was enthusiastic. Since Saenz was not particularly interested in writing a modern novel, his unparalleled interpretation of La Paz cannot be classified as avantgarde writing but instead as a traditional narration of a vigorous set of characters seen through the narrator's unifying point of view, which is dominated by the presence of alcohol and insanity.

Corsino Ordóñez's dark cellar, lost in the cold nights of the *aparapitas* (freeloaders) of La Paz, is the privileged meeting place for Felipe Delgado, the protagonist, and his humorous, eccentric friends. Here, while they consume alcohol by the gallons, they also reflect upon the world. It is in this incredible atmosphere that Felipe Delgado carries on the search for his meaningful self, guided by Christopher Columbus's indication that "navigare neccesere est, vivere non neccesere" (it is necessary to navigate, not to live), a phrase revealed to Delgado by his friend Juan de la Cruz Oblitas, a sorcerer according to some, a physician and philosopher according to others.

In this underworld Delgado engages in a tortuous search for identity, trying to interweave his life with the destinies of both the city and the country. This search is a failure, and Delgado disappears in the last chapters of this long novel, leaving his friend Oblitas to remind the other characters that Delgado's physical presence is neither necessary nor possible because he has, in his own particular way, "sacado el cuerpo" (taken off his body) and become invisible.

The opening scene of the novel is particularly useful to the study of the grotesque. Delgado's father is dying and Felipe searches for the priest that must administer the last rites. Delgado nevertheless feels strange, confusing impulses that obstruct his way to the convent. Sensing that he is being followed, he decides to enter a tavern and have a drink. While he is sitting there, remembering his childhood and trying to imagine the mother he never knew, he is unexpectedly interrupted by a pestiferous old man, a terrible and ridiculous figure who attacks Delgado and chases him away. Escaping from this apparition, Delgado finally gets to the convent but is unable to enter because the old man has already been there, dirtying the portico with his feces to the exasperation of the priest. A long, scandalous discussion between the priest and Delgado follows the sordid incident. The scene finishes with both characters arriving late at the bedside of Virgilio Delgado, who is already dead.

This scene introduces the notion of abjection, a theme that lies at the roots of the novel. Delgado's difficulty in complying with the paternal order and his sudden impulse to take a tortuous way to the convent are indications that his actions are not monitored by a stable, rational mind. To the contrary, the imaginary old man attests to the perilous, provisional nature of the rational control over the dispersing impulses of the hallucinatory drives that strive to break down Delgado's identity.

Delgado's destiny is marked by the desire for death as the primal instinct. Attacked by dreams, nightmares, and strange apparitions, the protagonist borders on insanity. This "maldición" (curse), his impulse for self-destruction, Delgado labels as a "deseo de eternidad" (longing for eternity). It seems that Delgado wishes to burn the demon that he carries within himself in order to purify himself and assume his deeper, truer essence.

The death drive persists in Corsino Ordóñez's cellar. Here Delgado fulfills the destiny of the alcoholic in search of his progressive wasting away of the body. Delgado's search for consumption is so similar to the setting that the cellar ends up being the inner self of the character, part of his death-driven deeper essence. Delgado vanishes in the last part of the novel at the same time that the cellar closes down with the death of its owner.

It is in the cellar passages of the novel that Saenz makes some original observations on the *aparapitas* of La Paz, the ideal models of corporeal destruction that Delgado emulates. Like his remarkable story "El aparapita de La Paz" (The Aparapita of La Paz, 1968), Saenz pictures these marginal rural settlers as the quintessence of the city of La Paz.

The *aparapitas,* destined to perish intoxicated, are what rational minds would consider the abject. People repudiate them; priests consider them possessed by the devil. For some they are beasts, for others repulsive lepers. High culture has deliberately forgotten them, while sociologists deem them a product of underdevelopment. For Saenz they are a source of veneration and fear, particularly the jackets they wear, "el saco de aparapita." When describing this incredible jacket in "El aparapita de La Paz," Saenz interprets the multiplicity and heterogeneity of the Andean cultures that the traditionally dominant social classes reject or at best unwillingly accept:

> La ropa que lleva en realidad no existe. El saco ha existido como tal en tiempos pretéritos, ha ido despareciendo poco a poco, según los remiendos han cundido para formar un saco, verdadero, pues no es obra del sastre, es obra de la vida un saco verdadero. Los primeros remiendos han recibido algunos otros remiendos; éstos a su vez han recibido todavía otros, y estos otros, todavía muchos más, y así, con el fluir del tiempo, ha ido en aumento el peso en relación directa con el espesor de la prenda, tanto más verdadera cuanto más pesada y gruesa . . .

> ( The jacket really does not exist. It existed a long time ago, but it has been disappearing little by little, being replaced by the patches that have been forming a new jacket, the real one, which is not tailor-made. The new jacket is a true jacket, made by life. The first patches have received new ones, which in turn have also received new ones. Thus the new jacket is the product of time, something that can only be proved by its weight. The value of the garment is in strict relation to its thickness. The more its weight, the more its worth . . . )

The jacket is a true symbol of the complexities of the disquieting world the official Spanish culture wishes to reject. For Saenz the jacket is not simply something the *aparapitas* wear; it is what they create throughout life. The final meaning of that life is the transcendence into death. When the *aparapita* de-

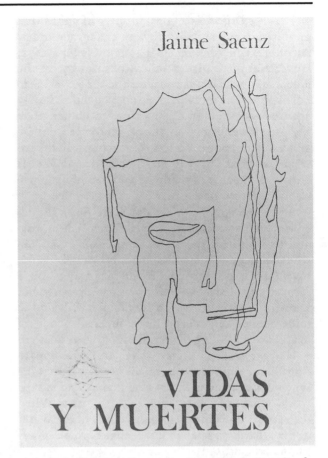

*Cover for Saenz's posthumous novel that includes portraits of twenty-four dead friends and autobiography*

cides that his time has arrived, he remains in the cellar and consumes alcohol uninterruptedly. Close to death, he leaves the cellar and throws his body in the street. This action, which Saenz calls "sacarse el cuerpo" (taking off the body), indicates a form of negation that brings back the notion of the abject.

*Felipe Delgado,* a novel of the ridiculous and the terrible, shocks the reader's consciousness and rationality because corporeal waste and refuse provoke cultural and individual horror and disgust symptomatic of the inability of Western culture to accept the body's materiality, limits, and mortality. Saenz knows that the most horrifying example of waste is the corpse, which is almost universally surrounded by taboos and rituals to prevent contamination of the living. He thus gives an interpretation of the *aparapitas* that is shocking because the "I" is expelled, rejected, and abandoned to the street. The corpse signifies the body's recalcitrance to consciousness, reason, or will, posing a danger to the ego insofar as it questions its stability and its control over itself. That is why Felipe Delgado is constantly attacked by apparitions that are a disturbance of the self.

*Felipe Delgado* is a constant play of masks that disguise identity and disturb both system and order. Alcohol is one such mask. Though it facilitates introspection, it is also a source of insanity. In the amounts in which it is consumed in the novel, alcohol deprives the individual of those qualities usually equated with human dignity or even human identity: the power to reason, the power to speak intelligibly, and the power to control emotions. In the extreme cases of Delgado and his friends alcohol is clearly the source of madness and the jubilant grotesque explored here.

Alcohol and madness also make *Felipe Delgado* a particularly interesting novel. If alcohol can suggest to a rationalist reader the animalistic, uncontrolled nature of humanity, madness can also fascinate, for it is a foreign and frightening way of life, a form of knowledge – alien knowledge certainly, but knowledge nonetheless. To take off the body and to understand the "cuerpo de la muerte" (body of death) are unsettling observations of the very otherness of the madman's view. The pestiferous apparitions that Felipe sees and smells are things that the sane human being with a vested interest in the sane world must ignore, repress, or flatly deny. When the reader confronts the primitive self, in the avatar of the lunatic, such alien knowledge becomes magical, marvelous.

In *Felipe Delgado* madness is also linked with the physical deformity of Peña y Lillo, the hunchbacked dweller of the cellar, and the generally bizarre appearance, dress, and behavior of the *aparapitas*. More daring, however, is the use of insanity as a point of view, a means of transforming the literal world of surfaces that Saenz leaves behind into a fluid, deranged, magical world populated by grotesques. Among this bizarre gallery of deranged characters, however, Felipe Delgado is unique and preeminent because it is through his perspective that the reader sees events ranging from the highly improbable to the utterly impossible in the known world. Through such incidents Saenz transforms the historical Bolivian world of the 1930s, dominated by the senseless Chaco War (1932–1935) between Bolivia and Paraguay, into the grotesque private world of Delgado and his doubles.

Doubles, however, is a misnomer: the narrator's ego is so fractured in this novel that it is not possible to say with certainty how many Felipe Delgados there are. He is not only the old man who haunts him, but also Ramona Escalera, his lover, and Ramón, his lover's lover. Felipe is also the cellar, its dwellers, and the city. Finally, his unique perspective derives from his being simultaneously a

lunatic and an artist of the grotesque. These roles, of course, are not experienced separately but are parts of a unified character, whose most important instrument is the central image of the *aparapita*. To the artist it is both muse and medium of expression, to the lunatic a weapon by which he wields magical control over the urban, structured world of larger, fiercer beings.

The cellar in *Felipe Delgado* is similar to the rooms in *Los cuartos* (The Rooms, 1985), a short novel set again in the margins of La Paz and inhabited by cripples and drunkards. Saenz repeats his terrible and ridiculous vision of the world and directs the reader's attention to the undignified, perilous, even gross physicality of existence, emphasizing it by exaggeration and distortion. In this work he gives significance to his observation of the thresholds of the rooms. They divide the outside, dominated by corporeal death and disintegration, and the inside, marked by the purified, immortal "cuerpo de la muerte." In *Los cuartos* destiny sometimes hinders the characters from crossing the threshold that will give them happiness and maybe immortality. Soledad Vaca, for example, is a destitute young girl who has been lodged in a convent by some compassionate nuns. When one of the rooms is offered to her by "la tía" (the aunt), the protagonist of the novel, she happily accepts and prepares to move. Destiny, though, gets in her way, and poor Soledad Vaca is struck by a car, suffering instant death. "La tía" is the only immortal character of *Los cuartos*. Through her, Saenz fictionalizes someone of great importance in his personal life, his aunt Esther, and explores the body of death as the main theme of the novel.

Saenz's literary universe cannot be separated from his eccentric, solitary life, overseen only by the solicitous care of his aunt Esther. In some chapters of *La piedra imán* (The Stone Magnet, 1989), his posthumous autobiographical narrative, Saenz indicates to us his contempt and his constant rejection of any form of compromise with everyday life. Though he seems to have a deep respect for marriage as an institution, his constant bouts with alcoholism and above all his desolate search for truth in the horrors of the night show a serious impediment to a stable, lasting relationship. Indeed, *La piedra imán* reveals some shocking aspects of Saenz's personal life. His marriage crumbled under the "signos de violencia y miedo" (signs of violence and fear) while he and his German wife lived in a "vieja y misteriosa casa" (old and mysterious house) in La Paz. Saenz indicates that the relationship was always troubled by alcohol, wrath, and some "espíritu maligno" (malign spirit) that conspired against the couple and ruined their marriage. When Saenz asks himself why he behaves as he does, he replies with his usual tautologies: "Soy así porque soy así. Seguramente por eso bebo . . . Y bebo porque soy un pobre carajo. Lo sé. ¿Y qué busco? El júbilo y el horror que andan juntos con el alcohol" (I am like this because I am like this. Surely that is why I drink . . . And I drink because I am a poor devil. I know. And what do I search for? The ecstasy and horror that go together with alcohol). Saenz never changed. His final days were marked by this marginal, asocial, nocturnal errancy, with no place for human love. He died from malnutrition in 1986, three years before the publication of *La piedra imán*. It is no revelation to indicate that the fragmented ego in *Felipe Delgado* is not only the narrator's but also the author's split point of view of the corporeal. Saenz created and monitored his own form of liberty with a pride that turned despotic in the last days of his life. He asked total allegiance of his friends and young followers, who found a source of knowledge in his at times disarmingly charming personality.

*Vidas y muertes* (Lives and Deaths, 1986), another autobiographical narrative, was published two months after Saenz's death. This book is a portrait of twenty-four friends who had died, plus a self-portrait. Some of these friends are unknown; others are well-known artists from the not so well-to-do Bolivian middle class. Saenz steps again into the nocturnal to explore his common themes of life, death, solitude, and what is and is not real.

Though the book does not touch on any new themes, *Vidas y muertes* is interesting because it gives added importance, particularly in the introductory essay, to the disturbance that the grotesque introduces to system and order. The serious and the ludicrous are again present in this book along with the suggestions Saenz gives to achieve the deep essence of being, overcoming the surface of things.

First, says Saenz, is humor. In the midst of the greatest spiritual or material sorrow, humor brings back reality and dissipates confusion. Humor synthesizes everything: tears, laughter, pain, and anguish. In his approach to humor Saenz also touches on the inexplicable interweaving of totally disparate elements, producing a strange and often unpleasant and unsettling conflict of emotions. Indeed, the coexistence of humor and terror cannot be described as funny. Likewise, the list of other requirements, such as haughtiness combined with humility, creates that special impact of the grotesque that would be lacking if the conflict were resolved, if the narra-

*Portrait of Saenz by Enrique Arnal*

tion concerned would prove to be just humorous after all, or if it turned out that the reader was in the presence of stark horror. Implicit in *Vidas y muertes* is the unresolved nature of the grotesque, its unsettling ambivalence that helps distinguish the grotesque from other modes or categories of literary discourse.

Irrationality is in essence what guides the search for meaning beyond the surface of things. In *Vidas y muertes* Saenz indicates that humanity is irrational by nature and that humanism is just an insincere way of masking reality. *Los papeles de Narciso Lima-Achá* (The Papers of Narciso Lima-Achá, 1991), his last posthumous novel, reinforces his view of the irrational nature of life. The novel, set again in the 1930s, is important because it reveals aspects left unanswered by *Felipe Delgado*, particularly the nature of the disquieting attacks the abject inflicts on the fragmented self. In dealing with this problem the narrator of *Los papeles de Narciso Lima-Achá* makes some candid revelations on the relationship between narcissism and homosexuality.

Narciso Lima-Achá, the protagonist, embarks with his uncle, Luis Lima-Achá (the name by which he masks his Aymara Indian origins of "Limachi") on a long cruise to Europe. While on board the *Sajonia* Narciso meets many young men. Some are handsome, clean, and neatly dressed, others nauseating and disgusting. Narciso is particularly attracted to a young German, Elbruz Ulme, the name by which he masks his true one, Wolfgang. Elbruz and Narciso become lovers during the voyage. As the journey comes to an end Elbruz stays in Vigo, Spain, while Narciso and his uncle continue to Germany. In Hamburg, Narciso is troubled by some new revelations about his inner self: he is attracted to other men. In Germany, Narciso finds a new partner, Konrad Kluge, with whom he establishes a relationship while maintaining his previous love affair. As time goes by Narciso loses interest in both Elbruz and Kluge. Elbruz dies in a fire; Kluge simply goes away. After the death of his uncle, Narciso finds a new lover, Mariana Wolf, a Nazi radical, with whom he settles down. Though the relationship fades away just as inexplicably as the other two, she reveals Adolf Hitler to him. It is this model of irrationality, both demonic and ecstatic, that somehow sums up the universal love for which the novel and its protagonist have been looking. Narciso returns to Bolivia in the early 1950s; has a minor participation in the nationalist revolution of 1952; meets Jaime Saenz, his own author; and follows, until death, a demonic and jubilant search comparable to Felipe Delgado's. His papers, like the author's, are published posthumously. *Los papeles de Narciso Lima-Achá* and *Felipe Delgado* are two sides of the same coin. A true bildungsroman, the novel is a search for knowledge, a voyage of the self guided by the principle that also ruled Felipe Delgado. Narciso's search for identity, however, seems to be less tortuous.

Like Ovid's Narcissus, Narciso is more than the representation of egotism as a metaphorical expression: it is literally sexualized self-love. Narciso flirts with males and loves his own sex in loving himself, and once he has attained what he calls total homoerotic love, he is willing to perform with women. The indication is clear: once universal love, the love for love's sake, has been achieved, the object of love is insignificant, nonexistent. The void

nevertheless is still there, waiting to be filled by negativity and the death drive.

Well known for his poetry, Jaime Saenz created a unique and personal vision of the world, a vision in which the interplay between death and life is constantly present. As a fiction writer he transplanted his poetic universe into fiction, thus becoming a master of the grotesque. In his literary endeavors Saenz, the solitary scrutinizer of the night side of the city, was revered by his followers as a source of poetic knowledge. Though disquieting as his eccentricities may have been, they sustain his impressive literary production and make it impossible to forget him when selecting the best modern Bolivian fiction writers.

**References:**

Luis H. Antezana, "Hacer y cuidar" and "Felipe Delgado," in his *Ensayos y Lecturas* (La Paz: Altiplano, 1986), pp. 231–264, 333–354;

Leonardo García Pabón, "Las memorias y el lenguaje de Felipe Delgado," in *El paseo de los sentidos: Estudios de literatura boliviana,* edited by García Pabón and Wilma Torrico (La Paz: Instituto Boliviano de Cultura, 1983), pp. 259–267;

Eduardo Mitre, "Jaime Saenz: El espacio fúnebre," in his *El árbol y la piedra: Poetas contemporáneos de Bolivia* (Caracas: Monte Avila, 1988), pp. 26–34;

José Ortega, "Fantasmagoría boliviana: 'Felipe Delgado' de Jaime Saenz," in *El paseo de los sentidos: Estudios de literatura boliviana,* pp. 269–276;

Blanca Wiethüchter, "Las estructuras de lo imaginario en la obra poética de Jaime Saenz," in *Obra poética* by Saenz (La Paz: Biblioteca del Sesquicentenario de la República, 1975), pp. 275–425;

Wiethüchter, *Memoria solicitada* (Santa Cruz, Bolivia: Altiplano, 1989).

**Papers:**

Saenz's papers are held by Arturo Orías in La Paz, Bolivia.

# Luis Rafael Sánchez

*(17 November 1936 –    )*

Alvin Joaquín Figueroa
*Trenton State College*

BOOKS: *Los ángeles se han fatigado y Farsa del amor compradito* (Barcelona: Lugar, 1960);

*En cuerpo de camisa* (San Juan: Lugar, 1966); revised and enlarged (Río Piedras, P.R.: Cultural, 1984);

*O casi el alma: Auto de fe en tres actos* (Barcelona: Rumbos, 1966); republished as *Casi el alma: Auto de fe en tres actos* (Río Piedras, P.R.: Cultural, 1974);

*La pasión según Antígona Pérez* (Hato Rey, P.R.: Lugar, 1968);

*Los ángeles se han fatigado* (Río Piedras, P.R.: Cultural, 1976);

*Farsa del amor compradito* (Río Piedras, P.R.: Cultural, 1976);

*La guaracha del Macho Camacho* (Buenos Aires: De la Flor, 1976); translated by Gregory Rabassa as *Macho Camacho's Beat* (New York: Pantheon, 1980);

*La hiel nuestra de cada día* (Río Piedras, P.R.: Cultural, 1976);

*Teatro de Luis Rafael Sánchez* (Río Piedras, P.R.: Antillana, 1976);

*Fabulación e ideología en la cuentística de Emilio S. Belaval* (San Juan: Instituto de Cultura Puertorriqueña, 1979);

*Quíntuples* (Hanover, N.H.: Ediciones del Norte; San Juan: Cultural, 1985);

*La importancia de llamarse Daniel Santos* (Mexico City: Diana, 1989).

PLAY PRODUCTIONS: *O casi el alma: Auto de fe en tres actos,* San Juan, Teatro Tapia, 23 April 1964;

*La pasión según Antígona Pérez,* San Juan, Institute of Puerto Rican Culture, 30 May 1968;

*Quíntuples,* San Juan, Centro de Bellas Artes de Puerto Rico, 3 October 1984.

OTHER: "Apuntación mínima de lo soez," in *Literature and Popular Culture in the Hispanic World: A Symposium,* edited by Rose S. Minc (Gaithers-

*Luis Rafael Sánchez*

burg, Md.: Hispanoaméricas / Montclair, N.J.: Montclair State College, 1981), pp. 9–14;

"La literatura como traducción de una cultura," in *Translating Latin America: Culture as Text,* edited by William Luis and Julio Rodríguez-Luis (Binghamton, N.Y.: State University of New York at Binghamton, 1991), pp. 23–33.

SELECTED PERIODICAL PUBLICATIONS – UNCOLLECTED: "El trapito," *El Mundo* (San Juan), 22 June 1957, p. 23;

"La espera," *El Mundo* (San Juan), 28 December 1957, p. 25;

"Diario de una ciudad," *El Mundo* (San Juan), 4 August 1958, p. 14;

"Retorno," *El Mundo* (San Juan), 17 January 1959, p. 23;

"Destierro," *El Mundo* (San Juan), 4 July 1959, p. 9;

"Espuelas," *Revista del Instituto de Cultura Puertorriqueña,* 3 (January–March 1960): 27–32.

Luis Rafael Sánchez is the most renowned author in contemporary Puerto Rican literature. Playwright, essayist, and fiction writer, in his most significant work he harshly criticizes the island's colonial situation through the use of a baroque language that is significantly related to the carnival tradition. For him the carnival does not mean a celebration of life in Rabelaisian fashion but a farcical way to confront the excessiveness of political colonialism. His work forms a metaphoric way of describing the political and social chaos of the so-called Free Associate State of Puerto Rico. *En cuerpo de camisa* (In Short Sleeves, 1966; revised and enlarged, 1984) and *La guaracha del Macho Camacho* (1976; translated as *Macho Camacho's Beat,* 1980) are Sánchez's main fictional works. In these, linguistic degradation presents a fresh new style that opposes the euphemism and "purism" of the leading figure of the 1950s in Puerto Rican literature, René Marqués. Once past his mimetic stage, Sánchez uses exaggeration, hyperbole, and excessiveness to offer a grotesque style that satirizes the island's political system. Although his work reflects the main theme of the country's art, the defense of a national identity, it breaks away from the social realism and the existentialism of earlier generations, giving a new voice to Puerto Rican literature.

Sánchez was born in Humacao in southeastern Puerto Rico on 17 November 1936. In 1948 his family moved to San Juan, like many others participating in the working-class migration to the capital resulting from the rapid industrialization the Popular Democratic party sponsored during the 1940s. He started his artistic career as a student actor in the drama department of the University of Puerto Rico. Sánchez worked in radio and became a playwright after graduation.

In his plays and fiction are two phases: one of mimesis, in which Sánchez reproduces what Puerto Rican literary critics call the "Marqués discourse," and one that confronts this model. The author builds this phase around what he calls "la poética de lo soez" (the poetics of the low).

The first of these phases reproduces the discourse of the generation of the 1930s and 1940s in the island's literary tradition. This language is characterized by certain commonplaces in Puerto Rican literature that revolve around the search for a national identity, responding to a program Sánchez calls "literatura de la culpa" (literature of guilt). His first short stories, for instance, talk about a folkloric peasant environment, as in "El trapito" (The Rag, 1957) and "Espuelas" (Spurs, 1960), that represents the base of an obsessive nationality. The return to the exquisite, lordly Spanish world of the Puerto Rican past, which comes from the old fiction and its existentialist background, forms the basis of works such as "La espera" (Awaiting, 1957), "Destierro" (Exile, 1959), and "Retorno" (Return, 1959).

A process of linguistic rupture is initiated in his fiction with "Diario de una ciudad" (Diary of a City, 1958). With this essayistic story Sánchez enters a new phase in which he begins a confrontation with old codes. Parody becomes the axis around which most of Sánchez's subsequent work revolves. The story is a portrait of Puerto Rico in the 1950s, the Puerto Rico of Luis Muñoz Marín and of the social development projects of the Popular Democratic party. It does not have specific characters but a collective one: the life of the San Juan worker. Sentences are brief, explaining in a monotonous fashion how people get ready for their daily tasks. The vocabulary, eliminating the euphemism of earlier works, is less polished and closer to Puerto Rican usage. Sánchez also introduces the subject of mass communication and its impact on Puerto Rican society, a constant theme in his later work. This is the best short story of Sánchez's mimetic phase. With this new language Sánchez shows the baroque carnival of his later work.

A total rupture, however, takes place with the publication of "Aleluya negra" (Black Alleluia, 1961; collected in *En cuerpo de camisa,* 1966). The language of this story initiates a literary work that becomes antiliterary. The dialect of the island's social outcasts is given an artistic representation that Sánchez later calls literature "escrita en puertorriqueño" (written in Puerto Rican). Without trying to imitate the phonology of these groups, Sánchez tries to create a literary discourse based on their language. It becomes "plebian," according to Puerto Rican novelist José Luis González, when Sánchez eliminates the epic, euphemistic, and grandiloquent narrative of the moment.

"Aleluya negra" is a carnivalesque text that narrates the story of Caridad, a young mulatto girl of Loíza, a mainly black community on the northeastern coast. Her incipient sexual desires lead her to lose her virginity when Carmelo el Retinto (*retinto* means a black person of extremely dark complexion) rapes her during a rite to an African deity called Bacumbé. The story apparently takes place during the festivities for the patron saint of Loíza, where Catholic tradition mingles with African beliefs brought by slaves during Spanish colonialism.

The most evident note of the tale is the use of metaphors that point to sexuality. The story is also rich in musicality, but more important, "Aleluya negra" is a story of profusion. Caridad's rape forms part of the carnival, where the symbol of the town is a *vejigante,* a colorful masque made of coconut that emulates festive demons.

Sánchez's fiction is related to his essays, which form the theoretical skeleton of his fictional work and reflect his poetics. His nonfiction also presents two phases: a minor one, in which the author acts as literary, theatrical, and cinema critic; and an incisive, caustic one that sharply scolds the social evils of modern Puerto Rico, including government corruption, political mediocrity, racism, the stupefying effect of the mass media, linguistic deterioration due to American political influence, and Puerto Rican immigration.

"La guagua aérea" (The Flying Bus, 1983) combines fictional and essay techniques to produce one of the most amusing but at the same time serious expositive works by Sánchez. The argument parodies an airplane disaster film: two crabs escape from a suitcase inside an airplane that travels between San Juan and New York, threatening the life of the blond *gringa* stewardess. Far from a funny short story, it becomes a sociological analysis of the Puerto Rican way of life, the dialectics of the empire and its colony, and the island's immigration phenomenon. The passengers dramatize and establish the limits of their political situation. Their open ticket guarantees their return, so they do not put down roots in the United States in order to keep on being what they are, *puertorriqueños.* The narrator asks his neighbor what part of Puerto Rico is she from, to which she answers New York. Sánchez comments that this is the revenge of the invaded invading the invader.

"La guagua aérea" is a powerful, important product of Puerto Rican literature. The airplane suggests the coming and going of a people who defend their identity in spite of the colonial offense. The crabs that break up the harmony inside the plane are a challenge to power and represent the nonofficial story. This text sums up the sociocultural experience of a people not yet a people, a nation not yet a nation, or as Sánchez puts it, a floating nation among two shores of smuggling hopes.

*En cuerpo de camisa* is Sánchez's only short-story collection. It groups the most characteristic traits of

Cover for the 1993 edition of Sánchez's 1976 novel that tells about several characters caught in a traffic jam in San Juan

his narrative art: the use of the island's language; humor, farce, and parody; and literary self-consciousness. However, what is most evident in these stories (fifteen in its last edition of 1984) is the displacement of the language to re-create the grotesque. Eating, sexual acts, and other physical activities performed by his characters manifest the "low" in every moment. The characters are marginal elements of society: drug addicts, blacks, prostitutes, the unemployed, and homosexuals.

The characters always present an aspect of social degradation. In its most recent edition, *En cuerpo de camisa* represents a world where the inhabitants include a tender black prostitute who discovers sublime feelings of love and maternity ("Tiene la noche una raíz" [The Rooted Night]), a mulatto woman thirsty for physical love ("Aleluya negra"), a black and effeminate homosexual who is killed by his community "¡Jum!" [Hm!]), an old man who belongs to a lonely hearts club and commits suicide after learning about the death of his distant lover in

San Juan ("Memoria de un eclipse" [Memory of an Eclipse]), a group of junkies ("Que sabe a paríso" [Like Heaven, Man]), a sexual snooper ("Etc."), a beggar who pretends to be blind and does not know what to do when his parish collects the money needed for his operation ("La maroma" [Somersault]), and a mentally incompetent woman who reveals ugly facts to her daughter's lover.

Sánchez's treatment of the grotesque presents a conflict between opposite poles. For him the carnival is not a festivity but the masquerade of social reality. In this way the carnival is the camouflage of loneliness, prejudice, dictatorship, colonialism, and death. In using common language Sánchez does not try to provoke laughter but to make the reader reflect about what is exposed. His work possesses an important ethical element that places him in the more traditional camp of Puerto Rican literature, notwithstanding his challenging of the establishment.

"Tiene la noche una raíz" is one of the most beautiful stories of the collection. Gurdelia Grifitos, the town harlot, faces the unique experience of being solicited by a ten-year-old child, Cuco, who has arrived to buy the love that his father and other men in town say she sells. Gurdelia, without knowing how to react to the boy's demands when he starts crying and saying that he is already a man, takes him in her arms and cuddles him until he falls asleep. The prostitute reveals human qualities when Cuco awakes. Cuco leaves the house jumping and shouting that the experience has been divine. That night, Gurdelia turned the lights off early, and an old drunkard got tired of knocking at her door.

The narrator, without assuming a moralizing posture, shows the human side of this woman, who discovers her maternal instinct during this special night. She is the victim of the town's prejudice and even of witchcraft. However, Gurdelia keeps on selling her merchandise, a limited business. She is resigned to her role of poor harlot, exploited by a community that rejects her but uses her at the same time. Gurdelia charges just two dollars per service, and she does not make more because among other things she is very ugly. Even her last name, Grifitos, shows social prejudice, referring to her kinky or woolly hair. As with many of Sánchez's characters, her name serves to degrade her.

All his short fiction leads to the novel La guaracha del Macho Camacho (1976). The novel has a thesis, and even when the verbal artifice is its most evident feature — the book is a masterpiece of intertextuality — its ethical intention is clear. In this sense the novel, although exploring a series of narrative games by inserting material alien to that considered properly literary, still belongs to that common area of Puerto Rican literature that considers art as a weapon of social struggle. Sánchez does not form part of a "literature of guilt," but his narrative insists on making evident the ethical aspect of the text. According to Sánchez Puerto Rican literature is the backbone of its people, an ambassador of a country without embassies, of a nation that is still not a nation due to U.S. imperialism. Hence, the grotesque realism constitutes a way of seeing national reality. For Sánchez, the novel is a social fact and art a political commitment.

The setting of La guaracha del Macho Camacho is a traffic jam that parodies Julio Cortázar's "La autopista del sur" (The Southern Thruway, from Todos los fuegos el fuego, 1966; translated as All Fires the Fire, 1973), yet this parody is not the only evident aspect but a whole connotational process that links the text with a historical reality. The novel takes place during rush hour in greater San Juan during a Wednesday at five in the afternoon. Not by chance, this traffic jam takes place in the stretch from the Constitution Bridge up to Roosevelt Avenue along the old slaughterhouse route. These signs — constitution, Roosevelt Avenue, and slaughterhouse — allude to colonialism and the social stagnation Puerto Rico's political status generates.

The main characters include the tacky Mother or "China Hereje"; Sen. Vicente Reinosa; his pseudoaristocratic wife Graciela Alcántara y López de Montefrío; their son Benny, whose favorite hobby is to masturbate using his Ferrari as his sexual fetish; the working-class Doña Chon; and el Nene, the retarded son of China Hereje. All of these characters relate to this traffic jam physically and emotionally. While the senator is right in the middle of the congestion waiting for a way of getting out of it, China Hereje, his mistress, waits impatiently for him. Graciela waits in the psychiatrist's office. Doña Chon waits for the release of her son, accused of drug dealing, from jail. This motif of waiting, which can have political connotations, is absent in Benny, who, also trapped in the traffic jam and looking for a shortcut, runs over el Nene and kills him.

Each character's narrative is interrupted structurally by the intervention of a disc jockey who repeats the musical hit of the moment, "La vida es una cosa fenomenal" (Life Is a Phenomenal Thing). During the development of the novel the narrator inserts lines of the song's lyrics in order to create the illusion that it is being transmitted again and again. The structure of the novel proposes an oral reading in which the noise of *la guaracha* invades everything and repeats itself, annoying the reader. The end of the novel re-creates the entire lyrics of the song.

The characters represent the process of class struggle: the discourse of the outcasts, the non-whites (China Hereje, Doña Chon, and el Nene), confronts that of the white upper class (Vicente, Graciela, and Benny). The range of secondary characters – the psychiatrist Severo Severino, Graciela's maids, the Spanglish-speaking receptionist, the Cuban perfumists – goes from the working class to the upper middle class.

Intertextuality is always present, establishing a dialogue between the plot and the subtexts from movies, television, colloquialisms, political slogans, advertising, comics, and popular songs and literature, the last being the most important. There is a whole web of characters and situations that in one way or another, and sometimes illogically or anachronistically, are linked. Huey, Dewey, and Louie; Liz Taylor; Lope de Vega; Fulgencio Batista; Blondie; Little Lulu; Pluto; Luis Muñoz Marín; Federico García Lorca; and others share the plot of the novel. In all this parodic dialogue, something remains clear: the role of popular literature and mass media as generators of a literary discourse that, through an artistic game, tries to offer a portrait not just of Puerto Rico but of all the colonized part of North America.

*La guaracha del Macho Camacho* also re-creates and parodies the language of different social groups: the pseudopure Spanish of the senator, the euphemistic language of Graciela, the secretary's Spanglish, Benny's personal dialect, the vulgarity of China Hereje, and the clichéd language of Doña Chon. Given these features, *La guaracha del Macho Camacho* is Puerto Rico's contemporary novel par excellence. No other work in the island's literature describes the national situation better. Notwithstanding the laughter it provokes, the novel makes the reader see a pessimistic future with grief.

*La importancia de llamarse Daniel Santos* (The Importance of Being Daniel Santos, 1989), Sánchez's latest novel, is a baroque reflection on the many myths popular culture generates through a legendary figure in Puerto Rican popular music, Daniel Santos. Santos's tale personifies the hopes and dreams of those profane characters the author started to re-create in his early short stories and in *La guaracha del Macho Camacho*. The text itself represents a total rupture with tradition. Most critics consider it a novel, but it could be classified as an anti-novel, a long social essay, a collection of stories, or

LA IMPORTANCIA DE LLAMARSE DANIEL SANTOS

*LUIS RAFAEL SÁNCHEZ*

DIANA*bcdefghijk*LITERARIA

*Cover for the 1993 printing of Sánchez's 1989 novel, an experimental work about a popular singer*

an epic poem of Latin America's poor and exploited.

Similar to *La guaracha del Macho Camacho*, *La importancia de llamarse Daniel Santos* is structured as a dialogue between its narration – the author's omniscient reflections – and the lyrics of some of Daniel Santos's songs. This text starts with a section entitled "El método del discurso" (The Method of the Discourse), where the first short paragraph gives the reader a clear idea of the intent of the narration. The main body of the text is divided into three parts: "Las palomas del milagro" (The Miracle Doves), based on Santos's musical world; "Vivir en varón" (To Live within Macho Codes); and "Cinco boleros aún por melodiarse" (Five Ballads Waiting for a Melody). The last part is a brief grand finale whose title parodies the bolero singer's discourse: "Saqueos, discografía, muchísimas gracias" (Booty, Discography, Many Many Thanks). This last part repeats the initial statement of the introduction and then clarifies the mechanism of Sánchez's intertextual art.

In a way, the main character of the tale is the bolero and the myths it generates. This Caribbean tropical ballad that deals with broken hearts, passionate treason, and indolence in love places itself in the macho realm. In this way the text becomes a digression on the Spanish phenomenon of machismo. As a contemporary Don Juan with his many women, alcoholic habits, and "true" manliness, Daniel Santos camouflages Latin American social truth through the bolero.

Like *La guaracha del Macho Camacho,* the narration explores the languages of the masses. It is totally baroque and parodic, and it laughs but at the same time cries about Latin America's misery. Here the guaracha turns into the slow-beat bolero, but the intention is still the same: using popular music to approach not only Puerto Rico but all of Barefoot America.

In his works Luis Rafael Sánchez uses Puerto Rican and Spanish American popular language, humor, musical structures, parody, and literary self-consciousness. Although the continent is always present, Sánchez's main concern is Puerto Rico and its existence as a colonized society. From "Diario de una ciudad" to *La importancia de llamarse Daniel Santos,* his fiction, through baroque and carnivalesque language, enriches contemporary Caribbean literature.

### References:

Margot Arce de Vázquez, "Acotaciones a una lectura de *La guaracha del Macho Camacho," Revista Puertorriqueña de Ciencias Sociales,* 1, 2 (January–June 1977): 18–25;

María Arrillaga, "Enajenación social y lingüística en *La guaracha del Macho Camacho de Luis Rafael Sanchez," Hispamérica,* 12 (April–August 1983): 155–164;

Efraín Barradas, *Para leer en puertorriqueño: Acercamiento a la obra de Luis Rafael Sánchez* (Río Piedras, P.R.: Cultural, 1981);

Helen Calaf de Agüera, "*La guaracha del Macho Camacho:* Intertextualidad y ruptura," *Caribe,* 2 (Fall 1977): 7–16;

Eliseo R. Colón Zayas, "La problemática del ser puertorriqueño en los cuentos de Luis Rafael Sánchez," *Pensamiento Crítico,* 4, no. 26 (October–November 1981): 21–25;

Alvin Joaquín Figueroa, *La prosa de Luis Rafael Sánchez: Texto y contexto* (New York: Peter Lang, 1989);

Roberto González Echevarría, "La vida es una cosa fenomenal: *La guaracha del Macho Camacho* y la estética de la novela actual," in his *Isla a su vuelo fugitivo: Ensayos críticos sobre literatura hispanoamericana* (Madrid: José Porrúa, 1983), pp. 91–102;

Nélida Hernández Vargas and Daisy Caraballo Abréu, eds., *Luis Rafael Sánchez: Crítica y bibliografia* (Río Piedras: Editorial de la Universidad de Puerto Rico, 1985);

Carlos Roberto Morán, "Los lenguajes, la dependencia, el intento liberador," *Sin Nombre,* no. 1 (April–June 1977): 57–61;

Randolph D. Pope, "*La guaracha del Macho Camacho* y la contaminación de la mente," *The Bilingual Review,* 5, no. 1–2 (1978): 152–155;

*Revista de Estudios Hispánicos,* 5 (1978), special issue on Sanchez;

Loreina Santos Silva, "*En cuerpo de camisa* o los malamañosos," *Renacimiento,* 1, no. 2 (July–December 1981): 21–29;

Stacey Schlaw, "Mass Media Images of the Puertorriqueño in *La guaracha del Macho Camacho,*" in *Literature and Popular Culture in The Hispanic World,* edited by Rose S. Minc (Gaithersburg, Md.: Hispanoaméricas; Montclair, N.J.: Montclair State College, 1981), pp. 161–171;

Carmen Vázquez Arce, "Sexo y mulatería: Dos sones de una misma guaracha," *Sin Nombre,* 12, no. 4 (July–September 1982): 59–63;

Vázquez Arce, "Los medios de comunicación en *La guaracha del Macho Camacho* de Luis Rafael Sánchez," *Hispamérica,* 20, no. 5 (1987): 229–236.

# Rogelio Sinán

*(25 April 1904 –    )*

## Maida Watson Espener
*Florida International University*

BOOKS: *Onda* (Rome: Casa Edifrice, 1929);
*Incendios* (Panama City: Mar del Sur, 1944);
*Dos aventuras en el Lejano Oriente* (Panama City: Biblioteca Selecta, 1947);
*Plenilunio* (Panama City, 1947);
*Semana santa en la niebla* (Panama City: Ediciones del Departamento de Cultura y Publicaciones, 1949);
*La boina roja* (Panama City: Nacional, 1954);
*Los valores humanos en la lírica de Maples Arce* (Mexico City: Conferencia, 1959);
*Chiquilinga* (Panama City: Panamá, 1961);
*La poesía panameña* (Panama City, 1962);
*Cuna común* (Panama City: Tareas, 1963);
*A la orilla de las estatuas maduras* (Mexico City: Secretaría de Educación Pública, Subsecretaría de Asuntos Culturales, 1967);
*Saloma sin salomar* (Panama City: Ministerio de Educación, 1969);
*Cuentos de Rogelio Sinán* (San José: Editorial Universitaria Centroamericana, 1971);
*Teatro infantil* (Panama City: Géminis, 1976);
*La isla mágica* (Panama City: Instituto Nacional de Cultura, 1977);
*Los pájaros del sueño* (Guayaquil, Ecuador: Casa de la Cultura Ecuatoriana, 1978);
*El candelabro de los malos ofidios y otros cuentos* (Mexico City: Signos, 1982);
*Onda* (Panama City: Formato Dieciseis, 1983);
*El conejito; El Pato Patuleco; Motivo de Ratón Pérez; El caballito negro; El caballito del naranjal* (San José: Editorial Universitaria Centroamericana, 1985);
*La cucarachita Mandinga* (Panama City: Instituto Nacional de Cultura, 1992).

SELECTED PERIODICAL PUBLICATIONS – UNCOLLECTED: "Un modernista panameño, Darío Herrera," *Lotería*, 230 (1975): 55–64;
"Vivencia de la India," *Maga*, 5–6 (1985): 98–100.

Rogelio Sinán has been important to Panamanian literature not only as an innovative writer but

*Rogelio Sinán*

as a teacher and mentor to numerous writers during his many decades as the undisputed leader of the country's literary circles. Though best known for his short stories, his role as an innovator has been in the areas of poetry and the novel. He introduced avant-garde techniques in both genres and became known outside Panama for his use of Panamanian landscape and themes in literary creations ranging from surrealistic, cubist works in the 1930s to his use of magic realism in his epic novel *La isla mágica* (The Magic Island, 1977).

Sinán, whose real name is Bernardo Domínguez Alba, was born on 25 April 1904 on the island of Taboga, located off the coast of Panama City. When he was five his family moved to Panama City, but he returned to Taboga often during his childhood. The island became the setting for most of his literary creations. After receiving his *bachillerato,* the equivalent of a baccalaureate degree, from the National Institute in 1923, Sinán continued his university studies in Santiago, Chile, where among his friends he counted Pablo Neruda and Gabriela Mistral. According to Sinán, Mistral encouraged his vocation as a writer. Like Rubén Darío, whose first contact with the world of serious literature was through Santiago, Sinán fell in love with the ambience of a transplanted Europe that Santiago represented for him.

In 1926 Sinán embarked for Rome, where he continued his studies at the University of Rome. During this period the young author's pseudonym was conceived. Sinán explains that his name was based on a place in his beloved island, Taboga. His new last name is a version of Sinai, a hill on Taboga, to which he added his father's first name, Rogelio. In Rome Sinán became familiar with the works of the Spanish vanguardists through the pages of the Spanish literary magazines, just as he had become familiar during his stay in Chile with the writings of the Argentines Jorge Luis Borges and Ricardo Güiraldes.

In 1938 Sinán was named Panamanian consul to Calcutta, where he served for two years. Upon returning to the isthmus in 1941 he was made director of the newly created Department of Fine Arts. In the same year he founded the Biblioteca Selecta, a series of volumes showcasing the writings of Panamanian and other Latin-American authors. From 1953 to 1960 he lived in Mexico, fulfilling various diplomatic functions. Afterward he taught drama at the University of Panama and Spanish at the National Institute, where he continued his role as mentor to a younger generation of writers.

In Rome Sinán published his first volume of poetry, *Onda* (Wave), in 1929. This significant work was heralded by literary historians on the isthmus and elsewhere as marking Panama's break with modernism and its incorporation into the vanguardist movement. Other volumes of Sinán's poetry include *Incendios* (Fires, 1944), *Semana santa en la niebla* (Holy Week in the Cloud, 1949), and *Saloma sin Salomar* (Saloma without Salomar, 1969).

Sinán's poetry introduces themes developed in his short stories, just as his stories provide charac-

ters, themes, and techniques for his two novels. *Onda* uses Panamanian subject matter and folk language, a trait evident in all of Sinán's later works. In a manner reminiscent of the poetry of Nicolás Guillén, Sinán uses the rhythmic ingredients of drum beats to create an atmosphere of tropical sensuality. In *Saloma sin Salomar* he continues the use of rhythmic ingredients and Dantesque symbols. The pantheistic *Semana santa en la niebla* continues the use of symbols taken from the island setting.

Sinán's use of vanguardism in *Onda* fuses elements of French cubism, German expressionism, and Italian futurism with his own native themes and creative ability. He deliberately set out to break with all the traditional forms of poetry popular at that time in Panama, believing that for this reason his poetry would not have a mass audience. Recent critics have debated the extent of Sinán's influence on Panamanian poetry at that time, stating that Sinán, though evidently revolutionary in his own right, did not bring about the sweeping changes in Panamanian poetry once believed.

Instead, it was as a prose writer that Sinán made his mark. His important contributions to the short-story genre include "A la orilla de las estatuas maduras" (At the Edge of the Mature Statues, 1932), written upon the insistence of Alejo Carpentier; "Hechizo" (Bewitched, 1938), selected by Eduardo Mallea as one of Latin America's best short stories in the Argentine publication *La Nación;* and *La boina roja* (The Red Beret, 1953), included in Seymour Menton's *The Spanish American Short Story: A Critical Anthology* (1980). Other titles worthy of mention are "El sueño de Serafín del Carmen" (Serafín del Carmen's Dream, 1931), "Todo un conflicto de sangre" (All a Conflict of Blood, 1946), "Una cobra en mi cama" (A Cobra in My Bed, 1954), "Bobby" (1954), "Los pájaros del sueño" (The Birds in the Dream, 1957), "Cuna Común" (Common Cradle, 1963), "Eva, la sierpe y el árbol" (Eve, the Serpent, and the Tree, 1975), and "El candelabro de los malos ofidios" (The Candelabra of the Bad Ophidians, 1982). In 1971 the Editorial Universitaria Centroamericana (EDUCA) published an anthology of fourteen stories, *Cuentos de Rogelio Sinán* (Stories by Rogelio Sinán).

Unifying factors in Sinán's prose are the emphasis on the subconscious as conveyed via stream-of-consciousness and interior-monologue techniques, the prevalence of sexual and erotic themes, the frequent incorporation of dreamlike and surrealistic elements, and his penchant for infusing his fiction with delightful yet disconcerting ambiguity.

*Cover for Sinán's 1947 novel, one of the first in Central America to
break with regional realism in favor of
experimental techniques*

These aspects characterize not only Sinán's short stories but also his two novels, *Plenilunio* (Full Moon, 1947) and *La isla mágica.*

The eight short stories that Sinán wrote between 1924 and 1939 anticipate the main themes he develops in *Plenilunio:* obsession, especially sexual obsession; the importance of dream worlds; and the subconscious and the use of varying levels of space and time. The satire of the white Panamanian oligarchy and North American powers are also themes developed first in his stories.

In 1954 Sinán published *La boina roja,* perhaps his most famous story, in which the themes of dreams, the subconscious, and the use of interior monologues popular with the avant-garde appear. Many of its techniques anticipate what critics later called magic realism. In this story science is the element from which the author creates the surrealistic

techniques. He weaves the ocean, the tropical landscape, magic, and the importance of dreams into a mystery in which a famous scientist, Paul Eckerd, is accused of murdering his research assistant, Linda Olsen, on a secluded tropical island off the coast of Panama. Traditional Western science is represented by Eckerd, whose knowledge is counterposed to the folk magic of an old Haitian woman who practices voodoo on the island.

Sinán incorporates symbols from Greek mythology into his stories, particularly seductive sirens and river nymphs. Characters are changed from one physical state to another, usually as a result of magic or love. In *La boina roja* the American scientist and his research assistant are seduced by the tropical landscape. The research assistant may even have metamorphosed into a creature that is part fish and part human.

Sinán also introduces into this significant early story the use of multiple perspectives, a technique expanded later in his two novels. The story of the mystery murder on the island is narrated from several points of view: those of the scientist, the judge who interrogates him in the Panamanian courtroom, and the scientist's own recollection of previous dialogues. The varying interpretations of one event serve to underline the complexity of the situation in a style reminiscent of Borges's games with the reader.

Associated with metamorphosis in Sinán's work is the underlying theme of racial conflict. White oppressive foreigners or members of the upper class are challenged by the more-authentic values of a dark native class more in contact with nature. Sinán's writings identify darkness with indigenous values, whiteness with foreign and anti-native forces. In one of his plays for children, *La cucarachita Mandinga* (Mandinga the Cockroach, 1992), the heroine is courted by a white foreign suitor, but she chooses a dark native spouse instead. In *La boina roja* Linda Olsen is from the southern United States and displays strong negative feelings toward the blacks on the island but under the influence of the magic of the island has sexual relations with one of them. In "Todo un conflicto de sangre" the rich, white, upper-class woman, Mrs. Rosenberg, believes that she is turning black as the result of a blood transfusion from her black chauffeur. In Sinán's stories eros functions paradoxically both as a force to stimulate and to combat racial prejudice. Mrs. Rosenberg overcomes her guilt and hatred of her black chauffeur whom she has fired by making love to him. In "Bobby" Lucy Loving awakens the latent racial prejudice of the white sailors on the tropical island by falsely accusing the black Sid of trying to rape her.

Sinán's interest in the psychological is a constant in his prose. In almost all of his stories and novels there is a doctor or a psychiatrist. Sinán's grandfather was a country doctor who never charged for his services. In "Todo un conflicto de sangre" the story is told by a psychoanalyst who watches in horror as his patient begins to develop the traits of her black chauffeur. In "La noche buena de la doctora Duarte" (Doctor Duarte's Good Night, 1943) the main character is a doctor from the lower middle class who is married to a rich and degenerate member of the upper class. The story is told by a lawyer who says that the telling of the story will be a form of self-analysis. In *La isla mágica* is a doctor, Don Plácido, who studied medicine and works as a doctor on the island though he

never completed his degree. Like Sinán's grandfather, he never charges anyone.

Sinán's writings usually contain a strong vein of social protest, aimed primarily at North Americans or the white Panamanian upper class on the isthmus. In one of his earliest stories, "La nueva víctima de la revolución" (The New Victim of the Revolution, 1932), he uses the stream-of-consciousness technique to tell the story of an unemployed teacher, representative of a socio-economic group with whom Sinán has always identified, who decides to marry a rich old man in order to improve her social status. Once she decides to marry him, she finds to her horror that a social revolution has just taken place and that he is no longer rich.

The publication of *Plenilunio* was an extremely important event in the history of Central American fiction, since this was the first Panamanian novel — and the only one for decades afterward — to transcend the thematic and stylistic strictures of *criollismo* fully and feature the characteristics associated with "the New Novel." The use of multiple narrators and direct address to the reader (in this case, through a "lectora" [reader]) established different kinds of author/reader relationships.

The influences of Luigi Pirandello and Miguel de Unamuno y Jugo — specifically *Sei personaggi in cerca d'autore* (1921; translated as *Six Characters in Search of an Author,* 1922) and *Niebla* (1914; translated as *Mist,* 1928) respectively — are especially prominent in *Plenilunio;* Sinán had just spent five years in Italy when he wrote the novel and was familiar with Pirandello. As the novel begins the author converses with his reader, who is actually present in the room with him, in a familiar, provocative manner, inviting her to participate with him in the creative process. After the reader retires to the bedroom, the scene is interrupted by the arrival of three individuals. These visitors claim to be literary personages whom the author once created and then forgot: Don Céfaro Cunha, his granddaughter Elena, and Miguel Camargo, whose nickname is El Mack Amargo. After Elena refreshes the author's memory with an erotic evocation of the circumstances of her creation, the three characters relate what has happened to them since they were given life.

From this point the narrative is alternately supplied by one or another of the personages while the author occasionally interjects himself to seek clarification or to describe the sometimes heated verbal interactions that take place between the characters, a technique Sinán had used in his earlier short stories to provide varying perspectives. Don

Céfaro, eager to unburden himself of painful recollections, begins with an account of his turbulent, traumatic youth in Europe and of his marriage to a woman prone to episodes of murderous psychosis under the spell of the full moon. He tells how, after his wife dies in childbirth leaving him with an infant daughter to care for, he becomes involved in drug trafficking and white slavery. Eventually his daughter marries a wastrel from an upper-class family, and from this union Elena is born. Céfaro develops a strong bond with his granddaughter, but Elena's parents finally sever his relationship with her by taking her to Europe. This precipitates a severe depression in Don Céfaro. Sinking into alcoholism and drug abuse and unable to manage his affairs, he is swindled out of his riches by his trusted associate, a crafty, depraved individual named Crispín.

At this point the narrative is taken over by El Mack Amargo, who sketches the details of his life. El Mack's name is evidently influenced by Bertolt Brecht's *Die Dreigroschenoper* (1928; translated as *The Threepenny Opera,* 1933). The son of a prostitute, he never knows his father's identity. El Amargo explains that he worked at a series of menial jobs but squandered most of his earnings on prostitutes, lottery tickets, gambling, and liquor.

Fascinated by the Jewish experience during World War II and by the Jewish presence in Panama's upper class, Sinán creates Jewish characters in his fiction that are both attractive and repelling. When it is Elena Cunha's turn to tell her story, she relates that on the eve of World War II she met and fell passionately in love with a Jewish sculptor named Ninsky in Antwerp. Elena evokes the memory of their ardent romance, ended when her lover is gunned down by Nazis, and recalls how she would pose nude for Ninsky and make love to him under the rays of the full moon. Immediately after the death of her lover Elena flees Europe and joins her grandfather Don Céfaro in Panama. She describes her sense of alienation and despair on coming to Panama and relates that she soon retreated into a world of fantasy, clinging to the memory of happier days with Ninsky. Also, like her grandmother, she begins to experience disconcerting personality changes when the moon is full. Adding to her discomfort are the continuous amorous advances made by the unsavory Crispín, who is living in Don Céfaro's home and still exerting his malevolent influence on the old man. When this perverse, disgusting man proposes to Elena she is repulsed, but she nevertheless agrees to marry him in order to regain possession of the wealth he fraudulently has appropri-

ated from her grandfather and to obtain revenge by subjecting him to sexual humiliation.

But from the beginning the sexual relationship between Elena and Crispín is characterized by grotesquely neurotic interactions resulting in reciprocal degradation. Elena's susceptibility to severe personality disorders under lunar influence suddenly becomes more acute, the moon's rays precipitating her orgastic hallucinations during which she imagines herself possessed by her dead lover Ninsky. The theme of women who change into other creatures under the influence of erotic passion is one that Sinán has experimented with in several preceding short stories. Elena's paroxysms of lust for another man provide the element of deviance needed to stimulate Crispín's prurient instincts, and he frantically awaits the onset of her attacks. Continuing her narrative, Elena tells of her relationship with a famous international psychiatrist with whom she consulted and to whom she was drawn because of his uncanny resemblance to Ninsky.

The narrations of the three characters now converge in the masterfully constructed climax of the novel, which features layers of ambiguity. First Elena tells of her ruse to trick Crispín into assuming responsibility for her pregnancy by feigning a relapse of her moon-induced dementia, thereby inducing him to have sex with her. Naked in the moonlight and awaiting Crispín's stealthy approach, she is surprised in her garden by El Mack Amargo, who has come looking for Crispín in order to avenge his sister's murder. Excited by Elena's nudity and seizing the opportunity to gain retribution against Crispín by cuckolding him, El Amargo assaults her, overcoming her admittedly perfunctory resistance. Their "struggle" is interrupted by the sudden appearance of Crispín armed with a knife, and a violent confrontation ensues between him and Mack. During the scuffle Crispín is shot and killed. Contradictory indications as to who fired the fatal shot – Mack, Don Céfaro, or someone else – constitute the first of several ambiguous aspects in the intriguing denouement. Again Sinán uses the technique of multiple possibilities and varying solutions seen in his earlier works.

The story now comes full circle, and the three personages explain why they have come on this night to the home of their creator, the author. They contend that there was another witness present on the night of the shooting who can establish the identity of the real killer, the author himself. The author's denial of any knowledge of the crime leads to a heated discussion between him and the others.

Elena maintains that the author, having become a character in his own novel, is the real murderer. Her accusation stimulates the memory of the author, who now recalls that it was really Elena who killed her husband during a recurrence of her moon-induced illness. The validity of these assertions diminishes as the true nature of the characters' existence is called into question. Are they really nothing more than literary creations, or might they actually be autonomous flesh-and-blood entities? Perhaps, it is even argued, the author himself is fictitious, merely existing in someone else's novel or someone else's dream.

Don Céfaro, struggling like the others to make sense out of the baffling ambiguity of the situation, points out that it is exactly one year ago that the crime took place and that the moon is exactly where it was on that night. Responding to Don Céfaro's exhortation to reenact the pivotal episode, Mack is about to assault Elena but is temporarily prevented from doing so by the author. But Mack is intent on carrying out his role. In order to eliminate further interference, he restrains the author by tying a cord around his neck.

Suddenly the scene fades out, giving way to a stream-of-consciousness passage that culminates with a restoration of the reality that existed before the arrival of the three personages, leading the author to assume that he has dreamed the entire sequence. But this explanation is apparently belied by the painful scratches on his neck and the "claras huellas del vestido de Elena" (the clear signs of Elena's dress) left on the premises. The author remembers that the reader is still asleep in his bedroom and goes to wake her up. When she awakens, his neck pain is gone; thus he understands that his experience with Elena and the others was a dream within another dream originating in the subconscious of the reader. These contradictions remain unresolved, and the reader is left to puzzle over the knotty question of what constitutes reality within the context of the novel and how the reader figures in the creation of the meaning of a text.

Sinán claims *Plenilunio* was written in less than a month. His second novel, *La isla mágica,* was the product of a more involved process. Sinán began the work in 1943 but was forced to put the work aside after writing about seventy-five pages. It was only after his retirement from teaching in the 1970s that he was able to finish the novel.

Although there are important points of contact between *Plenilunio* and *La isla mágica* – both works employ dreamlike and surrealist elements, feature temporal experimentation, and are substantially infused with eroticism – the differences are more significant than the similarities. For example, *La isla mágica* is a far more complex work, structurally as well as thematically. In addition, it is much more heavily imbued with the characteristics associated with the magic realism of Carpentier and Gabriel García Márquez. A useful reference point for discussing *La isla mágica* is García Márquez's masterpiece, *Cien años de soledad* (1967; translated as *One Hundred Years of Solitude,* 1970) with which it shares some basic similarities. Like the imaginary village of Macondo in *Cien años de soledad,* Sinán's magic island – based on Taboga, although this is never stated specifically – is an enchanted place where reality and the supernatural are fused imperceptibly; where generation after generation lives in a unique, isolated environment that retains its anachronistic, even timeless nature despite frequent intrusions from the outside world; and where one is exposed to a metaphysical view of humanity, birth and death, and the comic and tragic aspects of life in an absurd world.

The basic theme of *La isla mágica* is that humanity is a slave to its instincts, which should not be repressed but allowed to be expressed. Incest and relationships between animals and humans abound. Another related theme is the identical nature of spiritual and physical love. Sex in the novel is the force that eliminates class barriers through the uncontrollable force of eros.

Another recurrent subject is that of the tropical landscape. Again Sinán uses the island of Taboga as the setting for his work. The novel, aptly titled The Magic Island, is set on an island like that of *La boina roja,* where magic and reality fuse. Time is also important. Sinán left Taboga when he was five and afterward only saw the island as a visitor. Holy Week is the most important week for tourists and returning natives to visit the island, and Sinán sets one of his collections of poems and part of *La isla mágica* during this festival.

In terms of narrative technique, Sinán again employs multiple perspectives in *La isla mágica* as he did in *Plenilunio* and various short stories to provide structural unity. The novel changes narrators even in the middle of a paragraph. The characters weave in and out of the narration, providing different perspectives on events.

Through his abundant use of intertextuality Sinán borrows characters and reemploys themes that have appeared previously in his literary creations. Goyo Gancho, who elopes with a village girl in one of Sinán's short stories, "A las orillas del río" (At the River's Edge), appears again in this novel.

Serafín del Carmen, the narrator in *La isla mágica,* is the main character in another story, "El sueño de Serafín del Carmen."

Prominent among the scores of colorful, memorable characters who populate the pages of *La isla mágica* are representatives of several generations of the Durgel clan: Juan (Juancho Hermoso), his son Goyo Gancho, and especially his grandson Juan Felipe. The latter could be considered the central character of the novel, for it is through his experiences, relationships, remembrances, hallucinations, and dreams that the crucial link between its numerous narrative strands is maintained. He is a delightful literary creation whose main attribute, his voracious, incorrigible sexuality, manifests itself in a multitude of erotic episodes.

*La isla mágica* is a complex novel with several interrelated story lines that demand a high degree of reader involvement if the novel is to be made comprehensible. In addition to chronicling the adventures of the Durgel family, the novel features an impressive array of other characters whose interactions, often tragicomic in nature, reflect the violence, pathos, superstition, mystery, and exoticism that characterize life on the magic island.

*La isla mágica* is divided into ten *decálogos* of ten chapters each – one hundred episodes in all. The inspirations for this structural format are of course Dante's *The Divine Comedy* (1321) and Giovanni Boccaccio's *The Decameron* (1351). Virtually every chapter in the novel can stand on its own as a self-contained short story. Each is also an integral part of the composite work.

The difficulty in reading the novel is due in great part to the author's virtuoso handling of extremely intricate configurations in time. The novel is based on three separate yet interrelated temporal frames of reference. Several early chapters as well as the concluding one take place ten years after the death of Chompipe Durgel. In the final pages of the novel the reader learns that the action depicted in these chapters, which cover approximately three hours, occurs just after the conclusion of World War II. A second time frame encompasses the events that occur during Holy Week of 1936 and that culminate with the bizarre death of Chompipe and another important character, Hipólito. The third temporal track of the novel, which intersects with the other two in often-confusing ways, covers approximately one hundred years – another point of contact with *Cien años de soledad* – beginning with the period of the California gold rush and ending in the 1940s. Many significant events in Panamanian history – the building of the Panama Railroad, the

French canal enterprise, the Thousand Days War, the armed conflict with Costa Rica over the disputed Cota region, and the United States presence on the isthmus – provide an effective backdrop for events depicted without ever becoming the main focus. The action of the novel is not presented chronologically; rather, the narration jumps back and forth in time and space, and from one story line to another, in such a way that the reader is frequently hard put to determine the many characters' relationships to one another or to place the events described in a coherent linear sequence.

Another factor adding to the complexity of the novel is the author's frequent ambiguity. Sinán's penchant for misleading the reader with conflicting versions of reality manifests itself from the start of the narration. The novel begins with a description of a ceremony in which a statue apparently representing Chompipe is being dedicated to honor him as a hero on the tenth anniversary of his death. Immediately the reader recognizes that he has entered a world where life is permeated with a sense of the absurd and where things are not always as they appear, for the panegyric offered to the deceased refers not to deeds normally considered heroic or worthy of praise but rather to his notorious sexual prowess. Furthermore, the reader learns that the statue does not necessarily represent Juan Felipe Durgel at all, but might instead be meant to symbolize either Francisco Pizarro or perhaps the sixteenth-century Spanish monarch Philip the Fair. At any rate, the scandalous eulogy is delivered by an emotionally disturbed schoolteacher initially referred to as la maestra Salerna and eventually identified as Cándida, whose relationship with Chompipe is one of the key plot ingredients of the novel. Such confusion is frequently encountered in the novel.

The reader's disorientation is further compounded by Sinán's custom of referring to many characters by two or more names. Thus sometimes only after many chapters have passed does one realize that what seems to be two or more people is actually one. It is only as *La isla mágica* approaches completion that the reader has sufficient data to solve the formidable problems presented by its complicated structure.

Rogelio Sinán has always believed that universal values in literature must spring from a thorough knowledge of the writer's own national reality. His poetry, fiction, and drama are permeated with a sense of Panama's history, landscape, and racial relations. At the same time, his many years spent living outside Panama and his vast readings in world literature offer him the perspective of an outsider.

Vanguardism, magic realism, and myth theory have all provided him with techniques and inspirations with which to express his own unique view of his recurrent symbol, the magic island. In Sinán's work the island of Taboga becomes generic, a metaphor for reality and a symbol for all islands ever conceived or dreamed about.

**Interviews:**

Dimas Lidio Pitty, "Entrevista a Rogelio Sinán," *Lotería,* 222–223 (1974): 61–68;

Dorothy Mull, "Conversación con Rogelio Sinán a la edad de 82," *Hispania,* 68 (1985): 568–570.

**References:**

Elsie Alvarado de Ricord, *Escritores panameños contemporáneos* (Panama City: Cervantes, 1962);

Ramón María Andreu, "Lo onírico y la ambigüedad en la obra narrativa de Rogelio Sinán," Ph.D. dissertation, University of Southern California, 1981;

Ciro Bianchi Ross, "Sinán: La magia de la tierra," *Cuba International* (September 1984): 58–63;

Gloria Guardia Zeledón, *Rogelio Sinán: Una revisión de la vanguardia en Panamá,* second edition (Panama City: Litho-Impresora Panamá, 1975);

Martín Jamieson Villiers, "Literatura panameña actual," *Cuadernos Hispanoamericanos,* 407 (May 1984): 108–117;

Teresa López de Vallarino, "Rogelio Sinán," *Atenea,* 89, no. 276 (1948): 470–481;

*Lotería,* special issue on Sinán, 370 (January–February 1988);

*Maga,* special issue on Sinán, 5–6 (1985);

Seymour Menton, "La narrativa centroamericana (1960–1970)," *Nueva Narrativa Hispanoamericana,* 2 (January 1972): 119–128;

Mirna M. Pérez-Venero, "A Novelist's Erotic Racial Revenge," *Caribbean Review* (October–December 1972): 24–27;

Rafael Ruiloba, "Rogelio Sinán o la muerte del Don Juan," *Lotería,* 320–321 (November–December 1982): 50–55;

Alicia Soto de Cáceres, "Breve viaje a la isla mágica de Rogelio Sinán," *Lotería,* 293–294 (1980): 20–30.

# Antonio Skármeta
*(7 November 1940 –   )*

### D. L. Shaw
*University of Virginia*

BOOKS: *El entusiasmo* (Santiago, Chile: Zig-Zag, 1967);

*Desnudo en el tejado* (Buenos Aires: Sudamericana, 1969);

*El ciclista del San Cristóbal* (Santiago, Chile: Quimantú, 1973);

*Tiro libre* (Buenos Aires: Siglo Veintiuno, 1973);

*Novios y solitarios* (Buenos Aires: Losada, 1975);

*Soñé que la nieve ardía* (Barcelona: Planeta, 1975); translated by Malcolm Coad as *I Dreamt the Snow Was Burning* (London: Readers International, 1985);

*No pasó nada* (Barcelona: Pomaire, 1980);

*La insurrección* (Hanover, N.H.: Ediciones del Norte, 1982); translated by Paula Sharp as *The Insurrection* (Hanover, N.H.: Ediciones del Norte, 1983);

*Ardiente paciencia* (Hanover, N.H.: Ediciones del Norte, 1985); translated by Katherine Silver as *Burning Patience* (New York: Pantheon, 1987; London: Methuen, 1988);

*Match Ball* (Buenos Aires: Sudamericana, 1989);

*Watch Where the Wolf Is Going,* translated by Donald L. Schmidt and Federico Cordovez (London: Readers International, 1991).

PLAY PRODUCTION: *Ardiente paciencia,* Berlin, Bat Theatre, June 1983.

OTHER: Elizabeth Bowen, *La casa en París,* translated by Skármeta and Cecilia Boisier (Santiago, Chile: Zig-Zag, 1969);

*Joven narrativa chilena después del golpe,* edited by Skármeta (Clear Creek, Ind.: American Hispanist, 1976);

"Al fin y al cabo, es su propia vida la cosa más cercana que cada escritor tiene para echar mano," in *Del cuerpo a las palabras: La narrativa de Antonio Skármeta,* edited by Raúl Silva Castro (Madrid: LAR, 1983), pp. 131–147; reprinted in *Más allá del Boom,* edited by David Viñas, sec-

*Antonio Skármeta ( photograph by Bartolo Ortiz)*

ond edition (Buenos Aires: Folios, 1984), pp. 263–285;

*Poesía joven de Chile,* edited by Skármeta (Munich: Federlese, 1985);

*Santiago Pena Capital,* edited by Skármeta (Santiago, Chile: Documentas, 1991);

"Tendencias en la más nueva narrativa hispanoamericana," in *Enciclopedia labor* (Barcelona: Labor, 1984), IX: 751–771.

SELECTED PERIODICAL PUBLICATIONS – UNCOLLECTED: "La novísima generación: Varias características y un límite," *Revista de Literatura Hispanoamericana,* 10 (1976): 9–18;

"Words Are My Home," *Review,* 27 (1981): 8–10.

Since winning the Casa de las Américas Prize in 1969 with *Desnudo en el tejado* (Naked on the Roof, 1969), Antonio Skármeta has been considered one of the foremost Spanish-American writers of fiction of his generation and perhaps the leading figure in the post-Boom. The birth of this movement may indeed come in time to be dated from the 1975 publication of his first novel, *Soñé que la nieve ardía* (translated as *I Dreamt the Snow Was Burning*, 1985). He has been praised by fellow writers such as Mempo Giardinelli and Ariel Dorfman and hailed by critics in Europe as well as in North and South America. His books and short stories have been translated into a dozen languages and in some cases filmed successfully. By 1992 four full-length critical books had been written about him, including one in English, as well as a flattering body of critical articles and introductions in several languages. A filmmaker of distinction, he has also won prizes in film festivals on both sides of the Atlantic and taught filmmaking in the Berlin Academy of Cinema and Television. Since returning to Chile from exile in 1988, he has devoted much time to encouraging younger writers through seminars and workshops and by editing their work. He also teaches and lectures regularly in the United States.

Skármeta was born on 7 November 1940 in Antofagasta in northern Chile, the grandson of Yugoslavian immigrants. As a young child he was taken by his parents to Buenos Aires and lived with them there until age twelve. Despite the family's difficult financial circumstances, he enjoyed the atmosphere of the great city, where he worked as an errand boy, and won his first literary prize with a comic poem in a radio contest. Back in Chile he quickly discovered his vocation as a writer and began devouring English and Russian fiction. At his secondary school in Santiago he organized a celebration of Charles Baudelaire, became the leading light of the school literary circle, and discovered Chilean poet Pablo Neruda, who remained a major influence on his work. Sports (basketball and soccer), pop music, and the youth culture of the 1950s and later, all of which loom large in his fiction, were important as he grew up. In 1959 he began an arts degree at the University of Santiago, where he soon began producing avant-garde plays (by writers such as Edward Albee, William Saroyan, and Eugène Ionesco) with the university drama group. The same year saw the publication of his first short story, "El Señor Avila" (Mr. Avila). After traveling widely in Latin America with a puppet-theater group, he graduated in 1961.

Two years later the best of his early short stories, "La Cenicienta en San Francisco" (Cinderella in San Francisco), won a prize. It was based on his experiences during a trip to North America, where he later earned an M.A. from Columbia University in New York with a thesis on Julio Cortázar. This success led to the writing and publication of his first collection of short stories, *El entusiasmo* (Enthusiasm, 1967). Meanwhile he taught philosophy and Spanish-American literature at his alma mater and helped edit literary magazines, notably *Ercilla*. His favorite writers at this time were Neruda, Franz Kafka, Jorge Luis Borges, Nicanor Parra, Ernest Hemingway, St. John Perse, and Juan Rulfo. During the 1960s he won more prizes with his short stories and saw the first English publication of one of them, "Entre todas las cosas lo primero es el mar" (translated as "First Comes the Sea") in *The Arizona Quarterly*. At this time he was also publishing translations of Norman Mailer, William Golding, Herman Melville, Jack Kerouac, Charles Webb, and F. Scott Fitzgerald.

A turning point in his career was the award of the Casa de las Américas Prize in Cuba for his second collection of short stories. At this time his political ideas were beginning to evolve. He had always belonged to the moderate Left, with strong ties to his proletarian origins, though these had been modified by his middle-class status as a university professor and an increasingly successful writer. The victory of Salvador Allende and his Popular Unity coalition in the Chilean elections of 1970 encouraged Skármeta to adopt a more open political stance. He affiliated himself with MAPU, a radical splinter party of the Christian Democrats, and eagerly embraced the new opportunities to bridge the gap between the intelligentsia and the workers. For example, he began to conduct writing workshops for young people, which he still was running more than twenty years later. This was a period of euphoria for him and his circle of friends, who discovered new areas of literary activity and social commitment. In an interview in 1986 he spoke of the importance of the Allende period in his development saying, "Antes de que se produjera la Unidad Política en Chile, mi literatura era individualista y egocéntrica. El auge del socialismo, por el contrario, conllevó la necesidad de hacer una apreciación realista de la situación política del país, y en el terreno personal me impulsó hacia lo 'otro' no sólo para amarlo, sino para abarcarlo en tanto que 'cuerpo social' " (Before Popular Unity arose in Chile my writings were individualistic and self-centered. The rise of socialism, however, forced me to make a realistic reevaluation of the political situation in the country and at the personal level pushed me toward the "Other" [the proletariat] not just to feel affection for it, but to incorporate it as part of the "body of society"). This evolution of attitude is clear in subsequent short stories such as "El cigarrillo" (The Cigarette) from his third collection *Tiro libre* (Fire at Will, 1973), the first of several tales that relate to political conditions in Chile. But it is best seen in his novels *Soñé que la nieve ardía* and *La insurrección* (The Insurrection, 1982).

In the meantime he published a series of articles and gave several interviews that help to situate him in the Spanish-American literary context of his time. The 1960s were the crucial period for the Boom writers in Spanish America. In the opinion of many critics, by the mid 1970s the movement had passed its creative peak. Skármeta clearly belongs to the group of writers, including Isabel Allende, Elena Poniatowska, Luisa Valenzuela, and others, who rejected certain aspects of Boom writing – especially its pessimism, its avoidance of emphasis on love as a major existential support, its sometimes-excessive experimentalism, and particularly its tendency to privilege the exploration of the human condition in general rather than the conditions prevailing in Spanish America – and went on to launch the post-Boom. Although he dislikes the term, preferring *hiperrealismo* (hyperrealism), Skármeta's nonfictional writings have been influential in helping to define it. They also suggest some approaches to his own work.

In an illuminating article called "Al fin y al cabo es su propia vida la cosa más cercana que cada escritor tiene para echar mano" (In the End, His Own Life Is the Nearest Thing That Every Writer Has to Make Use Of, 1983), Skármeta listed among the characteristics of his generation of writers the incorporation into fiction of characters and lifestyles drawn from the real working class: urban settings; exuberance and vitality (in contrast to the negativism and intellectualism of the Boom); spontaneity (in contrast to the emphasis in the Boom on "writerly" qualities in fiction); emphasis on the everyday, including colloquial speech; fantasy; and regional concerns (in contrast to the sometimes-portentous stress in the Boom on the problem of the human condition). He characterized his own work in this context as *infrarreal,* concerned with the smaller, apparently less important aspects of experience, in themes and characters, "pop" in attitude in line with the youth culture of the 1950s and 1960s, and lyrical and realistic in its use of language.

Skármeta has worked as a professional teacher and academic critic of Spanish-American literature.

His critical opinions are not those of a dilettante. In particular, in two important articles of the 1970s, "La novísima generación: Varias características y un límite" (The Most Recent Generation: Various Characteristics and a Limiting Factor) and "Tendencias en la más nueva narrativa hispanoamericana" (Tendencies in Contemporary Spanish-American Narrative), he criticizes the Boom writers for their obsession with technical innovation at the expense of plot, their tendency to subvert observed reality, and their lack of reader-friendliness.

By this time the Allende government had fallen, and Skármeta was forced to move abroad with his wife, painter Cecilia Boisier, and their two elementary-age children, Beltrán and Gabriel. They went first to Buenos Aires and then to West Berlin. For thirteen years he taught film and theater, wrote radio theater, and collaborated on films based on his own scripts with Peter Lillienthal and other German directors. For these he won several prizes, including one at the Prague Film Festival in 1974, the German Bundes Prize in 1976, and prizes at both the Rosario Film Festival and the Bordeaux Film Festival in 1985.

By this time Skármeta was one of the leading writers of his generation in Spanish America. Further, critics have seen a technical improvement between *Desnudo en el tejado* and *El entusiasmo*. Skármeta has stated that by 1970 he had begun to feel confident of his ability as a short-story writer. The real difference between *Desnudo en el tejado* and *El entusiasmo,* however, has to do with the treatment of reality. In two of the stories in particular, "El ciclista del San Cristóbal" (The Cyclist from San Cristóbal, filmed in 1988) and "Una vuelta en el aire" (A Spin through the Air) something magical seems to happen. In the former the cyclist taking part in a race not only wins but in some mysterious way also seems to have brought his sick mother suddenly back to health. Similarly, in "Una vuelta en el aire" normal relationships of cause and effect seem to be subverted. The result in each case is positive and reassuring; there is a sense of triumph over negative forces that runs counter to the predominant outlook of the Boom writers. In "Basketball" and "A las arenas" (Stuck in the Mud) the young protagonists also experience some kind of positive transformation of their situation and outlook, this time through sex, which produces in each case, as in other stories, an epiphanic moment.

It is not clear where this exploration of magical moments in individual lives would have led had the rise and fall of the Allende government in Chile (1970–1973), followed by Skármeta's exile, not in-

*Skármeta, circa 1989 (photograph by Gonzalo Cáceres)*

1975) and "La composición" (The Composition, 1978), each of which gives fascinating insights into life in Chile under the Pinochet regime and have been included in English in his book of translated stories *Watch Where the Wolf Is Going* (1991).

Skármeta's first novel, *Soñé que la nieve ardía,* was finished in exile in Argentina. Its theme is illustrated by the evolution of the young hero, Arturo, a would-be professional soccer player, from mere self-interest to political awareness and greater sympathy with the working class and the Left. As the novel progresses Arturo's experiences on and off the soccer field slowly bring him to a greater understanding of the need for human solidarity. As it ends he is arrested at the funeral of the Nobel laureate Neruda, which turned into a memorable left-wing demonstration. A feature of the novel is the symbolic role played by Arturo's virginity, which he does not succeed in losing until near the end of the novel, after his bid for stardom has failed miserably. In all Skármeta's work sexuality is prominent and full of symbolic overtones, sometimes producing an epiphanic moment of self-liberation and reconciliation with life. Here it is used to associate virile self-realization with left-wing political commitment. Commercialized, professional soccer, on the other hand, is used to symbolize the capitalistic practice of selling one's talents to the highest bidder in return for individual gratification.

In contrast to Arturo is a group of young left-wing activists with "Fatty" Osorio as their natural leader. Unlike Arturo, Osorio is emotionally involved with the others in his peer group and with his class, sexually fulfilled, and clear about his political stance without being in any way dogmatic or fanatical. It is largely his influence and example that set Arturo right. His turning point, however, does not come until Arturo finally manages to lose his virginity with Susana, another member of the group, whose embrace symbolizes the warm embrace of worker solidarity. Susana is an important character in her own right, seen by some as the first to break the mold of conventionality among female characters in contemporary Spanish-American fiction. In her independence and handling of her own sexuality, she is a forerunner of the strong new heroines popularized by Allende, Valenzuela, and other female novelists of the post-Boom. One can date from her appearance a change from Skármeta's earlier practice in the short stories, where semiautobiographical male figures predominate almost exclusively. *Soñé que la nieve ardía* still contains significant elements of fantasy in that its subplot, borrowed from an earlier short story, concerns a

tervened. The next collection of tales, *Tiro libre,* shows him moving in a more politicized direction. The longest of the stories, "Uno a uno" (One by One), is still in the line of quasi surrealism noteworthy in *Desnudo en el tejado,* but interestingly it ends tragically, as if to suggest that the author had somehow begun to lose the spontaneous youthful confidence that overflowed in his earlier work. At the same time a group of four stories with markedly political overtones illustrates the fact that a shift was taking place in the author's interests. "Primera preparatoria" (Taking the Plunge) deals with the divisive effect of political conflict inside the same family. "El cigarrillo" presents a young worker who betrays his class allegiances. "Balada para un gordo" (Ballad for a Fat Man) explores contradictions inside the political Left. "Enroque" (The Chess Move) describes the ideological and sexual confusion of an upper-class young man. More recently Skármeta has published "La llamada" (The Call, comedian's stooge who turns into a kind of guardian angel for his partner. No such mixture of techniques is as present in his later fiction, which illustrates the tendency in a large sector of post-Boom fiction to return to something closer to mainstream realism than the Boom writers normally had been willing to accept.

Skármeta's next novel, *No pasó nada* (Play On, 1980), the first of his novels to be written in Germany, is his contribution to the Spanish-American novel of exile. Presented from the standpoint of a teenage Chilean boy sharing his parents' exile in West Berlin, the plot shows Skármeta successfully solving the problem of relating the experience of exile to a theme of wider human significance. The stress here is on the boy, Lucho, and his developing awareness of the other sex. By linking exile to the problems of adolescence, Skármeta lifts the work above the level of mere protest, nostalgia, or exaltation of the preexile struggle.

Lucho's description of exile frames the core episode of this short novel, a fight between himself and a German youngster provoked by an altercation between Lucho and his opponent's younger brother. Behind this hovers Lucho's first girlfriend, who is largely responsible for the course of events. The fight itself and the reconciliation that follows are in part symbolic. Lucho discovers in himself qualities of courage, forbearance, and magnanimity that he associates with his Chilean heritage. An implicit lesson is that these qualities will eventually overturn the Pinochet regime and restore national unity. At the end of the novel Lucho's antagonist revises his opinion of the exile community in Berlin, and Lucho begins to court a more suitable German girlfriend. Thus the theme of exile merges with that of a rite of passage into young adulthood.

One of the motives that drew Skármeta to move to West Berlin was to collaborate with German filmmaker Lillienthal. They produced four films together with screenplays by Skármeta: the first, *La victoria* (Victory), won an award at the 1973 Prague Film Festival. Seven films with other collaborators followed, five written and directed by Skármeta, including the much-praised film version of his *Ardiente paciencia* (Burning Patience, 1985), which won a series of prizes. Nonetheless, Skármeta defines himself as a writer who occasionally makes films rather than the other way around. In 1979 he visited Nicaragua to make a film of the Sandinista rebellion, which eventually became *La insurrección*. It won an honorable mention in the Prix Italia competition the following year. In 1982 a novel of the same name appeared. In it Skármeta uses a collective protagonist, the inhabitants of a small neighborhood in the Nicaraguan city of León. Banding together, they heroically overcome the brutally repressive Somoza military regime. Just as in *Soñé que la nieve ardía,* in which collective values gradually prevail over the selfish, individualistic ones of Arturo, here they impose themselves on Agustín Menor, a young army recruit who eventually decides to desert, and on the local mailman, Salinas, who after trying to stand aside eventually becomes a leader of the rebellion.

The rebellion itself is not the main focus of most of the novel. Skármeta employs a deliberately fragmentary way of telling the story so that the reader is challenged to assemble the various elements. In the bulk of the novel Skármeta partly describes aspects of the oppressive Somoza regime and partly sets out the options open to individuals who are exposed to that sort of tyranny. These range from submission or collaboration to various kinds of opposition. Thus the reader gradually comes to understand the motivations underlying the final uprising. Skármeta rejects pamphleteering and militant protest writing, and he makes a real effort to present Captain Flores, the representative of the regime, in a humanly understandable light. He is less successful in other cases, such as Flores's brutal sergeant, a cardboard villain who rapes the heroine; the bishop of León, an easily ignored nonentity; and Leonel, the guerrilla poet, who seems rather idealized despite the author's attempt to present him with gentle irony. However, the heroine Victoria, like Susana in *Soñé que la nieve ardía,* is another of the strong — in this case firmly feminist — female figures in recent Spanish-American fiction. Also, the attack on the local barracks at the climax of the novel is led by a woman.

The shifting focus and the fragmentary technique reach a climax in the chapter in which an unarmed demonstration by a group of young townsfolk is bloodily repressed by Flores and his troops. These narrative strategies reflect Skármeta's vision of social change as brought about by creative interaction among a variety of human forces. Once this effect has been created, the plot moves to the uprising itself, in which the townsfolk and the guerrillas from the countryside successfully join forces. The liberation of the city is accompanied by the triumph of true, loving, and tender sexuality on the part of Leonel and Victoria symbolizing the emotional and sexual liberation that goes with political and social freedom. By contrast with other novels — such as Mario Vargas Llosa's *Historia de Mayta* (1985; translated as *The Real Life of Alejandro Mayta,* 1986), in which the would-be revolutionary protagonist fails miserably, or Allende's *De amor y de sombra* (1984; translated as *Of Love and Shadows,* 1987), in which the hero and heroine are forced into exile – *La insurrección* offers a confident message of faith in individual and collective libertarian effort.

Skármeta's most successful novel, the one which he believes will live on, is *Ardiente paciencia.* Set in Chile near the home of Neruda at Isla Negra, the time frame of the plot is deliberately made to coincide with the rise and fall of the Allende government. The story functions at three different levels. At the personal, human level, it is the story of the love affair and marriage of Mario, a young mailman, and Beatriz, who helps in her mother's bar. At a more aesthetic level, it concerns Mario's friendship with Neruda, who helps with the marriage, and the young man's discovery of his own love of poetry and his personal creativity. Finally, at the political level, the novel deals with the destructive effect of political tyranny on young love. Mario is to some extent intended to represent the Chilean provincial working class. He enjoys emotional, sexual, creative, and political liberation under Allende, only to see it snatched away when Pinochet seizes power. As in *La insurrección,* true love and fulfillment are linked with progressive forms of government, a theme that goes back to the beginning of modern fiction in Spanish America.

Two of the most attractive aspects of *Ardiente paciencia* are the strong presences of humor and sexual references in the text. Situational and verbal humor are both prominent. The former has to do chiefly with the growth of the relationship between Mario and Neruda and their joint problems with Beatriz's battle-ax mother. The contacts between the mailman and the famous poet are brilliantly comic almost to the end, when the latter is on his deathbed. There are memorable descriptions of the poet's resigned patience with his young protégé, the development of their mutual regard and friendship, and most unforgettably of Neruda dancing, like an enormous penguin, to the Beatles' version of "Please Mr. Postman." Similarly, the scenes between Doña Rosa and her daughter, to say nothing of her skirmishes with Mario and Neruda, are full of humor, something all too rare in Spanish-American fiction. Not just hilarity, it is functional in that it presents most of the characters in an attractive light and contrasts effectively with the oleaginous hypocrisy of the right-wing politician Labbé and the pathos and misery of the ending. Verbal humor sparkles in much of the dialogue and creates a sense of joie de vivre that is dramatically destroyed by the Pinochet coup. Unre-

strained sexuality, not only between the lovers but also among the bar's clientele as they celebrate Neruda's Nobel Prize, is part of the vitality and jollity that characterize life under Allende in the first part of *Ardiente paciencia.* The scene of the first love-making between Mario and Beatriz stands out as one of the high points of post-Boom fiction. As always in Skármeta, sexual activity is symbolic of breaking out of bourgeois prejudices and restrictions and achieving one's fullest potential.

Neruda looms over the whole novel, infusing it with poetry as well as bringing happiness to the young couple. Once he leaves for Paris the tone changes, if only because now Mario has to accept his responsibilities as a husband, father, and son-in-law. When the mortally ill poet returns and Allende falls, poetry, love, and freedom are all destroyed: the poetry contest in which Mario had intended to participate is canceled, the great poet dies, Mario is arrested and probably murdered, and military repression replaces democratic liberty. *Ardiente paciencia* is at bottom a kind of allegorical fairy tale with Neruda cast as the Good Fairy and Pinochet as the Demon King. A typical novel of the post-Boom, it is reader friendly in the best sense, full of fun and delightful people but ultimately deadly serious in intent.

In 1985, after twelve years in exile, Skármeta briefly visited Chile and three years later returned finally to Santiago. His marriage to Cecilia Boisier ended, and he began a new family with Nora Preperski, whom he had met in Germany. The first novel to appear after his return was *Match Ball* (1989), which illustrates the neo-romanticism of the post-Boom. Papst, the protagonist, abandons a flourishing practice as a physician in Berlin and an attractive wife because of an irresistible attraction to a teenage tennis champion, Sophie Mass. This infatuation leads him to wound a rival and to serve time in an English prison, but at the end of the novel Papst is still in its grip.

At times Papst's account of his experiences reads like a confession of his middle-aged illusions and follies. But this is in the end misleading. Like Josef von Sternberg's famous film *Der blaue Engel* (The Blue Angel, 1930), this is a Faustian story of love producing first rejuvenation and then self-destruction. The inner themes of the novel are connected with fear of growing old, frustration with the upper-middle-class lifestyle, and love in the fullest sexual sense as the ultimate source of vitality and self-fulfillment. Haunted by memories of his youth, Papst surrenders to the impulse to plunge back into a more "real" existence dominated by unrestrained emotion and desire despite a series of warnings and his half recognition that Sophie is a temptress who ultimately will play him false.

Like many of Skármeta's characters, Papst is a humanly attractive figure who retains enough droll self-awareness to keep some of the reader's liking and respect, while his actual behavior, especially his treatment of his wife, is unforgivable. His motivation is one with which any middle-aged reader, male or female, can sympathize: to identify love and enthusiastic sexuality with recovery of youth and a sense of living life to the fullest. As he and Sophie make love for the first and only time, he achieves one of those epiphanic moments that characterize Skármeta's fiction from the start. In this case it is made more intense by Papst's awareness of the risk involved. He never really loses sight of his situation, and though critical at times of his own behavior he remains under the spell of his illusion. Fifteen-year-old Sophie is the most enigmatic of Skármeta's heroines up to now. Her motives for leading on the fifty-two-year-old Papst remain mysterious. The reader does not know whether she is a capricious, manipulative, spoiled child or a fatherless girl caught up in a relentless round of competitive tournaments whose stress crushes her spirit as much as Papst's professional life crushes his. Perhaps she is reaching out for a father figure, but she also willfully victimizes the adoring Papst without ever attempting to explain her conduct.

In a 1991 interview Skármeta spoke condescendingly of Papst as a figure from a B movie, but for anyone who was young in the 1960s Papst comes close to being a modern archetype. His heroic, idiotic behavior is the last hurrah of a man who was young in the hippie era and is now in a society dominated by yuppies. In one sense *Match Ball* is the swan song of a generation.

In 1991 Skármeta published a brief anthology of some of his best short stories in English translation under the title *Watch Where the Wolf Is Going*. It contains "The Young Man with the Story," "Cinderella in San Francisco," and "Watch Where the Wolf Is Going" – his only story set in the colonial period of Chile (it includes an exposure of the rapacity of a Spanish conquistador who robs his own men) – from *El entusiasmo;* "The Cyclist from San Cristobal" and "Stuck in the Mud" from *Desnudo en el tejado;* "Fish," a story of generational conflict in an average Chilean family, "The Cigarette," and "Taking the Plunge," a tale of youthful political activism, from *Tiro libre;* "Man with a Car-

Cover for Skármeta's 1989 novel, about a married man who goes to prison for wounding the rival of a teenage tennis star with whom he is infatuated

nation in his Mouth," a moving story of a chance encounter between two exiles, from *Novios y solitarios* (Significant Others and Solitary Folk, 1975); and two late stories, "The Composition" and "The Call," about the dangers of daily life to people of all sorts under Pinochet. The collection offers an admirable cross section of this aspect of Skármeta's work.

Antonio Skármeta offers perhaps the clearest and, given his training in literary criticism, the most conscious example of what it is to be a fully post-Boom writer. Definitions of this new movement in Spanish-American fiction inevitably remain provisional, but a study of Skármeta's work and outlook offers unique insights into the progress of fiction in Spanish America in the last quarter of the twentieth century.

**Interviews:**

Jorge Lafforgue, "Antonio Skármeta, entrevista," *Hispamérica,* 7 (1974): 43–56;

John Mosier, "Art, Film and Reality: An Interview with Antonio Skármeta," *New Orleans Review,* 7 (Fall 1980): 257–260;

George Woodyard, "Entrevista a Antonio Skármeta, dramaturgo chileno," *Chasqui,* 14 (1984): 86–93;

Andrea Pagni, "Entrevista con Antonio Skármeta," *Discurso Literario,* 5, no. 1 (1985): 59–73;

Horacio Xaubet, *Entrevista con Antonio Skármeta* (Saint Louis: Washington University Occasional Paper, 1988);

Marcelo Coddou, "Sobre *Match Ball,* entrevista a Antonio Skármeta," *Revista Iberoamericana,* 151 (1990): 579–582;

Juan Andrés Piña, "Antonio Skármeta: Literatura, política y vitalidad," in his *Conversaciones con la narrativa chilena* (Callao, Peru: Los Andes, 1991), pp. 153–184.

**References:**

Monique Lemaitre, *Skármeta, una narrativa de la liberación* (Santiago, Chile: Pehuén, 1991);

Constanza Lira, *Skármeta: La inteligencia de los sentidos* (Santiago, Chile: Dante, 1975);

Donald Shaw, "La Cenicienta en San Francisco by Antonio Skármeta," *Revista de Estudios Hispánicos,* 21, no. 2 (1987): 89–99;

Shaw, "The Structure of *Soñé que la nieve ardía,*" in *Paradise Lost or Gained,* edited by Fernando Alegría and Jorge Ruffinelli (Houston: Arte Público, 1990), pp. 145–150;

Shaw, "Narrative technique in Skármeta's *La insurrección,*" *Antipodas,* 3 (1991): 191–204;

Shaw, "Skármeta and Sexuality," *Paunch,* 65–66 (1991): 11–29;

Raúl Silva Cáceres, ed., *Del cuerpo a las palabras: La narrativa de Antonio Skármeta* (Madrid: LAR, 1983).

# Mario Vargas Llosa

*(28 March 1936 – )*

César Ferreira
*University of North Texas*

BOOKS: *Los jefes* (Barcelona: Rocas, 1959); translated by Gregory Kolovakos and Ronald Christ in *The Cubs and Other Stories* (New York: Harper & Row, 1979);

*La ciudad y los perros* (Barcelona: Seix Barral, 1963); translated by Lysander Kemp as *The Time of the Hero* (New York: Grove Press, 1966; London: Cape, 1967);

*La casa verde* (Barcelona: Seix Barral, 1966); translated by Gregory Rabassa as *The Green House* (New York: Harper & Row, 1968);

*Los cachorros* (Barcelona: Lumen, 1967); translated by Kolovakos and Christ in *The Cubs and Other Stories* (New York: Harper & Row, 1979);

*La novela* (Montevideo: Fundación de Cultura Universitaria, 1968);

*La novela en América Latina,* by Vargas Llosa and Gabriel García Márquez (Lima: Milla Batres, 1968);

*Antología mínima de M. Vargas Llosa* (Buenos Aires: Tiempo Contemporáneo, 1969);

*Conversación en La Catedral,* two volumes (Barcelona: Seix Barral, 1969); translated by Rabassa as *Conversation in the Cathedral* (New York: Harper & Row, 1975);

*Los cachorros; El desafío; Día domingo* (Barcelona: Salvat, 1970);

*Literatura en la revolución y revolución en la literatura,* by Vargas Llosa, Oscar Collazos, and Julio Cortázar (Mexico City: Siglo Veintiuno, 1970);

*Día domingo* (Buenos Aires: Amadis, 1971);

*García Márquez: Historia de un deicidio* (Barcelona: Barral, 1971);

*La historia secreta de una novela* (Barcelona: Tusquets, 1971);

*El combate imaginario: Las cartas de batalla de Joanot Martorell,* by Vargas Llosa and Martín de Riquer (Barcelona: Barral, 1972);

*Los cachorros; Los jefes* (Lima: Peisa, 1973);

*Mario Vargas Llosa ( photograph by Tom Victor)*

*García Márquez y la problemática de la novela,* by Vargas Llosa and Angel Rama (Buenos Aires: Corregidor-Marcha, 1973);

*Obras escogidas: Novelas y cuentos* (Madrid: Aguilar, 1973);

*Pantaleón y las visitadoras* (Barcelona: Seix Barral, 1973); translated by Kolovakos and Christ as *Captain Pantoja and the Special Service* (New York: Harper & Row; London: Cape, 1978);

*La orgía perpetua: Flaubert y "Madame Bovary"* (Madrid: Taurus, 1975); translated by Helen R. Lane as *The Perpetual Orgy: Flaubert and "Madame Bovary"* (New York: Farrar, Straus & Giroux, 1986);

*La tía Julia y el escribidor* (Barcelona: Seix Barral, 1977); translated by Lane as *Aunt Julia and the Scriptwriter* (New York: Farrar, Straus & Giroux, 1982);

*Conversación en La Catedral; La orgía perpetua; Pantaleón y las visitadoras* (Madrid: Aguilar, 1978);

*José María Arguedas, entre sapos y halcones* (Madrid: Ediciones Cultura Hispánica del Centro Iberoamericano de Cooperación, 1978);

*La utopía arcaica* (Cambridge: Centre of Latin American Studies, University of Cambridge, 1978);

*The Genesis and Evolution of "Pantaleón y las visitadoras"* (New York: City College, 1979);

*Art, Authenticity, and Latin American Culture* (Washington, D.C.: Wilson Center, 1981);

*Entre Sartre y Camus* (Río Piedras, P.R.: Huracán, 1981);

*La guerra del fin del mundo* (Barcelona: Seix Barral, 1981); translated by Lane as *The War of the End of the World* (New York: Farrar, Straus & Giroux, 1984);

*La señorita de Tacna* (Barcelona: Seix Barral, 1981); translated by David Graham-Young as *The Young Lady from Tacna* in *Mario Vargas Llosa: Three Plays* (New York: Hill & Wang, 1990);

*Contra viento y marea,* 3 volumes (Barcelona: Seix Barral, 1983–1990);

*Kathie y el hipopótamo* (Barcelona: Seix Barral, 1983); translated by Graham-Young as *Kathie and the Hippopotamus* in *Mario Vargas Llosa: Three Plays* (New York: Hill & Wang, 1990);

*Historia de Mayta* (Barcelona: Seix Barral, 1984); translated by Alfred MacAdam as *The Real Life of Alejandro Mayta* (New York: Farrar, Straus & Giroux, 1986);

*La cultura de la libertad, la libertad de la cultura* (Santiago, Chile: Fundación Eduardo Frei, 1985);

*La chunga* (Barcelona: Seix Barral, 1986); translated by Graham-Young as *La Chunga* in *Mario Vargas Llosa: Three Plays* (New York: Hill & Wang, 1990);

*¿Quién mató a Palomino Molero?* (Barcelona: Seix Barral, 1986); translated by MacAdam as *Who Killed Palomino Molero?* (New York: Farrar, Straus & Giroux, 1987);

*El hablador* (Barcelona: Seix Barral, 1987); translated by Lane as *The Storyteller* (New York: Farrar, Straus & Giroux, 1989; London & Boston: Faber & Faber, 1990);

*Elogio de la madrastra* (Barcelona: Tusquets, 1988); translated by Lane as *In Praise of the Stepmother* (New York: Farrar, Straus & Giroux, 1990);

*El debate* (Lima: Universidad del Pacífico, Centro de Investigación, 1990);

*La verdad de las mentiras* (Barcelona: Seix Barral, 1990);

*A Writer's Reality* (Syracuse, N.Y.: Syracuse University Press, 1991);

*Lituma en los andes* (Barcelona: Planeta, 1993);

*El pez en el agua: Memorias* (Barcelona: Seix Barral, 1993); translated by Lane as *A Fish in the Water* (New York: Farrar, Straus & Giroux, 1994);

*El señor de los balcones* (Barcelona: Seix Barral, 1993).

OTHER: "Literature Is Fire," in *Doors and Mirrors,* edited by Hortense Carpenter and Janet Brof (New York: Grossman, 1972), pp. 430–435.

Few writers from Peru have achieved the literary status and international recognition of Mario Vargas Llosa. A writer of many talents, Vargas Llosa is the author of several books that include novels, short stories, plays, literary criticism, memoirs, and a prolific production of journalistic writings. Never afraid of intellectual controversy, he has always been outspoken on Latin-American cultural and political issues. Vargas Llosa's political stands have ranged from defending socialism and the Cuban revolution in the 1960s to embracing neoliberal economic thought and free-market economies in the 1980s. But in spite of his recent involvement in professional politics, literature remains his first passion, and it is in the art of storytelling where his talent has shone the most.

With few exceptions, Peruvian society has always been at the center of Vargas Llosa's literary universe. A country of enormous contrasts, Peru encompasses many racial backgrounds – a ruling white class, a vast Quechua-speaking Indian population, and smaller groups of Asians, blacks, and Amazon Indians – resulting in great social stratification and fragmentation. Such divisions are only further exacerbated by Peru's diverse geographical makeup: the coastal desert area, the Andean region, and the jungle of the Amazon, three separate worlds coexisting in one country with fragile political institutions that are often incapable of representing such a wide spectrum of differences. These many worlds and their conflictive coexistence are at the center of Vargas Llosa's many novels.

Vargas Llosa was born into a middle-class family on 28 March 1936 in Arequipa in southern Peru. The second most important city of Peru after

Lima, the capital, Arequipa is known for the local pride and rebellious nature of its people, who often boast of the natural beauty of their region, while holding a traditional rivalry with Lima as an economic and cultural center. Although middle-class when he was born, Vargas Llosa's family had an aristocratic background and hence held ties with the Peruvian ruling class.

The writer's childhood was marked by family turmoil. At the time of his birth his parents separated, leaving him to be raised as an only child in his maternal grandfather's home. Because of family connections, his grandfather held various government appointments, including diplomatic posts, which obliged the family to move frequently during Vargas Llosa's childhood years. His early schooling took place in Cochabamba, Bolivia, between 1937 and 1941. Later his grandfather moved to Piura, a city on the northern coast of Peru, where Vargas Llosa attended a private religious school.

In 1950, when Vargas Llosa was entering adolescence, his parents reconciled and moved once again, this time to Lima. Vargas Llosa recalls this period as a traumatic one that provided the roots of a rebellious character that aroused his first interest in literature. Although his father was a virtual stranger to him (as a boy he had been told his father was dead to avoid telling him he had abandoned his mother), Ernesto Vargas was intolerant and authoritarian with his son, constantly accusing him of displaying an unmanly personality due to his spoiled upbringing in his mother's family. As a result Vargas Llosa was sent by his father to the Leoncio Prado military academy, an experience that marked the future writer's life. The Leoncio Prado was not only Vargas Llosa's first experience outside his sheltered middle-class environment, it was also his first encounter with the institutional violence that affects the various social groups that make up Peru's ethnically diverse society.

Vargas Llosa spent two years at the Leoncio Prado, returning to Piura to finish his last year of high school at the Colegio Nacional San Miguel de Piura while living with one of his mother's brothers. By this time his literary vocation was maturing. He recalls his return to Piura as a time of discovery, greatly admiring the works of a variety of authors, Alexandre Dumas and Fyodor Dostoyevsky among others. While finishing high school Vargas Llosa worked for a local newspaper and wrote a play, *La huida del inca* (The Flight of the Inca), which, although never published, was staged at a theater in Piura. At the same time, he made repeated attempts at writing short stories.

In 1953 Vargas Llosa entered the University of San Marcos in Lima. He began his studies in literature and law during the dictatorship of Gen. Manuel Odría, who deposed the democratic government of President José Luis Bustamante y Rivero in a 1948 military coup and ruled Peru with an iron fist until 1956. Because San Marcos was a stronghold for clandestine opposition to Odría's dictatorship, it proved crucial in Vargas Llosa's intellectual formation. He joined Cahuide, a student cell of the Peruvian Communist party, which he later abandoned for the newly formed Christian Democratic party. While active in university politics, he also held part-time jobs as a newscaster, librarian, and journalist and worked closely with the historian Raúl Porras Barrenechea. In the 1950s Peruvian literature was greatly influenced by indigenist novels by Ciro Alegría and José María Arguedas, and a younger generation of writers such as Julio Ramón Ribeyro interested in portraying the changing social composition of modern Lima in urban-realist novels. However, none of these trends truly interested Vargas Llosa. Instead, he was more attracted by the rich narrative technique in the novels of William Faulkner, one of Vargas Llosa's first literary masters. Of the importance of Faulkner's style and structure for Latin-American writers, Vargas Llosa later commented in *A Writer's Reality* (1991):

> By reading Faulkner I learned that form could be a character in a novel and sometimes the most important character – that is, the organization of the perspective of the narration, the use of different narrators, the withholding of some information from the reader to create ambiguity. . . . he is probably the most important novelist of our time, the most original, the most rich. . . . But there are more specific reasons for which Faulkner has such appeal in Latin America. The world out of which he created his own world is quite similar to a Latin American world. In the Deep South, as in Latin America, two different cultures coexist, two different historical traditions, two different races – all forming a difficult coexistence full of prejudice and violence. There also coexists the extraordinary importance of the past, which is always present in contemporary life. In Latin America, we have the same thing. The world of Faulkner is preindustrial, or, at least, resisting industrialization, modernization, urbanization – exactly like many Latin American societies. Out of all this, Faulkner created a personal world, with a richness of technique and form.

Vargas Llosa's discovery of Faulkner was crucial in the experimental nature of many of his novels and his concept of the "total novel," an attempt to depict through writing as many facets of reality as possible.

*Vargas Llosa and his wife, Julia, at the French
Radio-Television Network in Paris, 1961*

At the same time, Vargas Llosa was also attracted to Jean-Paul Sartre's political commitment and the way literature could become a tool to pursue such a commitment. Of Sartre he wrote, "I liked Sartre's idea that literature is not and cannot be gratuitous, that it is unacceptable for literature to be purely entertainment, that literature is serious because a writer, through his books, can be a voice in society, can change things in life.... I also liked Sartre's idea that literature is intimately linked with contemporary time, that it is morally unacceptable to use literature to escape from contemporary problems."

At age nineteen Vargas Llosa married his aunt, Julia Urquidi Illanes, thirteen years his senior, an event that caused great family turmoil. They later divorced. As an aspiring intellectual seeking to broaden his horizons, he soon decided he needed to leave for Europe to pursue a career as a writer. While completing his degree in literature Vargas Llosa edited two literary journals, *Cuadernos de Conversación* and *Literatura,* and continued working on a book of short stories. One of the stories, "El

desafío" (The Challenge), won a short-story competition sponsored by the *Revue Française* in Lima; as a result he briefly visited Paris in 1958. In 1959, after a brief stay in Madrid, where he began doctoral studies at the Universidad Complutense, Vargas Llosa moved to the French capital, initiating a self-imposed exile that lasted several years. Meanwhile, his collection of short stories *Los jefes* (1959; translated in *The Cubs and Other Stories,* 1979) was awarded the Leopoldo Alas prize in Spain and published that year in Barcelona.

Survival in Paris proved difficult for Vargas Llosa in the early 1960s. While earning a living teaching Spanish at Berlitz schools and working as a journalist for Agence France-Presse and the French radio-television network, he finished a first draft of his first novel. Work at the network allowed Vargas Llosa to become acquainted with several Latin-American writers also living in Paris: Julio Cortázar, Alejo Carpentier, Miguel Angel Asturias, Carlos Fuentes, and others. Like Vargas Llosa, many of them were supporters of the 1959 Cuban revolution. In 1962 he also met Carlos Barral, the editor of the prestigious Spanish publishing house Seix Barral. Shortly after this he entered his manuscript in the competition for the prestigious Biblioteca Breve award, sponsored by Seix Barral, under the title "Los impostores" (The Imposters). He won, and in 1963 the novel was published in Barcelona as *La ciudad y los perros* (translated as *The Time of the Hero,* 1966).

*La ciudad y los perros* was soon acclaimed as a masterpiece, earning Vargas Llosa international recognition. It was one of many outstanding works that appeared in the 1960s written by an important group of Latin-American writers, including Cortázar's *Rayuela* (1963; translated as *Hopscotch,* 1966), Fuentes's *La muerte de Artemio Cruz* (1962; translated as *The Death of Artemio Cruz,* 1964), Guillermo Cabrera Infante's *Tres tristes tigres* (1967; translated as *Three Trapped Tigers,* 1971), and Gabriel García Márquez's *Cien años de soledad* (1967; translated as *One Hundred Years of Solitude,* 1970). Such novels brought Latin-American literature to international attention in what was later known as the Boom generation.

The publication of *La ciudad y los perros* was undoubtedly a turning point in the history of Peruvian literature. Inspired by Sartre's notion that the writer's role in any given society is to question the established social order relentlessly, *La ciudad y los perros* marked the appearance of Peru's most internationally renowned writer to date. On a personal level the novel proved that many of Vargas Llosa's early autobiographical experiences were to be crucial in the crafting of his fictional universe. Within the boundaries of traditional realism but pursuing many experimental modes of narration, Vargas Llosa's work denounced the violence that permeates all levels of Peruvian society.

In *La ciudad y los perros* Vargas Llosa comes to terms with his painful years at the Leoncio Prado military academy. Led by Jaguar, the leader of a gang of cadets, a first-year cadet named Cava steals an exam to share with his peers. Another cadet, nicknamed El Esclavo (The Slave), witnesses the theft, but the secret code of honor shared by the group silences all who know about the robbery. El Esclavo finally breaks down and reports the theft, and the school's military authorities launch an internal investigation. Shortly after, during military maneuvers, Jaguar kills the informer. While his murder is finally brought out into the open by another cadet, the superiors cover up the tragic events, fearing embarrassment to the institution and harm to the army's reputation. Only Lieutenant Gamboa insists on bringing out the truth, but he is soon silenced by his superiors to avoid a public scandal and is eventually sent to a remote region in the Andes as a form of punishment for his defiance.

The city of Lima and its neighborhoods are made to represent the different social classes of Peruvian society. But by sharing a common space within the closed boundaries of the school the Leoncio Prado cadets re-create a microcosm of Peru's potentially explosive society, marked by strong ethnic and social tensions that reproduce themselves on a larger scale in the open boundaries of the city. In the name of military discipline the cadets endure brutal physical and psychological acts. Degrading and dehumanizing, these acts are seen as rites of passage into manhood but are often fed by social prejudices. Hence, in many ways the novel is a statement about survival in a society that has lost its sense of human dignity, which has been replaced by a code of brutality to preserve a rigid and corrupt social order. *La ciudad y los perros* also reveals Vargas Llosa's strong antimilitaristic stance, a constant theme in his work. The novel's first appearance prompted a strong protest by the Peruvian army, which soon after its publication organized a book burning on the school's patio, which only helped its popularity.

The novel's literary mastery received unanimous critical praise. A turning point in contemporrary Peruvian literary history, *La ciudad y los perros* moves away from traditional linear narration, mixing interior monologue, omniscient narration, and

dialogue. The result is a rich mosaic that, although apparently chaotic, actually expands the boundaries of reality thanks to its rich psychological depth and experimental nature.

Vargas Llosa's early literary talent was confirmed by the publication of his second novel, *La casa verde* (translated as *The Green House,* 1968) in 1966. Two distinctive geographical regions of Peru, the northern coastal city of Piura where Vargas Llosa had lived with his grandfather, and Santa María de Nieva in the Amazon jungle serve as the settings. *La casa verde* traces the stories of two interconnected characters. Within this larger framework, the intricate plot and narrative structure divide the book into four chapters and an epilogue to develop a five-story line. Each chapter in turn is carefully crafted to include multiple stories that are fragments the reader must organize. However, the main points of reference for the novel's many characters are the lives of the two main characters, Sergeant Lituma and a girl named Bonifacia, who move in opposite geographical directions. Lituma is sent from Piura to an army post in Santa María de Nieva, while Bonifacia is sent from the Amazon jungle to the desert city. As a young girl Bonifacia had been taken away by a group of Spanish nuns who, with the support of soldiers, systematically kidnap native Aguaruna Indian girls from their jungle tribes to place them in their boarding school in Santa María de Nieva. There they are educated in Western ways and forced to integrate into civilization. Through the novel's careful interweaving of numerous stories in a complex use of time and space, the reader also learns of the rape of a blind girl, Antonia, who is the daughter of the musician Anselmo, the owner of the Green House, a brothel in Piura; and of the sale of the adolescent Lalita, who is to become the concubine of a Japanese outlaw and rubber lord of the area named Fushia. Fushia controls an island in the jungle and a personal army with which he raids the native villages in order to steal their rubber and women repeatedly. He eventually dies in a leprosarium in the jungle, while Bonifacia, after escaping from the convent and marrying Sergeant Lituma in a kind of domestic slavery, finally becomes a prostitute at the Green House on the outskirts of Piura.

All of the characters' lives are marked by a clear sense of determinism in spite of their attempts to escape their miserable existences. But power, money, human brutality, and violence prove overwhelming. Vargas Llosa's extraordinary overlapping of time and space allows each of these lives to be told in a multiple narrative, allowing the reader to learn about each of the character's lives from youth into adulthood and old age. By the same token, his strategy forces the reader to organize the linear sequence of the many fragmented stories that are presented simultaneously. Many bridges are built into the narrative structure to establish the various relationships among the characters. All of them eventually gather at the Green House, a microcosm of human degradation and despair. Lalita, for example, after escaping Fushia's domain and marrying Nieves, another of the brothel's musicians, introduces Bonifacia to Sergeant Lituma. Lituma returns to Piura when his post in the jungle is over and forces Bonifacia into prostitution at the Green House, where she is called La Selvática (Wildflower). At the brothel Bonifacia also meets Chunga, the new owner of the establishment; she is the daughter of Anselmo.

*La casa verde* is an all-encompassing novel in which narration, description, flashbacks, dialogue, and omniscient and first-person narration add to a torrential narrative through which the author's technical mastery emerges. *La casa verde* received unanimous critical acclaim soon after its release and in 1967 was awarded the prestigious Rómulo Gallegos Prize of Venezuela, at which Vargas Llosa delivered an important speech titled "Literature Is Fire," inspired by his admiration for Sartre's notion of the writer's commitment to social criticism.

Vargas Llosa returned to Lima's urban setting and the world of the Peruvian upper middle class in his third book, *Los cachorros* (The Cubs, 1967). A novella set in Lima in the 1950s, *Los cachorros* provides Vargas Llosa the opportunity to delve into the world of adolescence and its rites of passage into adulthood. While its events are relatively simple, this work is once again an extraordinary exercise in form and content carefully interwoven to create a masterpiece.

Inspired by a newspaper story Vargas Llosa once read, *Los cachorros* narrates the tragic story of a young boy emasculated by a dog. Cuéllar, the protagonist, struggles for acceptance among his peers, who, as they grow up from early childhood into adulthood, become his companions and who rebaptize him after his accident as "P. P. Cuéllar," to refer euphemistically to his lost manhood. The novella's six chapters chronicle the different stages of their development, emphasizing moments of crisis in the boys' personal development. Cuéllar is repeatedly hit the hardest. Always an outsider, he has not only been physically crippled through direct castration but is also progressively alienated by the strict social code of the Peruvian bourgeoisie. In a patriar-

chal society in which the exercise of a macho identity is essential for survival, Cuéllar's physical deformity symbolizes his moral defeat, eventually leading him to self-destruction in a car accident in his thirties.

Theme and technique are carefully balanced by Vargas Llosa to achieve a complete fictional universe. A multiple-narrative voice is carefully crafted to obtain such an effect, but in contrast to his two previous works, the various points of view this time all come together in one single text in a unique form of syntax that switches at will its grammatical subject, ultimately representing a collective consciousness. As a result multiple levels of reality are depicted, and the reader is soon placed in the center of the fictional world that is evoked. At the same time language emerges as the central element in the novel to express an ambiguous, rich context in which a rigid social code brings about personal alienation and defeat.

One of Vargas Llosa's most monumental works is *Conversación en La Catedral* (1969; translated as *Conversation in the Cathedral,* 1975). The backdrop is Vargas Llosa's experience as a university student during the dictatorship of General Odría. Odría's corrupt administration illustrates the authoritarian yet chaotic course of Peru's republican history, as expressed in one of Vargas Llosa's most quoted phrases: "¿En qué momento se había jodido el Perú?" (At what precise moment had Peru screwed itself?). Vargas Llosa often has acknowledged the traumatizing scars that Odría's repressive regime left on him and his entire generation.

*Conversación en La Catedral* centers on a four-hour conversation between Santiago Zavala, the black sheep of a well-to-do family, and Ambrosio, the family's former chauffeur, as they drink in a bar in Lima. At stake is Zavala's final outcome as a failed rebel or antihero, exemplified in his identity as Zavalita. Minimizing the presence of the omniscient narrator, the author has the conversation between Santiago and Ambrosio serve as a review of the two characters' lives and their thoughts and recollections of their individual lives as Odría's final days in power take place. At the same time, such a narrative structure triggers multiple dialogues in space and time between other characters in the novel. As many as six conversations are represented simultaneously on a page, but because of Vargas Llosa's masterful technique, the apparent juxtaposition of elements ultimately interact in a concert of narrative voices and dramatized episodes that slowly reveal the novel's happenings. The final result is the portrayal of a multiple canvas of interlocking realities about Peruvian society that redefines Vargas Llosa's art of the total novel.

Odría's dictatorship is seen as a manifestation of contemporary Peruvian society's deeply rooted ills. As the dialogue between Santiago and Ambrosio develops, the reader learns of Santiago's personal transformation and his total disillusionment with his country. Santiago's father, Don Fermín Zavala, is a rich, aristocratic entrepreneur who supports Odría and in return receives important favors for his business enterprises. He also holds close ties with the regime's minister of the interior, the mischievous Cayo Bermúdez, who is largely responsible for repressing the regime's political enemies. Santiago despises his father's wrongdoings and grows increasingly uncomfortable with his privileged social status. He attends San Marcos, where he joins a clandestine Marxist cell. When the group is discovered by Odría's secret police Santiago and his comrades are detained. But while the latter are punished, Santiago is freed in less than twenty-four hours because of his father's connections. Further enraged by the situation, Santiago abandons the paternal household, getting a job as a crime reporter for the daily *La Crónica*. Through his job he learns even more about the life of fear and violence that affects many Peruvians and becomes progressively skeptical about the society to which he belongs and his future in it.

Through Ambrosio's conversation Santiago learns how Don Fermín's alliance with the regime has required that his home phone be tapped by the secret police and of his father's sordid behavior behind public life. While leading a life of decency for the external world, Cayo Bermúdez also keeps two whores, La Musa and Queta, for his entertainment and to blackmail many of the upper-class men who support Odría. La Musa and Queta carry on a lesbian liaison that Cayo Bermúdez enjoys as a voyeur. Don Fermín frequently attends the minister's parties. One day Don Fermín elopes with Cayo Bermúdez's childhood friend and chauffeur, Ambrosio. In reality Don Fermín is a well-known homosexual, and Ambrosio soon becomes his lover. Santiago learns of his father's true identity when he investigates La Musa's murder and hears Queta tell the authorities that La Musa was killed by Ambrosio to protect Don Fermín from being blackmailed. Vargas Llosa once again depicts human violence, widespread corruption, and degradation at every level of Peru's institutional and social structure. Regardless of social class, however, all of the novel's characters lead an existence marked by defeat. As part of a system lacking any kind of basic

Cover for Vargas Llosa's 1977 novel, which combines autobiographical fiction and soap-opera melodrama

values, Santiago is no exception. He too becomes the victim of a society that engenders only mediocrity and personal failure. Zavalita's stubborn refusal to conform to the cheap values of his social class offers perhaps the novel's only hope in Vargas Llosa's otherwise pessimistic outlook for Peru's future.

Along with his prolific fictional production, Vargas Llosa has also proved to be a lucid literary critic. Many of his theories about the novel, particularly his idea of the total novel, can be traced back to his enthusiasm for novels of chivalry and for the works of Gustave Flaubert. In 1969 Vargas Llosa wrote the prologue for the first modern Spanish edition of the chivalric Catalan novel *Tirant lo Blanc* (1511) by Joanot Martorell. Vargas Llosa points to Martorell's great virtues as a storyteller: his talent as a narrator of adventures and his attempt to capture reality on more than one fictional level, two essential ingredients in the Peruvian writer's craft. Vargas Llosa further developed this idea of the totalizing vocation of the novel in two other books. In

*García Márquez: Historia de un deicidio* (García Márquez: The Story of a Deicide, 1971) he studies the entire canon of the Colombian author, using García Márquez's masterpiece *Cien años de soledad* as a prime example of the total novel. He also discusses his personal ideas on a writer's obsessions, what Vargas Llosa calls any novelist's demons. These demons, he claims, whether psychological, intellectual, autobiographical, or otherwise, inadvertently invade the writer's creative consciousness and ultimately surface in his fictional work. In his later study of Flaubert's *Madame Bovary* (1857), *La orgía perpetua: Flaubert y "Madame Bovary"* (1975; translated as *The Perpetual Orgy: Flaubert and "Madame Bovary,"* 1986), Vargas Llosa expands on these ideas, stressing the notion of the writer as a god, as a creator of fictional realities. For Vargas Llosa, Flaubert's writing is key to understanding realism and the modern novel. If the novel is a genre that captures all aspects of reality, the novelist should strive to represent all aspects of life with equal passion and persuasion. In his attempt to achieve this totality by exploring as many different planes of reality as possible, he becomes the invisible creator of a fictional world, a god that holds the ultimate power over a given reality. Such is the case, Vargas Llosa argues, of Flaubert's *Madame Bovary*.

After Vargas Llosa's narrative achievements in the 1960s and his important theoretical reflections on the novel, he returned to his familiar world of the Peruvian jungle and the army in *Pantaleón y las visitadoras* (1973; translated as *Captain Pantoja and the Special Service,* 1978). Abandoning the blunt realism he had used to explore these themes in his previous works, he turned to parody and satire. Captain Pantaleón Pantoja is a model officer who genuinely believes in the values of service, obedience, and discipline in the army. Commissioned by his superiors to organize a secret prostitution service for the sex-starved soldiers stationed in the Peruvian jungle, Pantaleón carries out his mission with military zeal, running the operation with enviable efficiency. He scientifically calculates the number of prostitutes needed, the number of soldiers to be serviced, and even the number of orgasms each man requires to satisfy his sexual appetite. Whether by boat or by plane, he arrives at every army post in the jungle punctually so that each man may have mathematically calculated equal time with the *visitadoras*.

Without realizing it, Pantaleón slowly becomes a glorified pimp in an army uniform. His dutiful conscience is burlesqued by the values of a religious sect that operates in the jungle whose proselytizing often disrupts the efficiency of his secret mis-sion. Led by Brother Francisco, the fanatical members of the esoteric Ark Brotherhood carry out strange cults, including infanticide. Eventually Captain Pantoja decides to have a taste of his own product, while the news of his enterprise is leaked by a radio broadcaster. The army's authorities quickly claim no knowledge of the clandestine operation because of the hypocritical public outcry, and the faithful captain is demoted by the army and sent to a remote post in the Andes.

Except for omniscience Vargas Llosa deploys an extraordinary montage of narrative techniques ranging from multiple dialogues to letters, radio news, official military bulletins, and scientific statistical discourse. Humor breaks through the rigid tone of all of these discourses, quickly revealing the crass absurdity of the protagonist's military operation, functioning as the main tool of criticism of the army as an institution.

Humor also serves as a key element in Vargas Llosa's fifth novel, *La tía Julia y el escribidor* (1977; translated as *Aunt Julia and the Scriptwriter,* 1982). Fictionalized autobiography and soap-opera melodrama construct a narrative that attempts to erase the borders between fact and fiction. Set in Lima in the 1950s, *La tía Julia y el escribidor* tells the story of Marito, an eighteen-year-old radio journalist and aspiring writer, who falls in love with and marries his thirty-two-year-old aunt. At the radio station Marito meets Pedro Camacho, an eccentric Bolivian soap-opera scriptwriter whose corny fantasies hold a high audience rating. Camacho is fanatical about the various stories of infanticide, incest, prostitution, religious fanaticism, and genocide that keep his audience glued to the radio. Such success contrasts with Marito's failed attempts to become a respected writer. However, both kinds of narration blend in the novel's plot, for Marito and Julia's crazy love affair could well be merely the product of Camacho's fantasies. Vargas Llosa takes his fictional enterprise a step further, often stretching the limits of fact and fiction by using not only the historical real names of his main characters, but many historical events and characters from Peruvian public life as well. The novel ends with the return of Marito from Paris as a famous writer and the deterioration of Pedro Camacho, who has gone crazy, confusing the lives of his characters to the point that he believes they actually exist.

*La tía Julia y el escribidor* is the story of fiction writing itself. Although seemingly opposites, Marito and Camacho are ultimately two versions of one authorial figure who, in contrast to his previous works, creates a larger presence for himself in his own fiction. At the same time, *La tía Julia y el escribidor* is in tune with the works of a new generation of writers that slowly emerged in the 1970s in Latin America – the so-called post-Boom generation that included Manuel Puig, Antonio Skármeta, Mempo Giardinelli, and Isabel Allende. Distancing themselves from the solemn issues of the novels of the Boom, these younger novelists vindicated elements of popular culture such as music, cinema, and soap operas, artistic expressions traditionally viewed as second-rate, giving them in their fiction a renewed artistic status.

Varga Llosa's artistic renewal in *Pantaleón y las visitadoras* and *La tía Julia y el escribidor,* which many argue were less-fortunate artistic endeavors, also coincided with his interest in new ideological trends. Throughout the 1970s Vargas Llosa became progressively disenchanted with the Cuban revolution he had supported since the early 1960s, becoming highly critical of Fidel Castro's regime as well as of right-wing totalitarian governments that appeared throughout Latin America. In 1971 when the poet Heberto Padilla and various other Cuban intellectuals critical of Castro's government were forced to apologize publicly for their criticism of the Cuban regime, Vargas Llosa resigned from the editorial board of Casa de las Américas, Cuba's most important cultural institution, of which he had been a member since the 1960s. Instead, thanks to his discovery of thinkers such as Isaiah Berlin, Jean-François Revel, and Karl Popper, he slowly moved from social-democratic ideas to more liberal-democratic ideas. These new tendencies began to emerge in his next novel.

While *La guerra del fin del mundo* (1981; translated as *The War of the End of the World,* 1984) is Vargas Llosa's only novel not set in Peru, the events – this time set in Brazil – can be read as representing Latin-American history as a whole. A historical novel of epic proportions, it is based on the Brazilian journalist Euclides da Cunha's *Os Sertões* (1902; translated as *Rebellion in the Backlands,* 1944), the account of a rebellion by a poverty-ridden peasant population in northeastern Brazil led by the fanatical preacher Antonio Conselheiro.

By the late nineteenth century, Brazilian society was making the transition from a monarchy to a newly born republic in the fever of European positivist thought. Conselheiro establishes on the backlands of the city of Bahía a community known as Canudos, where followers quickly increase, lured by his charismatic personality and his announcement of the end of the world. Vargas Llosa carefully narrates individual stories of how the Conselheiro's

prophetic word sparks spiritual hope among the poor that soon brings out religious fanaticism. As Conselheiro clashes with the state and with the authorities of the Catholic church, he is considered by the government as the tool of a monarchic subversion against the republic. The republican army is soon sent into Canudos to suppress the peasant subversion, and after several failed attempts and much bloodshed Conselheiro's followers are destroyed.

Though set in northeastern Brazil, the struggle of the people of Canudos can be read as the fight of a community of marginalized peoples. Their plight is contrasted to the narrow-minded concerns of Brazilian politicians who interpret the happenings in Canudos from their comfortable surroundings in Bahía and Rio de Janeiro, making every effort to protect their personal privileges. Along with many politicians and military commanders, Vargas Llosa includes important characters such as Galileo Gall, a wandering phrenologist, and a journalist, both of whom accompany the republican army in its mission into Canudos. Gall, caught between his intellectual ideals and reality, significantly never reaches Canudos. The journalist, however, known for his physical near-sightedness (resembling da Cunha himself) and lack of political commitment, symbolically loses his spectacles during the struggle, only to see and understand fully through the eyes of Conselheiro's followers the genuine nature of this rebellion in Canudos.

A tour de force, *La guerra del fin del mundo* is for many Vargas Llosa's masterpiece. It exemplifies a classical narrative style reminiscent of the great adventure novels of the nineteenth century and includes many naturalist touches whereby Vargas Llosa displays his talent as a storyteller. More important, the novel depicts an apocalyptic struggle of the marginal people of Latin America. Inspired by fanatical religious beliefs, Conselheiro and his followers clash with a conservative middle class, who must justify Canudos's bloody events with an equally fanatical faith in science and reason in order to protect the status quo.

The huge critical success of *La guerra del fin del mundo* was only the beginning of what proved to be an intense decade for Vargas Llosa both as a writer and an influential public figure in Peru in the 1980s. He added a new dimension to his literary career with the publication of three plays, *La señorita de Tacna* (1981; translated as *The Young Lady from Tacna,* 1990), *Kathie y el hipopótamo* (1983; translated as *Kathie and the Hippopotamus,* 1990), and *La chunga* (1986; translated as *La Chunga,* 1990). The first play is an intense work that probes the nature of the cre-

*Cover for Vargas Llosa's 1984 novel, about Peruvian politics in the 1950s*

ative act, an ever-growing intellectual preoccupation in Vargas Llosa's works. This is seen through the aspiring writer Belisario's attempts to save cherished moments of the past from oblivion through the recollections of his great-aunt, the aging Mamaé. *Kathie y el hipopótamo* is a comic farce about people who deceive themselves while living part of their lives in make-believe worlds created through stories in order to escape their own suffocating mediocrity and insignificance. In *La chunga* Vargas Llosa brings to the stage many of the characters from *La casa verde,* using melodrama and sordid eloquence to focus on capitalist exploitation from a sexual viewpoint.

In spite of the interesting combination of time and space and of fantasy and reality in each of these plays, their obvious narrative tendency is often disappointing from a theatrical point of view. Perhaps more important than the works themselves are Var-

gas Llosa's reflections about the nature of why human beings tell stories, leading to such universal questions as the need for art, its purpose in life, and the process involved in creating fiction. As a fiction writer and a playwright Vargas Llosa seeks to show his readers the many ways in which art contributes to the quality of life – particularly the human need to substitute fantasy for reality – in order to gain a better understanding of human nature's deepest concerns.

In 1983 Vargas Llosa began publishing many of his journalistic writings under the title *Contra viento y marea* (Against All Odds). A three-volume anthology, *Contra viento y marea* gives an overview of Vargas Llosa's political and literary ideas ranging from his early admiration for Sartre and Cuban socialism in the 1960s to his defense of neoliberal free-market capitalism of the 1980s. This shift to a conservative position often placed him at the center of intellectual controversy both in Peru and abroad. Peru itself had experienced a wide range of political changes. After a twelve-year left-wing military government led by Gen. Juan Velasco Alvarado and Francisco Morales Bermúdez, elections were held, and Fernando Belaunde Terry, ousted earlier by Velasco Alvarado's coup in 1968, returned to power. While remaining politically independent, Vargas Llosa maintained such close political ties to Belaunde's regime that he was offered the post of prime minister, which he did not accept. At the same time, El Sendero Luminoso (the Shining Path), a Maoist guerilla group, began operating in the southern highlands of the Ayacucho province, quickly making its violent presence known in Peru's major cities.

Vargas Llosa's political stands are present in his next novel, *Historia de Mayta* (1984; translated as *The Real Life of Alejandro Mayta,* 1986). In it he delves again into Peruvian history in the late 1950s and using real and imagined events tells the story of Alejandro Mayta, a Marxist revolutionary who organized a rebellion in the provincial city of Jauja in the southern Peruvian Andes. At the same time a contemporary novelist in the 1980s (like Vargas Llosa himself) is trying to track down information about the legendary Mayta who, as the novel progresses, becomes a character bigger than life. The novelist interviews Mayta's political allies, his leftist professors, a senator, Mayta's girlfriend, and even Mayta himself, who by this time is an older man who has chosen to forget his revolutionary past. The reader is often a close witness of the author's struggle to convert the facts of Mayta's failed revolution into fiction. At times the book's essayistic tone resembles that of a documentary repeatedly questioning the boundaries between fact and fiction, one of the novel's greatest virtues. Within this larger framework an ideological debate between Christianity and Marxism takes place. Ultimately, however, *Historia de Mayta* is an inquiry into and a reflection on the relationship between writing as a means of representation and reality itself. As in *La tía Julia y el escribidor,* the portrait of the author as artist and the mysterious craft of storytelling again become central issues.

Vargas Llosa's novella *¿Quién mató a Palomino Molero?* (1986; translated as *Who Killed Palomino Molero?*, 1987) can be seen as a return to the melodramatic ingredients based on the secret passions of men and women that make for good storytelling. Relying on proven narrative techniques that create layer upon layer of ambiguity and the conviction that reality and truth are indeed illusions, Vargas Llosa plays with the reader's curiosity from the outset by posing a question in the title of the novel that is never satisfactorily answered. In addition to asking who killed the protagonist, an innocent young man, the novel's characters ask themselves why he was killed in such a brutal manner and for what reason.

The action takes place in the northern Peruvian city of Talara, near Piura. Again Vargas Llosa includes a medley of characters who represent the gamut of social and economic levels in Peru. The novel is an entertaining piece of detective fiction. Sergeant Lituma of *La casa verde* reappears as a detective with his faithful companion, Lieutenant Silva. Lituma and Silva are portrayed as clumsy and inexperienced in their undertaking. In fact, they face great odds in discovering the truth, as certain individuals work to prevent the policemen from uncovering it. Although they are able to write a report to their superiors with the names of Palomino's murderers, larger questions loom heavily over the incident. In the end the reader is faced with the moral task of disentangling the elements that played a role in bringing about Molero's death: a pure, ideal love between a girl and a boy made impossible because of social mores based on racial and economic discrimination, unrequited love, incest, perversion, lust, and false illusions.

In *El hablador* (1987; translated as *The Storyteller,* 1989) Vargas Llosa returns to the Amazon jungle of Peru, adding another piece to the author's growing narrative mosaic of social, cultural, and literary concerns from previous novels. *El hablador* tells of an Amazon Indian tribe, the Machiguengas, and in particular the life of the community's storyteller, Saúl Zuratas. As in *Historia de Mayta,* the narrator-author closely resembles Vargas Llosa himself. The novel opens as the narrator wanders into a photo gallery in Florence, Italy, where an exhibition of old photographs of the Machiguengas is being held. The author remembers his college days with Zuratas before he abandoned his anthropological studies to live permanently with the Machiguengas. In a society without writing or rigid political or religious hierarchies, his role as a storyteller becomes crucial to remember the tribe's history. This metaliterary theme is not new in Vargas Llosa's work, and the relation between the primitive tribal storyteller and his community and a modern-day novelist and his society is easily made. In parallel fashion the novel communicates other themes Vargas Llosa has previously explored: the right to dissent, the right to tribal or ethnic autonomy, the clash between a dominant Western culture and a marginalized indigenous population, the novelist's responsibility to write history (not the official version, but the personal, unwritten human histories), and the art of fiction writing. In the case of the last theme, the novel's counterpoint structure becomes significant for the juxtaposed nature of two narrative lines — one characteristically realist and objective involving the narrator-author, who conjures up his memories of Zuratas, the other a construct around myth, magic, and legend, dealing with the storyteller. A felicitous blend of oral fiction, although at times lacking narrative tension, *El hablador* was a new inquiry into the multifaceted identity of Peruvian society, in which primitive and modern lifestyles are forced to coexist in conflict and contradiction.

In 1987 Vargas Llosa was unexpectedly placed at the center of political debate in Peru as he became an outspoken critic of President Alan García's reformist tendencies. García had achieved the presidency by an overwhelming margin in 1985, placing his center-left party in power for the first time in the country's history. Lured by the support of Peru's two oldest conservative parties, Vargas Llosa soon formed the Movimiento Libertad (Freedom Movement), a conservative coalition, and became an outspoken supporter of neoliberal economic ideas. In the meantime, he published a short novel in 1988, *Elogio de la madrastra* (translated as *In Praise of the Stepmother,* 1990), a successful but minor attempt at the erotic genre, and a book of essays on various American and European novels, *La verdad de las mentiras* (Lies That Tell the Truth, 1990), reflecting on various aspects of creative fiction.

Vargas Llosa's only incursion into professional politics was short-lived. He ran for the presidency of Peru in 1990 and, despite being heavily favored, lost in a second-round vote to the then-unknown Alberto Fujimori. His failed attempt for the presidency of Peru led him to produce a volume of memoirs in 1993, *El pez en el agua* (translated as *A Fish in the Water,* 1994). Using the counterpoint technique that had proved so successful in his previous works of fiction, the book is a behind-the-scenes look into Vargas Llosa's political campaign in the context of Peruvian political history as well as a biographical account of his childhood through young adulthood and his slow rise to literary stardom. A passionate and often bitter narrative, *El pez en el agua* provides the author's views on Peru's tumultuous history as a nation and his participation as a writer in its cultural development.

Since his political defeat in 1990 Vargas Llosa has lived in Europe, devoting himself entirely to writing with occasional visits to the United States to lecture at universities. He has also published a fourth play, *El señor de los balcones* (Lord of the Balconies, 1993), which tells the story of Prof. Aldo Brunelli, an Italian immigrant, who one day decides to save every old colonial balcony from being destroyed by Lima's growing modernity. Brunelli makes the preservation of colonial balconies a lifelong crusade, buying every balcony that he can and protesting the destruction of old buildings. Modernity, however, proves to be an overwhelming force against which Brunelli and his quixotic quest cannot compete.

Vargas Llosa's most recent novel is *Lituma en los andes* (Lituma in the Andes, 1993), which was awarded the important Planeta prize in Spain. Set in the small town of Naccos, in the central highlands of Junín province, it is Vargas Llosa's first work entirely set in the Andes. It revolves around the mysterious disappearance of three natives of the region. Lituma reappears as the central character, this time accompanied by his faithful subordinate Tomás Carreño. Although at first the plot resembles that of a detective novel, it slowly delves into the mythical psychology of Andean legends, superstitions, and demons. *Lituma en los andes* can be read as a remake of the Greek myth of Dionysus transposed to the Peruvian highlands, for as Lituma tries to shed light on the missing members of the community he soon discovers that the belief in local myths is responsible for many acts of violence. He eventually learns that a local bar owner, Dionisio, once a musician in remote towns of the region, has presided over the human sacrifice of the missing members of Naccos to the *apus* (Andean gods). *Lituma en los andes* plays out the struggle between rational Western thought and mythical nonrational beliefs in the context of Peru's recent violent history. What surfaces is a portrait of a world whose violent and barbaric manifestations (the Shining Path included) remain mysterious.

Vargas Llosa is without a doubt at the forefront of Latin-American literature. Constantly redefining the role of the writer in Latin-American society, he is very much a man of his time. His evolution from an interest in social criticism to a more conservative position parallels to some extent the evolution of Latin-American political ideology from Socialist and statist solutions to a tendency toward neoliberalism. Although immersed in the complex problems of Peru in particular and Latin America in general, his works also have a universal stature as they repeatedly examine social and ideological conflicts and the contradictory nature of human passions. Vargas Llosa's own relentless passion for the world of fiction and the multiple manifestations of reality make him a crucial protagonist in Spanish America's contemporary literary history.

**Interviews:**

Ricardo Cano Gaviria, *El buitre y el ave fénix: Conversaciones con Mario Vargas Llosa* (Barcelona: Anagrama, 1972);

Raymond L. Williams, William Gass, and Michel Rybalka, "The Boom Twenty Years Later: An Interview with Mario Vargas Llosa," *Latin American Literary Review,* 15, no. 29 (1987): 201–206;

Ricardo Setti, "The Art of Fiction: Mario Vargas Llosa," *Paris Review,* 116 (Fall 1990): 47–72;

Julia A. Kushigan, "Entrevista: Mario Vargas Llosa," *Hispamérica,* 63 (1992): 33–41.

**References:**

María Isabel Acosta Cruz, "Writer-Speaker? Speaker-Writer? Narrative and Cultural Intervention in Mario Vargas Llosa's *El hablador,*" *Inti,* 29–30 (1989): 133–143;

Carlos J. Alonso, "*La tía Julia y el escribidor:* The Writing Subject's Fantasy of Empowerment," *PMLA,* 106, no. 1 (1991): 46–59;

Alicia Andreu, "Pedro Camacho: Prestidigitador del lenguaje," *Modern Language Studies,* 16, no. 2 (1986): 19–25;

Birger Angvik, "La risa que se vuelve mueca: El doble filo del humor y de la risa: *Historia de Mayta* frente a la crítica en Lima," *Lexis,* 15, no. 1 (1991): 39–72;

Luis de Arrigoitia, "Machismo, folklore y creación en Vargas Llosa," *Sin Nombre,* 13, no. 4 (1983): 19–25;

Rosa Boldori de Baldusi, *Mario Vargas Llosa: Un narrador y sus demonios* (Buenos Aires: Fernando García Cambeiro, 1974);

Belén Sadot Castañeda, *Mario Vargas Llosa: Crítico, novelista y dramaturgo* (Madison: University of Wisconsin Press, 1987);

Castañeda, "El elemento añadido en *Historia de Mayta,*" *Confluencia,* 4 (Spring 1988): 21–28;

Debra Castillo, "The Uses of History in Vargas Llosa's *Historia de Mayta,*" *Inti,* 24–25 (Fall–Winter 1986–1987): 79–98;

Sara Castro-Klarén, "Fragmentation and Alienation in *La casa verde,*" *Modern Language Notes,* 87, no. 2 (1972): 286–299;

Castro-Klarén, "Humor and Class in *Pantaleón y las visitadoras,*" *Latin American Literary Review,* 7, no. 13 (1978): 64–79;

Castro-Klarén, "Locura y dolor: La elaboración de la historia en *Os Sertões* and *La guerra del fin del mundo,*" *Revista de Crítica Literaria Latinoamericana,* 10, no. 20 (1984): 207–230;

Castro-Klarén, *Mario Vargas Llosa: Análisis introductorio* (Lima: Latinoamericana, 1988);

Castro-Klarén, "Santos and Cangaceiros: Inscription without Discourse in *Os Sertões* and *La guerra del fin del mundo,*" *Modern Language Notes,* 101, no. 2 (1986): 366–388;

Frank Dauster, "Vargas Llosa and the End of Chivalry," *Books Abroad,* 44, no. 1 (1970): 41–45;

Mary E. Davis, "*Dress Gray* y *La ciudad y los perros:* El laberinto del honor," *Revista Iberoamericana,* 47, no. 116–117 (1981): 117–126;

Davis, "Mario Vargas Llosa: The Case of the Vanishing Hero," *Contemporary Literature,* 28 (Winter 1987): 510–519;

Rita De Grandis, "La problemática del conocimiento en *Historia de Mayta* de Mario Vargas Llosa," *Revista de Crítica Literaria Latinoamericana,* 19, no. 38 (1993): 375–382;

Luis Alfonso Diez, *Mario Vargas Llosa's Pursuit of the Total Novel* (Cuernavaca, Mexico: CIDOC, 1970);

Diez, ed., *Asedios a Vargas Llosa* (Santiago, Chile: Universitaria, 1972);

Inger Enkvist, *Las técnicas narrativas de Mario Vargas Llosa* (Göteborg, Sweden: Acta Universitatis Gothobugensis, 1987);

M. J. Fenwick, *Dependency Theory and Literary Analysis: Reflections on Vargas Llosa's "The Green House"* (Minneapolis: Institute for the Study of Ideologies and Literature, 1981);

Roland Forgues, "Lectura de *Los cachorros,*" *Hispamérica,* 5, no. 13 (1976): 34–49;

Carlos Fuentes, "El afán totalizante de Vargas Llosa," in his *La nueva novela latinoamericana* (Mexico City: Joaquín Mortiz, 1969), pp. 35–48;

Magdalena García Pinto, "Anatomía de la revolución en *La guerra del fin del mundo* e *Historia de Mayta* de Mario Vargas Llosa," in *The Historic Novel in Latin America,* edited by Daniel Balderston (Gaithersburg, Md.: Hispamérica, 1986);

Dick Gerdes, *Mario Vargas Llosa* (Boston: Twayne, 1985);

Helmy Giacoman and José Miguel Oviedo, eds., *Homenaje a Mario Vargas Llosa* (New York: Las Américas, 1971);

Rita Gnutzmann, *Cómo leer a Mario Vargas Llosa* (Madrid: Júcar, 1992);

Jorge Guzmán, "A Reading of Vargas Llosa's *The Real Life of Alejandro Mayta,*" *Latin American Literary Review,* 15 (January–June 1987): 133–139;

Hollis Huston, "Revolutionary Change in *One Hundred Years of Solitude* and *The Real Life of Alejandro Mayta,*" *Latin American Literary Review,* 15 (January–June 1987): 105–120;

Instituto de Cooperación Iberoamericana, *Semana de Autor Mario Vargas Llosa* (Madrid: Cultura Hispánica, 1985);

Julie Jones, "The Search for Paradise in *Captain Pantoja and the Special Service,*" *Latin American Literary Review,* 9, no. 19 (1981): 41–46;

Marvin A. Lewis, *From Lima to Leticia: The Peruvian Novels of Mario Vargas Llosa* (Lanham, Md.: University Press of America, 1983);

Stephen M. Machen, "Pornoviolence and Point of View in Mario Vargas Llosa's *Aunt Julia and the Scriptwriter,*" *Latin American Literary Review,* 9, no. 17 (1980): 9–16;

George McMurray, "The Novels of Mario Vargas Llosa," *Modern Language Quarterly,* 29, no. 3 (1968): 329–340;

Willy Muñoz, "La historia de la ficción de Mayta," *Symposium,* 44 (Summer 1990): 102–113;

Michael Moody, "Paisajes de los condenados: El escenario natural de *La casa verde,*" *Revista Iberoamericana,* 47, nos. 116–117 (1981): 127–136;

Marta Morello-Frosch, "Of Heroes and Martyrs: The Grotesque in *Pantaleón y las visitadoras,*" *Latin American Literary Review,* 7, no. 14 (1979): 40–44;

José Miguel Oviedo and others, "Focus: *Conversation in the Cathedral,*" *Review,* 14 (Spring 1975): 5–37;

Oviedo, ed., *Mario Vargas Llosa: El escritor y la crítica* (Madrid: Taurus, 1981);

Oviedo, *Mario Vargas Llosa: La invención de una realidad* (Barcelona: Seix Barral, 1982);

Michael Palencia-Roth, "The Art of Memory in García Márquez and Vargas Llosa," *Modern Language Notes,* 105 (March 1990): 351–366;

Antonio Pereira, *La concepción literaria de Mario Vargas Llosa* (Mexico City: Universidad Nacional Autónoma de México, 1981);

René Prieto, "The Two Narrative Voices in Mario Vargas Llosa's *Aunt Julia and the Scriptwriter,*" *Latin American Literary Review,* 11, no. 22 (1983): 15–25;

Angel Rama, "*La guerra del fin del mundo*: Una obra maestra del fanatismo artístico," *Eco,* 40 (April 1982): 600–640;

Susana Reisz de Rivarola, "La historia como ficción y la ficción como historia: Vargas Llosa y Mayta," *Nueva Revista de Filología Hispánica,* 35, no. 2 (1987): 835–863;

José Rodríguez Elizondo, *Vargas Llosa: Historia de un doble parricidio* (Santiago, Chile: La Noria, 1993);

Charles Rossman and Alan Warren Friedman, eds., *Mario Vargas Llosa: A Collection of Critical Essays* (Austin: University of Texas Press, 1978);

William Rowe, "Liberalismo y autoridad: Una lectura política de Vargas Llosa," *Nuevo Texto Crítico,* 4, no. 8 (1991): 91–100;

Joaquín Roy, "Mario Vargas Llosa," in *Narrativa y crítica de nuestra América,* edited by Roy (Madrid: Castalia, 1977), pp. 351–386;

Michel Rybalka, "Mario Vargas Llosa and *The Real Life of Alejandro Mayta* from a French Perspective," *Latin American Literary Review,* 15 (January–June 1987): 121–131;

Iván Silen, "El anti-Mayta," *Revista de Crítica Literaria Latinoamericana,* 11, no. 23 (1986): 269–275;

David Sobrevilla, "La nueva teoría de la novela de Mario Vargas Llosa," *Cuadernos Hispanoamericanos,* 496 (October 1991): 59–71;

Joseph Sommers, "Literatura e ideología: La evaluación novelística del militarismo en Vargas Llosa," *Hispamérica,* 4, no. 1 (1975): 83–117;

Peter Standish, *Vargas Llosa: La ciudad y los perros* (London: Grant & Cutler, 1983);

Eduardo Urdanivia, "Realismo y consecuencias políticas en *Historia de Mayta,*" *Revista de Crítica Literaria Latinoamericana,* 11, no. 23 (1986): 135–140;

Alvaro Vargas Llosa, *El diablo en campaña* (Madrid: El País/Aguilar, 1991);

Raymond L. Williams, *Mario Vargas Llosa* (New York: Ungar, 1986);

*World Literature Today,* special issue on Vargas Llosa, 52 (Winter 1978);

Roger A. Zapata, "Las trampas de la ficción en *Historia de Mayta,*" in *La historia en la literatura: Textos del XXVI Congreso del Instituto Internacional de Literatura Iberoamericana,* edited by Raquel Chang-Rodríguez and Gabriela de Beer (New York: Ediciones del Norte/City University of New York, 1989).

# Marcio Veloz Maggiolo

## (13 August 1936 – )

### Silvio Torres-Saillant
*Hostos Community College, City University of New York*

BOOKS: *El sol y las cosas* (Cuidad Trujillo, Dominican Republic: Arquero, 1957);

*El buen ladrón* (Cuidad Trujillo, Dominican Republic: Arquero, 1960);

*Intus* (Santo Domingo: Arquero, 1962);

*Judas; El buen ladrón* (Santo Domingo: Librería Dominicana, 1962);

*El prófugo* (Santo Domingo: Brigadas Dominicanas, 1962);

*Creonte; Seis relatos* (Santo Domingo: Arquero, 1963);

*La vida no tiene nombre; Nosotros los suicidas* (Santo Domingo, 1965);

*Los ángeles de hueso* (Santo Domingo: Arte y Cine, 1967);

*Arqueología prehistórica de Santo Domingo* (Singapore & New York: McGraw Hill, 1972);

*Cultura, teatro y relatos en Santo Domingo* (Santiago de los Caballeros, Dominican Republic: Universidad Católica Madre y Maestra, 1972);

*El precerámico de Santo Domingo, nuevos lugares, y su posible relación con otros puntos del área antillana,* by Veloz Maggiolo and Elpidio Ortega (Santo Domingo: Cultural Dominicana, 1973);

*Apuntes sobre la prehistoria de Santo Domingo* (Santo Domingo: Cultural Dominicana, 1974);

*Esquema para una revisión de nomenclaturas arqueológicas del poblamiento precerámico en las Antillas,* by Veloz Maggiolo and Plinio Pina (Santo Domingo: Fundación García-Arévalo, 1974);

*De abril en adelante* (Santo Domingo: Taller, 1975);

*Medioambiente y adaptación humana en la prehistoria de Santo Domingo,* 2 volumes (Santo Domingo: Taller, 1975, 1976);

*Sobre cultura dominicana y otras culturas* (Santo Domingo: Alfa y Omega, 1977);

*De dónde vino la gente* (Santo Domingo: Alfa y Omega, 1978);

*Novelas cortas* (Santo Domingo: Alfa y Omega, 1980);

*Sobre cultura y política cultural en la República Dominicana* (Santo Domingo: Alfa y Omega, 1980);

*Marcio Veloz Maggiolo*

*Las sociedades arcáicas de Santo Domingo* (Santo Domingo: Fundación Garcías-Arévalo, 1980);

*Vida y cultura en la prehistoria de Santo Domingo* (San Pedro de Macorís, Dominican Republic: Universidad Central del Este, 1980);

*La biografía difusa de Sombra Castañeda* (Caracas: Monte Avila, 1981);

*La fértil agonía del amor* (Santo Domingo: Taller, 1982);

*La palabra reunida* (San Pedro de Macorís, Santo Domingo: Universidad Central del Este, 1982);

*La arqueología de la vida cotidiana* (Santo Domingo: Taller, 1985);

*Apearse de la máscara* (Santo Domingo: Biblioteca Nacional, 1986);

*Cuentos, recuentos y casicuentos* (Santo Domingo: Taller, 1986);

*Florbella* (Santo Domingo: Taller, 1986);

321

*Poemas en cierne; Retorno a la palabra* (Santo Domingo: Taller, 1986);

*Materia prima* (Santo Domingo: Fundación Cultural Dominicana, 1988);

*Panorama histórico del Caribe precolombino* (Santo Domingo: Banco Central de la República Dominicana, 1991);

*Ritos de cabaret* (Santo Domingo: Fundación Cultural Dominicana, 1991).

PLAY PRODUCTION: *Y después las cenizas,* Santo Domingo, 15 January 1964.

OTHER: Carlos Esteban Deive, *Magdalena,* prologue by Veloz Maggiolo (Santo Domingo: Arte y Cine, 1964), pp. 5–10.

SELECTED PERIODICAL PUBLICATION – UNCOLLECTED: "El escritor dominicano y las presiones sociales de su medio," *Casa de las Américas,* 7, no. 43 (1967): 109–112.

Marcio Veloz Maggiolo, who has enjoyed literary prestige since his early twenties when his first book appeared, is the most prolific contemporary Dominican writer and is often hailed as the most impressive of his country's intellectuals. He was born in the city of Santo Domingo on 13 August 1936 to Francisco Veloz Medina, a self-taught scholar who authored an often-cited history of the Santo Domingo neighborhood of La Misericordia, and Mercédez Maggiolo, the devout daughter of Protestant Christians of Italian emigrant descent. Veloz Maggiolo grew up in an ambience that fostered reading and discussion of both religious and secular texts. The fierce dictatorship of Rafael Leónidas Trujillo, whose total hold of Dominican society began in 1930 and ceased only with his violent death in 1961, brought the young Veloz Maggiolo into contact with social and political imperatives. Overall, his works, despite the stylistic and thematic changes perceptible in successive titles over three decades of literary practice, consistently show a concern with the drama of individuals as they grapple with the forces that shape their reality.

Veloz Maggiolo received his primary, intermediate, and secondary education in his native city, where he also attended the University of Santo Domingo. He began higher education as a law student, then changed to humanities with a concentration in literature and history. After receiving his baccalaureate in 1961 he began a teaching career at his alma mater, where he still teaches and most likely will

continue, especially since the university has recently named him professor-in-residence for life, an honor previously conferred only upon the revered poets Pedro Mir and Aída Cartagena Portalatín. In 1963, with the fall of the Trujillo regime and the rise of the democratically elected president Juan Bosch, the twenty-seven-year-old Veloz Maggiolo accepted an appointment as Dominican ambassador to Italy, which began a diplomatic career that took him as ambassador to Mexico (1965–1966), Peru (1982–1983), and again to Italy (1983–1985). In 1968 Veloz Maggiolo went to Spain to complete a doctorate in the history of the Americas at the Universidad Complutense de Madrid, specializing in prehistoric archeology and pre-Columbian history. His doctoral dissertation was published as *Arqueología prehistórica de Santo Domingo* (Prehistoric Archeology of Santo Domingo, 1972).

His training in the archeology, anthropology, and prehistory of the Americas has brought Veloz Maggiolo recognition at home and abroad. Having served as his country's assistant secretary of education and as chairman of the Department of History and Anthropology of the Autonomous University of Santo Domingo, where he also served as director of anthropological research, Veloz Maggiolo headed the Museo del Hombre Dominicano from 1975 through 1978. His book-length scholarly publications written alone and in collaboration exceed twenty titles, including the two-volume work *Medioambiente y adaptación humana en la prehistoria de Santo Domingo* (Environment and Human Adaptation in Prehistoric Santo Domingo, 1975, 1976), *Las sociedades arcáicas de Santo Domingo* (Archaic Societies in Santo Domingo, 1980), *Vida y cultura en la prehistoria de Santo Domingo* (Life and Culture in Prehistoric Santo Domingo, 1980), *La arqueología de la vida cotidiana* (Archeology of Everyday Life, 1985), and *Panorama histórico del Caribe precolombino* (Historical Overview of the Caribbean before Columbus, 1991). His scholarship has made Veloz Maggiolo an authority on the archeology of the Caribbean area and has led to various scientific awards at home and the conferral of the Spinden Medal by the Smithsonian Institution in Washington. In regard to his literary practice, his scientific research has generated notable strategies and thematic options. The narrative forms he has termed *protonovel* and *archeonovel* seem to emulate a scientific reconstruction of textual canvases from dispersed fragments. His concept of *materia prima* (raw material) evolves naturally from his familiarity with archeological and anthropological methods. As is particularly evident in his recent work, Veloz Maggiolo often assumes the art of literary creation in the manner of an archeologist unearthing meaningful objects from an excavation.

Veloz Maggiolo's first book-length publication, a volume of verse entitled *El sol y las cosas* (The Sun and the Things, 1957), was saluted as a triumph of Dominican poetry by Antonio Fernández Spencer, then one of the most prominent men of letters in the country. With considerable maturity of vision, the volume advances a sustained reflection on the futility of language as a reliable means of communication while proclaiming the ultimate power of poetry as a trustworthy testament of the human experience. The volume also exhibits an insistent preoccupation with the divine. References to God recur throughout even while the dominant tone of the poetic voice avoids devotional diction.

Veloz Maggiolo's second book was a short novel entitled *El buen ladrón* (The Good Thief, 1960), which also earned Fernández Spencer's laudatory appraisal. The older writer celebrated the text as "la novela más hermosa y problématica de la literatura dominicana" (the most beautiful and problematic novel in Dominican literature). Set in ancient Judaea during Jesus' life, the novel enacts the drama of three individuals trapped within the rigid prison imposed by class origin and unfavorable social conditions. The first-person protagonist of the novel is a single mother whose destitution, combined perhaps with her admitted ineptitude, has made it hard for her to secure sustenance for her son, Denás, and her daughter, Midena. The story centers around the family's travail in meeting the challenges of survival in the midst of their circumstances.

Denás and Midena have had to support themselves since early childhood. An epileptic since age ten, Denás works to help his mother make ends meet. When menial jobs prove insufficient to support the household, he becomes a thief and Midena a prostitute. The mother's relaxed moral creed has clear political implications. She places her children's deviance within the framework of the oppressive forces that shape their everyday lives. She understands that their poverty is due to an unjust social system that deprives the weak of any control over their existence. When the Roman army needs their land to build a road, the family loses its house. Such social injustice explains her leniency toward her son even when he is believed to have committed murder. With Denás in hiding, the mother reflects on the questionable moral ascendancy of the soldiers who search the house, the servants of Caesar whose criminal record she deems no more pure than that

of her son. Midena also identifies the political structure as the cause of the family's misery.

Such an awareness of prevailing injustice and the perception of widespread social discontent draws Denás to a subversive Galilean preacher. Having first learned about the preacher from his partner Gester, Denás interprets Jesus' movements as a form of political upheaval, imagining that the general turmoil caused by the Galilean's entrance into Jerusalem would give him and Gester an opportunity to loot the main stores of the city.

As he gets closer to Jesus, Denás turns into a socially committed individual who advocates the well-being of the collective, much to the dismay of his mother, who sees him "convertido en hombre bondadoso y estúpido" (converted into a generous stupid man). Midena meanwhile has converted, seduced by the powerful spell of the preacher's teachings. Soon Denás, recognizing the spiritual rather than social texture of the revolution upheld by Jesus, becomes hopeless and angry, even vowing to kill the Galilean. Instead of killing him, however, Denás experiences a spiritual surrender and is miraculously relieved of his epilepsy. From then on Denás continues to steal but with a nobler purpose: to support the family and to share his bounty with the disinherited. Ironically, that benevolent state of mind leads to his demise. A poor man to whom Denás had given a yellow tunic reports him to the Roman authorities. Sentenced to death, Denás and another thief are crucified, each flanking Jesus, also sentenced to die on the cross.

Since the mother narrates the story after the fact, she enjoys the privilege of retrospection, which enables her to assess her son's decisions and actions in light of actual results. While she cannot share Midena's belief that Denás will come back to life, she reasons that if Jesus has returned from the dead, everyone who died for him should also. Nor does she have any qualms about vaunting her son's valor. She regards his death as a greater martyrdom than that of Jesus since the Galilean always knew he had the chance of coming back to life.

*El buen ladrón* moves with agility and occasionally achieves a moving lyrical tone, perhaps due to the author's poetic practice, as Carlos Esteban Deive has suggested. Veloz Maggiolo forges here a vigorous narrative through the felicitous device of the narrator's biased point of view and forceful voice. The novel constitutes a propitious beginning for the author as a fiction writer.

Veloz Maggiolo's work would seem to challenge the existence of a world where good always triumphs and evil always gets punished. In the early texts he wrestles with the concept of God and the existential problems derived from God's relationship to humanity. The poem "Piedad del viento" (Pity from the Wind) from *Intus* (Within, 1962), a second volume of verse made up mostly of sonnets, partly illustrates that state of mind. The poem "Antes" (Before), also from the volume, portrays the Almighty as an elusive entity who appears impervious to humanity's desperate spiritual search, a God that needs to be told such otherwise obvious propositions as "Señor, te busca el hombre" (Lord, man looks for you), as in the last line. The very notion of omnipotence appears reduced by God's own susceptibility to needs, desires, and other sublunary qualities. God is ontologically dependent upon humanity. With the world ruled by such an imperfect God, the speaker has grounds for dispensing with the idea of a higher principle that guarantees the preeminence of justice. The speaker's prevalent attitude is summed up in a line from "Pequeña biografía" (Little Biography), the sonnet that opens *Intus,* which presents art as his ultimate creed: "Creo en el arte, dudo de la vida" (I believe in art, I doubt life).

His novel *Judas* (Judas, 1962) earned Veloz Maggiolo the Dominican Republic's National Book Award for fiction, a distinction he attained simultaneously in the category of poetry for *Intus*. In 1962 he also received the William Faulkner Award granted by the University of Virginia for *El buen ladrón*. In remarkable ways *Judas* prefigures the author's archeological sense, a feature that became central to his works following his formal studies in Spain. Similarly, the tendency to narrate a marginal story that bears obliquely on a central story becomes perceptible here, having begun to show slightly in his earlier novel. Thus, in telling the biblical story of Judas Iscariot, who in the scriptures matters primarily because of his relationship with Jesus, Veloz Maggiolo focuses his attention principally on the family conflicts, personality clashes, and sibling rivalries that surround Judas's tormented existence. Both Judas here and Denás in the previous novel have pathetic human dramas of their own. Their ultimate connection with the Galilean preacher occurs naturally as a consequence of their lives.

*Judas* consists of four parts: an editorial commentary, an introduction to the voice of Judas, a posthumous letter from Judas to his father Simon, and a letter by Judas's brother Moabad. The opening section, spoken by a narrator-editor who identifies himself as "Marcio Veloz Maggiolo," says that the letter from Judas reached him through a friend who bought it as a papyrus in Tel Aviv twenty-four

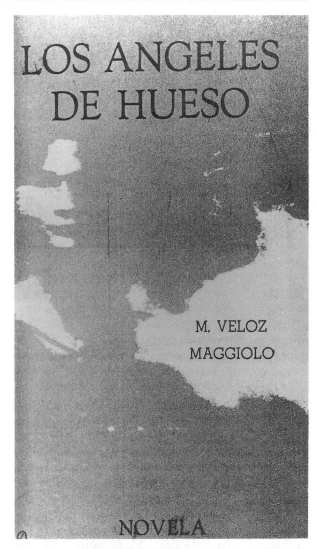

Cover for Veloz Maggiolo's highly experimental 1967 novel, which features a schizophrenic narrator

years before the discovery of the Dead Sea Scrolls. The letter of Moabad he inherited from a nineteenth-century Italian ancestor as a French translation of the ancient original. In commenting on the two texts, the narrator-editor claims not to have meddled with the first-person accounts of either Judas or Moabad, though he admits to having used his skills as a novelist in composing the introduction so as to give Judas a voice to ward off his unearned ill fame. The introduction permits Judas to set the record straight by claiming that he saved Jesus from degenerating into a common man. He decries the ingratitude of his colleagues, who found a substitute to occupy his position among the disciples after he hanged himself from a tree. In doing so, they undermined the fact that he, more than anyone else among them, helped Jesus to accomplish his divine mission.

In part three, which reproduces Judas's letter, the novel delves into the character's personal history and psychology. He tells how he suffered neglect and ill treatment from his father, who favored his brother Moabad in every respect, and how he nurtured feelings of jealousy and hatred that led to their violent break. Understood only by Olfa, who in time becomes his wife, he uses the money stolen from his father to try his luck in business in various Middle Eastern cities. He prospers cunningly in Bethsan and suffers failure in Otath, cities under foreign imperial domination. Moabad, feigning goodwill, catches up with him in Emat, where Judas has settled with wife and children. Judas's gullible welcoming of his brother leads to the loss of his business, wife, and children, which then causes in him a tortuous internal crisis. Self-critical and mortified, he undergoes a process of repentance and undertakes a search for God. He seeks spiritual cleansing by going on a pilgrimage and throwing his gold into the river Jordan.

Written after Judas's death from the privileged perspective afforded by the knowledge of his brother's letter, Moabad's missive to Simon, contrary to what one might expect based on Judas's portrayal of Moabad, contains a strikingly positive appraisal of Judas. Moabad tells of his own travail after robbing Judas's house. Having soon squandered what valuables he stole, he could not make Olfa happy, and she left him. He then heard of a miracle performed by Jesus during the wedding at Cana in Galilee and he had no objection to following Ezequiel, his young employer, when he left a prosperous business behind to join the Galilean preacher. The experience, motivated first by convenience since he would continue to receive his salary from Ezequiel, produced an earnest spiritual transformation and a desire to make amends for past evils, particularly against his brother Judas. Drawn to Jesus, Moabad comes upon none other than his brother Judas, who, already a disciple of Christ, treats him kindly.

The encounter allows Moabad to learn the details of his brother's conversion and of his close relationship with Jesus, who had talked him into serving as informer so as to fulfill the prophecy. Moabad claims to have partaken in easing Judas's concern about the "betrayal," reassuring him about the greatness of his divine complicity and its reward. Unfortunately, things do not turn out well for Judas. He commits suicide when, having completed his part of the deal by collecting the thirty silver pieces, he despairs at not seeing Jesus rise from the dead right away. Moabad closes his letter with the hope that his brother one day will be vindicated. In his final assessment of his brother, he likens him to a martyr, for Judas subjected himself to humiliation and historical disparagement for the sake of helping Jesus fulfill his divine purpose.

Like *El buen ladrón* and *Judas,* Veloz Maggiolo's *Seis relatos* (Six Tales, 1963), which appeared in the same volume with his play *Creonte* (Creon, 1963), treats biblical themes. It consists of a sequence of six short prose narratives related to the life of Christ. The first, "El joven rico" (The Young Rich Man), tells the pathetic story of Gedeón, the young man whom Jesus advises to get rid of his wealth as a prerequisite for leading a life of virtue. The biblical text does not expound on this episode, but Veloz Maggiolo prods into the young man's tragic end as he revolts against his father in order to fulfill Jesus' mandate. "La semilla y el árbol" (The Seed and the Tree) undertakes to capture through personification the drama of the tree chosen by Judas upon which to hang himself after selling out his master, just as "El pollino sagrado" (The Sacred Donkey) re-creates the background of the donkey ridden by the Savior to enter Jerusalem on Palm Sunday. "Dídimo" delves into the personal predicament of Thomas the Twin, the disciple who required concrete evidence to believe that the Lord indeed had risen from the dead. "Lázaro" provides a conclusion to the account of Lazarus following his having been raised from the dead, revealing that he returned to death shortly after Jesus left him and his sisters. Finally, in the sixth story, "Las bodas de Caná" (The Wedding at Cana), what interests the narrator is the very act of transformation of the water into wine, the concrete logistics of the miracle.

Each of the six stories shows Veloz Maggiolo's predilection for marginal and alternative stories. Moreover, their biblical subject matter provided a safe venue at the time for the author to comment on the relationship between the individual and the state without offending the Trujillo regime. In fact, *El buen ladrón* and *Judas* have been grouped together with *El testimonio* (Testimony, 1961) by Ramón Emilio Reyes and *Magdalena* (Magdalene, 1964) by Carlos Esteban Deive as forming a subcategory called the *biblical novel* in Dominican literature. Veloz Maggiolo has validated such a grouping, arguing that they used themes from the scriptures in order to disguise their opposition toward the oppressive regime then prevalent in the country.

Veloz Maggiolo admits the influence in his formative years of the Nobel Prize–winning Swedish novelist Pär Lagerkvist, author of *Barabbas* (1950), and the Polish-American novelist Sholem Asch, author of such biblical novels as *The Nazarene* (1939) and *The Apostle* (1943). In all likelihood this influence, combined with the deistic perspective on religion evident in his work as early as *El sol y las cosas,* helps to explain Veloz Maggiolo's peculiar approach to biblical subject matter.

With *Creonte,* a reworking of the Antigone legend from Sophocles, Veloz Maggiolo found another cultural artifact of the ancient world that would allow a Dominican author writing during the dictatorship to deal critically with political structures and oppressive regimes without fear of reprisal. The problems that afflict the characters in this play correspond to the existential dilemma of finding oneself in the midst of two clashing moral orders. The state must enforce its law so that society can function while Antigone must do what she thinks is right in the eyes of God. Both options represent a conflict between the individual and society. At a sociological level the plot, in presenting Hemon, who rebels against his father Creon in defense of his fiancée who has violated a royal decree, dignifies an act of blatant civil disobedience. Adarco's subversive statement, "Sólo dos cosas pueden contra la tiranía: la fuerza o la persuasión" (There are only two courses against tyranny: force or persuasion), gains import in light of the fact that all attempts at persuading Creon prove unsuccessful, leaving the insinuation that perhaps violence alone is ultimately the solution in dealing with a repressive regime. The author explained that the play, completed one year before the death of Trujillo, sought to re-create the moment when the dictatorship clashed with the power of the Church, foreseeing the crumbling of the tyranny.

With the death of Trujillo in 1961 and the eventual dismantling of the formal dictatorship, it became less necessary for Veloz Maggiolo and other Dominican authors to conceal their political criticism behind ancient Hebrew or classical Greek characters and situations. Their critical lens then turned to direct examination of their national drama with an eye toward deciphering the meaning of three decades of brutal oppression. They also developed a keen eye for scrutinizing their present political options and the extent to which their small society could aspire to a system of equality and justice. In this context Veloz Maggiolo's works reflect a vision of the future and a worldview that, while avoiding pessimism, remains reserved. On the whole he seems to sneer at all views that assume a fixed moral order in the world.

In Veloz Maggiolo's world justice does not guarantee success. Fairness and goodwill do not automatically bring reward. Often it is the contrary, as in his novella *El prófugo* (The Fugitive, 1962). The text does not constitute a considerable literary achievement, marred as it is by an overly rhetorical and journalistic prose, according to the author's own admission. It merits discussion, however, because of what it confirms about his worldview. Alberto, the main character, has killed Trujillo, the tyrant whose ruthless regime had brought plunder and death to his country for thirty-one years. Yet his heroic, patriotic action does not bring him glory or recognition. Instead, he suffers the most humiliating ostracism, for though the dictator has died, the political and military machinery of his government survives, now in the hands of "un presidente miedoso y una familia agresiva, temeraria y rica" (a fearful president and an aggressive, fearful, and rich family). The tyrant's family and associates orchestrate a violent, intensive search for all involved in the death of their chief, torturing and killing the ones they catch. Alberto, a character suggested to the author by the real-life odyssey of Juan Tomás Díaz, Antonio de la Maza, and the other men involved in the actual death of Trujillo, ends up hiding in the charcoal burner of a city house unbeknown to the household members. He eats by stealing the leftovers brought by the girl of the house to her dog Leal until Leal starves to death, and Alberto, his source of food gone, must venture to find another hideout.

The second part of *El prófugo* introduces Angel Hortón, a secret service agent who worked as a mason until he joined the Military Intelligence Service (SIM), the murderous secret police of the regime, in order to advance himself and his family. Subjected to the harsh reiterative criticism of his wife Matilde, who functions as a voice of conscience, Angel finds it hard to continue to rationalize his killings in the name of law and order or material need. Following a strenuous process of soul-searching, he consents to leave his job after he completes his last mission. In the meantime, Alberto appears in the dark of night on the way to a nearby church, seeking the protection afforded by the house of God. When he confesses to the priest that he has killed the dictator, the latter asks him to repent, but he refuses on the grounds that he did not kill a personal enemy but liberated his country. The priest absolves Alberto anyway and becomes in turn troubled by a heavy conscience for thinking he

*Veloz Maggiolo with Alejo Carpentier in Guanajuato, Mexico, 1968*

has done wrong. His sense of social justice has interfered with his theological judgment, causing him to consecrate a capital sin.

Meanwhile a paid informer named Alfonso Yañez recognizes Alberto and reports him to the SIM, hoping to collect a reward. Johnny, the chief agent in charge of the operation, selects Angel Hortón, whom he had started to distrust, to join the patrol to capture Alberto. The SIM agents force their way into the church. Angel hesitates before striking the priest and forcing him to reveal the fugitive's whereabouts, but the captain insists on his taking the lead. When Angel beats the information out of the priest, they easily track down Alberto and kill him. In the shoot-out that ensues Angel also falls, killed "accidentally" by friendly fire. Nobody hears his last words, as he gaspingly murmurs that it was his last night. The story closes with the priest praying before an image of Christ as he gratefully recalls Angel's hesitation before hitting him.

In *El prófugo* cruelty and depravity triumph. The SIM agents gloat at the sight of Matilde's sorrow as they heartlessly unfold before her eyes the dead body of her husband drenched in blood. The villainous Johnny ends up rewarded as he, with the informer Alfonso Yañez's mysterious death, manages to collect the reward offered for the capture of Alberto. By the same token, the priest's good intentions toward the fugitive prove too weak before the weight of violence and force. Angel becomes a victim of the murderous regime precisely at the point when he has chosen to dissociate himself from the path of evil. Clearly the cosmos in which the plot occurs does not obey the dictates of a morally consistent universe.

The volatility of perception, the difficulties of communication, personal greed, human frailty, downright evil, and the immeasurable role of chance all play a part in whatever aspirations people may have concerning their advancement and the betterment of society. Veloz Maggiolo's works tend to accord a reasonable space to those uncontrollable variables. In *Y después las cenizas* (Ashes to Ashes), a play first staged on 15 June 1964 (according to an entry in the author's diary), Captain Reines and his comrades conspire against a backward system but fail, ending up in hiding. Afraid that if found they might ruin their ultimate revolutionary purpose,

Reines prevails upon his associates to immolate themselves on behalf of the cause. Twelve years later, with Reines still living in concealment, the revolution triumphs, and Manuel Druso, the traitor who caused the failure of the original conspiracy, now reaps glory as a marshal of liberation. Eventually Druso pays for his deceit, but Reines, who kills himself right after Druso dies, attains no vindication. Instead, he leaves behind the perception that, an accomplice to Druso's treachery, he took his life for fear of facing the rightful judgment of the revolution.

A similar existential dilemma appears in the short novel *La vida no tiene nombre* (Life Has No Name, 1965), whose plot draws on the political situation of Dominicans during the United States occupation of the country from 1916 through 1924. The main character, Ramón, has fought the invaders successfully until personal circumstances work to his disadvantage and he ends up in the hands of the enemy. Told by the protagonist, who sits awaiting his impending execution, the story unfolds as the speaker, induced by the immediacy of his death, recollects the events that led to his present state. He recounts the family conflicts and rivalries of his youth in a manner that resembles the story of *Judas*. The speaker's forceful voice and biased viewpoint also bring to mind the mother in *El buen ladrón*. Ramón suffered a life of abuse at the hands of his Dutch father, who cared nothing either for him or for his Haitian mother. Carrying the nickname of El Cuerno on account of his illegitimate birth, he brings a heavy baggage of pain and injustice to his initial association with the insurgent troops then fighting for the cause of national liberation.

Thus positioned in a subversive political camp, Ramón opposes those in the country who side with the occupying American army, including his father, a landowner, and his brother Fremio, the legal heir to the old man's possessions. He also clashes with a host of Dominican soldiers who form the National Guard, the law enforcement body created by the American government during the occupation, among whom the young officer Trujillo figured prominently. Ramón recalls the young Trujillo personally leading the firing squad against Juan Crisóstomo and Mayí, two guerrilla fighters. The trauma of his dying mother in urgent need of costly medical help clouds Ramón's vision, and he goes to his father's house for help, a disastrous measure that leads to his captivity. In the hands of the National Guard and the American army, Ramón reflects on the awesome task before his comrades in arms. He can hold on only to the hope that they will

continue to reproduce themselves for as long as imperial abuse threatens the freedom of small nations. He prays that the feeling of patriotism and concern for national sovereignty overshadow the moral poverty of Trujillo and all others who find it easy to sell their souls as well as their people. However, he cannot avoid a deep sense of bitterness at having to die doubting the feasibility of his hope and his prayer.

*La vida no tiene nombre* fits naturally within the thematic continuum in Veloz Maggiolo's work; stylistically, it looks back to the earlier novels. *Nosotros los suicidas* (Suicidal Peers, 1965), another short novel, seems to point the way toward the formal explorations that typify his later work. The narration shifts perspectives to agree with the changing identity of the voice telling the story. Largely self-conscious, the narrator often addresses the reader or at times alludes to the process of composing the story being told. The setting of the story avoids a recognizable geography so as to accord with the otherworldliness of the dramatic situation since the characters are all dead. Reminiscent of Jean-Paul Sartre's *Huis clos* (1944; translated as *No Exit*, 1946), the tension of the plot revolves around existential questions concerning the ultimate meaning of human action. The dialogue form that pervades the book accentuates the many voices of the text and the dialectical texture of the issues examined by the speakers: whether certain individuals, such as Alejandro Rodrigues, have committed suicide and if they properly belong in the Federación Mundial de Suicidas. At another level the novel may be read historically as a satire of the Trujillo dictatorship.

*Nosotros los suicidas,* a thoughtful narrative that delves into profound moral and political questions, provides an existential rendering of death as ultimately and perhaps invariably a result of one's will in the context of one's relationship with society. In this sense the book provides a natural transition to Veloz Maggiolo's *Los ángeles de hueso* (The Bone Angels, 1967) another short novel in which he escalates his exploration of the formal possibilities of the genre and intensifies the self-consciousness of the text. The volume consists of a sustained utterance by a schizophrenic, unreliable first-person narrator who comments haphazardly on his dead brother, the political situation of his country, the intermittent company of his mother, the presence of his real or imagined wife, and his immediate physical surroundings.

The novel skillfully juxtaposes an aesthetic reflection on the literary form at hand with a thorough obeisance to a historical imperative that keeps the reader alerted to the political implications of human action in society. Enunciating what one might read as part of a poetics of the novel, the narrator begins in the opening paragraph of the first chapter decrying linear narrative constructions. At the outset and throughout the text he protests at the recurrence of "I" in his first-person account and speculates that he could begin his novel by narrating the most minute and least significant detail, such as George Washington's false teeth or Napoleon's stomachache at Austerlitz, just as the reader could begin this novel halfway through the text, as he asserts later. He thereby alludes to the multiple options available to the novelist at the moment of writing. Similarly, despite a hypersensitive perception that attributes significance to everything, often to the point of exaggeration, the speaker is not oblivious to the historical drama in which he is a player. He thinks of disturbances at the border with Haiti, Dominican soldiers shooting at Haitians as they try to cross. He thinks of Christopher Columbus loving the Dominican land but letting his hungry dogs devour its native inhabitants. He recalls the musical piece entitled *Nexus 16* by Loren Rush but reasons that his brother, Juan, killed at Las Manaclas by government soldiers, could never enjoy such music. He remembers the time when Juan joined the revolutionaries convinced that the country's honor, then trampled upon by a military junta, had to be redeemed. He saw their choice as an act of madness, but, he ponders, military coups do tend to drive people mad. The narrator chooses out of fear not to join his brother, and therein may lie the feeling of guilt that seems to take hold of him upon Juan's death and may be at the core of his troubled state of mind.

Probably a reworking in fiction of a brief one-act play Veloz Maggiolo published in 1965 under the title *La soledad* (Solitude), which featured more or less the same characters, *Los ángeles de hueso* displays a harmonious interaction of form and content. Edna Coll saluted the author for achieving in this book the popular "language novel" and doing so with originality while Manuel Valldeperes viewed the stylistic innovations as perhaps unnecessary at the time, given the writer's "ya seguro y original camino" (already secure and original path). Yet one can argue that the sense of balance outweighs all the other merits of the book. The subject matter – the social chaos born of the violent overthrow of the constitutional government and the crushing of the element that sought redress – finds a fitting medium of expression in a form that challenges its own structure. The story comes from a demented narrator whose account one can only partly accept. The

text contains empty spaces that signify moments of silence for the speaker and ultimately symbolize the desolation brought on by death and the reign of violence. The speaker's mental promenade goes around in circles, making possible a return to the point at which the narrative began, except that it is not a perfect circle but a coming to a halt. In the middle of a reflection on death and sleep, the last sentence begins but does not go on, leaving the suspicion that the narrator has ceased to exist. The undefined conclusion, however, allows for different interpretations, and some take its open-endedness as a reiteration of hope whereby Veloz Maggiolo conveys the sense of searching and expectation that still persists in Dominican society.

The historical events that fueled Veloz Maggiolo's imagination in composing *Los ángeles de hueso* – the coup d'etat against President Juan Bosch in 1963; the installation of puppet governments under direct orders from the Trujillista military elite and the American embassy; the uprising led by Manolo Tavárez Justo in the mountains of Las Manaclas, where many revolutionaries met their death at the hands of government forces; and the overall discontent that pervaded Dominican society – culminated in the armed struggle known as the Revolution of April 1965, headed by Col. Francisco Alberto Caamaño and a nationalist faction of the armed forces. Called *constitucionalistas* since they sought to restore the constitutionally elected president and his cabinet, the insurgents garnered considerable civilian support and virtually defeated the soldiers of the coup leaders. The arrival on 28 April 1965 of forty-two thousand U.S. Marines changed the course of events. Though President Lyndon B. Johnson authorized their intervention ostensibly to protect the lives of U.S. citizens in Santo Domingo, the American troops immediately aligned themselves with the right-wing military. The American presence, which Veloz Maggiolo protested energetically in an open letter addressed to President Johnson, put an end to the short-lived sense that Dominicans could have control over their own political destiny. This bitter turn, while not extinguishing the fire of revolutionary fervor, produced a mixed sense of resentment, confusion, and disillusionment. The following year, with Santo Domingo still occupied by foreign military units, Veloz Maggiolo, then Dominican ambassador to Mexico, continued to decry the intervention in an interview published by *El Día* on 16 February 1966. Later that month, attending a celebration of Dominican Independence Day, he covered his car partially with a black cloth to signify his country's continu-

*Cover of Veloz Maggiolo's 1988 novel, which combines
metafiction with Dominican history*

ous mourning due to the presence of the invading forces.

A visible figure as a diplomat and already celebrated as a brilliant, mature man of letters despite his youth, Veloz Maggiolo had a first-hand taste of the traumatic and turbulent events of the mid and late 1960s in Dominican society. The recollection and analysis of those events fueled his imagination once more in writing *De abril en adelante* (From April Onward, 1975), the work that has received the most critical attention of his writings. Like *Los ángeles de hueso,* this novel simultaneously launches a reflection on the act of writing and a dissection of the social structures and historical conjunctures that informed the April Revolution. These two lines of inquiry, the challenges of literary creation and the demands that political situations place on individuals, alternate in the mind of the narrator, who is equally dismayed at his inability to come up with a topic for his novel and at the reproachable exhibitionism of

many revolutionaries during April 1965. The shifting narrative voices face equally awesome tasks in both areas. Regarding literature, one reads about the aim to produce a novel strictly out of indigenous material. Concerning the speaker's historical reality, one reads that during their invasion of Santo Domingo the Americans divided the city in two fronts by drawing a line that even encompassed the sea. Both lines of inquiry merge in passages where the speaker reflects on their interaction. The reader thus hears his justification for combining subject matter from the April 1965 Revolution with the seventeenth-century rebellion of Hernando de Montero and the nineteenth-century War of Restoration on the grounds that his novel seeks to create a world that allows for the intermixture of diverse historical moments.

Ultimately *De abril en adelante,* as a speaker in the text says, deals with a novelist who speaks about a novelist who cannot write a novel because of the suffocating social milieu. That milieu consists of the concrete social reality in which the characters exist in combination with the political and economic structures that shape their material lives as well as their mental or spiritual growth. In staging the disintegration of the novel form – with the inclusion of "anti-chapters," shifting voices or narrative standpoints, inverted words, scrambled spelling, breaks in pagination, assorted typographical variations, and self-referential editorial pronouncements – *De abril en adelante* seems intent on reflecting structurally the sociopolitical chaos that ensued from the failure of the revolution.

If *De abril en adelante* and much of the author's earlier work manifest a kinship with the literature of the absurd, as Luis F. González-Cruz contends, the absurdity in question has a direct correspondence in true historical circumstances. In writing the novel Veloz Maggiolo was aware that on 1 June 1966 Dr. Joaquín Balaguer, Trujillo's puppet president when the dictator died in 1961, had been inaugurated as chief of the Dominican Republic after winning an infamous election with the full backing of the right-wing military and the United States Army. One can therefore understand the mood of despondency and helplessness prevailing in the novel. Yet one should note that its closing words voice a desire to change the prevailing mood. Veloz Maggiolo, like most Caribbean authors, refuses to make concessions to pessimistic visions of his people's future even before baleful circumstances.

Critics of *De abril en adelante* have overemphasized the uniqueness of its formal innovations, but in the context of Veloz Maggiolo's aesthetic development it is a natural step in a literary quest. In fact, the novel maintains an insistent intertextual dialogue with some of his earlier works, chiefly *Los ángeles de hueso* and the short story "El Coronel Buenrostro" (Colonel Goodface), published in the 1960s, from both of which it draws thematically as well as stylistically. All of the elements of narrative self-consciousness exhibited in *De abril en adelante* have antecedents in *Los ángeles de hueso* and partly in *Nosotros los suicidas*. Similarly, many of the remaining narrative techniques, such as stream of consciousness and the displacement of time and space, are successfully rehearsed in "El Coronel Buenrostro." Ramón Francisco, a fellow Dominican writer who shared with him and René del Risco Bermúdez the leadership of the literary group called "El Puño," had years before *De abril en adelante* highlighted Veloz Maggiolo's technical, thematic, and linguistic innovation, crediting him with bringing Dominican fiction to a level with the best and most

modern literary work in the rest of Latin America. Doris Sommer, who articulates her "high regard" for the book strictly on an appreciation of its "experimental narrative structure," is the most ardent critic of the novel in the United States. Her conviction that, on account of its deconstruction of form, the novel constitutes the finest product of modern Dominican fiction has compelled her to indict Dominican intellectuals and readers for "the cool response" and the critical objections the novel received when it was first published. Sommer praises *De abril en adelante* primarily because in her reading the text reveals an approach to history and literature that she espouses, which she says Dominicans would do well to uphold.

However, Sommer does not really harbor great respect for the book as a work of art. Dominican critics such as Héctor Incháustegui Cabral, José Alcántara Almánzar, and Bruno Rosario Candelier have lauded Veloz Maggiolo's talent, maturity, and importance in the country's literature, but Sommer discounts their judgments, saying, "Veloz is hardly an accomplished writer; his language is often cumbersome and redundant, although never pretentious; but the structure of his novel is remarkably adequate to its content." Her ambivalent appraisal has to do largely with her reading *De abril en adelante* in isolation from the author's work as well as from the social and cultural milieu from which it derives the paradigms of its significance.

Veloz Maggiolo once denounced the incommunication between Dominican writers and their people in "El escritor dominicano y las presiones sociales de su medio" (The Dominican Writer and the Social Pressures of His Environment, 1967), decrying the fact that in Santo Domingo literary artists wrote "from above" for "those above." Ironically, his *protonovel,* as he termed *De abril en adelante,* for the most part failed to speak to its home public, including an individual as cultivated as Juan Bosch, who declared his inability to finish reading it. One could speculate that, whatever slight to his artistic ego Veloz Maggiolo may have suffered, at heart he came to recognize that his failure to stimulate Dominican readers was at least partly due to a flaw in his aesthetic project. That recognition probably explains his return to the protonovel in *Materia prima* (Raw Material, 1988), a text that in many respects rewrites and improves on *De abril en adelante.*

Winner of the Dominican Republic's National Book Award for fiction and applauded by various literary reviewers, *Materia prima* takes up many of the characters and situations of the earlier work, spanning the Trujillo dictatorship, the revolutionary moment from Tavárez Justo through April 1965, and the populist regime that has dominated politics in the country since then. Stylistically the novel innovates as much as and probably more than *De abril en adelante,* but the innovation comes from the author's own aesthetic evolution rather than straight from importations. The writing of the novel, which is circular and self-referential, enacts Veloz Maggiolo's notion of raw material, a concept derived from first-hand experience during three decades of continuous literary work as well as from his anthropological and archeological expertise. The concept posits that a literary text need not emerge from a constant imaginative flow in the mind of the writer but may result instead from a concatenation of fragments salvaged from previous efforts. In other words, the raw material for literary creation may be found in the writer's archives as much as in the recesses of his or her imagination.

*Materia prima,* like its antecedent, proceeds with many voices, with the characters Persio and Papiro serving as the recognizable interlocutors. Many of its chapters take the form of epistles to Persio in which the narrative voice comments critically on the preceding chapters, focusing on such literary questions as the verisimilitude as well as the veracity of the affairs narrated, the author's biased or otherwise limited perspective, and the propriety of character portrayal. Narration and analysis of the dynamics of composition occur in quick succession. "He pensado que vale más la memoria que la invención, y he comenzado a sustituir la imaginación con el recuerdo" (I have thought that memory is more valuable than invention, and I have begun to substitute remembrances for imagination), the narrator explains, enunciating thereby the principle of coherence implemented in the novel. Veloz Maggiolo's active memory of the past and keen awareness of present conditions weave a tapestry in which fragments from earlier literary exercises can cohere with mental flashes from the author's childhood, adolescence, and adulthood, using the Santo Domingo neighborhood of Villa Francisca as his locus.

Evolving from the author's interest in history, the novel advances a critical view of the concept of world history, highlighting the arbitrariness of the people and episodes that normally are included or excluded from global accounts of human events. The narrator insists that the history of a neighborhood is the history of humanity, concluding that the story of Villa Francisca summarizes the human experience in all its depth and complexity as much as would the story of Paris, Rome, or any of the more internationally renowned geographical and political sites. In asserting for Villa Francisca, a Dominican neighborhood with its typically Antillean cultural accent, a rightful spot in the global scheme, the novel challenges ethnocentric views of world history that construe the West as the center of human society. In that respect, the social and aesthetic project informing *Materia prima,* which achieves originality by escaping the formal derivativeness of *De abril en adelante,* points to a concern for cultural authenticity. The affirmation of a Dominican place implies an acceptance of the milieu as holding the ultimate clue to the artistic and ideological significance of the novel.

This cultural self-assurance did not occur without a laborious process. A diverse list of titles in different genres occupied Veloz Maggiolo between *De abril en adelante* and *Materia prima. De dónde vino la gente* (Where People Came From, 1978), a prose tale intended for young readers, engaged him in the exploration of the magic and wisdom of the pre-Columbian inhabitants of Santo Domingo. He also published *Florbella* (1986), an "archeonovel" in a straightforward narrative style featuring an archeologist who falls in love with the bones of a Taino princess found in his excavation. The tension in this charming book comes from the clash between the scientist's creativity, which is vital in order to reconstruct a long-gone historical reality from the evidence of a few artifacts, and his emotional involvement, which in this case exceeds the limit. It also raises interesting questions about the dangers of the imagination.

Veloz Maggiolo also published three volumes of verse, *La palabra reunida* (The Collected Word, 1982), *Apearse de la máscara* (Giving Up the Mask, 1986), and *Poemas en cierne; Retorno a la palabra* (Nascent Poems; Return to the Word, 1986), which in their lack of a coherent thematic or stylistic center evince a state of unconcluded searching. They share a concern for the exploration of identity in the areas of concrete historical experience, cultural spaces, language, and the magic of artistic creation. Similarly, his short-fiction books *La fértil agonía del amor* (Love's Fertile Agony, 1982) and *Cuentos, recuentos y casicuentos* (Tales, Twice-Told Tales, and Almost Tales, 1986) include a greater formal and thematic versatility than a coherent aesthetic project could unify. Despite the National Book Award won by *La fértil agonía del amor* and the praise of Dominican reviewers for his short fiction, his merit in the genre consists primarily in his rehearsal of some of the stylistic devices and thematic variations that are more systematically developed in more ambitious and sustained later works.

As an essayist Veloz Maggiolo has sought to explore the elements of a Creole culture in the Dominican Republic. The essays compiled in his book *Sobre cultura dominicana y otras culturas* (On Dominican Culture and Other Cultures, 1977) variously contribute knowledge that aims to highlight the indigenous values of Dominican culture. In many respects they expand on his earlier exposition of the Caribbean nature of the Dominican experience and the cultural commonality of the Antillean region.

The most important milestone in Veloz Maggiolo's literary career in the years between *De abril en adelante* and *Materia prima* is the novel *La biografía difusa de Sombra Castañeda* (The Vague Biography of Sombra Castañeda, 1981), winner of the National Book Award for fiction, a text that marks an auspicious development in his search for a culturally authentic poetics of the novel. Combining political allegory with historical exploration along with the mythical richness of the Caribbean cosmology, the novel centers around the tyrannical figure of Sombra Castañeda. This autocratic chief evokes and transcends the historical Trujillo. At one level the narrative follows the dictates of verisimilitude in recounting the drama of Esculapio, a resident of Villa Francisca who has actively opposed the Trujillo dictatorship. Esculapio dies absurdly on the day when he should have started to live, when the radio announces the death of the tyrant. At a parallel level are the more-mythical adventures of Sombra Castañeda with his seat of power in El Barrero, a village at the foot of the Martín García mountain chain. This is a world of fantastic specters and hidden forces that possess otherwise real and recognizable places.

No matter how mythical the narrative, however, Veloz Maggiolo never steps entirely outside the realm of the historical. Symbolically, Sombra's loss of any trace of his navel at age seven might suggest an obliteration of evidence of his human birth and his temporality. His chronology even violates the limits of a normal human life span since he can boast about centuries of first-hand experience. Yet he remains cognizant of the political moment and the historical time transpiring simultaneously at the other level of the narrative. The two worlds actually move toward each other, as is evident when Serapio Rendón, who challenges Sombra's absolute power, becomes confused with Esculapio, the opponent of Trujillo. Similarly, the announcement of Trujillo's death coincides with Sombra's decomposition and evanescence. Sharon Keefe Ugalde classifies the novel as a dictator's novel, a subgenre that

many have noted in Latin American literature. More important, she highlights Veloz Maggiolo's exploration of a wide range of linguistic possibilities in the text.

The critical success of *La biografía difusa de Sombra Castañeda,* and perhaps also the reason it is the first novel by Veloz Maggiolo to have been translated into a foreign language, lies in its search for cultural authenticity, its earnest effort to convey the magic of the Dominican experience by evoking elements that tie the Dominican people to the Caribbean legacy.

Continuing the saga of Villa Francisca, the author's 1991 novel, *Ritos de cabaret* (Cabaret Rituals), features mostly strange characters going through uncommon situations against the backdrop of distinctly recognizable political events in recent Dominican history. While the novel does not compare with either of its two predecessors, it encompasses popular culture and aspects of the people's oral culture, thus furthering Veloz Maggiolo's ties with the Caribbean literary tradition. In addition, the book gives evidence of Veloz Maggiolo's continuous search for the precise mold in which to cast his understanding of the relationship between individuals and the society that both entraps them and gives them meaning. Most important, however, it shows the persistence of the complex creative drive that won him a high rank among Dominican writers when his first books appeared more than three decades ago.

**Interviews:**

Guillermo Piña Contreras, "Marcio Veloz Maggiolo," in his *Doce en la literatura dominicana* (Santiago de los Caballeros, Dominican Republic: Universidad Católica Madre y Maestra, 1982), pp. 193–213;

Bruno Rosario Candelier, "Entrevista a Marcio Veloz Maggiolo," in his *Tendencias de la novela dominicana* (Santiago de los Caballeros, Dominican Republic: Universidad Católica Madre y Maestra, 1988), pp. 340–371.

**References:**

José Alcántara Almánzar, *Los escritores dominicanos y la cultura* (Santo Domingo: Instituto Tecnológico de Santo Domingo, 1990);

Alcántara Almánzar, *Narrativa y sociedad en Hispanoamérica* (Santo Domingo: Instituto Tecnológico de Santo Domingo, 1984);

Héctor Incháustegui Cabral, *Escritores y artistas dominicanos* (Santiago de los Caballeros, Dominican Republic: Universidad Católica Madre y Maestra, 1979);

Diógenes Céspedes, "Muerte y violencia en la escrítura desigual de *La fértil agonía del amor* de Marcio Veloz Maggiolo," in his *Estudios sobre literatura, cultura e ideologías,* second edition (Santo Domingo: Taller, 1983), pp. 165-167;

Edna Coll, "Veloz Maggiolo, Marcio," in her *Indice informativo de la novela hispanoamericana,* volume 1 (San Juan: Editorial Universitaria, Universidad de Puerto Rico, 1974), pp. 217-220;

Carlos Esteban Deive, *Tendencias de la novela contemporánea* (Santo Domingo: Arquero, 1963);

Giovanni Di Pietro, "La novela bíblica y el fin de la era," *Cuadernos de Poética,* 6, no. 18 (1989): 7-76;

Antonio Fernández Spencer, "Prólogo," *El sol y las cosas* by Veloz Maggiolo (Ciudad Trujillo, Dominican Republic: Arquero, 1957), pp. 11-22;

Ramón A. Figueroa, "*Novelas cortas* por Marcio Veloz Maggiolo," *Sin Nombre,* 12, no. 4 (1982): 87-90;

Luis F. González-Cruz, "Desde el absurdo: La narrativa de Marcio Veloz Maggiolo," *Anales de la Literatura Hispanoamericana,* 7, no. 8 (1979): 119-125;

Neil Larson, "¿Cómo narrar el Trujillato?," *Revista Iberoamericana,* 54, no. 142 (1988): 89-98;

Bruno Rosario Candelier, "Marcio Veloz Maggiolo: La vida no tiene nombre," *Coloquio,* 29 (April 1989): 8-11;

Doris Sommer, "*De abril en adelante:* Can Narrative Survive the Death of Romance?" in her *One Master for Another: Populism as Patriarchal Rhetoric in Dominican Novels* (Lanham, Md.: University Press of America, 1983), pp. 197-228;

Sommer, "Good-Bye to Revolution and the Rest: Aspects of Dominican Narrative since 1965," *Latin American Literary Review,* 8, no. 16 (1980): 223-228;

Sharon Keefe Ugalde, "Veloz Maggiolo y la narrativa de dictador/dictadura: Perspectivas dominicanas e innovaciones," *Revista Iberoamericana,* 56, no. 142 (1988): 129-150;

Manuel Valldeperes, "*Creonte & Seis relatos* por Marcio Veloz Maggiolo," *Revista Iberoamericana de Bibliografía,* 15, no. 1 (1965): 59-60.

# Erico Veríssimo

### (17 December 1905 – 28 November 1975)

### Mary L. Daniel
*University of Wisconsin–Madison*

BOOKS: *Fantoches* (Pôrto Alegre, Brazil: Globo, 1932);

*Clarissa* (Pôrto Alegre, Brazil: Globo, 1933);

*Caminhos cruzados* (Pôrto Alegre, Brazil: Globo, 1935); translated by L. C. Kaplan as *Crossroads* (New York: Macmillan, 1943); republished as *Crossroads and Destinies* (London: Arco, 1956);

*Música ao longe* (São Paulo: Nacional, 1935);

*A vida de Joana d'Arc* (Pôrto Alegre, Brazil: Globo, 1935);

*As aventuras do avião vermelho* (Pôrto Alegre, Brazil: Globo, 1936);

*Um lugar ao sol* (Pôrto Alegre, Brazil: Globo, 1936);

*Meu ABC* (Pôrto Alegre, Brazil: Globo, 1936);

*Rosa Maria no castelo encantado* (Pôrto Alegre, Brazil: Globo, 1936);

*Os três porquinhos pobres* (Pôrto Alegre, Brazil: Globo, 1936);

*As aventuras de Tibicuera, que são também as aventuras do Brasil* (Pôrto Alegre, Brazil: Globo, 1937);

*Olhai os lírios do campo* (Pôrto Alegre, Brazil: Globo, 1938); translated by Jean Neel Karnoff as *Consider the Lilies of the Field* (New York: Macmillan, 1947);

*O urso com música na barriga* (Pôrto Alegre, Brazil: Globo, 1938);

*Aventuras no mundo da higiene* (Pôrto Alegre, Brazil: Globo, 1939);

*Outra vez os três porquinhos* (Pôrto Alegre, Brazil: Globo, 1939);

*Viagem à aurora do mundo* (Pôrto Alegre, Brazil: Globo, 1939);

*A vida do elefante Basílio* (Pôrto Alegre, Brazil: Globo, 1939);

*Saga* (Pôrto Alegre, Brazil: Globo, 1940);

*Gato preto em campo de neve* (Pôrto Alegre, Brazil: Globo, 1941);

*Viagem através da literatura americana* (Rio de Janeiro: Instituto Brasil-Estados Unidos, 1941);

*As mãos do meu filho* (Pôrto Alegre, Brazil: Meridiano, 1942);

*O resto é silêncio* (Pôrto Alegre, Brazil: Globo, 1943); translated by Kaplan as *The Rest Is Silence* (New York: Macmillan, 1946; London: Arco, 1956);

*Brazilian Literature: An Outline* (New York: Macmillan, 1945);

*A volta do gato preto* (Pôrto Alegre, Brazil: Globo, 1947);

*Ana Terra* (Pôrto Alegre, Brazil: Associados, 1949);

*Um certo Capitão Rodrigo* (Pôrto Alegre, Brazil: Globo, 1949);

*O tempo e o vento: O continente* (Pôrto Alegre, Brazil: Globo, 1949); translated by Linton Lomas Barrett as *Time and the Wind* (New York: Macmillan, 1951); revised and enlarged as *O tempo e o vento: O continente; O retrato,* 2 volumes (Pôrto Alegre, Brazil: Globo, 1951); revised and enlarged as *O tempo e o vento: O continente; O retrato; O arquipélago,* 3 volumes (Pôrto Alegre, Brazil: Globo, 1962);

*Lembrança de Pôrto Alegre* (Rio de Janeiro: Globo, 1954); translated by Iris Strohschoen as *Souvenir of Porto Alegre* (Rio de Janeiro: Globo, 1960);

*Noite* (Rio de Janeiro: Globo, 1954); translated by Barrett as *Night* (New York: Macmillan, 1956; London: Arco, 1956);

*Gente e bichos: Histórias infantis* (Pôrto Alegre, Brazil: Globo, 1956);

*México: História duma viagem* (Pôrto Alegre, Brazil: Globo, 1957); translated by Barrett as *Mexico* (New York: Orion, 1960; London: Macdonald, 1960);

*O ataque* (Pôrto Alegre, Brazil: Globo, 1959);

*O arquipélago,* three volumes (Pôrto Alegre, Brazil: Globo, 1961–1962);

*O continente* (Rio de Janeiro: Globo, 1962);

*O retrato* (Pôrto Alegre, Brazil: Globo, 1963);

*O senhor embaixador* (Pôrto Alegre, Brazil: Globo, 1965); translated by Barrett and Marie McDavid Barrett as *His Excellency, the Ambassador* (New York: Macmillan, 1967);

*Ficção completa,* five volumes (Rio de Janeiro: Aguilar, 1966–1967);

*O prisioneiro* (Pôrto Alegre, Brazil: Globo, 1967);

*Israel em abril* (Pôrto Alegre, Brazil: Globo, 1969);

*Incidente em Antares* (Pôrto Alegre, Brazil: Globo, 1971);

*Um certo Henrique Bertaso* (Pôrto Alegre, Brazil: Globo, 1972);

*Rio Grande do Sul* (São Paulo: Brunner, 1973);

*Solo de clarineta: Memórias,* part one (Pôrto Alegre, Brazil: Globo, 1973);

*Artistas gaúchos* (Pôrto Alegre, Brazil: Sociedade Israelita Riograndense, 1975);

*Solo de clarineta: Memórias,* part two (Pôrto Alegre, Brazil: Globo, 1976);

*Contos* (Pôrto Alegre, Brazil: Globo, 1978);

*Histórias infantis de Erico Veríssimo* (Pôrto Alegre, Brazil: RBS, 1978);

*Galeria fosca* (Rio de Janeiro: Globo, 1987).

SELECTED TRANSLATIONS: John Steinbeck, *Ratos e homens* (Pôrto Alegre, Brazil: Globo, 1940);

James Hilton, *Adeus, Mr. Chips* (Pôrto Alegre, Brazil: Globo, 1941);

Robert Nathan, *O retrato de Jennie* (Pôrto Alegre, Brazil: Meridiano, 1942);

Hilton, *Não estamos sós* (Pôrto Alegre, Brazil: Globo, 1943);

Aldous Huxley, *Contraponto* (Pôrto Alegre, Brazil: Globo, 1943).

Erico Veríssimo, who called himself a teller of stories and a painter with words, is a perennial favorite among Brazilian fiction readers of all ages. His literary career, which spanned nearly half a century from the early 1930s until his death in 1975, reflects the wide range of novelistic themes and stylistic innovations of a writer at once thoroughly integrated into the regional and national life of his own country and the greater Pan-American and international community.

Erico Lopes Veríssimo, son of Sebastião Veríssimo da Fonseca and Abigail Lopes Veríssimo, was born on 17 December 1905 in the small city of Cruz Alta in the southernmost Brazilian state of Rio Grande do Sul. His father, a pharmacist, died when Erico was quite young, and his mother sustained the family by working as a seamstress. After completing his elementary studies at a local school, he pursued secondary education at a boarding school in the state capital of Pôrto Alegre. He subsequently worked at a dry-goods shop in his hometown before attempting, in the family tradition, a career as a pharmacist. His love of art, music, and literature, however, soon lured him away from purely commercial pursuits, and his pharmacy became the gathering point for local students and teachers desiring to study English and debate literary issues. Veríssimo's own enthusiasms included the works of authors as diverse as Jonathan Swift, Anatole France, Oscar Wilde, and the nineteenth-century Brazilian psychological realist Machado de Assis.

Veríssimo's first short story, "Ladrão de gado" (Cattle Thief), was published in 1929 in the leading newspaper of Pôrto Alegre. Following the closing of his pharmacy due to financial problems in 1930 and his marriage to Mafalda Volpe on 15 July 1931, he moved to the state capital and began a career as caricaturist and short-story writer for two newspapers. His first published volume was *Fantoches* (Puppets, 1932), a collection of short stories in dramatic form. He became editor of the *Revista do Globo,* which subsequently expanded its sphere of influence to become a major Brazilian publishing house, the Editora Globo, directed by Henrique Bertaso. In the meantime Veríssimo and his wife had two children, Clarissa in 1935 and Luís Fernando in 1936, the latter becoming a popular

Brazilian writer of short fiction in his own right during the last third of the twentieth century.

In his early collaboration with Globo, Veríssimo devoted most of his time to translations of novels and detective stories from English, French, and Spanish; among the best known of these translations is that of Aldous Huxley's *Point Counter Point* (1928) as *Contaponto* in 1943. Early in his career Veríssimo established the pattern of doing his own original writing during evenings and weekends while carrying a full workload at the publishing house during the day. As he translated the works of other novelists, he customarily assimilated and sought to emulate narrative techniques that he found innovative and promising. One of the most productive of these was the "point counter point" structure of Huxley, which Veríssimo used in at least two of his own novels, *Caminhos cruzados* (1935; translated as *Crossroads*, 1943) and *O resto é silêncio* (1943; translated as *The Rest Is Silence,* 1946).

Veríssimo's career as a major Brazilian fiction writer was launched with the 1933 publication of his novel *Clarissa,* whose protagonist is a young girl on the verge of puberty. *Clarissa* was the first of five works dealing with the same group of urban, middle-class adolescents of both sexes; the others are *Caminhos cruzados, Música ao longe* (Distant Music, 1935), *Um lugar ao sol* (A Place in the Sun, 1936), and *Saga* (1940). The series or cycle of novels carries Clarissa, her boyfriend Amaro, her cousin Vasco, and other peers from early adolescence through their teen years, with their attendant problems, into the world of work as they follow various urban professions. The most troubled of these protagonists from a psychological point of view is Vasco, whose search for meaning in life takes him to Spain to fight on the democratic side in the Spanish Civil War, then back to Brazil and the challenges of reentry into a society that has changed during his absence.

*Caminhos cruzados* introduces Professor Clarimundo, a commentator on events, and an adult couple, Fernanda and Noel, to the cast of characters. *Um lugar ao sol* adds a wider gallery of actors, featuring adult individuals and couples from upper-to lower-middle-class urban families and various professions, seen in a series of scenes from everyday life in a small city. *Música ao longe* utilizes both musical motifs and the personal diary of Clarissa to convey a wistful glimpse of hope and decadence in the lives of former rancher João de Deus, the bankrupt Jovino and Amâncio, a couple whose twelve-year courtship remains unconsummated, an elderly woman living in the past, and various other locals.

Veríssimo's predilection for visual appeal through frequent, detailed, colorful, panoramic descriptions makes this novelistic cycle prime material for cinematic interpretation, and his sympathetic presentation of adolescent psychology and the daily problems of the silent majority of urban residents gives a Balzacian flavor to the entire series, as do most of his later novels. The five-work series is presented in a flowing, accessible prose style that created an enthusiastic public for these works and the author's later novels. From a critical point of view, *Saga* is the least well wrought piece of the series, while both *Caminhos cruzados* and *Música ao longe* won literary prizes.

Capitalizing on the wide juvenile public for his novels, Veríssimo branched out during the second half of the 1930s into children's literature, publishing nearly a dozen short books dedicated to historic events, science, and traditional children's stories. Among these popular volumes are *A vida de Joana d'Arc* (The Life of Joan of Arc, 1935); *As aventuras do avião vermelho* (The Adventures of the Red Airplane, 1936); *Meu ABC* (My ABCs, 1936); *Rosa Maria no castelo encantado* (Rosemary in the Enchanted Castle, 1936); *Os três porquinhos pobres* (The Three Poor Little Pigs, 1936); *As aventuras de Tibicuera* (The Adventures of Tibicuera, 1936), notable for its presentation of Brazilian geography; *O urso com música na barriga* (The Bear with Music in Its Tummy, 1938); *Aventuras no mundo da higiene* (Adventures in the World of Hygiene, 1939); *Outra vez os três porquinhos* (The Three Little Pigs Again, 1939); *Viagem à aurora do mundo* (Voyage to the Dawn of the World, 1939), a treatise on prehistoric creatures; and *A vida do elefante Basílio* (The Life of Basil the Elephant, 1939). The author's pedagogical purpose, communicated in charmingly attractive narrative style and graphic illustrations, was so successful that a children's radio series, *Amigo Velho* (Old Friend) hosted by Veríssimo was carried by the major station in Pôrto Alegre.

Two adult novels, *Olhai os lírios do campo* (1938; translated as *Consider the Lilies of the Field,* 1947) and *O resto é silêncio,* solidified his national and international reputation, and from approximately 1940 he was able to live exclusively on royalties from the sales of his books. Though not a pair in the strictest sense, these two novels have much in common. The first deals with professional and personal tensions in the life of a doctor, Eugênio Fontes, in his relationships with patients, family, and acquaintances, probing such areas as ethics, collegial relations, the disparity between medical services available to rich and poor, and the anguish of doctors facing life-and-

Cover for Veríssimo's 1967 novel, which criticizes war and
human-rights violations

death decisions in the operating room. The density of psychological penetration of this novel, couched in an easily flowing style characterized by ample use of the historic present, takes precedence over the panoramic views and gallery of socio-economic types that predominated in Veríssimo's earlier novels; the focus is now on dramas of conscience.

A similar equation characterizes *O resto é silêncio,* but in this work structural innovations also come into play as Veríssimo weaves multiple narrative threads that eventually bring together in a twenty-six-hour period a dozen individuals representing the gamut of Pôrto Alegre society, including businessmen such as Aristides Barreiro and Norival Petra, their wives, newsboy Sete Meis, ne'er-do-well Chicharro, councilman Lustosa, writer Tônio Santiago (Veríssimo's alter ego) and his family, Roberto the reporter, and orchestra conductor Bernardo Rezende and his wife Marina. All these characters, and several secondary figures as well, have seen or

been close to the suicide of a young woman named Joana, who leaped from a high building in the center of the city at dusk on Good Friday.

Using the "point counter point" technique of bouncing back and forth between and among the actors on this fictional stage, Erico traces each character's private life and public image, whether positive or negative, introducing the reader to a broad range of emotions, concerns, woes, pretenses, hopes, and fears. Little by little the individual threads begin to intertwine as people cross paths and compare versions of Joana's suicide and its probable cause. As more encounters occur, the characters are seen as complementary pieces in a meaningful puzzle, as though they had always been searching for each other but only at this point have been able to make contact as a result of yet another unknown person's tragedy. Special attention is focused on writer Tônio Santiago, for through him Veríssimo explores the issue of professional responsibility and the ethics of writing. If Joana, for example, had indeed begun to fantasize an amorous relationship with one of the fictional characters in Tônio's novels, suffering suicidal depression as a result of the character's failure to respond to her love letters and the author's own failure to answer her notes to him, to what degree is the novelist who created the fiction with which she identified responsible for her suicide? *O resto é silêncio* poses many such problems but does not offer easy answers. There is, however, the consolation that people in all professions may benefit by their mistakes and by those of others to learn sensitivity toward those who are unlike them. As the novel draws to a close in a concert hall on Holy Saturday night with Maestro Rezende leading the orchestra in Ludwig van Beethoven's Fifth Symphony, the main characters are spotlighted one by one as they listen to the masterpiece. The use of the music speaks of hope and strength in the midst of turmoil and courage in the face of trials, and the final message of the novel is one of human fulfillment and solidarity linking past, present, and future as Easter Sunday approaches.

*Olhai os lírios do campo* and *O resto é silêncio* focused public attention on Veríssimo's fiction in part because of the themes of ethics and individual conscience probingly treated in both; the incorporation of a microcosm of middle-class characters in partial contrast with the predominantly youthful cast of his earlier novels; and the unconventional structure of the second novel. Veríssimo received numerous invitations to lecture at universities in the United States and in 1941, 1943–1944, 1945, and 1946 made academic tours under the auspices of the U.S. Department of State, lecturing at the University of California, Berkeley; Mills College (where he received an honorary doctorate in letters in 1944); and other universities in California, Arizona, Indiana, and Texas. The literary results of these visits include the textbooks *Brazilian Literature: An Outline* (1945) and a pair of entertaining travel narratives depicting people and places encountered during his North American travels, *Gato preto em campo de neve* (Black Cat in a Field of Snow, 1941) and *A volta do gato preto* (The Return of the Black Cat, 1947). He returned for a more prolonged period of residence in Washington, D.C., in 1953 as director of the Department of Cultural Affairs of the Pan American Union (now the Organization of American States), a position he held until 1956. A 1955 trip to Mexico produced the travel book *México* (1957; translated as *Mexico,* 1960). In 1958 Veríssimo made his first trip to Europe, and in 1959 he returned for official literary appearances and

tourism in Portugal, Spain, England, France, Italy, Germany, and Holland.

During the 1950s, busy as he was with international travel, Veríssimo chose to devote himself to short fiction. His 1954 novelette *Noite* (translated as *Night,* 1956) is a kind of urban allegory of humanity lost in the crowd and seeking to discover its true identity. The nocturnal meanderings of the protagonist, an amnesiac, facilitate the surrealistic scanning of nightlife in all strata of society – parks, bars, brothels, a wake, a bazaar, a first-aid post, a cabaret, and confusing networks of streets – in an unnamed city. In 1958 he published a volume of short stories and other short fiction entitled *O ataque* (Attack), but his future focus was not on brief narratives but on a much broader fictional horizon, as had already been announced by the publication in 1949 of the first third of the work generally considered his masterpiece.

Veríssimo entered this "epic" phase with *O continente* (The Continent, 1949), a 670-page novel recreating the evolution of the politics, economy, and society of southern Brazil, especially the state of Rio Grande do Sul and the river Plate region, from approximately 1745 to 1895. Two extended families, or "clans" – the Terras and the Cambarás – form the nucleus of this panoramic work. Subsequent volumes in the cycle are *O retrato* (The Portrait), a 611-page novel published in 1951 which continues the history of the same clans from 1909 to 1915, a turbulent period in gaucho politics, and *O arquipélago* (The Archipelago), a gigantic 1,014-page work that brings the action up to 1945, the Getúlio Vargas period in Brazilian politics, and involves several real-life personalities on the national scene. The most imposing regional epic written to date in Brazil, these books bore the overall title of *O tempo e o vento* (Time and the Wind), with the individual works continuing to be published independently. Segments of *O continente* dealing with a pair of outstanding characters were compiled for publication as well under the titles *Ana Terra* (1949) and *Um certo Capitão Rodrigo* (A Certain Captain Rodrigo, 1949). The popularity of the trilogy is reflected in its serialization on Brazilian television in the 1980s.

*O continente,* the literary masterpiece of the trilogy, is a kind of chanson de geste of the southernmost region of Brazil. Tracing multiple generations of Terras, Cambarás, and neighboring families, the work introduces stoic matriarchal figures such as Ana Terra, Maria Valéria, and Bibiana, pioneer Jesuit missionaries, and such gaucho stalwarts as Pedro and Horácio Terra and Licurgo and Rodrigo Cambará. In broad splashes of prose suggestive of colorful mural paintings, Veríssimo re-creates the robust, sometimes-violent political and social history of his native Rio Grande do Sul during its formative period within the context of territorial occupation and Spanish-Portuguese relations as both nations sought to expand their colonial influence in the New World and their independent "offspring" began to assert their presence and jostle for power in the region of the river Plate. *O continente* is frontier literature at its best and serves as the undisputed masterpiece of historical regionalism dealing with southern Brazil and surrounding territory.

The second part of this trilogy, *O retrato,* continues the history of the Terra and Cambará clans from their rural origins toward increasing urbanization. The central character is Dr. Rodrigo Cambará, great-grandson of the original Captain Rodrigo of *O continente,* and events in the novel gravitate around the politics of the Pinheiro Machado period in regional and national politics. This period, immediately preceding World War I, is re-created not only politically but also culturally through the incorporation of such details as airplanes, movies, cars, and the ominous folklore surrounding the appearance of Halley's comet.

*O arquipélago* is the most wide-ranging of the three works that constitute "O tempo e o vento," composed as it was while the author was suffering increasingly severe heart problems. Treating the period from 1930 to 1945, dominated in Brazilian politics by the figure of Vargas, this massive novel follows a structural scheme rotating among historical narratives tracing the progression of Vargas's career in regional and national politics: six diarylike chapters entitled "Caderno de pauta simples" (Simple Lined Notebook) that trace individual reminiscences and poetic reflections; and six interspersed chapters entitled "Reunião de família" (Family Gathering) which serve to integrate the personal, regional, and national levels of the narrative. The novel ends with a chapter entitled "Encruzilhada" (Crossroads), which brings together the multiple strands of the work.

The Cambará family dominates this extensive novel, and the cardiac problems of the author are superimposed on politician Rodrigo Cambará, close ally of Vargas and protagonist of the work. The Cambarás, residing now in Rio de Janeiro as their star has risen in national politics, gather at the family home in Santa Fé in Rio Grande do Sul to confer and plan strategy in one of the segments entitled "Reunião de família." In the sections making up the "Caderno de pauta simples" the author engages in his most uninhibited poetic and prose digressions,

bringing together many diverse ideas, values, and reactions in a kind of free association of component elements. The novel thus runs along three simultaneous and intertwining tracks, evolving through a pattern of circular movement.

The element in this novel setting it apart from the other parts of the trilogy and from Veríssimo's earlier novels is the poetry and poetic prose of the "Caderno" segments, used to explore the author's most intimate and shifting sentiments on a variety of subjects running the gamut of human experience. The increasing fragmentation of modern society is a constant preoccupation reflected in the metaphoric evolution of the titles of the progressive segments of the trilogy. From the solid image of the eighteenth- and nineteenth-century continent with its robust expectation of expansion and growth to the fragmentation of the mid-twentieth-century archipelago, the trilogy reflects Veríssimo's increasing pessimism regarding human relations in general and Brazilian socio-economic and political life in particular. He ponders in the last volume whether the most important function of a mid-twentieth-century writer of fiction might be to construct bridges among the diverse fragments or islands of the modern "archipelago" of regional, national, and international life, thus promoting in some small measure a degree of mutual understanding.

Following the microcosmic focus of his initial series with its developing youthful protagonists and middle-class setting and the panoramic social and regional epic represented by the *O tempo e o vento* cycle, Veríssimo turned his attention to the international scene, reflecting his own experiences in cultural diplomacy and his increasing concern over the trends he observed in international relations during the 1960s. The literary results of this concern are the novels *O senhor embaixador* (1965; translated as *His Excellency, the Ambassador,* 1967) and *O prisioneiro* (The Prisoner, 1967). Here are dramas of conscience worked out in contexts that for the first time in Veríssimo's career are foreign to Brazil. It was inspired in part by his own experiences in Washington, D.C., during his years as director of cultural affairs of the Pan American Union and in part by developing events in Asia, specifically Vietnam, involving Western intervention. These two novels reveal an increasing pessimism in an author previously known for his unfailing optimism and altruism in the treatment of problematic situations and a broad cast of characters.

*O senhor embaixador* re-creates in almost caricatural manner the diplomatic merry-go-round of Washington. The microcosm of public and private

*Veríssimo in the early 1970s*

activities of the ambassador of the "Republic of Sacramento" and other members of the international diplomatic corps is seen within the macrocosm of the various nations represented. Reporter Bill Godkin, whose daily political column appears in a local newspaper, is the author's mouthpiece. As he circulates freely in governmental circles, Godkin ("little God?") observes and comments upon official activities, international intrigue, and the many faces of ambition, hate, and greed seen in both overt and covert settings. The novel ends violently with the death of the ambassador before a firing squad in his home republic. Replete with references to journalistic sources and actual Latin-American political developments of the post–World War II period, this novel is Veríssimo's thinly veiled commentary upon the state of affairs in the nations of the Western hemisphere and the fundamental inhumanity of even the most sophisticated members of officialdom.

The scene shifts to southeast Asia in *O prisioneiro,* written as Veríssimo recoiled before developing events in the Vietnam War and the aftermath of decolonization in the francophone nations of Africa. The characters of this novel are generally identified only by their function – such as colonel, lieutenant, sergeant, general, prisoner, medic, or teacher – never by name, giving the work a distinctly impersonal tone. All the actors are little pieces in the machine of war, and there is no time for compassion or mutual understanding among the group of whites, blacks, Jews, and Asians that Veríssimo has assembled for a work in which all of them are in one form or another victims of the system. Orders are followed because they have been given by superiors, and a single life is worth essentially nothing when compared with the hypothetical masses comprising various national populations and diverse ethnic groups. *O prisioneiro* is a kind of antiwar parable, an accessible and perhaps deceptively simple plea for human rights in the international context of deep-seated racism, ethnic zeal, and paranoia by an author moved by humanitarian rather than political motives.

Veríssimo accepted the invitation of the Israeli government for an official academic visit in 1966 and in 1969 published a travel narrative entitled *Israel em abril* (Israel in April). In 1967 he won the Juca Pato Prize as Brazilian intellectual of the year and began to write his memoirs, eventually published under the title *Solo de clarineta* (Clarinet Solo). Volume one of this two-volume work appeared in 1973, two years before the author's death, and volume two was published in 1976. However, it was his last work of fiction that drew the public's attention once again in a rather startling way even compared to the undying popularity of his early cycle of youthful protagonists. It continues the appeal of his epic panorama of gaucho and national history in the trilogy and the pointed critiques launched in his "international" novels of the 1960s. *Incidente em Antares* (Incident in Antares, 1971) introduces the element of magic realism, and in this work Veríssimo allegorically subverts the institutions and structures of Brazilian society of which he was generally more tolerant, or at least less overtly critical, in earlier novels.

Antares is the approximate equivalent in Brazilian literature of the Macondo of Gabriel García Márquez. A city located somewhere in the interior of Rio Grande do Sul, it serves as a microcosm of both contemporary and traditional Brazilian society. The main events of the ostensible plot of the novel occur nearly on the eve of the 1964 revolution (inauspiciously, on Friday, 13 December 1963), and they are of an uncommon variety. Seven citizens of the small city die on the same day and because of a grave diggers' strike are left unburied. They get together, decide to surprise the living citizens of the town, and take over the central bandstand in order to make their voice heard in a totally objective way and with impunity. A parallel and complementary subplot follows the research of Prof. Martim Terra, a teacher of sociology and, not surprisingly, a descendant of the Terra clan of the *O tempo e o vento* trilogy. Professor Terra is gathering statistics for his book to be entitled *Anatomia de uma cidade gaúcha de fronteira* (Anatomy of a Gaucho Border City), and his diary of snippets and valorizing comments serves as an external counterpoint to the main text. *Incidente em Antares* is, like *O arquipélago* but in an even more integrated fashion, a work of both fiction and metafiction with a weighty yet witty sociopolitical component.

The seven deceased protagonists of *Incidente em Antares* form a composite of the widely divergent classes, prejudices, and points of view that characterize the town's population; Quitéria, a member of the landed aristocracy; Dr. Cícero, a lawyer; Menandro Olinda, a professional musician; Barcelona, the anarchist shoemaker; João Paz, a factory worker; Erotildes, a prostitute; and Pudim de Cachaça, one of the town drunks. Once dead, these representative individuals are able, albeit with reluctance in some cases, to leave behind those things that have divided them in life and find their common humanity. As they are able to discern their mutual value as persons, they come to form an often accusatory voice concerning the ongoing tragicomedy that surrounds them in the land of the living.

Their public appearance in the bandstand in the main town square draws a huge crowd, at once curious and horrified, that represents a cross section of the local society. The group pulls no punches in its exposé of what is wrong in Rio Grande do Sul, in Brazil, and in contemporary society in general.

There is a dramatic quality about this novel reminiscent of the sixteenth-century morality plays, especially those of Gil Vicente, that influenced Brazilian theater of both the colonial and modern periods. Veríssimo has a message, or rather an appeal, in his last novel not radically different from the one that remained constant throughout earlier works: it is within the power of human beings to make or break their society, to weave or tear the sociocultural fabric of family, local, regional, national, and international life. Life is so important and intrinsically valuable that its maintenance and nurture merit the careful attention of all people, and an important component of the vocation of writers is to raise the consciousness of their readers. The inhabitants of the global village must care for one another if there is to be a future for humanity.

The fiction of Veríssimo – even in those works in which he is most exercised over personal, regional, national, or international injustice, misunderstanding, cruelty, inhumanity, or abuse – never loses its quiet elegance and balance. Never is there gratuitous bad taste, even in passages portraying violence. Never is the balanced marriage of content and form lost from view, even in novels verging on the experimental. Veríssimo does not engage in art for art's sake, although he takes pleasure in trying out innovations. The accessibility of his prose has been criticized by a few reviewers, though it has endeared him to the broad Brazilian reading public.

One other feature of much of his fiction, however, has been the target of considerable questioning by critics: the frequent inclusion of prolonged or recurring theoretical sociopolitical and/or philosophical debates within prose dialogues. The greatest offender in this regard is *O arquipélago,* though the tendency is present in most of his novels. He conceives of literature not only as "painting with words" or the "telling of tales" but as a stage for talking about and working out the fundamental concerns of individuals and their society. Even though he has no partisan ax to grind, he is a novelist with a deep sense of moral responsibility.

At his death Erico Veríssimo had achieved in Brazil a level of reader recognition and popularity unrivaled by any other writer with the possible exception of Jorge Amado. His urbane prose, gentle manner, warm humanitarianism, and broad thematic and stylistic perspective appear to have guaranteed him a secure place in Brazilian letters of the twentieth century.

## Interviews:

"Encontro com Erico Veríssimo," *O Estado de São Paulo,* literary supplement (28 August 1965);

Carlos Nobre, "A nobre entrevista de Erico," *Zero Hora* (2 December 1966);

Paulo de Almeida Lima, "John dos Passos visto por Erico Veríssimo," *O Estado de São Paulo,* no. 617, literary supplement (8 March 1969);

Carlos M. Fernandes, "Veríssimo: Evite o espelho mágico," *O Estado de São Paulo,* no. 763, literary supplement (12 March 1972);

Delmar Marques, "Estória dum contador de histórias," *Zero Hora* (2 December 1973);

Maria Abreu, "Veríssimo, último capítulo," *Ultima Hora* (1 December 1975);

"A entrevista inacabada," *Zero Hora,* special supplement (17 December 1975).

## References:

Maria da Glória Bordini, ed., *Erico Veríssimo: O escritor no tempo* (Pôrto Alegre, Brazil: Sulina, 1990);

Flávio Loureiro Chaves, ed., *O contador de histórias: Quarenta anos de vida literário de Erico Veríssimo* (Pôrto Alegre, Brazil: Globo, 1972);

Chaves, *Erico Veríssimo: Realismo e sociedade* (Pôrto Alegre, Brazil: Globo, 1976);

Daniel Fresnot, *O pensamento político de Erico Veríssimo* (Rio de Janeiro: Graal, 1977);

Oswaldo Antônio Furlan, *Estética e crítica social em "Incidente em Antares"* (Florianópolis, Brazil: UFSC, 1977);

Malory J. Pompermayer, *Erico Veríssimo e o problema de Deus* (São Paulo: Loyola, 1968);

José Clemente Pozenato, *O regional e o universal na literatura gaúcha* (Pôrto Alegre, Brazil: Movimento/IEL, 1974);

Joaquin Rodrigues Suro, *Erico Veríssimo: História e literatura* (Pôrto Alegre, Brazil: D. C. Luzzatto, 1985).

# Checklist of Further Readings

Abrahams, Roger D. *The Man-of-Words in the West Indies: Performance and the Emergence of Creole Culture.* Baltimore: Johns Hopkins University Press, 1983.

Alan, M., and Evelyn Rugg, eds. *Actas del Sexto Congreso Internacional de Hispanistas.* Toronto: University of Toronto Press, 1980.

Alegría, Fernando. *Literatura y revolución.* Mexico City: Fondo de Cultura Económica, 1971.

Anderson Imbert, Enrique. *El realismo mágico y otros ensayos.* Caracas: Monte Avila, 1976.

Aparicio López, Teófilo. *El "boom" americano: Estudios de crítica literaria.* Valladolid, Spain: Estudio Agustiniano, 1980.

Araújo, Elena. *La Scherezada Criolla.* Bogotá: Universidad Nacional de Colombia, 1989.

Avalle-Arce, Juan Bautista, ed. *Narradores hispanoamericanos de hoy.* Chapel Hill: University of North Carolina, Department of Romance Languages, 1973.

Bacarisse, Salvador, ed. *Contemporary Latin American Fiction.* Edinburgh: Scottish Academic Press, 1980.

Balderston, Daniel, ed. *The Historic Novel in Latin America.* Gaithersburg, Md.: Hispamérica, 1986.

Bassnett, Susan, ed. *Knives and Angels: Women Writers in Latin America.* London: Zed, 1990.

Bella, Jozef. *A mascara e o enigma: A modernidade da representação a transgressão.* Rio de Janeiro: Alves, 1986.

Benedetti, Mario. *Literatura uruguaya siglo XX,* second edition. Montevideo: Alfa, 1969.

Benitez Rojo, Antonio. *La isla que se repite: El Caribe y la postmodernidad.* Hanover, N.H.: Ediciones del Norte, 1989.

Beverley, John, and Marc Zimmerman. *Literature and Politics in the Central American Revolutions.* Austin: University of Texas Press, 1990.

Bleznick, Donald W., ed. *Variaciones interpretativas en torno a la nueva narrativa hispanoamericana.* Santiago, Chile: Universitaria, 1972.

Boldy, Steven. *Before the Boom: Four Essays on Latin American Literature before 1940.* Liverpool: Center for Latin American Studies, University of Liverpool, 1981.

Brushwood, John. *La novela mexicana (1967–1982).* Mexico City: Grijalbo, 1985.

Campos, Julieta. *Oficio de leer.* Mexico City: Fondo de Cultura Económica, 1971.

Carballo, Emmanuel. *Diecinueve protagonistas de la literatura mexicana del siglo xx.* Mexico City: Empresas, 1965.

Castro, Sílvio. *A revolução da palavra.* Petrópolis, Brazil: Vozes, 1976.

Chang-Rodríguez, Raquel, and Gabriella de Beer, eds. *La historia en la literatura iberoamericana*. Hanover, N.H.: Ediciones del Norte, 1989.

Chevigny, Bell Gale, and Gari Laguardia, eds. *Reinventing the Americas: Comparative Studies of the Literature of the United States and Spanish America*. New York: Cambridge University Press, 1986.

Cornejo Polar, Antonio. *La novela peruana: Siete estudios*. Lima: Horizonte, 1977.

Cornejo Polar. *Sobre literatura y crítica latinoamericanas*. Caracas: Ediciones de la Facultad de Humanidades y Educación, Universidad Central de Venezuela, 1982.

Coutinho, Afranio, ed. *A literatura no Brasil,* 6 volumes. Rio de Janeiro: Sud Americana, 1968–1971.

Dacanal, José Hildebrando. *Nova narrativa épica no Brasil*. Pôrto Alegre, Brazil: Sulina, 1973.

Dacanal. *Realismo mágico*. Pôrto Alegre, Brazil: Movimento, 1970.

DeCosta, Miriam, ed. *Blacks in Hispanic Literature*. Port Washington, N.Y.: Kennikat Press, 1977.

Díaz, Nancy Gray. *The Radical Self: Metamorphosis to Animal Form in Modern Latin American Narrative*. Columbia: University of Missouri Press, 1988.

Dorfman, Ariel. *Hacia la liberación del lector latinoamericano*. Hanover, N.H.: Ediciones del Norte, 1984.

Dorfman. *Some Write to the Future: Essays on Contemporary Latin American Fiction*. Durham, N.C.: Duke University Press, 1991.

Ellison, Fred P. *Brazil's New Novel*. Berkeley: University of California Press, 1954.

Erro-Orthmann, Nora, and Juan Cruz Mendizábal, eds. *La escritora hispánica*. Miami: Universal, 1990.

Fell, Claude. *Estudios de literatura hispanoamericana contemporánea*. Mexico City: Sepsetentas, 1976.

Fitz, Earl E. *Rediscovering the New World: Inter-American Literature in a Comparative Context*. Iowa City: University of Iowa Press, 1991.

Fleischmann, Ulrich, ed. *El Caribe y América Latina: Actas del III. Coloquio Interdisciplinario sobre el Caribe*. Frankfurt am Main: Vervuert, 1987.

Foster, David William. *Alternate Voices in the Contemporary Latin American Narrative*. Columbia: University of Missouri Press, 1985.

Foster. *Gay and Lesbian Themes in Latin American Writing*. Austin: University of Texas Press, 1991.

Foster and Virginia Ramos Foster, eds. *Modern Latin American Literature,* 2 volumes. New York: Ungar, 1975.

Gallagher, David Patrick. *Modern Latin American Literature*. London: Oxford University Press, 1973.

García Pinto, Magdalena. *Historias íntimas: Conversaciones con diez escritoras latinoamericanas*. Hanover, N.H.: Ediciones del Norte, 1988.

Gazarian Gautier, Marie-Lise. *Interviews with Latin American Writers*. Elmwood Park, Ill.: Dalkey Archive Press, 1989.

Genro, Tarso Fernando. *Literatura e ideologia: Um novo romance latino-americano.* Curitiba, Brazil: Criar, 1982.

Gertel, Zunilda. *La novela hispanoamericana contemporánea.* Buenos Aires: Columbia, 1970.

Glantz, Margo. *Repeticiones.* Jalapa, Mexico: Universidad Veracruzana, 1974.

González Echevarría, Roberto. *Myth and Archive: A Theory of Latin American Narrative.* Cambridge & New York: Cambridge University Press, 1990.

González Echevarría. *The Voice of the Masters: Writing and Authority in Modern Latin American Literature.* Austin: University of Texas Press, 1985.

Guelfi, Maria Lucia Fernandes. *Novíssima: Contribuição para o estudo do Modernismo.* São Paulo: Universidade de São Paulo, Instituto de Estudos Brasileiros, 1987.

Heise, Karl H. *El grupo de Guayaquil: Arte y técnica de sus novelas sociales.* Madrid: Playor, 1975.

Jackson, David, ed. *Transformations of Literary Language in Latin American Literature: From Machado de Assis to the Vanguards.* Austin, Tex.: Abaporu, 1987.

Jackson, Richard. *Black Literature and Humanism in Latin America.* Athens: University of Georgia Press, 1988.

Jackson. *Black Writers in Latin America.* Albuquerque: University of New Mexico Press, 1979.

Jara, René, and Hernán Vidal, eds. *Testimonio y literatura.* Minneapolis: Institute for the Study of Ideologies and Literature, 1986.

Kulin, Katalin. *Modern Latin American Fiction: A Return to Didacticism,* translated by Aszter Molnar. Budapest: Akademiai Kiado, 1988.

Lagunas, Jorge Román, ed. *La literatura centroamericana.* New York: Edwin Mellen, 1994.

Larson, Neil, ed. *The Discourse of Power: Culture, Hegemony, and the Authoritarian State.* Minneapolis: Institute for the Study of Ideologies and Literature, 1983.

Leite, Dante Moreira. *O amor romantico e outros temas.* São Paulo: Conselho Estadual de Cultura, 1964.

Lewis, Marvin. *Treading the Ebony Path: Ideology and Violence in Contemporary Afro-Columbian Prose Fiction.* Columbia: University of Missouri Press, 1987.

Lima, Luís Costa. *A metamorfose do silêncio.* Rio de Janeiro: Eldorado, 1974.

Lindstrom, Naomi. *Women's Voice in Latin American Literature.* Washington, D.C.: Three Continents, 1989.

Lockert, Lucía Fox, ed. *Mitos en Hispanoamérica Interpretación y literatura.* East Lansing, Mich.: Imprenta la Nueva Crónica, 1989.

Losado, Alejandro. *Creación y praxis: La producción literaria como praxis social en Hispanoamérica.* Lima: Universidad Nacional Major de San Marcos, 1976.

Luis, William. *Literary Bondage: Slavery in Cuban Narrative.* Austin: University of Texas Press, 1990.

Luis, ed. *Voices from Under: Black Narrative in Latin America and the Caribbean.* Westport, Conn.: Greenwood Press, 1984.

Magnarelli, Sharon. *The Lost Rib*. Lewisburg, Pa.: Bucknell University Press, 1985.

Marting, Diane E., ed. *Spanish American Women Writers: A Bio-Bibliographical Source Book*. New York: Greenwood Press, 1990.

Martins, Heitor, ed. *The Brazilian Novel*. Bloomington: Indiana University Press, 1976.

McDuffie, Keith, and Alfredo Roggiano, eds. *Texto/Contexto en la literatura iberoamericana*. Madrid: Artes Gráficas Benzal, 1981.

Menton, Seymour. *Historia crítica de la novela guatemalteca,* second edition. Guatemala: Editorial Universitaria de Guatemala, 1985.

Menton. *Prose Fiction of the Cuban Revolution*. Austin & London: University of Texas Press, 1975.

Meyer, Doris, and Margarite Fernandez Olmos, eds. *Contemporary Women Authors of Latin America*. Brooklyn: Brooklyn College Press, 1983.

Miller, Yvette E., and Charles M. Tatum, eds. *Latin American Women Writers: Yesterday and Today*. Pittsburgh: Latin American Literary Review, 1977.

Minc, Rose, ed. *The Contemporary Latin American Short Story*. New York: Senda Nueva de Ediciones, 1979.

Minc, ed. *Literature and Popular Culture in the Hispanic World: A Symposium*. Gaithersburg, Md.: Montclair State College/Ediciones Hispamérica, 1981.

Minc, ed. *Literatures in Transition: The Many Voices of the Caribbean Area – A Symposium*. Gaithersburg, Md.: Montclair State College/Ediciones Hispamérica, 1982.

Mohr, Eugene. *The Nuyorican Experience: Literature of Puerto Rican Minorities*. Westport, Conn.: Greenwood Press, 1982.

Mondragón, Amelia, ed. *Cambios estéticos y nuevos proyectos culturales en Centroamérica*. Washington, D.C.: Literal, 1994.

Nunes, Benedito. *O dorso do tigre*. São Paulo: Perspectiva, 1969.

Oropeza, José Napoleón. *Para fijar un rostro: Notas sobre la novelística venezolana actual*. Valencia, Venezuela: Vadell Hermanos, 1984.

Ortega, Julio. *Crítica de la identidad: La pregunta por el Perú en su literatura*. Mexico City: Fondo de Cultura Económica, 1988.

Ortega. *La imaginación crítica: Ensayos sobre la modernidad en el Perú*. Lima: Peisa, 1974.

Ortega. *Poetics of Change: The New Spanish-American Narrative*. Austin: University of Texas Press, 1984.

Osorio, Nelson, ed. *La formación de la vanguardia literaria en Venezuela*. Caracas: Academia Nacional de la Historia, 1985.

Patai, Daphne. *Myth and Ideology in Contemporary Brazilian Fiction*. Rutherford, N.J.: Fairleigh Dickinson University Press; London: Associated University Presses, 1983.

Paz, Octavio. *El signo y el garabato*. Mexico City: Joaquín Mortiz, 1973.

Perez, Renard. *Escritores brasileiros contemporâneos.* Rio de Janeiro: Civilização Brasileira, 1960.

Perus, Francoise. *Historia y crítica literaria: El realismo social y la crisis de la dominacion oligárquica.* Havana: Casa de las Américas, 1982.

Picón Salas, Mariano. *Estudios de literatura venezolana.* Caracas: Edime, 1961.

Quinlan, Susan Canty. *The Female Voice in Contemporary Brazilian Narrative.* New York: Peter Lang, 1991.

Rincón, Carlos. *El cambio de la noción de la literatura.* Bogotá: Instituto Colombiano de Cultura, 1978.

Rodríguez de Laguna, Asela, ed. *Images and Identities: The Puerto Rican in Two World Cultures.* New Brunswick, N.J.: Transaction, 1987.

Rodríguez Monegal, Emir. *El Boom de la novela latinoamericana.* Caracas: Tiempo Nuevo, 1972.

Rodríguez Monegal. *Narradores de esta América.* Montevideo: Alfa, 1969.

Rodríguez-Luis, Julio. *Hermenéutica y praxis del indigenismo.* Mexico City: Tierra Firme, 1980.

Rodríguez-Luis. *La literatura hispanoamericana entre compromiso y experimento.* Madrid: Espiral, 1984.

Rosas, Patricia, and Lourdes Madrid. *Las torturas de la imaginación.* Mexico City: Premiá, 1982.

Roy, Joaquín. *Narrativa y crítica de nuestra América.* Madrid: Castalia, 1977.

Ruffinelli, Jorge. *Crítica en marcha: Ensayos sobre literatura latinoamericana.* Mexico City: Premiá, 1979.

Santiago, Silviano. *Nas malhas da letra: Ensaios.* São Paulo: Companhia das Letras, 1989.

Siemens, William L. *Worlds Reborn: The Hero in the Modern Spanish American Novel.* Morgantown: West Virginia University Press, 1984.

Silva-Velázquez, Caridad, and Nora Erro-Orthmann, eds. *Puerta abierta: La nueva escritora latinoamericana.* Mexico City: Joaquín Mortiz, 1968.

Silverman, Malcolm. *Moderna ficção brasileira,* translated by J. G. Linke. Rio de Janeiro: Civilização Brasileira, 1978.

Smart, Ian I. *Central American Writers of West Indian Origin: A New Hispanic Literature.* Washington, D.C.: Three Continents, 1984.

Sole, Carlos A., ed. *Latin American Writers,* 3 volumes. New York: Scribners, 1989.

Sommer, Doris. *One Master for Another: Populism as Patriarchal Rhetoric in Dominican Novels.* Lanham, Md.: University Press of America, 1983.

Souza, Raymond D. *Major Cuban Novelists: Innovation and Tradition.* Columbia: University of Missouri Press, 1976.

Torres Fierro, Danubio. *Memorial plural: Entrevistas a escritores latinoamericanos.* Buenos Aires: Sudamericana, 1986.

Umaña, Helen. *Literatura hondureña contemporánea: Ensayos.* Tegucigalpa, Honduras: Guaymuras, 1986.

Viñas, David. *De Sarmiento a Cortázar: Literatura argentina y realidad política*. Buenos Aires: Siglo Veinte, 1971.

Virgillo, Carmelo, and Naomi Lindstrom, eds. *Woman as Myth and Metaphor in Latin American Literature*. Columbia: University of Missouri Press, 1985.

Volek, Emil. *Cuatro claves para la modernidad*. Madrid: Gredos, 1984.

Williams, Raymond L. *Una década de la novela colombiana: La experiencia de los setenta*. Bogotá: Plaza y Janés, 1981.

Williams, ed. *Ensayos de literatura colombiana*. Bogotá: Plaza y Janés, 1985.

Yates, Donald A., ed. *Otros mundos otros fuegos: Fantasía y realismo mágico en Iberoamérica*. East Lansing: Michigan State University Press, 1975.

# Contributors

Ana Luiza Andrade .................................................*Universidade Federal de Sta Catarina*
Eduardo Béjar ............................................................................*Middlebury College*
Steven M. Bell ...................................................................*University of Arkansas*
Amanda Castro-Mitchell ..................................................*Westminster College*
Carmen Chaves Tesser .......................................................*University of Georgia*
Margaret B. Crosby ..........................................................*University of New Mexico*
Julia Cuervo Hewitt ......................................................*Pennsylvania State University*
Mary L. Daniel .........................................................*University of Wisconsin–Madison*
Angela B. Dellepiane ..........................................................*City University of New York*
Fred P. Ellison..............................................................*University of Texas at Austin*
Nora Erro-Peralta .............................................................*Florida Atlantic University*
Margarite Fernández Olmos .....................*Brooklyn College, City University of New York*
César Ferreira ...................................................................*University of North Texas*
Alvin Joaquín Figueroa .........................................................*Trenton State College*
Ann González ...........................................*University of North Carolina at Charlotte*
Michael Handelsman ...........................................*University of Tennessee at Knoxville*
Regina Igel .........................................*University of Maryland at College Park*
Efraín S. Kristal ....................................................*University of California, Los Angeles*
Dante Liano ...........................................................*Università degli Studi de Milano*
M. Angélica Lopes........................................................*University of South Carolina*
Rick McCallister .......................................*University of South Carolina at Spartanburg*
Adriana Méndez Rodenas........................................................*University of Iowa*
John C. Miller ...........................................*University of Colorado, Colorado Springs*
Ardis L. Nelson............................................................*East Tennessee State University*
Gustavo Pérez Firmat ........................................................*Duke University*
Ineke Phaf.........................................*University of Maryland at College Park*
Rubén Ríos Avila ...............................................................*University of Puerto Rico*
Carmen S. Rivera...........................................*University of North Carolina at Charlotte*
Lorraine Elena Roses...........................................................*Wellesley College*
Javier Sanjinés C. ...........................................*University of Maryland at College Park*
D. L. Shaw.......................................................................*University of Virginia*
Elzbieta Sklodowska ...............................................................*Washington University*
Ian Isidore Smart.................................................................*Howard University*
Silvio Torres-Saillant .................*Hostos Community College, City University of New York*
Nicasio Urbina ...................................................................*Tulane University*
Hugo J. Verani........................................................*University of California, Davis*
C. Michael Waag...........................................................*Murray State University*
Maida Watson Espener ..........................................*Florida International University*

# Cumulative Index

*Dictionary of Literary Biography,* Volumes 1-145
*Dictionary of Literary Biography Yearbook,* 1980-1993
*Dictionary of Literary Biography Documentary Series,* Volumes 1-11

# Cumulative Index

**DLB** before number: *Dictionary of Literary Biography*, Volumes 1-145
**Y** before number: *Dictionary of Literary Biography Yearbook*, 1980-1993
**DS** before number: *Dictionary of Literary Biography Documentary Series*, Volumes 1-11

Cumulative Index

# C

# S

# U

# V

Cumulative Index